The Hudson River
Guidebook

THE STATUE OF LIBERTY resplendently refurbished for her Centennial Celebration flourishing a new gold-leaved flambeau.
Photo: © Gretchen McHugh.

The Hudson River Guidebook

Second edition,
fully revised and newly illustrated

Arthur G. Adams

FORDHAM UNIVERSITY PRESS
New York
1996

Designed and typeset by TechType of Ramsey, NJ

"Journey to the Source of the Hudson River," which previously appeared in *The Riverdale Press* and the Hudson River Clearwater *Navigator*, is copyright 1996 by Gretchen McHugh.

Oil paintings by marine artist William G. Muller.
Front: View looking north up Hudson River from West Point Hill in 1915. Day Line steamer *Robert Fulton* rounding the Point. © William G. Muller.
Back: Cunard Liner *Mauretania* leaving New York on a night sailing in 1932.

Library of Congress Cataloging-in-Publication Data

Adams, Arthur G.
    The Hudson River Guidebook / Arthur G. Adams. — 2nd
ed.
      p. cm.
    Includes index.
    ISBN 0-8232-1679-9 (hardcover). — ISBN 0-8232-1680-2 (paperback)
    1. Hudson River—Guidebooks. 2. Hudson River Valley (N.Y. and
N.J.)—Guidebooks. I. Title.
F127.H8A22 1996
917.47'30442—dc20   96-1894
                                                    CIP

Printed in the United States of America

To Daryl

Contents

Maps

Key Map

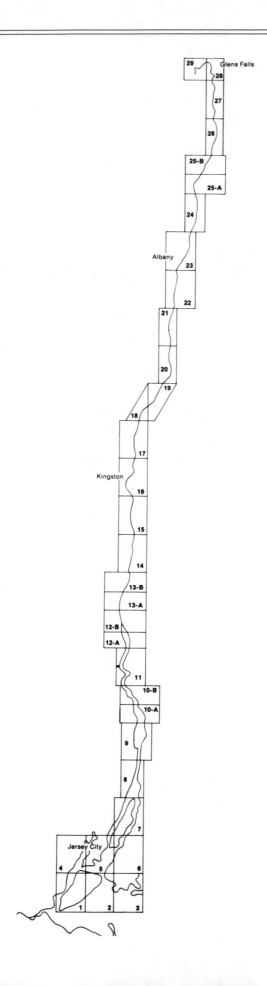

Acknowledgments

Numerous people and institutions have been helpful in the research and writing of this book—and they all have my grateful thanks. However, I would like to give particular thanks to the following people and organizations: to Dr. Alfred H. Marks, of the State University of New York, New Paltz, for encouragement and constructive criticism; to Mrs. Frances Reese, of Scenic Hudson Preservation Conference, for encouragement, good advice, and putting me in touch with other people who have been very helpful; to the late Mr. Charles Keppel for well-informed constructive criticism and evaluation; to the late Mr. Alfred Van Santvoordt Olcott, Jr., for encouragement, valuable information, and the use of unique material from his personal collection and the archives of the original Hudson River Day Line, which his family founded and operated for many years—and simply for his friendship; to the Steamship Historical Society of America, for information from its membership (some of whom have insisted upon remaining anonymous); to Mr. William G. Muller, Marine Artist, for use of his paintings; to Mr. Leon R. Greenman, of Walking News Press, for advice on map work; to Bob Tebbenhoff for planning the layout of this complex book; and finally to my wife Daryl, children Christopher and Cynthia, and my mother, for their help, patience, and encouragement.

Arthur G. Adams

Preface

Over the course of the years there have been numerous books about the Hudson River. Guidebooks were popular in the nineteenth century. In our own times history books, photographic albums, and accommodation and dining guides have predominated. All these books served a good purpose, and some, such as Benson Lossing's *The Hudson, From the Wilderness to the Sea,* have intrinsic literary value. The guidebooks of Walton Van Loan, Wallace Bruce, and Ernest Ingersoll were popular until just after the turn of the century. However, since their books went out of print before 1940, there has not been a good, detailed, point-by-point guide available.

It is the purpose of this book to fill this need. There is renewed interest in the Hudson. People are again beginning to travel upon it, as well as along the roads that follow its banks. This book describes the river and shorelines point by point, with historical background. Emphasis is upon points as seen from the water. Inland points of interest are also covered in self-guiding road routes along either shore. These road routes take in all major scenic and historical attractions and also follow some intriguing and picturesque by-ways. For good measure, there are descriptions of the views along the railroad routes on either shore.

Arthur G. Adams

It is the intention of both the author and the publisher to keep this reference book permanently in print. Therefore, occasional reprintings are anticipated. As we wish to make this publication as accurate, up-to-date, and useful as possible, we invite our readers to send us any corrections of fact or news of changes. Appropriate documentation will be appreciated. You may send this information, or any other communication, to either:

Arthur G. Adams
116 Deerfield Terrace
Mahwah, New Jersey 07430-2825
Telephone: 201-825-0743

or

Loomis Mayer
Fordham University Press
University Box L
Bronx, New York 10458-5172
Telephone: 718-817-4788
Fax: 718-817-4785

How to Use This Guidebook

Measurement System

All distances in this guidebook are measured in land miles using a decimal system of notation carried generally to the tenth of the mile but occasionally to the hundredth of the mile, where features crowd close upon one another (Examples: 1.00 = 1 mile; 1.40 = 1⁴/₁₀ mile; 2.45 = 2⁴/₁₀ and ⁵/₁₀₀ miles, etc.) The ¹/₁₀-mile readings are fairly accurate, but the ¹/₁₀₀ readings are "by convention," meaning that the distances are not to be taken literally, but only to differentiate from other very nearby features, such as several houses next door to one another, or sharp bends in a road only a few feet apart.

Water measurements were obtained from marking large-scale United States Coast and Geodetic Survey navigation charts. The distance from the base point is measured along the main steamboat channel, which is not necessarily in midstream. Points on the shore are measured by dropping a line perpendicular to the direction of the steamboat channel at the nearest point. Therefore, if one is traveling upstream, a feature designated for a stated river mileage will be 90° either to right or left, designated always as east or west. Distances and directions are often deceiving on bodies of water such as the Tappan Zee or Newburgh or Haverstraw Bay, and often the steamboat channel is not running parallel to the shoreline. Therefore, one should use the simple rule of first looking directly ahead up the channel, and then at right angles right or left to find a place listed at a specific distance.

Road distances were measured (and checked at least twice in different vehicles) by odometer. Measurement is accurate within one tenth of a mile, but the readings in one hundredths are by convention. Frequently distances will vary with the distance being traveled in different directions. This can come about because of differences in distance at interchanges, cloverleafs, or traffic circles, and sometimes by the necessity of using alternate one-way streets or park drives. Weighted averages have been used where appropriate, our purpose being to simplify matters for the user of the guide.

Railroad mileages are those given in operating employees timetables and engineering charts, and these will sometimes vary slightly from published public timetables (which tend to round off distances to the nearest full mile from major terminals) and from actuality. These later variations have usually come about from minor changes in track alignment and are not of any real significance.

Calibration

This guide describes five possible routes for the tourist:

1. Directly up the main steamboat channel;
2. Along a selected scenic road route along the east shore;
3. Along a selected scenic road route along the west shore;
4. Along the West Shore Railroad (Delaware & Hudson Railroad further upstream, above Albany);
5. Along the Grand Central Terminal and Hudson Divisions of the former New York Central Railroad from Manhattan to Albany, which is the route used by M.T.A. commuter and Amtrak long-haul trains.*

Consequently it has been necessary to correlate distances along the different possible routes. Distance along the river has been used as the standard, and every measurement along the road or rail routes has been assigned an equivalent river mileage, or E.R.M. number. Thus, when following any given land route, it will be possible to find what is on the opposite shore by looking up what features share the same E.R.M number.

In assigning distance designations along a river whose vestiges can be traced from the Adirondacks to Bermuda, and whose precise source is a point of some

---

*Recently Amtrak trains have been rerouted to Penn Station via the Manhattan West Side Line.

dispute, it was necessary to assign some baseline for measurement. I have chosen a line running exactly east and west along 42nd Street in Manhattan as the 0.00 base line. While it might be argued that Sandy Hook, the Narrows, or the Battery would be more suitable, I believe that the following practical reasons are sound. Most tourists of the Hudson River start their tour from this line, as Grand Central Terminal is located on 42nd Street, the Day Line operated from Pier 81 at the foot of West 41st Street, and the Circle Line Sightseeing Yachts operate from Pier 83 at the foot of West 43rd Street. Also the New Port Imperial Ferry operates from the Weehawken terminal site to West 38th Street. All of the latter are reached by the 42nd Street crosstown bus, which passes Grand Central terminal. The former West Shore Ferry terminal was at 42nd Street and the passenger rail terminal was almost directly across the river at Weehawken. The railroad measured all distances from Weehawken Terminal. Many motorists will wish to use the Lincoln Tunnel, which runs between 40th Street and Weehawken. The junction of Boulevard East and 48th Street in Weehawken has been chosen as the 0.00 point for the west side road route, as it is very close to the Weekawken Railroad and Ferry Terminal, which is reached by Pershing Avenue, an eastern extension of 48th Street. The streetcars also descended the Palisades at this point, and it is possible to drive from the Lincoln Tunnel Administration Building to this point, along the foot of Kings Bluff, via Baldwin Avenue and up the Palisades on Pershing Avenue, or along an upper route following the Boulevard East.

Concurrently on the east shore, the junction point of West 42nd Street Manhattan and Twelfth Avenue is directly on the scenic route and convenient to the Lincoln Tunnel and midtown Manhattan hotels.

Use of this baseline has necessitated use of negative numbers south of here as far as − 910.00 at Bermuda; − 21.5 at Rockaway Point, on the eastshore road route, and − 23.0 at the Twin Lights at Atlantic Highlands. For simplicity, point measurements on the scenic lower east and west side road routes are given in positive distances measured from Rockaway Point and from the Twin Lights (but the negative E.R.M. numbers are intercalated).

In several instances alternate routes are indicated, each utilizing the same base points. Because of one-way streets and prohibitions on left turns in many cases, and in order to obtain the most striking vantage points, it is highly recommended that the lower road routes be traversed from south to north—indeed, it is almost impossible to do otherwise in Brooklyn and lower Manhattan. To expedite this, an alternative express route has been shown from the 42nd Street baseline, south

to both Rockaway Point and the Twin Lights. These express routes also serve as interesting alternates and can be used in either direction.

Practical Notes

The Henry Hudson Drive, along the base of the Palisades, is closed during much of the winter and early spring because of danger from falling rocks, and at various other times for the exclusive use of bicycles, joggers, and pedestrians. Hook Mountain and Tallman Mountain Parks are closed in wintertime. Rockland Cemetery and Greenwood Cemetery are private property. One enters as a guest, and the sanctity of the grounds must be respected. Often it is not possible to follow the direct route through the United States Military Academy Grounds at West Point. The Storm King Highway makes an attractive alternate.

Amtrak Hudson River Line and Empire Service trains presently (since April 10, 1991) operate from Penn Station.

Various new ferry lines have been re-established from points in lower Manhattan to:

Weehawken
Hoboken
Newport City
Harborside Terminal
Paulus Hook   ⎫
Liberty State Park   ⎬   Jersey City
Port Liberté   ⎭
Bayonne
Elizabethport
Newark Airport
Brooklyn
Port Monmouth
Atlantic Highlands
Highlands
Long Branch

All provide excellent scenic views of the lower river and bays.

The M.T.A. operates local train service between Grand Central and New Haven which makes an easier connection for those connecting with their Hudson River Line. Remember that trains no longer stop in downtown Albany, but at the Albany-Rensselaer station, which is a short taxi ride across the river. There is no scheduled service on the West Shore Railroad. Excursions in the past have operated from the Erie-Lackawanna N.J. Transit Terminal at Hoboken and followed the Jersey

Junction Line to the former site of Weehawken Terminal. Tourists without an automobile can also avail themselves of New Jersey Transit-North Jersey Shore trains from Penn Station Manhattan to Perth Amboy, South Amboy, Mattawan, Middletown, Red Bank, and Long Branch. Several city subway lines operate to Coney Island, and some BMT Division trains operate across the Manhattan Bridge, offering good views. The IND Division trains also operate to Rockaway via Jamaica Bay. Staten Island Rapid Transit trains operate on an above-ground route from St. George Ferry Terminal to Tottenville. There is no longer any ferry service across to Perth Amboy.

Introduction to the Hudson River

The Hudson River
(A Trip Downstream)

The Hudson rises from numerous springs in the Adirondack region that feed three of its principal branches. Lake Tear of the Clouds, at an elevation of 4,322 feet on the southwestern slope of Mount Marcy, is generally recognized as the river's principal source.

Feldspar Brook is the outlet of Lake Tear of the Clouds. It in turn flows into what is today called the Opalescent River. This is called the Main Branch of the Hudson. The West Branch has its source in Hendrick Spring, northeast of Long Lake, whose waters flow north to the Saint Lawrence River. The waters of Hendrick Spring are first collected in Fountain Lake. The West Branch continues south through Round Pond and Catlin Lake and then turns east and flows through Rich Lake and Harris Lake to a junction with the Main Branch near Newcomb, which is about fifteen miles from Lake Tear of the Clouds. A third branch, known as the North Fork, has its head at Henderson Lake and joins the Opalescent River at the outlet of Sanford Lake to form the Main Branch.

From Newcomb, the Hudson flows generally southeast to the community of North River, receiving on the way the waters of the Boreas River. It then continues south to Riparius, below which it combines with Mill Creek, coming from the southwest. It continues south

SPRING ON MT. MARCY, alleged highest source of the Hudson River. Photo: Courtesy of Alfred V. S. Olcott, Jr.

past The Glen to Thurman Station, where it receives the waters of the Schroon River from the northeast. From here the river continues south, bowing slightly to the west, to take up the waters of Stony Creek. Below Luzerne it receives the waters of the Sacandaga River from the west. From here south to Corinth, at the head of Jesup's Great Falls, the river is broad and smooth-flowing. Below the falls the river starts to curve first east and then northeast, flowing through Lake Moreau and making several loops before arriving at the dam and falls at Glens Falls. It is crossed by the bridge of Routes 9 and 32 just below the dam and above the falls.

This is the northern terminus of our detailed descriptions. It is 115 miles from Lake Tear of the Clouds. Outside of the dam, the principal feature here is the Pruyn's Island log pool, just above it. In the years when the upper Hudson was an important logging river, logs were driven down and collected at the great boom here. Much of the water is diverted along power canals of the Finch Pruyn Co. on the north side of the falls, and frequently the flow of water over Glens Falls is disappointing, though there is sometimes a spectacular scene during the spring runoff. Before the reconstruction of the highway bridge, it was possible to descend a stairway from the midpoint of the bridge to one of the numerous rocky islands in the falls, where the cave that was described by James Fenimore Cooper in *The Last of the Mohicans* is located. All access to this famous cave is now closed off. To this point, the Hudson has flowed primarily through wilderness. From here to its mouth, it will flow through a densely populated region with intensively cultivated lands. It is a "river of history," and was for many years the nation's greatest commercial artery. It is with this lower portion that we shall concern ourselves.

The next seven miles to Fort Edward are full of rapids, most prominently Baker's Falls, just above the town of Hudson Falls. Its banks are crowded with industry, including pulp and paper mills and chemical plants. (The notorious PCBs came from a General Electric Co. plant at Hudson Falls.) At Fort Edward the river turns decisively south. It continues straight south for the next forty-four miles to the Government Lock at Troy, at the head of

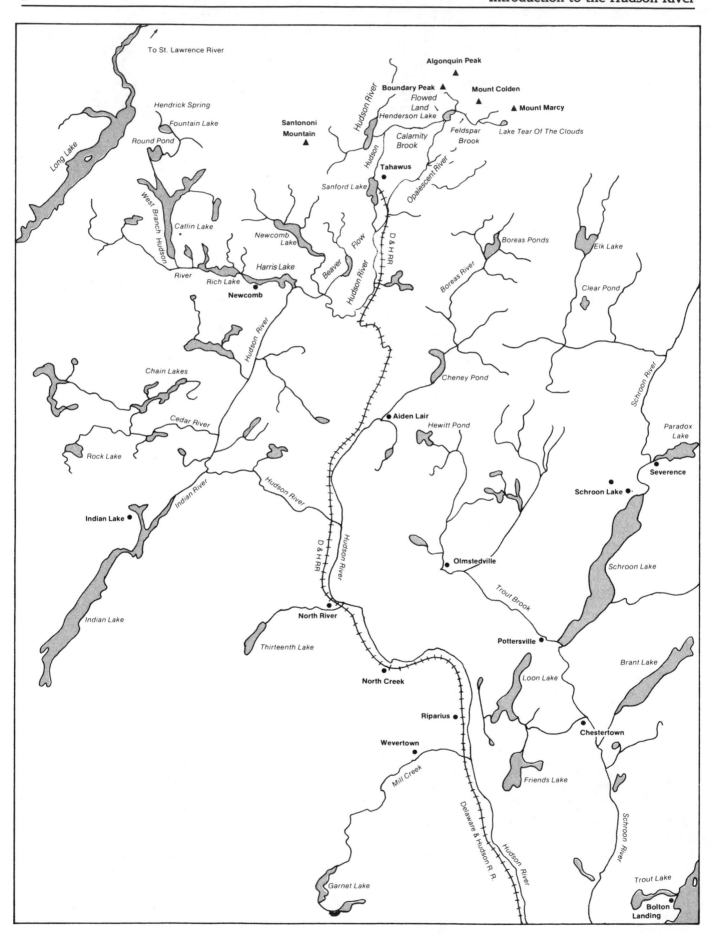

To St. Lawrence River

Hendrick Spring

Fountain Lake

Round Pond

Long Lake

West Branch Hudson River

Catlin Lake

Newcomb Lake

Harris Lake

Rich Lake

Newcomb

Santononi Mountain

Algonquin Peak

Boundary Peak

Mount Colden

Mount Marcy

Flowed Land

Henderson Lake

Calamity Brook

Feldspar Brook

Lake Tear Of The Clouds

Tahawus

Sanford Lake

Opalescent River

Hudson River

Hudson

Beaver Flow

Hudson River

D & H RR

Boreas Ponds

Elk Lake

Boreas River

Clear Pond

Chain Lakes

Cheney Pond

Cedar River

Rock Lake

Hudson River

Aiden Lair

Hewitt Pond

Schroon River

Paradox Lake

Severence

Schroon Lake

Indian River

Indian Lake

Olmstedville

Schroon Lake

D & H RR

Hudson River

Trout Brook

North River

Thirteenth Lake

Pottersville

Brant Lake

North Creek

Loon Lake

Riparius

Chestertown

Wevertown

Mill Creek

Friends Lake

Delaware & Hudson R. R.

Hudson River

Schroon River

Garnet Lake

Trout Lake

Bolton Landing

HEADWATERS OF THE HUDSON

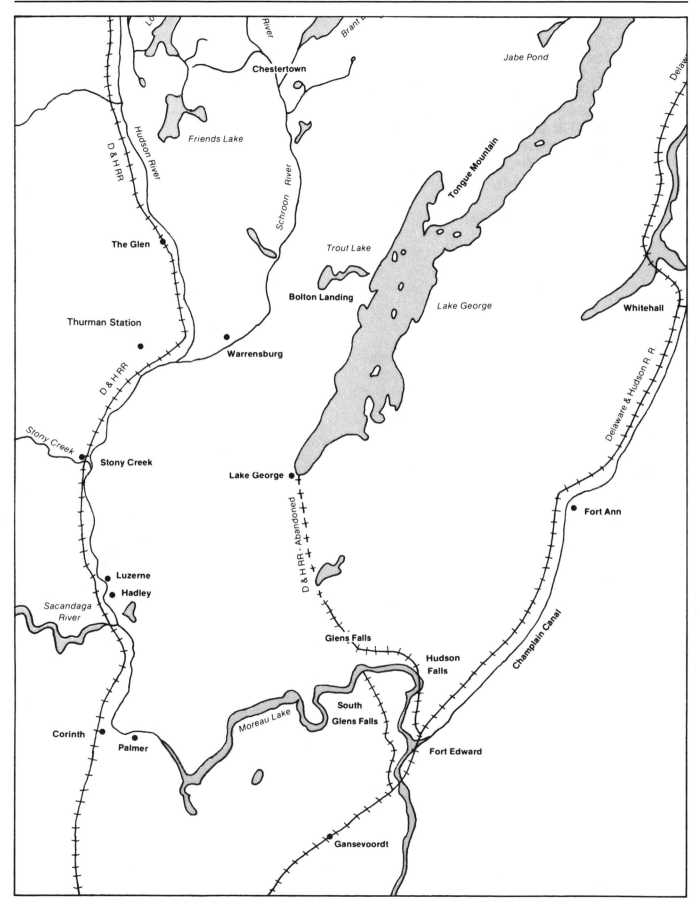

HEADWATERS OF THE HUDSON

SUMMIT OF MT. MARCY from Lake Tear of the Clouds. Photo: Courtesy of Alfred V. S. Olcott, Jr.

tidewater. This stretch passes through a broad pastoral valley given over largely to dairy farming in its upper reaches and industry in its nether ones. It is in fact a canalized river, forming a part of the Champlain Canal, and there are several dams and locks along the way. It flows past Fort Miller, Thomson, and Northumberland, where it receives the waters of the Batten Kill from the east. Next is Schuylerville, where it is fed by Fish Creek from the west. Along the right bank, running south from here to Bemis Heights, is the Saratoga Historic Battlefield Park, where a decisive battle of the American Revolution was fought in October of 1777, in which the British, under Gen. John Burgoyne, were forced to surrender to Gen. Horatio Gates.

Near Stillwater, the Hudson receives the waters of the Hoosic River from the east. Then it flows south past Mechanicville and Waterford, where the New York State Barge Canal (successor to the Erie Canal) enters from the west. Between here and the city of Cohoes, the Mohawk River—called the Maquaas Kill in early times—flows into the channel west of Van Schaick and Simmons Islands. On the east shore is the Lansingburgh section of Troy. South of Van Schaick Island is Green Island. The Federal Lock is located between Green Island and Troy, on the east bank.

From here to the south, the river is tidewater—salty as far north as Newburgh and brackish to just above Poughkeepsie, although, in some conditions, fresh water can be drawn from the Hudson at Chelsea, ten miles below. North of there, it is quite fresh.

From Troy, the river flows through broad flats, and until 1930, when extensive dykes were built, it was often quite shallow, with a shifting channel. The Berkshire Mountains are visible to the east, and the Helderbergs to the southwest.

Below Troy, the river flows almost directly southward, with only a few short and sharp bends near West Point and Bear Mountain in the Highlands. The principal

broader stretches, from north to south, are Newburgh Bay, Haverstraw Bay, and the Tappan Zee. From Athens, on the west bank, south to the Highlands just below Newburgh, the banks are precipitous. The river is paralleled to the east by the Taconic Range and to the west by the Catskill Mountains, and further south by the Shawangunk Mountains and Plattekill Hills. Below Newburgh, at Cornwall, the Hudson breaches the main chain of the Appalachian Mountains in what are called the Hudson Highlands. The range to the east is called the Taconics, and the one to the west the Ramapos. South of the Highlands, the east bank remains relatively high all the way to Manhattan Island. The west bank immediately below the Highlands is made up of a series of low mountains: Buckberg, Little Tor, and High Tor are the principal ones, below which are Hook, Clausland, Nebo, and Tallman mountains. The Palisades run from just below Sneden's Landing to Jersey City, with the highest portion extending from the New York–New Jersey state line to Weehawken. The Highlands served as an important military bulwark during the Revolution, and West Point remains an important military base to this day.

The Hudson River below the George Washington Bridge, connecting Manhattan to Fort Lee, is often called the North River, which was a name that was originally given to it to distinguish it from the East River and the South River (Delaware). At the foot of Manhattan Island, the river is joined by the East River and opens out into Upper New York Bay. To the southeast is Brooklyn, located on Long Island. To the west is a low peninsula terminating at Bergen Point in Bayonne and separating New York Bay from Newark Bay, which in turn has collected the waters of the Passaic and Hackensack river systems. Bayonne is separated from Staten Island by the Kill Van Kull, a tidal estuary that connects New York and Newark bays. Another estuary called the Arthur Kill separates Staten Island from the New Jersey mainland and connects Newark Bay with Raritan Bay. There are several high hills on Staten Island: Todt Hill, Grimes Hill, and Latourette, in the Dongan Hills.

The Upper Bay narrows between Brooklyn and Staten Island and is simply called the Narrows. It is spanned by the great Verrazano Narrows Bridge. Below the Narrows is Lower New York Bay. To the east is Coney Island, separated from Brooklyn by Gravesend Bay. To the west is Raritan Bay, at the mouth of New Jersey's greatest river, of the same name. To the south are Sandy Hook Bay and the Atlantic Highlands of New Jersey. The long sand spit of Sandy Hook extends almost four miles due north from Atlantic Highlands and separates the mouth of the Shrewsbury River and Sandy Hook Bay from the open sea. Here the Hudson seems finally to lose its identity. About 10,000 to 15,000 years ago, however, prior to the last glacial period, the entire land mass was

UNITED STATES COAST GUARD ICEBREAKING CUTTER *RARITAN* in typical Hudson River ice conditions in 1986. A channel is kept clear to the Port of Albany each winter. Photo: Walter Plankl.

higher, and the Hudson extended another 120 miles further out to sea. A submerged trough, known as the Hudson Canyon, has left vestiges half-way to Bermuda, another 330 miles beyond the continental shelf.

The principal tributaries on the west bank south of Albany are the Norman's Kill, Catskill Creek, Esopus Creek, Rondout Creek, Black Creek, Quassaic Creek, Moodna Creek, Popolopen Creek, Minisceongo Creek, and the Sparkill. The principal tributaries on the east side are Papscanee Creek, Moordener Kill, Vlockie Kill, Schodack Creek, Stockport Creek, Roeliffe Jansen Kill, Landsman Kill, Indian Creek, Wappinger's Creek, Fishkill Creek, Indian Brook, Annsville Creek (Peekskill Creek), Croton River, Pocantico River, and the Neperhan or Saw Mill River. The Spuyten Duyvil Creek, which separates Manhattan from the mainland to the north, is not, properly speaking, a tributary but rather a tidal estuary, as is also the East River. The East River and Spuyten Duyvil

Creek are connected by the Harlem River, which is another tidal estuary that separates Manhattan from the Bronx on the mainland.

The larger towns and cities past which the Hudson flows are Glens Falls, Hudson Falls, Fort Edward, Waterford, Cohoes, Troy, Albany, Rensselaer, Hudson, Catskill, Saugerties, Kingston, Poughkeepsie, Newburgh, Peekskill, Haverstraw, Nyack, Yonkers, New York City, Weehawken, Hoboken, Jersey City, and Bayonne.

The Hudson is actually a fjord or drowned river. Taking 42nd Street in Manhattan as a base line, we can consider that the Hudson has a length of 314 miles from Lake Tear of the Clouds to the north, and 580 miles to its last vestige in the Southwestern Canyon to the south, beyond the continental shelf, which is a total identity of 894 miles. The section of the river that most people think of is the 200 miles from Manhattan to Glens Falls. It is sometimes remarked that the Hudson is a very big river for its size. Taking this grand total length into consideration, we can understand why this is the case.

Journey to the Source
of the Hudson River
by Gretchen McHugh

Some say the Hudson River begins at perfectly-normal-looking Lake Henderson, a mere 1,800 feet above sea level in the Adirondacks. But for those of us under the river's spell, its real, or highest, source is a tiny, cloud-shrouded lake halfway up Mt. Marcy, New York's

highest peak. The Indians' romantic-sounding name for this body of water almost 4,500 feet above sea level is Lake Tear-of-the-Clouds.

And hereby beginneth a tale. You can drive to Henderson Lake, but you have to walk to Lake Tear.

I used the excuse of having to take a photograph of the Hudson's source for this book to make my first pilgrimage to Lake Tear. Three friends from Albany joined me, each with a reason for the climb. We'd all hiked in the Adirondacks' high-peak region, so we knew the requirements: sturdy boots with heavy soles, pack frames filled with necessities for three days, a topographical map showing the trails.

And courage. None of us was properly conditioned,

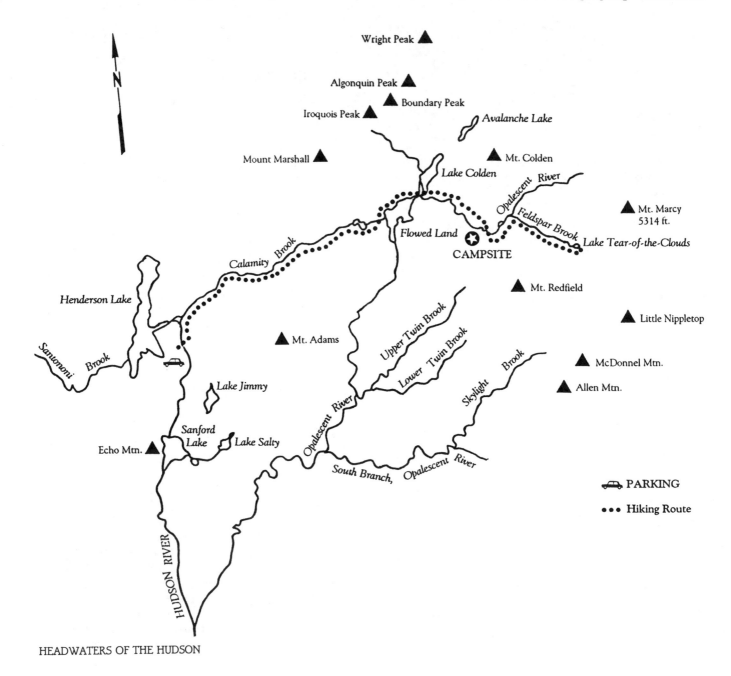

HEADWATERS OF THE HUDSON

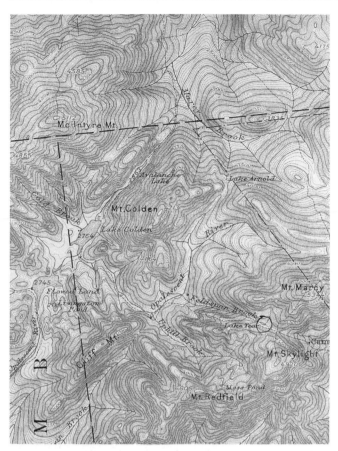

Topo map of Mt. Marcy Headwaters region.

and we would hike 2,500 feet uphill to the source of the Hudson, carrying our heavy packs the first 1,000 feet. At the end of our first day's hike, we aimed to make a base camp at the foot of Mt. Marcy, then climb to Lake Tear-of-the-Clouds the next day, and pack out the third day.

Calamity Brook

The high-peak region of the Adirondacks is laced with well-travelled foot trails kept up and marked by the New York Department of Environmental Conservation. No one I know has ever hiked them in a dry condition. I wrote in my notebook, "Trail was wet and muddy, rutted, rooty, rocky."

The first of three suspension bridges swayed madly when we crossed it, one at a time, urging our companions to heed the sign "Do not jiggle the bridge while someone else is on it," and trying hard not to giggle.

The hiker is a bundle of mixed exhilarations when crossing one of these foot bridges. First, of course, it's the Hudson you're crossing: coursing downhill eight miles from its source, the river, here called Calamity Brook, tears along under you singing gaily as it frolics over rocks and around corners. Then there is the physical thrill of

making sure to balance a heavy pack, hiking stick, and tripod well enough to get a good grip on the wire "handrail." The river is eight feet straight down.

Helping to make sure the trail doesn't dry out are more than a hundred tributaries to the three streams we followed—Calamity Brook, the Opalescent River, and Feldspar Brook. Each tributary adds its own song to the general theme. There is the roar of a torrent falling steeply over rocks, the quiet trickling of a rivulet on gravel, the spooky hum of a cascade gone suddenly underground. Sometimes the trail veers away from streams, leaving the only sounds to break the forest's quiet calls from chickadees or white-throated sparrows, or the sharp scolding of a squirrel.

"Some leaves falling. Some rain," say my notes. "Sometimes you can see mountains. The trail smells like Christmas, and occasionally of strawberries." It is a magical place.

Sharing Bread with Thelma

My hiking partner opened the door of the tent at our base camp on the second morning of the trip and cried, "My pack is gone!"

He had propped it against a tree just outside the tent, after covering it with a plastic bag to keep it dry. Whoever took the pack was a bold burglar, to lift it away just inches from the tent. We had not heard a sound. Five hikers came by, saw us puzzling over the theft, and told us that their 30 pounds of food, hung carefully in a tree to keep it safe from bears, had been stolen. The burglar had untied the rope and carted off the entire cache. They had had to abort their trip as a result.

We all commiserated. Our own food, tied between two trees, had escaped the felon, but Bob wanted his expensive pack back, and his spare glasses, compass, toothbrush, and commemorative bowie knife with personally-inscribed sheaf. We figured that some mad, impoverished hiker had lifted the pack and then filled it with our acquaintances' 30 pounds of provisions, giving himself a week of carefree fun at our expense.

Then the ranger showed up and restored our faith in human nature. The culprit, he told us, was most certainly Thelma, a black bear who made her living by lifting food from unwary, sleeping hikers. Bob then admitted to having left a loaf of brown bread with raisins in the side pocket. We fanned out and rescued the pack, which Thelma had carted 100 feet up the hillside. She had neatly ripped the bread out of the side pocket, leaving Bob's stuff strewn around. She also left an avocado he'd forgotten to put in the food cache, badly smushed. I added that to our lunch pack for the day.

Climb to Lake Tear

Thelma's escapade delayed the start of our final climb to Lake Tear. Meanwhile, I discovered a handkerchief belonging to my friend Tom Berry in my pack. An ecologian who heads the Riverdale Center for Religious Research, Tom published his book The Dream of the Earth last year. Sometimes when he comes to our house for dinner, he forgets his handkerchief. I had borrowed one of these as an all-purpose photographer's tool. Knowing Tom would understand the significance of such a ritual, I decided to baptize his handkerchief in the headwaters of the Hudson.

With hopes that it wouldn't rain too hard on us, and that the mist might even lift to give us a glimpse of the magical lake, we started climbing Mt. Marcy shortly before noon. We met two young climbers coming back from Marcy's summit as we crossed the Opalescent.

"Too foggy to see anything from the top," they panted. They seemed to have loped up the trail, and were fairly galloping back to their base camp, where Fettucini Alfredo awaited them, they informed us happily.

The trail steepened. The thick mist turned to thin rain. The mix of hardwoods and hemlock gave way to solid hemlock. The tops of the taller trees were eaten away, by

FELDSPAR BROOK drains Lake Tear of the Clouds and empties into Opalescent River. 1989. Photo: © Gretchen McHugh.

OPALESCENT RIVER is among the highest tributaries of the Hudson River. 1989. Photo: © Gretchen McHugh.

acid rain, we presumed, and gave the forest a spooky look.

At the junction of Feldspar Brook with the Opalescent, the brook could be seen tumbling down the steep slope of the mountain. We turned to follow it, in the home stretch now. The trail became nearly vertical in places, and consisted principally of rocks of every description, all slippery. We stopped talking and concentrated on climbing.

We met a small group of people who said it was impossible to see much of the lake through the mist. Then the last of their party, coming down a bit later, said he was writing a story on the Hudson for The Poughkeepsie Journal, and could he interview us. Why were we there? We answered his questions and sent him off, worrying about the long descent his party had before them. They hoped to reach the main trail head, nine miles down, before dark.

It was 3:30 when we reached the outflow of Lake Tear-of-the-Clouds. That was thrilling, but more thrilling was the prospect of lunch. We hurried along the shore of the lake for five minutes to the bog at its far tip, and hunkered down under the very wet sky for a repast of salami, cheese, crackers (Thelma had the bread), and bear-smushed avocado. This will be, I know, one of my all-time memorable meals.

Tom Berry's Magic

It was time for pictures. Because the wind blew precipitation straight into the lens, I focused with the filter on, then turned away, took it off, swung around and shot. The only thing was, I couldn't tell where the lake was, it was so misty. "Lake Tear, indeed," Bob sniffed.

Then it was time for ceremony. We traveled back to the outflow of the lake. I climbed out to a rock—it didn't matter that one foot slipped entirely into the water, since I was drenched already—and whipped Tom's handkerchief out of my pocket. After dipping it three times and wringing it out, I turned back to the lake for a last look.

The mist had lifted.

Revealed was a tiny, tear-shaped lake surrounded by fir trees. In the silence, it had the primeval, mysterious aspect that the Indians must have known. Its icy water, collected from springs even higher up the still-hidden Mt. Marcy, and from under the bog at its other end, would tumble down the mountain, join with salt water from the sea, and pass back and forth in front of our homes with the tides, sustaining creatures only dreamt of here.

I went back to the bog to shoot another roll of film, this time of the lake revealed.

It's a lot faster to descend a trail than to climb it, and we made base camp in about half the time of our climb. The next day, we would have emerged at the trail head, too, in less than half the time it took to come in. But the sun finally came out. We stopped to sun like seals on the rocks in Calamity Brook, enjoying another version of the wild Hudson's beauty, among mountain peaks where no cars will ever go.

This story was first published in *The Riverdale Press*.

In 1625, Johannes De Laet, in his *New World*, or *Description of West-India* (Amsterdam, n.d.), tells how the early Dutch explorers and settlers had divided the Hudson into "reaches." These are stretches of the river, all of which could be seen point to point, and on which sailing conditions were somewhat uniform. Their names remained in common use all through the age of sail and into the early steamboat days. They had fallen into such disuse, however, that when in 1975 we asked Capt.

LAKE TEAR OF THE CLOUDS (1989). Photo: © Gretchen McHugh.

William O. Benson (d1986) of Sleightsburg, a noted authority on steamboating who had been active on the river for forty-five years, to clarify a point, he wrote, "During my day on the Hudson the only reaches I ever heard older men speak about was 'Percey's Reach' between Hamburg and Hudson Lighthouse." This was not very helpful, for Captain Benson was not a young man, and the name Percey's Reach seems rather new and does not belong in the traditional canon—it is frankly apocryphal. The exact definition of the reaches is hard to relate to present-day place names; however, after much study of various authorities, I will venture the following breakdown:

1. The Great Chip Reach: The Palisades were known by the old Dutch settlers as the "Great Chip." This extended from Weehawken to the New Jersey–New York state line for about 18 miles.
2. Tappan Reach: Equivalent to the Tappan Zee. From state line to Verdrietege Hook (that is, Tedious Hook or Hook Mountain).
3. Haverstroo Reach: Equivalent to Haverstraw Bay. From Verdrietege Hook to within view of Pyngyp or Timp Mountain on the west side. The Old Dutch mariners used to change tack when they were within range of Pyngyp Mountain, and the booms of the sloops would sound a "ping" or "pyngyp" when they swung over. In modern parlance this would be from Hook Mountain to Stony Point.
4. Seylmakers' Reach, or Sailmakers' Reach: Stony Point to Peekskill.
5. Crescent Reach or Cook's Reach: A crescent-shaped stretch from Peekskill to Manitou through the Kittatinny Mountains or Highlands. The Indian name Kittatinny is no longer applied to the Highlands but is preserved in the name of the southern part of the Shawangunk Mountains in New Jersey. The Indians applied the name to the entire Ramapo and Highland Mountains.
6. Hoge's or High Reach: Manitou to Gee's Point, opposite Constitution Island at West Point.
7. Martyr's Reach: Also called Martelaire's Reach. Between Constitution Island, which the Dutch navigators called Martelaer's Island, and Storm King Mountain, which they called Klinkersberg. It is claimed that a French family named Martelaire lived on Constitution Island about 1720. A variation on this was Martyr's Reach. The word "martyr" as used in this connection signifies "contending" or "struggling," as vessels coming up the river with a fair wind would frequently find themselves, immediately after passing Constitution Island, struggling with the wind right ahead. Possibly it was an allusion to perilous sailing with downdrafts from the mountains and a rocky

shoreline. Vorsen or Foxes' Reach were still other names that were applied to Martyr's Reach between Constitution Island and Storm King Mountain.
8. Fisher's Reach: Storm King to Wappinger's Creek; includes Newburgh Bay.
9. Lange Rack or Long Reach: Wappinger's Creek to Crum Elbow and possibly as far north as Whiskey Point.
10. Vasterack or Vaste Reach: Whiskey Point to Athens. Refers to the great width of Hudson around Inbocht Bay. Rodger's Island was formerly called Vasterack Island.
11. Kleverack or Claverack: Clover Reach: Athens to Fourmile Point. This was also the name of Van Rensselaer's lower manor house near Hudson.
12. Backerack or Baker's Reach: Fourmile Point to Fordham Point.
13. Jan Playsier's Reach: Fordham Point to Hinnenhoeck (Nutten Hook).
14. Hart's or Hunter's Reach: Hinnenhoeck to Kinderhoeck (Nutten Hook to Stuyvesant).

Changes in the channel, islands, and shorelines, as well as of place names, make it extremely difficult to determine accurately the limits of these reaches, yet they remain a pleasant subject for speculation.

The Hudson was known by many names, and the Indians had various ones. To the Iroquois it was the Cohohatatia, or "place to catch shad." To the Lenapes and Mahicans it was the Muhheakunnuk or Mahican-nittuck, or "great waters constantly in motion" (referring to the tides), which came to have the secondary meaning, "place where the Mahicans dwell." The Mahicans also called it the Shatamuc, Shattemuc, or Shattemuck. In 1524 Verrazano called it simply the Grande Rivière, or Angoleme. In 1525 Gomez dubbed it the Rio San Antonio, and it was later called the Rio de Gomez, or Guamas. About 1569 it appears on several maps as the Norumbeza. In 1609 Henry Hudson called it the Manhattes, from the tribe at its mouth. In 1611 the Dutch named it the Mauritius River or Mauritz Rivier, or River of the Prince, after Prince Maurice of Nassau. In 1625 Johannes DeLaet called it the Rio de Montaigne or River of the Mountains. The Dutch also used the name the Nassau River, also in honor of the prince, but soon came to call it simply the Groote or Great River. The English called it variously the Manhattan River, Great River, River of the Mountains, North River (Noordt in Dutch), or, most commonly, Hudson's River, which name ultimately remained, shortened to simply Hudson River.

Tides are felt as far north as the Federal Lock at Troy, where the tide rises six inches and at Albany, where it rises two feet. Highest tides occur when the moon is in the southeast or the northwest. A log would take almost a year to float from Troy to the sea. Normally, it would be carried eight miles downstream and seven and a half miles back upriver each day. Some authorities give the figures twelve miles down and seven to nine miles up per day; much depends upon the rate of stream flow. Wallace Bruce has said that a drop of water would take three weeks to get from Albany to New York City.

The salt line or wedge is normally at Newburgh, but in recent years it has ranged as far north as Poughkeepsie in 1966, and as far south as the Battery in New York in 1968. Normally, salt is $^{30}/_{1000}$ parts at New York City. The river is most salty from late summer to early spring, when runoff from the mountains commences. It is saltier at lower depths.

There are considerable shoals at Edgewater that are caused by a process called flocculation, wherein salinity causes silt in suspension to precipitate to the extent of 4,000,000 cubic yards per year. To remove this material and keep the channels to sufficient depth for shipping, the United States Army Corps of Engineers maintains large dredges. One of these, the *Driftmaster*, which is based at Gravesend Bay, removes 24,000 tons each year. The great new dredge *Essayons* went into operation in 1950. It is 525 feet long and cost $11,500,000. Two huge pumps attached to long tubes can pick up 8,000 cubic yards per shipload. The material is then taken six and a half miles southeast of Ambrose Light and dumped through twenty-four trap doors in the bottoms of the hoppers. The river is navigable by large river steamers to Troy, and by ocean-going vessels to the Port of Albany. "The Hudson Tide," a short article from the 1901 edition of Wallace Bruce's *Hudson by Daylight* is of interest:

The tide in the Hudson River is the continuation of the tidewave, which comes up from the ocean through New York Bay and is carried by its own momentum one hundred and sixty miles, growing, of course, constantly smaller, until it is finally stopped by the dam at Troy. The crest of this wave, or top high water is ten hours going from New York to Troy. A steamer employing the same time (ten hours) for the journey and starting at high water in New York, would carry a flood tide and highest water all the way and have an up-river current of about three miles an hour helping her. On the other hand, the same steamer starting six hours later, or at low tide, would have dead low water and an ebb-tide current of about three miles against her the entire way. The average rise and fall of the tides in New York is five and one-half feet, and in Albany two feet.

The flood tide may carry salt water, under the most favorable circumstances, so that it can be detected at Poughkeepsie, but ordinarily the water is fresh at Newburgh.

To those who have not studied the tides the following paragraphs will also be of interest.

The tides are the semi-diurnal oscillations of the waters of the ocean, caused by the attraction of the moon and sun.

The influence of the moon's attraction is the preponderating one in the tide-rising force, while that of the sun is about two-fifths as much as that of the moon. The tides therefore follow the motion of the moon, and the average interval between the times of high water is the half length of the lunar day, or about twelve hours and twenty-five minutes.

The tide-waves always travel west. When the configuration of the coast line drives it into a corner, as in the Bay of Fundy, or the mouth of the Severn, the tides rise to very great heights—fifty, seventy-five, or even one hundred feet. The lowest regular tides are on the islands in mid-ocean.

(Bruce, *Hudson by Daylight*,
New York: Bryant Literary Union, 1901, p. 306.)

Geology of the Hudson

In addition to various geological references scattered through these pages, the following facts from the *American Geological Railway Guide*, by James Macfarlane, quoted in Bruce's *Hudson by Daylight*, (pp. 307–309), will be of interest.

The State of New York is to the geologist what the Holy Land is to the Christian, and the works of her Palaeontologist are the Old Testament Scriptures of the science. It is a Laurentian, Cambrian, Silurian and Devonian State, containing all the groups and all the formations of these long ages, beautifully developed in belts running nearly across the State in an east and west direction, lying undisturbed as originally laid down.

The rock of New York Island is gneiss, except a portion of the north end, which is limestone. The south portion is covered with deep alluvial deposits, which in some places are more than 100 feet in depth. The natural outcroppings of the gneiss appeared on the surface about 16th street, on the east side of the city, and run diagonally across to 31st street on 10th avenue. North of this, much of the surface was naked rock. It contains a large proportion of mica, a small proportion of quartz and still less feldspar but generally an abundance of iron pyrites in very minute crystals, which, on exposure, are decomposed. In consequence of these ingredients it soon disintegrates on exposure, rendering it unfit for the purpose of building. The erection of a great city for which this island furnishes a noble site, has very greatly changed its natural condition. The geological age of the

New York gneiss is undoubtedly very old, not the Laurentian or oldest, nor the Huronian, but it belongs to the third or White Mountain series, named by Dr. Hunt the Montalban. It is the same range which is the basis rock of nearly all the great cities of the Atlantic coast. It crosses New Jersey where it is turned to clay, until it appears under Trenton, and it extends to Philadelphia, Baltimore, Washington and Richmond, Va., and probably Boston, Massachusetts, is founded on this same formation.

On the opposite side of the river may here be seen for many miles the Palisades, a long, rough mountain ridge close to the water's edge. Its upper half is a perpendicular precipice of bare rock of a columnar structure from 100 to 200 feet in height, the whole height of the mountain being generally from 400 to 600 feet, and the highest point in the range opposite Sing Sing 800 feet above the Hudson, and known as the High Torn [sic]. The width of the mountain is from a half mile to a mile and a half, the western slope being quite gentle. In length it extends from Bergen Point below Jersey City to Haverstraw, and then westward in all 48 miles, the middle portion being merely a low ridge. The lower half of the ridge on the river side is a sloping mound of detritus, of loose stones, which has accumulated at the base of the cliff, being derived from its weathered and wasted surface. This

talus and the summit of the mountain are covered with trees, with the bare rocky precipice called the Palisades between, and many fine country residences may be seen on the level summit, from which are beautiful views of the river, the harbor and City of New York. Viewed from the railroad or from a steamboat on the river this lofty mural precipice with its huge weathered masses of upright columns of bare rock, presenting a long, straight unbroken ridge overlooking the beautiful Hudson River, is certainly extremely picturesque. Thousands of travelers gaze at it daily without knowing what it is. This entire ridge consists of no other rock than trap traversing the Triassic formation in a huge vertical dike. The red sandstone formation of New Jersey is intersected by numerous dikes of this kind, but this is much the finest. The materials of this mountain have undoubtedly burst through a great rent or fissure in the strata, overflowing while in a melted or plastic condition the red sandstone, not with the violence of a volcano, for the adjoining strata are but little disturbed in position, although often greatly altered by the heat, but forced up very slowly and gradually and probably under pressure. Subsequent denudation has laid bare the part of the mountain now exposed along the river. The rock is columnar basalt, sometimes called greenstone, and is solid, not stratified like water-formed rocks, but cracked in cooling and of a

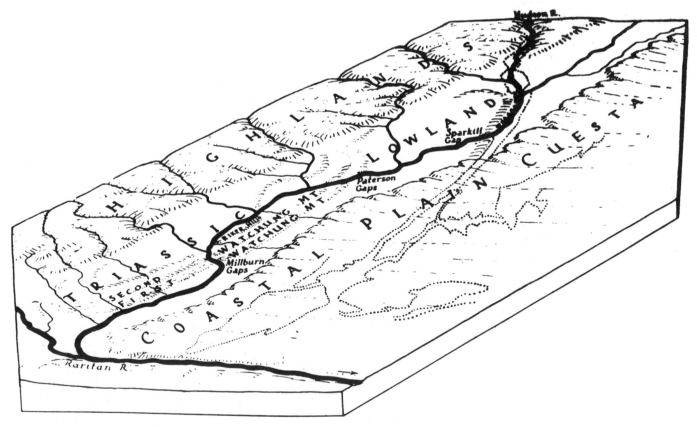

Hypothetical course of the Hudson River in Schooley Time according to the theory of superimposed subsequent drainage. (*The Geology of the Hudson River*—A. Van Santvoord Olcott, Jr.)

crystalline structure. Here is a remarkable but not uncommon instance of a great geological blank. On the east side of this river the formations belong to the first or oldest series of Primary or Crystalline rocks, while on the west side they are all Triassic, the intermediate Cambrian, Silurian, Devonian and Carboniferous formation being wanting. This state of things continues all along the Atlantic coast to Georgia, the Cretaceous or Jurassic taking the place of the Triassic farther south.

Montrose to Cornwall. This celebrated passage of the Hudson through the Highlands, is a gorge nearly 20 miles long from 3 miles south of Peekskill to Fishkill, and is worn out of the Laurentian rocks far below mean tide water. The hills on its sides rise in some instances as much as 1800 feet, and in many places the walls are very precipitous. The rock is gneiss, of a kind that is not easily disintegrated or eroded, nor is there any evidence of any convulsive movement. It is clearly a case of erosion, but not by the present river, which has no fall, for tide water extends 100 miles up the river beyond the Highlands. This therefore was probably a work mainly performed in some past period—when the continent was at a higher level. Most likely it is a valley of great antiquity.

Opposite Fishkill is Newburgh, which is in the great valley of Lower Silurian or Cambrian limestone and slate. North of that, on the west side of the river, the formations occur in their usual order, their outcrops running northeast and southwest. On the N.Y.C. & H.R.R.R., on the east side, the same valley crosses, and the slates from Fishkill to Rhinebeck are about the same place in the series; but being destitute of fossils and very much faulted, tilted and disturbed, their precise geology is uncertain. See the exposures in the cuts at Poughkeepsie. The high ground to the east is commonly called the Quebec group.

A series of great dislocations with upthrows on the east side traverse eastern North America from Canada to Alabama. One of these great faults has been traced from near the mouth of the St. Lawrence River keeping mostly under the water up to Quebec just north of the fortress, thence by a gently curving line to Lake Champlain or through Western Vermont across Washington County, N.Y. to near Albany. It crosses the river near Rhinebeck 15 miles north of Poughkeepsie and continues on southward into New Jersey and runs into another series of faults probably of a later date, which extends as far as Alabama. It brings up the rocks of the so-called Quebec group on the east side of the fracture to the level of the Hudson River and Trenton.

Catskill Mountains. For many miles on this railroad are beautiful views of the Catskill Mountains, 3,800 feet high, several miles distant on the opposite or west side of the river, and which furnish the name for the Catskill formation. The wide valley between them and the river is composed of Chemung, Hamilton, Lower Helderberg and Hudson River. The geology on the east or railroad side is entirely different.

Albany. The clay beds at Albany are more than 100 feet thick, and between that city and Schenectady they are underlaid by a bed of sand that is in some places more than 50 feet thick. There is an old glacial clay and boulder drift below the gravel at Albany, but Professor Hall says it is not the estuary stratified clay.

The foregoing article can be very briefly summed up in the following simple statements:

(1) The Palisades are composed of metamorphic basalt or diabases. (2) The Highlands are composed primarily of granite and gneiss with various intrusions. (3) From Beacon to Albany the composition is of shales and limestones, or mainly sedimentary rock, with contorted strata resulting from the Taconic revolution in the late Ordovician period.

AGE	YEARS AGO	PRINCIPAL ACTION
Pre-Cambrian Period		
Archean	more than 1,000 million	Grenville sediments layed down
Algonkian	1,000 million	" " " "
Paleozoic Period		
Cambro-Ordovician	500 million	Ramapo fault formed
Late Ordovician	400 million	Taconic revolution
Silurian Devonian	300 million	Storm King and Fishkill faults
Permian	200 million	" " " " "
Post-Paleozoic Period		
Triassic	175 million	Lava intrusions: Palisades formed
Cretaceous	100 million	
Tertiary	35 million	General rising of area
Quarternary	1 or 2 million	Ice ages: area depressed. Hudson filled with silt, and sea intrudes

It has been stated that the Hudson is actually a fjord. The only other true fjord on the North American east coast is Somes Sound on Mount Desert Island in Maine.

Basal Biology of the Hudson

The Hudson River is a particularly rich estuary in respect to the many varieties of life its waters sustain. In order to properly appreciate this richness it is appropriate to quote here in their entirety two short articles by Dennis Mildner of the Hudson River National Estuarine Research Reserve, which administers and monitors 4,000 acres of tidal brackish and freshwater marshes, intertidal flats, swamps, river islands and wooded uplands. The Reserve was established by the *Coastal Zone Management Act of 1972* to set aside in perpetuity representative tidal wetlands as long-term field laboratories for estuarine research and education. The Hudson River Reserve was established in 1982 as a network of four distinct estuarine sites—Piermont Marsh, Iona Island, Tivoli Bays, and the Stockport Flats. Their field station is located at Bard College, Annandale, N.Y. 12504. Various field programs are conducted and information on current programs may be obtained by telephoning them at 914-758-5193.

Mr. Mildner writes:

The Hudson's floating gardens—its vast, aquatic meadows of microscopic plants called phytoplankton—are impossible to see with the unaided eye, but not easily dismissed because they are the very foundation of all aquatic life in the estuary.

Phytoplankton provide the link between the sun's energy and myriad life forms that reside in the Hudson's waters. These plants, through the process of photosynthesis, are the primary producers, converting the sun's light energy into organic matter, the chemical energy that fuels the river's life processes.

The solar energy locked up by these microscopic plants is transferred throughout the estuary via the food chain. The plants are fed upon by herbivorous zooplankton—plant-eating microscopic animals—and certain species of fish such as menhaden, herring and anchovies. These fish and zooplankton in turn are fed upon by even larger fish and aquatic invertebrates. Eventually the sun's light energy is passed along to life forms at the top of this energy pyramid, to species like bald eagles, ospreys, and man.

These free-floating plants begin tremendous blooms of production in the spring when environmental conditions—light, temperature, and available nutrients—are just right. These blooms, occurring in the portion of the water column where light penetrates, may contain one or

several species, again depending on environmental conditions.

There are four basic groups of these microscopic plants—the diatoms, green algae, blue-green algae, and dinoflagellates—although the latter might more accurately be described as aquatic organisms, since dinoflagellates exhibit characteristics of both plants and animals. The diatoms that prevail in the estuarine environment have siliceous walls, and may be known in the form of diatomaceous earth or as a component of the white cliffs of Dover.

The green algae are characterized by an abundance of the green pigment chlorophyll and in the simplest form are single oval cells. Some species also exist as filamentous and non-filamentous colonies. The blue-green algae are not necessarily blue-green and lack the complicated cell structure of the green algae. Nor are they especially common as a free-floating plankton, but tend to appear as broad mats covering flats exposed at low tide.

A second, and probably dominant energy pathway in the river—the detrital food chain—based on decomposition of organic materials, is one that is less popularly understood, and one with its foundation in the tidal marshes of the Hudson.

Detritus is made up of the decaying remains of dead plants. The source of this plant material in the Hudson estuary is the tons of cordgrass, cattail, and other emergent plant species produced by the river's tidal marshes. These particles are colonized by bacteria and fungi that provide nutrition to the detrivores, the organisms that ingest the detritus.

The Hudson supports a wide variety of detritus-consuming animal species, among them worms, crustaceans such as shrimp and crabs, insect larvae, and the young and adults of fish species such as bay anchovies, killifishes, silversides and menhaden. These species represent the first-order consumers and form the link between the detritus produced in the tidal marshes and the higher consumers-predaceous fish, birds and man.

The first-order consumption process is simple. Bacteria and fungi, the agents of decomposition, break down fragments of dead plants into smaller particles. These particles are ingested by the detrivores, the bacterial and fungal colonies removed as nutritious food, then the remainder passed out as yet smaller particles of detritus.

Bacteria and fungi attack these, which are again consumed by detritivores, but this time by different species that ingest smaller particles. Eventually, most of the solar energy harvested by the living green plants has been harnessed, for use throughout the estuarine system, by the bacterial and fungal agents.

It is not difficult to appreciate the vital role the Hudson estuary's tidal marshes play in the ecology of the river.

The decomposing detritus produced by these emergent marshes join the floating gardens of phytoplankton in harnessing the sun's energy and supplying the fuel that keeps the river as biologically productive as it is.

Pollution

For many years raw sewage and industrial wastes have been poured into the Hudson. In recent years treatment plants have been built and marine life such as crabs is returning to the river. The water is noticeably clearer. However, marine boring worms cannot live in New York Harbor. Possibly the most polluted points on the river are the Albany Pool and the raw sewage outlets in Manhattan. Among the worst are those at 59th Street and 96th Street. The 172d Street outlet, known as the Medical Center Sewer, has a coliform bacteria count of 10M/100ML and the 72nd Street outlet spouts straight, untreated sewage. Manhattan sewage takes six days to reach the sea and sometimes penetrates upriver to the Tappan Zee. A large new treatment plant is presently under construction on filled land between 137th and 145th Streets. In 1977, 175 million gallons of raw sewage per day were poured into the Hudson at Manhattan.

Other sources of pollution are piers where garbage scows are loaded (to be emptied just outside the lower bay) and various industrial sources including refined syrups and sugar wastes at Yonkers, paint from the General Motors plant at Tarrytown, oil from the railroad yard at Harmon, and wastes from the paper mills near Glens Falls.

Sometimes the river is afflicted by the red tide, which consists of microscopic dinoflagellates called Glenodinium and Prorocentrum. These cause the eyes, nose, ears, and throat to burn. As this penetrates along the shoreline it is a menace to Long Island and Jersey Shore resorts. However, the local variety is not the same as the more virulent Florida variety, which is called Gymnodinium Breves.

So-called thermal pollution is not, strictly speaking, pollution. It is simply the raising of the water temperature above normal, caused by outflow of cooling water from power plants. This causes significant changes in marine life.

In addition to the organic polluting agents described above, the Hudson has suffered significant contamination from inorganic and man-made substances. Metals such as aluminum, barium, chromium, lead, and manganase enter the Hudson from runoff and discharges, and are sometimes found at detectable levels in ambient water quality testing in the lower Hudson. Studies show that between 1970 and 1984 lead accounted for 58.5% of violations of Department of Environmental Conservation (DEC) wa-

ter quality standards for the protection of human and aquatic life, cadmium for 6.1%, and mercury for 4.7%, out of a total 2,123 water quality violations in the Hudson River. Among the most common contaminants the following health effects are observed:

Arsenic—Cancer-related. Damage to digestive tract, kidneys, liver, lungs, skin.
Cadmium—High blood pressure, kidney disease, emphysema, testicular cancer.
Chromium—Cancer-related.
Lead—High blood pressure, decreased immunity, nervous system damage, mental retardation.
Mercury—Damage to nervous system.
Oil—Toxic compounds, cancer-related.
CHPs—Cancer-related.
PCBs—Cancer-related. Damage to liver, kidneys.

NOTE: CHPS:—Chlorinated hydrocarbon pesticides, including Endosulfan, Endrin, Kelthane, Lindane, Methocyclor, and Toxaphene.
PCBs:—Polychlorinated biphenyls. Used in transformers and other heavy electrical equipment.

Petroleum companies and other industries along the Hudson River are point dischargers of oil and grease, the most frequently discharged pollutants of the river, accounting for 25% of the toxic discharges identified in a 1986 study. In 1982, 771,007 pounds of oil and grease were discharged and urban runoff is estimated to have contributed 9,262,620 pounds in the same year. Spills and accidents, common on a river so heavily trafficked as the Hudson, number in the hundreds each year, and pose unpredictable and unexpected threats. In 1987 an oil tanker crashed in the Bear Mountain area, releasing 102,000 gallons of unleaded gasoline in the river. Unlike oil, which can be actively cleaned up, gasoline removal is dependent upon vaporization, which depends largely upon weather conditions. Other petroleum derivitive pollutants include such toxics as toluene, benzene, and xylene.

The Hudson River has been characterized as one of the country's worst cases of PCB contamination. Over a period of thirty years, General Electric facilities, located forty miles north of the Troy dam, discharged approximately 1.2 million pounds of PCBs into the Hudson.

PCBs, a class of stable and long-lasting organic chemicals, are damaging to the liver and kidneys and are a suspected human carcinogen. They pose the greatest danger when accumulated in the body through fish consumption, but consuming them in drinking water may also cause health problems; blood samples taken from people exposed to PCBs in drinking water for over twenty years showed abnormalities in liver function, glucose metabolism, and red blood cell reproduction. The presence of PCB's in the Hudson, from samples taken at Chelsea, show fourteen parts per trillion. US Environmental Protection Agency standard maximum allowable concentration is ten parts per trillion.

There are also agricultural runoffs such as phosphates and salt from road and highway sanding. The heaviest cadmium pollution is in Cold Spring Bay from a former battery factory. It settles to the bottom and is found in such bottom-feeding fish and crustaceans as eels and crabs, and it is now unsafe to eat these taken from the Hudson because of the danger of cadmium buildup.

Heaviest known PCB concentrations are above the Troy dam, in the fresh water section, immediately below Albany, and in the Weehawken Channel, where it has apparently precipitated upon meeting denser salinity. There is a continuing fight to get Federal funds for an adequate cleanup. However, some specialists think it better not to stir up the settled contaminants and there is much controversy on the subject.

Population and Developmental Pressures

Although the New York City Metropolitan Area, including Northern New Jersey, and the Albany Capital Area have long been among the most densely populated parts of the entire world, the Hudson River Valley, north of New York City, has managed until quite recently to remain rather rural—particularly above the Troy-Waterford area. However, in recent years the area has been subject to strong developmental pressures between New York and Albany on both banks. This is proving detrimental to agriculture and the environmental purity and aesthetics of the Valley. There is constant pressure for the placing of power plants, pumped storage power facilities, and coal ports along both banks. Spreading suburban development is eating up farmlands and open areas and requiring construction of additional roads and highways, and putting strains on fresh water supplies and creating additional sewage and garbage disposal problems. The most scenic open areas along the river are being gobbled up for developments—often high-density and high-rise. The scenic quality of the region is under great attack. In 1963 Consolidated Edison Company proposed construction of a massive pumped storage power facility at Storm King Mountain in the Highlands. This would have defaced one of the most impressive scenic wonders of the region and opposition was immediately organized with the formation of the Scenic Hudson Preservation Conference. Scenic Hudson went to court to block the project and won an environmental landmark decision when the Supreme Court granted it status under law to speak for the environment. Much of the present-day environ-

mental movement can thank Scenic Hudson's efforts for obtaining court standing for the public in protecting the environment. Other issues, such as the atomic power plant at Indian Point and efforts to build high-rise apartments along the Yonkers waterfront, have been major issues confronted by Scenic Hudson. At the present time New York City is seeking to make major withdrawals of drinking water from the Hudson rather than enacting strong conservation measures such as metering and fixing leaks, or going further afield, such as to Canada, for drinking water. Taking of fresh water from the Hudson would upset the entire ecological balance of the river and is strongly opposed by most environmentalists. Furthermore, the water of the Central Hudson is not particularly attractive for drinking in light of the pollution and possible health hazards.

Environmental Organizations

The pollution of the water and developmental pressures have led to the creation of a great many organizations with the basic purpose of preserving and restoring the purity and natural beauty of the Hudson River Valley. Here is a partial list of the most well-known ones:

Scenic Hudson, Inc.
9 Vassar Street
Poughkeepsie, NY 12601   914-473-4440

As described in the above article, Scenic Hudson was formed in 1963 initially to combat the Storm King Pumped Storage project, and celebrated its 25th anniversary in 1988 with a special chartered train trip along the Hudson. While almost all the distinguished citizens of the Hudson Valley have at some time been active with Scenic Hudson, the lady who really got the project going is Frances Reese (Mrs. Willis Reese), who is now Chairman Emeritus. In 1987 the New York State Bar Association awarded her a special award for "significant contribution to the development of environmental law." This was the first time this prestigious award was given to a non-lawyer. Ironically, the presentation was made by G. S. Peter Bergen, the attorney who had represented Consolidated Edison in the landmark Storm King case. Later the organization continued under the very able leadership of Alexander Zagoreos as Chairman and Klara B. Sauer as Executive Director. Scenic Hudson remains deeply involved in many environmental issues and often seeks court standing. It is a membership organization and members enjoy receiving their excellent quarterly newspaper, *Scenic Hudson News*—the source of many facts stated in the preceding articles.

Hudson River Sloop Clearwater, Inc.
112 Market Street
Poughkeepsie, NY 12601   914-454-7673

In 1966 folk-singer-poet Pete Seeger, long a "fan" of the Hudson River, became very concerned about the encroaching pollution and environmental degradation of the Hudson. He had always been a great admirer of pictures of the graceful sloops that had once sailed the Hudson in great numbers. He conceived the idea that the recreation of a full-sized classic Hudson River sloop would help to draw the public's attention to the plight of the river. Within three years he had succeeded in forming an organization and launching the *Sloop Clearwater* in 1969. Since then she has sailed the river regularly, carrying cargoes of pumpkins and Christmas trees to New York City and countless thousands of students and environmentalists as passengers to get a closer and slower look at the river than is readily available elsewhere these days. The organization remains active in environmental advocacy and education and runs the annual Hudson River Revival Festival, a mecca for all river lovers. Clearwater is a volunteer membership organization and among the privileges of membership is the right to serve as crew aboard the *Clearwater*.

Ferry Sloops, Inc.
P. O. Box 534
Hastings-on-Hudson, NY 10706   914-478-1557

This is a more intimate version of Clearwater and is actively engaged with sloop clubs along the Hudson from New York Harbor to Albany and with environmental education, sail-training programs, and small boat construction and maintenance. Their vessels are the *Woody Guthrie* and *Sojourner Truth*. Ferry Sloops is also a major sponsor of the annual June Great Hudson Revival Festival and is generally involved in many river activities, and sponsors an annual Hudson River Photography Competition and salon. Their President is Robert Walters. Membership is a good way to gain close touch with the river.

Hudson River Foundation for Science
    and Environmental Research, Inc.
122 East 42nd Street
Suite 1901
New York, NY 10168   212-949-0028

The Hudson River Foundation supports scientific and public policy research, environmental education programs, and physical improvement projects on the Hudson River. The Foundation was established in 1981

SLOOP CLEARWATER off Piermont, with Tappan Zee Bridge in background. Photo: © Gretchen McHugh.

FERRY SLOOP *SOJOURNER TRUTH* off Hastings-on-Hudson with the Palisades in background. Photo: © Gretchen McHugh.

under the terms of an agreement among environmental groups, government regulatory agencies, and utility companies seeking a constructive resolution of a long series of legal battles over the environmental impacts of power plants on the Hudson River. The Foundation's principal endowment is the Hudson River Fund, which was created in recognition of the critical need for a new, independent institution to sponsor scientific and educational programs that would contribute to the understanding of public policy issues related to the river's ecological system. In 1985 the Foundation established the Hudson River Improvement Fund, a separate endowment supporting projects that stress the enhancement of public use and enjoyment of the river's natural, scenic, and cultural resources. Much of the funding came from General Electric Company and Consolidated Edison. The Foundation is a good source of information on all scientific matters concerning the Hudson. The Chairman is William S. Beinecke and Clay Hiles is Executive Director.

Hudson River Greenway Council
2 City Square
Albany, NY 12207   518-426-0667

As the river has become cleaner and as the Valley's unique cultural and historic resources have become more widely recognized, more and more people and businesses want to share in our quality of life. The pressure to develop the Valley's resources has become intense. The creation of a Greenway would help to ensure that the very qualities that attracted residents and visitors alike to the Valley are not lost.

In his 1988 State of the State address, Governor Mario Cuomo called for the creation of a Hudson River Greenway that would "link the extraordinary environmental, cultural and historic heritage of the Hudson River Valley—in the process, fostering a sense of regional identity while protecting a Greenway of national and international significance."

The New York State Legislature agreed with the Governor and formed the Hudson River Valley Greenway Council. "A Greenway," the legislators said, "is an approach that can link and relate the Hudson River with the parks and protected areas, including historic sites, wetlands, wildlife habitats, urban cultural parks and scenic settings, within the Hudson River Valley for the beneficial enjoyment of the public." The Legislature directed the Council to formulate a plan for the creation of a Greenway by November of 1990. The study area runs from the Battery to just north of Troy and east to the Taconic Parkway and west to the Shawangunk Mountains and northern Catskills. The Council is charged to do the following:

1. Make a brief and general historical overview regarding the lands considered for inclusion in the Greenway.
2. Make an inventory of all public lands and protected private land eligible for conservation easements in the study area.
3. Make recommendations for utilizing the state designated urban cultural parks in the Valley as a focal point for visitation, planning, and development in appropriate urban settings within the Valley.
4. Make recommendations including draft legislation for designation of the lands and waters that will make up the proposed Greenway and guidelines for future designations.
5. Make recommendations for heritage or historical trails in urban settings as part of the Greenway.
6. Make suggestions for overall management guidelines for preservation and beneficial use of the Greenway.
7. Make recommendations for actions to rehabilitate facilities and natural areas.
8. Make recommendations for heritage and environmental education.
9. Prepare a financial statement estimating the necessary costs and potential funding sources to carry out recommendations in the study over a five-year period.

Much impetus for the Greenway legislation came from Ulster County State Assemblyman Maurice D. Hinchey. The Chairman of the Council is Barnabas McHenry and David S. Sampson is Executive Director. As this book is being revised, hearings are being held throughout the Hudson Valley and testimony and suggestions solicited from the public on all aspects of the Greenway project. (Final report issued February 1991.)

Hudson River National Estuarine Research Reserve
Bard College Field Station
Annandale, NY 12504   914-758-5193

This organization is described in detail in the preceding article. Please see above. The Reserve Educator is Dennis Mildner and the Reserve Manager is Betsy Blair. They should be contacted for more information on field programs, teacher workshops, curriculum guides, and research opportunities at any of its four tidal wetland sites.

Friends of the Shawangunks, Inc.
P. O. Box 177
Accord, NY 12404   914-687-9051

The Friends was formed to oppose out-of-scale resort development of the scenic Shawangunk Mountains on the west bank of the Hudson and to undertake preservation and conservation of other wild lands along the Shawangunk Ridge. They were largely instrumental in creation of the Minnewaska State Park and were generally active in obtaining scenic easements and acquiring land through their subsidiary Shawangunk Conservancy. For further information contact Chairman Keith LaBudde.

Mohonk Consultations on the Earth's Ecosystems
Mohonk Mountain House
New Paltz, NY 12561   914-255-1000

While largely involved with international ecological issues, the Mohonk Consultations has a Hudson River Basin Program and serves as an information clearinghouse for ecological information in the Hudson Valley. Whatever your interest, they can refer you to the proper organization. Chairman is Albert Keith Smiley, Jr.

Whether it is at the local, the national, or the international level, Mohonk Consultations considers that its role will be to provide a forum for groups with varied viewpoints to discover common ground for needed action on the basis of a common aim—to maintain planet Earth as a livable home for all people and for other life.

The Hudson Valley: A Very Special Place

Excerpts from remarks by Robert Muller, Assistant Secretary General of the United Nations:

Well, to go from the global to the local, I have the definite impression that there could be something very great evolving here in the Hudson Valley. We are here in Mohonk, a very beautiful place, a very unique place. Throughout history, it was always river valleys which have been at the origin of great civilizations, and I have the feeling that something is happening along this great river that emerges in New York because at the end of it you have the United Nations, which is now the convergence of thinking of the entire planet. Along with a city which is definitely the center of the world in terms of thinking, power, and commerce and trade—and that is really a lot—and there you have the United Nations.

And as you go up this valley, you have some phenomena which I consider very important. For example, Westchester County has now become the greatest concentration of multinational business in the world. It has become a completely different center. Also you have the natural beauty of the valley. It is also a valley where great writers were born, at the beginning of America. Washington Irving is an example. It was a civilizing valley for America itself, and I think it could become again a civilizing valley and river for the world. And also take the universities. Consider how many universities you have now in Westchester County, as well as all those extending from the top to the bottom of this river. I will say it is also prophetic that just here, across the river, you have one of the greatest cosmic thinkers ever who is buried there, and very few people know that he is buried there. I refer to the famous Jesuit philosopher, Teilhard de Chardin.

I think that one could revive this valley as a particular center of world consciousness of arts and of poetry. You had beautiful painters in this valley. You have composers; you have writers. I think a river, a great river, has this characteristic. It symbolizes the flow of life. I think the flow of life is always inspiring. I remember that Secretary General U Thant lived in Riverdale and he once said to me, "I need to live on the bank of a river." He had to see the sunrise and the sunset on the river; he couldn't live elsewhere. And there are many people who have the same feeling because a river gives you a sense of freedom. There is at least one area where there is no building. Others like the oceans, for exactly the same reason. So I believe that with very little doing—with very little doing indeed—you could revive the forces which have accumulated in this valley.

I believe that here we have a global conjunction of

elements that would help give the world a new myth, as you call it, or a new vision, or a new hope, and I know that you have been thinking of this here at Lake Mohonk. You have been concerned first with the environment of the Hudson Valley, but very soon you discovered that the problem was infinitely broader and you came to the conclusion that you may perhaps offer your facilities here for something which is truly universal and world-wide. I believe that you have the ingredients. You have the participants right here because in the United Nations and in New York City and in the intellectual community of this valley, you have probably the highest concentration of brain power and knowledge in the entire world. I think this region is very unique in terms of world knowledge; so, I think whatever you may plan in this direction, I would welcome it very much.

Rockland County Conservation Association, Inc.
P. O. Box 213
Pomona, NY 10970   914-354-1071

This is one of the early pioneer environmental organizations in the Hudson Valley. Founded in 1930, it has actively fought to preserve the Palisades and Highlands of the Hudson and is now working toward the preservation of the large Sterling Forest tract. This local group has been in the forefront of such issues as recycling of solid wastes and preservation of wetlands and has exerted an influence out of all proportion to its size. Their excellent newsletter is a benefit of membership and of interest to all residents along the Southern Hudson Valley interested in environmental matters. Chairman is Jeanne Nelson and President Betty Hedges. Their list of directors and honorary directors includes such famous pioneers in the movement as Eleanor Burlingham, Lois Jessup, and Zipporah Fleisher.

The Hudson Waterfront Museum
P. O. Box 1602
West New York, NJ 07093   201-662-1229

Founded in 1985 by tug and barge dwellers, this museum is now located on their barge at the foot of Newark Street in Hoboken, immediately north of the Erie-Lackawanna Terminal.

After twenty years of stagnation, vast areas of the waterfront have now become available for redevelopment. As plans are being made to revitalize New Jersey's waterfront with multi-billion-dollar commercial and residential development, the Hudson Waterfront Museum believes an essential element of appreciating this progress is to offer the people of today an understanding of the people of our past who struggled, persevered, and succeeded in making this progress possible. The museum seeks to preserve some of the flavor of an earlier life along the Hudson River when railroads and shipping were the key to local economies, shad fishing flourished, and steamboat trips provided recreation and transportation. Through a series of floating, pier-side, and land-based spaces, the museum will serve local families, school groups, tourists, and the people whose livelihoods have been tied to waterfront-related industries. It will provide a reference to work, life, and transportation along the Hudson during its commercial heyday. This museum sponsors a varied program giving a good insight into many aspects of environmental concern and river history. President is Captain Anthony Rondinone. Executive Director is David Sharps.

South Street Seaport Museum
South Street
New York, NY 10038   212-669-9400

Although not an "environmental organization," the various programs of South Street impinge upon such concerns and they have undertaken major efforts in preservation of regional maritime history and several visits are essential for an understanding of the Hudson River. Their curator of ships and marine historian, Norman Brouwer, is one of the greatest present-day experts on Hudson River navigation and shipping.

There are innumerable other organizations and museums concerned with various aspects of the ecology such as the Hudson River Fisherman's Association, whose President, Robert Boyle, has written the definitive books on the biology of the Hudson; the Hudson River Maritime Museum at Kingston, whose shop built the *Riverkeeper*, the environmental patrol-boat manned by John Cronin; the actual "Riverkeeper," who works for the Hudson River Foundation and the Fisherman's Association; and Wave Hill in Riverdale (Bronx), located in a beautiful riverfront mansion with extensive arboretum and gardens, and which also undertakes an extensive Hudson River environmental education program under the able direction of Uta Gore. There is a great deal of excellent work being done on the subject of restoring and enhancing the environment of the Hudson Valley by many smaller organizations and individuals. However, since the list would be very long, and the above-listed organizations can provide almost any needed information, we will now proceed to our actual point-by-point survey of significant points along the river.

1

From the Ocean's Depths to New York Bay

—580.00 **The Abyssal Plain.** The last significant vestiges of the Hudson Canyon are discernable in the debris at the bottom of the Continental Shelf, more than halfway to Bermuda.

—241.00 **Rim of the Continental Shelf—the Hudson Canyon.** Eleven thousand years ago, before the last glacier retreated, the continental shelf was above sea level. Before entering the Atlantic, the Hudson River then ran 120 miles farther southeast than it does at present. The old channel is now smothered with silt and is not discernable northwest of Mud Hole, near Ambrose Light. From Ambrose Light (about 26 miles from shore) to about 131 miles from shore, the Hudson Channel is noticeably deeper than the rest of the ocean floor. From 131 miles to the rim of the continental shelf (and beyond) it is much deeper and is known as the Hudson Canyon. At the rim of the continental shelf the bottom of the canyon is 1½ miles below the surface of the water and five miles wide.

With today's concerns about the ecological systems of the Huson estuary, adequate navigational clearances to accommodate the new tankers and cargo vessels, and safe locations for depositing dredging spoils without damage to the environment, there is a renewed interest in the offshore canyon.

In 1930, the United States Coast and Geodetic Survey made echo soundings and found the canyon to be 9,000 feet deep near the rim of the shelf and 15,000 feet deep 160 miles beyond the shelf, just before it disappeared in the abyssal plain sloping toward Bermuda. This canyon was formed by turbidity currents. Sediments disclose shallow water shells. Dr. William Beebe studied the canyon's life forms in the 1920s and described his findings in *Arcturus Adventure.* He called the canyon the "Hudson Gorge." It was his opinion that "long after the last animal and insect from the heart of Africa and New Guinea has been collected and named, and the north and south poles have been crossed and recrossed with tourist planes, strange fish and other creatures will still be brought to light within a day's motor boat run of New York City" (William Beebe, *Report on the Eleventh Expedition of the Department of Tropical Re-*

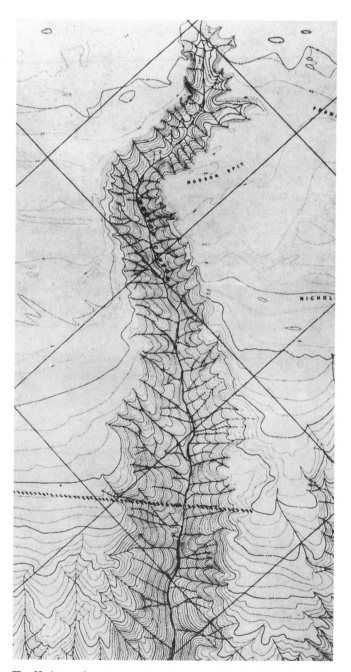

The Hudson submarine canyon as contoured by A. C. Veatch on the basis of echo sounding by the U. S. Coast and Geodetic Survey. Streams are shown and contours drawn in accordance with Veatch's belief that submarine canyons represent submerged subaërial valleys. Courtesy of the Geological Society of America.

21

search of the New York Zoological Society, New York, 1928).

Among these strange fish are Bathytractes drakei, Haplophryme hudsonius, Dragonfish (Chanliodus sloanei), and Stylophthamus, which has a bill like a duck, eyes on the tops of long stalks, and a long, threadlike body lined with what looks like scores of glowing portholes.

– **131.00 Inland End of the Hudson Canyon--Outer End of the Hudson Channel.** The submerged Hudson Channel is here nearly five miles wide and two-thirds of a mile deeper than the ocean floor.

– **116.00 The Gully.** A deep hole in the former delta--now submerged.

– **26.00 The Inland End of Submerged Hudson Channel.** Here the submerged channel is only twenty feet deeper than the ocean floor.

– **26.00 The Dumping Grounds.** In this vicinity are various dumping grounds for garbage and other types of waste, brought out to sea in scows. Among them are: Doorknob Grounds, filled with rubbish from the Manhattan East Side Urban Renewal; Subway Grounds, filled with material excavated in building the Eighth Avenue Subway; New or Seagull Grounds, where organic garbage from New York City is dumped (scavenging gulls hover over this area). Acid Grounds is to the east of the main shipping channel. Here are dumped sulphuric acid and iron sulphate wastes from the National Lead Company plant at Sayreville, New Jersey. Special dumping barges now make two trips a day. Formerly the wastes were dumped directly into the Raritan River. Acids have killed all marine life near the Acid Grounds. Certain of the other grounds attract fish, however.

– **25.75 The Ambrose Light Tower** (40°27' N × 73° 49' W), east of the Channel. This tower marks the outer end of Ambrose Channel, which is the main approach to New York Harbor. Built in 1966, it has two decks and a helicopter pad and is permanently manned. Built in 190 feet of water, it rises 75 feet above the surface. The tower replaces lightships that were previously anchored here. The original red-painted lightship (now on display at the South Street Seaport Museum), built in 1907 at Camden, New Jersey, by the New York Shipbuilding Company, measured 135 by 29 feet, was designated Light No. 87 of the former United States Lighthouse Service. It was manned by civilians. The service was later taken over by the United States Coast Guard, which operates the present light tower. The original lightship was in use here until 1932 and subsequently was

AMBROSE CHANNEL LIGHTSHIP. Floating lighthouses such as this were used from 1907 until 1966, when a permanent light tower was built at 40°27' N × 73°49' W, 15 miles southeast of the Narrows, to mark the east side of the outer end of Ambrose Channel, the main approach to New York Harbor. There were a number of such vessels, measuring 135 ft by 29 ft and painted red. They were designated Light No. 87 by the United States Lighthouse Service and manned by civilians. They were later taken over by the United States Coast Guard. The original lightship is on display at the South Street Seaport in Manhattan. Author's collection, from an old postcard.

stationed at other stations until retirement in recent years. Other similar lightships served the Ambrose Station until erection of the present tower in 1966.

From here to just below Sneden's Landing, eighteen miles north of Forty-second Street, Manhattan, where the New Jersey–New York state line is located, all the land to the west of the channel belongs to New Jersey, except for Swinburne, Hoffman, Staten, Liberty, and Ellis Islands, which belong to the State of New York. All land on the east side belongs to New York. North of Sneden's Landing, which is in New York State, the Hudson flows entirely within New York State. North of Paulus Hook, the middle of the river serves as the state line. The present boundaries were established in 1719 and were formally ratified in 1772.

New York State

New York State is the thirtieth in size and second in population of all the states in the United States. Its area is 49,576 square miles, its 1990 population, 17,990,455. Its capital is Albany, and its largest city is New York, with a population of 7,322,564. The eleventh state to be admitted to the union, its total road and highway mileage is 107,743, and its total railroad mileage is 5,578.

New Jersey

New Jersey is the forty-sixth state in size and ninth in population. It is the most densely populated state in the

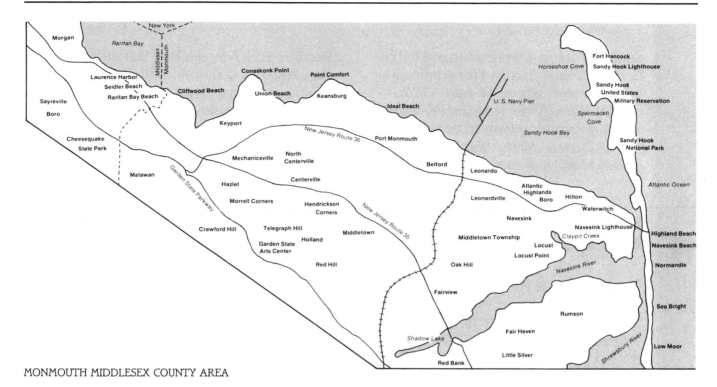

MONMOUTH MIDDLESEX COUNTY AREA

Union with 933.7 persons per square mile. Area: 7,836 square miles. Population in 1990: 7,730,188. Capital: Trenton. Largest city: Newark. Third state to be admitted to the Union. Total road and highway mileage: 32,704. Total railroad mileage: 1,838.

On 24 June 1664 the land now known as New Jersey was sold by the Duke of York (later King James II of England) to John, Lord Berkeley and Sir George Carteret. Originally called Scheyichbi by the Indians, it was renamed New Caesarea or New Jersey in honor of Sir George Carteret, who had been Governor of the Isle of Jersey. The first governor of New Jersey was Philip Carteret. The Proprietors divided the new colony into East Jersey and West Jersey on 1 July 1676. Berkeley sold his undivided share of West Jersey in 1674 to John Fenwick in trust for Edward Byllinge, a Quaker. Byllinge assigned his share to William Penn and other Quakers. Carteret's widow sold her share in East Jersey to William Penn and eleven others in 1680. Ultimately there were twenty-four proprietors. From 1688 till 1689 the Jerseys were annexed to the Colony of New England for administrative purposes, but on 17 April 1702, under Queen Anne, New Jersey became a royal province. However, between 1702 and 1738 New Jersey shared the same governor as New York.

Monmouth County New Jersey

The land on the New Jersey shore, adjacent to the lower New York Bay and Raritan Bay and including Sandy Hook, is designated Monmouth County. On 17 April 1665, Governor Richard Nicolls of New York granted a patent to a group of Englishmen who were mainly Baptists and Quakers from Rhode Island and the settlement of Gravesend in New York. This patent embraced all of present Monmouth County and large parts of Ocean and Middlesex Counties. Principal early settlements were between the Shrewsbury and Navesink rivers and at Middletown, on the south shore of Raritan Bay. Population 552,124.

Long Island

The land on the east of New York Bay is a large, fish-shaped island, 118 miles long, known as Long Island. It was called Paumanok by the Indians. It varies from twelve to twenty miles in width and extends east-northeast from the mouth of the Hudson River. It is separated from Staten Island by the Narrows, and from Manhattan and the Bronx by the East River. It is separated from the New York mainland and Connecticut by Long Island Sound, to the north. To the south is the Atlantic Ocean. The two "tail fins" are at the east end. The more northerly and shorter one is known as Orient Point, and the longer southern one is Montauk Point. Between these points, from west to east, are Great Peconic Bay, Little Peconic Bay, Noyack Bay, Gardiners Bay, Napeague Bay, and Block Island Sound. Islands in these bays, from west to east, are Shelter Island, Ram Island, and Gardiners Island.

The north shore is hilly and strewn with boulders. A glacial terminal moraine runs the length of the island. The central section is flat and sandy with pine growth predominant. The southern portion is low and sandy. There are long and narrow barrier reef islands along the southern shore, separated from the main island by the broad, shallow Jamaica Bay, Zacks Bay, Great South Bay, Moriches Bay, and Shinnecock Bay.

The island was first settled by the Dutch in 1636. Present population is about five million. The western end belongs to New York City, the borough of Brooklyn (Kings County), and the Borough of Queens (Queens County). East of Queens is Nassau County, and Suffolk County is at the eastern end of the island. The eastern end of the island is largely devoted to agriculture, resorts, and oyster fishing. Whaling was formerly important; many early settlers came from New England and Nantucket. Much of the eastern end remains rural. Famous resort towns include Southampton, East Hampton, and Amagansett. The central portion is devoted to suburban homes, light industry, aviation plants, and test airfields. Jones Beach is a large south shore resort for day-trippers that is located on a barrier island. Fire Island, to the east, caters to a more Bohemian element. Many wealthy society people have estates along the scenic north shore. The western end is more industrialized and has many row houses and apartment houses in Queens and Brooklyn. LaGuardia and Kennedy International (formerly Idlewild) airports are in Queens County. The island was also known as Nassau Island in early times. It is served by the New York City subway system and lines of the Long Island Rail Road. There are ferry steamers from Port Jefferson to Bridgeport, Connecticut, and from Orient Point to New London, Connecticut. Long Island belongs entirely to New York State.

Lower New York Bay

Lower New York Bay is an arm of the Atlantic Ocean that is enclosed by the shores of northeastern New Jersey, Staten Island, and Long Island. It is separated from the open sea by Sandy Hook Bar, which runs six miles between Sandy Hook and Rockaway Point along the southeastern edge of the bay. The bar is breached by Ambrose Channel, opened in 1907 and named for Dr. John Wolfe Ambrose, Irish physician and engineer. It is 45 feet deep and 2,000 feet wide. The western portion is also known as Raritan Bay. Tributaries are, clockwise from Sandy Hook, the Shrewsbury–Navesink rivers, Raritan River, Arthur Kill (separating Staten Island from mainland New Jersey), and the Narrows (separating Staten Island from Long Island), which connect with Upper New York Bay. Van Der Donck's map of New Netherlands calls it Port May, or Godyns Bay. See James

Fenimore Cooper's *Water Witch* and James Kirke Paulding's *New Mirror For Travellers,* for excellent descriptions (quoted in the author's anthology: *The Hudson River in Literature.* New York: Fordham University Press, 1988).

– **23.00 The Highlands of the Navesink and Twin Lights.** *The Neversink Highlands hold a position of honor among the American hills. They stand near the principal portal of the continent—the first land to greet the curious eyes of the stranger and to cheer the heart of the returning wanderer. The beauty of these wooded heights, the charming villas that stud their sides, the grace of their undulating lines, give to the traveller prompt assurance that the country he visits is not only blessed with rare natural beauty, but that art and culture have suitably adorned it. The delight with which the wearied ocean-voyager greets the shores that first rise upon the horizon has often been described; but, when these shores have a rare sylvan beauty that opens hour by hour to view as the vessel draws near—when, instead of frowning rocks or barren sands, he beholds noble hills clothed to their brows with green forests, fields and*

WEST TOWER OF TWIN LIGHTHOUSES at Atlantic Highlands. The tower is 50 ft high and built of red sandstone. Photo: Alfred H. Marks.

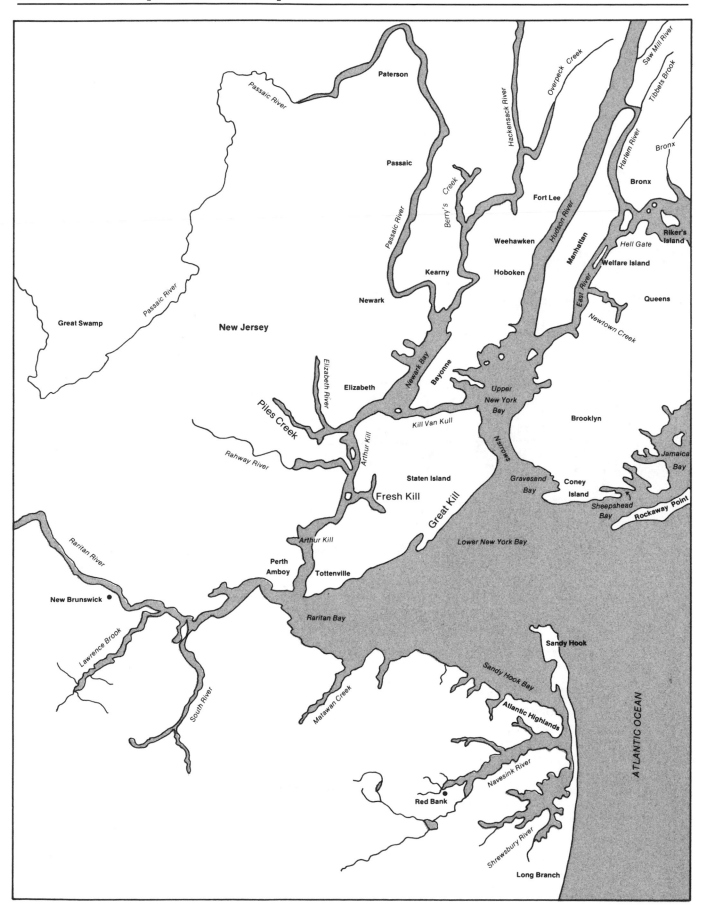

NEW YORK HARBOR AND ADJACENT WATERS

BEACON HILL, ATLANTIC HIGHLANDS with Twin Lighthouses. Entrance to the Shrewsbury River and neck of Sandy Hook, with tracks of former Southern Railroad of New Jersey, are in foreground. Beacon Hill has an elevation of 266 ft. The present twin lights were built in 1862. Author's collection.

meadows basking with summer beauty in the sun, cottages nestling amid shrubbery, and spires lifting above clustering treetops—the picture possesses a charm which only he who first beholds it can fully realize. It is such a green paradise that the Neversink Hills offer to the gaze of every ocean-wanderer who enters the harbor of New York. These highlands are situated in New Jersey, extending several miles along the coast in a southerly direction. At their feet flows the Shrewsbury River—beyond the river stretches a narrow strip of sand, upon which the surf of the Atlantic ceaselessly beats. This strip or tongue of sand extends northerly into the sea, somewhat beyond the reach of the hills, which, suddenly trending westward, form, in connection with the Hook, what is known as Sandy-Hook Bay. The ship entering from the sea stretches past this point of sand, leaving the hills to the left—but from their receding forms the voyager soon turns to greet the rising shores of Staten Island.... The outer bay or Lower Bay, as it is commonly called, has upon its west side a deep estuary, between the New Jersey and Staten Island shores, known as Raritan Bay. Shrewsbury River, which is probably more an estuary than a river, enters the sea between Raritan Bay and the Hook.

This description, written in 1872 by O. B. Bunce for *Picturesque America*, edited by William Cullen Bryant (New York: D. Appleton, 1872, pp. 173–174) still holds true today. The highest of the elevations is Beacon Hill, which is 266 feet above sea level. This is the highest location along the Atlantic coastline south of Mount Desert Island in Maine immediately at the ocean's edge. Todt Hill on Staten Island (410 ft.), is one mile inland. There is considerable confusion about the proper name of these hills. Verrazano called them the Montagne di S. Polo. Often they are simply called the Atlantic Highlands. However, the name Atlantic Highlands more properly belongs to the small town at their feet on the south shore of Sandy Hook Bay. The name Navesink is in general use today among cartographers. Most Jerseyites simply refer to "the Highlands" (never meaning the

Highlands of the Hudson, which they inclusively call "Bear Mountain"). Even in 1872, there was much confusion, and we shall again quote Mr. Bunce:

In regard to the designation of these hills, there exists a fearful orthographical confusion. The word is sometimes spelled "Navasink," sometimes "Navisink," then again as "Nevisink," and lastly as "Neversink," as in Philip Freneau's poem "Neversink". The correct method can be determined only by a knowledge of its origin, and of this there appears to be some doubt. "Navasink" is supposed to be an Indian word, meaning "fishing-place," and, of course, applied to the river; but others claim that this is simply a common instance of a natural desire to find an aboriginal root for our nomenclature, and that the term is really "Neversink," having been bestowed by the sailors, as expressive of the long time which these hills remain in view to the outward voyager. There is more romance and originality in the Indian term, but, so far, the weight of authority does not appear to be in its favor.

We disagree with this last affirmation, having in mind the Neversink River in the Catskills, which is and was a fishing place par excellence, and whose name is of undoubted Indian derivation. Other Indian names such as Matawan, meaning "place of the beaver," are found both on the shores of Raritan Bay and along the mid-Hudson.

These Navesink Highlands offer fine views of the Atlantic, Sandy Hook, Long Island, New York Bay, Staten Island, and much of New Jersey, and, in clear weather, of Manhattan, the Verrazano-Narrows Bridge, and the Watchung Mountains of New Jersey. They are still "dotted with villas and cottages" and have many picturesque winding roads and small chapels and crossroad hamlets on the banks of the Navesink and Shrewsbury rivers. The peninsula between these two rivers is occupied mainly by large estates with beautiful landscaping and architecture. The bustling town of Red Bank, formerly an important point for shipping oysters to the New York market, is at the head of navigation on the Navesink River. Formerly served by steamboats from New York, it may be reached by N.J. Transit North Jersey Shore trains from Penn Station and Newark.

The most interesting feature of the Highlands of the Navesink is the historic Twin Lighthouse. This ridge, the highest point found on the shore of the Atlantic, emerged from the sea about 125 million years ago and resisted erosion because it was capped with ironized conglomerate stone. Beacon Hill and the rest of the ridge is an erosional remnant, or cuesta. Because of this advantageous elevation

near the entrance to New York Harbor, it was considered a suitable location for a major lighthouse, and as early as 1764 a beacon was erected here. This was replaced in 1828 by a double lighthouse, which served until construction of the present Twin Lights in 1862. The early lighthouses were lighted by tallow candles. After 1812 the Argand lamp was in general use until about 1852, when the Fresnel lens came into use. The Argand lamp, named for its inventor, the Swiss chemist Aimé Argand (1755–1803), made use of circular wicks that admitted air to the center of the flame and thereby increased the intensity of combustion. These lamps burned either spermaceti oil or gas and were the brightest lights known at the time. The Fresnel lens is named for its inventor, the Frenchman Augustin Jean Fresnel (1788–1827). It is a circular compound lens that polarizes light in the horizontal axis and can send beams a great distance. It has generally superseded the use of mirrors in lighthouses and for beacon lights. The United States Lighthouse Service (now incorporated into the Coast Guard) was organized in 1852, and this was the immediate impetus for the construction of the great new Twin Lights in 1862. Writing of these lights, in 1872, Mr. Bunce notes

We soon reach Beacon Hill, crowned by a double-towered lighthouse furnished with "Fresnel" lights of remarkable capacity. The square tower has the most powerful light on the coast, the rays of which reach a distance of thirty-five miles, or as far as the altitude of the tower lifts the horizon. This light gives the mariner the first intimation of his nearness to our shores, just as the green slopes of the hill it surmounts greet him with the first show of land. This magnificent light is of French construction, was exhibited and secured the prize at the great French exposition (Paris 1867), and was purchased by our government at a cost of thirty thousand dollars. The light in the corresponding tower was manufactured in imitation of it, and although upon the same principle, is scarcely so powerful. A visit to this lighthouse will repay us; the view from the tower is superb, and the magnificent lenses of the lamp are well worth our curious attention. The obliging lighthouse keeper will draw the curtain, and show, reflected upon the convex central crystal, an exquisite miniature of all the expanse of land and sea and sky—such a landscape as the most gifted painter would despair of being able to imitate.

The northwestern tower is octagonal, and the southeastern one is square; each is 50 feet high. They are constructed of red sandstone and linked by a gabled central pavilion, forming a total frontage of 300 feet.

The entire structure is crenellated. The towers and facade are of rusticated sandstone, but the back is built of red brick. Since World War II, the lights have been superseded by radar and are not operational. The Twin Lights are now a museum. Visitors may climb the octagonal tower. This museum is maintained by the Navesink Twin Lights Historical Society and is open from Memorial Day to Labor Day. Also on view are the first United States Life Saving Station of 1842 (moved here from another location) and Marconi's radio tower, from which he made the first successful transatlantic radio transmission in 1907.

— **21.50 Sandy Hook (W).** Sandy Hook is a long, low, and narrow strip of sandy land, about five miles in length, extending north by northwest from the mouth of the Shrewsbury River east of Beacon Hill. It separates the Atlantic Ocean on the east from Sandy Hook Bay on the west. It is the southern cape of Raritan Bay. While now a peninsula, it has been an island or barrier reef at various times in the fairly recent past. Originally, the Shrewsbury and Navesink Rivers each emptied directly into the Atlantic farther south, near Rumson. In 1778 an inlet was cut through by the sea during a gale, but this was closed again in 1800. Another was cut in 1830, of such size that steamboats passed through, but this was closed by 1866. At present, the shoreline is continuous and unbroken from Shark River inlet to the tip of Sandy Hook, which is about 13 miles. The Navesink River empties into the Shrewsbury River east of Rumson, and the Shrewsbury flows north to empty into Sandy Hook Bay (part of Raritan Bay) inside Sandy Hook at the foot of the Highlands.

This long and strongly curved hook was built up by currents in Sandy Hook Bay in stages that have resulted in coves on the inland side. A seawall has been built along the ocean side to prevent future erosion. A government bulletin notes that

Technically, Sandy Hook is a compound, complex, recurved barrier sand spit. It was formed from a series of currents eroding both the ocean and bay shore-lines. For nearly 10,000 years these currents have continually worked on changing the Sandy Hook Shoreline. The currents create a constantly changing beach area by removing sand from the south end of the hook and transporting it northward. This sand is deposited at the northern tip of Sandy Hook where it widens and elongates the Hook.... The waves generally strike the shoreline from the southeast. This produces a deflected runoff of water toward the north. This littoral current transports sand northward and has led to the present spit formation.

In geological terms a spit which curves toward the mainland is called a hook. This particular formation has grown over 7,000 feet since 1764, and because of this constant growth, the Sandy Hook Channel, just off the northern tip of the Hook, must be dredged periodically in order to keep the channel open to ship traffic.
(Sandy Hook Visitors Information, National Park Service. Washington: US Government Printing Office, 1978)

Construction of the present seawall from Sea Bright to the Hook was started after a violent storm in 1914. The work was completed in 1921. It utilized in part material excavated in construction of the Holland and Lincoln tunnels. It is continually being strengthened. The central portion of the Hook is composed of sand dunes, and the western border of salt marsh, tidal pools, and coves. Typical vegetation includes cordgrass, sea rocket, salt hay, seaside goldenrod, poison ivy, holly trees, foxtail reeds, bayberry, prickly pear cactus, beach plums, sumac, eastern red cedar trees, wild black cherry, golden heather, Indian fig, tree of heaven, green briar, groundsel, apple trees, shad bush, high bush blueberry, privet, and honeysuckle. Because of driving salt spray, there are few large trees.

Principal features on the inside of the Hook from south to north are: Plum Island (now joined to the Hook by a narrow isthmus); Spermaceti Cove (partly enclosed by small, crescent-shaped Skeleton Hill Island); and shallow, open Horseshoe Cove. Fort Hancock and the United States Coast Guard Station are at the northern tip.

Sandy Hook has long been closed to the public, as it was an Army Base. In recent years, portions of the Hook have been set aside as a state park, part of the new Gateway National Recreation Area, which is administered by the National Park Service. There are bathing beaches and nature trails. Inquiries may be made to Area Manager, P. O. Box 437, Highlands, New Jersey 07732; or telephone (201) 872-0115. Caution: the beaches become extremely crowded in July and August, and tourists should check traffic conditions in advance.

Sandy Hook Lighthouse

The first Sandy Hook lighthouse began operation on 11 June 1764. It was built by Isaac Conro of New York City with money collected from the merchants of that city. It was 103 feet tall with an oil-burning lantern that was 7 feet high. Originally, the lighthouse was only 500 feet from the end of the Hook, but the continual buildup of

SANDY HOOK LIGHTHOUSE in 1866 as sketched by Benson Lossing. The original lighthouse was built ty Isaac Conro in 1764 and was 103 ft tall with an oil-burning lantern 7 ft high. Originally the lighthouse was only 500 ft from the end of the Hook, but is now 7,000 ft from the end owing to sand buildup.

sand now leaves it 7,000 ft. (one-and-a-half miles) from the tip. In 1950 the light was listed as "45,000 candle-power, third-order electric light, fixed white, in a white stone tower, 85 feet above ground and 88 feet above water, visible for 15 miles."

Historic Fort Hancock

One of the first important military actions on the Hook was on 5 July 1778, when the forces of the British General Sir Henry Clinton, retreating after the Battle of Monmouth Courthouse, embarked from here to New York City in barges. The following are extracts from the brochure "Sandy Hook's Bicentennial Story," distributed by the Gateway National Recreation Area.

As the threat of a second war with England grew, the Federal Government purchased all the land north of the lighthouse in 1806 to build the preliminary fortifications for New York Harbor defense. ... a "massive log fort" was constructed half a mile north of the lighthouse. The fort was manned by the Monmouth County Militia during the War of 1812. Plans for a more permanent fortification on Sandy Hook were made in 1847 by Army Captain Robert E. Lee, then Recorder for the Engineer Board. ... Work began on a massive granite star-shaped fort in 1859 and

continued intermittently until construction was suspended in 1869. It was never completed largely because the technical improvements of weapons and explosives during the Civil War made granite forts obsolete. During the 1890s most of the fort walls were partially dismantled for various Army building projects around the Hook. Construction of the first heavily fortified solid-concrete shore batteries were begun in 1890. The Mortar Battery (1890–1892) mounted 16 12-inch breech-loading Sea-coast mortars which could fire 700 lb. projectiles in high arcs that would descend almost vertically on the lightly armored decks of warships. They were clustered in four pit-like emplacements and manned by almost 200 men. Battery Potter (built 1890–1898) mounted two 12 inch high power guns mounted on a hydraulic lift barbette carriage and had a useful range of eight miles using a 1,000 lb. projectile—which was sufficient distance to match or out-shoot the guns of contemporary battle-ships. This remained operational until 1903.

From 1876 until after the First World War, when all operations were moved to Aberdeen, Maryland, the Army used Sandy Hook for its proving grounds.

In 1950, while a missile was being developed that could destroy a high-altitude aircraft, the Army established ARAACOM (Army Anti-aircraft Command). A unit of this defense command, consisting of various battalion batteries of the 52nd Artillery Brigade, was assigned the primary mission of defending the New York area in 1952. Initially armed with 90 mm and 120 mm anti-aircraft guns, the Brigade later received the Nike Ajax, the first missile to protect American cities against air attack, in 1954–1955. The Nike Ajax had a range of over 30 miles and an altitude of 60,000 ft.

By 1957 most of the remaining gun batteries were deactivated. A year later the Nike Ajax were replaced by the Nike Hercules, which had a range of 96 miles and an altitude of 100,000 ft. and was designed to use either a conventional or nuclear warhead. Aircraft nearing this area could be detected by the radar tracking post at Fort Hancock. If identified as hostile, the radar post would coordinate the firing of Nike Hercules from the launching area against approaching aircraft. In recent years the continuing technical development of missiles has made the Nike Hercules obsolete. This has led to the removal of these weapons from Sandy Hook and the deactivation of Fort Hancock in 1974.

For many years fortifications at Sandy Hook were simply officially designated "Fort at Sandy Hook." On October 30, 1895, General Army Order #57 designated the fortification at Sandy Hook as Fort Hancock, thus honoring Major General Winfield Scott Hancock of Civil War fame (1824–1886). Around the turn of the century the officers-row of houses was constructed. By the time of the First World War, Fort Hancock had become a formidable coastal defense site bristling with heavy ordnance. World War Two saw the post expand into an anti-aircraft site and an eastern staging area for troops being readied for European duty. The post was also a primary reception center in the New York area at the end of the war for returning European theater veterans.

Historical Incidents

On New Years Eve day in 1783 H.M.S. *Assistance*, a British warship, sent a detachment of fourteen men to the Hook to round up some deserters. Led by twenty-year-old 1st Lt. Hamilton Douglas Halyburton, the group met a tragic fate when a blizzard trapped them on the Hook.

A similar incident is recounted by Benson Lossing in his book, *The Hudson—From the Wilderness to the Sea*:

About a mile below the pier near the lighthouse, on the inner shore of the Hook, once stood an elegant monument, erected to the memory of a son of the Earl of Morton, and thirteen others, who were cast away near there, in a snow storm, during the revolution, and perished. All but one were officers of a British man-of-war, wrecked there. They were discovered, and buried in one grave. The mother of the young nobleman erected the monument, and it remained, respected even by the roughest men of the coast, until 1808, when some vandals from a French vessel-of-war, landed there, and destroyed that beautiful memorial of a mother's love.

(Troy, N.Y.: H. L. Nims & Co., 1866, p. 464.)

Sandy Hook seems to have been a place of ill omen. In 1609, one of Henry Hudson's crewmen, John Coleman, was the first white man to be killed in this area by an Indian. He was shot through the throat with an arrow while exploring the Kill van Kull in a small boat. To preserve his body, his fellow crew members buried him on Sandy Hook, which long bore the name Coleman's Point.

In 1620 a Dutch immigrant ship bound for New Amsterdam was wrecked on Sandy Hook. The passengers and crew got ashore and decided to walk to Manhattan, because they were afraid of Indians. However, Penelope van Princis, who was only eighteen years old, refused to leave her seriously wounded husband, and she stayed to care for him in the bitter winter cold. They were found by local Raritan Indians, who killed her husband and left Penelope for dead with a fractured skull and serious wounds of the left arm and abdomen. She crawled into a hollow tree and hid for days, living on bark and frozen tree gum, until two Indians found her. One expressed the wish to kill her; the other prevailed upon him to take her to a nearby village, where she was nursed back to health. Word of her plight reached New

Amsterdam, and she was soon ransomed. Four years later, she married an Englishman, Richard Stout, and moved with him back to New Jersey, to be among the first settlers of Middletown. The Indian who had befriended her visited them often. Once, at considerable risk to himself, he warned them of an intended massacre. Penelope lived to the age of 101 and left 502 direct descendants when she died.

In the early 1870s the Southern Railroad of New Jersey was built south from Spermaceti Cove to Long Branch. When Spermaceti Cove was found to be too shallow for the connecting steamboats, the terminal was moved to Horseshoe Cove. Eventually these services were absorbed by the New York & Long Branch and Central Railroad of New Jersey. The former railroad right-of-way is now part of the Salt Marsh Hiking–Nature Trail. There is an unsubstantiated belief that Captain Kidd buried treasure on Sandy Hook.

– **21.50 Rockaway Beach, Long Island (east).** Popular seaside resort and residential area.

– **21.25 Sandy Hook Bar.** Sandbar extending from Sandy Hook on the west to Rockaway Point on the east, separating Lower New York Bay from the open Atlantic Ocean. It is breached by the Sandy Hook and Ambrose Channels, which are the major shipping lanes. The natural depth of water is twenty-one feet, but it was deepened to twenty-three feet in 1837.

Since 1694, ships have taken on their harbor pilots here and the pilot boats are stationed here as well. Members of the two separate associations, the United New Jersey Sandy Hook Pilots Benevolent Association and the United New York Sandy Hook Pilots Benevolent Association, used to race each other to get the job as each ship appeared. These days, they have made peace and take alternate

SEABROOK HOMESTEAD, also known as Shoal Harbor Marine Museum, at Port Monmouth on the south shore of Sandy Hook Bay. Built in 1664, it has been a private home and stage-coach tavern. Dunes in foreground were once typical of the coastline but are now rare, endangered, and protected. Photo: Alfred H. Marks.

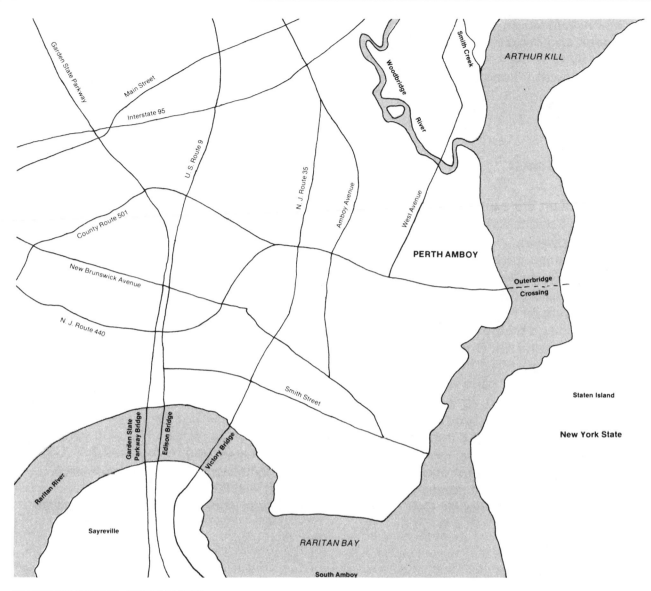

MIDDLESEX COUNTY—PERTH AMBOY

turns. They take the ships as far up the Hudson as Yonkers, where members of the Hudson River Pilots Association, based in that city, take over from them.

— **21.25 Keansburg, New Jersey (west).** On south shore of Raritan Bay, beyond Sandy Hook.

— **20.00 Raritan Bay.** This heavily polluted body of water is the western extremity of the Lower New York Bay and the outlet of the Raritan River. It is bounded on the north by Staten Island and on the west by Middlesex County, New Jersey (population 671,780), and on the south by Middlesex and Monmouth Counties (population 553,124), New Jersey. The cities and ports of Perth Amboy (population 41,967) and South Amboy (population 7,863) are at the head of the bay, and the city of New Brunswick is ten miles up the Raritan River. Principal tributaries are the Arthur Kill to the north, the Raritan River to the west, and Matawan, Chingarora, Thornes, Waycake, Pews, and Comptons Creeks, and the Shrewsbury River to the south. The southeastern portion of Raritan Bay, inside Sandy Hook, is also known as Sandy Hook Bay.

Raritan River

All thy wat'ry face
Reflected with a purer grace,
Thy many turnings through the trees,
Thy bitter journey to the seas,
Thou Queen of Rivers, Raritan!

John Davis—1806
"Ode to the Raritan, Queen of Rivers"

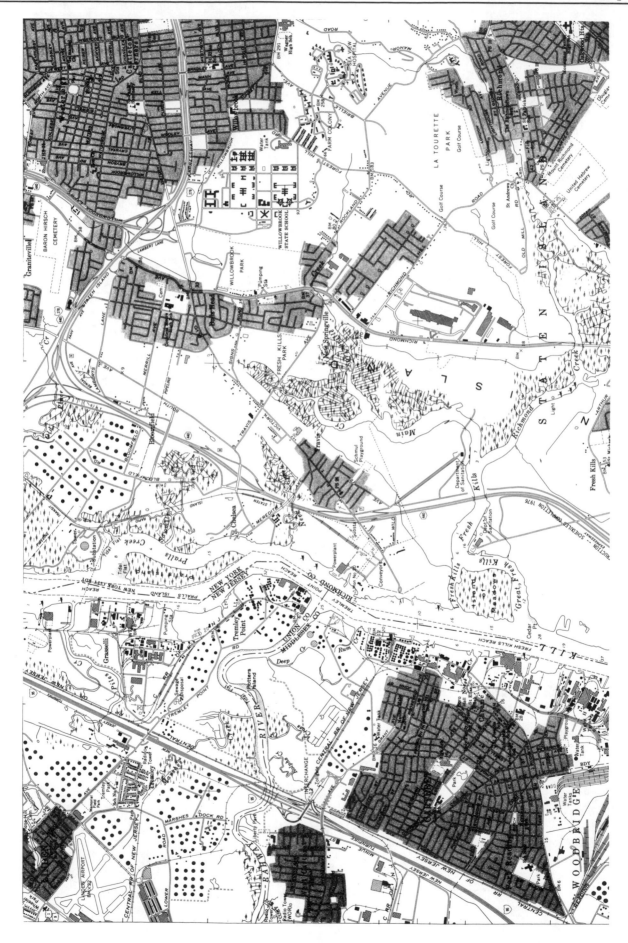

The Raritan is the largest river entirely within the state of New Jersey. It is roughly 100 miles from the headwaters of the south branch at Budd Lake in Morris County to Raritan Bay at Perth Amboy. It drains more than 1,000 square miles. The first white settlers were Dutch. They moved in prior to 1650. The name Raritan comes from the Indian word Laletan, meaning "forked river." This has also been interpreted as "gentle" or "smooth-running." All are accurate descriptions of the river. The local Indians were called Raritangs or Naraticongs. They grew maize, pumpkins, beans, and fruit. The early settlers found the region good for growing grain and raising cattle.

The South Branch starts at Budd Lake in Morris County and flows south past Schooley's Mountain through Bartley, Naughtright, Long Valley, Middle Valley, and High Bridge. It continues past Clinton and Hamden. Here the river turns east and flows past Flemington Junction, Three Bridges, Woodfern, Neshanic, and South Branch. The North Branch starts at Ralston, in Morris County, at the confluence of Burnett and Indian Brooks. It flows southeast past Pleasant Valley and south into Somerset County past Peapack, Gladstone, Far Hills, Pluckemin, and Burnt Mill, where it is joined from the west by the Lamington River. It continues south past North Branch and Milltown to its junction with the South Branch, just west of Raritan. The combined stream, now officially known as the Raritan River, flows east past Raritan, Somerville, and Finderne to Manville and Zarephath, where it is joined from the south by the Millstone River. Continuing east, we pass Bound Brook, Piscataway, Fieldville, and Somerset before coming to New Brunswick on the south shore and Highland Park on the north shore. We are now in Middlesex County. This is now a tidewater area and the river is navigable by ships to New Brunswick. Continuing east we pass Weston's Mills on the south shore and Greensand, Bonhamtown, and Nixon on the north.

Lawrence Brook and South River enter the Raritan just west of Sayreville on the south shore. The river here is quite wide, with extensive salt marshes and abandoned claypits on either side, the remnants of a once extensive brick-making industry. We pass Phoenix on the south and finally enter Raritan Bay at the confluence of the tidal estuary Arthur Kill from the north. Perth Amboy is on the north shore and South Amboy on the south.

At New Brunswick, the Raritan is crossed by high bridges of the Pennsylvania Railroad, Route 1, and the New Jersey Turnpike, and by a lower-level bridge of Route 27 between New Brunswick and Highland Park. Just west of Perth Amboy, it is crossed by the twin high-level Governor Alfred E. Driscoll Bridge of the Garden State Parkway and the Thomas A. Edison Bridge used by U.S. Route 9, immediately to the east. Also at Perth Amboy are the long, low-level, swing, Victory Vehicular Bridge, and that of the New York & Long Branch Railroad—the outermost bridge on the river, at its confluence with Raritan Bay. Crab Island is located north of Sayreville. Also near Sayreville is the large plant of the National Lead Company. There is a large power generating station at South Amboy and several railroad car dumpers. South Amboy was the terminal of the pioneer Camden & Amboy Railroad across New Jersey. The Delaware & Raritan Canal parallels the south bank of the Raritan from Zarephath to New Brunswick, where the last lock lowers it to tidewater.

The Arthur Kill

Formerly known as the Achter Kil, the Arthur Kill is a deepwater tidal estuary separating Staten Island and New Jersey. The state line runs down the middle of its channel. It empties into Newark Bay at the north and Raritan Bay at the south. From south to north the principal tributaries are: Woodbridge Creek, Smith Creek, Rahway River, Pile's Creek, Morse's Creek, and Elizabeth River, on the west bank. Fresh Kills (fed by Richmond Creek from the south) and Old Place Creek are on the Staten Island side. Principal islands, both in New York State, are the Island of Meadows, at the mouth of Fresh Kills, and Prall's Island near Tremley Point and the mouth of the Rahway River.

Principal locations from south to north along the New Jersey side are: Perth Amboy, Barber, Sewaren, Woodbridge, Port Reading, Tufts Point, Chrome, Carteret, Tremley Point, Warner's Station, Grasselli, Bayway, and Elizabethport. On the Staten Island side: Tottenville, Richmond Valley, Charleston, Port Mobil (formerly Port Socony), Smoking Point, Rossville, Linoleumville; Fresh Kills, Island of Meadows, Travis, Bloomfield, Pralls Island, Gulfport, Port Ivory, and Howland Hook. Bridges from south to north are: Outerbridge Crossing, between Perth Amboy and Tottenville; Goethals Bridge, between Elizabeth and Howland Hook; and the lift bridge of the Staten Island Rapid Transit Railroad (freight only), between Elizabeth and Howland Hook. There were formerly ferries between Tottenville and Perth Amboy and Port Ivory and Elizabethport. The Arthur Kill was part of the popular inside or north shore route between New Brunswick and the Amboys and Newark, Manhattan, Jersey City, and Hoboken in the early days of steamboating.

The Central Railroad of New Jersey (Conrail) parallels the Arthur Kill on the New Jersey side. This was formerly the Elizabeth & Perth Amboy Railroad. The Sound Shore Branch and Chrome Branch also serve the area. An electrified branch of the Pennsylvania Railroad (Conrail), used by North Jersey Shore Trains, connects the Pennsylvania Mainline at Rahway with Perth Amboy, via Woodbridge. At Perth Amboy, both the Central of New Jersey and Pennsylvania lines connect with the New York & Long Branch, which is also electrified across the Raritan River Drawbridge to Long Branch.

The New Jersey Turnpike and U.S. Routes 1 and 9 parallel the Arthur Kill inland from the Central of New Jersey tracks. Major oil refineries of Gulf Oil Corporation, Socony-Mobil Corporation, and Standard Oil of New Jersey (Esso-Exxon) are located along the estuary and are served directly by deepwater tankers. There are major plants of the Nassau Smelting & Refining Division of Western Electric Company and of Proctor & Gamble, Ivory Soap Division, at Tottenville and Port Ivory on Staten Island. The shores are marshy and largely devoted to heavy petrochemical industry, tank farms, and cemeteries. The area was formerly a resort that was popular with fishermen, crabbers, and marsh hunters. There is considerable heavy-tonnage shipping, and these waters are not recommended for pleasure cruising in small boats. The upper reaches of the Rahway River, near Rahway and Cranford, are very scenic. They are kept as parkland and are popular for canoeing. The Elizabeth River is littered with trash and is given to violent flooding after heavy rains or snow.

The Rahway Reformatory, a major state prison and prison farm, is at Rahway. The Raritan Arsenal is located at Carteret. The west bank is bounded by Middlesex County to the south and Union County to the north. Elizabeth is the county seat of Union County (1990 population 493,819) which was settled from New England in 1664. The tall, white office tower is the Union County Court House, built in 1903 by the architects Ackerman & Ross.

Outerbridge Crossing

Named in honor of Eugenius H. Outerbridge, first chairman of the Port of New York Authority, the Outerbridge Crossing and the similar Goethals Bridge were the first facilities constructed by the Port Authority. In conjunction with the Verrazano-Narrows Bridge, these bridges provide access from New Jersey to Long Island and serve as part of the metropolitan area's southerly highway bypass system.

Length of Center Span	750 ft.
Total Length of Truss Spans	2,100 ft.
Length of New Jersey Viaduct	4,758 ft.
Length of Staten Island Viaduct	1,920 ft.
Total Length of Elevated Structure	8,778 ft.
Width of Bridge (Main Span)	62 ft.
Width of Roadway (Main Span)	42 ft.
Width of Roadway (Viaducts)	50 ft.

Outerbridge Crossing. Courtesy of Port Authority of New York and New Jersey.

Channel Clearance at Midspan	135 ft.
Opened to Traffic 29 June, 1928	

Goethals Bridge

Goethals Bridge was built as a memorial to Maj. Gen. George W. Goethals, builder of the Panama Canal and first consulting engineer of the Port Authority.

Length of Center Span	672 ft.
Total Length of Truss Spans	1,152 ft.
Length of New Jersey Viaduct	2,831 ft.
Length of Staten Island Viaduct	3,126 ft.
Total Length of Elevated Structure	7,109 ft.
Width of Bridge (Main Span)	62 ft.
Width of Roadway	42 ft.
Channel Clearance at Midspan	135 ft.
Opened to Traffic 29 June, 1928	

Goethals Bridge. Courtesy of Port Authority of New York and New Jersey.

FIRST PRESBYTERIAN CHURCH, ELIZABETH. Present building was erected in 1724 on site of earlier building of 1668. It was destroyed by the British in 1780 and rebuilt, and again destroyed by fire in 1947 and rebuilt. One of its early pastors was Jonathan Dickinson, 1st President of the College of New Jersey, now Princeton. Photo: © Uta Gore.

BELCHER-OGDEN MANSION, ELIZABETH. This is the pre-1742 home of Jonathan Belcher, Governor of the Provinces of New Jersey, and later of Aaron Ogden, a later Governor of New Jersey active in steamboat enterprises and one of the litigants in the famous patent case Gibbons vs Ogden of 1824. Photo: © Uta Gore.

Kill van Kull

The Kill van Kull is a deepwater tidal estuary connecting Newark Bay and the Arthur Kill with Upper New York Bay. It separates the north shore of Staten Island from Bayonne, in Hudson County, New Jersey. It was while sailing through this estuary in a small boat, making explorations in 1609, that John Coleman, one of Henry Hudson's crew members, was shot through the throat by an Indian. This was the first recorded incident of bloodshed in the New York area. Coleman was buried on Sandy Hook.

Shooters Island (one-third of which is in New Jersey and two-thirds in New York) is at the west end at the mouth of Newark Bay. The Kill van Kull serves as the state line between New Jersey and New York. It is one of the entrances to the busy ports of Newark Bay. From

west to east, these are its principal points: on Staten Island there are Mariners Harbor, Arlington, Elm Park, Port Richmond, West New Brighton, Livingston, Sailors Snug Harbor, New Brighton, and St. George. In New Jersey, there are Bergen Point, Port Johnson, and Constable Hook. Robbins Reef with its light is at the junction with Upper New York Bay. It is crossed by the Bayonne Bridge between Bayonne and Elm Park. There was formerly a ferry here.

The Bayonne Bridge

The Bayonne Bridge is the longest steel arch bridge in the world. The mid-span clearance of 150 feet permits ocean-going vessels to use this entrance to Port Newark and the Elizabeth–Port Authority Marine Terminal without interference.

Length of Arch Span	1,675 ft.
Length of New Jersey Viaduct	3,010 ft.
Length of Staten Island Viaduct	2,010 ft.
Total Length of Elevated Structure	6,695 ft.
Width of Bridge	85 ft.
Width of Roadway	40 ft.
Channel Clearance at Midspan	150 ft.
Height of Arch above Water at Crown	327 ft.
Opened to Traffic 15 November, 1931	

The south shore of the Kill van Kull is paralleled by the freight-only branch of the Staten Island Rapid Transit line between St. George and Port Ivory. The waterway can best be seen by driving along Richmond Terrace on Staten Island. Sailor's Snug Harbor is worth a visit. The currents of the Kill are swift, and there is considerable ship traffic. It is not recommended for small boats, however.

Staten Island

Staten Island is the large island on the west side of the narrows (1990 population 378,979). Roughly oval in shape, it incorporates an area of fifty-seven square miles with a maximum length of fourteen miles and breadth of eight miles. On the north, it is separated from Bergen Point (Bayonne), New Jersey by the Kill van Kull. On the west, it is separated from the New Jersey mainland by Newark Bay and the Arthur Kill. Raritan Bay is to the south, and Lower New York Bay and the Narrows are to the east. Upper New York Bay is to the northeast.

The western portion of the island is low and swampy. It is drained by Old Place Creek, the Fresh Kills, and Richmond Creek. The remainder of the island consists of indeterminate hills and upland. One principal ridge runs from southwest to northeast along the eastern side of the island. Its principal elevations are Latourette (241 feet), Grimes Hill (370 feet), and Todt Hill (410 feet). Todt Hill is the highest point on the Atlantic Seaboard south of Mount Desert Island in Maine. Principal indentations on the southeastern shore are Princess Bay and Great Kills Harbor, both oyster ports until 1916. Ward's Point at the confluence of the Arthur Kill and Raritan Bay is the southernmost point in New York State.

The original inhabitants were the Raritan and Hackensack tribes of the Lenni-Lenape Indians. They called the island Eghquaons, which means "place of high sandy banks." At the time of European discovery, the island was heavily wooded. For a more detailed description of early topography, the reader is referred to James Fenimore Cooper's "Water Witch," quoted in the author's *The Hudson River in Literature*, Fordham University Press, 1988.

In 1609 Henry Hudson named the island Status Eylandt in honor of the States General of the Nether-lands, which had financed his voyage. In 1630 the Dutch West India Company granted Staten Island to Michael Pauw, who also held extensive grants at the present site of Jersey City. However, in 1634 title reverted to the Dutch West India Company because Pauw had failed to plant any settlements.

Planting settlements was not so easy a matter because of Indian hostility. In 1639 David Pietersen De Vries received a grant and started a colony at the Watering Place, near present-day Tompkinsville. This was named from the fact that there were several good springs where ships replenished their water supplies. This settlement was wiped out by Indians in 1641.

In 1640 Cornelis Melyn attempted to establish a patroonship and planted a colony that was destroyed in 1643. He made a second attempt at the Watering Place in 1650, but this too was destroyed in 1655. In 1659 Melyn gave up his patroonship.

Peace with the Indians was established by a treaty in 1660, and, in 1661 Governor Peter Stuyvesant gave permission to nineteen Dutchmen and Frenchmen from the Palatinate to settle at Oude Dorp, or Old Town, just inland from present-day Fort Wadsworth. The leader of this colony was Pierre Billeau, a Walloon. A small garrison was established for its protection, and there were church services every two months. These were conducted by Dominie Drisius, who preached in English, French, and Dutch. The Dutch generally accepted French settlers so long as they made no attempts at claiming French sovereignty.

The English conquered the island in 1664 and renamed it Richmond, in honor of the Duke of Richmond, second son of Charles II. All settlers were required to take an oath of allegiance. Long Island and Staten Island were incorporated together into the West Riding of Yorkshire. The seat of government was established at Gravesend on ᷅Long Island, and court continued to be held there until 1675.

In 1670 Governor Francis Lovelace made a "final purchase" from the local Indians. He required that the young Indians also sign the deed, so that it would not quickly be forgotten. This same year it was estimated that there were about one hundred families, mainly Dutch and French, settled on Staten Island. In 1668, some Waldensians had settled and established a church near Stony Brook; and some Huguenots had settled at Fresh Kill, which is now known as Greenridge.

The original settlers lived in cabins of squared logs, but these were gradually replaced by more substantial stone houses of long and low massive construction. Stone, timber, and shingles were easily procured, and lime was made from oyster shells collected along the shore. The stonework was irregular, and door and window placement was asymmetrical. The houses were usually only one room deep and had no hallway. Steep gables were favored, but the houses differed from those elsewhere in the colony in that they lacked the graceful overhanging eaves and, also, the original unit was usually the largest section.

In 1671 the village of New Dorp was settled on the shore, east of the present village of that name. Also that year, the settlement of Oude Dorp spread to the nearby fertile valley, and this new section was laid out as the New Lots of the Old Town, now known as Dongan Hills. In 1682 Thomas Dongan became governor of the province of New York. He would hold this office until 1688. He lived for some time on Staten Island but later returned to Ireland where he became the Earl of Limerick, dying there in 1715 at the age of eighty-one. In 1683 Governor Dongan called the first Provincial Assembly, and Staten Island was organized into Richmond County. The county seat was established at Cuckold's Town, near New Dorp, which was given the more dignified name of Richmond Town.

It was the English custom to give grants of eighty acres, or multiples thereof, to settlers and speculators. In 1684 Governor Dongan granted two large manorial estates on Staten Island, one near Ward's Point to Christopher Billopp and one, located in the central part of the island, to John Palmer. Dongan himself shortly thereafter acquired the Palmer manorial lands. This immense tract became known simply as The Manour.

After Louis XIV of France revoked the Edict of Nantes in 1685, there was a considerable influx of French Huguenot settlers to Staten Island. Also about this time, a dispute arose between the colonies of New Jersey and New York for possession of the island. The Duke of York, according to an old tradition, offered title to whichever colony boasted a native son who could first circumnavigate the island within twenty-four hours. The honors went to Capt. Christopher Billopp of New York in 1687, and Staten Island has belonged to New York ever since. In 1688 the four townships of Northfield, Southfield, Westfield, and Castletown were established, corresponding to the earlier precincts and Castleton Manour.

In 1775 the New York City Council chartered a ferry route to Manhattan. This was served by small sailing boats known as piraguas. During the American Revolution, the British took control of Staten Island in the summer of 1776 and held it until the autumn of 1783. The state of New York established a quarantine station on the northern extremity of the island in 1799. In 1858 the locals burned it down in protest of the fact that two years earlier there were over five hundred cases of yellow fever held at the station. The facility was then replaced by a hospital ship anchored in the Upper Bay. However, today there is again a quarantine station located at Rosebank.

The island was devoted to fishing and agriculture until the 1830s. The principal crops were corn, wheat, and rye. Some grapes were grown for wine, and there were extensive cherry and apple orchards and many cider mills. From the 1830s on, the island became popular as a resort and suburban residence for wealthy New Yorkers. Many large villas were erected, enjoying the fine views of the harbor and Narrows. The great landscape architect, Frederick Law Olmstead, creator of Central Park, made his home on Staten Island and developed plans for a greenbelt, which was never created during his lifetime. Today his plans are being implemented, and a scenic hiking trail system has been named the Olmstead Trailway. Among the famous nineteenth-century residents were Francis Parkman, Giuseppe Garibaldi, and Cornelius Vanderbilt. Vanderbilt was a native of Staten Island and started his vast transportation empire with a small ferryboat plying between there and Manhattan. The elaborate Vanderbilt family mausoleum in the Moravian Cemetery near New Dorp is one of the island's most interesting sights.

During the Civil War, Staten Island was a pocket of Southern sympathy, and there were particularly violent draft riots. After ferry and railroad services were consolidated at St. George in 1886, that town rapidly became the principal community and county seat. In 1898 Staten Island was consolidated with New York City as the Borough and County of Richmond. Some heavy industry settled along the western shore, including a smelting plant at Richmond, refineries along the Arthur Kill, and a large soap factory at Port Ivory. However, most development has been residential, Richmond being the most rural of the New York boroughs. The island is served by the Staten Island Rapid Transit Railroad, which provides freight service and passenger service between St. George and Tottenville. In past years, ferry lines have operated to Perth Amboy, Elizabeth, Bayonne, and Brooklyn, as well as to Manhattan. Today only the St. George line to Manhattan survives, the others having been replaced with the Outerbridge Crossing, Goethals Bridge, Bayonne, and the Verrazano-Narrows bridges. This last great bridge across the Narrows was completed in 1965, and the island's population has boomed since then to 378,917 in 1990. Interstate Highway 278 connects the Goethals and Verrazano-Narrows bridges and serves as an important southern bypass around New York City, connecting New Jersey with Long Island.

Silver Lake, near Stapleton, is the southern termination of the Catskill aqueduct system. The recreational facilities offered by Staten Island include many beaches along the eastern shore. Midland and South beaches are connected by the Franklin D. Roosevelt Boardwalk, which offers superb views of the Lower Bay. Among the many parks are Wolfe's Pond Park, Great Kills Park, New Springville Park, Latourette Park, and golf course, Willowbrook Park, Clove Lakes Park, Silver Lake Park, and Barrett Park with the Staten Island Zoo, which contains one of the largest snake collections in the world. Also of interest are the High Rock Nature Conservation Center, Moravian Cemetery, and the Jacques Marchais Center of Tibetan Art with its oriental garden. Old Richmondtown is a historic restoration with three dozen buildings recreating a seventeenth-century village. There is a historical museum, several old churches and homes, and a lighthouse in the vicinity. This complex is operated by the Staten Island Historical Society.

Staten Island is particularly rich in educational institutions, hospitals, and asylums for the aged and infirm. Among the more notable institutions are Saint Paul's Seminary, Augustinian Academy, Notre Dame College, Willowbrook State School, Saint Francis Seminary, Wagner College, Staten Island Community College, Mount Loretto Academy, Staten Island Academy, Saint Joseph-by-the-Sea Home, Sailors' Snug Harbor, The Goodhue Home, Staten Island Hospital, United States Public Health Service Hospital at Rosebank, and the United States Quarantine Station. There is a major military base at Fort Wadsworth, overlooking the Narrows, and a United States Coast Guard station at Saint George. Principal historic landmarks include the Billopp Conference House, Voorlezer's House, Saint Andrew's Church, the Moravian Church at New Dorp, and the Stillwell-Perrine House at Dongan Hills.

At the present time there are plans to make Stapleton a new Homeport for the Atlantic Fleet, which will bring considerable Naval activity to Staten Island. Also, the City of New York has commenced building a "garbage mountain" at the Great Fresh Kills and Island of Meadows landfill site on the Arthur Kill. It is planned to use the most modern compacting techniques and earth-covering methods and tap the methane gases generated by the disintegration of the organic material. It is planned to build the "mountain" to a height of 500 feet, which will make it the highest point on the Atlantic shoreline south of Maine and overtop Todt Hill (410 ft) on Staten Island, the presently highest point, and Beacon Hill (266 ft) in the neighboring Atlantic Highlands. It will be used for such recreational activities as skiing.

Newark Bay
(formerly Arthur Cull Bay)

Newark Bay is a deepwater bay, five miles long by one and a half miles wide to the west of Bayonne and Upper New York Bay. It is the outlet of the Passaic and Hackensack rivers in New Jersey. It lies entirely in New Jersey, although it debouches into both the Arthur Kill and Kill van Kull, north of Staten Island, at its south end. It is bounded on the east by Bayonne and Jersey City, and on the west by Elizabethport and Newark. Kearny is

PORT NEWARK—CONTAINERPORT. Newark Bay is in the background. Across Newark Bay is the Bayonne Peninsula with the towers of lower Manhattan and the twin towers of the World Trade Center beyond. Bayonne and Manhattan are separated by Upper New York Bay, not visible in this picture. Photo: Courtesy of Port Authority of New York and New Jersey.

NEWARK BAY LOOKING NORTH. This view is taken from between Port Newark and Bayonne Park. The cantilever-arch highway bridge in the foreground belongs to the New Jersey Turnpike Jersey City Extension. The railroad lift bridge beyond is the former Pennsylvania RR–Lehigh Valley RR bridge now owned by Conrail, connecting the Oak Island and Garden Yards on the left with the Greenville Yard on the right. Photo: © Uta Gore.

at the north end, between the mouths of the Passaic and the Hackensack. Bayonne, Jersey City, and Kearny are in Hudson County. Newark is in Essex County (1990 population 493,819), and Elizabethport is in Union County.

Elizabeth Port Authority Piers are bounded on the north by the Elizabeth Channel, and Port Newark is bisected by City Channel, also known as Port of Newark

Channel. Both port complexes are on the west shore. Behind the massive port complexes are the Newark Branch of the Central Railroad of New Jersey (Conrail), the New Jersey Turnpike, and Newark International Airport. This is the busiest part of the entire Port of New York and is equipped to handle container ships. Principal features on the eastern shore from south to north are Bergen Point, City Park, Bayonne Park and Lagoon, Roosevelt Stadium, Droyer's Point, and the Hackensack River. On the west shore are Elizabethport, Port Elizabeth, Oyster Creek, Elizabeth Channel, Port Newark, City Channel, Passaic Valley Sewage Plant, the Passaic River, and Newark. There was formerly a large lift bridge of the Central Railroad of New Jersey across the mouth of the bay. This bridge carried four tracks and was an engineering marvel of its day. It was removed by dynamiting to provide access to the Bay by the new giant ships, and alternate rail routes are now used. Further north, between Port Newark and Jersey City, are another railroad bridge of the Pennsylvania Railroad and Lehigh Valley (Conrail) and the Newark Bay Bridge of the New Jersey Turnpike's Holland Tunnel extension, the latter of which offers good views. Newark Bay is busy and dirty, and the water can be rough. It is not recommended for small boats.

The Passaic River

The Passaic is one of the major rivers of New Jersey. It rises near Mendham in Morris County and flows east past Ledell's Pond at Washington Corner, near Jockey Hollow in Morristown National Historical Park (Washington spent a winter here during the Revolution) to Van Doren's Mill, Osborn Pond, Osborn Mill, and the Great Swamp National Wildlife Refuge near White's Bridge in Millington. This is the vast remains of the former large Lake Passaic, which was once contained by the Watchung Mountains.

Here the river has been trending southeastward, but after passing Millington it makes a sharp bend and starts to flow northeast past Stirling, Gillette, Meyersville, Berkeley Heights, New Providence, Chatham, Florham Park, and Hanover. Much of this area has a New England aspect and is a popular suburban neighborhood. It can be seen best from an Erie-Lackawanna N.J. Transit Gladstone Branch train. Flowing north from Hanover, the river passes Swinefield Bridge, Hanover Neck, and Rockaway Neck, where the Passaic is joined by the waters of the Rockaway River from the north. Here the Passaic makes a great loop to the west around the Great Piece Meadows, passing Pinebrook Bridge, Horseneck Bridge, and Two Bridges, where it is joined from the north by the Pompton River. The Pompton itself has been formed by the junction of the Ramapo River, which

rises west of the Hudson Highlands, and the Pequannock River, which rises in the eastern hills of Sussex County. The Pequannock also receives the waters of the Wanaque River, which is the outlet of Greenwood Lake which lies half in New Jersey and half in New York State, south of Monroe, New York.

By the time the Passaic River reaches Two Bridges, it is at the junction of Morris, Essex, and Passaic Counties, and is flowing east. It passes Fairfield and North Caldwell on the south and the Borough of Totowa on the north to the falls at Little Falls, where much water is diverted to old power canals. Here it turns northeast past West Paterson to the Great Falls at Paterson. This portion is beautiful slack water, rimmed by Pennington Park on the south and Westside Park on the north. In this calm stretch of the river, in May 1881, John P. Holland launched the first successful submarine, the *Fenian Ram*, named for the Irish Fenian Society which financed the venture. In a subsequent test on the Hudson River it was

LITTLE FALLS OF THE PASSAIC RIVER at Little Falls, New Jersey. Once important for their water power, the falls will make an attractive view for the new condominium apartments being created from the old carpet factory shown in the picture. Photo: © Gretchen McHugh.

GREAT FALLS OF THE PASSAIC RIVER AT PATERSON. Photo:
© Gretchen McHugh.

rammed and sunk by a Weehawken ferryboat! The periscope had not yet been invented and the *Fenian Ram* was running "blind." It was raised and is now on view in Paterson's Westside Park.

The Great Falls at Paterson are 70 feet high and were a famous scenic destination in the eighteenth and early nineteenth centuries, visited by such notables as Washington Irving, who was inspired to write a poem entitled "The Falls of the Passaic." The abundant water power inspired Alexander Hamilton to found the Society for Useful Manufactures in 1791 to exploit the water power, and this organization controlled it until 1946. The industrial city of Paterson grew up around the falls, named for Governor William Paterson of New Jersey (1745–1806). This was a great center of the cotton, locomotive, armaments, and silk industries. Between Two Bridges and Paterson the Passaic River was paralleled by the Morris Canal, which operated from 1836 to 1924, connecting the Delaware and Hudson rivers across northern New Jersey.

Below the Great Falls at Paterson the Passaic makes a great loop to the north, enclosing Paterson on its right bank, and with Prospect Park, Hawthorne, and Fairlawn

on its left bank. It receives the waters of Goffle Brook at Hawthorne. Heading south between Paterson on the west and Elmwood Park (formerly East Paterson) on the east, it enters Dundee Lake, formed by the Dundee Dam between Clifton and Garfield. There was formerly a power and navigation canal to bypass the dam. Bergen County is now on the east and Passaic County on the west. Tidal action is felt up to the Dundee Dam, and the Passaic is open to commercial navigation up to Wallington, a half mile below the dam. Between Garfield and Wallington, opposite Passaic, it receives the waters of the Saddle River, which rises between Tallman and Monsey in New York State and flows south through Bergen County, receiving the waters of Hohokus Brook, rising in Franklin Lakes, New Jersey. The Passaic River makes an "S" loop at Passaic, which is on the west bank, and then continues south to Newark Bay as a navigable tidal waterway. Below Passaic is Delawanna, in Passaic County, and Nutley, Belleville, and the City of Newark in Essex County on the right or west bank. On the left or east bank are Wallington, Carlton Hill, Rutherford, Lyndhurst, and North Arlington in Bergen County, and Arlington, East Newark, Harrison, and Kearny in Hudson County. At Nutley the Yantacaw Brook flows in from the west and between Belleville and Newark the Branch Brook, or Second River, also enters from the west. Below Newark the banks are heavily industrialized and the river makes several loops through mud flats and railroad yards between Newark and Kearny. This stretch between Passaic and Newark was once very beautiful, flanked by plantations and fine homes famous in the eighteenth and early nineteenth centuries. In 1798 Robert R. Livingston, Colonel John Stevens, John Stoudinger, and Nicholas J. Roosevelt participated in the construction and operation

PASSAIC RIVER AT NEWARK, LOOKING NORTH. The large lift bridges in the foreground carry the tracks of Amtrak's Northeast Corridor and PATH rapid transit from Harrison, on the right, to Penn Station Newark, on the left. The large square highrise building on the left is the new headquarters of Public Service Electric & Gas Company. Photo: © Uta Gore.

of a small steamboat called the *Polacca* at Belleville, on the Passaic River, and are reputed to have sailed it under steam to Manhattan via the Passaic, Newark Bay, Kill Van Kull, and Upper New York Bay, and back—nine years before Fulton's *Clermont*!

The Hackensack River

The Hackensack River was originally called the Demarest Kill after a family of Huguenot settlers. The east branch of the Hackensack River rises in Rockland Lake (also known as Snedeker's Pond) atop the Palisades at Hook Mountain in Rockland County. It meanders west, down off the Palisades, through Swartwout Lake and Congers Lake, thence south through Valley Cottage and southwest into Lake DeForest, an artificial reservoir formed by damming the West Branch of the Hackensack River. It is named for Robert W. DeForest, former President of the Hackensack Water Company.

The west branch rises in a bog south of Little Tor Mountain east of Pomona. It meanders eastward to near New City and then turns directly south and flows into the northern end of Lake DeForest. From Lake DeForest it flows south past historic Clarksville and West Nyack into Lake Tappan (another artificial reservoir) at Orangeburg. This section, also known as Blue Hill, is on the border between Rockland County, New York, and Bergen County, New Jersey. It is the heart of the old Dutch settlement area. From Lake Tappan it continues south past Rivervale, New Jersey, and Harrington Park into the artificial Oradell Reservoir at Closter. Here it receives the waters of the Dwarskill from the slopes of the Palisades to the east, the Tenakill from the south, and Dorotockeys Run from the north.

The Pascack rises near Spring Valley in New York and flows south past Pearl River, New York, and Montvale, Park Ridge, and Woodcliff Lake, New Jersey, before entering the large Woodcliff Lake Reservoir. At Montvale, it receives the waters of the small Pearl River

OVERPECK CREEK at Leonia, New Jersey. This view is taken in Overpeck County Park looking north from Fort Lee Road. Teaneck is across the river. Photo: © Gretchen McHugh.

(now ingloriously renamed Muddy Creek) from the east. South of Woodcliff Lake the Pascack continues south and east past Hillsdale, Westwood, and Rivervale to Oradell Reservoir.

Below the dam at Oradell, the Hackensack continues south past New Milford and River Edge, where tidewater navigation begins. From here south we pass New Bridge, Teaneck, and Bogota on the east side; and Hackensack, county seat of Bergen County, South Hackensack, and Little Ferry on the west. At Ridgefield Park (here confusingly known as Little Ferry Station) the Overpeck Creek enters from the east. The Overpeck in turn receives the waters of Wolf Creek. From here south the Hackensack flows through the vast Hackensack Meadows, which are swampy areas of marsh grass and cattails that are now being filled in to make land for industry and provide garbage dumping area. In colonial times, this was a

DROYERS POINT REACH OF THE HACKENSACK RIVER. Looking north we see the Routes 1 and 9 Lift Bridge and Pulaski Skyway in the distance. Photo: © Uta Gore.

HACKENSACK RIVER AND MEADOWS AT SECAUCUS. This view, taken looking north from Harmon Cove, shows typical, fast disappearing, marsh vegetation. Distant highway bridges carry NJ Route 3 across Hackensack River to Meadowlands Sports Complex. Photo: © Gretchen McHugh.

swampy cedar forest. From here south, we have Moonachie, Carlstadt, East Rutherford, Kingsland, North Arlington, Arlington, and Kearny on the west; and North Bergen, Secaucus, and Jersey City on the east bank. (During the Revolutionary period, Dow's Ferry crossed from the foot of Saint Paul's Avenue in Jersey City to Kearny.) Here it enters the north end of Newark Bay. Principal tributaries south of Overpeck Creek are Losen Slote, Moonachie Creek, Bashe's Creek, Cedar Creek, Berry's Creek Canal, Berry's Creek, Kingsland Creek, and Saw Mill Creek on the west. On the east are Bellman's Creek, Paunpeck Creek (also known as Cromakill Creek), Mill Creek, Fish Creek, and Penhorn Creek. Droyer's Point is on the east side of the junction with Newark Bay. Laurel Hill, also known as Snake Hill and mentioned by Washington Irving, is on the east bank between Secaucus and Penhorn Creek, near the New Jersey Turnpike and the Pennsylvania Railroad. It is nearly half quarried away.

For all its proximity to densely populated areas, the Hackensack is a difficult river to see. Its northern reaches can be seen from local roads, but the large reservoirs are fenced off. The Pascack Branch and the stretch between Hackensack and Oradell can be seen from trains of the Pascack Branch of New Jersey Transit (formerly the New Jersey & New York Railroad). The lower reaches can best be seen from the New Jersey Turnpike and local roads near Secaucus. The stretch from Overpeck Creek to Bogota can be seen from either the West Shore Railroad or the New York, Susquehanna & Western, neither of which presently offers passenger service. The Hackensack is navigable for small pleasure boats north to New Milford. Above there, it is largely controlled by the Hackensack Water Company, and all trespassing is forbidden.

HACKENSACK RIVER BRIDGES. This view is taken looking north with Kearny on the left and Jersey City on the right. The confused-looking tangle is actually four separate bridges close together. From front to back they are respectively:
1) PATH Rapid Transit, former Hudson & Manhattan RR
2) Pennsylvania RR, now Conrail, leading to Meadows Yards on the left. This was once the main line leading to the Manhattan ferries at Exchange Place, Jersey City, on the right.
3) Newark Turnpike Highway Bridge.
4) Delaware, Lackawanna & Western RR (Morris & Essex Div.), now owned by New Jersey Transit.
All are lift bridges, creating a considerable obstacle to the navigation of large vessels on the upper Hackensack River. Photo: © Uta Gore.

— **19.00 Romer Shoal is to the southwest.** It is named for the former pilot boat *William J. Romer* which struck a submerged reef and sank with loss of one pilot in 1863. There are rich pastures of plankton in the area, and consequently excellent striped bass fishing.

— **17.10 Romer Shoal Light to the west.** Bend in channel to the north.

— **17.00 Fort Tilden to the east.** Located on Rockaway Beach Point in Queens County, New York. It is an active military installation and the home of the 99th Army Signal Battalion, 411th Army Engineer Brigade, Army 306th Engineer Company, and a United States Coast Guard Station.

— **17.00 Ward's Point, Staten Island, and Tottenville Beach to the west.** This is the southernmost point in New York State.

— **16.00 Rockaway Point and Lighthouse, Queens County, to east.**

— **16.00 Old Orchard Shoal Light to west. Seguine Point, Staten Island, to west.**

— **15.60 Great Kills Light to west, offshore. Huguenot Beach, Staten Island, to west.**

— **15.50 Crooke's Point, Staten Island, to west.**

GENERAL PULASKI SKYWAY CROSSING HACKENSACK RIVER. This view is taken looking south in the Marion Reach. Public Service Electric & Gas Company's Kearny Power Plant is on the right and the Jersey City marshes are visible on the left. Named for Polish patriot Casimir Pulaski (1748–1779), who fought in the American Revolution, the Skyway is 3.5 miles long and rises 145 ft above both the Hackensack and Passaic Rivers. It cost $21,000,000 when built in 1927. It carries U.S. Routes 1 and 9. Photo: © Uta Gore.

— **15.50 Breezy Point, Queens County, to east.**

— **15.50 West Bank Light offshore to west.** 70 ft. high.

— **15.00 Great Kills Beach, Staten Island to west.**

— **15.00 Rockaway Inlet to east.** This is the entrance to Jamaica Bay, spanned by the Marine Parkway Lift Bridge—it separates Rockaway Beach Point and Queens County on the south from Brooklyn and Kings County to the north.

— **14.60 Oakwood Beach, Staten Island, to west.**

— **14.60 Manhattan Beach, Brooklyn, to east.**

— **14.50 Brighton Beach, Brooklyn, to east.**

— **14.50 New Dorp Beach, Staten Island, to west.**

— **14.10 Northern end of Ambrose Channel.**

— **14.10 Coney Island Beach, Brooklyn, to east.**

— **14.10 Northern end of East Bank Shoals to east.** They extend south to − 16.50.

— **14.10 Elm Tree Light on Staten Island to west.**

— **14.10 Miller Field, Staten Island, to west.**

— **14.10 Swinburne Island, to west, at southern end of West Bank Shoals.** Formerly a quarantine detention station with crematorium and pesthouse.

— **14.00 Latourette Hill on Staten Island (241 ft.) to west.**

— **14.00 Richmond, Staten Island, to west.** This is a site of historic restorations.

— **14.00 New Dorp, Staten Island, to west.** An early settlement.

— **13.50 Midland Beach, Staten Island, to west.**

— **13.00 Norton Point and Lighthouse, Coney Island, Brooklyn, to east.** The 75 ft. steel frame tower has a 70,000 candlepower light and is the last manned lighthouse in the area.

— **13.00 Seagate, Coney Island, Brooklyn, to east.** An exclusive residential area.

— **13.00 Coney Island to east.** This island, once separated from the mainland, is part of Brooklyn. Famous for bathing beaches, amusement parks, and its Boardwalk, in the nineteenth century this was a fashionable resort with large summer hotels served by many steamboats and railroads. Among the railroads were the Manhattan Beach Railroad; Sea Beach Railroad; Long Island Rail Road; Brooklyn, Bath and Coney Island Railroad; Brooklyn, Flatbush and Coney Island Railroad; and Prospect Park and Coney Island Railroad. This gives some measure of the popularity of the beach. Today all these lines are part of the subway system. Steamboats ran to Locust Grove, Norton Point, and the great tubular iron pier that was built out into the ocean. The early trains had open cars with striped red and white awnings and were pulled by steam locomotives known as dummy engines. Because the tracks ran down carriage roads and streets, the engines were disguised as passenger cars in order not to frighten the horses. Principal resorts were Brighton Beach, Manhattan Beach, and Coney Island Beach. The principal amusement parks were Luna Park, Dreamland Park, and Steeplechase Park. Originally, the island was covered with sand dunes, and wild rabbits were abundant, thence the name Coney Island.

— **12.80 Hoffman Island to west.** At midpoint of West Bank Shoal. There was formerly a small coastal

SWINBURNE ISLAND. This grim picture taken c1900 shows the facilities of the Quarantine Detention Station. From left to right the buildings are a) physician's house, b) pest houses, c) crematorium. Most visitors left the island via the smokestack. Today the buildings have been leveled and the island is a unit in the Gateway National Recreation Area. Photo: Smith's New York Harbor Guide.

defense battery located here, as well as a military prison and a quarantine detention station.

- **−12.75 West Bank Shoals to west.**

- **−12.50 Grant City, Staten Island, to west.**

- **−12.25 Dongan Hills, Staten Island, to west.**

- **−12.25 Gravesend Bay to east. Separating Coney Island from the mainland.**

- **−12.25 Gravesend to east.** A section of Brooklyn and an early settlement.

- **−12.20 Bensonhurst to east.** Residential section of Brooklyn.

- **−12.20 Bensonhurst Park to east.** Waterfront recreational area.

- **−12.00 Bath Beach to east.** Residential section of Brooklyn that was formerly a summer resort.

- **−12.00 South Beach, Staten Island, to west.**

- **−11.50 Arrochar, Staten Island, to west.** A residential community.

- **−11.50 New Utrecht, Brooklyn, to east.** An early settlement.

- **−11.25 Dyker Heights, Brooklyn, to east.** Elevation 106 feet.

- **−11.25 Dyker Beach Park, east.** A large city park. Formerly the eight-story Grand View Hotel was built on piles out over the water here. There were four levels of balconies running around the building that had a mansard-roofed tower. The view was out over the lower bay and the Narrows.

- **−11.20 Fort Hamilton, Brooklyn, to east.** The name applies to a residential neighborhood and a military installation. The original fort stood upon the heights and was built in 1832. It was enlarged and strengthened during the Civil War and mounted sixty heavy guns, some of them *en barbette*. It remains an active army base with a chaplains' school and Veterans' Administration Hospital.

- **−11.00 The Narrows.** This is a channel separating upper and lower New York Bay. Staten Island to the west, Long Island to the east.

- **−11.00 The Verrazano-Narrows Bridge.** Connecting Brooklyn and Staten Island. This is the world's longest suspension bridge. Its center span is 4,260 feet, and its side spans are each 1,215 feet. Its total length, including approaches, is 13,700 feet. The bridge is 103 feet wide, with two levels of six traffic lanes each. The towers are 690 feet above mean high water. Clearance at the center is 228 feet above mean high water. The deepest foundation is 170 feet below mean high water. It is supported by four cables of 35⅞ inches in diameter, consisting of sixty-one strands, with 428 wires per strand or 26,108 wires per cable. Each cable is 7,205 feet long, and the total length of wires comes to 143,000 miles. There are 161,000 tons of steel in the structure, and 724,600 cubic yards of concrete in the anchorages, tower piers, roadway, and approaches. The bridge was opened in November of 1964, and the lower level was completed in 1969. It carries Interstate Route 278. It was used by 61,800,000 vehicles in 1991. It is a toll bridge and is operated by the Triborough Bridge and Tunnel Authority. The bridge was designed by Othmar H. Ammann of the firm of Ammann & Whitney. Milton Brumer was the chief construction engineer.

- **−10.75 Fort Lafayette, east.** This fort formerly stood on Hendrick's Reef, 200 yards from the Brooklyn shore and was originally called Fort Diamond. Its construction was begun in 1812 but was not completed until the start of the Civil War. It mounted 75

VERRAZANO-NARROWS BRIDGE spanning the entrance to New York Harbor. The main span is 4,260 ft long. The bridge was opened in 1964. Photo: Courtesy N. Y. Convention & Visitors Bureau.

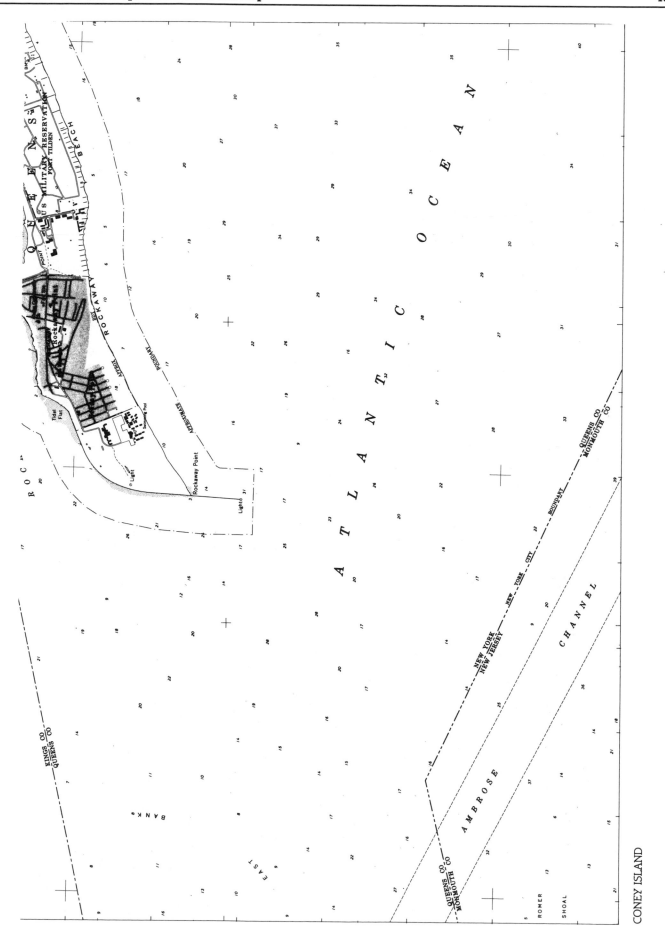

CONEY ISLAND

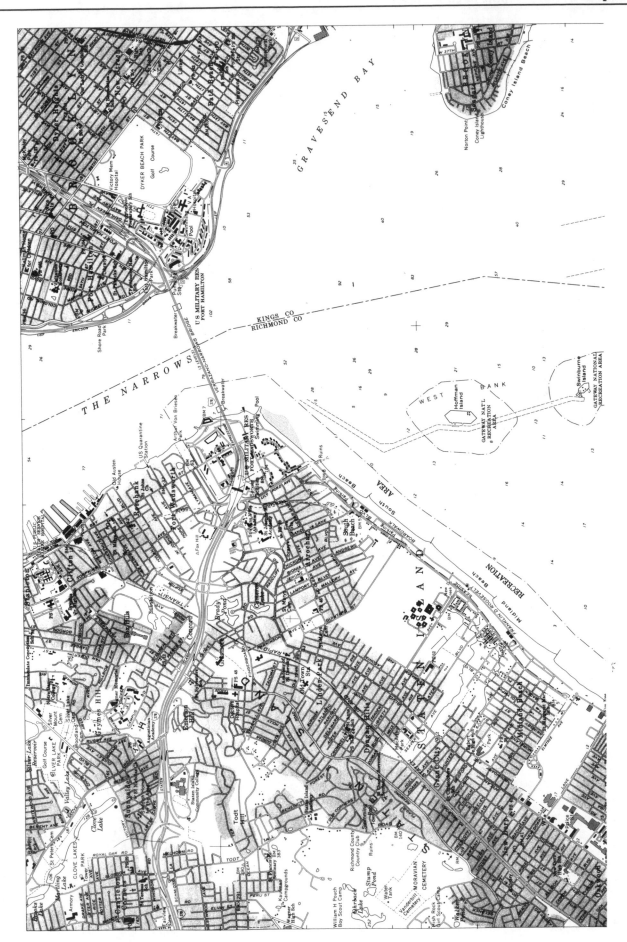

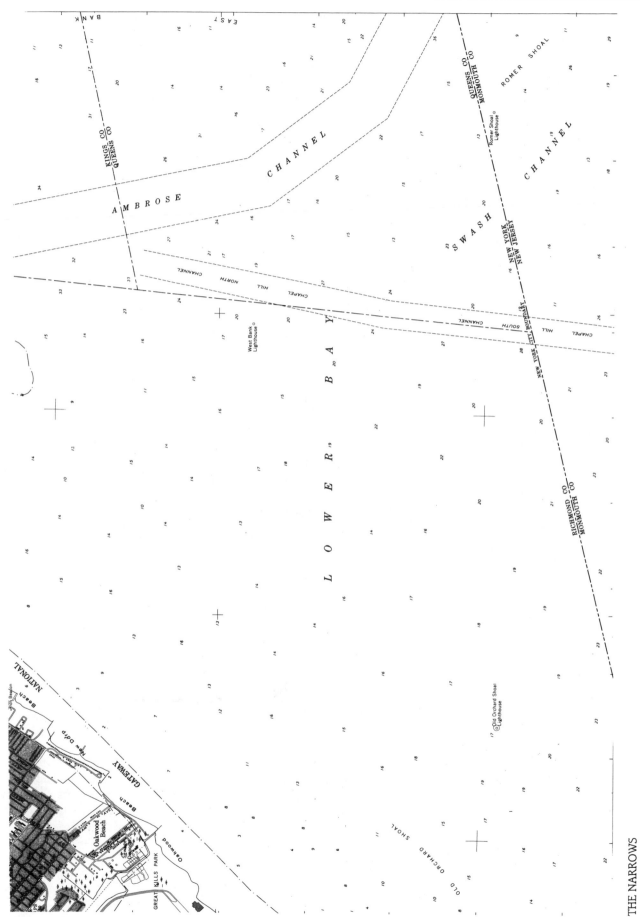

THE NARROWS

heavy guns and also served as a political state prison during the Civil War.

— **10.75 Hendrick's Reef, to east.**

Brooklyn

The Borough of Brooklyn in Greater New York City occupies the southwestern tip of Long Island on the east side of the Narrows. It is oval in shape, occupying an area of seventy-one square miles. Its greatest lengths are eleven miles from north to south and ten miles east to west. It is bounded on the north by Newtown Creek and the English Kills. On the north and east, it is bounded by the Borough of Queens, Old Mill Creek, Jamaica Bay, Pumpkin Patch Channel, Rulers Bar Hassock, and The Raunt, and, on the south, by Rockaway Inlet and Lower New York Bay. On the west, it is bounded by Gravesend Bay, the Narrows, upper New York Bay, Buttermilk Channel, and the East River.

Principal waterways and bays are Wallabout Bay, Newtown Creek, and the English Kills which are either on or empty into the East River; Sheepshead Bay, Gerritsen Creek, Mill Creek, Gerritsen Inlet, Mill Basin, East Mill Basin, Paerdegat Basin, Fresh Creek, Hendrix Creek, and Old Mill Creek, emptying into Jamaica Bay; Gravesend Bay abutting on the Narrows; Gowanus Bay and Canal, Erie Basin, and Red Hook Basin abutting on Upper New York Bay; and Buttermilk Channel, separating Brooklyn Heights and Governor's Island. The East River separates Brooklyn from Manhattan.

The Borough is broken into the following thirty-one recognized sections: northwestern quadrant: Greenpoint, Williamsburgh, Brooklyn Heights, South Brooklyn, Red Hook, and Park Slope; northeastern quadrant: Bushwick, Bedford-Stuyvesant, East New York, Brownsville, Crown Heights, Prospect Park, and Flatbush; southeastern quadrant: Borough Park, Kensington, Flatlands, Bergen Beach, Canarsie, and Sheepshead Bay; southwestern quadrant: Sunset Park, Bay Ridge, Fort Hamilton, Dyker Heights, New Utrecht, Bath Beach, Bensonhurst, Gravesend, Seagate, Coney Island, Brighton Beach, and Manhattan Beach.

Coney Island, once a true island on the southern shore facing on lower New York Bay, has since become attached to the mainland by means of land fill. Sheepshead Bay and Gravesend Bay are at the east and west end of the former channel that separated the island from the mainland. Norton Point is at its west end in the Seagate district and separates Gravesend Bay from lower New York Bay.

The Borough of Brooklyn is congruent with Kings County (1990 population 2,300,664). The southern portion is low ground. The early settlers found it sandy but fertile. The southeastern section had large grassy plains

ROW HOUSES ON 8TH AVENUE, BROOKLYN. Typical of comfortable residences in "The City of Homes." Photo: Alfred H. Marks.

that were devoid of forest. This land, especially around Canarsie, was good for growing maize. The western end of a terminal moraine that ran east and west traversed the southern portion of the region. This moraine extends far east out onto Long Island and there are numerous erratic boulders in this belt.

In the north-central region is a long ridge of medium height running roughly east and west, known as Crown Heights. Grand Army Plaza and the Brooklyn Museum now crown this ridge. In early times, this was stony and densely forested. It served important defensive purposes in the Battle of Long Island in 1776. Its western terminus, known as Brooklyn Heights, fronts on Buttermilk Channel and the East River. Further south, fronting on Upper New York Bay, are Cowans Heights, which are now inside the limits of Greenwood Cemetery, and 106 feet high Dyker Heights, facing on Gravesend Bay and the Narrows near Fort Hamilton. The northeastern and far northern sections were originally densely wooded. Most of Brooklyn is now well built over.

The aboriginal inhabitants of Brooklyn were the Canarsie Indians, whose Sachem was Sessys. Ownership of parts of the area was disputed by the neighboring Rockaway Indians, whose principal settlements were in present-day Queens.

As early as about 1624, there were scattered Dutch settlements at New Amersfoort near Flatlands, facing on Jamaica Bay. An Indian pathway, which much later developed into Flatbush Avenue, ran from Bergen Island, on Jamaica Bay, to opposite Manhattan, at the later site of Fulton Ferry, which is a distance of 10½ miles. Soon after settlement, Flatlands became a palisaded village. Between 1634 and 1636, scattered settlements were made in the section then called Midwout, which is now part of Flatbush. In 1636 Jacob Van Curler made extensive land purchases from the Indians.

Twenty-two Dutch and Walloon families settled at Gowanus in 1636 and at Wallabout Bay in 1637. Also, between 1638 and 1639, the Dutch West India Company acquired the Indian title from the Canarsie tribe for most of present-day Brooklyn. In 1642, a Cornelius Hooglandt was licensed to operate a flat-bottomed rowboat ferry across the East River from New Amsterdam. The landing on the Long Island side soon became known as "The Ferry." Between 1641 and 1650, numerous Swedes and Normans settled along Newtown Creek in what was then called Woodtown or Bushwick. This is now part of present-day Williamsburgh. Later, Frenchmen settled in this same area.

In 1643 a patent was granted to Lady Deborah Moody, widow of Sir Henry Moody of Garsden in Wiltshire. In 1640, she had moved to Massachusetts for religious reasons. Because of their non-conforming views, she and her son, Sir Henry, were excommunicated and sought asylum in the New Netherlands. The settlement at Gravesend was "dedicated to freedom of religion." Forty house plots were set out in a palisaded enclosure, with forty farms located outside the stockaded area. The enclosure contained sixteen acres. In 1644 the settlement was almost wiped out by Indians but managed to hang on. Lady Moody died in 1658, and Sir Henry moved on to Virginia. In 1645 or 1646, the settlement at "The Ferry" on the East River was incorporated as Breuckelen, which is Dutch for "broken ground." Also in 1646, a settlement was made in "The Clove" at present-day Bedford. A patent was granted for a settlement at Flatbush in 1651, and a Dutch church was established in 1654.

Land near the Narrows and Gravesend Bay was informally settled as early as around 1643, but in 1652 the Nyack Patent was granted to Cornelius Van Werckhoven, schepen of Utrecht in Holland, and a member of the Dutch West India Company. He repurchased this land from the Indians. He died in either 1655 or 1656, before he could establish his patroonship. However, in 1657 Jacques Cortelyou, who had been the tutor

of his children and manager of his estates, purchased this tract and founded the village of New Utrecht. This was a palisaded village consisting of twenty plots and a blockhouse. It was surrounded by twenty fifty-acre farms. In 1675, a disastrous fire almost destroyed the settlement. In 1677, a Dutch church was organized. By 1661 five Dutch towns and one English town had been established in Brooklyn.

New Amsterdam was conquered by the English in 1664. That same year a twenty-year lease of the Brooklyn ferry was given to William Merritt, at the rental of twenty pounds per year. He was to operate flat-bottomed scows powered by oars and sometimes by sail. These boats had no keels. Also, the name of Breuckelen was officially changed to Brooklyn. In 1665 a conference was called at Hempstead and the Dukes Laws were promulgated by Governor Richard Nicolls. Long Island and Staten Island were incorporated into the West Riding of Yorkshire, with the seat of government at Gravesend. In 1670, the Rockaway Indians made claim to the Flatbush area, and the town was repurchased and a firm eastern boundary established. Shortly thereafter, in 1671, a new settlement, known then as Oostwoud (East Woods), or the New Lots of Flatbush, was established in the area later known as New Lots or East New York.

The first Colonial Assembly was called in 1683. The ridings were abolished, and counties were established. Brooklyn became Kings County, possibly because it was the richest and most fertile part of the colony. There were further minor reorganizations after the Jacob Leisler Rebellion in 1691. During the American Revolution, Brooklyn was the site of the important and disastrous Battle of Long Island. After 1776, Brooklyn remained in British control. The infamous prison ships were anchored in Wallabout Bay, and those who died in them were buried in shallow graves on the site of the present Navy Yard.

The first steam ferry, owned by Robert Fulton and his

FORT LAFAYETTE. Formerly this fort stood on Hendrick's Reef, 600 ft from the Brooklyn shore at the Narrows, but was demolished in 1962 to make way for the eastern tower of the Verrazano-Narrows Bridge. The fort was completed 1861. Photo: Smith's New York Harbor Guide.

BROOKLYN

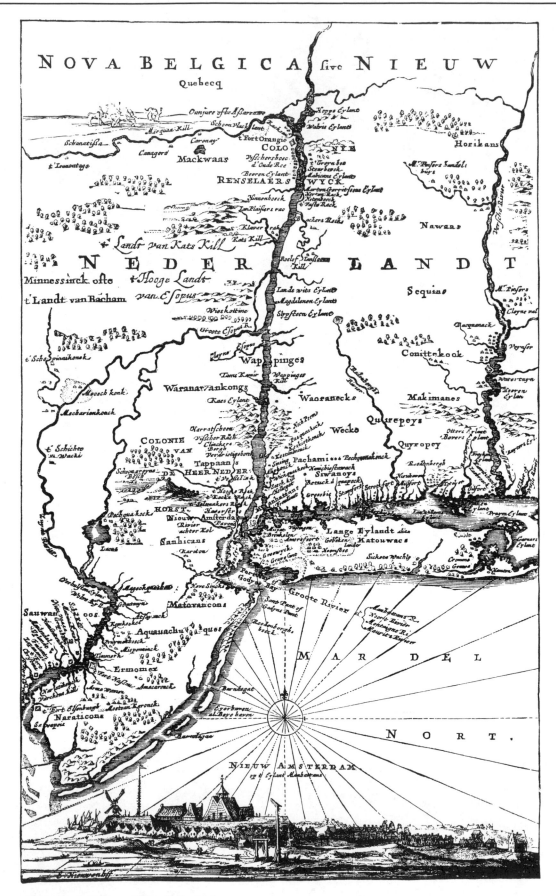

Van Der Donck's map of New Netherlands.

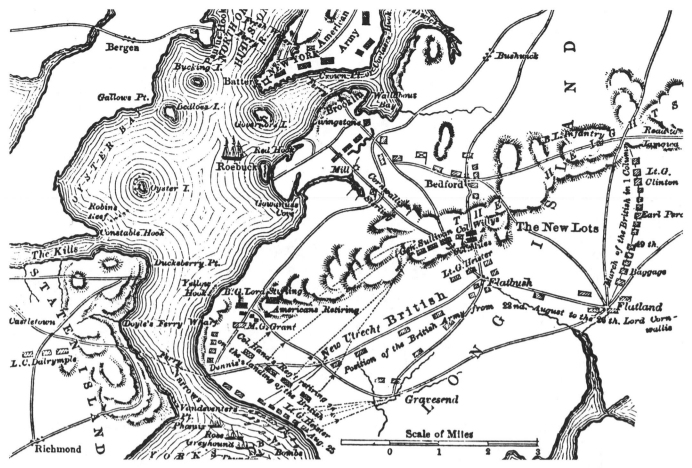

New York Bay and Narrows in 1776.

brother-in-law, William Cutting, was put into service to Manhattan in 1814. It was double-ended and named the *Nassau*. Fulton Ferry operated until 1924.

In 1816 Brooklyn was formally incorporated as Brooklyn Ferry, and again incorporated as a city in 1834. In 1841 the *Brooklyn Daily Eagle* was formed, of which Walt Whitman served as editor from 1846 to 1847. From here on, Brooklyn grew rapidly. Williamsburgh was absorbed in 1855, making it the third largest city in the United States. The Brooklyn Bridge was under construction from 1869 till 1883. It was designed and constructed by John and Washington Roebling at a cost of $15,500,000. The main span is 1,595 feet. The new bridge and steam ferries gave terrific impetus to Brooklyn's growth. Handsome Greek Revival houses were built on Brooklyn Heights, and Brooklyn fast became a fashionable suburb. Finally, in 1898, with a population of around one million, Brooklyn became a borough of the city of New York. The 1990 population is 2,300,664.

With construction of rapid transit lines and subway tunnels to Manhattan, Brooklyn became a city of fine homes and mansions. It was frequently called the City of Homes or the City of Churches. Among the more prominent churches are the Reformed Protestant Dutch Church at Flatbush, organized in 1654 (the present building was built 1796); Saint Ann's Episcopal Church, established in 1784; and the Plymouth Church where Henry Ward Beecher preached from 1847 onward. In the twentieth century agriculture gave way to apartment houses and private home development in southern and eastern Brooklyn, and the great main streets were laid out. It is interesting to note that the early colonial homes in Brooklyn were mainly built of wood and lath, owing to a shortage of building stones. The graceful curved eaves and porticos of Dutch Colonial architecture reached a high point of perfection in Brooklyn. The Lefferts Homestead in Prospect Park is a beautiful example of this. Unfortunately, very few of these homes survive.

Trade and industry also developed in the nineteenth century. The Erie Canal Basin was established in 1825 with extensive warehouses. In the early 1860s the great India Docks and Atlantic Docks, with substantial granite warehouses covering over forty acres, were erected. The great brick Empire Stores were built on the East River in the 1870s. These were the forerunners of the later tremendous Brooklyn Eastern District and Bush

Terminals and present-day Port Authority Ocean Terminals. Brooklyn alsodeveloped extensive machinery, textile, paper, and chemical goods industries. It is served by the Brooklyn Branch of the Long Island Rail Road, with a major terminal at Flatbush Avenue, numerous elevated and subway lines, and the freight-only branch of Conrail (formerly New York Connecting Railroad), from Bushwick to Bay Ridge, near the Brooklyn Army Terminal. The former New York Naval Shipyard, which once handled the Navy's heaviest work, is greatly reduced in size; its facilities on Wallabout Bay are leased to private operators.

The great Verrazano-Narrows Bridge, completed in 1965, replaces the former Sixty-ninth Street Ferry to Staten Island. Brooklyn is joined to Manhattan by the Brooklyn (1883), Manhattan (1909), and Williamsburg (1903) Bridges across the East River—all of the suspension type, and also by the Brooklyn-Battery Tunnel. The Williamsburg and Manhattan Bridges carry subway trains as well as motor vehicles. The Kosciusko Bridge across Newtown Creek carries Interstate 278-A, the Brooklyn-Queens Expressway, into Queens. The Marine Parkway Bridge carries Flatbush Avenue across Rockaway Inlet to the Rockaway Peninsula in Queens County. Other principal highways in Brooklyn are the Gowanus Expressway along the Upper New York Bay, and the Belt Parkway (Route 27-A), also called the Shore Parkway, along the shores of the Narrows and Gravesend and Jamaica Bays. Floyd Bennett Field, the former New York Naval Air Station, is located in the southeasternmost portion of the Borough near Jamaica Bay. Fort Hamilton, built originally in 1831 as a harbor defense at the entrance of the Narrows, now serves as an administrative center and school for military chaplains. The former Manhattan Beach Civil Defense Training Center is now given over to the Kingsborough Community College.

A now extinct, unique Brooklyn institution was Ebbets Field, the former home of the Brooklyn Dodgers baseball team. The team was originally called the trolley dodgers because of the plethora of streetcar lines that once operated in Brooklyn. They are now gone, along with the ball club.

Brooklyn was also once a fashionable resort, with large hotels at Manhattan Beach and Brighton Beach. The great Manhattan Beach Hotel, Hotel Brighton, and Oriental Hotel were colossuses of their day. An iron pier out into the ocean accommodated the landing of excursion steamers of the Iron Steamboat Co. and other lines from such points as Manhattan, Newark, and Jersey City, bringing day-trippers to the famous surf bathing beaches of Coney Island. Later, these fashionable hotels gave way to the boardwalk, bathhouses, and amusement parks such as famous Luna Park, Dreamland Park, and Steeplechase Park, with its great parachute jump tower and roller coaster rides. Sheepshead Bay was the center for party

fishing boats and such large seafood restaurants as F. W. I. L. Lundy's.

Among Brooklyn's cultural attractions are the Brooklyn Museum of Art, the Brooklyn Academy of Music, with both an opera house and concert hall, and the Brooklyn Public Library. The Brooklyn Botanical Garden is possibly the finest in the United States. There is also a small zoo. Prospect Park is in the center of the city, and the Grand Army Plaza, at its northern end, with its monumental arches and colonnades, is reminiscent of the Arc de Triomphe in Paris. A fine formal Parade Ground is adjacent to the southern end of 526-acre Prospect Park.

Other major parks include Brooklyn Marine Park on Jamaica Bay, Dyker Beach Park near Gravesend, McGolrick Park, McCarren Park, Fort Greene Park, Tompkins Park, Bushwick Park, Lincoln Terrace Park, Sunset Park, Owl's Head Park overlooking the Narrows, Manhattan Beach Park, the Jamaica Bay Wildlife Refuge Islands, Canarsie Park, Plum Beach, McKinley Park, and Shore Road Park overlooking the Lower Bay. The very extensive and beautiful Greenwood Cemetery on Cowans Heights also served as a park in the nineteenth century.

The principal educational institutions include Brooklyn College of CUNY, Polytechnic Institute of Brooklyn, Pratt Institute, St. John's University, St. Joseph's College for Women, Packer Collegiate Institute, Long Island University, and Kingsborough Community College.

– **10.75 Vandeventer's Point on Staten Island, west.**

– **10.75 Grasmere, Staten Island, to west.** Residential neighborhood.

– **10.75 Fort Wadsworth, Staten Island, to west.** Active military base. Part of harbor defenses started ca. 1812. Originally called Fort Richmond, but later renamed in honor of General Peleg Wadsworth (1749 – 1829), who served in the Battle of Long Island. The massive waterfront bastions were never completed, such type of construction having been outmoded by heavy artillery. However, the area of the fort bristled with cannon.

– **10.65 von Briesen Park on west.**

– **10.50 United States Quarantine Station on west.**

– **10.00 Rosebank, Staten Island, on west.**

– **9.75 Catskill Aqueduct** passes water from Brooklyn to Staten Island in a bell-and-spigot pipeline.

– **9.75 Todt Hill, Staten Island, on west.** Elevation 410 feet. Highest point on Atlantic shoreline south of Mount Desert Island, Maine.

— 9.70 **Clifton, Staten Island, west.**

— 9.70 **Pouch Terminal docks and warehouses on west.**

— 9.70 **Shore Road Park, Brooklyn, on east.**

— 9.65 **Foreign Trade Zone No. 1 on west.**

— 9.60 **Stapleton Port Authority Trailership Terminal on west.**

— 9.60 **Stapleton, Staten Island, on west.** Site of former Doyle's Ferry Wharf and early steam ferry lines run by Daniel Tompkins and Cornelius Vanderbilt. It is the proposed new Home Port for the Navy's Surface Action Group—including nuclear ships.

— 9.00 **Sand Bay, Staten Island to west.**

— 9.00 **Bayridge Section of Brooklyn on east.**

— 9.00 **Bennett Point on east.**

— 9.00 **Tompkinsville, Staten Island, on west.** Formerly known as the Watering Place, because in early days sailing ships filled their water casks from springs in the neighborhood.

— 8.75 **Yellow Hook, Brooklyn, to east.**

— 8.75 **Owl Head to east.**

— 8.50 **Sixty-ninth Street, Brooklyn.** Former terminal of ferry from Staten Island.

— 8.50 **Ducksberry Point on west.**

— 8.50 **Emerson Hill on west.**

— 8.50 **St. George, Staten Island, on west.** Seat of Richmond Borough and county government. Commercial center of Staten Island. Terminal of ferry from Manhattan and of Rapid Transit lines.

— 8.25 **Owl's Head Park, Brooklyn, east.**

— 8.25 **Kill van Kull, west.**

— 8.20 **66th St., Bay Ridge, Brooklyn, east.**

— 8.20 **Constable Hook and Point, Bayonne on west.** Site of many oil refineries.

Bayonne, New Jersey

Bayonne occupies a low peninsula separating Upper New York and Newark bays. It is three miles long by less than one mile average width, widening out at the south end into Bergen Point on the west and Constable Hook on the east. It is bounded on the north by the Greenville section of Jersey City, on the west by Newark Bay, on the south by the Kill van Kull, which separates Bayonne from Staten Island, and on the east by Upper New York Bay.

It was first settled in 1646 by Dutch traders under a grant to Jacob Roy, Chief Gunner, or Constable, to the Dutch West India Company. Later, in 1654, the Pamrapo Section was settled by small farmers and fishermen who lived along the shore, but the area was largely undeveloped until the nineteenth century. During the Revolution Fort DeLancey was situated at Bergen Point on the Kill van Kull, and was in British hands during much of the war.

An early road ran from Bergen (present-day Jersey City) to the ferry between Bergen Point and Staten Island. This was part of a major stagecoach route between New York City and Philadelphia. This early road was later developed into Hudson County Boulevard, which has since been renamed Kennedy Boulevard. In the nineteenth century, the Central Railroad of New Jersey was built south from Jersey City to the tip of the peninsula and then crossed Newark Bay to Elizabethport on a long bridge. This railroad extended eventually to Allentown and Wilkes-Barre, Pennsylvania, with important connections to Philadelphia and Harrisburg. Trains of the Reading Company and Baltimore & Ohio also operated over the Jersey Central. Today it serves as a secondary line of Conrail. The Lehigh Valley and Pennsylvania Railroads also built a jointly shared bridge across Newark Bay to Port Newark from the north end of Bayonne. This is also part of the Conrail system today.

Victor Dupont arrived from France and settled in Bayonne in 1800. He called his home facing the Kill van Kull "Bon Sejours." In 1845 David La Tourette purchased the mansion and built a dock. He reconstructed the mansion into a large Gothic Revival resort hotel. It operated for many years and was finally razed in 1926.

This was the beginning of Bayonne as a society resort. Many wealthy New Yorkers took advantage of the pleasant seaside atmosphere and built large suburban homes overlooking the water. There were numerous golf courses, bridle trails, picnic groves, and tennis courts and clubs. The town even boasted an opera house. Many large mansions and churches from this era remain. In 1840 Hudson County was split off from Bergen County. The City of Bayonne was incorporated in 1869.

In 1875 the first oil refinery was established in Bayonne. Soon the Standard Oil Company of New Jersey came to occupy much of Constable Hook. Deepwater docking for tankers and oil barges, good rail connections, and proximity to the New York and New England markets favored the further development of refineries. However, these had the unpleasant consequences of polluted waters and malodorous vapors that destroyed Bayonne's desirability as a resort or suburban area for the affluent. The wealthier residents moved

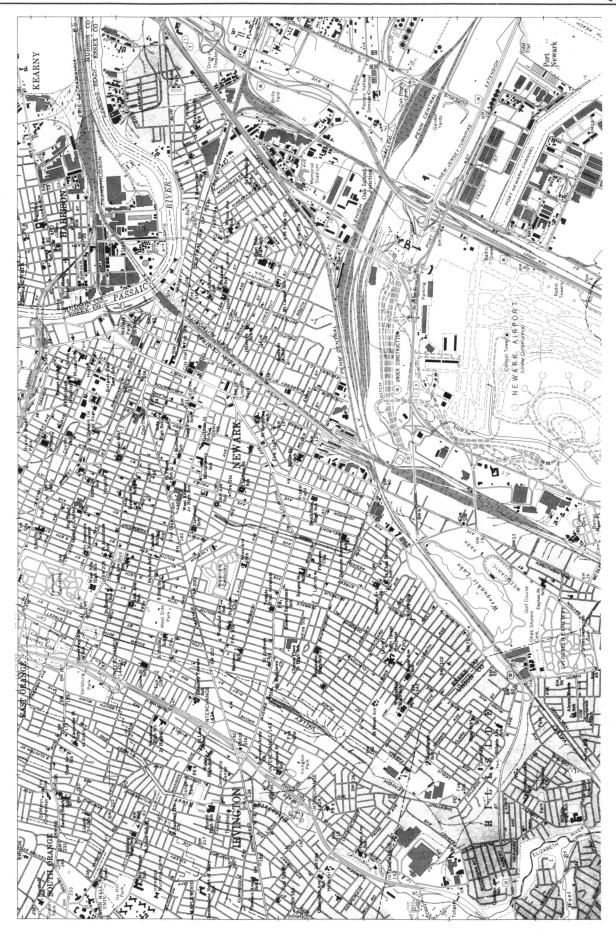

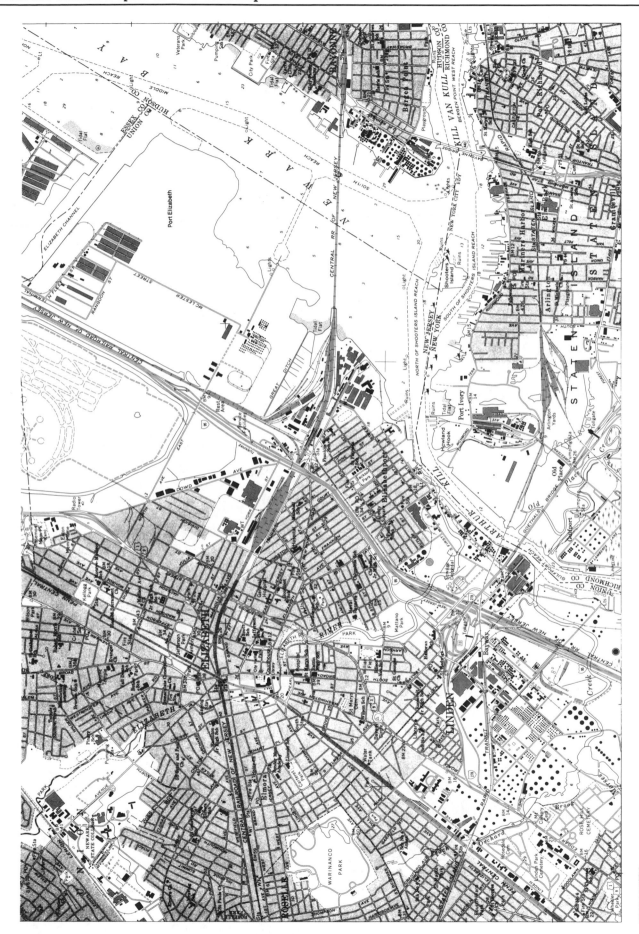

ELIZABETH

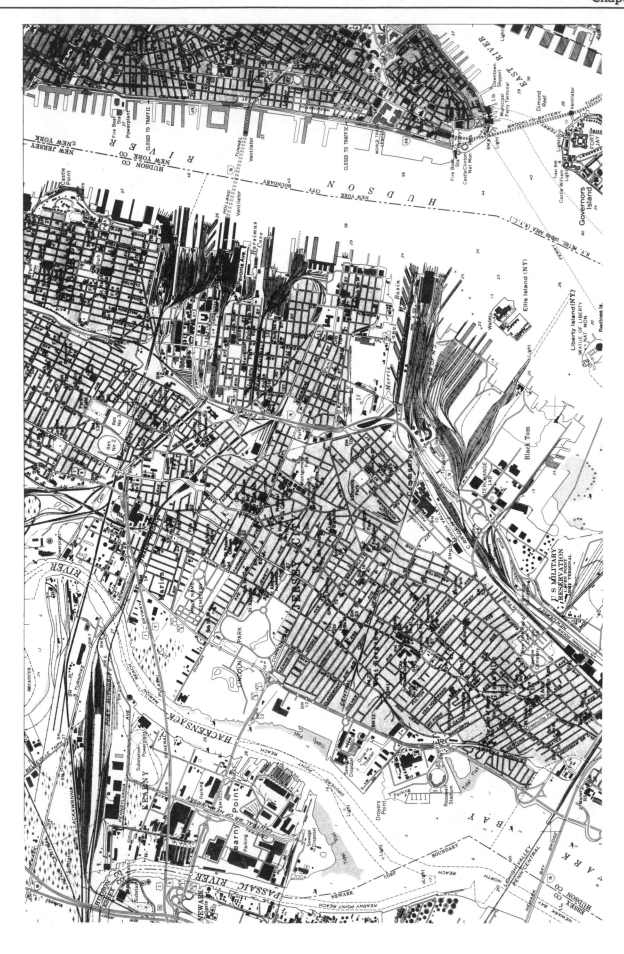

JERSEY CITY

farther west along the Jersey Central to such towns as Roselle, Cranford, Plainfield, and Somerville. Immigrant labor flowed in to work on the Hook, and inexpensive row houses and tenements were built to accommodate them. Refinery activity was at its zenith during World War II when the Big Inch Pipeline was completed from the southwest with Bayonne as its eastern terminal. At the present time Texaco and Richfield Oil have facilities at Bergen Point, and Asiatic Oil, Tide Water Oil, and Exxon have large facilities at Constable Hook. Other major industries are Baker Castor Oil, General Cable, National Sulphur, Bergen Port Chemical, and American Radiator. Conrail serves Port Johnson on the Kill van Kull on Constable Hook and has extensive marshalling yards. The United States Army Military Ocean Terminal occupies a long pier on Upper New York Bay; this was formerly occupied by the United States Naval Supply Center.

Generally speaking, residential areas are west of the railroad, and heavy industry is east of it. Bayonne is connected to Staten Island by the Bayonne Bridge across the Kill van Kull, and with Port Newark by the high-level bridge of the New Jersey Turnpike Hudson County Extension across Newark Bay. There are three major parks along Newark Bay. The population of Bayonne in 1990 was 61,444.

− **8.18 Upper New York Bay.** This was called the Bay of Santa Margarita by Verrazano.

− **8.15 Robbins Reef and Light west.** There is also the outflow from the Hudson County sewage trunk line several hundred feet offshore. Bass caught near here taste oily and seals play on the surrounding rocks.

− **8.15 Constable Hook on west** is the site of oil refineries. There were many beached shipwrecks and barges in the cove north of the point, which has very shallow draft.

− **8.10 Bay Ridge Carfloat Terminal on east.** This is the eastern terminus of the crossbay railroad carfloat operation of the New York Cross Harbor Railroad.

− **8.00 Former Brooklyn Army Terminal on east.** These large concrete buildings were designed so that ships could be loaded in secret with no lights showing. They are now occupied by commercial tenants. The thick concrete walls and floors and low ceilings make them perfect to insulate computer equipment. Known as U. S. Military Ocean Terminal.

− **8.00 Bayonne on west.**

− **7.75 Oyster Island on west.** Very tiny.

− **7.75 Pamrapo on west.** Section of Bayonne settled in 1654.

− **7.70 U.S. Military Ocean Terminal on west.** Formerly known as U. S. Naval Reservation Bayonne Supply Center. There is a large basin-type drydock at the end of the point known as Graving Dock.

− **7.50 Bay Ridge Channel on east.** Close in to Brooklyn shore.

− **7.50 Bush Terminal Docks and Warehouses on east.** The piers are in a state of decay, but the massive loft buildings are well maintained with many commercial and industrial tenants.

− **7.50 Tidal Flats on west.**

− **7.40 Cowan's Heights on east.** Elevation 220 feet. Now included in grounds of Greenwood Cemetery.

− **7.40 Bayonne-Jersey City Line on west.**

− **7.25 Greenville Channel on west.**

− **7.25 Port Authority Greenville-Port Jersey on west.** This is on the site of the former Pennsylvania Railroad Greenville Yards. It is currently the location of the western carfloat bridges used by the New York Cross Harbor Railroad. There are tentative plans to develop this area as a coal port, but there is much resistance by the local residents.

− **6.75 Gowanus Cove on east.** A Port Authority Marine Terminal.

− **6.70 Gowanus Bay and Creek on east.** Leading to Gowanus Canal with its several basins. Gowanus is a corruption of "Cowan's." The canal is notably malodorous with constricted navigation.

− **6.65 Port Authority Columbia Street Marine Terminal on east.**

GOWANUS CANAL, BROOKLYN. Viaduct carries the Independent Division 6th Avenue Subway line, served by the F and GG trains. The Smith–9th Street station straddles the canal. Photo: Alfred H. Marks.

−6.65 Claremont Channel on west. Leads to former Lehigh Valley Railroad float bridges and Claremont Freight Yard and Terminal.

−6.60 Claremont Section of Greenville Section of Jersey City to west.

−6.50 Caven Point to west. This section of Jersey City was settled as early as 1643 by Dirck Straatmaker, who was struck by a poisoned arrow by Lenni Lenape Indians during an uprising in retaliation for a massacre of innocent Indian women and children, ordered by Governor William Kieft, who was later recalled for mismanagement.

Early in this century the area was used as a terminal and was a U. S. Military Reservation known as the Caven Point Army Terminal. A long pier was built out along the northern side of the Claremont Channel for loading deep-draft ships. Today the Point is occupied by the luxurious Port Liberté residential development. There are "Venetian" canals for docking private pleasure craft and a private ferry to Manhattan.

−6.50 Greenville Section of Jersey City on west. The village of Greenville was separately incorporated in 1863 and was a section of luxurious private residences, and was the site of the large Bayview and New York Bay Cemeteries, where the Cunard Line, which originally docked in Jersey City, maintained a plot for its employees. The area was first settled in 1654 and was called Minkakwa. The entire Bayonne Peninsula was originally part of Bergen County, before the erection of Hudson County.

−6.50 Oyster Bay on west. Once the most prolific spawning grounds for said delicious mollusc on the East Coast. According to James Kirke Paulding, in the early nineteenth century oysters from this bay were sold in Manhattan on every street corner for 5¢ per dozen. Landfilling of the bay by the railroad companies diminished the breeding area in the late nineteenth century, and the twentieth century has finished the job of killing off the oysters with pollution.

−6.50 Erie Basin on east. Former eastern terminus for canal boats traversing the Erie Canal and Hudson River, the basin was completed in 1825 using fill from the canal to create the breakwater. The outside of the breakwater was called the Breakwater Terminal, and the portion facing the east was called Brooklyn Basin or Henry Street Basin at various times. There are small drydocks within the Erie Basin, which has a very narrow entrance, to provide protection for the small canal boats, which often wintered here while the Captain's children attended

school in the Red Hook section of Brooklyn. Ocean-going sailing ships also used the basin.

Today the Basin is the site of the Port Authority Erie Basin Marine Terminal/Fishport, a fish harvesting, processing, and distribution center. This $30 million project already has five tenants with leases totaling 180,000 sq. ft, and is expected to generate regional sales of $130 million and annual payrolls of $23 million. There was formerly a grain terminal on the east side of the basin.

−6.50 Red Hook Section of Brooklyn on east. Still a residential area popular with marine workers.

−6.50 Red Hook Channel on east. Close to Brooklyn shoreline and connecting Bay Ridge Channel on the south with Buttermilk Channel on the north. Depths to 42 feet. Controlling 33 ft.

−6.45 Red Hook on east.

−6.35 Port Authority Red Hook Container Port on east.

−6.00 Black Tom Island on west. Now part of the mainland. During World War I (August 1916) there was a terrific ammunition explosion at a warehouse here. Sabotage was suspected.

−6.00 Gallows Point on west. During Colonial times criminals were hung here prior to having their remains left hanging in chains on nearby Gibbett (now Ellis) Island. Later the area was acquired by the National Docks Corporation subsidiary of the Lehigh Valley Railroad for a freight yard. Today the area is a very attractive part of the Liberty State Park with extensive views of the Upper New York Bay and with ferry service to Liberty Island, Ellis Island and the Battery (foot passengers only).

Jersey City

Jersey City occupies a peninsula between the Hudson River and Upper New York Bay on the east and the Hackensack River and Newark Bay on the west. The portions bordering the water are low and were originally swampy. A rocky ridge runs down the center; it is low at the south end and gains height and breadth at the north end. It constitutes the far southern end of the Palisades. At Jersey City the top forms a plateau about a mile wide. Jersey City is bounded on the north by Penhorn Creek, a tributary of the Hackensack, and the municipalities of Secaucus, North Bergen, Union City, and Hoboken. To the south it is bounded by the City of Bayonne, which occupies the southern tip of the peninsula.

The Hudson shoreline is indented, from north to south, by Harsimus Cove, Morris Canal Basin, and the Tidewater

Basin. Jersey City measures four miles from north to south and about two and a half miles from east to west, or roughly ten square miles. It is densely built up with homes and offices. Principal industries were meat-packing, ink, chemicals, steel and large plants owned by Continental Can and Colgate-Palmolive Soap Company. It was formerly a major steamship terminal and was Cunard's original terminal in the Port of New York. Harborside Terminal was one of the world's largest warehouse structures. It fronts on the Hudson River. Formerly there were major passenger train and ferry terminals of the Central Railroad of New Jersey, Pennsylvania Railroad, and Erie Railroad along the Hudson. All these lines have been absorbed into Conrail, and the trains have been rerouted to Penn Station in Manhattan and the Lackawanna Terminal in Hoboken. No ferry routes remain. Two subway tunnels of the PATH rapid transit system connect with downtown and midtown Manhattan. PATH trains also operate to Newark and to Hoboken from four stations in Jersey City: Pavonia, Exchange Place, Grove-Henderson, and Journal Square, site of the modern PATH Intermodular Transportation Center that includes a bus terminal and a large parking garage for private automobiles. There remain numerous freight yards, including the Pennsylvania's former Greenville and Harsimus Cove yards, and the Erie's Croxton Yard, in the Hackensack Meadows. Jersey City is also served by the New York, Susquehanna & Western Railroad.

The Holland Tunnel provides vehicular access to downtown Manhattan and connects with the Hudson County Extension of the New Jersey Turnpike. Major highways to the west are the Lincoln Highway (Routes 1 and 9), the Pulaski Skyway (Routes 1 and 9A), and the Jersey City and Newark Turnpike (Route 7). Principal north-south arteries are Kennedy Boulevard, atop the plateau, and Tonnele Avenue (Routes 1 and 9) along the western foot of the ridge. Residential and commercial areas predominate atop the plateau, with industry in the lower areas, although there is considerable residential development there as well. Much area is devoted to outmoded railroad freight yards that are being gradually redeveloped.

Jersey City's population in 1990 was 228,537—the second largest in the state after Newark. Major sections are Greenville, a residential area at the southern end of town; Caven Point, devoted to industry along Upper New York Bay; and Black Tom, which is also on the Upper Bay. Formerly it was largely devoted to railroad yards of the Jersey Central System. During World War I Black Tom was the site of a large and famous ammunition explosion. Bergen, atop the plateau, was the early nucleus of the city and one of the first parts settled; Communipaw, van Vorst, Paulus Hook, Harsimus, and Pavonia range along

the Hudson shoreline. Commercial centers are at Exchange Place in Paulus Hook, on the Hudson shoreline, where there are banks, warehouses, and the giant Colgate-Palmolive headquarters and plant; and at Journal Square, north of old Bergen, where there are the PATH Transportation Center, many banks and office buildings, and the large and palatial Loew's and Stanley theaters. Roosevelt Stadium is located on Newark Bay at Droyer's Point. The Medical Center, one of the largest hospitals in the New York metropolitan area, is near Bergen and Communipaw.

The largest of the many parks are the still-developing Liberty Park on the Upper Bay and Lincoln Park on the west side, which runs down to the Hackensack River. Here is located J. E. Fraser's famous statue of Lincoln, executed in 1929. Other major parks include County Park, Columbia Park, Bayside Park, Audubon Park, Grand Park, Lafayette Park, Leonard Gordon Park, and Montgomery Park.

Principal cemeteries include Saint Peter's and Holy Name on the West Side, and Jersey City Cemetery, New York Bay Cemetery, and Bayview Cemetery on the east side. These all provide significant open areas with long vistas. Squares are of importance in Jersey City and form the nucleus of residential areas consisting of brownstone and similar row houses, some of which are of considerable distinction. Many are being renovated and restored. Principal squares are Hamilton Park Square, van Vorst Park Square, and Washington Park Square at the junction of Grand and Washington Streets in the Paulus Hook section.

Saint John's Roman Catholic Church, on Kennedy Boulevard north of Journal Square, is of architectural interest with its massive limestone and granite construction and high campanile. Other landmarks are the former Brunswick Laundry, Jersey Central Terminal, and Fairmont Hotel, and Saint Peter's Preparatory School and College.

Jersey City had an exciting past. According to Robert Juet, who chronicled Henry Hudson's voyage of 1609, the crew was met by friendly Lenni-Lenape Indians on 3 September at Gamoenipa (now called Communipaw.) This name means "over the river." This region was occupied by the Hackensack Indians, who belonged to the Lenni-Lenape nation.

In 1610 the first permanent settlement was made at Ahasimus (now called Horsimus or Harsimus). An attempt at settlement had been made at Communipaw in the previous year, but this was probably simply a temporary trading post. Oloffe Van Cortlandt was among the first settlers in the Jersey City area. In either 1616 or 1618 a village was planted at Bergen by the Dutch East India Company. The meaning of the name Bergen has always been an enigma. Some authorities claim that it was named for Bergen in Norway, as there were possibly some Norwegians among the early settlers. Another theory is that it was named for Bergen-op-Zoom in Holland, which is much more likely. A third theory posits that the name is derived from the word *bergen,* denoting a "ridge between two marshlands." As this describes the situation perfectly, it is the most likely origin. In 1621 the Dutch West India Company acquired the lands of the Dutch East India Company, and in 1630 they granted the Pavonia patroonship to Michael Pauw. This grant also included Staten Island. By 1636 Cornelius van Vorst was in command of the Pavonia settlement. It consisted of thatch-roofed houses and was palisaded and well armed. In 1641 Myndert Myndertsen van der Horst was also given a grant in Jersey City.

Trouble soon developed with the Indians, aggravated by the stupid and stubborn attitude of the company's director, William Kieft. Bloody Indian raids in 1643 virtually destroyed the settlements on the New Jersey side of the Hudson. The problems between the Indians and the settlers were resolved in 1658 when Kieft's successor, Peter Stuyvesant, repurchased the lands from them.

By 1660, Bergen had become a palisaded village with a Dutch Reformed Church, which was the first in New Jersey. That same year Jacques Cortelyou was laying out a village at Communipaw, and William Jansen was being granted a charter to operate a horse ferry from there to New Amsterdam. Security was gained by following Governor Stuyvesant's order to concentrate the settlements, although by this time the local Indians were not causing any serious trouble.

Bergen's first municipal government was established in 1661, and the first school was built in 1662. In 1664 the English gained control. In 1675 Bergen was unofficially designated a county, and this was made official in 1683. Development was gradual under the English, who allowed the Dutch ways to continue. In 1762 a line of stages was established from Paulus Hook to New Bridge on the Hackensack River. A race track was established at Paulus Hook in 1771, which was popular with "bloods" from Manhattan. The English began to call Paulus Hook "Powles Hook," and both spellings have been used interchangeably to this day. Originally the Powles Hook area was a small island, separated from the mainland by marshes. During the American Revolution a small redoubt or fort was built there. It was commanded by the patriot general Hugh Mercer. On September 23, in 1776, it was cannonaded by the British, who gained command that day and were to hold it for the rest of the war, with one notable exception. On August 18, in 1779, Major "Lighthorse" Harry Lee recaptured the fort from the British, but he immediately abandoned it as difficult to hold and of little strategic value. It was mainly a moral victory, similar to Wayne's capture of Stony Point.

After the war, in 1804, Anthony Dey acquired property at Powles Hook, which was soon taken over by a group called Associates of the Jersey Company. The population then was only twenty persons. Major impetus to growth came in 1812 when Robert Fulton established a steam ferry from Powles Hook to Cortlandt Street in Manhattan. This latter evolved into the important Pennsylvania Railroad ferry route. Fulton lived in Jersey City until his untimely death in 1815. Establishment of the steam ferry assured the future growth and importance of Jersey City. In 1820 a "City of Jersey," or "Jersey City within Bergen County" was incorporated, centering at Powles Hook. A revised charter was granted in 1829, and the town was reincorporated simply as Jersey City in 1838. In 1837 Passaic County had been split off from Essex County because of a desire for more manageable political units setting a precedent. In 1840 Hudson County (1990 population 553,099), including all that area within present-day Jersey City, was split off from Bergen County (1990 population 825,380). The villages of van Vorst, Hudson City, and Bergen were annexed in 1851 and 1869. In 1873, the village of Greenville was also annexed, and a new charter was granted.

Shortly after 1824 the Morris Canal was completed, with its terminus in Jersey City, south of Powles Hook. The Erie Ferry at Pavonia was established in 1859 and the Jersey Central Ferry in 1902 from Communipaw. The Hudson and Manhattan subway tubes were completed in 1908 to Morton Street in Manhattan and to downtown Manhattan in 1909. The Holland Tunnel was completed in 1927.

Historic landmarks are:

(1) Dr. Barrow's Mansion, Ionic House, 85 Wayne Street. A restored Greek Revival mansion built in the 1830s. Five Ionic columns support a flat pediment across facade.

(2) Robert Fulton House, 77–79 Grand Street.

(3) Governor Ogden-Conrad Home, 248 Ogden Avenue.

(4) Hampton Court, 1–7 Wayne Street.

(5) Schurmann House, 240 Ogden Avenue.

(6) Saint Mary's Residence, 240 Washington Street.

(7) van Vorst Farmhouse, 531 Palisade Avenue.

(8) van Wagenen-Quinn Home, 298 Academy Street. Formerly called the Apple Tree House. Washington and Lafayette planned strategy here.

(9) Old Bergen Reformed Church, 797–809 Bergen Avenue. Greek revival, 1841.

(10) Grace van Vorst Church, 264 Erie Street. Gothic revival designed by Detlef Lienau, 1853.

(11) City Hall, Mercer and Grove Streets. Limestone and granite eclectic designed by Lewis H. Groome, 1895.

(12) New Jersey Title Guarantee & Trust Co., 83-85 Montgomery Street, 1888. Yellow brick with cast terra-

cotta ornaments and Art Deco portal added in 1931. Now an apartment house.

(13) Hudson County Courthouse, 591 Newark Avenue. Granite-faced classical structure. Designed by Hugh Roberts; completed in 1910.

(14) Jersey Central Railroad Depot, at the foot of Johnston Avenue. French Chateau styling, 1902–1914; handsomely restored.

Liberty Island

— **5.50 Liberty Island and Statue of Liberty to west.** Liberty Island is in New York State and was originally called Bedloe's Island after Isaac Bedloe, who had obtained a patent for it under Governor Francis Nicholson (1688-89). It has an area of 10.38 acres. The island served as New York's first quarantine station, established by Dr. John Bard (1716–1799). Between 1811 and 1841, a strong fortification named Fort Wood was erected on the island.

In 1875 the historian Edouard de Laboulaye conceived the idea of a monument commemorating the alliance of France and the United States in achieving American independence and symbolizing the friendship of the two nations. This monument was to be a

STATUE OF LIBERTY. This view shows Miss Liberty as rejuvenated for her centennial celebration. Note new gold-leaved flambeau. Photo: © Gretchen McHugh.

gift from the people of France. He organized the Franco-American Union and had raised about $250,000 by 1882. The promoters turned to Frederic Auguste Bartholdi (1834–1904), an Alsatian sculptor who had already earned a name for himself for such colossal monuments as *Switzerland Succoring Strasbourg; Vercingetorix*, at Clermont-Ferrand; and the gigantic *Lion of Belfort* at the Citadel in Belfort, which commemorated the heroic defense of that fortress from 1870 to 1871 during the Franco-Prussian War. Bartholdi conceived the idea for the statue as he sailed into New York Harbor. The statue was to be called *Liberty Enlightening the World*. It was to be the figure of a woman lifting a lighted torch in her right hand. The statue was to be 152 feet tall and made of copper sheets, which would soon oxidize to a green patina in the salt air. It was to be supported by a wrought iron armature.

First Bartholdi made a model nine feet high. Today this model stands near the Pont de Grenelle on a small island in the Seine in Paris. Workmen then hand hammered copper sheets ³⁄₃₂″ thick on wooden forms. The supporting armature was designed by Alexandre Gustave Eiffel (1832–1923), who was to build the famous Eiffel Tower in 1889. A circular stairway with 168 steps leads to an observation platform in the diadem, with a straight ladder branching off near the top and ascending through the uplifted right arm and hand, then through the base of the torch, to a circular platform around the flame of the torch. The entire statue weighs 225 tons and was shipped from France in 214 cases in 1885.

Joseph Pulitzer, editor of the *New York World*, organized an American subscription to build a suitable base. He raised $225,000 and engaged the American architect Richard Morris Hunt (1828–1895) to design the base. Hunt had been the first American to study architecture at the Ecole des Beaux-Arts in Paris, and he was later one of the organizers of the American Institute of Architects. He designed a pedestal 154 feet high in neo-Greco style built of concrete faced with granite. This sat atop the eleven-pointed rampart of Fort Wood, dating from 1811. The statue was formally presented to the United States in 1884, shipped in 1885, and assembled in less than 18 months. It was dedicated by President Grover Cleveland on October 28, 1886. It was designated a national monument in 1924 and put under control of the National Park Service in 1937. Over the years time, wind, and salt air had taken a great toll on the giant statue and there was need for extensive renovation. The Veterans of Foreign Wars had long adopted the Statue as a pet interest under the guidance of Mildred Peterson, their local coordinator, and were seeking to raise funds for renovation. A committee was formed and Lee J. Iacocca, the former head of Chrysler Corporation, was appointed Chairman and conducted an international drive. A new Museum of Immigration was built at the base of the Statue and both the base and the figure were given complete overhauls. The old glass torch, which was illuminated from within, was falling apart and it was decided to build a new flame, according to Bartholdi's original conception, as a solid, gold-leafed entity, lit from without by spotlights. This concept had not worked well originally owing to lack of suitable lighting equipment and the interior illumination had been substituted. With today's new high-intensity floodlights, the original conception now became feasible. The complicated job of building a new solid gold-leafed flame according to Bartholdi's original conception was entrusted to Les Metalliers Champenois, a Rheims-based French artistic metal working firm that had done much restoration work for the French Government. The project was put under the supervision of a talented young French metal artisan named Jean Wiart. The new flame is a thing of great beauty; a duplicate has been made and is now installed in Paris. Completion of the restoration was celebrated by great festivity, a naval parade, and fireworks on October 28, 1986, the statue's centennial. An elevator rises through the pedestal, but it

is necessary to climb the circular stairway to ascend to the observation platform in the head. This climb is not recommended for anyone who has a weak heart or who suffers from vertigo. The ladder to the torch is closed to the public because the extra weight and vibration in the arm (which is not in plumb with the rest of the statue but shoots up at an angle) would create dangerous stress in the framework. Only workmen ascend to maintain the powerful lights that illuminate the torch.

There is an American Museum of Immigration in the base, with both permanent and changing exhibits. The statue is open daily year around. Ferries leave from the Battery hourly between 9:00 A.M. and 4:00 P.M., with extra sailings in July and August.

In 1886 the Jewish-American poetess Emma Lazarus (1849–1887), who was a native of New York, wrote a sonnet eulogizing the monument.

The New Colossus

Not like the brazen giant of Greek fame,
With conquering limbs astride from land
to land;
Here at our sea-washed, sunset gates
shall stand
A mighty woman with a torch,
whose flame
Is the imprisoned lightning, and her name
Mother of Exiles. From her beacon-hand
Glows worldwide welcome; her mild
eyes command
The air-bridged harbor that twin cities
frame.
"Keep, ancient lands, your storied pomp!"
cries she
With silent lips. "Give me your tired,
your poor,
Your huddled masses yearning to breathe
free,
The wretched refuse of your teeming
shore.
Send these, the homeless, tempest-tost
to me
I lift my lamp beside the golden door!"

-5.10 Atlantic Terminal—India Wharf, Brooklyn to east.

-5.00 Baltic Terminal Brooklyn to east.

-5.00 Buttermilk Channel to east. Between Governor's Island and Brooklyn. So named because in Dutch times the channel was so shallow that the women of the island were able to walk across to Brooklyn at low tide to buy their buttermilk. In 1776 General Israel Putnam stretched a *chevaux de frise*

BUTTERMILK CHANNEL AND ATLANTIC BASIN. Buttermilk Channel separates Governor's Island from Brooklyn, seen on the right. The octagonal structure on Governor's Island is a ventilator tower for the Brooklyn-Battery Tunnel. Lower Manhattan and the East River are in the distance. All the large piers are operated by the Port Authority. Photo: Courtesy Port Authority of New York & New Jersey.

across the channel to impede British vessels from entering the East River and force them to pass beneath the guns on Governor's Island and the Battery.

— **5.00 Governor's Island.** Located to the east at the mouth of the East River. Separated from Brooklyn by Buttermilk Channel, the island has an area of 173 acres and maximum elevation of 40 ft. It was originally called Nutten or Nooten Island by the Dutch (this means Nut Island). In 1637 Governor Wouter Van Twiller purchased it from the Indians for a few trinkets, allegedly two axeheads and a few nails. In 1638, its rents were reserved as a perquisite of the governor; thus the name Governor's Island, which became official, however, only in 1784.

Fortifications were first authorized in 1703 but were not undertaken until the time of the Revolution. In 1784 a Dr. Price of Brooklyn built a racetrack on the island. This operated only until 1797, because it was inconvenient to bring the horses across on barges. Fort Jay was commenced in 1794 on a knoll near the center of the island. It was not completed until the early nineteenth century. In 1800 General Ebenezer Stevens took command of the fortifications and expanded them greatly in 1812. The original fort, later to be renamed Fort Columbus, was shaped like a five-pointed star. A second major fortification, now called Castle William, was built between 1807 and 1811 to the plans of Lt. Col. Jonathan Williams. It was circular, with a diameter of 200 feet and a height of 40 feet. The walls were 8 feet thick. In the nineteenth century it was nicknamed "the cheese box" because of its shape. While originally an important fortification, Castle William was later changed to a disciplinary barracks. Fifteen hundred Confederate prisoners were held in it during the Civil War, and in 1863 draft rioters attempted to storm the castle and free them.

In 1878 Fort Jay became the headquarters of the 2d Corps Area, and shortly after 1900 the federal government reclaimed much eroded land around the perimeter. A small fortification at the southern tip of the island was called South Battery. In 1906 Fort Columbus was described as shaded with old Lombardy poplars. Eventually a nine-hole golf course was laid out around the fort, and this is still in existence. For many years, until 1964, Fort Jay occupied the entire island and was the principal military installation in New York City, where it served as headquarters of the 1st Army Command. During the days of army occupancy, there was also a polo field on the island. Today the principal occupant of Governor's Island is the Coast Guard. It is the largest Coast Guard base in the United States, with 6,000 people working there on weekdays. It is the headquarters of the 3rd Coast Guard District and home port to several large cutters. There is also a Coast Guard training center. A medical air reserve unit is based on the island, and some of Fort Jay is devoted to government housing. Governor's Island is linked to Manhattan by two ferry boats making the 1,500 foot crossing to the foot of Whitehall Street. Access to the island is controlled, but open house is held on weekends during the summer. A large, white brick ventilator tower for the Brooklyn-Battery Tunnel is located just offshore from the northeastern corner of the island.

— **5.00 Brooklyn Heights on east.** Residential district of fine homes, many dating from Greek Revival period and the brownstone era. Excellent views from the public terrace.

— **4.80 Brooklyn Port Authority Fulton Marine Terminal to east.**

— **4.80 Ellis Island to west.** Ellis Island, known to the Indians as Gull Island, to the Dutch as Oyster Island, and to the English as Gibbet Island and Ellis Island, has grown from 3.7 acres to 27.5 acres by means of landfill. The English used to hang pirates on the island, which originally belonged to New Jersey. In 1794 it was purchased by the wealthy merchant Samuel Ellis and at that time reverted to the state of New York. At the time of purchase, it was called Bucking Island. Fort Gibson was established in 1808 when the United States Government purchased the island. Fort Gibson served both as a fortress and naval munitions magazine. In 1892 the United States Immigration Service established its major immigration depot here. The monumental buildings on the island date from 1898. The island served this function until 1943. From 1943 to 1954, it served as a detention station for enemy aliens and more recently as a holding station for immigrants with some defects in their credentials. In 1956 Ellis Island

ELLIS ISLAND. It is almost impossible to get a full view of the buildings from any angle because of the large trees on the waterfront esplanade. The scaffolding was erected for renovation work. Photo: © Gretchen McHugh.

was declared surplus property and offered for sale. Various proposals have been put forward for use of the island, but the general consensus is that it should be preserved as a museum or national monument to the immigrants who helped to build America. In 1965 President Lyndon Johnson signed a bill making Ellis Island a part of Liberty National Monument. On 5 November, 1975, a rededication ceremony was held. Over 15,000,000 new Americans had entered the "golden door" and passed through Ellis Island. New York is still the largest immigration port of entry, welcoming over 100,000 new arrivals each year. However, most of these enter through airports and the new liner piers. Ellis Island is accessible by passenger ferry from the Battery, Liberty Island, and Liberty Park in Jersey City.

In 1989 Ellis Island underwent a thorough restoration to be used as a museum of immigration. A temporary wooden trestle was built to the New Jersey shore for construction access.

— **4.70 Fish Point on west.**

— **4.70 East River on east.**

— **4.50 Communipaw Bay on west.** Largely filled in.

— **4.00 The Battery to east.** Southern tip of Manhattan Island at confluence of Hudson and East Rivers. Known to earliest settlers as Kapsee, the Dutch named it Schreyer's, or Weeper's Point (perhaps from gallows and gibbet erected here around 1650). The name Battery derives from a strong battery of ninety-two cannon lined up along the waterfront in 1693 by the British, in fear of a French attack. Ultimately a stone fort with four bastions was

erected. This was called Fort George, and its precincts included the governor's house and most of the government offices. As described by Benson Lossing:

At the beginning of the war for independence, Fort George and its dependencies had three batteries—one of four guns, near the Bowling Green; another (the Grand Battery) of twenty guns, where the flag-staff on the Battery now stands; and a third of two heavy guns at the foot of Whitehall Street, called the White Hall Battery. Here the boldness of the Sons of Liberty was displayed at the opening of the revolution, by the removal of guns from the battery in the face of a connonade from a British ship of war in the harbor. From here was witnessed, by a vast and jubilant crowd, the final departure of the British army, after the peace of 1783, and the unfurling of the banner of the Republic from the flag-staff of Fort George, over which the British ensign had floated more than six years. The anniversary of that day, "Evacuation Day" (the 25th of November) is always celebrated in the City of New York by a military parade and feu de joie....

At White Hall, on the eastern border of the Battery, there was a great civic and military display, at the close of April 1789, when Washington, coming to the seat of government to be inaugurated first president of the United States, landed there. He was received by officers and people with shouts of welcome, the strains of martial music, and the roar of cannon. He was then conducted to his residence on Franklin Square, and afterwards to the Old Federal

BATTERY AND LOWER MANHATTAN c1650. This is the famous Prototype View in watercolor by an anonymous artist. It clearly shows the church in the fort and the Governor's house and the windmill in the background and the "gallows" crane and settlers' houses in the foreground. Courtesy: General Government Archives of the Netherlands.

BROOKLYN BRIDGE. Completed in 1883, this beautiful, large suspension bridge crosses the mouth of the East River. Note 110-story twin towers of the World Trade Center in background. Photo: Courtesy New York Convention & Visitors Bureau.

Hall on Wall Street, where Congress held its sessions...

The present Battery or park, looking out upon the bay of New York, was formed early in the present century, and a castle, pierced for heavy guns, was erected near its western extremity. For many years, the Battery was the chief and fashionable promenade for the citizens in summer weather, and State Street, along its town border, was a very desirable place of residence. The castle was dismantled, and became a place of public amusement. For a long time it was known as Castle Garden; but both are now deserted by fashion and the Muses. All of old New York has been converted into one vast business mart, and there are very few respectable residences within a mile of the Battery. At the present time [September 1861], it exhibits a martial display. Its green sward is covered with tents and barracks for the recruits of the Grand National Army of Volunteers, and its fine old trees give grateful shade to the newly-fledged soldiers preparing for the war for the Union.

Castle Clinton was designed by a certain Colonel Jonathan and erected between 1808 and 1811 a bit off-shore—connected by catwalks with the mainland. It was built in the style of French military architecture. When it was turned into a concert hall and opera house in 1823, a roof was added. The Swedish soprano Jenny Lind made her American debut here on September 11, 1850 under the auspices of P. T. Barnum. The top price ticket sold for $250 and the concert brought in a total of $18,000. Miss Lind contributed her share of the receipts to various New York City charities, thus winning the hearts of her hosts.

In 1851 a great celebration was held here upon the opening of the Erie Railroad from Piermont to Lake Erie. President Millard Filmore embarked upon the steamboat *Erie*, along with many other dignitaries, to start a ceremonial journey the entire length of the new line.

Castle Garden served as the principal immigration station from 1855 to 1892, when Ellis Island became the principal depot. It was next remodeled, in 1896, by McKim, Mead & White, as an aquarium, and was used as such until 1941 when the aquarium was moved to Coney Island. It is now restored as a fortress.

Passenger ferries leave from the Battery to Liberty Island, and there are loading gates of steamboats along the seawall.

2

New York City and the New Jersey Palisades

The largest metropolis of the United States and the fifth largest city in the world, New York City's 1977 population figures were: New York, 7,646,818; metropolitan area, 9,634,400 (1990 New York City, 7,322,564; metropolitan area, 14, 622,000).

The following tabulation of comparisons will be of interest:

World's Largest Cities	1992 Population
1 Tokyo, Japan	26,952,000
2 Mexico City, Mexico	20,207,000
3. Sao Paulo, Brazil	18,052,000
4 Seoul, South Korea	16,268,000
5 New York, New York (metro area)	14,622,000

The area of New York City, including water surfaces, is 365 square miles. The city comprises five boroughs, each co-extensive with a county:

1990 Populations

Manhattan, New York County (an island)	1,487,536
Bronx, Bronx County (on the mainland)	1,203,789
Brooklyn, Kings County (on Long Island)	2,300,664
Queens, Queens County (on Long Island)	1,951,598
Richmond, Richmond County (Staten Island)	378,977
1990 Total	7,322,564

The Island of Manhattan is the center of the city. It is separated from the Bronx by the Harlem River, New York Ship Canal, and Spuyten Duyvil Creek, and from Queens and Brooklyn by the East River. It is separated from Staten Island by Upper New York Bay. Brooklyn and Staten Island are separated by the Narrows, connecting upper and lower New York Bay. New Jersey is to the west of Staten Island and Manhattan. Major islands belonging to the city are: in the East River: Rikers Island, Hart Island, City Island, Randall's Island, Roosevelt Island (formerly Blackwell's and Welfare Island), Ward's Island, and Governor's Island; in New York Bay: Ellis Island, Liberty Island (formerly Bedloes Island), Hoffman Island, Swinburne Island, and West Bank Island; in the Kill van

Kull: Shooter's Island. There are also many islands and pols in Jamaica Bay. Coney Island is now connected with the mainland of Brooklyn.

New York City was the provincial capital and became the state capital until 1797. It was the capital of the United States from 1789 to 1790. It was here that George Washington was inaugurated in 1789. By 1790, New York had outstripped Philadelphia and had become America's largest city, with a population of over 33,000. By 1800, the population was up to 60,515. The first of the great bridges, the Brooklyn Bridge, was built in 1883, and this paved the way for the formation of the present city. Until 1898, Brooklyn was a separate city. In 1898, New York took one of the most significant steps in its history and adopted a new charter, which transposed it into a metropolis of five boroughs, with a hugely increased population. Blessed with one of the world's finest harbors, with over 500 miles of waterfront, it expanded rapidly upon completion of the Erie Canal in 1825 and subsequently of the New York Central and New York & Erie railroads to the interior and became the nation's principal seaport. Today much of this port activity has moved to the New Jersey shoreline on the mainland on Newark Bay.

In 1946, New York was chosen as the permanent headquarters of the United Nations. The nation's financial center, New York is a leading center of manufacture and commerce. Among its principal industries are clothing, textiles, printing, publishing, machine shop and metal products, food, and chemicals. As center of the garment industry, it is an important fashion center. The headquarters of many large industrial firms are located here, as well as the stock and commodity exchanges and a Federal Reserve Bank. The World Trade Center and the World Financial Center facilitate international trade.

While the traditional Broadway theater has been somewhat in eclipse because of high production costs and grossly inflated ticket prices, New York remains an important theatrical center with many off-Broadway and off-off Broadway theaters. New York is also a major art and music center with many famous museums, two major opera companies, and a half-dozen orchestras. Columbia University, New York University, and C.U.N.Y are among the city's many institutions of higher learning.

THE MOUTH OF THE HUDSON. The Hudson River is on the left and the East River on the right as we look north from Upper New York Bay. Large twin towers belong to World Trade Center. Photo: © Air View Aerial Photography, Ossining, NY.

The first subway was built in 1904, and New York now has the nation's largest rapid transit system. Principal railroad depots are Grand Central Terminal, Pennsylvania Station, 125th Street Station (Amtrak and MTA), Flatbush Avenue, Hunter's Point, and Jamaica (Long Island Rail Road) and Hudson Terminal, located at the World Trade Center (PATH transit to New Jersey). The Hoboken, N.J., terminal of New Jersey Transit also serves as a major gate of entry. Principal bus terminals are at 41st Street (Port Authority), and at the George Washington Bridge. The three major airports serving the city are John F. Kennedy International Airport (formerly Idlewild), LaGuardia Airport, and Newark International Airport in New Jersey. Ocean steamships and cruise liners leave for all parts of the world from the Hudson River Passenger Terminal. Excursion boats of the Hudson River Day Line and Circle Line leave from the foot of 42nd Street. The Staten Island Ferry and Statue of Liberty Ferry depart from the Battery.

The problems that have beset all large American cities are especially acute in New York. Because of high costs, labor difficulties, and taxes, much industry has left the city. This is also the case with many industrial office headquarters, resulting in unemployment, with its related welfare costs and high taxes. Although the city continues to exert its attraction on the affluent, many middle-class people have fled to the suburbs.

For many years, the New York metropolitan area's transit and commuter railroad systems have been breaking down, making working in the city less attractive to commuters. The private corporations providing these services were hard hit by government subsidized truck and air competition and ill able to support the losses of running a large commuter operation, and even less able to keep it modern and attractive to riders. Only with recent infusions of state and federal funds has it become possible to begin to rehabilitate and modernize these services. In the meantime, many large firms, such as Western Union, Pepsico, and IBM, have moved to the suburbs.

Other problems are related to the obsolescence of the old-fashioned finger piers in Manhattan which required transshipment from truck or rail to ship by means of expensive lighterage operations and carfloats. Gradually much of this activity has been moved to the "Jersey Side." Also, with the grave financial problems and attendant breakdown of reliable and competitive freight services of the railroads serving the Port of New York, much traffic has been lost to other ports such as Halifax, Baltimore, Boston, Norfolk, and Philadelphia. There was also an unusually high level of theft and damage at the New York docks, which made it an unattractive gateway for high-value merchandise. However, the recent predominance of freight containerization has greatly mitigated this problem. Another factor is the jet plane, which has largely replaced transatlantic ocean liners. Vacationers no longer visit Manhattan before boarding ship. At most, the traveller has a few hours' lay-over at Kennedy Airport. This has hurt the city's hotel and entertainment industries.

Racial tensions, drugs, and their related problems, coupled with a shortage of affordable housing and homelessness and street-begging by "bag women" released from closed mental and custodial institutions, are reducing large areas of the city to barbarism and making them unsafe for civilized persons. People are viciously attacked on the streets and in the parks and subways, and many residents have adopted a garrison mentality in their homes and refuse to patronize the city's extensive public transit system, leading to loss of revenue and financial problems.

The great amount of promiscuous sexual activity and prostitution has encouraged spread of the dreaded AIDS syndrome, while the grossly polluted air (far below federal standards) has increased incidence of cancer and pulmonary disorders, and threatens a federally mandated moratorium on new building.

The city is in a chronic financial crisis and cases of political corruption or suspected corruption are not uncommon. The great landlords have obtained tremendous concessions and bounties from the city government and have become a law unto themselves with ever steeply increasing residential and commercial rents driving people out of the city and often out of their homes and onto the streets. Many small service businesses such as barbershops, tailors, grocery stores, etc. can no longer survive and many residents now shop regularly in New Jersey where these services are still readily available at lower cost and without the stiff sales tax on many items.

With all this loss of revenue and jobs, the city's tax base has been eroded, and the city has gone into debt and had to curtail basic services such as police, fire, and sanitation. All of this leads to a dirty city where crime is less well contained than previously.

New York City still has the seeds of greatness. It is still the mecca for active, intelligent, and creative people from all over the world. It has tremendous reservoirs of talent and ability. It has a fine and extensive infrastructure of public utilities and transport facilities. It has a remarkable bank of buildings that can be renovated and recycled. It can once again become the greatest city in the world.

The Port of New York and the Port Authority

With 500 miles of deepwater shoreline along protected waters, not more than ten miles from the open sea, and located at the mouth of a great navigable river, it is natural that New York grew into the world's largest seaport. Completion of the Erie Canal in 1825, and the New York Central and Erie Railroads shortly thereafter, caused New York to become the principal seaport for the eastern United States. The Port of New York includes facilities located in both New York and New Jersey, along the Hudson and East Rivers, New York Bay, Newark Bay, and adjoining estuaries. Port statistics are compiled by the Port Authority of New York and New Jersey. The following statistics will give an overview of present-day (1987) port activity:

Port of New York and New Jersey Statistics

1987
Oceanborne Foreign Trade: $50.3 billion
                                             53.7 million long tons

Oceanborne Foreign General Cargo: $44.6 billion
    Imports   10,304,025
    Exports   2,742,310
    Total   13,046,335 long tons

Oceanborne Foreign Bulk Cargo: $5.7 billion
    Inbound   33.4 million
    Outbound   2.3 million
    Total   40.7 million long tons

Total Overseas Passenger Arrivals
    & Departures by ship: 398,686
    (Compare with 1,039,838 in 1964)
    Airborne Foreign Cargo: 924,000 tons
    Airborne Overseas Passengers: 19,151,000
    Airline Overseas Flight Movements: 107,000

Distribution of Oceanborne Overseas Commerce:
    Europe   40.2%
    Far East   32.0
    South America   12.6
    Misc.   15.2

Principal Imports:
    Petroleum products, road motor vehicles, steel ingots, bananas, sugar, coffee, vegetables and vegetable preparations, Brazilian orange juice concentrate, wine, gypsum, salt, cement, lime, clay construction material, toys, and sporting goods.

Principal Exports:
    Iron and steel scrap, anthracite coal, non-ferrous scrap, slag, inedible tallow, garbage, sludge.

In the clipper ship days, the favored docking spaces were along South Street on the East River, in lower Manhattan. Auxiliary docking was in Brooklyn. With the coming of the steamboat, ships tended to dock in lower Manhattan along the North or Hudson River. Even ships coming in from Long Island Sound via the East River often docked at North River piers. With the development of ocean-going steamships, the piers along the Hudson in midtown Manhattan became popular, as did those in Jersey City and Hoboken. This remains true for large passenger liners. Through the years, traffic has shifted to terminals on the New Jersey shores because of more modern facilities, easier access to railroads and highways, and elimination of lighterage and shoreside vehicular congestion. Principal marine terminals now operated by the Port Authority are:

1. New York City Passenger Ship Terminal
2. Brooklyn Marine Terminal—Fulton Marine Terminal
3. Red Hook Container Terminal—Brooklyn
4. Erie Basin Marine Terminal—Fishport—Brooklyn
5. Columbia Street Marine Terminal—Brooklyn
6. Greenville—Port Jersey—Jersey City
7. Howland Hook Marine Terminal—Staten Island
8. Elizabeth Marine Terminal—Elizabethport
9. Port Newark

In addition, the United States Army has its extensive military ocean terminal in Bayonne, on Upper New York Bay. The privately operated Bush and Brooklyn Eastern District Terminals are in Brooklyn, on Upper New York Bay and the East River, respectively, and the private Pouch Terminal at Clifton on Staten Island, just above the Narrows. The refineries tend to be concentrated on Constable Hook in Bayonne and along the New Jersey shore of the Arthur Kill.

The Port Authority of New York and New Jersey is a self-supporting corporate agency of the two states. Functioning without burden to the taxpayer, it was created as the Port of New York Authority in 1921 by treaty between the two states, to plan, develop, and operate terminal, transportation, and other facilities of commerce and to improve and protect the commerce of the bi-state port. In 1972 the Authority's name was changed to identify more accurately its status as a bi-state agency of New York and New Jersey. Port Authority commissioners, six from each state, are appointed by the governors of New Jersey and New York. They serve without pay for overlapping terms of six years. The Port Authority is responsible for the operation of six interstate tunnels and bridges, a regional system of four airports and two heliports, nine marine terminals, two bus terminals, and two union motor truck terminals. In 1962 the Port Authority Trans-Hudson Corporation (PATH), a subsidiary of the Port Authority, assumed responsibility for operation and rehabilitation of the former Hudson Tubes, a vital rapid transit system which links Newark, Jersey

City, and Hoboken with lower and mid-Manhattan. The first element of the Journal Square Transportation Center was opened in December 1973.

The World Trade Center, under construction since 1966, opened its doors to its first tenants in 1970. The Trade Center, principal headquarters for international trade activities in the New York/New Jersey area, also houses the Port Authority administrative staff. These facilities represent an investment of over $3.4 billion. The Port Authority and its rail subsidiary, PATH, employ a career staff of over 8,000 people in the development and operation of the following facilities:

Rail & Bus Commuter Facilities
Port Authority Bus Terminal (Midtown)
George Washington Bridge Bus Station
Port Authority Trans-Hudson System (PATH)
Journal Square Transportation Center

Air Terminals
John F. Kennedy International Airport
LaGuardia Airport
Newark International Airport
Teterboro (N.J.) Airport (for private aviation)
Port Authority-Downtown Heliport
Port Authority-West Thirtieth St. Heliport

Marine Terminals
As listed above

Tunnels and Bridges
Bayonne Bridge
George Washington Bridge
Goethal's Bridge
Holland Tunnel
Lincoln Tunnel
Outerbridge Crossing

Miscellaneous Facilities
World Trade Center
Development offices in Chicago, Cleveland, Washington, New York, London, Tokyo, Zurich
Teleport Complex—Staten Island
Legal & Communications Center—Newark

Manhattan

Manhattan Island is 12½ miles long and 2½ miles wide at its widest point (1990 population 1,487,536). It is bounded on the west by the Hudson or North River, on the north by Spuyten Duyvil Creek, on the east by the Harlem River (called Muscoota by the Indians), Hell Gate, and the East River, on the south by the East River and Upper

Bernard Ratzen's Map of New York by James Lyne in 1728.

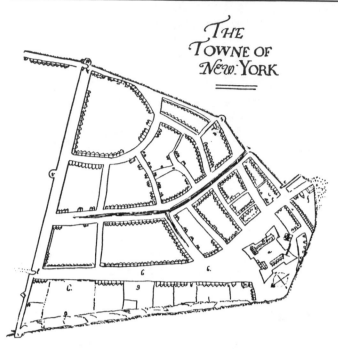

Sketch Plan of New York City 1664–1668 by Nicoll.

New York Bay. The far northern portion of the Harlem River and eastern reaches of Spuyten Duyvil Creek are also known as either the New York Ship Canal or the Harlem River Ship Canal, as its present navigable condition is the result of dredging a shallow backwater.

The point at the far southern tip of the island, known today as the Battery, was known to the earliest settlers as Kapsee. It was originally a semi-detached rocky point, the intervening space being filled-in land. The Dutch also called it Schreyer's Hook, or Weeper's Point in English. On the Hudson side, Greenwich Point was at present-day Gansevoort Street and Jeffrey's Hook under the approach of the George Washington Bridge. On the East River, Horn's Hook is just below Hell Gate at 89th Street, and Corlear's Hook is just south of the Williamsburg Bridge. Turtle Bay was located on the East River at the present United Nations site. Much of the present shore-line is filled land, both along the East River (south of Corlear's Hook) and along the Hudson River (north as far as Gansevoort Street, the former Greenwich Point). This process is continuing today between the Battery and Canal Street. This last-named street is named for an actual former canal. Cooper described it in his novel, *The Water Witch* (New York: G. P. Putnam's Sons, pp. 21–22), which is set before the Revolution.

A deep, narrow creek penetrated the island at this point, for the distance of a quarter of a mile. Each of its banks had a row of buildings, as the houses line a canal in the cities of Holland. As the natural course of the inlet was necessarily respected, the street had taken a curva-

ture not unlike that of a new moon. The houses were ultra-Dutch, being low, angular, fastidiously neat, and all erected with gables to the street. Each had its ugly and inconvenient entrance, termed a stoop, its vane or weathercock, its dormer-windows, and its graduated battlement-walls. Near the apex of one of the latter, a little iron crane projected into the street. A small boat, of the same metal, swung from its end,—a sign that the building to which it was appended was the ferry-house.

An inherent love of artificial and confined navigation had probably induced the burghers to select this spot as the place whence so many craft departed from the town; since it is certain that the two rivers could have furnished diverse points more favorable for such an object, inasmuch as they possess the advantage of wide and unobstructed channels.

Fifty blacks were already in the street, dipping their brooms into the creek, and flourishing water over the sidewalks, and on the fronts of the low edifices. This light, but daily duty was relieved by clamorous collisions of wit, and by shouts of merriment, in which the whole street would join, as with one joyous and reckless movement of the spirit. The language of this light-hearted and noisy race was Dutch, already corrupted by English idioms, and occasionally by English words....

As the movement of the ferryboat was necessarily slow, the alderman and his companion were enabled to step into it before the fasts were thrown aboard. The periagua, as the craft was called, partook of a European and an American character. It possessed the length, narrowness, and clean bow of the canoe, from which its name was derived, and the flat bottom and lee-boards of a boat constructed for the shallow waters of the Low Countries. Twenty years ago vessels of this description abounded in our rivers, and even now their two long and unsupported masts, and high narrow-headed sails, are daily seen bending like reeds to the breeze, and dancing lightly over the billows of the bay....

Though, in some respects, of singular aquatic habits, the original colonists of New York were far less adventurous, as mariners, than their present descendants. A passage across the bay did not often occur in the tranquil lives of the burghers; and it is still within memory of man, that a voyage between the two principal towns of the State was an event to excite the solicitude of friends, and the anxiety of the traveller. The perils of the Tappan Zee, as one of the wider reaches of the Hudson is still termed, were often dealt with by the good wives of the colony, in their relations of marvels; and she who had oftenest encountered them unharmed, was deemed a sort of marine Amazon.

This canal has been filled in for many years. However, the filled-in land made poor footing for the former elevated West Side highway, and the former canal location was spanned by a large and easily distinguished arch bridge.

The island is blessed with few natural watercourses. Minetta Brook flowed from the center of the island to the Hudson near 40th Street, but today it is merely a covered sewer. Another stream flowed from the vicinity of Fifth Avenue and 59th Street to the East River. A small natural pond, named Collect Pond, was near Foley Square. It has been filled in. The present ponds, lakes, and reservoir in Central Park are artificial. Manhattan Island is quite rocky, but formerly contained some rather fertile farmland. The southern portion is fairly level, but the central portion is covered with indeterminate hills. Among these are Murray Hill, Lenox Hill, Mount Morris, and Harlem Heights. Further north are Morningside Heights, Mount Washington (highest point in Manhattan), Washington Heights, Morris Heights, and Inwood Hill, at the northernmost tip of the island. There are several low traverse valleys. The most prominent are at Harlem, where the fertile Harlem Plains bordered the East River, and at Dyckman Street between Fort Tryon and Inwood Hill. Cooper's novel *Satanstoe* (New York: G. P. Putnam's Sons, pp. 81–82) gives a good description of the topography immediately prior to the Revolution:

The roads on the island of Manhattan were very pretty and picturesque, winding among rocks and through valleys, being lined with groves and copses in a way to render all the drives rural and retired. Here and there, one came to a country-house, the residence of some person of importance, which by its comfort and snugness, gave all the indications of wealth and of a prudent taste.

Early villages on the island were Kingsbridge, on the Harlem River near the bridge that still bears that name; Carmansville, atop Mount Washington; Manhattanville, on the Hudson near present-day 130th Street; Elm Park, near 110th Street and Broadway; Bloomingdale, near Columbus Circle; Harlem, on the Harlem River near 125th Street; Yorkville, near the Harlem River and 89th Street; Murray Hill, near Park Avenue and 40th Street; Greenwich Village, at its present location; and New Amsterdam, at the foot of the island. Broadway follows the former Bloomingdale-Manhattanville and Manhattanville-Kingsbridge roads.

New Jersey is to the west, across the Hudson River. Riverdale and Marble Hill are to the north, across the Spuyten Duyvil Creek. The Bronx, Randalls Island, and Wards Island are to the east, across the Harlem River. The Astoria and Long Island City sections of Queens are to the east, across the East River, as are the Greenpoint and Williamsburg sections of Brooklyn. Downtown

Brooklyn, Brooklyn Heights, and Governors Island and Upper New York Bay are to the south.

Manhattan is the principal borough of New York City, with a population of 1,487,536 and an area of twenty-two square miles. It is the governmental, financial, cultural, and commercial center of the city. The Borough of Manhattan is coextensive with New York County, which is not, as generally thought, confined to Manhattan Island. Both the Borough of Manhattan and County of New York include a small enclave on the mainland, north of Spuyten Duyvel Creek, known as Marble Hill. This is completely surrounded by the Bronx.

Formerly, Manhattan Island was connected to the mainland and adjacent islands by an extensive network of ferry routes. Today those to Hoboken and Weehawken, and to Staten Island and Governor's Island from the Battery remain in service, along with passenger launch service to Liberty and Ellis Islands. The first bridge to the mainland was a royal monopoly. It was called the Kingsbridge, and crossed the Harlem River near Marble Hill. Today there are twenty bridges connecting Manhattan with New Jersey and the other islands and boroughs: one water aqueduct, one footbridge, two

AERIAL VIEW OF MANHATTAN and surrounding waters, c1938. Photo: Hudson River Day Line, courtesy of Alfred V. S. Olcott, Jr.

AERIAL VIEW OF HELLGATE AREA. The waterways shown in this view are tidal estuaries. In the foreground is that section of the East River known as Hell Gate because of former submerged reefs (since removed), strong tides, and difficult sailing conditions. In the upper portion of the picture is the Harlem River, separating Manhattan on the far left from Wards Island in the immediate foreground, Randall's Island, and the Bronx, at the top of the picture. Randall's Island is separated from the Bronx by the small Bronx Kills, barely visible. The land in the immediate foreground is the Astoria section of Queens, on Long Island. The large buildings on Ward's Island belong to Manhattan State Hospital, a facility for the mentally ill. The large Downing Stadium, with a capacity of 20,000, is seen on Randall's Island. The railroad bridge with the long trestle approaches and large arch over the East River is the famous Hell Gate Bridge of the New York Connecting Railroad, part of Amtrak's Northeast Corridor Route. The highway bridge is the Triborough Bridge. Photo: Triborough Bridge & Tunnel Authority.

railroad bridges, and sixteen vehicular bridges, two of which also carry subway trains. There are also four vehicular, two railroad, and thirteen subway-rapid transit tunnels, not to mention aqueduct, power, and telephone wire tunnels. The principal railroad depots are Pennsylvania Station, Grand Central Terminal, and 125th Street Station. Principal bus depots are the Port Authority Bus Terminal in midtown and the George Washington Bridge Bus Terminal. The Port Authority operates a heliport at Thirtieth Street on the Hudson River. Steamship piers are located along the East River between Corlear's Hook and the Battery, and along the Hudson River from the Battery to 59th Street.

Principal remaining open areas on Manhattan are the following parks: Central, Riverside, Fort Washington, Fort Tryon, Inwood Hill, Highbridge, Colonial, Hudson, St. Nicholas, Morningside, Mt. Morris, Thomas Jefferson, Hamilton Fish, W. H. Seward, Gabriel's, Carl Schurz, Franklin, DeWitt Clinton, City Hall, Corlear's Hook, Bryant, Bowling Green, and Battery. There are also several squares (Tompkins, Union, Stuyvesant, Madison, Manhattan, Washington, and Gramercy) and such green spaces as Baker Field, the United Nations Plaza, Trinity and St. Paul's churchyards, and Trinity Cemetery. Fine panoramic views are obtained from many office buildings and bridges.

Manhattan has an interesting history. The name is a corruption of the Mohican word "Menohanet," meaning "people of the islands." Three groups of the Manhattan Indians lived on Manhattan Island. The Werpoes, with

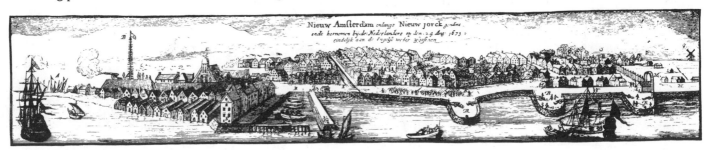

NEW AMSTERDAM IN 1673. From *Totius Neobelgii nova et accuratissima tabula…Typis Caroli Allard, Amsterdami,* with engraving attributed to Romeyn de Hooghe. View is from the East River side. Author's collection.

their Sachem Meijeterma, lived near present-day Foley Square and the former Collect Pond on the lower portion of the island. Rechewac was the sachem of the Rechewanis, who occupied the middle east side of the island. Their name means "little sand stream." The Inwood section of upper Manhattan was the home of the Weckquaesgeeks. The original Indian purchase of the island was made by Peter Minuit in 1626 for $24 worth of hardware, kettles, and rum. In 1715 the freeholders of New Harlem, by special tax, raised a fund with which Col. Stephen Van Cortlandt made a final settlement with the Manhattan Indians. The last bears and wolves had been driven from the island in 1686.

The first permanent settlement on the island was made under the auspices of the Dutch West India Company in 1625. The plan of the city was drawn by Cryn Fredericksz. The first street laid out was Pearl Street. The first church was built in 1633 at what is now 39 Pearl Street. Fort Amsterdam was built in 1635. This consisted of the Director's House, a barracks, a guard

house, and a block house, all surrounded by palisades. In 1638 the first sale of property was made to a private owner, the Dutch West India Co. having held title to all land until this time. A strong palisade or wall was erected along the present course of Wall Street in 1653; this was the upper limit of New Amsterdam. Above this were the commons. During the remainder of the seventeenth and early eighteenth centuries, the other villages mentioned above were founded and individual farmsteads were settled throughout the island.

Under British rule after 1664, New Amsterdam became New York and Fort Amsterdam became Fort James. In 1693, under threat of French invasion, a battery of ninety-two cannons were lined up along the Kapsee, thus giving the Battery its name. The first Trinity Church was erected in 1696. The present structure dates from 1830 and is the third on the site. The oldest building in the city is Fraunces Tavern, which was built in 1719 as a townhouse for Stephen DeLancey. It was converted to a tavern in 1762. The present St. Paul's Chapel was built

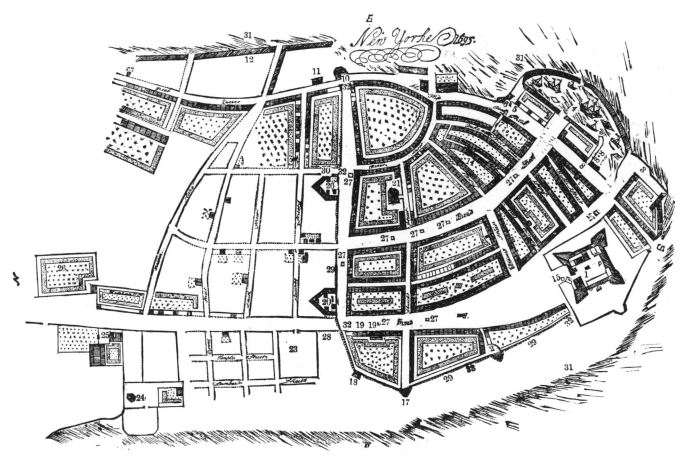

CITY OF NEW YORK. Plan by James Lyne in 1728. Key: 1) chapel in the fort of New York; 2) Leysler's half-moon; 3) Whitehall battery of 15 guns; 4) old dock; 5) cage and stocks; 6) stadt-house battery of guns; 7) stadt or state house; 8) custom-house; 8) bridge; 9) Burgher's or the slip battery of 10 guns; 10) the fly block-house and half-moon; 11) the slaughter-house; 12) new docks; 13) French church; 14) Jews' synagogue; 15) fort well and pump; 16) Ellet's alley; 17) works on the west side of the city; 18) northwest block-house; 19) Lutheran church and minister's house; 20) stone points on the north side of the city; 21) Dutch Calvinists' church, built 1692; 22) Dutch Calvinists' minister's house; 23) burying-ground; 24) wind-mill; 25) king's farm; 26) Col. Dungan's garden; 27) wells; 28) plat of ground designed for the E. minister's house; 29) stockado, with bank of earth on the inside; 30) ground proper for the building an E. church; 31) showing the sea flowing about New York; 32) city gates; 33) postern gate.

THE STADTHUYS IN NEW YORK, 1679. This view is from *Journal of a Voyage to New York 1679–80* by Jasper Dankers and Peter Sluyter. Engraving by J. Carson Brevoort. Note cannon mounted on primitive timber battery fortification. Author's collection.

between 1764 and 1766, and the spire erected in 1794. George Washington worshiped there while living in New York as President. Manhattan was in British control from 1776 until the end of the Revolutionary war. It was the capital of the United States from 1789 until 1790. George Washington was inaugurated as the first president of the United States in 1789 at Federal Hall, on the site of the present Sub-Treasury Building at Broad and Wall Streets.

We cannot continue the story of the growth of Manhattan into the great metropolis it is today. However, it should be observed that this greatness was achieved because of its unrivaled harbor, the access to the interior provided by the Hudson River and later by the Erie Canal and the railroads that paralleled them.

In three of his novels, *Satanstoe, The Water-Witch,* and *Afloat and Ashore,* James Fenimore Cooper gives some interesting descriptions of early New York. *Satanstoe* takes place in 1757, *The Water-Witch* in around 1708, and *Afloat and Ashore* after the Revolution (ca. 1814).

I dare say there were fifty young ladies promenading the churchwalk when I reached it, and nearly as many young men in attendance on them; no small portion of the last being scarlet-coats, though the mohairs had their representatives there too. A few blue-jackets were among us also, there being two or three king's cruisers in port. As no one presumed to promenade the Mall who was not of a certain stamp of respectability, the company were all gayly dressed; and I will confess that I was much struck with the air of the place, the first time I showed myself among the gay idlers. The impression made on me that morning was so vivid that I will endeavor to describe the scene as it now presents itself to my mind.

In the first place there was the noble street, quite eighty feet in width in its narrowest part, and gradually

expanding as you looked towards the bay, until it opened into an area of more than twice that width, at the place called the Bowling Green. Then came the fort, crowning a sharp eminence*, and over-looking everything in that quarter of the town. In the rear of the fort, or in its front, taking a water view, lay the batteries that had been built on the rocks, which were black and picturesque, and over the batteries they supported, was obtained a view of the noble bay, dotted here and there with some speck of a sail, or possibly with some vessel anchored on its placid bosom. Of the two rows of elegant houses, most of them brick, and, with very few exceptions, principally of two stories in height, it is scarcely necessary to speak, as there are few who have not heard of, and formed some notion of Broadway; a street that all agree is one day to be the pride of the Western world.

In the other direction, I will admit that the view was not so remarkable, the houses being principally of wood, and of a somewhat ignoble appearance. Nevertheless, the army were said to frequent those habitations quite as much as they did any other in the place. After reaching the Common, or present Park, where the great Boston road led off into the country, the view was just the reverse of that which was seen in the opposite quarter. Here all was inland and rural. It is true the new Bridewell had been erected in that quarter, and there was also a new jail, both facing the Common; and the king's troops had barracks in their rear; but high, abrupt, conical hills, with low marshy lands, orchards and meadows, gave to all that portion of the island a peculiarly novel and somewhat picturesque character. Many of the hills in that quarter, and indeed all over the widest part of the island, are now surmounted by country-houses, as some were then, including Petersfield, the ancient abode of the Stuyvesants, or that farm which, by being called after the old Dutch governor's retreat, has given the name of Bowery, or Bouerie, to the road that led to it; as well as the Bowery House, as it was called, the country abode of the then lieutenant-governor, James De Lancey; Mount Bayard, a place belonging to that respectable family; Mount Pitt, another that was the property of Mrs. Jones, the wife of Mr. Justice Jones, a daughter of James De Lancey, and various other mounts, houses, hills and places, that are familiar to the gentry and people of New York.

But the reader can imagine for himself the effect produced by such a street as Broadway, reaching very nearly half a mile in length, terminating at one end in an elevated, commanding fort, with its background of batteries, rocks, and bay, and at the other with the Common, on which troops were now constantly parading, the Bridewell and jail, and the novel scene I have just mentioned. Nor is Trinity itself to be forgotten. This edifice, one of the noblest, if not the most noble of its

---

*The Kapsee

kind in all the colonies, with its Gothic architecture, statues in carved stone, and flanking walls, was a close accessory of the view, giving the whole grandeur and a moral.

As has been said, I found the Mall crowded with young persons of fashion and respectability. This Mall was near a hundred yards in length; and it follows that there must have been a goodly show of youth and beauty. The fine weather had commenced; spring had fairly opened; Pinkster blossoms (the wild honeysuckle) had been seen in abundance throughout the week; and every thing and person appeared gay and happy.

(*Satanstoe*, pp. 98–101)

Here he soon stopped before the door of a house which, in that provincial town, had altogether the air of a patrician dwelling.

Two false gables, each of which was surmounted by an iron weathercock, intersected the roof of this building, and the high and narrow stoop was built of the red freestone of the country. The material of the edifice itself was, as usual, the small, hard brick of Holland, painted a delicate cream color.

A single blow of the massive glittering knocker brought a servant to the door.

(*The Water-Witch*, p. 15.)

New York, in that day, and on the Hudson side of the town, commenced a short distance above Duane Street. Between Greenwich, as the little hamlet around the State prison was called, and the town proper, was an interval of a mile and a half of open fields, dotted here and there with countryhouses. Much of this space was in broken hills, and a few piles of lumber lay along the shores. St. John's Church had no existence, and most of the ground in its vicinity was in a low swamp. As we glided along the wharves, we caught sight of the first market I had ever seen—such proofs of an advanced civilization not having yet made their way into the villages of the interior. It was called "The Bear," from the circumstance that the first meat ever exposed for sale in it was of that animal; but the appellation has disappeared before the intellectual refinement of these later times— the name of the soldier and statesman, Washington, having fairly supplanted that of the bear! Whether this great moral improvement was brought about by the Philosophical Society, or the Historical Society, or "The Merchants," or the Aldermen of New York, I have never ascertained. If the latter, one cannot but admire their disinterestedness and modesty in conferring this notable honor on the Father of his Country, inasmuch as all can see that there never has been a period when their own board has not possessed distinguished members, every way qualified to act as godfathers to the most illustrious markets of the republic. But Manhattan, in the way of

taste, has never had justice done it. So profound is its admiration for all the higher qualities, that Franklin and Fulton have each a market to himself, in addition to this bestowed on Washington. Doubtless there would have been Newton Market, and Socrates Market, and Solomon Market, but for the patriotism of the town, which has forbidden it from going out of the hemisphere in quest of names to illustrate. Bacon Market would doubtless have been equivocal—too much so to be tolerated under any circumstances....

We passed the Albany basin, a large receptacle for North River craft, that is now in the bosom of the town and built on, and recognized in it the masthead of the Wallingford.... We rounded the Battery, then a circular strip of grass, with an earthen and wooden breastwork running along the margin of the water, leaving a narrow promenade on the exterior. This brought us to Whitehall, since so celebrated for its oarsmen, where we put in for a haven.

(*Afloat and Ashore*, pp. 38–39.)

– **3.80 Pier A Manhattan to east.** Presently serving as a fireboat station for the Fire Department Marine Division, this interesting old pier was built between 1884 and 1886, making it the oldest in the city. It is also the only surviving specimen of block and bridge construction. It has a seventy-foot-high lookout tower with a clock, built by Seth Thomas, which strikes ship's bells. It was originally entirely clad in galvanized sheet iron and decorated with classical zinc ornaments. Originally housing the city's Department of Docks, it has since housed the city's Marine and Aviation, and Ports and Terminals Departments, the harbor police, and the fire department as well as serving as landing place for excursion steamers. In

STATEN ISLAND FERRY TERMINAL AND BATTERY. Photo: Courtesy New York Convention & Visitors Bureau.

1964 the entire exterior of the pier was covered with aluminum sheet metal. It is an official New York City landmark and is listed in the National Register of Historic Places. It is presently undergoing restoration.

– 3.80 New York Custom House visible to east.

– 3.75 Battery Place to east. Communipaw to west.

– 3.74 Whitehall Building to east. The Whitehall Building houses many shipping and maritime firms and social clubs. It was the site of the original New York weather station.

– 3.74 Former Central Railroad of New Jersey Ferry and Railroad Terminal to west. This palatial terminal was built in 1889 to replace a former terminal built on filled land. It was enlarged in 1914 and had 20 tracks covered by Bush Train Sheds and covered 7.07 acres. In its heyday it served long-distance trains of the Baltimore & Ohio and Lehigh Valley railroads as well as the numerous commuter trains of the Jersey Central, New York & Long Branch, Lehigh Valley, and New York & Newark lines. Steamboat ferries operated to Whitehall Street, Liberty Street, Clarkson Street, and West 23rd Streets in Manhattan. Service was discontinued on April 25, 1967, and all trains rerouted to Penn Station in Newark, where passengers transferred to PATH transit trains to reach Manhattan. The Central Railroad of New Jersey was bankrupt and was eventually absorbed into the new Conrail system and the entire Jersey City Terminal property became redundant. The site and building were acquired by the Liberty State Park. The yards were removed and landscaped and dilapidated structures, including the former ferry terminal front house, were removed.

THE STRAND, NEW WHITEHALL STREET, NEW YORK, c1686. The central house, with three windows in the roof, was the earliest brick house built in the town, and was at one time the dwelling of Jacob Leisler, and had been built by his father-in-law, Vanderveen. From Gay's *Popular History of the United States.* Author's collection.

The train concourse measured 383 ft by 75 ft, and the upper level provided access between the upper decks of the ferryboat and trains via ramps and escalators. Four double-decked steel buildings adjoined the ferry slips to accommodate the baggage room, mailroom, local ferry waiting room, and stationary department. The entire service was operated with great elegance. The steel buildings were removed after the Park acquired the property, but the ferry slips and bridges remain preserved.

The main building resembles a great French chateau, with its mansard roof, cupola, and gilded steeple. The main waiting room has a gabled ceiling three stories high and today opens out onto tremen-

UNITED STATES CUSTOMS HOUSE 1901–1907. This building was designed by Cass Gilbert. The statues on the facade are by Daniel Chester French. Photo: Author's collection.

CENTRAL RAILROAD OF NEW JERSEY train and ferry terminal, Jersey City. Built in 1889 and enlarged in 1914, it had four ferry slips, twenty tracks, and covered seven acres, and also served the Lehigh Valley, Baltimore & Ohio, and Reading Co. railroads. Remains of the ferry bridges are seen in the foreground. Today it has been restored to serve as a Visitors Center for the Liberty State Park. Photo: © Gretchen McHugh.

AERIAL VIEW OF CENTRAL RAILROAD OF NEW JERSEY terminal and yards. This view is taken from the opposite side (west) from the preceding picture and shows the massive extent of the facility. The towers of lower Manhattan are in the background. Photo: Courtesy Central Railroad of New Jersey. Author's collection.

dous views of the Manhattan and Brooklyn skylines and the entire Upper Bay. The State of New Jersey has completely restored the terminal to its original beauty as a visitor's center for the Liberty State Park. The waiting room is used for special events; the author and his wife have spent several delightful evenings attending formal fund-raising balls for the New Jersey Society of Architects and New Jersey Institute of Technology. Various railroad-related festivals and events are held here and it is hoped to develop an operating railroad museum and short tourist railroad on the site. Ferryboat service, by smaller diesel boats, has been resumed from an adjacent terminal in the Tidewater Basin, to the north. It is possibly the best vantage-point to see the harbor from the New Jersey side.

– 3.74 New landfill to old pier line on east.

– 3.73 Tidewater Basin and Morris Canal Basin to west.
This is the former eastern terminal of the old Morris & Essex Canal which formerly operated across the entire northern part of New Jersey from the Delaware River at Phillipsburg, NJ. It carried mainly coal from the Pennsylvania coalfields to New York City by barge. The barges were tied up in the basin prior to being towed by towboats to various parts of the harbor. There were numerous marine repair yards in the basin until 1988. It is now used by passenger ferryboats of the Circle Line. The Basin has been renamed and "gentrified" to Clermont Cove

to make it more attractive to prospective purchasers of adjacent luxury apartments.

Thus we erode our sense of history.

– 3.72 Liberty Harbor North to west.
Large new luxury apartment development on New Jersey's "Gold Coast," which extends from Caven Point to Fort Lee.

– 3.72 Battery Park City to east.
This large mixed-use residential and commercial development is built upon landfill extending out to the former pierhead line. There are marina coves to both the south and north, and the entire development is surrounded by an elegant promenade atop a seawall and offering fine water views.

– 3.71 Paulus Hook (Powles Hook) to west.
This former point of land, which was almost an island at high tide, was bounded originally by Communipaw Bay on the south and Harsimus Cove on the north. The Indians called it Aressick, meaning "a sandy hillock." The adjacent waters were exceptionally rich in bivalves and large middens of oyster and clam shells, evidence that the Indians made good use of this natural largess.

It is generally believed, although poorly documented, that there were traders settled here as early as 1618. It is, however, documented that by 1633 there was a small settlement led by Michael Paulaz or Paulsen, agent of the Dutch West India Company. Records show that in 1638 Abraham Isaacsen Plank purchased the hook. More than a century later, in 1769, Cornelius Van Vorst owned the land and opened a racetrack with weekly meets that were popular with the sporting element of Manhattan. As it is the closest land to Manhattan on the west bank of the Hudson, it became a focal point of roads from the interior, including the important one to Philadelphia, and the Hook became an important ferrying point.

During the Revolution the British erected a fortification upon this strategic point, which was then surrounded by water at high tide. On August 19, 1779, Major Henry Lee of the Continental Army succeeded in temporarily capturing the fort, but could not properly garrison it and subsequently let it revert to the British. Congress granted him a medal for this exploit which was important in raising American morale.

After the War, in 1804, Van Vorst sold the Hook to a consortium including Anthony Dey, Richard Varick, Jacob Radcliffe, John B. Coles, Joseph Bloomfield, then Governor of New Jersey, and twenty-nine other investors, who layed out building plots and streets and built the Hudson Hotel. They formed the Associates of the Jersey Co.

After the successful inauguration of his steamboat in 1807 Robert Fulton established a shipyard here, and the Hook became a center of steamboat activity. In March 1811 Robert Fulton and a consortium including the Associates, Elisha Boudinot of Newark, and Nicholas Roosevelt of New York, assumed the lease of the Paulus Hook Ferry. The Fulton shipyard, active until his death in 1815, built engines for his vessels. Fulton resided at 77-79 Grand Street in Paulus Hook. The Associates put one of Fulton's new steam ferryboats on the Paulus Hook line in 1812. Paulus Hook became a railhead on October 14, 1836 when passengers of the Morris & Essex Railroad commenced using the new Exchange Place Terminal and Paulus Hook Ferry. Over the years many railroad companies controlled and used the terminal and operated the ferry. In the twentieth century the Pennsylvania Railroad was the dominant company and operated the terminal and ferries to various points in Brooklyn and Manhattan—most particularly to Cortlandt Street. They also owned vast acreages of adjacent waterfront to use as freight yards and operated a large fleet of railroad carfloats and lighters from this area, and built the tremendous Harborside Warehouse Terminal. With construction of first the Hudson & Manhattan (PATH) tunnels and construction of a direct trans-Hudson railroad tunnel to midtown Manhattan and Penn Station in 1906, Paulus Hook Terminal lost its importance as a passenger depot, and the Pennsylvania Railroad gradually phased themselves entirely out of the ferry business. On December 31, 1949 all ferry service was discontinued, and the terminal was demolished in the 1960s, after falling into decrepitude.

For a number of years in the nineteenth century Paulus Hook served as the American Terminal of the Cunard Line, and is mentioned in Jules Verne's *Around the World in Eighty Days* as a major transfer point. The large Colgate-Palmolive soap and cosmetics plant is located at Paulus Hook, but is being renovated into offices and apartments. Paulus Hook is presently undergoing extensive renovation as a residential community with easy access to Manhattan and Newark via PATH and renewed ferry services. History repeats itself.

– **3.71 Colgate-Palmolive plant and ten-story office building on west.** The plant was established in 1847. Atop it was the world's largest conventional clock with a face fifty feet in diameter and a minute hand

twenty-six feet long. It was erected in 1924 and demolished in 1991.

– **3.70 Exchange Place, Jersey City, to west.** Former site of Cunard Line piers and Jersey City Depot of Pennsylvania Railroad and ferries. It was the eastern depot for various other railroads, and was the western terminus of Robert Fulton's first steam ferry line. Exchange Place is the site of the new office tower headquarters of the National Westminster Bank—New Jersey's highest building. It was designed by the Grad Partnership of Newark and offers spectacular harbor views from its upper floors.

– **3.70 Cortlandt Street to east.** Robert Fulton's first successful trip in the *Clermont* started from this site on September 4, 1807. Later it served as Manhattan terminal for Fulton's steam ferry to Paulus Hook, and for Pennsylvania Railroad and West Shore Railroad ferries until March 24, 1959, when the *S.S. Stony Point* made her last sailing. This area was known as Messier's Dock during Fulton's time and the actual dock was inland of the present West Street. All vestiges of the aboriginal marine terminals have been effaced by construction of Battery Park City, North Cove Marina, and landfill.

– **3.70 World Financial Center to east.** These large office buildings house financial institutions and are built upon landfill between West Street and the old pierhead line and are consequently west of the World Trade Center on the new waterfront. American Express Company is a major tenant. The adjacent quay is the terminal of the new restored ferry service to Lackawanna Terminal Hoboken.

– **3.70 PATH Downtown Twin Tubes.** Twin rapid transit single track tunnels connecting the World Trade Center in Manhattan with Journal Square and Exchange Place in Jersey City. Each tube is over a mile long. They were originally built by the Hudson & Manhattan Railroad, which was organized in 1901, and were completed on July 17, 1909. PATH stands for Port Authority Trans Hudson, as the former Hudson & Manhattan Raiload is now owned and operated by the Port Authority of New York & New Jersey. The downtown terminal is deep below the World Trade Center and reached by a gang of long escalators.

– **3.70 The World Trade Center and the Twin Towers.** This facility of the Port Authority of New York & New Jersey occupies a sixteen-acre site in Manhattan bounded by Liberty Street on the south, Church Street on the east, Vesey Street on the north, and West Street on the west. The project includes two 1,350-foot, 110-story tower buildings, two nine-story buildings, a new eight-story U.S. Customs building, and a five-acre landscaped plaza. It also serves as the downtown terminal for the PATH rapid transit system. It stands on the site of the former Hudson Terminal Buildings and Washington Market. There are nine million square feet of office space in this complex. Each floor in the twin towers is approximately one acre in size and is column-free to assure flexibility in layout. There is below-grade parking for almost 2,000 cars. An enclosed observation deck is located on the 107th floor, and an open promenade is on the 110th floor (roof) of the South Tower of the World Trade Center. The maximum observation point elevation is 1,377 feet. Observation decks are open from 9:30 A.M. until 9:30 P.M. every day of the year. There is a charge.

More than 1.2 million cubic yards of earth and rock were excavated to make way for the Trade Center. This material was placed in the Hudson River to create 23.5 acres of new land deeded to the City of New York, and which ultimately became part of the Battery Park City Project. Construction of the Trade Center utilized more than 200,000 tons of steel and 425,000 cubic yards of concrete. At peak construction periods, 3,500 workers were on jobsite. There are 43,600 windows with over 600,000 square feet of glass in the twin towers. Automatic window washing machines on stainless steel tracks clean the exterior. There are 102 passenger elevators in the project. More than 6,500 sensors throughout the Center register temperatures, pressures, power consumption, and other variables and feed data into a computer which provides instantaneous information for any necessary remedial action.

The architects were Minoru Yamasaki and Associates of Troy, Michigan, and Emery Roth and Sons of New York. Engineering was: Structural—Skilling, Helle, Christiansen and Robertson of New York and Seattle; Electrical —Joseph R. Loring and Assoc. of New York; Mechanical—Jaros, Baum and Bolles of New York; Functional Planning—World Trade Center Planning and Construction Division of Port of New York Authority; Foundations—Engineering Department, Port of New York Authority. General Contractor was Tishman Realty and Construction Co. of New York.

— **3.69 Harborside Terminal to west:** When built by the Pennsylvania Railroad in 1929 this was the world's largest warehouse and provided rail to keel transshipment facilities. Today it is undergoing con-

version to office space and residential apartments with its own private ferry service to Manhattan.

— **3.40 Harsimus Cove to west.** This area was part of the original Patent granted to Michael Pauw, a burgomeister of Amsterdam, by the Dutch West India Company in 1624, who purchased it from the Indians Aeomeauw, Tekwappo, and Sackwomeck in 1630. The section was originally called Ahasimus, later corrupted to Harsimus, and was part of the much larger Pauw Patent, called Pavonia. This section originally consisted of mudflats at low water and a shallow bay at high water, with a few higher pieces of ground along the base of the Palisades. Paulus Hook was to the south and the high ground of what later was called Castle Point in Hoboken to the north. The entire area has been filled in over the years. In 1630 Pauw sent his agent Cornelius Van Vorst, a Walloon, to oversee the settlement of farmers and conduct the fur trade. He built a home on the south shore of Harsimus Cove, in the section of Jersey City still called Van Vorst. The Patent passed to Nicholas Pauw who sold it back to the Dutch West India Company (for 26,000 florins) in 1638. Van Vorst then rented the farm from the Company and continued to reside there. It is recorded that in 1641 "the family of Cornelius Van Vorst, deceased, at the head of which was Jacob Stoffelsen, who had married Van Vorst's widow, was living at Ahasimus."

The settlement was destroyed in the Indian War of 1644. It was resettled, but again, in 1665, was attacked and destroyed by Indians. Under the Duke of

HARBORSIDE TERMINAL, JERSEY CITY. World's largest warehouse when built in 1929 by the Pennsylvania Railroad. Presently undergoing conversion to residential and office space. Note twin towers of World Trade Center in Manhattan in background left. The large structure behind Harborside on the right is the new headquarters of National Westminster Bank at Exchange Place, Jersey City. Photo: © Gretchen McHugh.

ABANDONED POWER PLANT OF HUDSON & MANHATTAN RR. Jersey City. This massive structure awaits "creative re-use." Photo: © Gretchen McHugh.

York (1664–1685) this neighborhood was again resettled into small bouweries and became known as "The Duke's Farms." Around 1802 Nathaniel Budd was operating a ferry from here to the foot of Cortlandt Street and in 1804 John B. Coles, a New York Alderman and flour merchant, purchased the area for development. In subsequent years various railroads, ultimately controlled by the Pennsylvania Railroad, purchased the entire region and filled it in to accommodate freight terminals and rail yards. For many years the Pennsylvania Railroad had its carfloat bridges located here. As of this writing the area has been cleared for more new apartment development south of the Newport City complex.

— **3.00 Pavonia to west.** This area shared a similar history to Harsimus as described above, and was, of course, part of the large Pavonia Patent of 1624. In the mid-nineteenth century streets were layed out inland and in 1855 Homer Ramsdell, then President of the Erie Railroad, quietly purchased 212 acres of land and water frontage a half-mile into the Hudson River between Jersey City and Hoboken. Erie then formed the Long Dock Company, which was incorporated by the New Jersey Legislature. The Long Dock Company was empowered to improve the property south of the center line of Pavonia Ferry in the Fourth Ward of Jersey City, to purchase other lands, and to establish a ferry. In 1856 the Long Dock Company commenced driving an 8,000 ft. tunnel through the Palisades under the direction of the brilliant engineer James B. Kirkwood. The tunnel is still in use by Conrail freight trains. The original charter for the Pavonia Ferry had been granted by King George II in 1733, but had lain dormant for 128 years until brought to reality by the Erie Railway Co.

in 1861 and operated by them until December 12, 1958. Routes were to Chambers Street and West 23rd Street Manhattan. The Erie maintained a large passenger terminal at the foot of Pavonia Avenue, a giant grain elevator on Pier 1, to the south of the ferry, and carfloat bridges and piers to the north. In September 1939 the grain elevator was destroyed in a spectacular fire. In later years the Erie's marine department yards occupied the site, and the McAllister Towing Company after cessation of Erie marine operations. Taylor's Hotel was an important landmark here during the early Erie years. Today the inland portion of Pavonia is devoted to brownstone row houses around Hamilton Square Park. The waterfront has been luxuriously redeveloped under the name Newport City, and includes apartments, stores, and theaters, and a private ferry to Manhattan.

— **2.50 Canal Street to east.** Built upon site of an early Dutch period canal draining westward from the Collect Pond near present-day New York Municipal Building. It is well described by James Fenimore Cooper in his novel *Water Witch,* quoted under the preceding article entitled *Manhattan.*

— **2.50 The Holland Tunnel.** This is another facility of the Port Authority, and was the first Hudson River vehicular tunnel. It connects Canal Street in Manhattan with Twelfth and Fourteenth Streets in Jersey City. The tunnel was opened November 13, 1927, when President Calvin Coolidge, in Washington, D.C., pushed an electric button which caused two huge American flags to part at each entrance to the tunnel. The $70 million tunnel was named for its chief construction engineer, Clifford M. Holland, who died of exhaustion in 1924 just two days before sandhogs digging from each side met in one of the tunnel's two tubes. His bust and a memorial plaque are at the Manhattan entrance. This was the first major tunnel to pose a ventilation problem. It was solved by construction of four ventilation buildings, two on each side of the Hudson River, housing immense fans which can provide a change of air every ninety seconds. This was, then, the first tunnel with forced ventilation.

The length of the tunnel (portal to portal) is 8,588 feet in the north (westbound) tube and 8,371 feet in the south (eastbound) tube. Each roadway is 20 feet wide with an operating headroom of 12'6" and an external diameter of roughly 30 feet. Maximum depth from mean high water to roadway is 93 ft. 5 in. There is a toll, which is collected eastbound only on the New Jersey side. Between 1987 and 1989 the tunnel underwent extensive renovations and refurbishment.

—**2.38 PATH Uptown Tubes.** These first railroad tunnels under the Hudson River, completed on March 11, 1904, were opened on February 25, 1908 from Hoboken to Morton St., Manhattan (extended uptown to West 33rd Street in 1910). Originally constructed by the Hudson & Manhattan, owing to an engineering miscalculation, the two shafts did not quite meet in the middle of the river, and it was necessary to connect them with an S curve halfway under the river. To this day, operating speeds are therefore restricted. Each tube is single-track. The rail tunnels were conceived by D. C. Haskins in 1874 and completed by William Gibbs McAdoo. The chief engineer was Charles M. Jacobs. The line is operated by the Port Authority of New York & New Jersey.

—**2.38 Morton St. to east.**

—**2.20 Hoboken to west.** Hoboken is a city comprising exactly one square mile between the Hudson River and the foot of the Palisades. Population in 1990 was 33,397. The name is derived from the Indian name *Hoboghan-Hackingh,* meaning "the place of tobacco pipes," because of the red clay found here out of which the Indians fashioned their pipes. The region was originally quite picturesque. As late as 1840, the landscape painter Asher B. Durand wrote in his *Journal,* "...for real and unalloyed enjoyment of scenery, the rocks, trees and green meadows of Hoboken will have a charm that all Switzerland cannot boast." While this is obvious hyperbole, many other early writers testify to the rural charms of the area.

In 1640 Aert Teunissen Van Putten leased a farm here from the Dutch West India Company, becoming the first white settler. By 1642 the Dutch had established a settlement and a brewery. In 1658 Governor Peter Stuyvesant procured a deed from

HOBOKEN STREET SCENE 1989. The City of Hoboken covers exactly one square mile and is largely residential. Photo: © Gretchn McHugh.

the Indians, after an unfortunate event in 1643 described by Benson J. Lossing:

The low promontory below Castle Point was the site of the large Indian village of Hobock. There the pleasant little city of Hoboken now stands [1866], and few of its quiet denizens are aware of the dreadful tragedy performed in that vicinity more than two hundred years ago. The story may be related in few words. A fierce feud had existed for some time between the New Jersey Indians and the Dutch of Manhattan. Several of the latter had been murdered by the former and the Hollanders had resolved on vengeance. At length the fierce Mohawks, bent on procuring tribute from the weaker tribes westward of the Hudson, came sweeping down like a gale from the north, driving great numbers of fugitives upon the Hackensacks at Hobock. Now was the opportunity for the Dutch. A strong body of them, with some Mohawks, crossed the Hudson at midnight, in February, 1643, fell upon the unsuspecting Indians, and before morning murdered almost one hundred men, women and children. Many were driven from the cliffs of Castle Point, and perished in the freezing flood. At sunrise the murderers returned to New Amsterdam, with prisoners and the heads of several Indians.

(Lossing, *The Hudson,* pp. 450–451.)

In 1663 Governor Stuyvesant granted a deed to Nicholas Varlet and in 1711 the land in the vicinity passed into the hands of Samuel Bayard, a wealthy New York merchant. In 1771, title passed to William Bayard, a loyalist in the Revolution. The land was confiscated and valued at $90,000. On May 1, 1784, John Stevens purchased 564 acres for £18,340 and established his home on what is now known as Castle Point in 1787.

Originally much of Hoboken was an island surrounded by swamps, but this had been gradually filled in through the years. In 1804 John Stevens laid out a town and a pleasure garden to the north, known as the Elysian Fields, which operated until about 1839 and was a popular resort for New Yorkers. Ferry services were established at an early date. In 1825 John Stevens built 630 feet of circular track on his estate and operated a "steam wagon" thereon—the first steam railroad in America. John Jacob Astor built a home here in 1828, which was a gathering place for authors, including Fitz-Greene Halleck, Washington Irving, Gulian Verplanck, and William Cullen Bryant. John Stevens died in 1838, but in 1850 his son Edwin Stevens hired Alexander Jackson Davis to build him a castle, which soon gave its name to the promontory on which it stood. This building served as the administration building of the Stevens Institute of Technology until 1959, when it was torn down to make room for the present high-rise building. Only the gatehouse remains. It is built of irregularly cut greenish stone and has crenellated towers and stepped gables.

Although the Stevens's developed the town through the Hoboken Land & Improvement Company (1838–1946), which had broad chartered powers for developing streets, sewers, and other infrastructure improvements, Hoboken was formally incorporated as a city on March 28, 1855. The new city attracted many German immigrants and seamen and the Hamburg American and North German Lloyd steamship lines established their American terminals here. At the time of the outbreak of the First World War in 1914 the great *Vaterland* of the Hamburg-American Line was tied up at Hoboken. She remained tied up there until after she was taken over by the U. S. Navy on July 25, 1917, becoming the *U.S.S. Vaterland.* She was subsequently renamed *Leviathan* and used as a troop ship. After the War she remained in the hands of the new United States Lines and operated again as America's largest luxury liner.

As late as the 1920s and 1930s, it was a common excursion to visit the German beer cellars at "Hoboken, where German is spoken." The south end of town was soon pre-empted by the Morris & Essex Railroad (later Delaware, Lackawanna & Western, Erie-Lackawanna, and Conrail) freight and passenger yards and terminals. Rows of brownstone houses (many now undergoing restoration) stood near the river, and light industry and boiler and machine works were located further inland and on the site of the former Elysian Fields. There were also shipyards at the north end, and the Hoboken-Port Authority Marine Terminal was located between Stevens Institute and Lackawanna Terminal.

Ferry service to downtown Manhattan resumed in 1989, maintaining Hoboken's close connection with the Hudson River. The first formal ferry service was operated by Hermanus Talman in 1774. In 1789 John Stevens first became involved in ferry operation and in 1811 established the world's first steam ferryboat service, which operated under the banners of the Hoboken Ferry Company, the Delaware, Lackawanna & Western RR, and the Erie–Lackawanna Railroad until November 22, 1967.

– **2.00 Lackawanna Terminal (west).** A large passenger terminal and ferry depot, this is the last remaining example of this monumental type structure. Built by the Delaware, Lackawanna & Western Rail-

road in 1907, this green copper-sheathed structure once boasted an impressive 203 ft. high campanile tower, which has since been replaced by a utilitarian microwave tower. This caused writer Christopher Morley, a sometime Hoboken resident, to dub the adjacent Ferry Plaza the Piazza San Lackawanna, as the tower was copied after that of St. Mark in Venice. (As a sidelight, Morley called Hoboken a "Seacoast in Bohemia," which was an entirely inland nation, now part of Czechoslovakia, and, as a "never-never land," was used by Shakespeare as the setting for his *The Winters Tale.* Morley was engaged in an early off-off-Broadway theatrical venture involving an endless run of the Victorian melodrama *The Black Crook* at a Hoboken Theater.) The terminal's architect was Kenneth M. Murchison and the structural engineer was Lincoln Bush. It incorporates many important developments in marine and railroad terminal design, including upper deck ferry loading ramps and the so-called, "Bush train sheds." The ferry terminal has six slips and a river frontage of 566 feet. The entire terminal structure, except for the train shed, is built out over the water. There are fourteen tracks. It remains an important and very busy railroad station and ferry terminal, and its unique neo-classic architecture is worthy of renovation and preservation. In 1979, the State of New Jersey D.O.T. undertook a $3,700,000 restoration program. The final cost of the completed restoration project was $4 million and the terminal was rededicated on October 3, 1981.

– **1.80 Hoboken-Port Authority Marine Terminal (west).** This facility was financed and developed by the Port Authority under a fifty-year, three-party lease, effective in 1952, among the U.S. Maritime Administration, the city of Hoboken, and the Port

LACKAWANNA FERRY TERMINAL, HOBOKEN. This massive ferry and railroad terminal was built in 1907, designed by Kenneth M. Murchison in the Beaux Arts style for the Delaware, Lackawanna & Western Railroad. It has six ferry slips and fourteen tracks, with a river frontage of 566 ft. Most of the terminal is built out over the water. The terminal is still in use and is undergoing restoration. Photo: © Uta Gore.

Authority. There are three modern cargo piers with 5,952 linear feet of wharfage. In 1975 it handled 121,096 long tons. The movie *On The Waterfront,* with Marlon Brando, was filmed here. This terminal is on the site of the former North German Lloyd, Hamburg-American, and Holland-American steamship terminals. The piers are presently in a state of disuse and advanced decay. Political disagreements are hampering definite planning for redevelopment.

— **1.50 14th Street Manhattan to east.** Consolidated Edison Building: 37 stories, 475 ft. with a clock in the tower.

— **1.50 Castle Point (west), also known as Stevens Point.** Former site of the home of Edwin Stevens, which was designed by Alexander Jackson Davis in Gothic Revival style and stood from 1850 to 1959. Now a high-rise building occupies its site, the property of Stevens Institute of Technology. Formerly the marine shops of the Pennsylvania Railroad stood at the foot of the promontory. During the years of activity of the Elysian Fields recreation grounds (1804–1839), the Sibyl's Cave, under Castle Point, a cool, rocky cavern containing a spring, was a popular resort point.

— **1.50 Former site of Greenwich Point on east.**

— **1.20 – 1.70 Old Chelsea Piers on east:** Fourteenth to 23rd Streets. This group of piers, numbered 54 through 62, were a set of unified piers for ocean liners. Their period of greatest activity was in the period 1920–1945 when the Cunard Line, French Line, and the United States Line all used their facilities. They were superseded by new piers north of 42nd Street after the mid-thirties and the development of new giant liners. They are presently in a state of ad-

vanced decay and scheduled for demolition as part of the waterfront renovation. The city uses some of them for storage purposes.

— **1.10 23rd Street Manhattan to east.** Site of former large ferry terminals of Jersey Central, Lackawanna, Erie, and Pennsylvania railroads. Formerly a copper-sheathed campanile tower. Visible on 23rd Street are the massive London Tower Apartments, the Starret-Lehigh Warehouse, and the Metropolitan Life Insurance Building (48 stories, 658 feet, with clock in tower). Built in Italian Rennaissance Eclectic style in 1908–1909, it was designed by N. LeBrun and Sons. The former Union Ferry Terminal matched the architecture of the Lackawanna Terminal at Hoboken, and was also designed by Kenneth M. Murchison. The site is now occupied by World Yacht Cruises, who operate a marina for large private yachts and also their own extensive fleet of luxury charter yachts and dinner cruise boats—a delightful way to view the Port of New York.

— **1.00 Elysian Fields (west):** Former pleasure grounds, operated from 1804–1839, was developed by John and Robert Stevens. They erected an early form of ferris wheel and roller coaster. On June 19, 1846 the first baseball game of record was played at Elysian Fields between two amateur teams, the Knickerbockers and the New Yorkers. The New Yorkers won, 24 to 1. Only a tiny remnant survives as a public park at the corner of Hudson and Tenth Streets.

— **1.00 Port Authority-West Thirtieth Street Heliport (east).** At foot of West 30th Street and Hudson River. Leased from the city of New York, it accommodates general and corporate helicopter operations. It opened in 1956. Facilities include a paved area 400 feet by 70 feet with two concrete landing pads, each 80 feet square, projecting 40 feet out over the water on steel "H" piles. The Terminal building is at the northern end.

— **1.00 New York Life Building (east).** Massive tower with golden spire (34 stories, 617 feet tall).

— **0.75 Weehawken Cove to west.** Today the cove is largely filled in. It was the outlet of Sluice and Weehawken Creeks, both now reduced to underground drains. As early as 1888 there were three shipyards here, and it was the site of the famous Teitjen & Lang Dry Dock Company. Todd Shipyards Corporation operated here from 1916 to 1965. All shipyards are now gone.

HOBOKEN LINE PIERS c1900. Today these are known as the "Old Port Authority Piers." For many years the *Leviathan* was moored here, and in more recent times they were used by the Holland America Line. They are currently abandoned. Photo: Author's collection.

— **0.65 Dea's Point to west.**

CHELSEA TRANSATLANTIC PIERS at 23rd Street, c1900. These piers were in use through the 1930s. View from Smith's New York Harbor Guide. Author's collection.

UNION FERRY TERMINAL at West 23rd Street, Manhattan, c1909. These handsome buildings were designed by Kenneth M. Murchison and served ferryboats of the Erie, Pennsylvania, Lackawanna, and Central Railroad of New Jersey. View from Smith's New York Guide. Author's collection.

– 0.60 **Former Erie Railroad Weehawken Yards.** Later site of the Sea Train containerport terminal. Later A.E.A. Fuel Ownership Co. acquired the 80-acre site for $45 million to build a coalport, projected to handle 10 million tons each year. Subsequently the property has been acquired by commercial developers.

– 0.55 **Lincoln Harbor to west.** A large new office development built by Hartz Mountain Industries. Passenger ferry to Manhattan.

– 0.50 **Foot of Baldwin Avenue Weehawken to west.** Former site of Electric Ferry line to Manhattan between 1926 and 1943. This section was known as Undercliff. At the present time there is a popular tourist restaurant at the end of a long pier with great views of the Manhattan skyline and passing river

traffic. It is quite incongruous to the surroundings but has a type of unique funky charm. It is very popular and always crowded.

– 0.50 **Entrance approach ramps for Lincoln Tunnel to west.**

– 0.50 **Empire State Building to east.** (102 stories, 1,265 feet to tip of tower). Completed 1931, this was for a long period the world's tallest building. Shreve, Lamb and Harmon were the architects. It has sixty-three passenger and four freight elevators.

– 0.50 **33rd Street Manhattan to east.**

– 0.50 **Pennsylvania Railroad Tunnel.** Twin single-track railroad tunnels completed in September and October of 1906. They are built of cast-iron rings 2½ feet long and 23 ft. in diameter, each composed of eleven segments and a key, and of a total weight of 11½ tons, embedded in loosely compacted riverbed silt. They are lined with concrete, leaving 18 feet clear internal diameter. A concrete walk 6 feet in width at the height of the car windows extends along each side of the tube, in which are imbedded the conduits for the water pipes, the power cables, and the signal wires. As there is but six inches clearance above the car roof, ventilation is assured merely by the trains forcing the air ahead of them and fresh air following. The tubes are 6,000 feet long, with the western portal in the Hackensack meadows west of the Palisades. Penn Station is at the eastern end.

– 0.35 West 38th Street Manhattan to east.
Terminal of New York Waterways Ferry to Weehawken.

– 0.35 Jacob Javits New York Convention & Visitors Center on east. This large structure occupies the blocks between West 34th and West 39th Streets and 11th and 12th Avenues. Opened in 1984, it was designed by I. M. Pei & Partners in association with Lewis, Turner Partnership. The center cost $375 million. The multi-level center has a total floor area of 1.8 million square feet, containing two major exhibition halls. Located on the upper level is the largest single exhibition hall in the U. S. to be built on one floor. This 500,000-square-foot hall is adjacent to the skylit central entrance hall. On the lower level is a 250,000-square-foot exhibition hall and 100,000 square feet of meeting and special events rooms and 35,000 square feet of restaurant facilities. The 90-foot-wide concourse level runs north-south for the length of the building and is located at a level equidistant of both exhibition halls. A skylit galleria, running the full length of the center's east-west spine, forms a mezzanine bridge overlooking the upper level exhibition hall and culminating in a view of the waterfront. The center presents a reflecting façade behind which can be seen the latticework of the steel space frame. The roof over the central hall is formed by faceted cubes piled one on top of the other, ranging in height from 100 to 180 feet. Three types of reflective glass cloak the cubes. Structural engineers were Weidlinger Associates in association with Salmon Associates. Syska & Hennessy in association with Pierre A. Dillard were the mechanical and electrical engineers.

– 0.25 40th Street Manhattan to east.
Outlet Minetta Brook to east. Covered over.

– 0.25 Lincoln Tunnel. Ventilator towers to east and west.

– 0.25 Lincoln Tunnel. A facility of the Port Authority of New York and New Jersey, it is the world's only three-tube vehicular tunnel. The width of the roadway in each tunnel is 21 feet 6 inches, with an operating headroom of 13 feet. External diameter of each tunnel is 31 feet and maximum depth from mean high water to roadway is 97 feet.

	North Tube	Center Tube	South Tube
Date opened	1945	1937	1957
Length	7,482 ft.	8,216 ft.	8,006 ft.

Direct ramps connecting the Lincoln Tunnel with the Port Authority Bus Terminal facilitate the handling of commuter buses by removing them from Manhattan streets, and provide direct access for automobiles to the three-level roof parking.

– 0.10 Site of former piers to west. In the nineteenth century there was a depot for barges from the Delaware & Hudson Canal Co. Subsequently the Erie and New York Central railroads occupied the location and in the 1950s the United Fruit Company had a large facility to unload bananas from their ships. The old piers have been removed and property acquired by ARCORP Corp., for residential and commercial redevelopment. The banana boats now continue upriver to unload at the Port of Albany.

– 0.10 Kings Bluff, Weehawken. This bluff was named for James Gore King, whose estate, Highwood, occupied the site. The duel between Aaron Burr and Alexander Hamilton on July 11, 1804, in which Hamilton was killed, took place on

VILLA ON THE HUDSON, near Weehawken. This view, taken by William Bartlett in 1836 for N. P. Willis's *American Scenery*, is looking north over the now-filled-in Weehawken Cove and shows us the home of James Gore King on King's Bluff. The foreground is now filled in with the approaches to the Lincoln Tunnel, railroad tracks, and the Lincoln Harbor development. Compare with the following picture taken in 1989. Author's collection.

FORMER WEEHAWKEN FERRY AND RAILROAD TERMINAL 1957. This large terminal served trains of the West Shore and New York, Ontario & Western Railway. It was abandoned in 1959 and has been razed to make way for the Port Imperial development of ARCORP. A new passenger ferry operation now operates from this same location and a much smaller terminal. Photo: Arthur G. Adams.

KINGS BLUFF, WEEHAWKEN. Note helix trestle leading to the entrance to the Lincoln Tunnel and tunnel ventilator towers behind trees at right. View is looking northwest from the present waterfront, well out into the former Weehawken Cove. Photo: © Gretchen McHugh.

the grounds of this estate, which was a recognized dueling ground. There were at least fifteen recorded duels at this place. On September 2, 1799, Burr fought another duel with John B. Church, in which neither was hurt. On November 23, 1801, Hamilton's son Philip was killed in a duel with a certain Mr. Eaker. The same set of dueling pistols was used in all three duels. Other notable duels fought here were between DeWitt Clinton and John Swartwout on August 1, 1802 in which Swartwout was wounded; and between Oliver Hazard Perry and John Heath on October 19, 1818, in which neither was wounded. The actual dueling ground was near the river bank at the foot of the bluff. It was blasted away during the construction of the New Jersey Junction Railroad (now Conrail).

0.00 40th Street Manhattan: Pier 81.
Former Hudson River Day Line terminal.

0.00 42nd Street Manhattan. Grand Central Terminal.

0.00 43rd Street Manhattan. Pier 83, Circle Line sightseeing yachts.

0.00 Former site of West Shore Railroad Terminal and Bonn's elevator on west. This large railroad-ferry terminal operated 1884–1959 with routes to West 42nd Street and various downtown terminals, most lately at Cortlandt Street. It was a shared facility with the New York, Ontario & Western Railway. In later years the West Shore was acquired by the New York Central. Also, in 1892 John Hillaric Bonn, a real estate and railroad promoter, constructed the North Hudson Railroad atop the Palisades. Its Guttenberg Steam Railroad had its terminal located atop a spectacular 148-foot-high and 900-foot-long viaduct running out at right angles from

near the top of the Palisades, from the portal of a short tunnel, to the shores of the Hudson at the ferry terminal. Passengers were lifted from the ferries to a complete station atop the two-track viaduct by three of the largest passenger elevators ever built. The station atop the tower was a four-story structure surmounted by a high flagpole. This unique structure was dismantled in 1897 when the railroad was electrified and began using another route to the ferry terminal. Gustave Eiffel was the designer.

Today the entire terminal area and adjacent rail yards have been acquired by ARCORP Corporation for commercial and residential redevelopment. A new passenger ferry service has been established from the site to West 38th Street and downtown Manhattan and the locality renamed Port Imperial. All the former rail facilities and lines, except a single track leading to the tunnel beneath the Palisades to North Bergen, have been removed.

0.00 Weehawken to west. (1990 population 12,385) The Weehawken Grant was given to Martyn Andreaensen by the Dutch West India Company in 1647. Development of the area was slow and a township was not incorporated until 1859. In the late eighteenth and early nineteenth centuries Weehawken was a popular picnic ground for New Yorkers. Fitz-Green Halleck wrote in his poem "Fanny,"

"Weehawken! in thy mountain scenery set,
All we adore of Nature and her wild
And frolic hour of infancy is met."
From "Fanny" by Fitz-Green Halleck,
George Dearborn, NYC, 1819

In the late nineteenth century, with the construction of railroads and streetcar lines, residential development was very rapid. Many German and Swiss immigrants settled here. Here were located the picnic ground, casino, and amphitheater of Eldorado Park, owned by the Palisades Amusement & Exhibition Company, John H. Bonn, President. The park offered such spectacles as Franko's Brass Band and such stage shows as "Egypt Through the Ages," "King Solomon," and "The Destruction of Jerusalem," with one thousand performers, camels, horses, and elephants. Strudel, pretzels, beer, and Rhine wine abounded. In later years Italians settled in the area, and today many Cuban refugees live in the neighborhood. Luxury homes and apartments are again being built, enjoying the spectacular views of the Hudson River and Manhattan.

The name comes from the Indian word for a "palisaded place" or one surrounded by "rows of trees." This analogy probably arose from the peculiar columnar basalt formations of the Palisades.

The New York, Ontario & Western Railway and West Shore Railroad built a 4,225-foot-long two-track tunnel from the water's edge to North Bergen in 1883. This is still in use with only one track by Conrail, but there are plans afoot to utilize it soon for an electric light rail system to give access to the restored ferry operation and new waterfront development. The entire waterfront, once occupied by railyards and terminals, was acquired from the Penn-Central Corporation by Arthur Imperatore for a rather modest sum and his ARCORP Corporation is in process of clearing and redeveloping the area.

0.00 The dome, visible atop the cliffs, back from the edge, belongs to the church of St. Michael's Monastery in Union City. Former Headquarters of the Passionist order.

0.30 Site of former New York Central RR Pier 7 grain elevator to west. This gigantic structure stood from 1884 to 1962 and had a capacity of 2 million bushels. It was built atop 7,000 piles 152 feet deep.

0.30 Passenger ship terminal. Operated by the Port Authority since 1974, its construction involved the rebuilding of three obsolete piers dating from 1933 between 48th and 52nd Streets to provide six ship berths with the most modern passenger facilities. The second level of the terminal is heated or air conditioned year round and is used for passengers and baggage. The ground level is used as a service area for delivery of equipment and ships' stores. Flat roofs provide parking for 1,000 vehicles. The terminal cost was in excess of $2 million and employs 171 people with an annual payroll of $2,145,000. It handled 433,050 passengers in 1975.

0.60 Old steamship "finger piers" on east. These piers, formerly used by small transatlantic liners and cruise ships,, are in an advanced state of decay and scheduled for demolition. They are used for storage of automobiles towed away for illegal parking.

1.00 Former site of New York Central Carfloat Bridges and Slips on east. The former railyard between here and Eleventh Avenue has been acquired by developer Donald Trump from the estate of the Penn-Central Corporation for development of a project called Television City. He has been hindered in his plan by various opposition and it is uncertain if and when the project will proceed. He planned very high buildings for the site.

1.00 Slough's Meadow to west. Once site of large New York Central freight yards, has again been cleared preparatory to commercial and residential redevelopment. At base of Palisades. The New York Central also operated a marine repair yard here, and the original Weehawken Ferry operated from here.

1.00 Day's Point to east.

1.50 Guttenberg on west: A town with a heavy German population. There was formerly a brewery here. The town has very short frontage on the Hudson River. It runs far west with a residential section atop the palisades.

The Palisades

This striking series of cliffs along the western shore is composed of columnar basalt and is named for their similarity in appearance to a wooden palisaded fortification. Their geology is described in detail in Chapter 1. The actual geological formation is more extensive than the section commonly designated the Palisades, running from Bayonne, New Jersey to the vicinity of Pomona, New York, about forty-eight miles. Generally speaking, they are said to start at Kings Bluff on the south end and continue north to Tallman Mountain, just south of Sparkill Creek near Piermont, New York. The highest point is Indian Head, opposite Hastings-on-Hudson, with an elevation of 522 feet. The top of the Palisades is generally level for about a mile back from the cliffs, and slopes from there down to the valley of the Hackensack River. Originally densely wooded throughout, the southern end is now devoted to dense residential development, while the northern end remains in forest devoted to recreation and conservation. The northern cliffs are park land and are under the protection of the Palisades Interstate Park Commission, formed in 1900 to preserve this unique area against quarrying and other unsightly encroachments. In past years, wealthy New Yorkers purchased extensive wood lots atop the Palisades to supply themselves with heating wood. The logs were pitched down from atop the cliffs to docks below. Many of these pitching places are

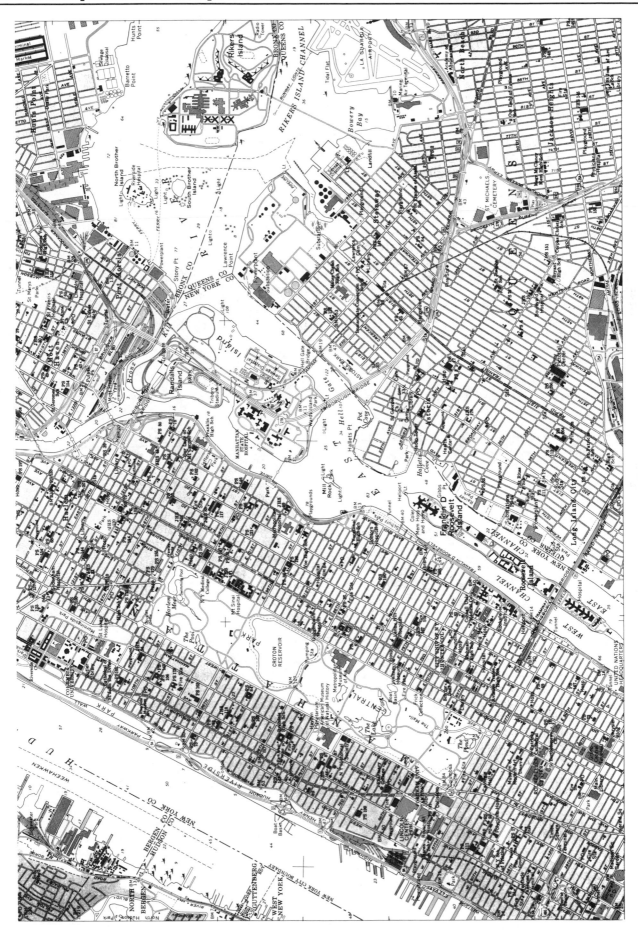

UPPER MANHATTAN

MANHATTAN TRANSATLANTIC LINER PIERS c 1950. This type activity was not untypical from 1940 until 1970. Ships shown are the *Independence, America, and United States,* with the *Queen Elizabeth* docking. Author's collection.

known as "gutters," and the names of these former docks are still used by hikers as landmarks. Until the formation of the Palisades Interstate Park, there were small farms at the base of the cliffs and on terraces above the river. Pears were one of the staple crops, and many of the "Undercliff" dwellers also pursued shad fishing, stone quarrying, and logging. Today the entire area is devoted to recreation. The Henry Hudson Drive runs beneath the cliffs and the Palisades Interstate Parkway and Route 9W run along the top. From Fort Lee south to Weehawken, many large high-rise apartment houses have been built in recent years. They offer their tenants spectacular views. However, while attractive enough in themselves, their erection is changing the character of the area and is tending to dwarf the Palisades themselves.

1.85 79th Street Yacht Basin on east.

1.85 Riverside Drive. This famous street runs from 72nd Street north to Dyckman Street. Its embankments, terraces, and pergolas were designed by the noted landscape architect Frederick Law Olmstead (ca. 1909) in the classic eclectic style. It is fronted by gracious townhouses and apartment buildings and is

separated from the river by Riverside Park. In the 1930s, the Hudson Division of the New York Central Railroad south of 123rd Street was covered over by landscaped terraces and the Henry Hudson Parkway constructed from the north end of the West Side Elevated Highway at 72nd Street to the Henry Hudson Bridge at the north end of Manhattan. This parkway runs closer to the river edge than does Riverside Drive and is a limited-access highway.

1.85 Boulevard East. This street runs along the top of the Palisades from King's Bluff to Hudson Heights at the Hudson-Bergen County Line. Many luxurious highrise apartments are being constructed along it.

1.85 Conrail (former West Shore Railroad/New York Central) freight yards along the foot of the Palisades. Site of former marine shops of the New York Central Railroad and coal piers of the New York, Ontario & Western and New York, Susquehanna & Western Railroads. During the 1940s and 1950s, many shanty dwellers lived aboard decaying barges aground on the shallow flats.

2.45 Block House Point on west. Site of a Revolutionary War blockhouse. Benson Lossing tells its history succinctly in *The Hudson* as follows:

In the summer of 1780, a few weeks before the discovery of Arnold's treason, that block-house was occupied by a British picket, for the protection of some woodcutters, and the neighboring New Jersey loyalists. On Bergen Neck, below, was a large number of cattle and horses, belonging to the Americans, within reach of the foragers who might go out from the British post at Paulus's Hook, now Jersey City. Washington's head-quarters were then inland, near Ramapo. He sent General Wayne, with some Pennsylvanian and Maryland troops, horse and foot, to storm the block-house and to drive the cattle within the American lines. Wayne sent the cavalry, under Major Henry Lee, to perform the latter duty, whilst he and three Pennsylvanian regiments marched against the block-house with four pieces of cannon. They made a spirited attack, but their cannon were too light to be effective, and, after a skirmish, the Americans were repulsed with a loss of sixty men, killed and wounded. After burning some wood-boats near, and capturing those who had them in charge, Wayne returned to camp with a large number of cattle driven by the dragoons.

This event was the theme of a satirical poem, in three cantos, in the ballad style, written by Major Andre, and published in Rivington's Royal Gazette *in the city of New York.*

(Lossing, *The Hudson*, pp. 439–441.)

2.45 Soldiers and Sailors Monument to east.
At corner of 89th Street and Riverside Drive. Designed by Charles W. and Arthur A. Stoughton in the Beaux Arts Eclectic style. Constructed between 1900 and 1902, it is dedicated to soldiers who lost their lives in the Civil War. It is in the form of a Greek temple with a peristyle of twelve Corinthian columns. Sculptural work is by Paul Duboy.

3.00 Bergen County. (1990 population, 825,380, county seat; Hackensack) extends from here to the New York State line at mile 18.00 along the west shore.

3.00 Shadyside on west. Named for former Shady Side Hotel. Formerly known as Bull's Ferry. Presently an industrial area.

3.30 Former Ford Motor Company assembly plant on west. Now a deepwater terminal and warehouse, being developed into a residential complex. This is the south end of the village of Edgewater. A tunnel of the New York, Susquehanna & Western RR pene-

SOLDIERS AND SAILORS MONUMENT. This monument was designed by Charles W. and Arthur A. Stoughton with sculptural work by Paul Duboy. It was dedicated in 1902 to men who had lost their lives in the Civil War, and is lcoated at Riverside Drive and West 89th Street. Photo: © Gretchen McHugh.

trates the Palisades here to the Hackensack Meadows.

3.30 Former site of Stryker's Bay on east.
Now filled in by construction of Riverside Park and Henry Hudson Parkway.

4.30 Sunnyside on west. A section of the village of Edgewater. Possibly named in contradistinction to Shadyside? In the late 1980s there were plans for construction of a large coal port here, but nothing has developed yet as we go to press. Former Seatrain Lines terminal. Citrus Port also being considered.

4.30 Riverside Church and Interchurch Center on east. At corner of 122nd Street and Riverside Drive. This is one of the largest churches in New York. Built 1930 in neo-Gothic style with a twenty-four-story, four hundred foot tower housing the seventy-four-bell Laura Spellman Rockefeller Carillon. The nineteen-story Interchurch Center is faced

RIVERSIDE CHURCH. This modern church, inspired by the Cathedral of Chartres, was designed by Allen, Pelton & Collens, and completed in 1930. Located at Riverside Drive and 122nd Street, the 400-foot tower houses the 74 bells of the Laura Spellman Rockefeller carillon. Photo: © Gretchen McHugh.

with Alabama limestone and houses church and church-related organizations of the Orthodox and Protestant religions. Columbia University is located behind the church and center.

4.40 Grant's Tomb on east. Tomb of General and President Ulysses Simpson Grant (1822-1885), located at the corner of 123rd Street and Riverside Drive. It houses President Grant and his wife Julia Dent Grant. There are also reliquary rooms displaying Civil War flags and other mementoes. The tomb is officially called the General Grant National Monument. Built between 1892–1897, it was designed in competition. The winning architect, John H. Duncan, chose to build in the classic eclectic style. The square base in the Doric mode is surmounted by circular peristyle in the Ionic mode with a stepped conical dome. The structure is reminiscent of the tomb of King Mausolos at Halicarnassos. The interior is similar to Napoleon's tomb in the chapel of the Hotel des Invalides in Paris, but is much smaller. It is built of white granite and cost $600,000. The apex of the memorial is 280 feet above the river.

4.40 Former Lackawanna ferryboat *S.S. Binghamton* is anchored along the shoreline at Edgewater to the west. Converted to a floating restaurant and supper club, it operates under the tradename *Binghamton's.* It is the only remaining typical large steam ferryboat on the Hudson. It has been added to the National Register of Historic Places.

4.40 Former Aluminum Company of America Plant—Alcoa—to west. This large poured concrete building was a can factory for many years. It was planned to convert it into a condominium apartment building, but PCB contamination has halted the project.

4.75 Site of former Jack Frost Sugar Refinery on west.

4.75 Formerly swimming baths were moored in the Hudson here on the east side. They were partially submerged barges with lattice bottoms to permit ingress of the river water. It is ironic that this was the most highly polluted place in the river with untreated sewage entering here.

4.75 Site of former Recreation Pier at end of 130th Street. This was also used by the Hudson River

GRANT'S TOMB. Located on Riverside Drive, this tomb designed by John H. Duncan was completed in 1897 and houses the bodies of General and President Ulysses Simpson Grant and his wife, Julia Dent Grant. Photo: Author's collection.

Day Line and Night Line and various excursion boats, and by the Iron Steamboat Company.

4.75 Riverside Drive Viaduct on east. Between 129th and 135th Streets (length 1,688 feet), it carries a 60-foot-wide roadway and two sidewalks 10 feet wide. It is built of steel girders and masonry at the southerly end. Opened for traffic in 1903. In 1987 the entire viaduct was dismantled, piece by piece, like a child's Erector or Meccano set, brought to a factory, sand-blasted, repainted, and reassembled onsite. This was more efficient than working on it *in situ.*

4.75 Visible behind the Riverside Drive Viaduct is the high 125th Street viaduct of the Broadway Line of the I.R.T. Division of the New York subway system. This is a large steel arch viaduct. The 125th Street station is atop the viaduct.

4.80 Site of former 125th Street Ferry to Edgewater on east. It is a peculiarity that West 125th Street and West 130th Street come together at an angle at the riverfront. Thus 130th Street pier and 125th Street Ferry were next to each other, with the 130th Street pier to the south.

4.80 Edgewater, N.J., to the east. Village at foot of the Palisades. Largely residential at the northern end, it has retained a rural atmosphere (population 5,001). The southern end is devoted to industry, and there were formerly large plants of the Jack Frost Sugar Company and Alcoa located here. Served by New York, Susquehanna & Western Railroad, it is the former terminus of the 125th Street Ferry and numerous electric interurban lines serving northern New Jersey. At one time shad fishing was a major local industry. The old Ox Hill Road was one of the pioneer roads up the Palisades.

4.80 Cliffside Park, N.J., residential community atop the Palisades. The section along the cliffs is known as Grantwood, after the tomb across the river. The very large apartment houses are known as the Winston Towers and stand on the site of the former large Palisades Amusement Park. This was one of America's largest amusement parks and featured a giant salt-water pool with machinery to simulate ocean waves, three giant roller-coasters (the Scenic Railway, the Sky Rocket, and the Bob-Sled), which were located dramatically atop the Palisades cliffs, and a large ferris wheel, also located at the edge of the cliffs.

The development of both the residential area and the amusement park was fostered by the ferry and various trolley lines crossing here.

4.80 Harlem section of Manhattan, to the east. Originally a valley of rich farms known in colonial days as Marritje David's Vly, it later became the location of luxurious country estates and later an area of stylish townhouses and apartment flats. As the wealthy white population moved further uptown and across to New Jersey, the area became popular with Blacks, and is now the largest single Black community in the United States. As the Blacks are becoming more affluent and moving farther afield, Hispanic people are gradually moving into Harlem, particularly along the East Side and Riverside Drive north of 125th Street.

4.90 Manhattanville section of Manhattan to east.

4.95 Site of the Grange, home of Alexander Hamilton, to east.

5.00 Undercliff section of Edgewater to west. Originally a colony of fishermen, and later of summer villas and bungalows. With commencement of regular ferry service it attracted permanent residents. In 1911 Lorentz Kleiner, or Cleiser, began making tapestry, and for more than 20 years Edgewater Looms tapestries, handwoven and handsewn, were produced on order for state capitols, museums, hotels, private clubs, expositions and prominent individuals here and abroad. Forced out of business in 1933 as a result of lack of demand and the importation of less expensive European articles, the Edgewater Looms had turned out thousands of pieces valued at from $300 to $2,000 each. The four buildings that made up its plant contained facilities for every phase of the work, from drawing designs to finishing huge textile mosaics that sometimes took as long as a year to weave. At the Newark Museum are two of the chief works of the looms—one depicting the life of the Hackensack Indians and the other showing Newark in 1826. After the closing of the looms the buildings were occupied by a number

EUREKA SPRING GROVE HOUSE, Edgewater. This old tavern was typical of the New Jersey waterfront establishments catering to fishermen and excursionists. Note the shad nets drying in the foreground. Photo: Courtesy of Claire Tholl.

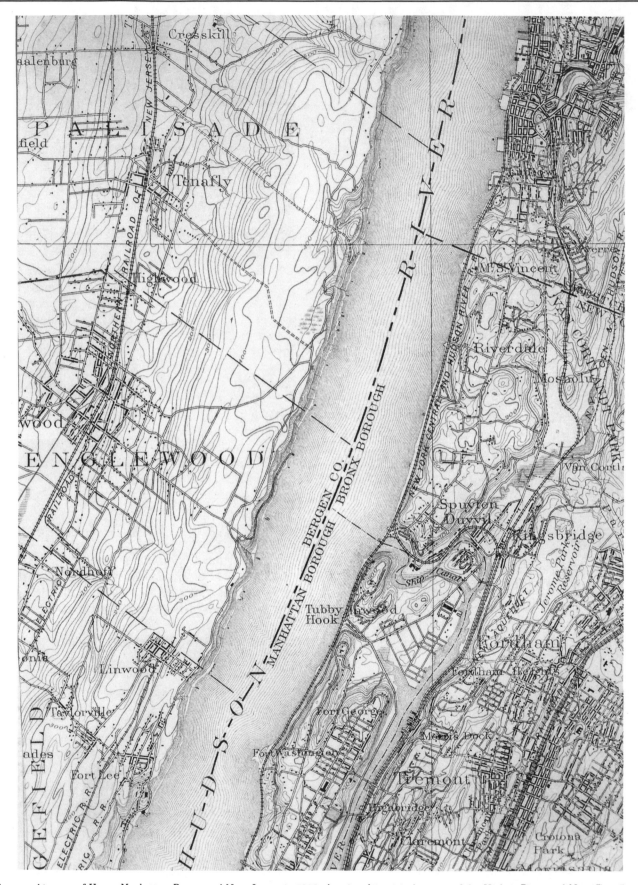

Topographic map of Upper Manhattan, Bronx, and New Jersey in 1905, showing the original course of the Harlem River and New Ship Canal.

of artists and the architect James MacGrath. Today the Undercliff area retains considerable charm, but is under development pressure by the many new high rise apartments that have been constructed in the last two decades.

5.00 Large new sewage treatment plant to east.

Along the river on the east. Site was once occupied by yards and docks of the Iron Steamboat Company and various coal companies.

7.00 Carmansville section of Manhattan.

Named for colonial era builder, developer, and merchant Richard F. Carman who owned extensive tracts in the area and developed village of Carmansville. Well-known inhabitants of this section were Roger Morris, Madame Jumel, the widow of Aaron Burr, and John James Audubon. The section is sometimes known as Audubon Heights or Audubon Park.

7.10 Columbia-Presbyterian Medical Center on east.

Large complex of buildings devoted to the care of the sick, medical research, and teaching. Completed in 1928 and designed by James Gamble Rogers, it is the site of the famed Harkness Pavilion. The medical center is to the north of the site of the early New York Institution for the Deaf and Dumb, founded in 1817.

7.10 Burdett's Landing on west.

This location has also been known through the years as Burdett's Ferry, Tillie Tudlem, Tilly Toodlum, Pleasant Valley, and Fort Lee Park. At the bottom of a clove giving easy access to the top of the Palisades and at the outlet of a small watercourse known as Dead Brook. In 1653 Etienne Burdett, a Manhattan merchant of Huguenot parentage, established a trading post and built his home, a picturesque gambrel-roofed struc-

TILLIETUDLEM. Country estate of the late Francis R. Tilliou, Esq. This is located immediately south of Burdett's Landing. From an old print. Courtesy Claire Tholl.

ture, which stood until about 1900, in a forest clearing at the foot of the gorge. In later years the Hackensack Turnpike, now called Hudson Terrace, became a major route to the hinterlands and farmers brought their product here for transshipment on Burdett's boats to the Bloomingdale section of Manhattan, thus establishing "Burdett's Ferry." During the Revolution Burdett's Ferry offered the only communication between Forts Washington and Lee. Troops, ammunition, and supplies were brought and sent from here. Etienne Burdett's brother, Peter, was then running the ferry and was an ardent patriot, and it is recorded that his wife often cooked flapjacks for General Washington and other of the Continental officers. It is recorded in Arthur C. Mack's *The Palisades of the Hudson* (privately printed, 1909), that:

"Burdett's Ferry has the distinction of having two miniature engagements of its own in the Revolution. Early on the morning of August 18, 1776, the British ships Phoenix *and* Rose, *which had previously passed up the river, stood down stream. When abreast of the ferry the* Rose *was hulled by a shot from General Mercer's Battery located there, firing grape shot in return. Again on October 27, at seven o'clock in the morning, two British frigates moved up the river and anchored off Burdett's Ferry, apparently to cut off communication between the forts. The barbette battery on Fort Lee Bluff opened fire and two 18-pounders brought down to the ferry landing from Fort Lee and planted opposite the ships repeatedly hulled and partially disabled one of the vessels. "Had the tide been flood one-half hour longer," wrote General Greene, "we should have sunk her."*

BRITISH FLEET FORCING THE HUDSON RIVER PASSAGE at Burdett Landing. This engagement on the morning of October 9, 1776, was depicted by Dominic Serres, the elder. Fort Lee is seen above the landing. Courtesy U.S. Naval Academy Museum.

After the Revolution some attempts were made to grow grapes on the adjacent hillsides and the farm trade continued at the ferry. Gradually the neighborhood developed as a resort and, in the mid and late nineteenth century a number of large hotels were built, including the Bluff Grove, Pavilion Hotel, Octagon House, and the Fort Lee Park Hotel. Transportation was required and a Union Steamboat Wharf was built for use of such local lower Hudson steamboats as the *Crystenah* and Burdett's Landing's own Fort Lee & New York Steamboat Company, also known as The People's Ferry Company, which operated between 1832 and ca. 1910. Its boats included the *Edwin*, the *Thomas E. Hulse*, the *Fort Lee*, the *Pleasant Valley*, and the *Shady Side*. Its route ran from here to Edgewater, Shadyside, Bulls Ferry, Guttenberg, Weehawken, and West 22nd Street, Spring Street, and Canal Street in Manhattan. Many summer commuters used the line, and there have been recent (unsuccessful because of high costs and fares) attempts to restore this service. With use of larger ships with lower fares it is quite likely that such a service will soon succeed again.

7.15 Site of former Powder Dock, or Dupont Dock on west. This was formerly operated by the DuPont Chemical Company for delivery of blasting powder to the former nearby quarries. It is now within the bounds of the Palisades Interstate Park, which runs from here northward to the New York State Line.

7.20 Site of Hazard's Dock on west. Also used for delivery of blasting powder to the quarries.

7.30 Fort Lee and Fort Washington

1776—A Year of Trial

Fort Lee found its place in American History during the 1776 British campaign to control New York City and the Hudson River. This was a year that saw: America for-

PLEASANT VALLEY LANDING (also called Burdett's Landing). Octagon House Hotel and Union Steamboat Dock in foreground. Photo: Courtesy Claire Tholl.

mally declare its independence; a great British invasion; retreats and defeats for the American forces; the outnumbered American Army meeting the British on the field of battle and surviving, to turn the tide with Washington's crossing the Delaware and capturing the garrison at Trenton.

Washington Acts to Defend New York

After the siege of Boston, where the British were forced to evacuate, George Washington, Commander-in-Chief of the American Army, turned his attention to the defense of New York and the Hudson Valley. Along with the construction of fortifications at New York City and Long Island, Washington felt it imperative to construct new fortifications along the Hudson River.

British Strategy

The British plan was to control the length of the Hudson with the overwhelming dominance of its Royal Navy; the plan, if successful, would split the colonies in half and hopefully bring an early end to the revolution.

The Americans Build Their Defenses

In July of 1776 work was begun on this site, which was eventually named for General Charles Lee, who aided in the defense of New York City. On the opposite New York shore, work had already begun on Fort Washington.

On July 12 Admiral Richard Howe sent two British naval vessels north up the Hudson. The cannon fire from Fort Washington had little effect upon their passage. General Washington then ordered that work on Fort Lee continue as quickly as possible. Upon Major General Israel Putnam's suggestion, the river was obstructed by placing sunken ships in the river channel. With these obstructions in place, in conjunction with the artillery fire from the sister forts of Lee and Washington, it was felt that no British shipping could sail up river without sustaining severe losses.

The Blow Against New York

King George III, wanting to end the revolution as quickly as possible, sent the largest armada of British ships and troops that had ever left England's shores. By mid-August Sir William Howe, the British Commander-in-Chief, had assembled an army of over 31,000 British, Hessian and loyalist troops on Staten Island.

On August 22 the British landed on Long Island and five days later forced the Americans to retreat to New York City. Through September and October the British and American forces were involved in battles at New York City, Harlem Heights, and White Plains. The British then turned their forces against Fort Washington. On November 16, Fort Washington fell to the overwhelming assault by the British force, which captured over 2,000 American troops.

The Fall of Fort Lee

General Washington, realizing that with the loss of Fort Washington Fort Lee was now of little military value, made preparations to evacuate his remaining army through New Jersey. An orderly retreat, however, was not in store for the Americans. On November 20, General Cornwallis ferried between 6,000 and 8,000 men across the Hudson about five miles to the north of Fort Lee. When word of the crossing reached Washington, he ordered an immediate retreat before his now-demoralized army was cut off and captured by the advancing British. Most of the American supplies and artillery had to be left behind. These were indeed the darkest days for the Revolution and led to Thomas Paine's famous words: "These be the times that try men's souls."

7.30 Fort Washington on east. Atop Washington Heights, the highest point in Manhattan (elevation 268 feet). The name now applies to the entire neighborhood of apartment houses. Originally named for a Revolutionary War fortification, this location is described by Benson Lossing in *The Hudson:*

...we reach the station-house of the Hudson River Railway, which stands at the southern entrance to a deep rock excavation through a point of Mount Washington, known for a hundred years or more as Jeffery's Hook. This point has an interesting revolutionary history in connection with Mount Washington. At the beginning of the war, the great value, in a strategic point of view, of Manhattan Island, and of the river itself—in its entire length to Fort Edward— as a dividing line between New England and the remainder of the colonies, was fully appreciated by the contending parties. The Americans adopted measures early to secure these, by erecting fortifications. Mount Washington (so named at that time) was the most elevated land upon the island, and formidable military works of earth and stone were soon erected upon its crown and upon the heights in the vicinity from Manhattanville to Kingsbridge. The principal work was Fort Washington. The citadel was on the crown of Mount Washington, overlooking the country in every direction, and comprising within the scope of vision the Hudson from the Highlands to the harbour of New York. The citadel, with the outworks, covered several acres between One Hundred

and Eighty-first and One Hundred and Eighty-sixth Streets.

On the point of the chief promontory of Mount Washington jutting into the Hudson, known as Jeffery's Hook, a strong redoubt was constructed, as a cover to chevaux-de-frise and other obstructions placed in the river between that point and Fort Lee, to prevent the British ships going up the Hudson. The remains of this redoubt, in the form of grassy mounds covered with small cedars, are prominent upon the point.... The ruins of Fort Washington, in similar form, were also very conspicuous until within a few years, and a flag staff marked the place of the citadel. But the ruthless hand of pride, forgetful of the past, and of all patriotic allegiance to the most cherished traditions of American citizens, has levelled the mounds, and removed the flag-staff, and that spot, consecrated to the memory of valorous deeds and courageous suffering, must now be sought for in the kitchen-garden or ornamental grounds of some wealthy citizen, whose choice celery or bed of verbenas has greater charms than the green sward of hillock beneath which reposes the dust of a soldier of the old war for independence!

"Soldiers buried here?" inquires the startled resident. Yes; your villa, your garden, your beautiful lawn, are all spread out over the dust of soldiers, for all over these heights the blood of Americans, Englishmen, and Germans flowed freely in the autumn of 1776, when the fort was taken by the British after one of the hardest struggles of the war. More than two thousand Americans were captured, and soon filled the loathsome prisons and prison-ships of New York.

Fort Washington mounted twenty heavy cannon and several smaller pieces and mortars. Its chief strength consisted in its position. The fort was commanded by Colonel Magaw of Pennsylvania, assisted by Lambert Cadwalader of that same state. The total American force was 2000 men, including those driven in from Ft. Tryon and Cock Hill Fort.

The British and German combined forces was about 5000 men; the British under Sir William Howe and the Hessians and Waldeckers under Baron Wilhelm von Knyphausen. The decisive action was on the morning of November 16, 1776, at which time Generals Greene and Washington were at Fort Lee, watching the battle from across the river. Knyphausen led 500 Hessians and Waldeckers from the north, having first taken Cock Hill and Fort Tryon. A Division of 800 English and Hessians under Lords Percy and Cornwallis, and Colonel Stirling and Brigadier Matthews attacked from the south and east. Despite hard fighting Magaw had to surrender by 1:30 P.M. when the Union Jack was raised over the fort—which was shortly thereafter renamed Fort Knyphausen.

7.30 Jeffery's Hook on east. Site of revolutionary fortification and of Jeffry Point Lighthouse. The lighthouse is no longer operational. It is located directly beneath the George Washington Bridge. When it was proposed to dismantle the red lighthouse, public feeling led to its permanent preservation. Hildegarde Swift wrote a children's story entitled "The Little Red Lighthouse and the Great Gray Bridge," which sold 2 million copies. Both the spelling Jeffery's Hook and Jeffry Point are used officially by different government agencies. The first lighthouse was erected here in 1885. The present one was built in 1920 and operated until 1951. Hildegarde Swift's story was first published in 1942.

7.30 Fort Lee to west (1990 population 31,997). Today largely devoted to highrise apartment houses and highway interchanges funneling into the George Washington Bridge, Fort Lee was originally called Pickletown. It is at an elevation of 260 feet and offers commanding views to both east, over the Hudson River to Manhattan, and to the west over the Hackensack Valley to the Watchung and Ramapo Mountains. In the early days of the movie industry many studios were located here and films shot in the surrounding area included the famous Pearl White *The Perils of Pauline* serials of "cliff hangers," which were actually filmed on the Palisades around 1918. In the mid 1930s the industry moved to California, but films were still processed here until the 1960s. Today the area is extremely popular with people of Japanese descent.

Fort Lee takes its present name from a fortification erected here in July 1776 on a bluff then called Mt. Constitution at an elevation of 250 ft. overlooking the Hudson. The fort was first named Fort Constitution, but on October 18, 1776, it was officially renamed Fort Lee, in honor of General Charles Lee, who had aided in defense of New York City. The fort was built by General Hugh Mercer. The principal fortification was located between the present Parker Avenue and Cedar, English, and Federspiel Streets with other works on Bluff Point, to the east of Hudson Terrace, the site of the present Fort Lee Historic Park.

Prior to construction of the fort the troops had spread out over an area known as Nolan's Ground and set up hut villages toward the west where was located another brook called Dead Bridge Brook. This was to the west of present Lemoine Avenue, south of Whiteman Street.

Colonel Rufus Putnam suggested that the Hudson be obstructed by placing sunken ships in the channel. These, in conjunction with Forts Lee and Washington, would prevent British ships from sailing upriver. The entire complex of Forts Washington and Lee was erected under the supervision of General Nathaniel Greene. The *chevaux-de-frise* consisted of two sunken sloops, two sunken brigs, two large ships mounted with heavy guns and swivels, "two hundred iron fraise of 400 weight each," besides sundry logs and other impedimenta. The *chevaux-de-frise* ran across beneath the present George Washington Bridge, and were covered by the batteries on the Bluff and at Fort Washington.

On August 16, 1776 the British warships *Phoenix* and *Rose* were attacked by American fireships and galleys just off Fort Lee. However, to quote from Arthur C. Mack's *The Palisades:*

"Colonel Putnam's elaborate obstruction had been proved vulnerable, for on the morning of October 9th, the British men-of-war Roebuck, Phoenix and Tartar, with all sail set to a fresh south wind, got under way from their anchorage in the lower river, and swept through the obstructions in gallant style, notwithstanding bombardment from the two shore defenses. Later, on the night of November 14th, a fleet of the enemy's flat boats passed in spite of the obstructions, and proceeded into the Harlem River."

However, in the interim, on October 27, the barbette battery at Fort Lee had driven off two British frigates anchored off Fort Lee.

After November 14, Washington ordered General Greene to evacuate Fort Washington and withdraw from Fort Lee. As the orders were of a somewhat discretionary nature, and Greene and Putnam were both sanguine of their ability to hold the forts, they decided to remain. Furthermore, Congress had sent instructions "not to evacuate the forts except in case of 'direst necessity.'"

On November 13 Washington arrived from Stony Point, reviewed the works at Fort Lee, and retired to his headquarters at Hackensack. On November 15 the attack on Fort Washington began in earnest. To quote Mack again:

"At four o'clock in the afternoon of the same day Greene sent a hurried message requesting the presence of Washington at Fort Lee. The General galloped over the Hackensack Turnpike and reached the fort at nine o'clock in the evening. Greene had already crossed the river. Down the Gorge road Washington hurried, and, boarding a boat, was rowed

across toward Jeffrey's Hook. When half-way across, as Washington himself puts it in his journal, "I met Generals Putnam and Greene, who were just returning from thence (Fort Washington) and they informed me that the troops were in high spirits and would make a good defense, and it being late at night, I returned." That night Washington slept at the Burdett house."

"Early the next day, after morning mists had cleared away, the boom of cannon and crack of musketry announced the opening of hostilities. From the lofty eminence of Fort Lee the entire scene of battle was visible....Across on the heights on the opposite island (Manhattan) these watchers could now clearly see the beginning of the greatest battle ever fought upon Manhattan Island."

Here the reader is referred to the article on Fort Washington at the same river mileage. The decisive action at Fort Washington was on November 16. Again let us quote Mack:

"Upon the crest of the Palisades stood Washington and his officers gravely watching the tide of battle. As the attacking columns worked nearer and nearer to the defenders, a look of anguish overspread the Commander's strong face. Taking paper and pencil he hastily wrote a message to Magaw. Washington had already seen that the defense was hopeless, but he believed that the little army might still be rescued. He implored Magaw to hold on till night when a rescuing force from Fort Lee would attempt to bring his men across the river.

Captain Gooch, of Boston, took the message from the General's hand, and dashed down to the river bank with it. Here he leaped into a boat and rowed across to Jeffrey's Hook. He landed, leaped up the rocky bank, rushed into the fort and in person handed the message to Magaw. Then the messenger ran out from the fort, reached his boat and rowed across to the western shore, which he regained in safety.

Washington's urgent instructions reached Magaw too late. He had found his position untenable before they had reached his hands. He had fought a battle against odds of three to one, but he had a still more serious handicap, William Demont, one of his own adjutants, the first traitor in the American Army, having supplied the enemy with the complete plans of Fort Washington.

In despair the Commander-in-Chief watched the last act in the tragedy being enacted before his eyes. Finally the firing ceased, and he saw the white flag flutter from the flagpole of Fort Washington. He

dropped his field glass, and in the agony of his soul 'wept with the tenderness of a child.' But in this, the hour of grief and discouragement, Washington never lost sight of the immediate danger to the force about him. He saw that further holding of Fort Lee was hopeless, that at any hour the British might cross and capture it.

The British losses were 500, the American losses 150. The British captured 3,000 men, besides valuable stores."

The evacuation of Fort Lee, which now followed, was accomplished with desperate haste. Greene took flight, leaving blankets and baggage except what his few wagons could bear away, more than three month's provisions for 3,000 men, camp kettles on the fires, above 400 tents standing and all his cannon except two twelve-pounders.

On the evening of November 19, Lord Cornwallis crossed the Hudson from the east bank with a force of 6,000 men, including the first and second battalions of light infantry, two companies of chasseurs, two battalions of guards, and the 33rd and 42nd regiments of the line. This formidable army was landed at the present Huyler's Landing. By the following morning the army had gained the crest of the Palisades, and after a two hours' march reached Fort Lee. However, the position did not prove so valuable from a strategic point of view as both sides had supposed. Meanwhile Washington's army had retreated to Hackensack via New Bridge and ultimately across New Jersey to Pennsylvania.

The fortifications on the bluff have been reconstructed, and there is a visitors center, museum, and scenic overlooks. Fort Lee Historic Park has its entrance on Hudson Terrace and is open daily 9:30 till 5:00 (201-461-3956).

7.30 George Washington Bridge. This bridge was built and is operated by the Port Authority of New York and New Jersey. It was designed by Othmar H. Ammann. Ground was broken in October 1927. It was opened for traffic on October 25, 1931. An additional two lanes were added to the upper deck in 1946. Construction of the six-lane lower level started in September 1958. The steelwork for the lower level was completed at 10:45 A.M. on June 16, 1960 when the seventy-sixth and final section, weighing 62 tons and measuring 108 feet wide and 60 feet long, was raised from a barge below the center of the bridge and fitted into the gap between the previously erected sections. The writer, quite unexpectedly, personally witnessed this final operation from the deck of the sidewheel steamer *Alexander*

GEORGE WASHINGTON BRIDGE. View from Ross Dock looking south. Photo: Courtesy Port Authority of New York & New Jersey.

GEORGE WASHINGTON BRIDGE TOWERS. Photo: Courtesy Port Authority of New York & New Jersey.

Hamilton. No doubt the construction crews purposely awaited the passing of the daily "up boat" to complete this historic operation. No previous public notice had been given. The lower deck was opened to traffic in 1962.

The George Washington Bridge spans the Hudson River between West 178th Street Manhattan and Fort Lee, passing directly over Jeffery's Hook and lighthouse. It forms part of Interstate Highway I-95. Upon its completion, it became the world's only fourteen-lane suspension bridge. Total bridge investment by 1975 came to $215,800,000.

Bridge Statistics:

Cost of bridge—$59 million
Length of river span—3,500 ft.
Length of main span between
    anchorages—4,760 ft.
Width of bridge—119 ft.
Width of roadway—90 ft.
Height of towers above water—604 ft.
Channel clearance of bridge at midspan
    under lower level—212 ft.
Bridge is supported by four main cables—
    two on each side.
There are sidewalks on either side of the
    upper level.

Provision was made in the tops of the towers for restaurants and observation platforms to be reached by elevators from the sidewalks, but these were never completed. The American Society of Civil Engineers has designated the bridge a National Historic Civil Engineering Landmark.

7.30 George Washington Bridge Bus Station to east. Operated by the Port Authority, it replaces various former bus sidewalk loading areas. It was designed by Dr. Pier Luigi Nervi and was opened on January 17, 1963. It can accommodate 200 buses and 10,000 passengers in a peak hour and has direct passageways to the IND subway station. The terminal measures 400 feet by 185 feet on three levels and cost $15,400,000. On a typical weekday, it handles 28,000 passengers on 1,200 buses. In 1975 it handled ten million passengers on 440,000 bus movements.

7.40 Taylorville section of Fort Lee to west atop Palisades.

7.50 Coytesville section of Fort Lee to west atop Palisades.

7.50 Carpenter's Beach to west.

7.60 Ross Dock to west. Has parking facilities and recreation fields.

7.60 Floraville to west. On western slope of Palisades.

8.00 The Miraculous Glen to west.

8.00 Linwood section of Fort Lee to west atop Palisades.

8.00 St. Michael's Villa and St. Peter's College atop Palisades to west.

8.05 Site of Palisades Mountain House (elevation 375 ft.). This was a large brick-and-stone, four-story hotel built atop the Palisades. It had porticos on three sides and towers and a mansard roof in the best Victorian style, and commanded a fine view up and down the river. It was located south of Palisades Avenue, on the edge of the cliffs. It was built by a syndicate headed by Andrew D. Bogert, and also including William B. Dana, William Walter Phelps, George S. Coe, Garret A. Lydecker, Jacob S. Wetmore, and Sen. Cornelius Lydecker. The hotel opened on June 7, 1860. The operating lessee was Dave Hammond, who also managed the stylish Murray Hill and Plaza Hotels in Manhattan. He installed William Perry as acting manager at the Mountain House. The hotel attracted a high-class clientele, and to make access easier, the hotel, through a subsidiary company, built a road down the cliff (the present Palisades Avenue, then called Palisades Turnpike) and a steamboat dock. It also built a well-

PALISADES MOUNTAIN HOUSE (1860–1884), 375 ft above the Hudson at Englewood Cliffs. Photo: Author's collection.

THE PALISADES. This view shows typical detail of columnar basalt scarp and talus consisting of fallen broken rock. Photo: Alfred V. S. Olcott, Jr.

constructed footpath down the cliffs. The hotel burned down in 1884 and was not rebuilt. The property was sold to William Outis Allison, who built a mansion on the site which stood until 1903. The location was known as Allison Point. St. Joseph's Orphanage acquired the property in 1907, and it now belongs to St. Peter's College.

8.10 Allison Point to west.

8.20 Fort Tryon to east. Located atop ridge in Fort Tryon Park north of intersection of Fort Washington Avenue and West 193rd Street. This Revolutionary War redoubt mounted two guns. Commanded by Colonel Rawlings, a small American force yielded to greatly superior Hessian forces under Baron Knyphausen on the morning of November 16, 1776. It was subsequently occupied by the British until the end of the war and was greatly strengthened by them.

8.30 The Cloisters to east. Atop ridge in Fort Tryon Park, the site was formerly occupied by a small castle built by A. C. Richards in 1864 and known as Wood Cliff. The property belonged to C. K. G. Bill-

ings until 1926. The Cloisters, which is now a branch of the Metropolitan Museum of Art, was presented to the city by John D. Rockefeller, Jr. It is a museum of medieval art incorporating whole sections of abandoned European monasteries, which have been brought here and reassembled.

8.70 Tubby Hook to east. Named for early ferryman

THE CLOISTERS. Photo: © Gretchen McHugh.

named Tiber. Site of former Dyckman Street Ferry to Englewood Cliffs.

8.75 Inwood Hill Park on east. Inwood Hill formerly called Cock Hill. A high wooded land incorporating a climax forest—on Manhattan Island! This is the site of a former Indian village called Shorakapkok, or "as far as the Sitting-Down Place."

9.70 Englewood at western foot of the Palisades. (1990 population 24,850) **and Englewood Cliffs atop Palisades** (1990 population 5,812) **to west.** Mainly a residential community with most of the homes located on the gentle western slopes of the Palisades, and in the Northern Valley. The business center is in the western part of town. There are numerous corporate headquarters office buildings along Route 9W atop the Palisades. Prior to the Revolution, Englewood was known as English Neighborhood, to distinguish it from the predominantly Dutch surrounding area. During the Revolution, a Liberty Pole was erected here, and for a while the town was called Liberty Pole. With the coming of the Northern Valley Railroad of New Jersey, the name Englewood was adopted. The southwestern part of town was called Nordhoff, and the northwestern part was called Highwood.

9.70 Devil's Elbow to west. A sharp hairpin turn in the old Englewood or Palisades Turnpike.

9.70 Englewood Creek to west. A small stream with waterfalls down the Palisades.

9.70 Englewood Yacht Club to west. Former landing of the Dyckman Street Ferry. Small excursion steamers used to land at the two-story pier here until the 1940s. The area is now surrounded by Palisades Interstate Park.

9.70 Site of Cock Hill Fort to east. On the northernmost tip of Manhattan Island, this was a small Revolutionary redoubt mounting two guns, captured by the Hessians under Baron Knyphausen on November 16, 1776.

9.70 Spuyten Duyvil Creek to east. Separates Manhattan Island from the mainland and connects the Hudson and Harlem Rivers (also called Harlem River Ship Canal). The name was also spelled Spitondivell, or "Spitting Devil," possibly from the strong currents. Another derivation is "in spite of the Devil," and derives from Washington Irving's story about Peter Stuyvesant's trumpeter, Anthony Corlear, as told in his *Knickerbocker History of New York:*

It was a dark and stormy night when the good Anthony arrived at the famous creek (sagely denominated Haerlem river) which separates the island of Manna-hata from the main land. The wind was high,

SPUYTEN DUYVIL CREEK c1872. Railroad bridge to Berrian's Neck and Palisades in the distance. View looking westward. From *Picturesque America 1872.* Author's collection.

the elements were in an uproar, and no Charon could be found to ferry the adventurous sounder of brass across the water. For a short time he vapoured like an impatient ghost upon the brink, and then, bethinking himself of the urgency of his errend, took a hearty embrace of his stone bottle, swore most valorously that he would swim across, "en spijt den Duyvel" (in spite of the devil!) and daringly plunged into the stream.—Luckless Antony! Scarce had he buffetted half way over, when he was observed to struggle most violently as if battling with the spirit of the waters—instinctively he put his trumpet to his mouth and giving a vehement blast—sunk forever to the bottom!

The potent clangour of his trumpet, like the ivory horn of the renowned Paladin Orlando, when expiring in the glorious field of Roncesvalles, rung far and wide through the country, alarming the neighbors round, who hurried in amazement to the spot. Here an old Dutch burgher, famed for his veracity, and who had been a witness of the fact, related to them the melancholy affair; with the fearful addition (to which I am slow of giving belief) that he saw the duyvel, in the shape of a huge Mossbonker with an invisible fiery tail, and vomiting boiling water seize the sturdy Antony by the leg, and drag him beneath the waves. Certain it is, the place, with the adjoining promontory, which projects into the Hudson, has been called Spijt den duyvel, or Spiking devil, ever since.

> (Washington Irving, *Knickerbocker History of New York*, New York: G. P Putnam's Sons, 1880, pp. 497–498.)

On June 12, 1693, William and Mary granted to Frederick Philipse authority to build a bridge at "a certain neck or island of land called Papparinnomo and to collect tolls." This was the origin of the present Kingsbridge. This place was also called "The Wading Place." It was the southern end of the East Side Kings Highway, which ran from King's Bridge to the ferry at Crawlier, over against Albany.

During the French and Indian Wars, Lord Loudon had broadened an old Indian trail. Under later Royal authority, it was widened to "The Queens Road, to be forever the Highway, of the breadth of four rods, English measurement, at the least." In 1703 the New York Provincial Assembly authorized improvements of the Kings Highway from Kings Bridge to Albany. The road was much used by cattle drovers in early days. This crossing was at the junction of Spuyten Duyvil Creek and the Harlem River.

9.70 Baker Field. The football stadium of Columbia University is visible to the east at the far tip of Manhattan Island.

KING'S BRIDGE c 1820. This bridge connected Manhattan Island and the mainland. Strong current at junction of the Harlem River and Spuyten Duyvil Creek is apparent. The course of the waterway has since been diverted by the New York Ship Canal. Picture attributed to William Bartlett. Author's collection.

MOUTH OF SPUYTEN DUYVIL CREEK and Henry Hudson Bridge c1950. Note railroad bridge and Berrian's Neck. Photo: Courtesy Triborough Bridge & Tunnel Authority.

9.70 Railroad Bridge to east. An opening swing bridge of the Hudson River Railroad (Conrail and Amtrak) across the mouth of Spuyten Duyvil Creek. It is used by Amtrak passenger trains operating to and from Penn Station. This line runs down along the west side of Manhattan. Passenger trains, bound for Grand Central Terminal, swing east here and follow the north bank of Spuyten Duyvil Creek, as do most freight trains. The original bridge on this site was built in 1848, and the present one erected in 1900. It was designed by Robert Giles, Staff Engineer of the New York Central RR. It consists of three fixed spans of truss construction (one on the Bronx side and two on the Manhattan side) with a central horizontal swing section, with 100 ft. wide channel clearance on each side of the central pivot support. The bridge allows 5 ft. clearance above high water—inadequate for commercial navigation. The turntable was originally steam-powered, but was electrified in 1963. It was withdrawn from train service in 1969, and after being hit by a boat in 1983, it was then left in the open position.

In 1988 the West Side rail line was finally linked with Penn Station for the first time and was acquired by Amtrak to operate their long distance trains into Penn Station to consolidate their services in Manhattan, facilitate transfer of through passengers and cars, and centralize maintenance. Local trains will continue to operate to Grand Central. This plan necessitated rehabilitation of the Spuyten Duyvil Bridge. Upon beginning work, it was found that the metal was so corroded that very extensive sandblasting and replacement of many plates would be required. The entire metalwork was removed, leaving only the masonry foundations. After repairs it was replaced and returned to operation in 1991.

9.70 Henry Hudson Bridge to east (across Spuyten Duyvil Creek). Operated by the Triborough Bridge and Tunnel Authority, this is a fixed arch bridge designed by Robinson and Steinman and Madigan-Hyland. Chief Construction Engineer was Emil Praeger. Construction started June 1935. Opened to traffic December 12, 1936. Length of arch span 800 feet. Length each side span 300 feet. Total length of structure, including approaches, 2,000 feet. There are three traffic lanes on the upper level and four on the lower. Clearance above the mean high water at midspan 142.5 feet. Total cost was $4,949,000. It carries the Henry Hudson Parkway. Its total traffic in 1972 was 15,480,762 vehicles.

9.75 Bloomer's Dock to west.

9.80 High Tom Rock to west (elevation 360 feet).

9.85 Berrian's Neck to east. At junction of Spuyten Duyvil Creek and Hudson River, near the present Spuyten Duyvil railroad station. This was the site of a small Revolutionary War fortification.

9.85 The Bronx to east. This is both a borough of New York City and a county of New York State. It stretches along the Hudson from here to River Mile 12.30, and embraces the neighborhoods of Riverdale and Mount Saint Vincent along the riverfront with a population of 1,203,789 in 1990.

It is bounded on the north by Westchester County, on the east by Long Island Sound, and on the south by the East River and Bronx Kills. The western boundaries are the Harlem River, Spuyten Duyvil Creek, and the Hudson River. Three major watercourses run from north to south within the Bronx. Tippetts Brook or Creek rises east of Yonkers and flows into the Spuyten Duyvil Creek near its junction with the Harlem River. This was known to the Indians as Moshula, and its banks were favorite camping grounds of a warlike Mohegan tribe. The Bronx River flows south to the East River from Kensico Reservoir, north of White Plains. The Hutchinson River rises in the town of Eastchester and flows into the East River near its junction with Long Island Sound.

The first recorded settler was Jonas Bronck, a Dane, who received his grant from the Dutch West India Company in 1641. The name Bronx is a corruption of his name. This family also settled upriver near Coxsackie. The next major settlement was a patent given to Adriaen van der Donck in 1646. Donck's Colony sold 7,708 acres of this patent to Frederick Philipse and two associates in 1672. Frederick Philipse was the first lord of the neighboring manor of Philipsborough. In 1686, he bought out his two associates, and the Philipse Manor then extended from Manhattan to the Croton River and east to the Bronx River, which flows for approximately 20 miles. He established his manor

houses at Yonkers and on the Pocantico at North Tarrytown. His adopted daughter, Eva, and son-in-law, Jacobus Van Cortlandt, were the first Van Cortlandts to own property in the Bronx. The present manor house, located in Van Cortlandt Park, was erected in 1748 by their son Frederick Van Cortlandt. Other English manorial grants were: Fordham in 1671; Pelham in 1687; and Morrisania, granted in 1697 to Lewis Morris (1671–1746), first lord of the manor. These were all considerably east and south of the Hudson River.

Originally the Bronx was part of New York and Westchester Counties. Eventually, the entire area became part of New York County, which had been originally erected in 1683. The present Bronx County was taken from New York County in 1914. Principal elevated areas are Tetard's Hill, along the Hudson; University Heights, along the Harlem River; and Fordham Heights, between the Harlem and the Bronx Rivers.

The Bronx has three large parks: Van Cortlandt Park in the north, which embraces the Van Cortlandt manor and the cottage where Edgar Allan Poe lived from 1846 to 1849 and where he wrote his famous poem "The Raven"; Pelham Bay Park; and Bronx Park with its large and famous zoological and botanical gardens. Yankee Stadium is located along the Harlem River. Major educational establishments include Fordham University, New York University (with its Hall of Fame on University Heights), Lehman College of CUNY, Manhattan College, and the New York State Maritime College at Fort Schuyler. Railroad service is provided by the former Hudson River, Harlem and Putnam Divisions of the defunct New York Central, and the New York, New Haven & Hartford, now all part of Conrail. Passenger service is provided by Metro-North Commuter Railroad. It was also served by the abandoned New York, Westchester & Boston Electric Railroad which had its southern terminus here. This line never got out of Westchester County, much less to Boston. Numerous subway and elevated lines serve the borough.

The Bronx is mainly a residential community. Large tenement and apartment buildings are prevalent in the south and central sections and private homes in the east, northern, and western sections. There are many fine private mansions in Riverdale, and this section was the home of former mayor Fiorello LaGuardia and Arturo Toscanini, the conductor.

There are important produce and lumber markets here, and clothing, textiles, food products, chemicals, machinery, bank notes, and musical instruments are manufactured.

3

The Hudson Below the Highlands

9.90 Tetard's Hill to east. Here, in 1608, Henry Hudson skirmished with Indians.

9.90 Site of former Fort Independence on Tetard's Hill near present Henry Hudson Monument. A smaller Continental Army fortification abandoned on November 2, 1776, before the Battle of Fort Washington.

9.90 Henry Hudson Monument. Statue atop tall column to east.

9.90 University Heights in the Bronx can be seen by looking east up Spuyten Duyvil Creek.

10.30 Undercliff to west. This is the site of a former settlement of fishermen, and was simply called "under the mountain." The Van Wagoner family was the largest in the vicinity. When the Palisades Interstate Park was created, the village was gradually abandoned as the residents died. There is a cemetery here, but no live residents today. There is a picnic area on the old village site, which used to be popular with artists because of the picturesque nature of the old waterfront houses, drying fishing nets, and beached boats usually encountered.

10.75 Powder Dock to west.

10.75 Clinton Point atop Palisades to west.

WAVE HILL MANSION in the Bronx. Photo: © Gretchen McHugh.

11.00 Riverdale to east. Wealthy residential section of the Bronx. Area called Nipnichsen by Indians and Constable's Point by Dutch.

11.50 Wave Hill to east. Wave Hill is a public garden on 28 acres overlooking the Hudson River. Set with more than 350 varieties of trees and shrubs, a number of formal gardens, two greenhouses, and two manor houses, it is a unique setting for art exhibitions, concerts, American landscape history programs, and nature studies.

Wave Hill House was built in 1843 by jurist William Lewis Morris. Publisher William Henry Appleton purchased the property as a summer home in 1866. Between 1893 and 1911, financier George W. Perkins assembled several separate properties into Wave Hill, an eighty-acre estate. Wave Hill's quiet beauty has nurtured a number of distinguished temporary residents including Theodore Roosevelt, Samuel Clemens, Arturo Toscanini, and Bashford Dean. Dean, the first Curator of Armor at the Metropolitan Museum of Art, built The Armor Hall at the north end of Wave Hill House in 1928. In 1960, the Perkins-Freeman family gave 28 acres of the original estate to New York City for use as a horticultural garden and cultural and educational institution. Visitors now enjoy planted exhibitions, weekly garden and forest walks, an acclaimed outdoor sculpture show, indoor exhibitions, and indoor and outdoor concerts—all set off by the backdrop of the Hudson River and Palisades.

Wave Hill's grounds include an English-style wild garden, a shaded garden, an herb garden, an old-fashioned flower garden, and an aquatic garden. The greenhouses contain widely representative collections of tropical, temperate and succulent plants. The T. H. Everett Greenhouse is a new solar-heated greenhouse which contains a collection of alpine plants. Exhibits at Wave Hill have ranged from photography and painting to sculpture and the artistic aspects of the environment. Nature and gardens are predominant themes.

The Education Department at Wave Hill offers programs ranging from weekend events for adults and families to natural history field explorations, workshops, and training for New York City school and day care teachers.

12.20 Mount Saint Vincent College to east. This interesting location is well described by Benson Lossing in his *The Hudson* of 1866:

A mile and a half below Yonkers, on the bank of the Hudson, is Font Hill, built in 1848, formerly the residence of Edwin Forrest (1806–1872), the eminent

MOUNT ST. VINCENT COLLEGE with Font Hill Castle in foreground. Photo: Courtesy of College of Mount St. Vincent.

American tragedian. The mansion is built of blue granite, in the English castellated form, a style not wholly in keeping with the scenery around it. It would have been peculiarly appropriate and imposing among the rugged hills of the Highlands thirty or forty miles above. The building has six towers, from which very extensive views of the Hudson and the surrounding country may be obtained. The flag, or stair tower, is seventy-one feet in height.

To this delightful residence Mr. Forrest brought his bride, Miss Catherine Sinclair, daughter of the celebrated Scotch vocalist, in 1838, and for six years they enjoyed domestic and professional life in an eminent degree. Unfortunately for his future peace, Mr. Forrest was induced to visit England in 1844. He was accompanied by his wife. There he soon became involved in a bitter dispute with the dramatic critic of the London Examiner, *and Macready the actor. This quarrel led to the most serious results. Out of it were developed the mob and the bloodshed of what is known, in the social history of the City of New York, as the "Astor Place Riot," (1849) and with it commenced Mr. Forrest's domestic troubles, which ended, as all the world knows, in the permanent separation of himself and wife. [Ed. note: She brought a divorce suit against him in England in 1852.] Font Hill, where he had enjoyed so much happiness, lost its charms, and he sold it to the Roman Catholic Sisters of Charity, of the Convent and Academy of Mount St. Vincent. This institution was founded in 1847, and the academy was in 105th Street, between the Fifth and Sixth Avenues, New York. It is devoted to the instruction of young ladies. The community, numbering about two hundred Sisters at the time of my visit (1865), was scattered. Some were at Font Hill, and others were at different places in the city and neighborhood. The whole* were under the general direction of Mother Superior Mary Angela Hughes. At Font Hill they erected an extensive and elegant pile of buildings in 1857, of which they took possession, and wherein they opened a school, on the 1st of September 1859. It was much enlarged in 1865. They had, in 1860, about one hundred and fifty pupils, all boarders, to whom was offered the opportunity of acquiring a thorough education. The chaplain of the institution occupies the "castle."

Today Mount St. Vincent is a full-fledged coed Catholic college. There is a local railroad station here.

12.20 Near this point the steamer *Henry Clay* burned and ran aground with great loss of life on Wednesday, July 28, 1852. The story is shortly told by John H. Morrison in his *History of American Steam Navigation*. The *Henry Clay* had left Albany that morning and was racing the *Armenia* downstream:

When a short distance below Yonkers, caught fire and was burned to the water's edge. The vessel was run ashore about two miles below Yonkers dock, in the vicinity of Forrest's Castle, or Riverdale. It was one of those accidents on the water which seem to electrify the community and cause them to ask, if there is any safety from such appalling disasters.

Morrison describes the steamboat race with the *Armenia* and a slight collision between them near Rhinebeck. He continues:

The effect of the collision was to cause the Armenia to drop astern, and the Henry Clay then took and maintained the lead, increasing the distance between them up to the time of the breaking out of the fire at 3:15 P.M. It is supposed that just previous to the fire, the blower having been put in operation for increasing the draft of the furnaces, and that the furnace doors not being securely fastened, the strong blast from the blower had forced open the furnace doors and drove the flames from the furnace against the wood-work in the vicinity of the boiler, that was in the hold of the vessel, which took fire immediately and burned with alarming rapidity The vessel was run ashore head on, but the larger number of passengers being aft of the engine and boiler were obliged to take to the water, which was here very deep almost to the shore, though a number remained on board the vessel until actually forced by the fire to take to the water. It is believed that over one hundred lives were lost by this lamentable occurrence; should not be called an accident.

(John H. Morrison, *History of American Steam Navigation*. New York: W. F. Sametz, 1903, p. 108.)

This seems to be an unlucky place on the river. On Saturday, August 28, 1965 the writer was aboard the southbound paddle steamer *Alexander Hamilton*, Captain Edward Grady, when it hit some large debris which jammed the paddle wheels and broke the paddle shaft bearings. The *Hamilton* drifted onto the same place where the *Henry Clay* had burned. Fortunately no great damage was done and we were towed home eventually by the tug *Carol Moran*. The damage was repaired overnight and the *Hamilton* made its scheduled run the next day.

12.20 Lambier Dock to the west.

12.30 Tenafly to the west. This New Jersey residential community was first settled by the Dutch in 1640. It was incorporated in 1894. The construction of the Northern Valley Railroad provided the first real impetus to its residential growth, which continues today. Present population is 14,827. This is double what it was just after World War II. The village proper is at the west foot of the Palisades in the Northern Valley. The west slope of the Palisades was devoted to luxurious homes and estates at the lower levels and forest on the upper slopes and plateau on top. To this day, only Clinton Avenue connects the village in the valley with Route 9W near Clinton Point. Most recent growth has been development of the middle western slopes. The Highwood House Hotel was a famous resort in the nineteenth century, as was the estate of the Lyle Family. The architecturally notable Gothic Style railroad station was designed by Josiah Cleveland Cady.

12.30 Greenbrook Falls to west. Greenbrook arises

OLD TRADING POST AT LAMBIER DOCK, Tenafly. Photo: Courtesy of Claire Tholl.

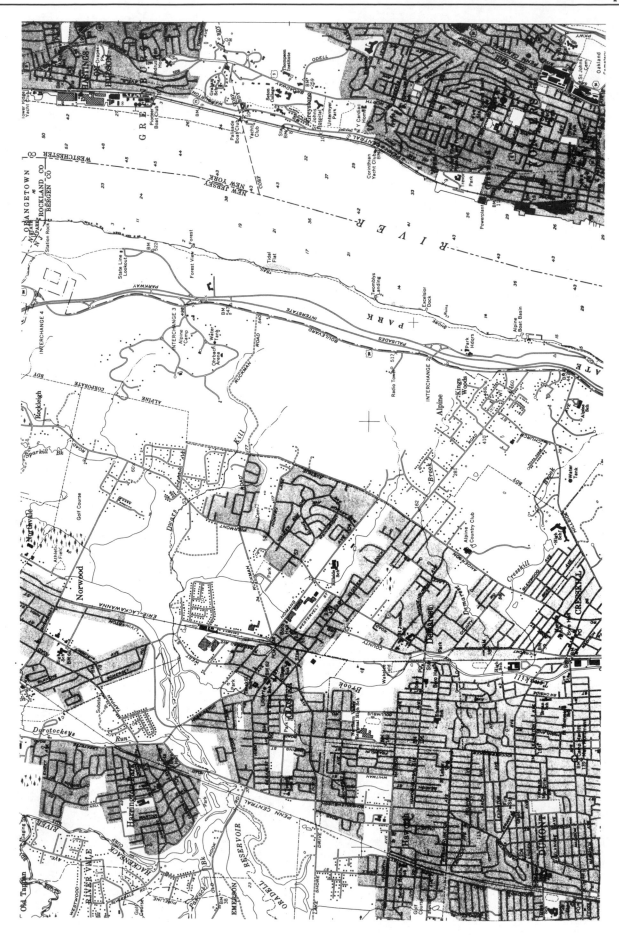

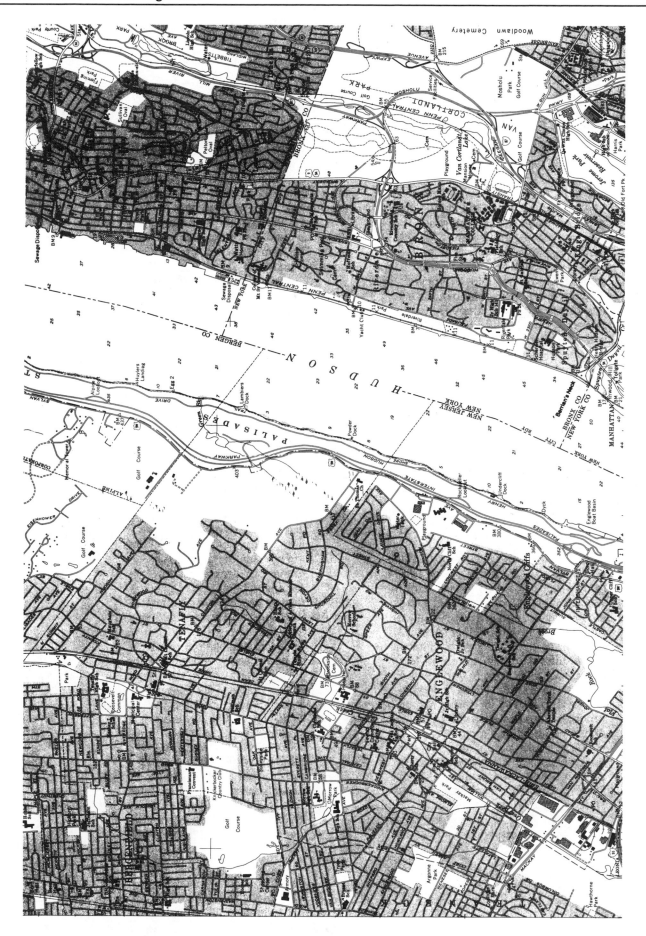

in the Kelder's Pond in Greenbrook Sanctuary atop the Palisades.

12.30 New York City/Westchester County line to east.

12.30 Westchester County (1990 population 874,866). From here to 42.60, the Putnam County line, Westchester County occupies the east shore of the river. Westchester County is bordered on the west by the Hudson River, on the north by Putnam County, on the east by Fairfield County, Connecticut, and on the south by Fairfield County, Connecticut, Long Island Sound, and the Bronx.

The county covers an area of 435 square miles. It is largely residential in character, but has several large cities in the southern part and is rural in the northern and eastern parts. It is home to many Manhattan commuters who travel the rail lines of the former New York Central Hudson and Harlem Divisions and the main line of the former New York, New Haven & Hartford, which runs along the Long Island Sound shoreline on its way to New Haven and Boston. The former New York & Putnam line of the New York Central formerly ran from the Bronx to Brewster, but has been abandoned north of Elmsford and handles only freight on the southern portion. All remaining lines are now part of the Conrail System.

The County of Westchester was established in 1683 and named for Chester in England. The present county seat is White Plains. Yonkers is the largest city.

The Indians called the tract stretching from Spuyten Duyvil Creek to Hastings-on-Hudson and between the Hudson and Bronx Rivers, Kekesick.

Early Dutch settlement was along the Hudson shoreline. New Englanders soon moved in along the eastern borders of the county, and French Huguenots settled around New Rochelle on Long Island Sound. Under the English several manor grants were established: 1693—Philipsburg; 1697—Van Cortlandt (stretching along the Hudson from Croton River to Anthony's Nose); 1701—Scarsdale, and the small Ryck's Patent enclave near Peekskill.

In his 1821 novel, *The Spy*, James Fenimore Cooper describes Westchester County in the following terms:

The country which lies between the waters of the Hudson and Long Island Sound, is, for the first forty miles from their Junction, a succession of hills and dales. The land bordering on the latter then becomes less abrupt, and gradually assumes a milder appearance, until it finally melts into the lovely plains and meadows of the Connecticut. But as you approach the Hudson the rugged aspect increases, until you at length meet with the formidable barrier of the Highlands. Here the neutral ground ceased....

The county of Westchester, after the British had obtained possession of the Island of New York, became common ground, in which both parties continued to act for the remainder of the war of the Revolution. A large proportion of its inhabitants, either restrained by their attachments, or influenced by their fears, affected a neutrality they did not feel. The lower towns were, of course, more particularly under the dominion of the crown, while the upper, finding a security from the vicinity of the continental troops, were bold in asserting their revolutionary opinions, and their right to govern themselves. Great numbers, however, wore masks, which even to this day have not been thrown aside; and many an individual has gone down to the tomb, stigmatized as a foe to the rights of his countrymen, while, in secret, he has been the useful agent of the leaders of the Revolution; and, on the other hand, could the hidden repositories of divers flaming patriots have been opened to the light of day, royal protections would have been discovered concealed under piles of British gold....

The royal army held the two points of land that commanded the Southern entrance of the river into the mountains [Stony Point and Verplanck's Point]; but all the remaining passes were guarded by the Americans.

We have already stated that the pickets of the continental army were sometimes pushed low into the country, and that the hamlet of the White Plains was occasionally maintained by parties of its troops. At other times, the advanced guards were withdrawn to the northern extremity of the county, and, as has been shown, the intermediate country was abandoned to the ravages of the miscreants who plundered between both armies, serving neither.... [These later were known as "Cowboys" and "Skinners."]

(James Fenimore Cooper, *The Spy*. New York: G. P. Putnam's Sons, undated, pages 2 and 306.)

12.50 Chimney Rock to west.

12.50 Hawthorne section of Yonkers to east. A residential area of private detached homes. Fay Park is in the vicinity.

13.00 Ludlow section of Yonkers to east. There is a local railroad station in this mixed residential and commercial neighborhood. It is named for a former large land owner, Thomas W. Ludlow.

13.00 Cresskill to west. This town, located in the

Northern Valley of Tenakill Brook to the west of the Palisades, was formerly called Schrallenburgh Station. It is a strictly residential bedroom community.

13.00 Huyler's Landing to west. Formerly called Lower Closter Landing. An old house built here in 1840 was an important transfer point. On the night of November 19, 1776, Lord Cornwallis landed here with 6,000 troops. He climbed the Palisades during the night and marched south to Fort Lee the following day.

13.50 Walker Hollow to west. A low point on the Palisades.

14.00 Yonkers (population 188,082). Residential and industrial city located at junction of Hudson River and the Saw Mill River (formerly known as Neperah or Neperhan River), whose water power gave impetus to industrial growth. Locust Hill and Rose Hill front along the Hudson and are backed by Nodine Hill and Valentine Hill, upon whose slopes a skirmish was fought after the Battle of White Plains.

An Indian village by the name of Nappeckamack was located here. West of the Saw Mill River is a large rock called Meech-keek-assin, or A-mac-ka-sin. The Indians paid reverence to this stone as an evidence of the permanency and immutability of their deity. The name Nappeckamack signified "the rapid water settlement," taken from the cascades of the Neperahan River.

In 1639 the Dutch West India Company purchased a tract of 24,000 acres hereabouts called the Kekeskick Tract from the Indians. In 1646 a patent was confirmed to Adriaen Cornelissen Van der Donck. He was a learned man, the first lawyer and historian in New Netherlands. He was given the nickname "jonker" or "yonkeer," meaning "the young lord," from which the present name of Yonkers is

PHILLIPSE MANOR HOUSE, YONKERS. Photo: © Gretchen McHugh.

derived. Van der Donck named his colony "Colen Donck," meaning "Donck's Colony." Van der Donck died in 1655 and Colen Donck was broken up after arrival of the British in 1664. Frederick Philipse and two associates purchased 7,708 acres, running along the Hudson from Spuyten Duyvil Creek to his other property near the Pocantico River at Castle Philipse. By 1686, he had bought out his two associates. On April 1, 1688, he purchased the Pocantico tract from the Indians, and by 1693, when he was created lord of the manor of Philipsburgh, his land extended from Spuyten Duyvil Creek to the Croton River and east to the Bronx River and covered 90,000 acres or about 200 square miles.

The history of this notable Hudson Valley family is worthy of note. Frederick Philipse I (1626–1702) was born and baptized in Bolswaert, Friesland, Netherlands, the son of a slater. He came to New Amsterdam with his family in 1647, and by 1653 was serving as carpenter and architect for Peter Stuyvesant. He commenced trading and purchasing land. In 1662 he married a rich widow, Margaret Hardenbroeck, relict of Peter Rudolphus de Vries. He then commenced trading on a worldwide scale in furs, whale oil, tobacco, sugar, cocoa, sassafras, logwood, grain, breadstuffs, animals, lumber, cloth, spices, ivory, slaves, wampum, rum, brandies, wine, tinware, molasses, flour, and manufactured goods. He established profitable mills upon his estates, and by 1674 he was the wealthiest man in New Amsterdam. He was named alderman by Governor Andros and also served as a member of the governor's council from 1675 to 1698.

On June 12, 1693 William and Mary granted him a royal charter for the erection of the manor of Philipsborough. In return for the status of lord of the manor, he owed the crown an annual fealty of fourteen pounds, twelve shillings. He held absolute title to the

OLD TRADING POST AT HUYLER'S LANDING, Alpine. Photo: Courtesy of Claire Tholl.

land except for any findings of gold or silver, which remained vested in the crown. He had the rights of Court Baron and Court Leet, having jurisdiction over all civil and criminal matters except treason.

By about 1680 he had three mills. The upper mill was on the Pocantico, the lower mill at Yonkers, and a third on the upper Nepperhan River. There were 40 families or about 200 individuals at the upper mill alone.

Frederick Philipse I had four children—Philip, Adolph, Annetje, and Rombout. In 1692, one year after the death of his first wife, he married Catharine Van Cortlandt Derval, daughter of Oloff Stevense Van Cortlandt. After his death in 1702, the upper mills were inherited by Adolph (1665–1750). He held the posts of member of the King's Council, judge of the Supreme Court, representative and speaker of the assembly and Westchester County Highway Commissioner. In 1720 he enlarged the upper manor. Among his occupations were the bolting of wheat and baking of ship biscuits. His tenants held only verbal leases.

Frederick Philipse II (1695–1751) inherited the lower mills at Yonkers upon his grandfather's death in 1702 and the balance of the family property upon Adolph's death in 1750. In that year he also acquired the so-called Highland Patent, incorporating most of present-day Putnam County. He married Joanna Brockholls, daughter of Lt. Gov. Anthony Brockholls. He served as Justice of the Supreme Court from 1731 to 1751. His elder daughter Susannah married Col. Beverly Robinson and lived on the Highland Patent. His younger daughter Mary was a great beauty, and it was rumored that George Washington considered proposing to her. She eventually married Roger Morris, one of Washington's associates on Braddock's staff. Frederick Philipse II greatly enlarged and beautified the original Manor House of 1681 at Yonkers. He added a stone section to the west and in 1745 built a brick north wing. These additions created a stately Georgian country seat. He planted boxwood hedges, flower gardens, trees, and ornamental shrubs and created a deer park. His establishment numbered thirty white and twenty black servants.

His son Frederick Philipse III, the last lord of the manor, also lived at Yonkers, leasing the upper mills to William Pugsley for £200 per year. He married Elizabeth Rutgers, a widow. Frederick III was a royalist and in 1776 was arrested and banished to Connecticut. He was attainted of treason in 1779 and his property confiscated and sold. In 1783 he sailed for England, where he died at Chester on April 30, 1785. That same year the Yonkers manor house, along

with 300 acres, was sold to Cornelius P. Low. In 1865 the manor belonged to W. W. Woodworth and in 1868 was acquired by the village of Yonkers to serve as village hall. In 1872 major interior changes were made to create a large Gothic council chamber. Recently it has been acquired and restored by the New York State Division for Historic Preservation, and it is now open as a museum.

The upper manor was purchased at auction by Gerard G. Beekman, Jr. in 1784. Upon the death of his widow in 1822, the upper manor was broken up. The manor house and the immediately adjacent property passed through the hands of many owners until 1937. At that time, the property was being foreclosed by a bank and in danger of being sold to developers. John D. Rockefeller Jr. intervened to save the historic site and established the Sleepy Hollow Restorations, which has now returned the manor mill to its earliest condition and operates it as a museum. The rest of the estate was sold in odd parcels to 287 different individuals in 1784.

Returning to the history of Yonkers proper, we note that 16,000 British troops camped here in 1780. By 1781 American soldiers were encamped on Locust Hill. A battle took place just off Yonkers between American gunboats and the British frigates *Rose* and *Phoenix*. The Hudson River Railroad reached Yonkers in 1849 and the town grew rapidly as a suburb popular with wealthy New York City merchants. Business also came, and in 1854 Elisha G. Otis established his elevator works as a principal Yonkers industry. In 1857 David Saunders opened a large machine shop, and in 1865 Alexander Smith and Halcyon Skinner revolutionized carpet manufacturing with introduction of the first Axminster power loom. The carpet mills grew to enormous size along the Neperhan River. Today they are no longer used for carpet manufacturing, but are rented out as loft space. Other manufactured products include clothing, books, patent medicines, refined syrups and sugars, and insulated wire and cable produced by the Habirshaw Cable & Wire Division of the Phelps Dodge Corporation.

Yonkers was incorporated as a village in 1855 and chartered as a city in 1872. The first American golf game was played here on the St. Andrew's golf course on November 1, 1888. As recently as 1940, Yonkers was served by fourteen passenger railroad stations. Today service is provided only on the former Hudson River Railroad line of Conrail, by the Metropolitan Transportation Authority, and Amtrak. Once an important river port, the municipal pier is undergoing restoration. The former ferry to Alpine has been discontinued.

14.10 Demarest to west. Located in the Northern Valley on Tenakill Brook and the Northern Railroad line on the western slopes of the Palisades. It is a strictly residential community. There is a Gothic Revival railroad station by Josiah Cleveland Cady, similar to that in Tenafly, but smaller. The top of the Palisades and shoreline belong to the Borough of Alpine. Near the Demarest station is an attractive artificial lake. In the nineteenth and early twentieth century the Murray Hill Home, resort hotel, with eight acres of lawn terraces, drew a considerable patronage.

14.10 Yonkers Municipal Pier on east.

14.20 Outlet of Nepperhan, or Saw Mill River, to east. Now covered over as a storm sewer. A mill was built here in 1646.

14.30 Former Alpine Ferry terminal on east.

14.30 Philipse Manor on east.

14.40 Otis Elevator Company plant on east.

14.40 Alpine, New Jersey, on west. Rural residential town atop Palisades. Former ferry to Yonkers.

14.40 Alpine Grove to west. Also formerly known as Occidental Grove or Riverview Landing (at base of Palisades); a former popular destination for excursion boats.

14.40 Closter to west. Closter is also in the Northern Valley of the Tenakill near its junction with the Dwars Kill, which flows west off the back of the Palisades, and on the line of the Northern Railroad of New Jersey. It is a mixed residential and commercial town, and like Cresskill and Demarest is bordered by Alpine atop the Palisades and along the waterfront. Closter is named for the former Patroon Frederick

OLD TAVERN AT ALPINE LANDING. Long incorrectly called General Cornwallis's Headquarters. Photo: Alfred H. Marks.

Closter. An important road, called Old Hook Road, ran from the Pascack Valley to the present Alpine Landing and was the main route to Manhattan via sloop and steamboat from the Pascack and upper Hackensack Valleys in New Jersey.

14.45 Alpine boat basin to west.

14.45 Alpine Landing to west. There is an old colonial tavern at the foot of the Palisades and the road up the cliffs through Alpine Gorge that was used in Revolutionary days. It is supposed that the British spent a night here preparatory to scaling the cliffs to take Fort Lee. Here Lord Earl Grey disembarked in October 1778, and crossed to the Hackensack Valley, surprising and massacring Colonel Baylor's patriots, despite their surrender and calls for mercy. Major General "No Flint" Grey killed thirty continental soldiers under Col. George Baylor at River Vale, New Jersey, after they had surrendered. This location was known as Closter Dock, taking its name from the early Closter Patent and the village of that name at the west foot of the Palisades. Patroon Frederick Closter had a sloop ferry. Today there is a boat basin and picnic facilities. This was the former western terminal of the Yonkers-Alpine Ferry, operational between 1876 and 1956.

14.50 Glenwood section of Yonkers on east.

14.50 Former New York Central Railroad electric power plant on east.

14.50 Cape Fly-Away on west. High crag of the Palisades.

14.60 Trevor Park and Hudson River Museum and Planetarium to east. In old Trevor Mansion.

MUNICIPAL PIER AT YONKERS. Photo © Gretchen McHugh, 1988.

14.60 Boar's Hill to east.

14.70 Armstrong FM radio tower to west. (See west side road 15.50.)

14.70 Excelsior dock on west. Site of Excelsior Grove, another former popular steamboat excursion park.

15.00 Grey Crag to west. Largest separated section of cliff on Palisades. Measures about 300 feet long by ten to twenty feet wide. Reached by a footbridge from top of Palisades. In winter and spring, 300-feet-high ice columns appear where the water plunges over the cliffs.

15.50 Twombly Landing to west. Named for a former owner who gave property to Palisades Interstate Park. Because of layers of oyster shells found here, this is believed to have been the site of Indian camps.

15.80 Bombay Hook to west (elevation 500 feet). Also called Boompes Hook, a corruption of the Dutch "Boomje" meaning "little tree," the highest, most isolated and conspicuous pillar of rock in the Palisades, literally curving 70 feet high between two large slides. Also formerly called Point Comfort. A face of a "man in the rock" can allegedly be seen near the base of the north face.

16.00 Untermyer Park to east. Named for Samuel Untermyer (1899–1940) who developed gardens and landscaped grounds around his former home. The site of former home of New York governor and United States presidential candidate Samuel J. Tilden, it was originally built for hat manufacturer John Waring. The house is now razed, its grounds being maintained by the city of Yonkers.

16.10 Greystone section of Yonkers to east. Seton Academy and Thompson Institute are located here. The remains of the Old Croton Aqueduct may be seen.

16.40 Ruckman Point to west (elevation 520 feet).

17.00 Forest Dock to west.

17.00 Yonkers/Greenburgh town line to east.

17.75 Villard Hill to east.

17.75 Hastings-on-Hudson to east. This residential community, with a 1990 population of 8,000, is named for the English birthplace of William Saunders, a local manufacturer. It was incorporated in 1879 and was the home of Dr. John W. Draper (1811–1882), President of New York University Medical School. In 1841 he took the first outdoor photograph of the human face in direct sunlight, on the

RUCKMAN POINT, "THE MINARETS," AND FOREST DOCK, Alpine, c1905. Photo: Courtesy of Claire Tholl.

roof of the University in New York. He and his family made significant contributions to the fields of astronomy and photography at Hastings. Chemicals, copper, and paving blocks were once manufactured here. The large riverfront plant of Anaconda Wire & Copper Company (formerly National Conduit & Cable) was closed in 1975 and the site is undergoing redevelopment. The famous Mount Hope Cemetery is located east of town in the unincorporated Town of Greenburgh. St. Matthew's R. C. Church is prominent from the water.

During the Revolution a party of 23 Hessian mercenaries was surprised and cut to pieces by dragoons under the command of Major Henry Lee, in what is known as the Battle of Edgar's Lane. On November 19, 1776 General Cornwallis and 6,000 British troops crossed to Huyler's Landing on their way to capture Fort Lee.

17.75 Indian Head to the west. Highest point on Palisades (elevation 522 feet.).

17.90 Giant's Stairway to west. Natural stone stairway up cliffs, used as a hiking route. The borough of Rockleigh, New Jersey lies on the west slope Palisades.

17.90 Point Lookout to west.

18.00 Station Rock to west. New Jersey/New York state line. Here, atop the cliffs, is a 6 foot memorial shaft erected in 1882.

18.25 High Gutter Point to west.

18.30 Skunk Hollow to west. This clove in the Palisades was the site of a free black community settled by Jack Earnest in 1806 and active until 1886.

18.35 Former Estate of C. F. Park to west. Located above Skunk Hollow.

18.65 Lamont Geological Observatory of Columbia University to west. Located atop the Palisades, the Lamont-Doherty Geological Observatory is an institute of Columbia University dedicated to research in earth sciences. The estate on which it is located has an interesting history. More than a hundred years ago, John Torrey, a famous botanist, discovered a wealth of plant life on top of a rocky cliff above Sneden's Landing. Torrey admired the beauty of the spot and splendid view of the Hudson and acquired a few acres upon which he built himself a summer home near the edge of the cliffs, and over the years he accumulated a herbarium of many thousands of botanical species which he presented to Columbia University in 1860. In 1928 Thomas W. Lamont, the financier, acquired Torrey Cliff and adjacent pieces of land and built up an estate of more than one hundred acres. In 1948, after his death, his widow gave the estate to Columbia. The University designated the use of the estate for research in earth sciences and Professor William Maurice Ewing founded the Lamont Geological Observatory in 1949. It has grown into one of the leading institutions of its kind in the world. In addition to seismology, marine geology, geophysics, and geochemistry, scholars at the Observatory are active in such diverse fields as atmospheric and space sciences, biological, physical, and chemical oceanography, paleoclimatology, polar studies, tectonophysics, geodesy, structural geology, and petrology.

18.70 Cliffside to west. Cliffside was the estate of Lydia G. Lawrence. It is located on a low plateau south of Sneden's Landing. It was best described by Arthur C. Mark in 1909:

"Of all the imposing homes of the Hudson Valley few command a grander view than this, overlooking the broad expanse of the Tappan Zee, and the lower river. A woodland path leads southward from the house to a pergola standing on the river's edge, modeled after a similar structure at Amalfi, Italy. Behind this pergola a cascade falls down the perpendicular side of the Palisades into a beautiful grotto with pools, fountains and statuary. The owner of "Cliffside" has recently given a large and valuable tract of her estate to the Palisades Interstate Park Commission."

18.90 Rockland County (1990 population 265,475). Running along the west bank of the Hudson for 24.6 miles, from ERM 18.00 to 42.60, from the New Jersey state line to Popolopen Creek, is Rockland County, embracing an area of 173 square miles, one-third of which is given over to park lands and wilderness areas. This was formerly a part of Orange County and was known as "Orange County under

the mountains." On February 23, 1798 it was separated from Orange and erected as The County of Rockland, well named after its topography. It had been difficult to administer the area from Goshen, the Orange County seat, and the economy of Rockland was more similar to that of adjacent Bergen County in New Jersey. The present New Jersey/New York boundary was determined in 1687.

The first recorded visitation of the area by a white man was that of Henry Hudson on September 15, 1609, when he dropped anchor off Tappan Slote (Piermont). This was the first time recorded that a white man set foot on New York soil, as his previous landings had been on present-day New Jersey territory.

An abortive settlement was made in April 1640 when David Pietersen De Vries attempted a colony again at Tappan Slote. He purchased land from the Lenni Lenape Indians and erected buildings and a trading post. He called his colony Vriesendael. In 1641 Myndert Myndersten Van Der Horst established another small settlement several miles west of Vriesendael. At first things went well with the friendly Indians, but when the Indian Wars began in 1643 the colonies were burned to the ground and De Vries returned to Holland.

In 1666, Balthazar De Harte purchased some land from the Indians in the vicinity of Haverstraw, and this was confirmed by a Patent on April 10, 1671.

The first recorded permanent settlements were in 1683 near Tappan. This land was purchased from the Indians in 1681 and 1682 and the Indian Deed was acknowledged by Governor Carteret of New Jersey on July 1, 1682. On March 24, 1686, Governor Dongon of New York granted a patent to sixteen Dutch farmers including Lambert Adriaense Smidt, Adriaen Lambertse Smidt, and Hendrick Gerritse Blauvelt, who owned the land in common until divisions were made in 1704 and 1721. This was known as the Tappan Patent. A Dutch Church was organized in 1694 and the first house of worship built in 1716. The Tappan Patent stretched from the Hudson to the Hackensack. Another tract near Snedens Landing was granted on February 20, 1685 to George Lockhart. This was again confirmed as a patent on June 27, 1687. Another major early grant was the Kakiat Patent, granted on June 25, 1696 to Daniel Honan and Michael Hawdon, speculators. This stretched west from the Hackensack to the vicinity of present-day Tallman, and north to the foot of the Ramapo Mountains. It was settled by people from Hempstead, Long Island, and they established their seat at New Hempstead—now New City, the present county seat. Other early settlements were at Jan Claus's land, near Greenbush, which is near present-day Blauvelt and Orangetown. The Tappan settlement included what is presently Old Tappan, New Jersey. Present-day Rockland County is abutted on the east by the Hudson River, on the southwest by Bergen and Passaic counties in New Jersey, and on the northwest by Orange county in New York. It is roughly an equilateral triangle. Principal watercourses are the Hackensack River and its tributaries, including Pascack Brook, Saddle River, Mahwah River, and Ramapo River, which all ultimately empty into Newark Bay. Minnisceongo Creek, Cedar Pond Brook, and Sparkill Creek empty into the Hudson River. Principal natural lakes are Rockland Lake and Swartwout and Congers Lakes, at the headwaters of the East Branch of the Hackensack River, and Hessian Lake near Bear Mountain. Most of the other large "lakes" are actually artificial reservoirs or recreational lakes of a manmade type. They include Lake De Forest and Lake Tappan on the Hackensack River (built by the Hackensack Water Company), and Owl Swamp, Lake Welch, Cranberry Lake, Pine Meadow Lake, and Lake Sebago in Harriman Interstate Park. There is an escarpment along the Hudson—a sort of northern continuation of the Palisades. The Ramapo Mountains cover the northwestern part of the county. The central portion is a high plateau and rolling hills drained by the Hackensack, Saddle, and Ramapo rivers. Principal parks are Tallman Mountain State Park, Blauvelt Interstate Park, Nyack Beach State Park, Rockland Lake State Park, Hook Mountain State Park, High Tor State Park, Bear Mountain State Park, and Harriman Interstate Park, all under the Palisades Interstate Park Commission. There are also the Kakiat and Pomona County Parks and Tackamack Town Park near Blauvelt and the Stony Point Battleground Reservation. Almost one-third of the county is devoted to parkland and reservations, thus preserving the original natural beauty of the area.

The County is divided into five townships: Haverstraw, Orangetown, Clarkstown, Stony Point, and Ramapo. Principal towns and villages are: Tappan, Nyack, Nanuet, Haverstraw, Pearl River, Spring Valley, New City, Sloatsburg, and Suffern. The county is largely residential, with some farming and small-scale industry. Principal rail lines are the West Shore line of Conrail (formerly New York Central), running north and south between Tappan and Bear Mountain through the Hackensack and Hudson valleys, the old Erie Mainline from Piermont to Suffern (now largely abandoned between Blauvelt and Nanuet), the Erie Mainline (former Erie–Lackawanna, now Conrail) along the Ramapo Valley between Suffern and Sloatsburg, the former New Jersey &

New York line from Pearl River to Nanuet (formerly with branches to New City and Thiells and West Haverstraw), now the Pascack Line of New Jersey Transit, and the former Northern Railroad of New Jersey from the New Jersey State Line to Nyack (now abandoned from Sparkill to Nyack), also part of the Conrail system. Passenger service is available only on the former Erie Mainline and the Pascack Line between Pearl River and Spring Valley. Principal highways are the New York Thruway from South Nyack to Sloatsburg, the Palisades Interstate Parkway from Palisades to Bear Mountain, Route 9W from Palisades to Bear Mountain along the Hudson River, and Route 17 from Suffern to Sloatsburg.

18.90 Sneden's Landing to west. This is located in the village of Palisades, New York and was formerly known as Dobb's Ferry, Paramus, and Rockland over the years, causing much confusion to historians. It was the western terminus of Dobb's Ferry, which operated from the present Dobbs Ferry on the eastern shore, and the name Dobb's Ferry was indiscriminately applied to both the actual boat operation and both eastern and western terminals.

On June 27, 1687 a patent of 3,410 acres was granted to George Lockhart. In 1698 William Merritt, who held the mortgage, assumed title and was known to be occupying the site in 1701. On May 14, 1705 it was sold to John Corbett, an English sea captain, who built a home here called "Cheer Hall." Corbett died in 1717 and left the property to his daughter, Mary Corbett Ludlow.

The present name of the community comes from the Sneden family, who descended from Jan Snedick who emigrated from Holland to New Amsterdam in 1657. The orthography of the family name has had many variants over the years, including: Sneeding, Sneydon, Sneyden, Snyden, Suyden, Sueden, and Snyding.

About 1740 Robert Sneden, Jr. settled here near the landing. He was a carpenter by trade and came from Eastchester, across the river. He was married to Mary, or "Molly" Dobbs, the daughter of John and Abigail Dobbs. John Dobbs had settled at Dobbs Ferry, across the river, in 1698, and started a ferry shortly thereafter. At this time his son William Dobbs, Mary's brother, was operating the ferry. In 1745 an improved road was built down the Palisades to the ferry landing and the ferry was prospering. In 1752 Robert Sneden purchased 120 acres and the ferry from his brother-in-law, William Dobbs. However, Robert died the next year, 1753, and his widow turned the ferry operation back to her brother,

William Dobbs, who operated it until 1759, when "Molly" herself took over.

Mary, or "Molly" Sneden was a famous personage in the area and lived from 1709 to 1810—101 years. Robert and Mary had five sons—John, Dennis, James, William, and Samuel. During the Revolution the entire family, with the exception of John, who was a strong patriot, were Tories. Therefore the Committee of Orange County prohibited them from operating this vital facility during the war, and operation was turned over to John, who was well trusted. During the Revolution Molly Sneden lived in a white frame house on the road by the river with her son Dennis, a bachelor. The story goes that a British soldier was pursued down the gully by some patriots; she hid him in her house in a large chest on which she set pans of cream to rise. When the patriots arrived she misinformed them. They were tired and asked for refreshment, and she offered them all the milk she had, but told them not to disturb the pans of cream which she had just set out. In the evening she is said to have ferried the soldier across the river. Some of her sons settled in Nova Scotia after the war, and, as loyalists, received grants of land there. After the war, John continued to operate the ferry. Later on Captain Lawrence J. Sneden (1800–1871), who was also a shipbuilder and assemblyman, operated the ferry. The steam ferryboat *Union* was built at the landing and put into operation on the line in 1832. With development of other more direct routes, the business languished for many years and was finally discontinued when the last boat was wrecked in the hurricane of September 14, 1944.

During the Revolution, in early December 1775, Martha Washington and her son John Parke Custis and his wife crossed on their way from Mt. Vernon to join General Washington in Cambridge, Massachusetts, travelling in the Washington family "Chariot" with postilion and footmen. Also, Aaron Burr, then in the Continental Army stationed at White Plains, frequently crossed the ferry when courting Mrs. Theodosia Prevost, widow of a British Army officer, living at the *Hermitage* in Hohokus. Both Sneden's Landing and Hohokus were known as Paramus at that time and were in disputed neutral ground. His nocturnal trips through this area, plagued with Skinners and Cowboys, and across the Hudson, patrolled by enemy warships, in a light skiff with his horse, must have been quite an adventure.

On November 8, 1776 General Nathaniel Greene and his troops retreated across the Hudson to here from Tarrytown.

David Cole, in his 1884 *History of Rockland County*, gives the following information:

To protect the landing place at Sneden's the Americans erected a work, which was visited by a British spy on June 27th, 1781, and thus described: "It is a redoubt about a mile and half from the landing, on a very rough rocky height, picketted in all around with tops of trees and branches; no way to get in without climbing over; about four rods within this circle is a round breastwork running quite round the height, eight feet high, with a gate to pass in on the west side. Within that circle, about three rods, is another breastwork running round the top of the height, about the same height as the other, on which is wooden embrasures built, in which they have one piece of cannon on a travelling carriage. On the south side of the inward work a gate opens into the first breastwork. The rise of the height is so much as to cause the top of the first breastwork to be no higher than the bottom of the second. At this time it was commanded by a Lieutenant, two Sergeants, two Captains, and twenty-five men in the works.

At one time during the war Garret O'Blenis and a half-dozen comrades were watching a British vessel, which had anchored off Sneden's Landing—now Palisades. At last their watch was rewarded by seeing a barge filled with men start for the shore. Concealing themselves behind the rocks, the Americans permitted the barge to approach within a few yards of the landing, and then fired into her. After the first surprise the enemy endeavored to force a landing, assisted by the guns of the ship. For a few moments the conflict was severe, but, unaware of the numerical strength of the shore party, the foe at length withdrew. The only man seriously wounded among the patriots was Garret O'Blenis, who had a ball pass through his right arm and completely through his body, smashing two ribs and perforating the right lung in its course. His wound was regarded as mortal, but, after several months' illness, he entirely recovered.

(David Cole, *History of Rockland County*, New York: J. B. Beers & Co., 1884.)

In the nineteenth century the landing was a busy place. There was a 300 ft. pier out to deep water and many sloops landed here to carry farmers' produce to market. With the development of steamboats, the ferry would take passengers from either shore out to mid-stream to board the big New York-to-Albany boats that would not deign to put in to such small landings. The same procedure was used at Nyack and Tarrytown.

There was a store at the landing and a quarry and shipyards near by. The shipyards were operated by "Boss" Sneden, J. Van Orden, and J. Waldron. Many large sailing ships were constructed here. The last vessel built in Sneden's Landing was the 150-ton schooner *Brave*, built in 1844.

Today the landing is a quiet backwater with numerous attractive older homes.

19.00 Dobbs Ferry to east (1990 population 9,940). Residential suburb in the Greenburgh Hills. The original Indian name was Weec-ques-guck, or Wecquaskeck, meaning "place of the bark kettle." It was originally part of the Phillipse Patent, but when the manor was confiscated and sold in 1785, the property here was acquired by Philip Livingston and two associates. By 1796 Livingston had sole possession.

One of the earliest settlers was an Englishman named John Dobbs, who, with his wife Abigail, settled near Willow Point in 1698 and established a ferry to Sneden's Landing, then called Paramus. (See previous article for history of the ferry.) His son William Dobbs later succeeded to the ferry, which operated until 1944.

In 1781 Washington established headquarters here and met with the Count de Rochambeau to plan the Yorktown campaign, which ended the Revolution. Also, in 1780, General Nathaniel Greene met the chief of three commissioners from General Henry Clinton in conference at Tappan concerning Major John Andre.

The British fleet lay in these waters and on May 7, 1783 Sir Guy Carlton entertained General Washington aboard *H.M.S. Perseverence* anchored offshore, and for the first time the British honored the new nation with a 17-gun naval salute. They had met the previous day at Tappan to discuss plans for British evacuation of New York and protection of American property (meaning slaves).

Interesting points in Dobbs Ferry include Zion Episcopal Church at Cedar and Main Streets, erected in 1834. Washington Irving was a vestryman here from 1837 to 1843. The church is built of stone. In 1854 the tower was heightened and mullions and buttresses added. *Estherwood*, now owned by the Masters School, is a large mansion. Built in 1895 by James Jennings McComb, a wealthy New York merchant, it is in the French Renaissance style, with turrets, carved balconies, and a glass conservatory. Buchman and Deisler were the architects. In the Victorian period there was a popular summer hotel called the *Glen Tower*. Mercy College was founded here in 1959.

19.25 Willow Point to east.

19.50 Wickers Creek to east. Name derived from Indian Wysquaqua.

19.50 Piermont Salt Marsh to west. A significant marine habitat administered by the Hudson River National Estuarine Research Reserve.

19.50 Crumkill Creek to west.

19.50 Tallman Mountain Interstate Park to west. A recreational park with picnic facilities and fine views of the river. Named for Hermanus Tallman (also spelled Taulman), an early settler. Elevation 160 ft.

20.10 Ardsley-on-Hudson on east. A residential area formerly called Abbotsford after Sir Walter Scott's ersatz castle, where the great poet and novelist attempted to live like a laird despite his bankruptcy, and to fulfill his dream of bourgeois romanticism. This image appealed to wealthy merchants of the late nineteenth century and many of them built imposing homes here in the baronial style. Among these imposing homes are Graytowers, or Belzover Castle, and Cottenet House. Cyrus West Field (1819–1892), who completed laying of the Atlantic cable after twelve years of effort, built a large mansion here in about 1860. This baronial approach is reflected in the Ardsley Club, built in monastic style, and the railroad station, which was built to harmonize with Stanford White's Casino, with its Tudor timbering. The casino was demolished in the 1930s to make way for an apartment complex. Nevis, the home of James Alexander Hamilton (1788–1878), third son of Alexander Hamilton, was named after his father's birthplace in the British West Indies. It was originally a simple Greek revival building with Doric columns, but was extensively remodeled by Stanford White in 1889. It has an Early Republican garden. Mrs. T. Coleman DuPont gave the estate to Columbia University in 1934 for establishment of a horticultural and landscape architecture center. There are over 2,640 trees of 56 varieties and 1,928 ornamental shrubs on the property, making it one of the largest arboretums in the United States. It now houses the Columbia University Nevis Laboratories for Physics Research.

20.80 Sparkill Creek on west. The name is a redundancy, as "kill" means "creek." It was formerly called Tappan Slote, as was the village at its mouth. It rises in Sparkill Brook in Rockleigh and Cooper Pond in Northvale, both in New Jersey. Thence it flows northeast into the Hudson through a gap between Tallman and Nebo Mountains. This is the only sea-level gap in the Palisades range between Bayonne and Bear Mountain. Some geologists believe that Sparkill Creek and the Hackensack River once formed a secondary channel of the Hudson, flowing west of the Palisades. As the general level of the land rose, the waters of the Hudson receded, leaving only the present small creek, with no connection with the Hackensack. In 1841 the Erie Railroad took advantage of this natural gap to gain the Hudson without tunneling or going over the mountain. Ice was once cut from the creek just west of the Route 9W viaduct, where remains of dams and forms can still be seen.

On November 8, 1776 troops landed here on retreat from Croton Point. On May 6, 1783 General Washington met Sir Guy Carleton here prior to conducting negotiations with him concerning the evacuation of New York City by the British. The negotiations were held at Tappan.

20.80 Barney Brook to east.

20.80 Irvington-on-Hudson on east (population 6,348). Area about 2,000 acres. This land was originally part of the Philips manor. In later years it belonged to Justus Dearman and was called Dearman's Station. In 1850, streets were laid out and parcels sold at auction, and, in 1854, the name Irvington was adopted in honor of its most famous resident, Washington Irving. Ironically, Irving's home, Sunnyside, was pulled into the incorporation of adjacent Tarrytown in 1870, prior to the incorporation of the village of Irvington in 1872. In the mid-nineteenth century the entire Irvington-Ardsley area was known as Abbotsford.

Early settlers included Wolfert Ecker (sometimes spelled Acker), Barent Dutcher, Captain John Buckout (who lived to the age of 103), and Captain Jan Harmse. The Harmse-Conklin-Odell Tavern on Broadway was built in 1690. During the Revolution this was neutral ground. British troops under Gen. Sir John Vaughan (famous for burning Kingston) camped near the Odell Tavern in 1776. The British burned the Wolfert Ecker home, which then belonged to Jacob Van Tassel. It was a favorite hangout of the patriots and a real thorn in the side of the British. This house was later made famous by Washington Irving under the name Wolfert's Roost. He later purchased the house in 1835 and rebuilt it into the famous Sunnyside. This house is now within the Tarrytown corporate limits.

The Abbotsford area attracted wealthy and romantic people who proceeded to act out their architectural dreams. François Cottenet built a two and one-half story French Victorian chateau named Nuits in 1892. It was built with stone from a quarry at

Nuits on the Côte d'Or in France. Strawberry Hill, a stone mansion in Norman Victorian Gothic style on North Broadway, was built in 1849. This was named after the home of English novelist Horace Walpole. Another extravaganza was the Octagon House built in 1860 on West Clinton Avenue by wealthy meat packer Philip Armour. This was built according to the ideas of Orson Fowler who, around 1849, wrote articles extolling this type of design. In more recent years it belonged to the well-known Hudson River historian Carl Carmer. He believed the house was haunted. It features a great octagonal dome and cupola. Louis Comfort Tiffany lived in Irvington and, about 1870, built some cottages for his employees that are still standing. They are two-story stone with mansard roofs. He also designed the stained-glass windows in the Presbyterian Church on Broadway.

The various developments were all called parks. They included Spiro Park, Ardsley Park, Joffrey Park, Matthiessen Park, and Barney Park. Very exclusive cooperative apartments, known as the Half-Moon Apartments, were built in Ardsley in the 1930s. An interesting building on Broadway is Villa Lewaro. It was built in 1917, at the cost of $350,000, by Sarah J. Walker, a black woman who had amassed a fortune from the sale of a patent hair straightener. It was designed in Anglo-Palladian style by Vertner Tandy, the first black admitted to the American Institute of Architects. It was built despite the strong opposition of the wealthy white neighbors. However, Madame Walker soon won their admiration and respect, as she was a real lady. The unusual name was coined by her friend Enrico Caruso, from the name of her daughter, A'Lelia Walker Robinson. Today it is the Anna E. Poth Home for Convalescent and Aged Members of the Companions of the Forest in America. Among the other prominent residents of the area were Cyrus W. Field, layer of the Atlantic Cable; Chauncey M. Depew, president of the New York Central Railroad, United States senator, and celebrated wit and after-dinner speaker; Amzi Lorenzo Barber, the asphalt magnate; and Albert Bierstadt, the noted landscape painter. Other interesting local structures include: Abercombie House (1850), carpenter Gothic; Buckout-Jewell House (pre-Revolutionary); Eliphalet Wood House (1869), Victorian with tower; Irvington Presbyterian Church (1869), Romanesque by James Renwick; and St. Barnabas Episcopal Church (1853), stone Gothic. The Brisbane-Walker Building, three-story stone Beaux Arts, was designed early in the century by Stanford White for Cosmopolitan magazine. It can be seen from the river. Just below it, near the railroad, at the foot of Main Street, is the red brick factory of Lord

& Burnham, one of the first manufacturers of green-houses and glass, boilers, heaters, and other horticultural equipment.

21.20 Erie Pier to west. A mile-long pier built in 1841 as a railroad and steamboat terminal by the Erie Railroad. The pier is no longer used by the railroad. Lamont Observatory keeps its oceanographic ship moored here. There is a small lighthouse.

At the present time the pier is a town park, and a large apartment development has been built near the inland end on the former Clevepac Corporation property. The pier has caused considerable siltation of the waters north of it.

21.25 Piermont to west. In early days this village was known as Tappan Slote or Tappan Landing, and sometimes as Bogerttown. Prior to the Revolution, a grist mill was built here, and a store was operated by Abraham Mabie, who kept it until the close of that war. About 1783 the store was acquired by Major Abraham Taulman, who managed it until his death in 1835. This was the first port of entry in Rockland County and an important point of access to the interior. During this period, the name of Tappan fell into disuse, and the place came to be called either Taulman's Landing or simply The Landing. Besides the Taulmans, other prominent early families included the Haddocks and the Myers, and an industrious African-American named John Moore, who built a saw mill. In 1815, William Ferdon built a woolen mill which spun yarn and manufactured blankets. The growth of Piermont depended almost entirely upon the opening of the Erie Railroad in 1841. It served as eastern terminus, and there were locomotive and car works here. Eventually two round houses, a machine, car, and paint shop, foundry, and planing mills were built.

The railroad facilities eventually covered four acres. This was the period of Piermont's greatest prosperity. In 1860 its population reached 2,426. The village of Piermont was organized in 1850. The name Piermont was coined in 1839 by Eleazor Lord, the first president of the Erie. It combined the name of the long pier with the mountainous nature of the surrounding country. At this time, Tappan Slote came to be called Sparkill. In 1852 the directors of the Erie obtained permission to relocate their terminal at Pavonia, and Piermont fell into decline. Today there are many quaint old corners and charming vistas. The Arie Smith, or Onderdonck, House near the upper landing was often fired upon by British ships during the Revolution. Paradise Lane has several mid-nineteenth century homes with good potential for restoration. Castlewood, the 1850 home of Eleazor Lord, and the 1840 Verdon-Blauvelt

house are also notable. McKelvin's Summer Hotel was operative here in the nineteenth century.

21.25 Tappan to west. This village, several miles inland from Piermont, is chiefly notable for its Revolutionary War associations. On July 4, 1774, local settlers gathered to sign the Orangetown Declarations, expressing Patriotic sentiments. Tappan is located in the Township of Orangetown. In July 1775 a closer Association of Patriots was also organized here. This was important because of proximity to the British lines.

George Washington made his headquarters in the Johannes DeWindt House, built in 1700. His first visit was from August 8–23 in 1780. He also stayed here from September 28 to October 2 that same year during the trial in Tappan of Major John André. On May 6, 1783, Washington and his staff met at the DeWindt House with Sir Guy Carleton to discuss plans for the British evacuation of New York and protection of American property.

Major André's court martial for spying was held in the Tappan Church (predecessor to the present building on the same site) from September 28 to October 2, 1780, on which date he was hanged on Treason Hill in Tappan, now marked by a small park and monument. He was originally buried at Tappan but, in 1821, was disinterred and removed to the south aisle of Westminster Abbey. During his trial André was incarcerated in the Mabie House Tavern, built in 1755 and now known as the "76 House," and still operating as a popular restaurant. The DeWindt House has been restored as a museum and is operated as the Masonic Washington Shrine by that order.

21.45 Tappan Zee. We are now in the Tappan Zee, which is 12 miles long by 2 to 2.4 miles wide. The bottom is composed of shells, mud, and glacial rubble, and bedrock is 500 feet farther down. There are oyster seedbeds here. The name Tappan Zee is derived as follows: Tappan is the Indian word for "cold springs" and zee is Dutch for "sea," a term they freely gave to any large body of water. Some Mohegan Indians dwelt on the eastern shore, but the western was inhabited by the Tappan and Saulrikan subtribes of the Unami Lenni Lenapes. The name was sometimes corrupted to Topan.

In his *History of Rockland County*, David Cole tells of military activity in this area:

As early as September 8th, 1776, Washington ordered the removal of his sick to the neighborhood of Tappan. Later when General Scott encamped in Haverstraw to protect the stores which were there, he ordered ten tons of lead moved from Tappan to

Major Smith's at Upper Nyack—the property now [1884] owned by Joseph Hilton. When Colonel Tyler had ceased to harry the Tories in Orangetown for a moment, and had withdrawn to Ramapo, Abraham Post, of Tappan, was ordered to remove eleven chests of armorer's tools, with bellows, anvils, &c, to the store of Abraham Mabie at the Slote. In 1780, General Greene had his headquarters in the stone house near the old road, which led from Sneden's Landing to Orangeburg, and which is now occupied by E. N. Taft and owned by Wm. Peet....

The River shore from Taulman's Point at Piermont, north, was much exposed to the depredations of foraging forces from the enemy's ships, and the chief duty of Colonel Hay and the Minute Men was to guard this long and exposed line. On the first appearance of the British vessels, on July 12th, 1776, the enemy made two attempts to land at Nyack, but were repulsed through the watchfulness of Colonel Hay's men, who, by reason of their small number— only 400—and the distance to be patroled, were on duty night and day. On July 16th the fleet sailed up as far as Haverstraw and anchored off Kiers' landing, but here, too, their attempts to land were prevented. So deficient was the guard in the necessary munitions of war that Hay appealed for powder and ball to supply his men. Fortunately General George Clinton was able to reinforce him at the time, and shortly after he was sent twenty pounds of powder. For nine days the vessels remained off Haverstraw, but only once succeeded in obtaining provisions from the west shore. On that occasion they burned the house of a man named Halstead and took his pigs.

At last, on July 25th, the vessels sailed slowly down the river, anchoring for a time off Teller's, now Croton Point, to obtain some provisions from the Westchester shore. But their presence had roused the spirit of battle in the patriots, and on August 3rd, 1776, the American galleys, Lady Washington, Spitfire, Whiting, and Crown, under Benjamin Tupper, attacked their vessels, Phenix, Captain Parker, and Rose, Captain Wallace, off Tarrytown and fought them for two hours.

This is perhaps a good time to retell the old Dutch Storm Ship legend as told by Washington Irving. This mysterious ship was often supposed to have been sighted in the Tappan Zee:

The Storm Ship legend harks back to the early days before the English came to bedevil the Dutch calm on the river. Then a mysterious ship, flying the Netherlands color is said to have been seen entering the river with sails bellied by winds nowhere else apparent, riding forward against a strong ebb tide. The astonished burghers signaled a command to her to stop and show her papers; but the ship sailed on. Then a gun at the Battery sent a ball thundering toward her. But her hull did not stop the ball, nor did the ball check her course. On she sped past the Palisades, straight up the Tappan Sea, around the frowning heights of Verdrietege Hook, until she disappeared from sight and for ever. She was never seen to pass down-river and out to sea. But that is not the last of her here, as many Tappan fisherman has attested, for she is the Storm Ship, says Bacon, that makes mysterious journeys, never heeding shoal or headland, tacking when the wind is fair and running free in the teeth of a gale, with never a concession to any weather that mortals give heed to. Into the moonlight she comes suddenly from some unknown quarter and as suddenly, while the eye is fixed upon her, vanishes completely as a bubble that floats for a moment where a wave has broken, and then, in a twinkling, is dissipated.

(Tales from Irving, New York: Bryant Literary Union, 1902, p. 30.)

There is another legend of a certain Rambout Van Dam of the Bronx, who, after carousing all one Sunday morning at a party in the Rockland Hills near Piermont, swore to row all the way back to Spuyten Duyvil, and was drowned by the devil for his blasphemy. Clearly this, and the legend of Anthony Van Corlear at Spuyten Duyvil, all hark back to the old Dutch legend of the Flying Dutchman— Vanderdecken—whose story is used as the basis of Richard Wagner's opera Der Fliegende Hollander. It is interesting to see how the Dutch colonists fleshed out the old legend to suit their new surroundings.

21.45 Sunnyside on east. The home of Washington Irving from 1835 until his death in 1859. It was built by Wolfert Ecker sometime in the seventeenth century and was owned by Jacob Van Tassel during the Revolution. Irving loved the old house, which he called Wolfert's Roost, and remodeled it extensively between 1835 and 1837. He turned the old farmhouse into a romantic dwelling "made up of gable ends...full of angles and corners as an old cocked hat."

It combines features of English, Spanish, Dutch, and Hudson River Gothic architecture into a happy and very personal blend, reflecting the personality of its owner. Irving never married, but he lived here with his brother Ebenezer and his nieces. He entertained greatly and Oliver Wendell Holmes, William Makepeace Thackary, and Louis Napoleon were

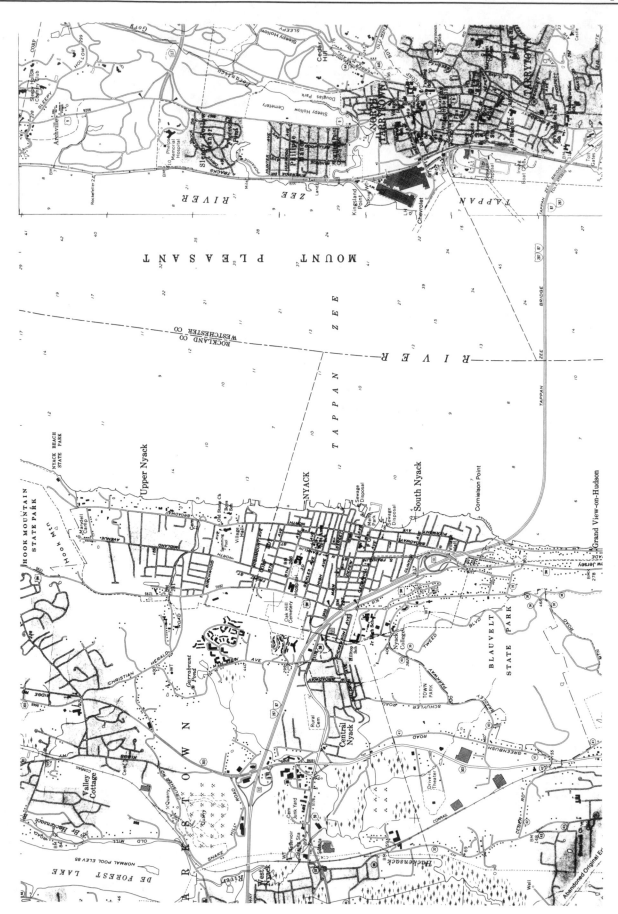

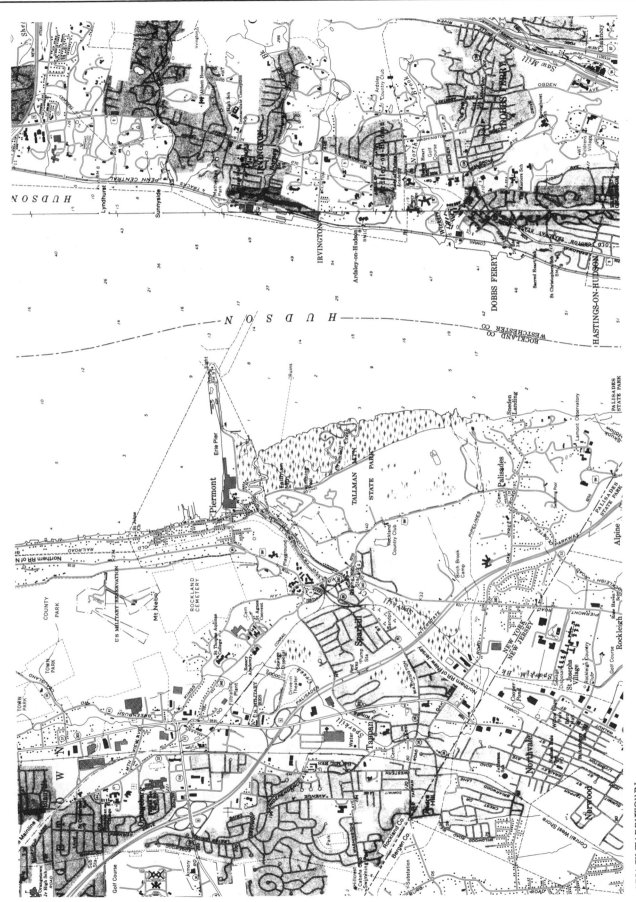

SUNNYSIDE—HOME OF WASHINGTON IRVING c1850. Currier & Ives print. Author's collection.

among his guests. He took meticulous interest in care of the grounds. The study, in particular, reflects the great author's personality. The house has been restored by Sleepy Hollow Restorations and is maintained as a museum. I recommend it very highly. Formerly some New York Central local trains used to stop at Sunnyside.

21.50 Mount Nebo to west (elevation 672 ft.).

21.50 Rockland Cemetery on upper slopes of Mount Nebo. (For further details see article on west side road route, mile 21.10.)

22.00 Grand-View-on-Hudson to west. Residential community, formerly served by the Northern Railroad of New Jersey, Nyack Branch.

22.00 Clausland Mountain to west (elevation 500 feet). The name is a corruption of "Jan Claus's land"—an early name for Greenbush, to the west of the mountain.

22.25 Requa Landing to east.

22.25 Lyndhurst to east. Lyndhurst is one of the finest and most important private estates extant along the Hudson River. Along with Sunnyside, Philipsburg Manor, Van Cortlandt Manor, Boscobel, and the Vanderbilt Mansion at Hyde Park, it serves as excellent documentation of both a period and style of architecture and decoration. Lyndhurst has been restored by the National Trust for Historic Preservation in a style reconciling the contributions of the three families who lived in it—the Pauldings, the Merritts, and the Goulds.

Lyndhurst is a Gothic Revival residence in the Pointed style. It was designed in 1838 by Alexander Jackson Davis (1803–1892), who was the greatest exponent of the Gothic Revival style in America, for

Gen. William Paulding. Paulding was a former New York congressman and ex-mayor of New York City. He lived at Lyndhurst with his son Philip Rhinelander Paulding.

In 1864 Lyndhurst was purchased by a New York City merchant named George Merritt. He retained Alexander Jackson Davis to further enlarge the house. During the 1865 enlargement, the house lost its symmetrical layout and became asymmetrical, which was more typical of the Gothic Revival style. At this time, a tower was built on the west and a porte cochère on the east, with a new large wing to the north which almost doubled the size of the house. The house was built of Sing Sing marble. The interior details such as the ribbed and vaulted ceilings, the stained glass windows, parquetry floors, door and window trip, mantles, and even the furniture, were all designed by Davis and presented a unified conception. The great taste-maker of that time, Andrew Jackson Downing, wrote of Lyndhurst: "The eye is struck by the picturesque outline of towers, turrets, gables, and pinnacles; and with the pleasing variety afforded by the windows decorated with mullions and tracery."

In 1880 Lyndhurst was purchased by the railroad financier Jay Gould. He and his daughters, Helen and Anna, respected the integrity of Davis's design and embellished the property with objets d'art and established a library. In 1964 Anna, Duchess of Talleyrand-Pèrigord, left Lyndhurst to the National Trust to be operated and maintained in memory of her parents as a non-profit museum.

The mansion is not the only attraction at Lyndhurst. In 1870 George Merritt had a gigantic greenhouse built for him by Lord and Burnham of neighboring Irvington. It was modeled after

LYNDHURST MANSION AT TARRYTOWN. Home of Jay Gould. View from the river side. Photo: Courtesy of National Trust for Historic Preservation.

Roulault's Conservatory in the Jardin des Plantes (1833) in Paris. The cupola was reminiscent of John Nash's Royal Pavilion of 1818 at Brighton and Samuel Sloan's Longwood at Natchez, Mississippi, sometimes known as "Nutt's Folly," of 1861. The greenhouse was 380 feet long. The central section was 95 feet wide and 80 feet long, and the wings on the east and west measured 148 feet each and were 36 feet wide. A 100-foot-high tower rose from the dome of the central section and was topped by a glass cupola 25 feet in diameter. Facilities included reception rooms, sleeping quarters, billiard room, bowling alley, gymnasium, carpenter shop, and seed rooms. In the cellar were coal rooms, boiler rooms, water tanks, store rooms for materials and potting tools, and a mushroom cellar.

The tower was surmounted by a bulbous, Saracenic, onion dome-shaped cage, used as an aviary. Shortly after Jay Gould purchased the property in 1880 this Arabian Nights creation burned. Gould had Lord and Burnham reconstruct the greenhouse, but without the Moorish tower. Gould specialized in the growing of orchids. The greenhouse is presently dilapidated, but restoration work is under way.

23.10 Tappan Hill to east (elevation 400 feet).

23.20 Tappan Zee Bridge. This bridge carries the mainline of the New York State Thruway between Tarrytown and South Nyack. It is one of the largest bridges in the United States; total length is 15,764 feet, or almost three miles. The main structure is a cantilever through truss span of 1,212 feet (two cantilevers @ 340 ft. and 532 ft. suspended span), with anchor spans of 602 ft. The remainder of the west end consists of conventional steel stringer design and the east end of deck truss design. There are

TAPPAN ZEE BRIDGE. View looking south from sidewheel steamer *Alexander Hamilton* c1960. Note double wake of paddle steamer. Photo: Arthur G. Adams.

153,900 cubic yards of concrete, 14,610 tons of reinforcing steel and 59,250 tons of structural steel (including railing). A total of 132,050 square yards or 27¼ acres of pavement comprises the roadway. This required 714,285 cubic feet or 26,455 cubic yards of concrete. Some 42,702 cubic yards were used in the eight foundation caissons alone. In the bridge foundations, a total of 1,602,200 feet (303 miles) of timber piles were used, as well as 330,500 feet (62.5 miles) of steel "H" piles and 33,400 feet (6.3 miles) of 30-inch steel pipe piles filled with concrete.

The bridge's roadway comprises six lanes, three in each direction, separated by a 10-foot center mall, which can be used for emergency parking except around the curve on the westerly end where 3,233 feet of median barrier has been installed.

Overall width of the structure is ninety feet between railings, with each roadway thirty-seven feet wide. An emergency walk three feet wide runs along each side of the bridge. The height of the bridge pavement above the river at the center of the main span is 157.3 feet; the clearance from the river to the bottom of the steel is a minimum of 138 feet in the channel, and the height of the two main towers above the river is 293 feet.

In 1991, a total of 40,750,000 vehicles crossed the bridge although peak capacity is estimated at 27,000,000 per year. The structure cost $80,800,000. The first test borings were sunk in June 1951, and actual construction begun in March of 1952. The bridge opened on December 15, 1955.

Designers were Madigan-Hyland consulting engineers. Major contractors were: American Bridge Division—U.S. Steel Corporation, Merritt, Chapman and Scott, Garafano and Eyclid, and Construction Aggregates Corp.

One of the unique features of the bridge is the use of eight concrete caissons supported on steel piles driven to rock, which serve as buoyant underwater foundations to support approximately seventy per cent of the structure's dead weight. The largest of these caissons is half the size of a city block and weighs 15,000 tons. The two caissons supporting the main piers measure 190 × 100 × 40 feet. The concrete caissons were poured in molds at Bowline Point, above Haverstraw, and floated downriver into place.

While the bridge is an engineering masterpiece, the writer cannot help but feel that it is unfortunately situated and destroys one of the finest water vistas in the world.

23.20 Carroll Castle to east. Prominent on a small hill south of Hackley Hill, this castle, originally called

"Carrollcliffe," was built in 1900 by newsman and playwright General Howard Carroll. This castle, with its crenellated towers, now serves as offices for the Axe-Houghton Investment Group.

23.25 Hackley Hill to east (elevation 450 feet).

23.50 The Bight to west. An old name for a small cove.

23.60 Cornelison Point on west.

23.60 South Nyack on west. The earliest settlers were John Claesen Kuyper and Theunis Roelofse Van Houten, who settled here in 1686. The Michael Cornelison House, dating from 1770, was often fired upon by British ships, and was briefly occupied by the enemy early in the war. The area is now entirely residential in character.

24.00 Tarrytown on east (population 10,739). There was formerly a ferry here to Nyack. This area was originally part of the Philips manor. In later times, the Beekmans were the large landowners in the vicinity. Incorporated in 1870, the town's famous residents have included Commodore Oliver Hazard Perry (1785–1819), the hero of the battle of Lake Erie in the War of 1812; his brother Commodore Matthew Calbraith Perry (1794–1853), who opened up Japan to United States trade in 1853 and was an early advocate of naval steamships; and General John C. Frémont (1813–1890), the "Pioneer Pathfinder of the West."

There are two theories of how Tarrytown got its name. The more prosaic, and more likely, theory is that it derives from the Dutch word "tarwe," which means "wheat," which was grown here. Washington Irving would have us believe that it got its name because the local farmers, when they went to market here, would tarry at the local taverns. Who knows? Maybe Irving was correct!

Marymount College (Catholic, women) is located here, as was the famous Miss Mason's Castle School for Girls, which operated from 1891 to 1933 in a crenelated castle, built as a private home in 1856, and razed in 1944. Of particular architectural and historic interest is Christ Church on Broadway at Elizabeth Street. It is a small brick church built in 1838. Washington Irving worshiped here from 1843 till his death in 1859. He was a warden, and his funeral was held here. The Warner Library on North Broadway was built in 1928 in the Beaux Arts style. It has a frieze, decorated cornice, formal portico, and arched windows set in recessed panels. The massive cast bronze bas-relief doors were taken from a Renaissance Italian baptistry.

On September 23, 1780, a most significant event in American history took place on North Broadway when John Paulding, David Williams, and Isaac Van Wart captured Major André. Wallace Bruce, in his *Guide to the Hudson*, tells the following story:

The following quaint ballad-verses on the young hero give a realistic touch to one of the most providential occurrences in our history:

> *He with a scouting party*
> *   Went down to Tarrytown,*
> *Where he met a British officer*
> *   A man of high renown,*
> *Who says unto these gentlemen,*
> *   "You're of the British cheer,*
> *I trust that you can tell me*
> *   If there's any danger near?"*
>
> *Then up stept this young hero,*
> *   John Paulding was his name,*
> *"Sir, tell us where you're going*
> *   And also whence you came?"*
> *"I bear the British flag, sir,*
> *   I've a pass to go this way*
> *I'm on an expedition,*
> *   And have no time to stay."*

Young Paulding, however, thought that he had plenty of time to linger until he examined his boots, wherein he found the papers (plans of the fortifications at West Point), and, when offered ten guineas by André, if he would allow him to pursue his journey, replied: "If it were ten thousand guineas you could not stir one step."

Young André was very much of an aristocrat and, while stationed down in New York, had written a long satiric doggerel poem entitled "The Cow Chase," concerning an episode near Bulls Ferry, New Jersey, and mocking the American patriots, and their leader, General Anthony Wayne. It closed with the following verse:

> *And now I've closed my epic strain,*
> *   I tremble as I show it,*
> *Lest this same warrior-drover Wayne,*
> *   Should ever catch the poet.*

The "Cow Chase" was given wide circulation. When André was captured by the Americans, some anonymous wag wrote the following verse, which was widely sung:

> *When the epic strain was sung*
> *   The poet by his neck was hung—*

And to his cost he finds too late
The dung-born tribe decides his fate.
(Bruce, *Hudson by Daylight*, pp. 88–96)

24.10 Chevrolet Motors assembly plant to east. A Maxwell plant until 1916, this is one of the largest assembly plants in the east. Closed by GM in 1996.

24.20 André Brook to east.

24.25 Tarrytown Lighthouse to east. On a small island a short distance offshore, this 56-ft.-high ironclad tower was completed in 1883 and operated until 1955. It had a 15-mile beam.

24.30 Kingsland or Beekman's Point to east.

24.50 Nyack to west (population 6,558). This residential village was incorporated in 1833. Claes Jansen Kuyper von Purmarent obtained a New Jersey patent for two tracts in this area in 1671. It was later settled by his son Cornelius Cuyper. The first recorded settler was Harman Tallman in 1675. His father, Douwe Harmanszen Tallman, joined him sometime between 1678 and 1686. Another early settler was Michael Cornelison. The Salisbury House on Piermont Avenue dates from 1770.

During the Revolution, Nyack saw some interesting skirmishing. The following extract is from David Cole's *History of Rockland County*.

Nyack, then but a hamlet of perhaps a dozen houses, became, before the end of the war, an object of the enemy's bitter aversion. This was partly due to those patriotic actions of its inhabitants, which ended in the repulsion more than once of their forces when they attempted to land for fresh provisions or water; partly because it was a rendezvous for the whale boat fleet, which patroled the river, and partly because of the residence at this place of Henry Palmer who had rendered himself obnoxious to the British.

Captain Palmer had owned a vessel and been employed in the carrying trade for one of the largest firms in New York, before the Revolution. When the news of the Battle of Bunker Hill reached that city, he was offered great financial advantages to serve the cause of the King but refused absolutely. Shortly after he conveyed two cargoes of arms and ammunition, which had been seized by the Sons of Liberty, from New York to the camp of the Continental Army. New York soon became uncomfortable for this patriot, and he removed with his family to a house, which formerly stood in Upper Nyack, on the east side of Broadway, opposite the old mountain road, by Garret E. Green's residence.

Owing to these causes, the British vessels, when-

ever they passed up the river greeted the residents of the Nyack valley with a shotted salute from their guns. For their protection, those residents erected an earth work on the land east of the Methodist Church and just north of Depew Avenue, which covered the first dock in the village; while the section known as Upper Nyack, was defended by a swivel mounted on Major John L. Smith's place, and a company of Minute Men, under his and his brother—Captain Auri Smith's command.

As soon as hostilities had begun in this Colony the Shore Guard was placed on duty; this following order governing those stationed at Nyack.

Haverstraw, October 16th, 1776.

General orders for the commanding officers at the place called the Hook.

Guards to mount daily at 4 or 5 o'clock in the afternoon, with sentries fixed as the commanding officer sees expedient. No soldier to fire a gun unless a sentry after hailing a craft or person three times, or at the enemy, or on an alarm. On every alarm, twenty hands to be sent to the commanding officer with intelligence. No person to pass without a permit from some commanding officer, or the committee from whence he came. No craft to be taken without liberty from the officer of the party of the place where said craft is. No liquor to be sold after 7 o'clock at night unless to a traveller, and none to be sold to any person in liquor. No sentry to leave his post until relieved. The commanding officer at the Hook to consult with the Major of the Riflemen, at New York, about the countersign. These orders to be read morning and evening to the guards until further orders.

A. Hawkins Hay
Commanding Officer

In October 1776, the enemy attempted to land at Nyack, but were repulsed by the Shore Guard, not however till their cannon balls had marked Sarvent's house. In December of the same year, they effected a foot-hold and, besides looting a house, took off some cattle. In the summer of the following year—1777—two boats attempted to land at the present Piermont, at the point now known as the upper dock, at daybreak. After a sharp conflict with the Shore Guard they were repulsed with three killed. Several of the Shore Guard were wounded, but none fatally. (Cole, *History of Rockland County*.)

During the nineteenth century, Nyack was a resort. Popular hotels of that era were the Mansion House, Pavilion, Clarendon, Smithsonian, Tappan Zee House, also operated as the Rockland Female Institute, and

Prospect House, formerly called the Palmer House. Many of these hotels doubled as young ladies' finishing schools during the winter.

Through the years, principal industries have included the manufacture of organs, sewing machines, and leather goods. There was a ferry to Tarrytown until 1941. Nyack was formerly the terminus of the Northern Railroad of New Jersey.

24.50 Pocantico River to the east. Also formerly called Gory Creek. The present name is derived from the Indian "pocanteco" or "weehkanteco," meaning "deep woods." It rises in the Pocantico Hills near the large private estate of the Rockefeller family named Kykuit, which means "lookout point." It then flows southwest through Sleepy Hollow and empties into the Hudson through a small cove, now largely silted up into marshland, just below the mill dam erected by Frederick Philipse I.

This area was part of the Philipse Manor, and the upper mill was built here in about 1680 by Frederick Philipse I. He erected a dam and a mill which ground corn and wheat. Sloops anchored just below the dam, and the location also became an important trading post. Shortly after settlement, there were two hundred settlers, making up about forty families. The manor house was also built to serve as a fortress. It was built of roughhewn blocks of native stone and fieldstone, mortared with riverbank clay. It was whitewashed. It had leaded glass casement windows with heavy wooden shutters. The dam served to create a millpond to create water power and also allowed the cove to silt up to create marshland for the growing of salt hay, then an important commodity. Frederick Philipse I also built a church in 1697 or 1699. Adolph Philipse inherited the upper mills in 1702, and they passed to Frederick Philipse II in 1750. His son Frederick Philipse III was a Royalist and his property was confiscated and sold at auction. The upper mill property was purchased in 1784 by Gerard G. Beekman Jr. After the death of his widow in 1822 the property passed through many hands until it was purchased by John D. Rockefeller, Jr., in 1937, and the present restoration work was subsequently commenced by the Sleepy Hollow Restorations.

It has been completely restored and operates as a museum. A visit is highly recommended, as it gives one an excellent idea of early life along the river. 914-965-4027

24.75 Philipse Manor to east. The name refers to a railroad station and a twentieth-century residential neighborhood. This is officially known as North Tarrytown. The large and beautiful Sleepy Hollow Cemetery is located here, with the graves of such notables as Washington Irving, Carl Schurz, Robert G. Ingersoll, Andrew Carnegie, and Whitelaw Reid.

25.25 Upper Nyack to west. This was also known in Revolutionary times as Sarvent's Landing. There is a "smuggler's tunnel" running from the river bank to Broadway, built about 1750. However, it is possible that this was actually built for use by the Shore Guard during the Revolution.

Toward the close of July, 1777, the British sent a galley ashore to destroy a sloop which was moored to a dock at Abram Sarvent's place in Upper Nyack. To oppose this endeavor Henry Palmer, Abram Sarvent, Cornelius Cuyper, Peter Freeland and Major Smith hastily collected, and concealed themselves in a quarry near the dock. Waiting till the enemy was within safe range, the patriots opened fire. The galley was at once put about and pulled out of gun shot for a time. A second attempt to force a landing, though assisted by the ship's guns, ended in failure. A third attempt was made, but the loss of the British was too great for further hope of success. The galley was then pulled up opposite Henry Palmer's house, and fire opened against that building from the bow carronade. So accurate was the aim of the gunners, that every shot struck the house or tore up the earth in the door yard. Mrs. Palmer, fearing each moment that a ball would pass through the building, took her infant in her arms and, creeping alongside the house, till out of range, at length crossed the mountain and found a safe asylum at the house of a friend. In her flight, a ball struck the bank so close to the fugitive as to spatter dirt over herself and child.

The morning after the fight at Sarvent's Landing, the bodies of nine British sailors floated ashore and were buried by the Americans.

On another occasion Captain Palmer with a few comrades fired into a British vessel which was becalmed and floating with the tide. Thirty-six of the enemy were killed or wounded in this slaughter while of Palmer's force but one man was injured. He was wounded by a splinter from the rock behind which he was concealed.

Dreadful warfare did the patriots wage against the enemy's ships with the swivel, which was mounted east of Broadway, in Upper Nyack, opposite the residences of Joseph Hilton and S. C. Eaton, on property now [1884] belonging to Wilson Defendorf. At best this famous gun would barely carry a ball a half mile, and as the ships kept in the channel, some two and a half miles away, no very great injury was done by this long range shooting. Once however, during the war, two boats attempted to land at this shore for water and the Shore Guard opened so hot a fire

*with muskets and swivel, that one boat's crew sur-
rendered at once while the other, braving the fire,
pulled for the ships. The captured crew was sent to
Tappan.*

(Cole, *History of Rockland County*)

The Old Stone Church on Broadway, oldest in
Rockland County, dates from February 1813. It is
built of red sandstone. Founders were William
Palmer, Nicholas Williamson, and John Green. Originally Methodist Episcopal, it is now Interdenominational. Upper Nyack is a residential community with
many large fine homes. Nyack Beach State Park is
located at the end of Broadway in the north end of
town.

26.50 Verdrietege Hook to west. Triassic red sandstone cliffs 730 feet high. There was formerly quarrying here prior to creation of the Palisades Interstate Park, which has subsequently acquired much of
the area and developed it for recreation. The name
derives from the Dutch and means "tedious hook,"
probably because it took so long for sailing craft to
pass it. As there is no single clearly defined point, it
was also called Point-No-Point. Still another early

name applied to the point was Calico Hook. Much of
the property in this area once belonged to Isaac I.
Blauvelt.

26.50 Ball Mountain (elevation 650 feet). Slightly to
the west of the southern end of Verdrietege Hook.

27.00 Hook Mountain to west. The northern part of
Verdrietege Hook, also sometimes called Diedrick
Hook.

27.50 Scarborough to east. A railroad station and a
fine residential area within the corporate limits of the
town of Briarcliff Manor.

27.60 Kemeyst Cove to east.

28.10 Sparta to east. Section within the town of
Ossining, with many fair to well-preserved buildings
from the early to mid-nineteenth century.

28.50 Sing Sing State Prison to east. The location of
New York State's famous electric chair, it presently
contains 2,719 prison cells.

*On the southern borders of the village of Sing
Sing (Ossining) is a rough group of small hills, called
collectively Mount Pleasant. They are formed of do-*

HOOK MOUNTAIN AND ROCKLAND LANDING. Photo: © Gretchen McHugh.

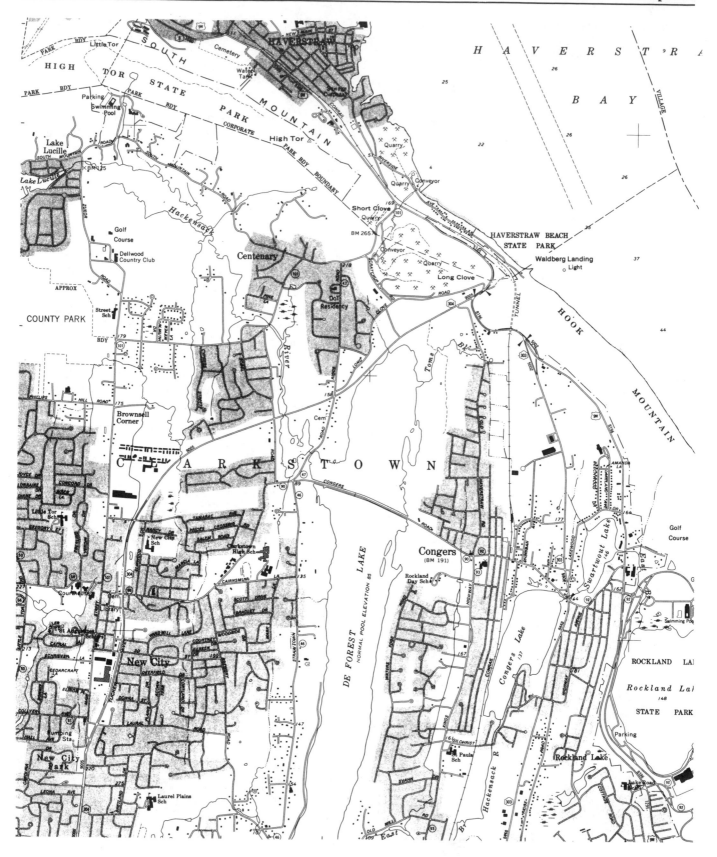

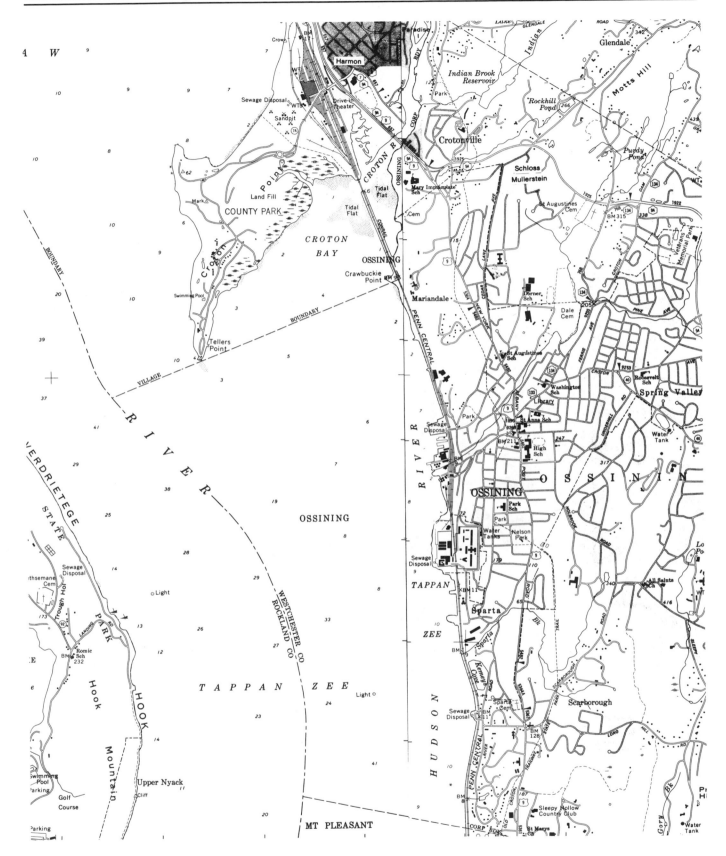

HAVERSTRAW/OSSINING SOUTH

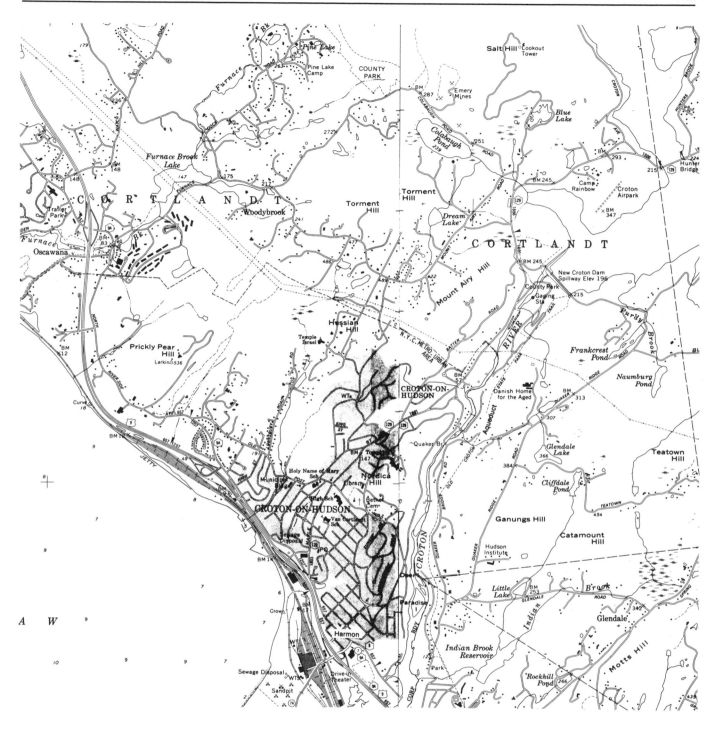

HAVERSTRAW/OSSINING NORTH

SING SING PRISON, Ossining. Photo: © Gretchen McHugh.

lomitic, or white coarse-grained marble, of excellent quality and almost inexhaustible quantity, cropping out from a thin soil in many places. At the foot of Mount Pleasant, on the shore of the river, is a large prison for men, with a number of workshops and other buildings, belonging to the State of New York. A little way up the slope is the prison for women, a very neat and substantial building, with a fine colonnade on the river front. These prisons were built by convicts about thirty years ago, when there were two establishments of the kind in the State, one in the city of New York, and the other at Auburn, in the interior. A new system of prison discipline had been adopted. Instead of the old system of indolent, solitary confinement, the workhouse feature was combined with incarceration in separate cells at night. They were made to work diligently all day, but in perfect silence, no recognition by word, look, or gesture, being allowed among them. The adoption of this system, in 1823, rendered the prison accommodation insufficient, and a new establishment was authorized in 1824. Mount Pleasant, near Sing Sing, was purchased, and in May, 1826, Captain Lynds, a farm agent of the Auburn prison, proceeded with one hundred felons from that establishment to erect the new penitentiary. They quarried and wrought diligently among the marble rocks at Mount Pleasant, and the prison for men was completed in 1829, when the convicts in the old State prison in the city of New York were removed to it.

It had eight hundred cells, but these were found to be too few, and in 1831 another story was added to the building, and with it two hundred more cells, making one thousand in all, the present number. More are needed, for the number of convicts in the men's prison, at the beginning of 1861, was a little more than thirteen hundred. In the prison for women there were only one hundred cells, while the number of convicts was one hundred and fifty at that time.

The ground occupied by the prisons is about ten feet above highwater mark. The main building, in which are the cells, is four hundred and eighty feet in length, forty-four feet in width, and five stories in height. Between the outside walls and the cells there is a space of about twelve feet, open from floor to roof. A part of it is occupied by a series of galleries, there being a row of one hundred cells to each story on both fronts, and backing each other. Between the prison and the river are the several workshops, in which various trades are carried on. In front of the prison for women is the guard-house, where arms and instructions are given out to thirty-one guardsmen every morning. Between the guard-house and the prison the Hudson River Railway passes, partly through two tunnels and a deep trench. Upon the highest points of Mount Pleasant are guard-houses, which overlook the quarries and other places of industrial operations.

In the prison for men, and in the workshops, everything is carried on with the most perfect order; every kind of labour, the meals, the religious exercises in the chapel, are all conducted according to the most rigid rules. The discipline is consequently quite perfect. Reformation, not merely punishment, is the great aim, and the history of the prison attests to the success of the effort. Severe punishments are becoming more and more rare, and the terrible Shower Bath, which has been so justly condemned by the humane, is now seldom used, and then in the presence of the prison physician. Only when all other means for forcing obedience have failed, is this horrid punishment inflicted. It is admitted, I believe, that the Mount Pleasant or Sing Sing prison is one of the best conducted penitentiaries in the world.

(Lossing, The Hudson, pp. 298-300.)

28.65 Rockland Lake Landing to west. This is at a clove called Trough Hollow. The Indians called the area Quaspeake, which gave its name to the original Patent to lands in the area. Later it was called Hunter's Landing, Slaughter's Landing, and Slauter's Landing. Originally this served the back country much as Huyler's and Sneden's Landings. In 1711 John Slaughter purchased a tract of land in the Clove, at the present Rockland Lake, and built a landing which bore his name until changed by Barmore, Felter & Co. in 1835.

In 1850 Francis Powley built a marine railway here to use for the construction and repair of vessels engaged in the ice and quarry business. In 1872 John Mansfield established a stone-crusher which he later sold to M. M. Miranda. Around 1884, an average of from 75 to 90 vessel loads of crushed stone were shipped annually, and employment was given to from 25 to 65 men according to the demand. In 1873 James W. Smith fitted up a pleasure ground known as Sylvan Grove. The Knickerbocker Ice Company built a gravity railroad from Rockland Lake atop the cliffs to the landing in 1858. In the 1860s this was the principal ice depot on the Hudson. In the nineteenth century Ackerson's Rockland Lake Hotel and Henry Vorratin's Hudson River Hotel operated at the landing.

28.65 Rockland Lake to west. Atop Hook Mountain (elevation 300 feet). This is an irregular ellipse, half a mile in length and three quarters of a mile at its greatest width and covers about 500 acres. It is supplied by springs in its own bosom, and clear mountain brooks. It is the headwater of the Hackensack River, which was originally known as the Demarest Kill, after a family of early settlers. The Indian name was Quaspeck Pond; but the name Quaspeck and also Snedecker's Pond were used interchangeably until the formal adoption of the name Rockland Lake in 1835. A post office of the later name was opened in 1842.

In 1694 the Pond or Quaspeck Patent was granted to Jarvis Marshall and William Welch, "speculators." The southern end of the pond was settled by Germans about 1711, although a certain John Hutchins had settled here as early as 1700. John Slauter settled on the west side in 1711 and Tunis Snedeker at the northern end in 1731. In 1775 John Ryder settled at the northeastern corner and Hermanus Hoffman at the southeastern one.

The water is of singular purity and has long been recognized as producing good ice. In 1835 John J. Felter, John G. Perry, and Edward Felter cut a sloopload of ice from the lake and sold it at an almost clear profit in New York. In 1836 they formed the firm of Barmore, Felter & Co., with a capital of $2,000. They purchased Slaughter's Landing and soon built a gravity railroad to lower the ice to boats in the river. Business grew rapidly, and the firm soon evolved into the Knickerbocker Ice Company, which was still doing business in New York City in 1978. During the heyday of natural cut ice, this was the largest of many such firms doing business along the river, and they also had other tributary lakes and ice depots along the Hudson.

28.75 Rockland Lighthouse to west. Built to guide traffic to Rockland Lake Landing.

28.75 Ossining to east (population 22,582). A large residential town and the site of Sing Sing Prison. The main portion of the village has an elevation of 100 ft. The name comes from the Indian "Sink-Sink"—also variously given as "Sin-Sing," "Sing-Sin," or "Sint-Sinck"—meaning "a stony place." Indeed, there are many stones here—mainly dolomitic marble. This is an excellent building material and formerly much was shipped from here. Also a great deal was burned to make builders lime. Other old spellings were: Cinque Singte, Cinque-single, Sinck Sinck, and Sin-sing. The name also applied to the brook which flows into the Hudson here. Silver was mined in the late eighteenth and early nineteenth centuries and copper was mined for a short time after 1820.

On August 24, 1685, Frederick Philipse purchased all the land along the Hudson River between the Pocantico and Croton Rivers from eight Indians—Weskenane, Keanarhan, Mamannane, Crawman, Wennicktanon, Weremenhore, Wappus and Aquaines—of the Sint-Sinck tribe. After the American Revolution, the Philipse lands were confiscated by the commissioners of forfeiture and sold off in much smaller freeholds, frequently to the former tenants of the patroon. At this period the locality was known as Hunter's Landing. The earliest settlement in the neighborhood was at Sparta, in the southern part of the present town, where there was a convenient natural dock. The southern portion of Ossining was known as Mount Pleasant.

The village of Sing Sing was incorporated in 1813. The Sing Sing prison was established in 1826. During the nineteenth century diverse manufacturing developed. The best known was the patent medicine works of Dr. Benjamin Brandreth, "the pill factory." Many Italian immigrants settled here to work in the marble quarries. In about 1900, many people were boycotting prison-made goods and mistook privately manufactured products made in the village of Sing Sing for prison-made merchandise. Naturally this hurt the local tradesmen. To end this confusion the name of the town was officially changed to Ossining in 1901, and the name Sing Sing applies only to the prison today. Ossining is the home of the Maryknoll Catholic Missions, which operates a large seminary and home for retired missioners. It is notable for its unique pagoda topped tower. The Maryknoll Fathers were particularly active in the Orient and today operate on a worldwide basis with particular activity in South America. Their Bishop Walsh was known for his long imprisonment by the Chinese Communist Government.

28.80 Sing Sing Brook to east. Also known as Sint-sinck Brook and Kil Brook. (Note the use of only one "l" in Kil.)

29.50 North Park to east. A residential area.

29.50 Crawbuckie Point to east. Former base of fishing operations.

29.50 Teller's Point to east. This is the dividing point between the Tappan Zee to the south and Haverstraw Bay to the north. Strictly speaking, Teller's Point is the southward-pointing tip of the larger Croton Point. It separates Croton Bay from the main channel of the Hudson. The present name comes from William Teller who purchased the point from the Indians for a barrel of rum and twelve blankets. It was also formerly called Sarah's Point in honor of his wife. The Indian name for the location was "Senasqua." In later years, the property passed into the ownership of R. T. Underhill, M.D., and his brother. Dr. Underhill had an Italian villa here and also operated a vineyard and winery. There were eighty acres devoted to the growing of Isabella and Catawba grapes, and, around the turn of the century, about 10,000 gallons were bottled annually. The old natives and the Indians both believed the point to be haunted by dead Indians, and "the Sachems of Tellers Point" were household words in the neighborhood. It is believed that there was once a great Indian battle here.

The British ship *Vulture* lay offshore here and was driven downstream by a cannonading. This was a proximate cause of Major André's capture at Tarrytown.

29.50 Croton Bay to east. An outlet of the Croton River, separated from the main channel of the Hudson by Teller's Point. Crawbuckie Point is at its eastern end. Henry Hudson anchored here in the *Half Moon* on the evening of October 1, 1609. This was once a great resort of canvasback ducks and other water fowl. Governor Thomas Dongan came here to hunt them in 1683. The bay was formerly quite deep and harbored great quantities of shad. However, the first Croton Reservoir Dam was swept away by a flood in 1841 and great quantities of earth were carried down which have silted up the bay to an average depth of only five feet. What is shown on modern charts as a tidal flat near the New York Central drawbridge across the Croton River used to be known as Dover Kill Island.

30.25 Croton River to east. This stream is almost 100 miles long, rising in the Pawling Mountains of Dutchess and Putnam Counties, and among the lakes of northern Westchester County. Another principal source is Lake Mahopac in Putnam County. This lake has an elevation of 800 feet, and was originally called Ma-cook-pake, which was Indian for "large inland lake." The last great convention of the Southern Tribes of the Hudson was held on an island in this lake. The Croton River flows generally southwesterly through a series of man-made reservoirs belonging to New York City. Principal tributaries are the Cross River and Mohansic River, sometimes called the Muscoot. The large Cornell or Croton Dam is about three miles upstream.

The Indian name for the river was the Kitchawan, or Kitch-a-wong, signifying "large and swift current." The Dutch renamed it Croton in honor of an Indian Sachem of that name. There is another theory that Croton is the corruption of another Indian name, Kenotin, signifying "wind or tempest."

The river drains an area of about 350 square miles. This, and its relative proximity to New York, made it an attractive place to build reservoirs. A dam was built in 1837, and construction commenced on a stone aqueduct to the city. The original dam was swept away by a flood in 1841, but it was immediately rebuilt to a higher level. Between 1884 and 1890 the system was again enlarged to the capacity of 100,000,000 gallons per day total. The 38-mile-long old aqueduct, opened for use 1842, is out of use, but the reservoirs continue to contribute their waters to the Catskill and Delaware Aqueduct systems. John Bloomfield Jervis (1795–1885) was the principal engineer. In early days, there was a very high covered bridge across the Croton Gorge at the head of navigation called Quaker's Bridge. Also, in the middle of the last century it was the location of an important iron foundry.

30.25 Crotonville to east. A small village on the south side of the mouth of the Croton River.

30.25 Van Cortlandt Manor to east. The seat of the Van Cortlandt family on the north bank of the Croton River (more fully described under east side road route mile 37.80), built in 1683.

30.50 Croton Point to east. Separating Croton Bay from main channel of the Hudson River, it projects southwesterly into the stream, its extremity, known as Teller's Point, pointing due south. Its average elevation is only twenty feet. The 504-acre Westchester County Croton Point Park is located here. (See Teller's Point.) Benson Lossing describes the area as follows:

A little west of the cemetery, at the neck of land which connects Croton Point with the main, stood the old fort or castle of "Kitch-a-wan," said to have been one of the most ancient Indian fortresses south of the Highlands. It was built by the Sachem Croton, when he assembled his parties for hunting or war. In a beautiful nook, a little east of the site of the fort, on the borders of Haunted Hollow, is the "Kitch-

a-wan" burying-ground. Around this locality hovers the memory of many a weird story of the early times, when the superstitious people believed that they often saw, in the groves and glens there, the forms of the departed red men. They called them the Walking Sachems of Teller's Point.

(Lossing, *The Hudson*, p. 315.)

In the nineteenth century, grapes, apples, and melons were grown here.

30.90 Enoch's Neck to east. Northern extremity of Croton Point.

31.00 Potato Rock to east. Small rocky island off Croton Point.

31.00 Collaberg Landing to east.

31.00 Harmon on east. Large yards and station on former New York Central Railroad. Here, electric locomotives are taken off long-distance trains and are replaced by diesel power (steam in the old days). Consequently, there are large locomotive shops here. The station has been renamed Croton-Harmon. Today this is an important station stop for both Metro North Commuter and Amtrak trains.

31.00 Harmon Park on east. A residential development built by aviation pioneer Clifford B. Harmon, part of Croton-on-Hudson.

31.50 Long Clove to west. The word comes from the Dutch "kloof," for cleft, gap, or ravine. We will encounter this name frequently along the Hudson. Route 9W comes through this Clove from the Hackensack to the Hudson Valley. It is at the north end of Hook Mountain. The West Shore Railroad also comes through a tunnel just to the south of Long Clove and runs northward along a ledge above the river.

31.50 Snedeker's Landing or Waldberg Landing on west. The land in this area originally belonged to Marshall and Welch's Pond's Patent of 1694. Tunis Snedeker settled in the neighborhood in 1707. In 1835 Abram B. Snedeker built a hotel here. In 1840 Abraham B. Conger purchased land in the area and eventually built a residence he named Waldberg. The name gradually spread to the entire neighborhood, and prior to 1860, had been adopted by the residents of the school district as the name of the locality. New Lake, somewhat inland, was renamed Congers Lake. The lack of sufficient depth of water at Haverstraw village led to the construction of a ship yard and marine railway here in 1845 for the repair of vessels engaged in the brick business. It

operated successfully until 1851 when it was superseded by other yards.

Snedeker's Landing derives historical interest as the landing place of the spy Major André on September 21, 1780. This is probably the best place to tell the story of the André incident, as we have been travelling through the scenes of its action since Dobbs Ferry and will continue to do so until we pass West Point.

Benedict Arnold was disaffected with his rank and command in the Continental Army and "sulking in his tent" like Achilles when he was given command of West Point.

The entire story is well told by Benson Lossing, in his *The Hudson*:

Arnold twice received honorable wounds during the war—one at Quebec, the other almost two years later at Saratoga; both were in the leg. The one last received, while gallantly fighting the troops of Burgoyne, was not yet healed when, in the spring of 1778, the British army under Sir Henry Clinton, evacuated Philadelphia, and the Americans, under Washington, came from their huts at Valley Forge to take their places. Arnold, not being able to do active duty in the field, was appointed military governor of Philadelphia. Fond of display, he there entered upon a course of extravagant living that was instrumental in his ruin. He made his headquarters at the fine old mansion built by William Penn, kept a coach and four, gave splendid dinner parties, and charmed the gayer portions of Philadelphia society with his princely display. His station and the splendour of his equipage captivated the daughter of Edward Shippen, a leading loyalist, and afterwards chief justice of Pennsylvania; she was then only eighteen years of age. Her beauty and accomplishments won the heart of the widower of forty. They were married. Staunch Whigs shook their heads in doubt concerning the alliance of an American general with a leading Tory family.

Arnold's extravagance soon brought numerous creditors to his door. Rather than retrench his expenses he procured money by a system of fraud and prostitution of his official power: the city being under martial law, his will was supreme. The people became incensed, and official inquiries into his conduct were instituted, first by the local state council, and then by the Continental Congress. The latter body referred the whole matter to Washington. The accused was tried by court-martial, and he was found guilty of two of four charges. The court passed the mildest sentence possible—a mere reprimand by the commander-in-chief. This duty Washington performed in the most delicate manner. "Our profession," he said, "is the chastest of all; even the shadow of a fault tarnishes the lustre of our finest achievements. The least inadvertence may rob us of the public favor, so hard to be acquired. I reprimand you for having forgotten that, in proportion as you had rendered yourself formidable to our enemies, you should have been guarded and temperate in your deportment towards your fellow citizens. Exhibit anew those noble qualities which have placed you on the list of our most valued commanders. I will myself furnish you, as far as it may be in my power, with opportunities of regaining the esteem of your country."

What punishment could have been lighter? Yet Arnold was greatly irritated. A year had elapsed since his accusation, and he expected full acquittal. But for nine months the rank weeds of treason had been growing luxuriantly in his heart. He saw no way to extricate himself from debt, and retain his position in the army. For nine months he had been in secret correspondence with British officers in New York. His pride was now wounded, his vindictive spirit was aroused, and he resolved to sell his country for gold and military rank. He opened a correspondence in a disguised hand, and in commercial phrase, with Major John André, the young and highly accomplished adjutant-general of the British army.

How far Mrs. Arnold (who had been quite intimate with Major André in Philadelphia, and had kept up an epistolary correspondence with him after the British army had left that city) was implicated in these treasonable communications we shall never know. Justice compels us to say that there is no evidence of her having any knowledge of the transaction until the explosion of the plot at Beverly.

Arnold's deportment now suddenly changed. For a long time he had been sullen and indifferent; now his patriotism glowed with all the apparent ardour of his earlier career. Hitherto he had pleaded the bad state of his wounds as an excuse for inaction; now they healed rapidly. He appeared anxious to join his old companions in arms; and to General Schuyler, and other influential men, then in Congress, he expressed an ardent desire to be in the camp or in the field. They believed him to be sincere, and rejoiced. They wrote cheering letters to Washington on the subject; and, pursuant to Arnold's intimation, they suggested the propriety of appointing him to the command of West Point, the most important post in the country. Arnold visited Washington's camp at the same time, and, in a modest way, expressed a desire to have a command like that of West Point, as his wounds would not permit him to perform very active service on horseback.

The change surprised Washington, yet he was unsuspicious of wrong. He gave Arnold the command of "West Point and its dependencies," and furnished him with written instructions on the 3rd August, 1780. Then it was that Arnold made his headquarters at Beverly, and worked vigorously for the consummation of his treasonable designs. There he was joined by his wife and infant son. He at once communicated, in his disguised writing and commercial phraseology, under the signature of "Gustavus," his plan to Sir Henry Clinton, through Major André, whom he addressed as "John Anderson." That plan we have already alluded to. Sir Henry was delighted with it, and eagerly sought to carry it out. He was not yet fully aware of the real character behind "Gustavus," although for several months he had suspected it to be General Arnold. Unwilling to proceed further upon uncertainties, he proposed sending an officer to some point near the American lines, who should have a personal interview with his correspondent. "Gustavus" consented, stipulating, however, that the messenger from Clinton should be Major André, his adjutant-general.

Arnold and André agreed to meet at Dobbs Ferry, twenty-two miles above New York, upon what was then known as neutral ground. The British waterguard prevented the approach of Arnold. Sir Henry, anxious to complete the arrangement, and to execute the plan, sent the "Vulture" sloop of war up the river as far as Tarry Town, with Colonel Robinson, the owner of Beverly, who managed to communicate with Arnold. A meeting of Arnold and André was arranged. On the morning of the 20th of September, the latter officer left New York, proceeded by land to Dobb's Ferry, and from thence to the "Vulture," where it was expected the traitor would meet him that night. The wily general avoided the great danger. He repaired to the house of Joshua Hett Smith [near West Haverstraw], a brother to the Tory chief justice of New York, and employed him to go to the "Vulture" at night, and bring a gentlemen to the western shore of the Hudson. There was delay, and Smith did not make the voyage until the night of the 21st, after the moon had gone behind the high hills in the west. With muffled oars he paddled noiselessly out of Haverstraw Creek [Minisceongo Creek], and, at little past midnight, reached the "Vulture." It was a serene night, not a ripple was upon the bosom of the river. Not a word was spoken. The boat came alongside, with a concerted signal, and received Sir Henry's representative. André was dressed in his scarlet uniform, but all was concealed by a long blue surtout, buttoned to the chin. He was conveyed to an estuary at the foot of Long Clove Mountain, a little below the Village of Haverstraw [Waldberg Landing].

Smith led the officer to a thicket near the shore, and then, in a low whisper, introduced "John Anderson" to "Gustavus," who acknowledged himself to be Major-General Arnold, of the Continental Army. There, in the deep shadows of night, concealed from human cognizance, with no witnesses but the stars above them, they discussed the dark plans of treason, and plotted the utter ruin of the Republican cause. The first faint harbingers of day began to appear in the east, and yet the conference was earnest and unfinished. Smith came and urged the necessity of haste to prevent discovery. Much was yet to be done. Arnold had expected a protracted interview, and had brought two horses with him. While the morning twilight was yet dim, they mounted and started for Smith's house. They had not proceeded far when the voice of a sentinel challenged them, and André found himself entering the American lines. He paused, for within them he would be a spy. Arnold assured him by promises of safety; and before sunrise they were at Smith's house, on what has since been known as Treason Hill. At that moment the sound of a cannon came booming over Haverstraw Bay from the eastern shore; and within twenty minutes the "Vulture" was seen dropping down the river, to avoid the shots of an American gun on Teller's Point. To the amazement of André, she disappeared. Deep inquietude stirred his spirit. He was within the American lines, without flag or pass. If detected, he would be called a spy—a name which he despised as much as that of traitor.

At noon the whole plan was arranged. Arnold placed in André's possession several papers—fatal papers!—explanatory of the condition of West Point and its dependencies. Zealous for the interests of his king and country, André contrary to the explicit orders of Sir Henry Clinton, received them. He placed them in his stockings, under his feet, at the suggestion of Arnold, received a pass from the traitor in the event of his being compelled to return to New York by land, and waited with great impatience for the approaching night, when he should be taking a boat to the "Vulture."

(Lossing, *The Hudson*, pp. 289–293.)

To conclude the story, André, in disguise, crossed the King's Ferry to Verplanck's Point and went by land to the old bridge across the Croton River where he was suspected. He was making his way by land back to New York when he was apprehended at Tarrytown. Arnold returned to the Beverly House, across from West Point, and was eating breakfast when word reached him of André's capture. He immediately left the table and ran to the river where

he was rowed downstream to the *Vulture*. Soon after this, he joined the British army and was sent on a marauding expedition up the James River in Virginia. He ended his days in England, an abhorred outcast.

31.50 to 32.40 Long Clove Mountain to west.

31.75 Nordica Hill on the east. Nordica Hill, named for opera singer Lillian Nordica (1859–1914), whose real name was Lillian Norton and who resided at Croton. She sang at the Metropolitan and was famous for Wagnerian roles.

32.00 Croton-on-Hudson on east (population 7,018). A residential community, first settled around 1609. Many Irish and Italian laborers working on the Croton Dam settled here. Incorporated in 1898, it had a separate local railroad station, in addition to the Croton-Harmon station (see 31.00). There was an artist's colony here after World War I, and an early "progressive" school, the Hessian Hills School, was opened in about 1932.

In the summer of 1996 the first elements of the New Netherland Museum is scheduled to open. This museum also operates the *Halve Maen*, a full-size replica of Hudson's ship.

32.00 Haverstraw Bay. This bay is six miles long, from Croton to Stony Point, and three miles wide. The Indian name was Kumachenack. The area on the east side was formerly called "Mother's Lap." High Tor and Hook Mountains are on the west side, and the Spitzenberg Mountains, Blue Mountain, Prickly Pear, Torment, Hessian, Airy, and Nordica Hills on the east side.

32.40 Short Clove on the west.

33.00 Mount Airy on the east (elevation 408 ft).

33.00 High Tor to the west (elevation 827 feet). A part of the Verdriedig Mountains, its geology is similar to that of Hook Mountain. There was formerly an airplane beacon atop the mountain. It is traversed by the Long Path hiking trail. Long a major landmark to navigators on the Hudson, it served as a beacon site during the Revolution. In the 1930s the New York Trap Rock Company started quarrying out the back of the mountain. The noted playwright Maxwell Anderson wrote a play entitled *High Tor* in 1937, which helped stimulate sentiment for preservation of the mountain. This verse play had a pessimistic ending, but the mountain had a happier ending. The Hudson River Conservation Society raised $12,000 and purchased the mountain from the heirs of Elmer Van Orden. In 1943 the property was acquired by the Palisades Interstate Park Commission. They removed the airplane beacon, which had been subject to repeated vandalism. Little Tor (elevation 710 feet) is to the north on the same ridge and is also reached by the Long Path. Everett Crosby's High Tor Vineyards are on the back slopes. Henry Varnum's painting of High Tor entitled *Grey Day* is in the Metropolitan Museum of Art.

33.10 Hessian Hill to the east (elevation 550 feet). Senasqua Beach to east.

33.20 Torment Hill to the east (elevation 600 feet).

33.25 Haverstraw to west (population 9,438). The name comes from the Dutch "haverstroo" or "oat straw," which grew abundantly in the swamps (the Dutch word is "hauver") along the Hudson and Minisceongo Creek. In 1671 two tracts were granted under New Jersey patents to Hendrick Van Bommel, and another to Balthazar De Hart and Nicholas DePew. Florus Willemse Crom and Minne Johannes settled here in 1681 and Reyn Van Ditmarsen in 1683. The Haverstraw Precinct was set off in 1719 and the first blacksmith established in 1720. In 1771 Jacob Van Dyke commenced the manufacture of bricks. On July 13, 1776 an attempted British landing was repulsed by local militia. After the Revolution, in 1825, followers of Robert Owen established the Franklin Community here, the first American Communist experiment. The town was incorporated in 1854.

In the 1820s red sandstone was quarried here in great quantities. Ten to twelve vessels a day would leave the docks beneath Hook Mountain.

In 1817 James Wood discovered the modern method of burning brick. As there was abundant good clay and straw (both necessary ingredients) in the vicinity, brick-making soon became an important industry. At first the bricks were mass produced in moulds compressed by a device known as Hall's Improved Machine. However, in the 1850s a local man, Richard A. Ver Valen, developed a better machine which was soon adopted and which gave great impetus to the brick industry. Coal dust and sand were mixed with the clay to impart durability to the bricks. This gave the industry a great advantage in the neighborhood, as there was also suitable sand in good quantity. It was also discovered that there were clay beds 200 ft. deep offshore beneath the river, and these were also mined. Cheap water transportation to New York also aided in growth of this major industry. In 1883 there were forty-two brick yards in operation between Long Clove and Jones Point, employing 2,400 men and with a production of 302,647,000 bricks. In 1884 there were forty-three yards between Long Clove and Tomkins Cove. At the height of production there were forty brickyards in Haverstraw alone, producing 326,000,000 bricks per annum. While bricks were also produced at other points upriver, Haverstraw was the capital of this industry. With the advent of poured concrete construction and the playing out of the clay beds the industry gradually faded away to nothing. Old clay pits, usually filled with water, can be seen in the grassy meadows between Haverstraw and Grassy Point along the Minisceongo Creek. There were major strikes in 1853 and 1877, and it was necessary to call in the militia. Both were caused by the manufacturers' cutting wages.

Today Haverstraw has light manufacturing and a large Hispanic population. Many row-type townhouses have been built in the outskirts in recent years.

33.50 Bowline Point to west. Slightly north of Haverstraw and between the Hudson and Minisceongo Creek. There is a recreation park here with a large lagoon. This is also the site of a large power plant owned jointly by the Orange & Rockland Utilities and Consolidated Edison Company of New York.

33.50 Prickly Pear Hill to east (elevation 536 feet). Washington encamped here in 1782 and used the peak as an observatory. The name comes from a species of cactus which grows abundantly here.

34.40 Oscawana to east. A small hamlet and local railroad station. End of third-rail electrification on railroad.

34.65 Oscawana Island to east. It has rocky ledges, now connected to the mainland by railroad causeways and siltation.

BOWLINE POINT POWER PLANT, Haverstraw. Photo: © Gretchen McHugh.

34.50 Little Tor to west (elevation 710 feet). See article on High Tor.

34.65 Samsondale to west. A residential section of Haverstraw inland from Bowline Point.

34.65 Garnerville to west. Inland from Samsondale, on Minisceongo Creek. This was a nineteenth-century "company town," centered around the Rockland Print Works (textile printing and dyeing). In 1828 a Scotchman named John Glass established the first works here for the printing of textiles. Later purchased by the Garner family. Red brick Gothic-style mill buildings were surrounded by rows of company houses for the workers and detached small villas for the managers. Brush Court, the Garner family mansion, was located in the west end of town. The textile operations moved south in the 1930s and the mills are sublet to a variety of light manufacturing firms. This is a good example of a Victorian factory community and is still largely intact.

34.70 Furnace Brook to east.

35.00 Grassy Point to west. This low point was originally very beautiful, being covered with a dense oak and chestnut forest and bordered by marshes and salt meadows. It is separated from the mainland by the serpentine Minisceongo Creek and Cedar Pond Brook. The mouth of this creek was crossed by what was called the Penny Bridge.

John Allison, who died in 1754, purchased the area from a certain Albert Minnie "and others." Allison left the tract to his son Joseph Allison, who in turn left it to his three sons, John, Joseph, and William. On April 9, in 1798, they sold this land to Jacob Sabriska, who shortly thereafter resold it to William Denning, Jr. On July 4, 1798, Mr. Denning sold it to his father, William Denning Sr., a wealthy lawyer, for use as a summer estate. Mr. Denning Sr. erected a handsome summer home which he used until his death.

After several years Denning sold ten acres at the south end to William Smith, a nephew of Joshua Hett Smith. Smith beautified the grounds and built a large two-story house which he called Rosa Villa.

After the death of Mr. Denning (who was a brother-in-law of Joshua Hett Smith), the property passed through the hands of Philip Verplanck, Isaac L. Pratt, and Dr. Lawrence Proudfoot. Later the property passed into the ownership of David Munn, Thomas Murphy, Abraham B. Conger, and others. It was eventually subdivided.

Dr. Lawrence Proudfoot built the first steamboat landing here in 1830. It was a popular landing because it offered adequate depth of water near the regular steamboat channel and was long an important way-landing, serving a considerable back country. Dr. Proudfoot also built a hotel and ran a bar room. In 1845 O. C. Gerow opened a general store, and James Creney opened a hotel in 1848. John I. Wiles opened a wheelwright shop and foundry in 1845, which was carried on for many years under the name of F. J. Wiles & Co. It specialized in manufacturing machinery for the quarry and brickmaking industry. During this period, there was also a shipyard and a marine railway.

A post office was established in 1834, which went under the name of North Haverstraw until 1836. In the late nineteenth and early twentieth centuries, the brick industry dominated and the forests were all cut down. Dun-colored sand hills, ugly clay pits, brick kilns, brick sheds, and tumbledown shanties covered the point, which was always under a pall of smoke and dust. Today there is a modern plant of the U.S. Gypsum Company. Several popular yacht clubs are located on the point, and, with the returning cleanliness of the waters, crabbing is again a popular pastime in the vicinity. It is an excellent place to recapture the old-time river flavor. According to an old legend, Captain Kidd buried treasure here.

35.00 Treason Hill to west. This is the hill upon which formerly stood the home of Joshua Hett Smith, which was visited by Major André on September 22, 1780. The house no longer exists. It stood on the present site of the Helen Hayes Hospital on Route 9W. (See article on André under mile 31.50, Snedeker's Landing.)

35.00 West Haverstraw to west (population 9,183). A residential community, formerly the northern terminus of the New Jersey & New York Railroad and of most West Shore Railroad commuter trains.

35.00 Crugers to east. A small hamlet and local railroad station named for John Peach Cruger, who was married to Elizabeth, granddaughter of States Morris Dyckman, owner of Boscobel on adjacent property. This place was also formerly called Cruger's Park.

35.25 Franklin D. Roosevelt Veterans' Administration Hospital on east. Formerly and more simply known as Montrose Veterans' Hospital, the hospital stands on the former estate of Boscobel, which belonged to States Morris Dyckman (1755–1806). The name means "beautiful woods" in Italian, and this name was most likely quite descriptive of the area in earlier times. In order to make room for new construction in the 1950s, the mansion was taken apart and moved and reassembled near Cold Spring (see mile 48.65). It has been completely restored with beautiful grounds and gardens and is now operated as a museum.

35.35 Minisceongo Creek to west. Also formerly known as Nappie's Kill, this creek rises in two major branches. The northern one rises in Palisades Interstate Park and is formed by the waters of Horse Chock Brook and Beaver Pond Brook. The artificial Lake Welch was formed by damming its waters. This branch flows southeastward to a junction with the southern branch near Letchworth village. The southern branch rises near Mount Ivy and flows northeastward to the junction. From Letchworth village, the stream flows east past Thiells and Garnerville to Samsondale, where it flows over Miner's or Minne's Falls to tidewater. It then turns northward behind Bowline and Grassy points and flows in a serpentine and meandering manner through garbage landfill and marshlands to an outlet at Stony Point Bay. Near its outlet, it receives the waters of Cedar Pond Brook. The old Penny Bridge crossed it near the outlet.

35.35 Cedar Pond Brook to west. Formerly known as Florus' Falls Creek and Flora's Falls Creek and also simply Cedar Brook, it rises in Lake Tiorati in Palisades Interstate Park and flows generally southeasterly as Tiorati Brook. Just west of Stony Point it is joined from the northwest by the waters of Timp Brook. It then flows east through a picturesque ravine near Stony Point village. This is now a park and is crossed by a viaduct on Route 9W. It then goes over some small falls to tidewater and meanders eastward through salt marshes to Minisceongo Creek, near its outlet into Stony Point Bay.

35.40 George's Island to east. Now attached to mainland by marshes. A public beach and park slightly to the north take their name from George's Island.

35.75 Montrose Point to east. Also known as Parson's Point. The Wagenals' House, a two-story clapboard with temple facade, ca. 1840, is on the south side of the point. The Montrose railroad station is located inland.

35.75 Stony Point Bay to west. Formerly known as Brewster's Cove. Between Grassy Point on the south and Stony Point on the north, it receives the waters of Minisceongo Creek. Home of Willow Cove Marina, Henry Corts–Prop.

35.75 Stony Point to west (village with population of 12,814). It was originally part of Haverstraw and was called North Haverstraw. In 1847 it was given a separate post office, and the name was changed to Flora Falls (a corruption of Florus' Falls). In 1865 Stony Point township split off from Haverstraw, and in 1870 the name of the village was changed to Stony

Point. The original owner of the land hereabout was Florus Crom, and the falls derived their name from him. There was a large iron works along Cedar Pond Brook in the mid-nineteenth century. A Methodist Society was formed in 1834. In 1844 William Knight opened a chemical works near Cedar Pond for the manufacture of pyroligneous acid, used at the Garnerville Print Works. Today the town is largely residential.

36.20 Stony Point to west. This is a high rocky headland jutting straight out into the river (elevation 150 feet). The river here is scarcely more than half a mile wide. Low, sandy Verplanck's Point is opposite to the northeast. Located at the southern gateway to the Highlands and commanding a narrow river pass, Stony Point was of considerable strategic military value during the Revolution. The Kings Ferry, which was a vital communications link, was located immediately to the north.

The Americans built a fort here early in the Revolution. They built another, called Fort Lafayette, on Verplanck's Point, just across the river. On June 1, 1779, both were captured from the Americans by British forces, which had been conveyed up the Hudson by Admiral Collier. Verplanck's Point, which was protected by only seventy men, was taken by Gen. Sir John Vaughan. Stony Point, which was garrisoned by only about forty men under Capt. Armstrong, was occupied by troops under the personal command of Sir Henry Clinton. The small American garrison did not attempt a defense, but retreated upon approach of the British, and the fort changed hands without bloodshed. The next morning, the British trained the cannons and guns of Stony Point upon Fort Lafayette on Verplanck's Point. Gen. Vaughan attacked Fort Lafayette from the rear simultaneously with the bombardment from Stony Point. The Americans surrendered themselves as prisoners of war.

The first months of 1779 found the British Commander, Sir Henry Clinton, located at New York City. George Washington and the Continental Army were encamped at Middlebrook, New Jersey, in the Raritan Valley, in the foothills of the Watchung Mountains. Clinton was playing a cat and mouse game, attempting to draw Washington into a full-scale battle that would be decisive. When he could not gain this end, he decided upon the campaign against the Highland fortifications. He decided to devote 6,000 troops to this venture, with a minimum goal of gaining control of the important King's Ferry, thus lengthening the American supply lines.

To strengthen the Highlands, Washington marched

his troops from Middlebrook to Smith's Clove in the Western Highlands. He posted troops at New Windsor and strengthened the garrisons of the various Highland fortifications. Lacking sufficient strength to penetrate farther up the Hudson, Clinton garrisoned Stony Point and Verplanck's Point with 1,000 troops and ordered raids on Connecticut coastal towns in another attempt to lure Washington into open field. Stony Point was garrisoned by men of the 17th Regiment of Foot, grenadier's companies of the 71st Regiment, and some artillery—all under the command of Lt. Col. Henry Johnson of the 7th Regiment. Washington burned to regain control of Stony Point, but felt that it was too strongly defended to be worth the attempt.

...General Anthony Wayne, known as "Mad Anthony," on account of his impetuosity and daring in the service, was then in command of the Americans in the neighborhood. Burning with a desire to retake the forts, he applied to Washington for permission to make the attempt. It would be perilous in the extreme. The position of the fort was almost impregnable. Situated upon a high rocky peninsula, an island at high water, and always inaccessible dryshod, except across a narrow causeway, it was strongly defended by outworks and a double row of abattis. Upon three sides of the rock were the waters of the Hudson, and on the fourth was a morass, deep and dangerous. The cautious Washington considered; when the impetuous Wayne, scorning all obstacles, said, "General, I'll storm hell if you will only plan it!"

Permission to attack Stony Point was given (July 10, 1779), preparations were secretly made, and near midnight, on the 15th of July, Wayne led a strong force of determined men towards the fortress.

(Lossing, The Hudson, pp. 282–283.)

At about 8 o'clock in the evening, on July 15, a force of one thousand picked men were formed into two columns near Springsteel's farm, back of Buckberg Mountain. One detachment, under the command of Colonel Richard Butler, had come from an encampment at Queensboro, in back of Bear Mountain, on the upper reaches of Popolopen Creek. That same morning, all the Massachusetts Light Infantry were marched to the headquarters of General Wayne at Sandy Beach, fourteen miles from Stony Point. It was a scorchingly hot day. At noon they started their eight-hour march over narrow trails over Dunderberg Mountain. Advance word had been sent to kill all the dogs in the vicinity so that their barking would not betray the troop movements.

Some advance espionage had been undertaken by a slave named Pompey, whose master was an ardent patriot. He had gotten into the habit of visiting Stony Point to sell fresh strawberries and cherries to the troops stationed there, and was able to obtain the countersign, "The fort's our own," of which good use was made in tricking the outlying sentries.

Shortly before midnight, when ebb tide was expected, Pompey led the troops toward Stony Point. Several outlying pickets were quickly dispatched and the troops soon arrived at the causeway.

Here the army split into three main parts. The southern group was under the overall command of Gen. Wayne and Lt. Col. De Fleury. The northern group was commanded by Col. Butler and Maj. Stewart. A small group under Maj. Murfee was to keep up a diversionary fire and attack the main landward approach. The two main bodies, under Wayne and Butler, were to skirt the southern and northern sides of the point and then turn to join in the middle of the fortifications. Each of the main columns was led by twenty picked men, under Lieutenants Gibbon and Knox, who cut through obstructions.

Because he believed that success demanded surprise and swift, close combat, Wayne ordered his men to carry unloaded muskets with fixed bayonets. No guns were to be loaded under penalty of death. Each soldier and officer put a piece of white paper in his hat to distinguish himself from the foe.

The attack began shortly after midnight. General Wayne forded the marsh on the south, covered at that time with two feet of water. The other column, under Colonel Butler and Major Murfee, crossed the causeway. They then split, with Colonel Butler going along the north side, and the men in the center, under Major Murfee, opening a diversionary fire.

...They advanced undiscovered until within pistol-shot of the picket guard on the heights. The garrison were suddenly aroused from sleep, and the deep silence of the night was broken by the roll of the drum, the loud cry "To arms! to arms!" the rattle of musketry from the ramparts and behind the abattis, and the roar of cannon charged with deadly grapeshot. In the face of this terrible storm the Americans made their way, by force of bayonet, to the center of the works. Wayne was struck upon the head by a musket ball that brought him upon his knees. "March on!" he cried. "Carry me into the fort, for I will die at the head of my column!" The wound was not very severe, and in an hour he had sufficiently recovered to write the following note to Washington:

"Stony Point, 16th July, 1779
2 o'clock, A. M.

*"Dear General,—The fort and garrison, with Colonel
Johnston, are ours. Our officers and men behaved
like men who are determined to be free.*
                                        "Yours most respectfully,
                                              "Anthony Wayne."
                            (Lossing, *The Hudson*, pp. 283–284.)

It is recorded that General Wayne was carried over
the rampart by his two aides, Fishbow and Archer,
after being wounded. Only fifteen minutes of bloody,
savage fighting brought the British to surrender. Only
fifteen Americans were killed and eighty-three
wounded. Estimates of the number of British killed
vary from twenty to sixty-three, with no count of
wounded. It is believed that about sixty escaped. We
took 543 prisoners.

The next morning the cannons were again turned
upon Fort Lafayette, which was then commanded by
Lt. Col. Webster. However, Sir Henry Clinton sent
relief, and the Americans did not succeed in recap-
turing Fort Lafayette. Lacking the men to hold Stony
Point, Wayne evacuated it three days later on the
night of July 18th, after destruction of the fortifications and removal of ordnance and stores to the
value of $180,000. These were loaded on a galley
and started for West Point. However, off Jones
Point, the galley was fired upon and sunk by the
British ship *Vulture*.

The main importance of this victory was to raise
American morale. It also removed about 600 British
troops from action. Most of the prisoners were in-
terned near Easton, Pennsylvania, whence they were
escorted by Count Casimir Pulaski and his cavalry
troop that was posted at Minisink, now known as
Port Jervis. Congress ordered a gold medal struck in
honor of the event and presented to General
Wayne. Silver copies of this medal were given to
two of the subordinate officers engaged in the enter-
prise. Cash was distributed to the troops.

Clinton immediately reoccupied Stony Point on
July 20th and built stronger fortifications. However,
he lacked the troops to penetrate further into the
Highlands and withdrew from Stony Point and Fort
Lafayette in October of 1779. He then turned his
attention to the war in the south.

A battlefield museum was opened in 1936, and the
area is now maintained by the Palisades Interstate
Park Commission.

The other major feature of Stony Point is the lighthouse. It was built of fieldstone in 1826 upon the site
of the old central powder magazine. It was thirty
feet high with a fixed white light, at an elevation of
179 feet above the water. It operated for one hundred years, when it was replaced with a small
modern electric light on the rocks nearer the water.
There was also a mechanical fog signal housed in a
pyramidal wooden housing. Old engravings show
what appears to be a weight suspended by a rope
running over a pulley, similar to the apparatus of
some grandfather's clocks. Possibly this activated a
bell or worked a bellows and trumpet.

36.25 Green's Cove to the east. It receives the waters of Meahagh Creek. Montrose Point is to the
south; Verplanck's Point is to the north.

36.50 Lake Meahagh to the east. This Indian name
stands for a creek which formerly meandered
through marshes east of Verplanck's point. It was
dammed for the purposes of cutting ice and was renamed Knickerbocker Pond, for the ice company
which operated there.

36.50 Collaberg Mountain to east. Also called
Coleberg Mountain.

36.75 King's Ferry. Former colonial ferry between
Verplanck's Point and Stony Point.

36.75 Verplanck Point on east. Formerly Verplanck's
Point, this is a broad and low sandy peninsula between the Hudson River on the west and south and
Meahagh Creek, or Knickerbocker Lake, now known
as Lake Meahagh on the east. It rises to elevations
of 100 feet at its northern end. The Indians called it
Meahagh Point. It was purchased from the Indians in
1683 by Stephanus Van Cortlandt. It next passed to
his son Johannes, whose daughter Gertrude married
Philip Verplanck, who gave it the present name.

It was the eastern terminus of the important
King's Ferry. Early in the Revolution, the Americans
built a fort near the southern extremity, overlooking
the Hudson, which they called Fort Lafayette. The
details of this fort's history have been told in the
preceding article on Stony Point, with whose history
it is inextricably joined.

After the withdrawal of the British from Fort
Lafayette in October 1779, the Americans again took
possession and put James Livingston in command.
On September 20 and 21, 1782, Gen. Washington
was encamped here and reviewed the American
troops and Rochambeau's French troops, and held a
large military banquet. This was also the place where
Henry Hudson first came to anchor after leaving the
mouth of the river. He attracted many Indians, one
of whom was shot and killed when he attempted to
steal a pillow and several other articles from a cabin.
Another Indian was drowned after his hand had
been cut off by a sword during an attempt to climb
into one of the ship's boats.

During a period of intense land speculation in 1836, a large village was mapped out and several fine mansions erected. Previously the area had been given over to the growth of corn and potatoes. Toward about the middle of the nineteenth century, the Cambrian limestone began to attract quarry operations. Brick making was also carried on for many years. Many fishermen of Italian descent live here now.

36.75 Former site of Sunset Park to east. This was a picnic reservation operated from 1924 to 1928 by the Central Hudson Steamship Lines. It was on the inner side of Verplanck Point.

36.80 Quarries to west. See article on Tomkin's Cove.

36.80 Ten Eyck's Beach to west. Named for an old ferryman named Tenyck whose family operated the ferry from 1784 until the mid-1860s and who lived here, at the western terminus of the King's Ferry.

37.00 Mountain panorama to west (from west to east). Pingyp Mountain (elevation 1,023 feet), Buckberg Mountain (elevation 793 feet), the Timp (elevation 846 feet), Bald Mountain (elevation 1,100 feet), and Dunderberg Mountain (elevation 1,086 feet). (Pingyp also spelled Pyngyp, and Buckberg was also known as Boulderberg.)

Pyngyp is from the Latin "piniger" or "pine bearing." Another possible explanation of the name Pingyp comes from an old Dutch nautical term, "pijngjip," which is an onomatopoeic word describing the sound made as the boom of a fore-and-aft-rigged vessel, such as a schooner or sloop, comes around on a tack. This is a cracking sound. Possibly the old Hudson mariners, who used the neighboring mountains to steer by, used this mountain as a point for changing course.

The name Timp comes from the Dutch "timpje," meaning a small cake or bun.

37.00 Mountain panorama to east (from west to east). Manitou Mountain (elevation 700 feet), Gallows Hill (elevation 400 feet), Jacob's Hill (elevation 600 feet), Fort Hill (elevation 320 feet), the city of Peekskill, Blue Mountain (elevation 640 feet), and Spitzenberg Mountain (elevation 560 feet). Both Blue Mountain and Spitzenberg are in what is called the Spitzenberg Mountains. Both lie within the limits of the Westchester County Park Commission's Blue Mountain Reservation. This is a forest preserve. The mountains are glacier-smoothed hogbacks. There are open bluestone ledges on the south side of Spitzenberg which offer a breathtaking view over Haverstraw Bay. The rock is norite, a blend of

hornblende and mica. It is gray colored with a pink tinge. There are also emory deposits.

37.35 Bulsontown to west. Inland beyond Buckberg Mountain.

37.35 Tomkin's Cove to west. This locality is noted for its limestone quarrying industry. As early as 1789, John Crom built a small lime kiln, but nothing much else developed during the next half century. In 1838, Daniel Tomkins discovered the limestone in this area only by searching carefully from Hoboken to the present Tomkin's Cove. During and after his search, he made several trips on foot between Haverstraw and Newark. The limestone beds which he discovered occupy a superficial area of nearly 600 acres, extending to the rear of Stony and Grassy Points, where they disappear beneath the red sandstone formation. They're traversed by white veins of carbonate of lime. Some of it is black and variegated, which makes pleasing ornamental "marbles," but most of it is blue.

"In the spring of 1838, having purchased twenty acres of land the year before for $100 an acre, Daniel Tomkins embarked at Newark, New Jersey, on board a sloop named Contrivance, *with sixteen men, one woman, one horse, one cow, and a small quantity of lumber, and set sail for his new home. Upon arriving at the now thriving hamlet of Tomkin's Cove, the men and woman were landed by small boat, while the animals were lowered into the water and allowed to find their own way to shore. A shanty for shelter was at once erected, and on the following day the work of quarrying out the limestone was begun.*

This branch of business proved a success from the outset, and has steadily continued to increase in importance. Beside the manufacture of lime, the company owning the cliff has added to its business by crushing limestone for macadamizing purposes.

When first begun, the business at Tomkins Cove was carried on under the name of Tomkins, Hadden & Co. At a later period, the firm was changed to Calvin Tomkins & Co., and the members were Calvin and Daniel Tomkins and Walter Searing. In 1859, the Tomkins Cove Lime Company was formed, and since that time the business has been conducted in its name."

(Cole, *History of Rockland County*)

The principal cliff workings were nearly 200 feet high and stretched along the river for one-half mile. Several wharves were erected for easy transfer to sloops and barges. The lime was slaked before shipment to prevent combustion. By 1865 the works were producing a million bushels per year and employed 100 men. Thousands of tons of stone annually were shipped to kilns in New

Jersey. Each year, 20,000–25,000 tons of "gravel" were shipped to New York City, where they were used to macadamise roads in Central Park and private driveways.

Calvin Tomkins & Co. opened a store near the landing in 1842. In 1850, a shipyard was started and a marine railway built. The post office was established March 15, 1860.

Calvin Tomkins was born in 1793 near Orange, New Jersey. He served in the War of 1812 and came to this area in 1834, after having established several successful businesses in Newark, New Jersey. His brother Daniel joined him in 1838, as described previously. Eventually their business included brick yards, plaster manufacturing facilities, and large real estate holdings, and extended as far away as New Brunswick, Canada. In 1858 Calvin Tomkins built a large private mansion for himself using poured concrete as the prime building material. It is believed that this was New York State's first poured concrete building. It is Gothic in style and is embellished by curved and carved bargeboards, diamond panes, and rich moldings. There is a central hot-air heating system employing sheetmetal-lined ducts embedded in the concrete walls. The interior is richly decorated. After Mr. Tomkin's death in 1892 at the age of 99, the property came into the hands of Charles S. Wood. For a period of time it was operated as the Boulderberg Manor Restaurant.

37.35 Ramapo Fault and Escarpment on east and west. Buckberg and Dunderberg Mountains represent the eastern end of the Ramapo Mountains, which extend southwest to the area of Oakland, New Jersey. The name was also spelled Ramapaugh, Remopuck, Remepog, Ramopog, and Ramapaw—which in Indian dialect means either "rugged country of the waterfalls" or "place of sloping rock." The fault line along its southern foot was created in the Cambro-Ordovician period. This has been supposed to be a relatively inactive fault line. However, in recent years, earthquakes in the vicinity of Mahwah and Oakland, New Jersey, have raised serious questions. The chief concern is that the Indian Point Nuclear Power Plant sits almost directly on top of the fault line.

37.36 Parc Marine and Villa Zagoreos to west. Former estate of Tomkins family.

37.37 Lovett plant of Orange and Rockland Utilities, Inc. on west. Originally designed to use coal brought in by seventy-five-car trains, it now burns low-sulphur oil, brought in by barge, to meet air environmental standards. Boilers and furnaces are designed so that they can operate on either fuel.

37.40 Overhead power cables across river.

37.40 Boulderberg Manor on west. See Tomkin's Cove article for details.

38.00 Former Reserve Fleet Anchorage on west. Between 1946 and 1971, 189 ships were anchored here. Most of them were Liberty Ship type freighters built for World War II, but a few fighting ships and passenger liners, including the big *George Washington,* were also stored here, anchored side to side in long rows perpendicular to the shoreline. Up until 1963, the ships were used to store surplus grain. Each ship could store 6,000 tons, or 225,000 bushels. Ninety-four men under a fleet superintendent kept watch over the "mothball fleet." Ships were reactivated for the Korean conflict, the Suez Crisis, and the Vietnam War. Ships were also stored here after World War I. This location was chosen because of the twice-daily alternation between fresh and salt water brought about by tidal action. This, plus low-voltage electric charges, inhibited build-up of marine incrustations such as barnacles.

38.25 Rose Town on west. Beyond the hill not visible from river.

38.25 Indian Point on east. Site of Indian Point Park, operated by the Hudson River Day Line. This park offered facilities for picnicking, dining in a cafeteria, swimming, strolling through the woods, or simply relaxing. The Day Line claimed that this property had been a meeting place for Indians. It covered 320 acres and included a farm for the raising of vegetables for use on the steamers. It opened for business in 1923. There were two piers here, and they were sometimes used for winter storage of ships. The Day Line steamers continued to call here until 1956. The property was then sold to Consolidated Edison Company for construction of a nuclear power plant.

The $90,000,000 nuclear reactor steam-electric generating station was scheduled for completion in 1960, but did not get into operation until 1963. In 1978 the plant was doubled in capacity. Tours of the

INDIAN POINT NUCLEAR POWER PLANT. Photo © Gretchen McHugh.

facility are available. Conservationists voiced concern about the warm water being returned to the river, and, in 1963, there was an incident where large numbers of striped bass fingerlings were drawn into the water intakes and killed. Many are concerned about the proximity of the Ramapo Fault.

38.50 Buchanan to east. A small residential community inland from Indian Point.

38.50 Caldwell's Landing to west. Formerly called Gibraltar. This was part of the Cheesecocks Patents of 1707. Joshua Colwil settled here before 1800. He was descended from John Cholwell, one of the original patentees. On March 19, 1800, he was granted by legislative act the right, in conjunction with Joseph Travis of Peekskill, to run a ferry across the river from his landing to that of Travis, in the south end of Peekskill. In the early nineteenth century there was a popular hotel located here. In his *New Mirror For Travellers* of 1828, James Kirke Paulding says of the Donderbarrack:

> ... at whose foot dwells in all the feudal majesty (only a great deal better) of a Rhoderick Dhu, the famous highland chieftain, Caldwell, lord of Donderbarrack, and all the little hills that grow out of his ample sides like warts on a giant's nose. To this mighty chieftain, all the steam boats do homage, by ringing of bells, stopping their machinery, and sending their boats ashore to carry him the customary tribute, to wit, store of visitors, whom it is his delight to entertain at his hospitable castle. This stately pile is of great antiquity; its history being lost in the dark ages of the last century, when the Indian prowled about these hills, and shot his deer ere the rolling wave of the white man swept him away forever.

(Paulding, *New Mirror For Travellers*, pp. 115–116.)

During the War of 1812, the Navy wished to establish a shipyard here, which would be less exposed to enemy attack than the one at Brooklyn. However, Colwil, or Caldwell, was a Federalist, and considered the war iniquitous. He placed so disproportionate a valuation upon his property that the government at once abandoned the project.

A post office was opened here in 1885. Shortly thereafter Charles H. Jones, a resident of Long Island, who owned some property in the vicinity, prevailed upon the postal and railroad authorities to give his name to the locale.

38.50 Jones Point to the west.

39.00 Lent's Cove to the east. The outlet of Dickey Brook. Indian Point is to the south and Charles Point to the north. British troops landed here for a raid on Peekskill in 1777.

39.00 Dickey Brook to the east. Rises on northern slopes of Blue Mountain and flows southwest, through Lounsbury Pond, to just north of Buchanan, thence northwest into Lent's Cove.

39.25 Charles Point to the east. Separates Lent's Cove on the south from the outlet of MacGregory Brook on the north. It was the site of the Fleischmann Yeast plant of Standard Brands, the largest of its type in the world. It was self-contained with 130 buildings and its own electric and steam plants. Today it is the site of a giant incinerator and cogeneration plant for the County of Westchester. New headquaters of the National Maritime Historical Society.

39.40 MacGregory Brook to east. Rises in eastern section of Peekskill, near Beecher Park, and flows west to Lake Penelope, thence southwest to Peekskill Bay.

39.45 Travis Point to east. This is a small point near southern end of Peekskill Bay, at foot of Mount St. Francis, the former eastern terminal of the ferry to Caldwell's Landing operated by Joshua Colwil and Joseph Travis.

39.50 Peekskill Bay to east. At outlet of Peek's Kill, or Annsville Creek. Roa Hook is to the north and Flatrock, Fort Hill, and the city of Peekskill are to the east. Travis and Charles Points are to the south. It is very shallow, varying from three to five feet in depth, save for a channel seven feet deep leading to the wharves. Some shoals have only one foot of water. Boatmen beware!

39.50 Peekskill to east. A city with population of 19,536, Peekskill is primarily residential, located at northern extremity of convenient rail commuting to New York City. There is some manufacturing as well as several foundries.

PEEKSKILL BAY. View is looking north. Mountains, from left to right, are Dunderberg, Bear, and Manitou. Photo: Alfred V. S. Olcott, Jr.

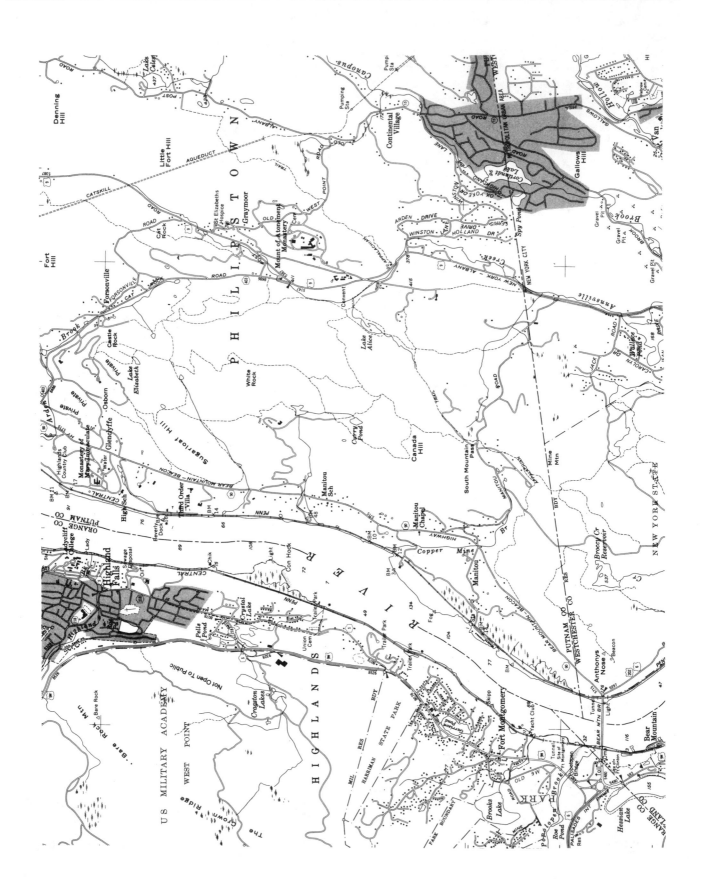

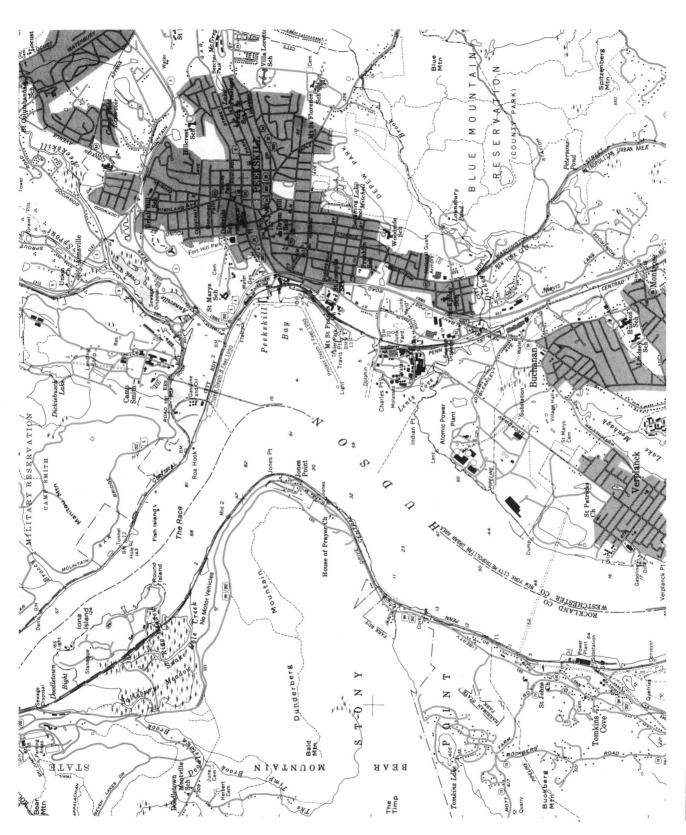

The Indians called this area Appamaghpogh, and the immediate vicinity of Peekskill Sackhoes. It belonged to the Kitchawong Tribe. In 1665 this area was granted as the Ryck's Patent and for many years formed an enclave in the surrounding Van Cortlandt Patent. A Dutch trader by the name of Jan Peek founded a trading colony here in 1697, on the banks of the creek which bears his name. He had sailed up this creek in the belief that it was the main channel of the Hudson. He was disabused when his ship hung up on a sandbar.

Neighboring Van Cortlandtville, two miles up the creek from the Hudson, was the seat of the Upper Manor of Van Cortlandt. In 1767 Catherine Van Cortlandt, daughter of the first lord of the manor, who was married to Andrew Johnson, founded St. Peter's Episcopal Church. It has recently been restored. In its churchyard are buried fifty-four Revolutionary soldiers and John Paulding, one of André's captors. This graveyard was established in 1752. Nearby is the family graveyard of the Van Cortlandt family.

Cornelia, daughter of Pierre Van Cortlandt, who was married to Gerard G. Beekman, lived at the Upper Manor. Her house served as George Washington's headquarters in 1776, 1777, and 1778. This area was used as a supply depot by the Americans and came to be called Continental Village. The depot and village were burned by the British on October 9, 1777. Across the creek, to the north, is Gallows Hill. Here, in August 1777, a British spy by the name of Nathan Palmer was hanged by General Israel Putnam. In response to a letter of inquiry from the British Command concerning Palmer's fate, Putnam answered: "Nathan Palmer was taken as a spy, tried as a spy, and will be hanged as a spy." P.S.—"He is hanged."

Peekskill was incorporated as a village in 1816 and as a city in 1940. The Peekskill Military Academy, which is over one hundred years old, was the first academy in the country after West Point to incorporate the military feature into its training. St. Mary's School for Girls occupies a conspicuous site atop Fort Hill.

Notable natives have been John Paulding, one of André's captors, Peter Cooper, early industrialist and philanthropist, Henry Ward Beecher, a famous preacher, and Chauncey M. Depew, president of the New York Central Railroad, senator, orator, and wit.

39.60 Fort Hill to east. This hill lies within Peekskill's city limits. St. Mary's School for Girls occupies its summit.

39.60 Flatrock to east. At the foot of Fort Hill, near the railroad.

39.75 Annsville Creek to east. Formerly called Peek's Kill and Peekskill Creek, its Indian name was Sackboes Creek. Its present name comes from the small community of Annsville, about one mile upstream on the north bank. It is tidal for about a mile upstream, where it is formed by three branches, all flowing generally from the northeast. The northernmost branch is simply called Annsville Creek and rises in Philipstown in the Manitou Mountains. The middle branch is called Sprout Brook in its lower reaches and Canopus Creek further upstream, and rises between the Taconic and Manitou Mountains, after which it flows southwest through Canopus Hollow. The southernmost branch, called Peekskill Hollow Brook, rises in Lake Peekskill, and flows southwest along the base of the Manitou Mountains.

This creek was originally named after early settler Jan Peek who mistook it for the main channel of the Hudson, until he ran aground on a sandbar. He established a trading post on its banks in 1697.

Its mouth is spanned by a railroad bridge and causeway 1,496 feet long called Cortlandt Bridge.

39.80–51.55 Putnam County on the east. 1990 population 83,941. Largely rural and mountainous.

4

The Highlands of the Hudson

40.00 Dunderberg Mountain to west (elevation 865 feet). This name is Dutch for "Thunder Mountain," as it was believed to brew storms. Another old Dutch name for it was Donderbarrack. According to Washington Irving, in his story "The Storm Ship,"

The captains of the river craft talk of a little bulbous-bottomed Dutch goblin, in trunk hose and sugar-loafed hat, with a speaking-trumpet in his hand, which, they say, keeps the Donder Berg. They declare that they have heard him, in stormy weather, in the midst of the turmoil, giving orders in Low Dutch, for the piping up of a fresh gust of wind, or the rattling off of another thunderclap. That sometimes he has been seen surrounded by a crew of little imps, in broad breeches and short doublets, tumbling head over heels in the rack and mist, and playing a thousand gambols in the air, or buzzing like a swarm of flies about Anthony's Nose; and that, at such times, the hurry-scurry of the storm was always greatest. One time a sloop, in passing by the Donder Berg, was overtaken by a thunder-gust that came scouring round the mountain, and seemed to burst just over the vessel. Though tight and well ballasted, she laboured dreadfully, and the water came over the gunwale. All the crew were amazed, when it was discovered that there was a little sugar-loaf hat on the masthead, known at once to be the

hat of the Heer of the Donder Berg. Nobody, however, dared to climb to the masthead, and get rid of this terrible hat. The sloop continued labouring and rocking, as if she would have rolled her mast overboard, and seemed in continual danger, either of upsetting, or of running on shore. In this way she drove quite through the Highlands, until she had passed Pollopel's Island, where, it is said, the jurisdiction of the Donder Berg potentate ceases. No sooner had she passed this bourne, than the little hat sprung up into the air like a top, whirled up all the clouds into a vortex, and hurried them back to the summit of the Donder Berg, while the sloop righted herself, and sailed on as quietly as if in a mill-pond. Nothing saved her from utter wreck but the fortunate circumstance of having a horse-shoe nailed against the mast—a wise precaution against evil spirits, since adopted by all the Dutch captains that navigate this haunted river.

There is another story told of this foul-weather urchin, by Skipper Daniel Ouslesticker, of Fish Kill, who was never known to tell a lie. He declared that, in a severe squall, he saw him seated astride of his bowsprit, riding the sloop ashore, full butt against Anthony's Nose, and that he was exorcised by Dominie Van Geisen, of Esopus, who happened to be on board, and who sang the hymn of St. Nicholas, whereupon the goblin threw himself up in the air like a ball, and went off in a whirlwind, carrying away with him the nightcap of the Dominie's wife, which was discovered the next Sunday morning hanging on the weather-cock of Esopus church steeple, at least forty miles off. Several events of this kind having taken place, the regular skippers of the river for a long time did not venture to pass the Donder Berg without lowering their peaks, out of homage to the Heer of the Mountains; and it was observed that all such as paid this tribute of respect were suffered to pass unmolested.

(Washington Irving, "The Storm Ship")

DUNDERBERG MOUNTAIN AND SLOOP *CLEARWATER*, 1969. Picture taken looking south from sidewheel steamer *Alexander Hamilton*. Photo: Arthur G. Adams.

Another interesting feature of this mountain is the uncompleted Dunderberg Spiral Railroad. It had been planned to hold the great Columbian Exposition on

Verplanck's Point in 1893. However, this plan fell through owing to a financial panic and ensuing depression. However, in 1889 a corporation had been formed by T. L. and H. J. Mumford of Mauch Chunk, Pennsylvania, to build a palatial hotel atop Dunderberg and a series of inclined planes and a gravity railroad on the southern and eastern faces of the mountain. There was such a system in operation at Mauch Chunk for many years and it was a great popular tourist attraction. There was nothing chimerical about this project. The hotel on the summit was to be reached by two inclined planes, such as operated on Mt. Beacon, totaling one mile in length. The cars were to return to the level of the river over a nine-mile course of loops and dips offering pleasant views of the surrounding countryside. They were to descend by gravity alone. Grading was begun in 1890; however, funds ran out in 1891 and the railway was never completed. Some of the grading, including a short tunnel, can still be seen by hikers on the mountain. The old highway skirted the foot of the mountain, near the present West Shore Railroad. The new Route 9W crosses a shoulder of the Dunderberg, offering fine views, particularly after the leaves are off the trees. The popular Dunderberg-Suffern hiking trail starts here.

Anthony Wayne's troops crossed the mountain on an old trail, somewhat inland from the river, prior to the attack on Stony Point, on July 15, 1779. Also, on the afternoon of October 6, 1777, British troops were led across this same trail, under cover of mist and fog, by a loyalist resident in the vicinity, on their way to attack Forts Clinton and Montgomery. A diversionary attack was made upon Fort Independence on Roa Hook, across the river.

40.20 Kidd's Point on west. This point takes its name from a curious and rather involved incident. Captain William Kidd was born near Greenock, Scotland, in about the middle of the seventeenth century. He later resided in New York City, near the corner of William and Cedar Streets, and here he was married. He made the acquaintance of Robert Livingston, the wealthy merchant, and it is believed that Livingston backed some of Kidd's later ventures. In April 1696 he sailed from England in command of the *Adventure Galley*, with full armament and eighty men. He captured a French ship, and, on arrival at New York, put up articles for volunteers. He remained in New York three or four months, increasing his crew to 155 men—mostly from above the Highlands. He sailed then to Madras, Bonavista, and St. Jago, Madagascar. He then went to Calicut and then back to Madagascar. After this he took the Moorish ship *Quedah Merchant.* Kidd kept forty shares of the

spoils, and divided the rest with his crew. He then burned the *Adventure Galley*, went on board the *Quedah Merchant*, and steered for the West Indies. Here he left the *Merchant*, with part of his crew, under one Bolton as commander. He manned a sloop and took his spoils to Boston, via Long Island Sound. It is claimed that he set goods on shore at different places. In the meantime, in August 1698, the East Indian Company informed the Lords' Justice that Kidd had committed several acts of piracy, including the taking of the *Quedah Merchant*. When Kidd landed at Boston, he was arrested by the Earl of Bellomont, and sent to England for trial in 1699. He was found guilty and executed at the Water Gate of the Tower of London in 1701. It is generally believed in the Hudson Highlands that the crew of the *Quedah Merchant*, which Kidd left at Hispaniola, sailed for their homes in the Highlands and further upriver, passing New York in the night, en route to Livingston Manor. They encountered a gale in the Highlands, and thinking they were pursued, ran her near the shore near Kidd's Point and scuttled her, the crew taking to the woods with such treasure as they could carry. It was believed that much treasure went down with the *Quedah Merchant*.

A modern tale of skullduggery is appended to this, as told by Benson Lossing, in his *The Hudson* of 1866:

...several years ago...the steam engine of an immense pumping apparatus was in operation at Donder Berg Point. Concerning that engine and its co-workers, there is a curious tale of mingled fraud, superstition, credulity, and "gullibility," that vies with many a plot born in the romancer's brain. It cannot be told here. The simple outlines are, that some years ago an iron cannon was, by accident, brought up from the river depths at this point. Some speculator, as the story goes, at once conceived a scheme of fraud, for the success of which he relied on the average ignorance and credulity of mankind. It was boldly proclaimed, in the face of recorded history, that Captain Kidd's piratical vessel was sunken in a storm at this spot with untold treasures on board, and that one of its cannons had been raised. Further, that the deck of his vessel had been penetrated by a very long augur, hard substances encountered by it, and pieces of silver brought up in its thread—the evidence of coffers of specie below. This augur with its bits of silver was exhibited, and the story believed. A stock company was formed. Shares were readily taken. The speculator was chief manager. A coffer dam was made over the supposed resting place of the treasure-ship. A steam engine and huge pumps, driven by it, were set in motion. Day after

day, and month after month, the work went on. One credulous New York merchant invested 20,000 dollars in the scheme. The speculator took large commissions. Hope failed, the work stopped, and nothing now remains to tell the tale but the ruins of the coffer dam and the remains of the pumps, which may be seen on a level with the surface of the river, at high water.

(Lossing, *The Hudson*, pp. 242–243)

Wallace Bruce adds the additional information that it was claimed that the ship could be seen on clear days, with her masts still standing, many fathoms below the surface; and that the Treasurer of the firm disappeared with $30,000.

Kidd's Point is also called Caldwell's Point, Jones Point, and Donder Berg Point.

40.30 Roa Hook on east. Also called Royer's Point, it is located at the northern side of the mouth of Annsville Creek.

40.30 Site of Fort Independence on east. On the high bluff at the western end of Roa Hook.

40.30 The Highlands. Ahead and on either side north to Newburgh Bay. These mountains were well described by Charles Callison, Executive Vice President of the National Audubon Society, while testifying against construction of a pumped storage facility at Storm King Mountain. He said:

...the Highlands are the most beautiful stretch of river scenery in the United States. [Its beauty is directly related] to the dominant geological feature of the eastern United States, the Appalachian Mountains. [It is] one of the very few places where the main chain of the Appalachians is broken by a river...the French Broad, at the base of the Great Smokies, cuts through the main chain. And the Susquehanna, starting in central New York's Otsego Lake, journeys southwest and then turns southeast to go through several of the Appalachian ridges of Pennsylvania. The Delaware, Connecticut, and James Rivers also cut through one or more of the main chains of the mountains, often with striking beauty. Yet nowhere, in my opinion, is the impact as great as it is through the Highlands. In the Smokies, of course, the French Broad cuts a deeper valley and is flanked by higher mountains. But there the river is shallow and narrow, a small stream practically hidden by the scale of the mountains. At the Delaware Water Gap there are also high hills. Yet in the Highlands—and only in the Highlands—the river cuts the Appalachian at sea level. And with a relative breadth it creates river scenery of an unequaled scale,

bounded on both banks by the precipitous hills. Here we have not simply a river, but an estuary...with the tides of the Atlantic literally cutting through the mountains. Here alone we have ocean-going vessels passing through a great mountain chain and traveling ninety miles on to the heartland. And here, too, and again here alone—we have Storm King Mountain—a headland unique in its height and sheer rise from the river.

(Federal Power Commission Hearing Testimony, November, 1966 *"Storm King Pumped Storage,"* U.S. Govt. Printing Office.)

At a much earlier date, James Fenimore Cooper observed in his novel, *The Spy* that:

To be seen in their perfection, the Highlands must be passed immediately after the fall of the leaf. The scene is then the finest, for neither the scanty foliage which the summer lends the trees, nor the snows of winter, are present to conceal the minutest objects from the eye. Chilling solitude is the characteristic of the scenery; nor is the mind at liberty, as in March, to look forward to a renewed vegetation that is soon to check, without improving, the view.

The Indians called these mountains the Kittatinny Mountains, a name since appropriated by the southern extension of the Shawangunks in New Jersey. Technically speaking, the mountains on the western side are the Ramapo Mountains, and those on the eastern side are the Manitou Mountains, a southern extension of the Taconic-Berkshire Chain.

The Appalachian Trail, affectionately known to hikers as the "A.T.," crosses the Hudson River here on the Bear Mountain Bridge. This trail, conceived by Benton Mackaye in 1921, runs from Mt. Katahdin in Maine to Mt. Oglethorpe in Georgia, along the crest of the Older Appalachians. The first section was completed in 1923, and the entire trail in 1937.

Old guidebook writers placed the Southern Gateway to the Highlands at Dunderberg, and the Northern Gateway at Storm King. This area was of great strategic importance during the Revolution, as the narrowness and bends of the Hudson made sailing ships vulnerable to gun batteries on shore. Principal fortifications in the area included Stony Point, Fort Lafayette, Fort Independence, Fort Clinton, Fort Montgomery, West Point, Fort Putnam, and Fort Constitution—not to mention numerous small gun emplacements and the various chevaux-de-frise and chains. Washington made his headquarters and chief supply depots here and just above at Newburgh, New Windsor, and Fishkill, and inland at Smith's Clove and Continental Village. The Highlands made possible keeping intact the lines of communications and supply between New England and the rest of the colonies, and kept the British from the breadbasket of the central Hudson region.

40.30 The Race. This is the stretch of river from here to Bear Mountain, also known formerly as the Horse Race, and the Devil's Horse Race, from the swiftness of the current here, the fastest on the river. This is one of the narrowest parts of the river below Albany, with depths up to 165 feet. The river here is only ⅜ mile wide.

40.30 Camp Smith on east. Above Roa Hook. This is the summer training grounds of the New York State National Guard. Infantry and artillery are trained here. The camp is named in honor of former Governor Alfred E. Smith, but is much older. Mine Mountain, at the northern end of the reservation, has abandoned iron mines.

40.50 Dickiebusch Brook on east. Rises in Dickiebusch Lake in Camp Smith Reservation and empties into Peekskill Bay at Roa Hook.

40.75 Fish Island on east. This is the smallest named island in the Hudson. Close to the eastern shore, it is little more than a rock awash in rough high water.

41.00 Flat Point on east. This bluff on Manitou Mountain was formerly tunneled by the New York Central Railroad. In the 1950s it was "daylighted," i.e., its top was blasted off to make it an open cut to improve clearance for automobile rack cars.

41.00 Deep Hole on east. 143 feet deep, just off Flat Point.

41.00 Round Island on west. The high, rocky southeastern tip of Iona Island, it is round in shape.

41.00 Hudson River National Estuarine Research Reserve. This organization manages several locations in the immediate area, including Salisbury Meadow, Ring Meadow, Snake Hole Creek, Round Island, Iona Island, and Doodletown Bight.

41.00 Snake Hole Creek on west. Between Iona Island and Dunderberg Mountain.

41.00 Salisbury Meadow on west. Between mainland and Iona Island. Drained to the south by Snake Hole Creek and to the north by Doodletown Brook, it was formerly called Salisbury Island. It is wet marshland, but has dry hummocks at low tide. There is a causeway from Route 9W on the mainland to Iona Island that affords good close views. The area is important in the incubation of marine life and the nesting of water fowl, and it is presently a wildlife refuge.

IONA MARSH AND RING MEADOW. View looking north from lower slopes of Dunderberg Mountain. Bear Mountain Bridge and Manitou Mountain in distance. Photo: Barbara Sandson.

41.00 Ring Meadow on west. This name refers to that portion of Salisbury Meadow on the southern end of Iona Island, east of Snake Hole Creek.

41.00 Manitou Mountain on east. With an elevation of 720 feet, Manitou Mountain lies within the Camp Smith Military Reservation.

41.50 Iona Island on west. Formerly known as Beveridge's Island and Weyant's Island, it is about 300 acres in size, 200 of which are marsh meadow. Only about 40 acres are suitable for cultivation. There are rocky outcroppings, and the maximum elevation, near the northern end, is 60 feet. It is separated from the mainland by Snake Hole Creek on the south and by Doodletown Brook and Doodletown Bight on the west and north. The West Shore Railroad cuts across the island, via a causeway and small bridge on the south and a long low trestle on the north. It is connected to Route 9W on the mainland by a low causeway across Salisbury Meadow. There was formerly a railroad station here. The sea breeze stops here, but its mild effect is visible upon vegetation. The spring season is two weeks in advance of that at Newburgh, only fourteen miles northward. In the mid-nineteenth century, C. W. Grant, M.D., a noted horticulturist and arborist, had extensive vineyards and orchards here. Twenty acres was devoted to the vine, and there were between 2,000 and 3,000 bearing pear trees and small fruit of every kind. According to Benson Lossing, Grant had eleven propagation houses, and produced more grapes and other fruit plants than all other establishments in the United States combined.

Later in the century the island served as a summer resort, and in the 1870s was a popular destination for excursion steamers from New York. The island served as a U.S. Naval Arsenal from 1900 until after World War II, and it was rumored to be strongly defended on the waterside by artillery. The government also stored rubber here. There was a circular iron shot tower with a conical top, painted with red and white checks which gave a picturesque effect, but has since been removed. The island is now under the jurisdiction of the Palisades Interstate Park Commission.

There was once a great railroad disaster here when an express train piled into the rear of a stopped passenger train made up of wooden coaches. One of the trains involved belonged to the NYO & W.

41.60 Broccy Creek and Reservoir to east.
Rising in Broccy Creek Reservoir at an elevation of 537 feet in a col between Anthony's Nose and Mine Mountain in the Camp Smith Reservation, it flows southwest to the Hudson. The name was corrupted from the Dutch Brocken Kill, or Broken Creek; an intermediately used name was Brockey Kill.

41.60 West Mountain to west. Elevation 1,257 feet. It is located at head of Doodletown Hollow and is traversed by the Timp-Torne and Suffern-Bear Mountain hiking trails. There is a shelter here.

41.60 Doodletown to west. This is the name of a hollow and village between Dunderberg on the south, West Mountain on the west, and Bear Mountain on the north. It is on the mainland behind Iona Island. The name most likely comes from the Dutch "Dooddel" or "Dead Valley." The name may have come from its dark and shadowy appearance, or dead trees in the vicinity. Many people think the name is derived from Yankee Doodle, but the name seems to have applied at an earlier date than that of the tune's original popularity. This land was part of the Richard Bradly Patent of 1743. The French Huguenot June family settled here in 1776. In the nineteenth century, the area was settled mainly by woodmen engaged in cutting and hauling wood to the landing northwest of Iona Island, for the boats and brickyards. When Mr. Beveridge bought Iona Island, he erected a church edifice here in 1851. This was called the Mountville Church. It was also used as a schoolhouse. In later years, around 1945, Doodletown had a population of about 100 persons, mostly working in the Palisades Interstate Park or on Iona Island at the arsenal. Today it is a ghost town. It is here that forces under Sir Henry Clinton, on their way to attack Fort Clinton, met their first American resistance. The American militia was composed of farmer lads, few of them over twenty-five years old.

41.60 Timp Brook to west. It rises in a col between the Timp and Bald Mountain and flows northeast into Doodletown Brook at Doodletown.

41.60 Doodletown Brook to west. Rising in a col between West Mountain and Bear Mountain, it flows east through Doodletown Hollow to Doodletown Bight near Salisbury Meadow.

41.75 Doodletown Bight to west. An outlet of Doodletown Brook, between Iona Island and Bear Mountain, it is a shallow bay. It is crossed at its mouth by a low and long trestle of the West Shore Railroad. It is also known as Doodletown Cove.

42.00 Chevaux-de-Frise across river. The name "chevaux-de-frise" is the French term for any sort of portable wire or metal entanglements. As part of the fortifications of the Highlands during the Revolutionary War, it was proposed that the Americans stretch chains across the Hudson to prevent British warships from sailing upriver. The first one was proposed by General G. M. Scott of the New York Militia, to be stretched from Fort Lee to Fort Washington. He proposed using heavy wooden beams shod with iron and bolted together in the form of tetrahedons, the ends of the beams extending beyond the joints into horns. They would be fourteen feet beneath the surface of the water and impale any wooden vessel running upon them. Robert Erskine, operator of the Ringwood iron mines and furnaces, and Washington's chief surveyor, undertook to manufacture such a chain. However, Forts Washington and Lee were lost to the British before anything could be done.

In 1776 Erskine undertook to manufacture a similar chain to be stretched across the Hudson between Bear Mountain and Anthony's Nose. This one was actually installed and consisted of heavy iron chain supported on wooden floats and protected on the downriver side by wooden booms. When the British captured Forts Clinton and Montgomery in 1777, they dismantled this chain and took it overseas where they used it for many years to protect the harbor at Gibralter. It had cost the Americans $250,000.

A second similar chain was installed between West Point and Constitution Island in 1779. These were manufactured in the Ramapo Mountains at the Sterling and Ringwood iron works and installed under direction of Captain Thomas Machin. A similar chain was proposed between Plum Point and Pollepel's Island.

42.10 Site of ice storage sheds on west. The Knickerbocker Ice Company used to cut ice from Highland Lake (Hessian Lake) and send it down long chutes to be stored in great sheds located on the shore of Doodletown Bight. It shipped 30,000 tons annually.

42.40 Bear Mountain to west. With an elevation of 1,284 feet, it was formerly called Bear Hill, or earlier, Bread Tray Mountain. It is supposed that bears were common in the vicinity. However, it is possibly a corruption of "bare" mountain, referring to its rather bald summit. It is the focal point of the Bear Mountain State Park section of Palisades Interstate Park. There is a large lodge here, administrative offices, an ice-skating rink, a ski run, ski jump, toboggan run, athletic fields, recreational lake, picnic grounds, swimming pool, museums, nature trails, and zoo. There were two steamboat piers and a railroad station here. It was a regular port of call for the Hudson River Day Line until 1989, and was a popular destination for other charter excursion boats. Bear Mountain Inn is open year round and has complete facilities. It used to be a popular training camp for athletic teams. The Pell and Harriman families formerly had residences near here, and Fort Clinton, the ruins of which can still be seen, was near the Bear Mountain Bridge. The Appalachian Trail crosses over Bear Mountain. The Perkins Memorial Drive goes to the summit where there is an observation tower. These are a memorial to George W. Perkins, who was president of the Palisades Interstate Park Commission until his death in 1920. The park took its present form under his direction.

Originally, in 1908, the state of New York had acquired the Bear Mountain area as a new site of Sing Sing Prison, and prisoners were actually moved here and work started on clearing the land. There was a great public outcry against this misuse of the area, and when Mrs. Mary A. Harriman gave her gift of 10,000 acres in the vicinity, she stipulated that the

prison project be abandoned. The Bear Mountain Inn was opened in 1922.

42.40 Site of Fort Clinton on the west.
Located on the bluff just to south of toll booths of the Bear Mountain Bridge, this was the site of exciting activity during the Revolution, as told by Benson Lossing in his *The Hudson.*

...Fort Montgomery was on the northern side of (Popolopen) the creek, and Fort Clinton on the southern side. They were constructed at the beginning of the war for independence, and became the theatre of a desperate and bloody contest in the autumn of 1777. They were strong fortresses, though feebly manned. From Fort Montgomery to Anthony's Nose a heavy boom and massive iron chain were stretched over the river, to obstruct British ships that might attempt a passage toward West Point. The two forts were respectively commanded by two brothers, Generals George and James Clinton, the former at that time governor of the newly organized State of New York.

Burgoyne, then surrounded by the Americans at Saratoga, was, as we have observed...in daily expectation of a diversion in his favour, on the Lower Hudson, by Sir Henry Clinton—in command of the British troops at New York. Early in October, the latter fitted out an expedition for the Highlands, and accompanied it in person. He deceived General Putnam, then in command at Peek's Kill, by feints on that side of the river, at the same time he sent detachments over the Donder Berg, under cover of a fog. They were piloted by a resident Tory or loyalist, and in the afternoon of the 6th of October, and in two divisions, fell upon the forts. The commanders of the forts had no suspicions of the proximity of the enemy until their picket guards were assailed. These, and a detachment sent out in that direction, had a severe skirmish with the invaders on the borders of Lake Sinnipink, a beautiful sheet of water lying at the foot of the Lofty Bear Mountain, on the same general level as the foundations of the fort (Clinton). Many of the dead were cast into that lake, near its outlet, and their blood so incarnadined its waters, that it has ever since been vulgarly called "Bloody Pond."

The garrisons at the two forts, meanwhile, prepared to resist the attack with desperation. They were completely invested at four o'clock in the afternoon, when a general contest commenced, in which British vessels in the river participated. It continued until twilight. The Americans then gave way, and a general flight ensued. The two commanders were among those who escaped to the mountains.

The Americans lost in killed, wounded, and prisoners, about three hundred. The British loss was about one hundred and forty.

The contest ended with a sublime spectacle. Above the boom and chain the Americans had two frigates, two galleys, and an armed sloop. On the fall of the forts, the crews of these vessels spread their sails, and, slipping their cables, attempted to escape up the river. But the wind was adverse, and they were compelled to abandon them. They set them on fire when they left, to prevent their falling into the hands of an enemy. "The flames suddenly broke forth," wrote Stedman, a British officer and author, "and, as every sail was set, the vessels soon became magnificent pyramids of fire. The reflection on the steep face of the opposite mountain (Anthony's Nose), and the long train of ruddy light which shone upon the water for a prodigious distance, had a wonderful effect; while the ear was awfully filled with the continued echoes from the rocky shores, as the flames gradually reached the loaded cannons. The whole was sublimely terminated by the explosions, which left all again in darkness."

Early on the following morning, the obstructions in the river, which had cost the Americans a quarter of a million of dollars, Continental money, were destroyed by the British fleet. Fort Constitution, opposite West Point, was abandoned. A free passage of the Hudson being opened, Vaughan and Wallace sailed up the river on their destructive errand to Kingston and Clermont.

(Lossing: *The Hudson*, pp. 262–264.)

Two of the ships the Americans lost were the frigate *Montgomery*, with twenty-four guns, and the frigate *Congress*, with twenty-eight guns. Sir Henry Clinton abandoned the forts after hearing of General Burgoyne's surrender at Saratoga.

Sir Henry Clinton's total force was about 4,000 men. He left 2,000 of them encamped below Peekskill and making feints on Peekskill and Fort Independence. Another 2,000 men, under his personal command, crossed to the west bank at Kings Ferry and marched north, across Dunderberg Mountain to Doodletown on October 6. They split into two groups. One division of 900 men went around the back of Bear Mountain to attack Fort Montgomery. They were met by American reinforcements of 400 men, but still managed to take the fort. The troops consisted largely of Hessians.

The other group of 1,100 men attacked Fort Clinton, after an active skirmish on the shores of Lake Sinnipink. The garrisons of the forts were composed mostly of untrained militia. They fought nobly and well, but could not stand up to the much larger force of disciplined troops. Many escaped, but a considerable number were slain or made prisoners. Governor George Clinton fled across the river from Fort Montgomery in a boat, and at midnight was with General Putnam at Continental Village. There is a persistent legend that he slid down the steep slopes from the fort to the shore on the seat of his pants. General James Clinton forced his way to the rear of Fort Clinton, where he received a bayonet wound in his thigh. However, he reached his home in New Windsor in safety.

42.40 Hessian Lake on west. Its elevation is 155 feet. Originally called Lake Sinnipink, it is called Hessian Lake or Bloody Pond after the battle of Fort Clinton. The bodies of Hessian troops were thrown into the lake and incarnadined the waters. In the nineteenth century it was called Highland Lake. During this period the Knickerbocker Ice Company cut 30,000 tons of ice here annually. Today it is a principal feature of Bear Mountain Park. There is a paved path around the lake, and its banks are popular for picnicking. There are rowboats for hire. The Bear Mountain Inn is at the south end and the new Lodge at the north end.

42.40 Anthony's Nose on east. Elevation 900 feet. There was an Indian settlement called Wiccapee here. The tip of the mountain is pierced by a tunnel of the New York Central Railroad over 200 feet in length. The most interesting feature of this promontory is its name.

Washington Irving, in his *Knickerbocker History of New York*, has a picturesque story to tell:

And now I am going to tell a fact, which I doubt much my readers will hesitate to believe, but if they do they are welcome not to believe a word in this whole history—for nothing which it contains is more true. It must be known then that the nose of Anthony the trumpeter was of a very lusty size, strutting boldly from his countenance like a mountain of Golconda, being sumptuously bedecked with rubies and other precious stones—the true regalia of a king of good fellows, which jolly Bacchus grants to all who bouse it heartily at the flagon. Now thus it happened, that bright and early in the morning, the good Anthony, having washed his burly visage, was leaning over the quarter railing of the galley, contemplating it in the glassy wave below. Just at this moment the illustrious sun, breaking in all his splendour from behind a high bluff of the Highlands, did dart one of his most potent beams full upon the refulgent nose of the sounder of brass—the reflection of which shot straightway down hissing hot into the water, and killed a mighty sturgeon that was sporting beside the vessel. This huge monster, being with infinite labour hoisted on board, furnished a luxurious repast to all the crew, being accounted of excellent flavour excepting about the wound, where it smacked a little of brimstone—and this, on my veracity, was the first time that ever sturgeon was eaten in these parts by Christian people. When this astonishing miracle became known to Peter Stuyvesant, and that he tasted of the unknown fish, he, as may well be supposed, marvelled exceedingly; and as a monument thereof, he gave the name of Anthony's Nose to a stout promontory in the neighbourhood, and it has continued to be called Anthony's Nose ever since that time.

The above refers to Anthony Van Corlaer, a real historical personage, who was allegedly drowned attempting to swim across Spuyten Duyvil Creek.

In his *New Mirror For Travellers* of 1828, James Kirke Paulding offers a few choice remarks:

Turning the base of Donderbarrack, the nose of all noses, Anthony's Nose, gradually displays itself to the enraptured eye, which must be steadily fixed on these our glowing pages. Such a nose is not seen every day. Not the famous hero of Slawkemburgius, whose proboscis emulated the steeple of Strasburg, ever had such a nose to his face. Taliacotius himself never made such a nose in his life. It is worth while to go ten miles to hear it blow—you would mistake it for a trumpet. The most curious thing about it is, that it looks no more like a nose than my foot. But now we think of it, there is still something more curious connected with this nose. There is not a soul born within five miles of it, but has a nose of most jolly dimensions—not quite as large as the mountain, but pretty well. Nay, what is still more remarkable, more than one person has recovered his nose, by regularly blowing the place where it ought to be, with a white pocket handkerchief, three times a day, at the foot of the mountain, in honour of St. Anthony. In memory of these miraculous restorations, it is the custom for the passengers in steam boats, to salute it in passing with a universal blow of the nose: after which, they shake their kerchiefs at it, and put them carefully in their pockets. No young lady ever climbs to the top of this stately nose, without affixing her white cambric handkerchief to a stick, placing it upright in the ground, and leaving it waving there, in hopes that all her posterity may be blessed with goodly noses. (p. 117)

There is an abandoned copper mine on the upper north slopes.

AERIAL VIEW OF BEAR MOUNTAIN BRIDGE, looking northward. Summit of Bear Mountain in foreground. Anthony's Nose to far right. Photo: Courtesy Hudson River Day Line, Alfred V. S. Olcott, Jr.

42.50 Bear Mountain Bridge overhead. When built in 1924, this was the world's longest suspension span. As early as 1889, a railroad bridge was projected for this "natural" bridgepoint. The present bridge was privately built at a cost of $5,000,000. It was designed by Howard Baird of New York City. Construction took place between April 1923 and November 1924. The central span is 1,632 feet long, and total length is 2,258 feet. It is 185 feet above the water. It was acquired by the state of New York in 1940 for $2,300,000. Routes U.S. 6 and U.S. 202 and the Appalachian Trail all make use of it. It is a toll bridge.

42.60 Orange County on west. From Popolopen Creek to Cedarcliff, the west bank is occupied by Orange County (1990 population 307,647). It is bounded on the south by Rockland County in New York and Passaic and Sussex Counties in New Jersey and by the State of Pennsylvania, and on the west by Sullivan and Ulster Counties in New York, and on the north by Ulster County. It covers an area of 829 square miles and embraces nineteen townships and five incorporated cities and villages.

It is one of the original counties of New York State, having been erected in 1683 by Governor Thomas Dongan. It was named in honor of King William III of England, who also was Stadtholder of Holland and Prince of Orange. Rockland County was taken from it in 1798, but some area was gained from Ulster County that same year. The county has two half-county seats, Goshen and Newburgh, but most official offices are at Goshen, the original shire town.

The original inhabitants were the Muncee Tribe of the Delaware Indians. They had all left the area by 1740. Orange County did not suffer from being pre-empted by gigantic patents. The largest was the Evans Patent, but it was revoked in 1699 by the lord of Bellomont, governor of New York, and the area was reissued in the form of eighty-two smaller patents between 1709 and 1775. Generally these were limited to 2,000 acres. However, several partners could group together to qualify for a larger patent. Among the larger ones were the Chesekook, Wawayanda, and Minisink patents. The so-called "German Patent" was promised to German Palatinate settlers by Queen Anne of England in 1708, but not confirmed until 1719, when they had already settled on the land.

The county is composed of the following townships: Newburgh, New Windsor, Deer Park, Mount Hope, Greenville, Wawayanda, Minisink, Goshen, Wallkill, Crawford, Warwick, Chester, Monroe, Tuxedo, Woodbury, Highlands, Blooming Grove, Hamptonburg, and Montgomery, and the incorporated cities and villages of Newburgh, Cornwall, Walden, Port Jervis, and Middletown.

Principal water courses are the Hudson on the east and the Delaware River on the southwest. It is also traversed from south to north by the Wallkill River, which rises in New Jersey and flows into Ulster County, and its tributary Shawangunk Kill, which rises on the eastern slopes of the Shawangunk Mountains within Orange County. The Neversink River rises in the Catskills and flows south to the Delaware at Port Jervis. Its tributary, the Basha Kill, flows south along the western foot of the Shawangunk Mountains. Moodna Creek is the principal outlet to the Hudson, along with Popolopen Creek. The former D & H Canal followed the western foot of the Shawangunk Mountains from Port Jervis to Ulster County. There is excellent fertile black dirt truck farming land along the Wallkill in southwestern Orange County, east of the Shawangunks.

Principal lakes include: Greenwood Lake (half in New Jersey), Lake Washington, Orange Lake, Chadwick Lake, Lake Tiorati, Lake Mombasha, Wickham Lake, Ramsdell Lake (also known as Beaver Dam Lake), and the smaller Silver Stream Reservoir, Popolopen, Stillwell, Silver Mine, Stahe, Island Pond, Cahasset, Massawippa, Long Pond, Round Pond, Tomahawk, Turkey Hill Pond, Skanatati, Skemonto, Tuxedo, Sterling, Sterling Forest, Walton, Round, Cromwell, Orange & Rockland Lake, Glenmere, Forest, Cranberry, Silver, Highland, Monhagen, Hessian, Shawangunk, Cahoonzie, and Big Pond Lakes.

Principal mountain ranges are the Shawangunks, running from southwest to northeast, along the

western portion of the county; the Catskills in the far western tip; the Plattekills, along the Hudson and the Highlands of the Hudson, actually the northern end of the Ramapo Mountains; as well as the isolated Schuenemunk Mountain near the Highlands.

Principal highways are Route 9W, along the Hudson; the New York Thruway, following Smith's Clove and paralleling the Hudson west of the Highlands and Plattekills; Interstate I-84 from the Newburgh Bridge to Port Jervis; and Route 17, the Quickway, from Harriman northwest to the Sullivan County border.

Principal railroads are the West Shore along the Hudson and the Erie, following the Ramapo River and Smith's Clove, heading west to Middletown and Port Jervis, thence up along the Delaware with former branches to Newburgh, Montgomery, and Pine Bush; the Middletown & New Jersey (part of the old Oswego Midland route) from Slate Hill to Middletown; the former Lehigh & Hudson from Maybrook south to New Jersey; and the former New Haven line from the Poughkeepsie Bridge to Maybrook. The now-abandoned Lehigh & New England ran from Maybrook to the New Jersey border near Pine Island, and the abandoned New York, Ontario & Western ran from the Hudson at Cornwall, westward to Middletown and thence over the Shawangunk Mountains into Sullivan County, with branches to Port Jervis and Kingston and Monticello.

Two noted early settlers were Sarah Wells and William Bull, whom she married. They were of Irish extraction. Later, the Frenchman Hector St. John de Crévecoeur purchased a farm near Goshen. He wrote the famous *Letters From an American Farmer*, describing agricultural life in the early nineteenth century. Famous native sons include Cadwallader Colden of Coldenham who lived in the county between 1727 and 1760 and served several terms as colonial governor of New York. William H. Seward, who later became Secretary of State of the United States and purchased Alaska ("Seward's Folly"), was born in Florida, near Goshen. Benjamin B. Odell, a shipping magnate of Newburgh, was governor of New York from 1900 to 1904; and W. Averell Harriman, of Harriman, was governor of New York from 1955 to 1958.

42.60 Popolopen Creek to west. Also formerly known as Popolopen's Kill, Pooploop's Kill and Fort Montgomery Creek or simply Montgomery Creek, it rises about six miles to the west in Popolopen and Stillwell Lakes in the Forest of Dean area behind the West Point Military Reservation. There was a dam at the head of navigation and the small lake behind it was known as Roe Pond. The area near Roe Pond is very rugged and picturesque, and was given the name "Hell Hole" by the West Point cadets who practiced summer manouevres there. Popolopen Torne rises 941 feet above it to the north. The creek is crossed near its outlet by the high viaduct of Route 9W and the low trestle of the West Shore Railroad.

In the past this area was known for its iron mining operations. Between 1746, when the first mining operations began in the Forest of Dean region, and 1934, when the last mine shut down, roughly 2,000,000 tons of high-grade ore were taken from these hills. The ore is a pinkish calcite with crystalized magnetite, producing between sixty and sixty-one percent iron, with a low sulphur content which was excellent for non-Bessemer production. Benson Lossing visited the area in 1865, the same year that commercial operations got under way on a large scale. He noted a mill dam, flume, and water wheel at the head of navigation, about one mile from the Hudson. The wheel was used to provide pumping and hoisting power for the Forest of Dean Iron Ore Company, who started operations that year. They ran the mine until 1894, when it was abandoned. In 1905, with modern electric equipment, the Hudson Iron Company found it profitable to re-open the mines. The business was taken over between 1914 and 1934 by the Fort Montgomery Iron Corporation. They used 2½-ton skips at the mine, where they had a tipple and crushing plant. From thence, the ore was taken three miles over a narrow-gauge steam railroad, along the creek to the head of the falls. Here the ore was dumped into large buckets on a suspended wire ropeway to be conveyed for 1¼ miles to either barges anchored in the creek or cars of the West Shore Railroad.

42.65 Site of Fort Montgomery to west. (See article on Fort Clinton.) The West Shore Railroad goes through a short tunnel here below the site of the fort.

42.65 Putnam County to the east. From here to Fishkill, just below Beacon, we have Putnam County on our right. It is one of the smallest in New York State, having only 235 square miles (1990 population 83,947). It is bounded on the south by Westchester County and on the east by Connecticut and the north by Dutchess County, from which it was taken in 1812. It was named in honor of Revolutionary War General Israel Putnam. The county seat is Carmel, well inland to the east. The county is quite mountainous, and largely devoted to country estates, parks, and small agriculture. The mountains are the southwestern end of the Taconics. Principal water

courses are the Croton River, draining the eastern precincts, and Fishkill Creek, draining northwest into the Hudson in Dutchess County. The Canopus Creek flows southwest into Annsville Creek and the Hudson. Principal towns are Brewster, Cold Spring, and Garrison. Major roads all run from north to south except interstate I-84, which runs from the Newburgh Bridge to the Connecticut border via Brewster. Route 9N follows the Hudson; Route 9 parallels it further inland (the old New York and Albany Post Road); the Taconic State Parkway bisects the county from north to south. The New York Central Railroad follows the Hudson, and the Harlem Division runs from south to north through the Croton River Valley. The now abandoned New York & Putnam ran from Westchester County to Brewster via Lake Mahopac. The former New Haven (now Conrail) has a line running from Poughkeepsie to Danbury, Connecticut, via Brewster. The most famous native son was Daniel Drew, who came from Carmel. It is a question whether he was famous or notorious. The countryside is very picturesque and the natives have a liking for dirt roads (well maintained and oiled) and actively work to preserve a rural atmosphere.

42.65 Popolopen Torne to west (elevation 941 feet).

42.75 Fort Montgomery village to west.

42.75 Sandy Beach. Here on the morning of July 15, 1779, General Anthony Wayne assembled the Massachusetts Light Infantry prior to marching upon Stony Point. Today there is a boatyard protected by unfriendly canines.

42.75 Brook's Lake to west. Behind village of Fort Montgomery.

43.40 Garrison Pond on west. In village of Fort Montgomery, along Route 9W.

43.40 Manitou on east. Formerly called Highland, it is a station on the railroad.

43.70 Mystery Point on east.

44.40 Canada Hill on east (elevation 820 feet).

44.40 South Mountain Pass on east. Between Canada Hill and Anthony's Nose, it leads to Canopus Hollow and was used by the old highway before construction of the highway along the ledges of Anthony's Nose. Now closed to through traffic

44.40 Copper Mine Brook to east. It rises in South Mountain Pass.

44.40 Manitoga Nature Conservancy to east. On slopes of Canada Hill. Entrance from Route 9D.

44.60 Curry Pond to east.

43.40 to 44.60 on west. Estates of John S. Gilbert, William Pell, and Arthur Pell. Active at turn of the century, they are now broken up into trailer home courts.

44.80 Con Hook on west. Formerly spelled Cohn's Hook, and pronounced Connosook, it is a low rocky headland jutting directly out into the channel with a 125 foot depth. The water immediately north and south is only one-half foot deep, sheerly dropping off to depths of 108 and 72 feet. A menace to navigation, it has a flashing beacon with a 2½-second signal. Henry Hudson anchored here on his way up river on September 14, 1609. The estate of J. Pierpont Morgan was located above the Hook.

45.00 Crown Ridge to west (elevation 1,000 feet).

45.00 Cragston Lakes to west. Atop the first bluffs, this is the site of the former estate of Alfred Pell.

45.00 Pell's Pond to west (up on ridges).

45.00 Crystal Lake to west (up on ridges).

45.00 White Rock to east (elevation 885 feet).

45.50 Bare Rock Mountain to west. Also called Mt. Eyrie, its elevation is 1,210 feet.

45.50 Former Estates on west of Charles Tracy, Captain Roe, "Benny" Havens, and John Bigelow, called "Squirrelwood."

45.50 Sugarloaf Hill to east (elevation 730 feet). Wallace Bruce says:

> ...so named as it resembles, to one coming up the river, the old-fashioned conical-shaped sugar-loaf, which was formerly suspended by a string over the centre of the hospitable Dutch tables, and swung around to be occasionally nibbled at, which in good old Knickerbocker days, was thought to be the best and only orthodox way of sweetening tea.
> (Bruce, *Hudson by Daylight*, p. 118.)

The Dutch was "Suycker Broodt."

45.50 Third Order Villa to east. Former estate of S. J. Livingston.

45.65 Glenclyfe Siding to east. Former home of Hamilton Fish.

45.70 Beverly Dock to east. Benedict Arnold escaped from here to the British ship *Vulture* on the morning of September 24, 1780, after he learned of the capture of Major André. Benson Lossing tells us that:

> ...His six oarsmen on that occasion, unconscious of the nature of the general's errand in such hot haste down the river, had their muscles strengthened by a promised reward of two gallons of rum; and the barge glided with the speed of the wind. They were awakened to a sense of their position only when they were detained on board the "Vulture" as prisoners, and saw their chief greeted as a friend by the enemies of their country. They were speedily set at liberty, in New York, by Sir Henry Clinton, who scorned Arnold for his meanness and treachery.
> (Lossing, *The Hudson*, p. 240)

45.70 Beverly Robinson House site to east. Located above Beverly Dock, it was burned in 1892. It was built in 1758 and belonged to the Tory Beverly Robinson. Benedict Arnold made it his headquarters while in command of West Point and escaped from here on the morning of September 24, 1780.

The scene is described in a lively manner by Wallace Bruce:

> ...Alexander Hamilton and General Lafayette sat gayly chatting with Mrs. Arnold and her husband (over breakfast) when the letter from Jamison was received. Arnold glanced at the contents, rose and excused himself from the table, beckoning to his wife to follow him, bade her good-bye, told her he was a ruined man and a traitor, kissed his little boy in the cradle, rode to Beverly Dock, and ordered his men to pull off and go down the river. The "Vulture," an English man-of-war, was near Teller's Point, and received a traitor, whose miserable treachery branded him with eternal infamy in both continents.
> (Bruce, *Hudson by Daylight*, p. 114.)

46.20 Highland Brook to west.

46.20 Buttermilk Falls to west. On Highland Brook, this site is well described by Benson Lossing:

> ...a small stream comes rushing down the rocks in cascades and foaming rapids, falling more than a hundred feet in the course of as many yards. The chief fall, where the stream plunges into the river, is over a sloping granite rock. It spreads out into a broad sheet of milk-white foam, which suggested its name to the Dutch skippers, and they called it "Boter Melck Val"—Buttermilk Fall. The stream affords water-power for flour-mills at the brink of the river. The fall is so great, that by a series of overshot water-wheels, arranged at different altitudes, a small quantity of water does marvellous execution. Large vessels come alongside the elevator on the river

front, and there discharge cargoes of wheat and take in cargoes of flour.

Rude paths and bridges are so constructed that visitors may view the great fall and the cascades above from many points. The latter have a grand and wild aspect when the stream is brimful, after heavy rains and the melting of snows.

On the rough plain above is the village of Butter-milk Fall.

(Lossing, *The Hudson*, p. 255.)

The mill that Lossing was referring to in 1865 was the grist mill of David Parry, built about 1838. It stood just south of the fall of the cascades into the Hudson. The water is ninety feet deep right off shore here. When the West Shore railroad was built, it was necessary to demolish the mill and hang bridges parallel to the cliffs out over the water to carry the railroad. Parry also operated a resort hotel called the Parry House above his mill, to the south of the falls. Buttermilk Falls are on private property and not open to the public. They can be seen only from the water or a West Shore train.

46.25 Highland Falls Village to west. Formerly called Buttermilk Falls, it is basically a service village for the adjacent United States Military Academy at West Point. It offers small stores, motels, and housing for base personnel. Ladycliff College was located here. It was formerly a resort town. The historical landscape painters Emanuel Leutze (1816–1868) and Robert W. Weir (1803–1889) both resided here.

46.40 Ladycliff College to west. Atop the cliffs north of Buttermilk Falls was this Catholic college, formerly Ladycliff Academy for Girls. It occupied the site of earlier Cozzens's Hotel and Cranston's Hotel. Cozzens originally operated a resort on the West Point grounds. In 1849 he built a much larger one south of the military reservation, somewhat north of the former Ladycliff College. In about 1860, it burned down, and he built a larger one on the high rocky bluff overlooking Buttermilk Falls. It was later oper-ated under the name Cranston's, and was acquired by a Catholic order in 1900 for use as an academy.

The hotel was situated 180 feet above the river and accommodated between 250 and 500 guests. It was visited by the Prince of Wales in 1865. There were cottages attached and extensive pleasure-grounds with walks, rustic bridges, etc.

46.40 Monastery of Mary Immaculate to east. This monastery is run by the Capuchin Franciscan fathers as a friary and convent. The southern end was built ca. 1890; it is four-story red brick with

copper-crowned cupola. The northern end was built in 1932; it is red brick, two-story.

46.40 Castle Rock to east. A spire-topped castle atop a 630-foot hill, it is three-story stone with tower and was built in 1881 for William H. Osborn.

46.70 Cozzens's or Cranston's Landing to west. (The Highland Falls railroad depot).

46.75 U. S. Hotel Thayer to west. On West Point grounds, this hotel is owned and operated by the United States government. It is open to the general public. Built in 1924 and renovated 1978, it was named in honor of Sylvanus Thayer, an early West Point superintendent.

46.75 Arden Point to east. It was named for the former estate of T. B. Arden, "Ardenia."

46.80 Arden Brook to east. It was formerly called Kedron Brook. In the mid-nineteenth century, there was a mill near the upper end of the ravine.

46.80 Fort Hill to east. Also known as Redoubt Hill, from Revolutionary War fortifications, its elevation is 810 feet.

47.35 West Point (United States Military Academy) to west. West Point has been called the Gibralter of America because of its strategic situation. In sailing days, ships had to change course here because of the sharp bends in the river, and virtually came to a halt. In the narrow waters, they became easy targets for guns on shore. Early in the Revolution, fortifica-tions were built both on West Point and Constitution Island on the opposite shore. Constitution Fort, on Constitution Island, was completed in September 1775. In 1778 a chain was stretched across the river from West Point to Constitution Island. Fort Clinton, originally called Fort Arnold, was completed at West Point in the spring of the same year. In 1779 Fort Putnam was built atop Mount Independence, behind Fort Clinton. It was on a virtually impregnable crag and provided covering protection to Fort Clinton. There were several smaller batteries. Battery Knox faced the river near Fort Clinton. Redoubt Wyllis and Redoubt Meigs both faced to the south and were located on lower ground southeast of Fort Putnam. In early Army orders this group of fortifications was designated as "the citadel and its dependencies." After the failure of Arnold's plan to hand it over to the British in 1780, West Point was never again threatened, and the American flag has flown over it since 1778. It was first occupied by the United States Army on January 20, 1778, making it the nation's oldest continually occupied military post.

In October 1776, Congress appointed a committee

to prepare plans for a military school. Shortly after the Revolution (1783), Washington suggested West Point as a possible site for a military academy. In 1793, in his annual message, Washington again recommended West Point as a location. In 1794 Congress organized a corps of artillerists to be stationed at West Point, with thirty-two cadets attached. In 1798 the number was increased to fifty-six cadets. On March 16, 1802, Congress formally authorized the founding of a military academy at West Point, and it opened on July 4 of that year with ten cadets. Under Major Sylvanus Thayer, who served as Superintendent from 1817 to 1833, West Point became a military school of the first order; the basic system established by Thayer is continued today.

The cadets live a strict military life in an atmosphere of learning. All cadets receive considerable basic military instruction, particularly in the last two years. The curriculum includes much mathematics, physics, and engineering, and leads to a B. S. degree. The graduates are then required to serve with the Army for a number of years. Graduation from West Point is held in great esteem in the Army and is often the key to high advancement in the ranks. Many graduates, and even dropouts, have gone on to great success in civilian life as well. Among the most famous graduates are Robert E. Lee, Ulysses S. Grant, "Stonewall" Jackson, Philip Henry Sheridan, Douglas MacArthur, George Patton, and Dwight D. Eisenhower. Edgar Allan Poe and James A. McNeill Whistler became famous, although they did not complete their terms. For many years West Point was the nation's premier school of civil engineering.

In the nineteenth century, West Point was a popular summer resort because of the attractions of the beautiful scenery and interesting historic associations. It is still a popular place for pleasure excursions, and visitors are always welcomed and treated with courtesy and respect. The regular outdoor band concerts and July 4th pyrotechnic displays are very popular with the natives of the surrounding towns. Athletic events draw large crowds—particularly football games at Michie Stadium. Reviews on the parade grounds are perhaps the most popular event, and the military museum and organ recitals in the chapel also draw large attendance.

Principal points of interest are as listed here. I shall give full descriptions only of those points not seen from the river. These latter will be fully described at the appropriate river mileage, although some of them are considerably inland.

1. Hotel Thayer—described at ERM 46.75.
2. Cavalry and Artillery Drill Field—now known as South Athletic Field—across from Hotel Thayer.
3. Michie Stadium—open only during games. This football field with seating capacity of 26,000 was named in honor of Dennis Mahan Michie, class of 1892, captain of the first West Point football team, killed in action at San Juan, Cuba, in 1898.
4. Redoubt Meigs—near junction of Wilson and Kinsley Hill Roads.
5. Redoubt Wyllis—immediately north of Redoubt Meigs.
6. Lusk Reservoir—opposite Michie Stadium on Mills Road.
7. Fort Putnam—on Mount Independence, north of Michie Stadium. Approached by a steep foot trail from Mill's Road, it was originally built in 1778 and partially restored in 1907–1910. Its elevation is 451 feet above the river. Completely restored 1975.
8. Cadet Chapel—the dominant structure on the reservation. Its elevation is 300 feet above the river. It is located on DeRussy Road.
9. Catholic Chapel of the Most Holy Trinity—on Washington Road near Mill Road. Modeled on an English Carthusian abbey church, it was consecrated in 1900.
10. Old Cadet Chapel—in the cemetery on Washington Road. Built in 1837 on the site of Jefferson Hall and moved to its present site in 1911, it is in Renaissance Revival style with a Roman Doric portico. Inside is an oil painting by Robert W. Weir entitled *Peace and War*. Black marble shields on the walls are inscribed in gold with the name, rank, and dates of birth and death of every Revolutionary War general. One bearing only a date of birth and rank, omits the name of Benedict Arnold.
11. Thayer Hall—near lower landing. (See article ERM 47.50.)
12. Grant Hall—opposite Administration Building on Thayer Road. Adjacent to the South Cadet Barracks, it is the cadet reception hall, built in Tudor Gothic style.
13. Administration Building—Thayer Road. Built in 1904. Designed by Cram, Goodhue & Ferguson—mainly work of Cram. Dark gray granite trimmed with limestone in Gothic style with a 160-foot tower keep on its southwest corner. Built of solid masonry, it has battlements, buttresses, and cross-mullioned and traceried windows. The entrance is ornamented with heraldic seals of the Government and the Washington coat of arms, and is guarded by a raised portcullis. It contains the Ordnance Museum.
14. Central Cadet Barracks (1851)—behind Grant Hall.
15. Washington Hall—Jefferson Road. Built in 1925–1929. Designed by Gehron & Ross architects. This is the cadet mess hall. In Gothic style, its large stained glass window depicts outstanding events in the life of Washington.
16. Superintendent's Quarters—Jefferson Road (ca.

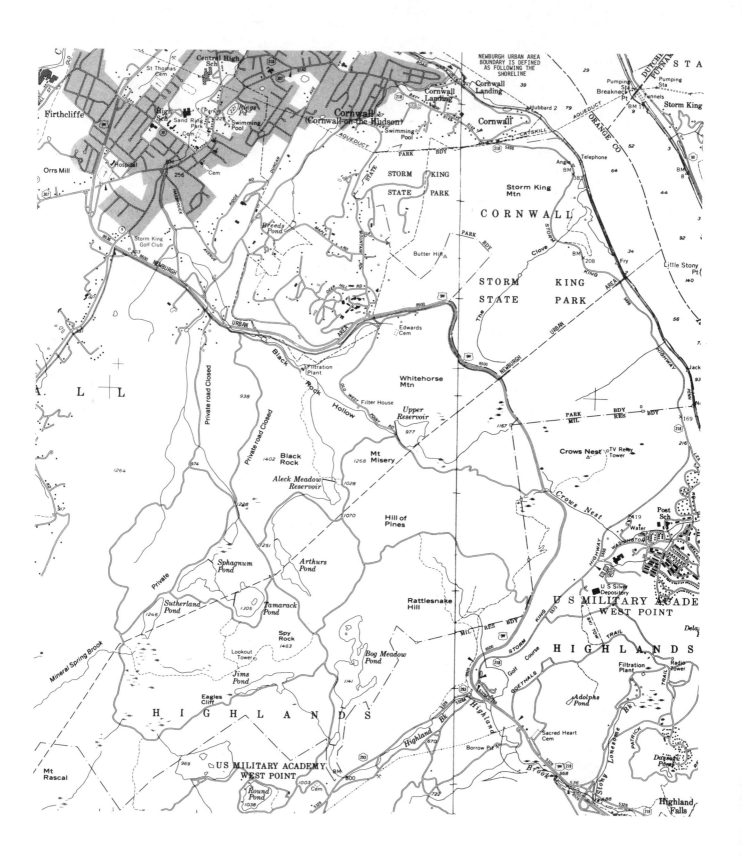

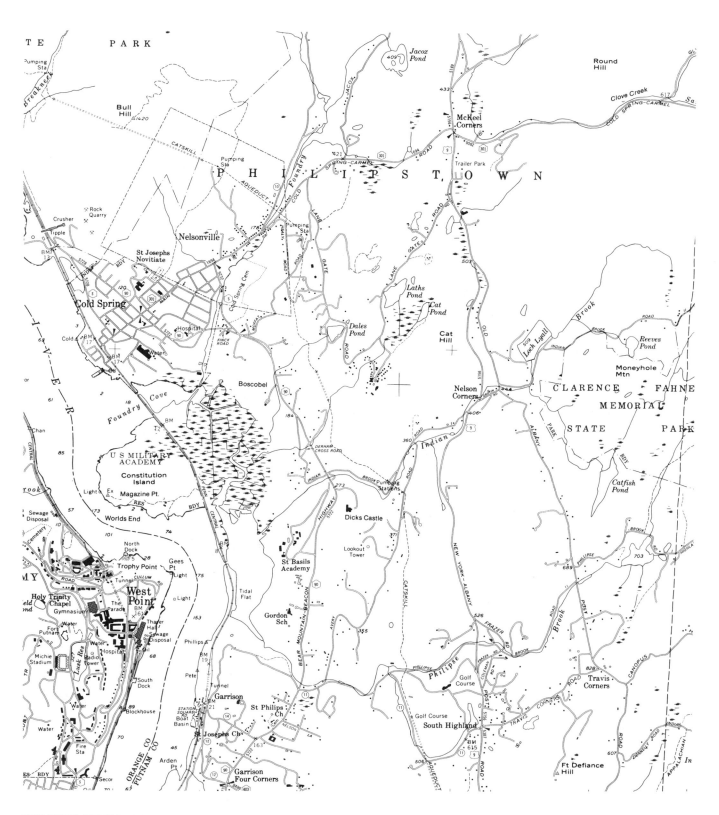

CORNWALL/WEST POINT SOUTH

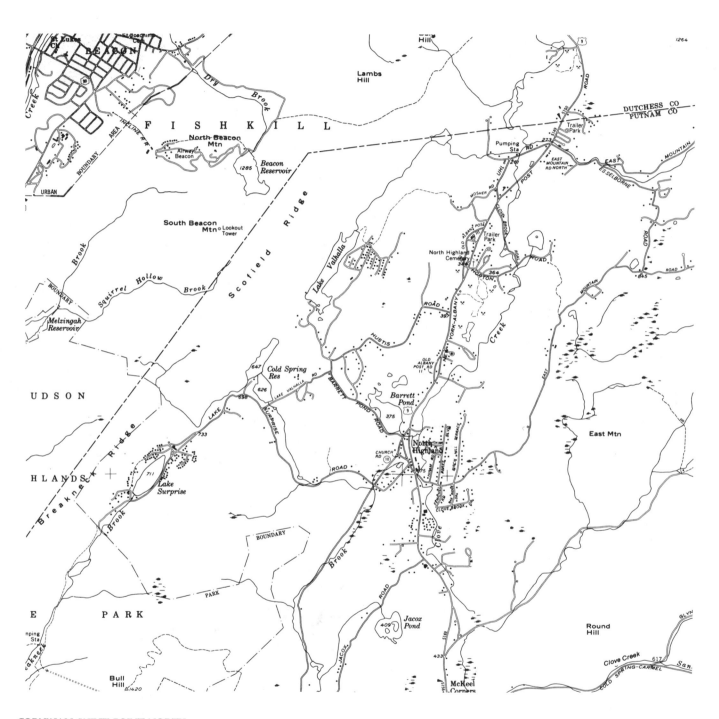

CORNWALL/WEST POINT NORTH

1820). This building was once occupied by Robert E. Lee.

17. Battle Monument—Trophy Point (off Washington Road). The monument was erected to the memory of the 2,230 officers and privates of the regular Army killed in action in the Civil War. A Roman Doric column, five feet in diameter and forty-six feet high, stands upon a five-step circular stairway broken by eight plain pedestals around the perimeter, each of which supports a sphere flanked by two cannons. The column supports a winged statue of Fame, by Frederick MacMonnies. The rest of the monument was designed by Stanford White.

18. Kosciusko Monument—Cullum Road, on site of old Fort Clinton. Designed by John H. Latrobe, class of 1822, it was erected by the corps of cadets in 1828. (See article ERM 47.76 for details about Kosciusko.)

19. Site of Fort Clinton (Fort Arnold). Cullum Road and Clinton Place. See article ERM 47.75.)

20. Officers' Club (mess)—Cullum Road. (See ERM 47.70.)

21. Bachelors' Building—Cullum Road. (See ERM 47.72.)

22. Cullum Memorial Hall—Cullum Road. (See ERM 47.71.)

23. Flirtation Walk—A gravel and rock foot trail which leaves Cullum Road just north of the Bachelors' Building and winds three quarters of a mile down the cliff to the river, past the lighthouse at Gee's Point, the beach where the western end of the great chain was anchored, the site of the chain battery, and the remains of the earthworks of Fort Clinton, and ends at Battle Monument. Just before passing the lighthouse the path is overhung by "Kissing Rock," so called because, according to tradition, if a cadet passes underneath with his best girl and fails to kiss her, the rock will crush them both.

24. Kosciusko's Garden—near south end of Flirtation Walk. According to Benson J. Lossing:

...a pleasant terrace in the steep bank of the river, which is called Kosciusko's Garden. At the back of the terrace the rock rises perpendicularly, and from its outer edge descends as perpendicularly to the river. This is said to have been Kosciusko's favourite place of resort for reading and meditation, while he was at West Point. He found a living spring bubbling from the rocks, in the middle of the terrace, and there he constructed a pretty little fountain. Its ruins were discovered in 1802 and repaired. The water now (1865) rises into a marble basin. Seats have been provided for visitors, ornamental shrubs have been planted, and the whole place wears an aspect of mingled romance and beauty. A deep circular indentation in the rock back of the fountain was made, tradition affirms, by a cannon-ball sent from a British

ship, while the Polish soldier was occupying his accustomed loitering place, reading Vauban, and regaled by the perfume of roses.

(Lossing, *The Hudson*, pp. 233–234.)

25. Battery Knox—formerly immediately above Kosciusko's Garden.

26. Site of West Point Hotel—was located on Trophy Point. It is also known as Roe's Hotel.

27. Stony Lonesome—desolate area west of Michie Stadium.

28. Benny Haven's—name of a bartender in village of Highland Falls who sold refreshment to the cadets in violation of the regulations. Affectionately mentioned in many old songs and jokes.

Visitors may call 914-938-5261 for information about visiting hours and all special events.

47.35 West Point South Dock and Depot to west.

This is not the original West Point landing. According to Benson Lossing, "The road from the plain to the landing at West Point was cut from the steep rocky bank of the river, at a heavy expense to the government. The wharf is spacious, and there a sentinel was continually posted (1865), with a slate and pencil, to record the names of all persons who arrive and depart. This was for the use of the Superintendent, by which means he is informed daily of the arrival of any persons to whom he might wish to extend personal or professional courtesies." The road to the landing is named Williams Road. When fresh recruits used to arrive at West Point by train, they were made to run up this hill as their first re-

UNITED STATES MILITARY ACADEMY AT WEST POINT from South Dock, 1952. At this period regualr day line steamers made this regualr landing. There has been considerable new construction around Thayer Hall on the hill to the west. Also, the railroad station is now used only by special trains. Much of the shallow water immediately beneath the *Riding Academy* and hill on the right has been filled-in to create athletic fields. Photo: Arthur G. Adams.

ception at the Point. The scene will be familiar to those who saw the motion picture *The Long Gray Line.* Note the Gothic railroad station. This was a regular landing of the Day Line. The schedule between here and New York City was the world's oldest scheduled passenger steamer route, having been established by Fulton's *Clermont.* Service ended 1989.

47.35 Fort Defiance Hill to east (elevation 900 feet).

47.35 Garrison to east A residential village with local railroad station and military-only passenger ferry to West Point (formerly vehicle ferry). Originally called Garrison's after a local family, it is in the town of Phillipstown, which was organized ca. 1858. Garrison was used as the site for filming some of the scenes of *Hello Dolly!* because of its supposed resemblance to Yonkers in the 1890s. There are many nineteenth-century buildings left in the village. Many Continental Army troops were stationed here during the Revolution.

47.50 Thayer Hall to west. Formerly the Riding Hall, it was designed by Cram, Goodhue & Ferguson and built in 1911. It rises from the river shore to the level of the east edge of the plain. Formerly an arena covering more than 16,000 square feet was provided for cavalry practice. There were stalls for 100 horses. The area has since been broken up and used for classroom space. It is of granite Gothic construction; a power house is located in the lower portion and the roof is used for parking.

47.50 Mount Independence to west (elevation 451 feet).

47.50 Fort Putnam to west. Atop Mount Independence. Built under the direction of Colonel Rufus Putnam in 1778–1779 by men of his Massachusetts regiment, it was partially restored 1907–1910. Totally restored 1975.

47.65 Site of Phillipse Manor to east. The seat of the Phillipse family's Highland Patent, this included most of present-day Putnam County.

47.70 Phillipse Brook to east.

47.70 Gordon School to east. The former home of M. P. Moore, it is in Stone Gothic (1847), designed by Richard Upjohn.

47.70 Duck Island to west. Formerly amidst ½-foot-deep shallows, now filled in to create athletic fields at the foot of the bluffs.

47.70 Officers' Mess to west. Atop the bluffs on Cullum Road, it is also known as the Officers' Club.

One of three neoclassic buildings in a row designed by McKim, Mead & White and built between 1898 and 1903, this is the most southerly of the three. It is built of granite and is two stories high. The Bachelor Officers' Mess is one of the oldest in the service. The river front has undergone extensive modifications in recent years, to add a ballroom.

47.71 Cullum Memorial Hall to west. The middle of the neoclassic group on Cullum Road, it is granite, two stories, with hipped roof. The main facade is adorned with four three-quarter engaged Ionic columns.

47.72 Bachelors' Building to west. This is the most northerly of the neoclassic group.

47.73 Site of Battery Knox to west. Atop bluffs.

47.75 Site of Fort Clinton to west (originally Fort Arnold). Atop bluffs. Built in the spring of 1778 under the direction of Thaddeus Kosciusko, then colonel in Continental Army and chief of the Engineers' Corps, it was 600 yards around within the walls with embankments 21 feet thick at the base and 14 feet high. It was 180 feet above the river and could accommodate 600 persons. It has been partially restored.

47.76 Kosciusko's Garden to west. Partway up bluffs. (See item 24 under West Point article, ERM 47.35, for details.)

47.76 Kosciusko's Monument to west. Atop bluffs on site of Fort Clinton. Designed by John H. Latrobe, class of 1822, it was erected by the corps of cadets in 1828. I quote from Lossing with reference to Thaddeus Kosciusko:

Kosciusko was much beloved by the Revolutionary Army, and his memory is held in reverence by the American people. He was only twenty years of age when he joined that army. He had been educated at the Military School of Warsaw. He had not completed his studies, when he eloped with a beautiful girl of high rank. They were overtaken by the maiden's father, who made a violent attempt to seize his daughter. The young Pole was compelled either to slay the father or abandon the daughter. He chose the latter, and obtaining the permission of his sovereign, he went to France, and there became a student in drawing and military science. In Paris he was introduced to Dr. Franklin, and fired with a desire to aid a people fighting for independence, he sailed for America, bearing letters from that minister. He applied to Washington for employment. "What do you seek here?" asked the leader of the armies of the revolted colonies. "I come to fight as a volunteer for

KOZIUSKO'S GARDEN AT WEST POINT c1870. Drawing by Harry Fenn. Author's collection.

American independence," the young Pole replied. "What can you do?" Washington asked. "Try me," was Kosciusko's prompt reply. Pleased with the young man, Washington took him into his military family. The Congress soon afterwards appointed him engineer, with the rank of colonel. He returned to

Poland at the close of the Revolution, and was made a major-general under Poniatowski. He was at the head of the military movements of the Revolution in Poland, in 1794, and was made a prisoner, and carried to St. Petersburg.... After the Empress Catherine died, the Emperor Paul liberated him, offered him command in the Russian service, and presented him with his own sword. He declined it, saying, "I no longer need a sword, since I have no longer a country to defend." He revisited the United States in 1797, when the Congress granted him land in consideration of his services. He afterwards lived in Switzerland, and there he died in 1817. A public funeral was made for him at Warsaw. Twelve years afterwards, the cadets of West Point, actuated by love for the man and reverence for his deeds, erected a beautiful marble monument to his memory, within the ruins of Old Fort Clinton, at a cost of about $5,000.

(Lossing, *The Hudson*, pp. 229–232)

47.76 There are eddies in the channel here, caused by the bend in the river and water entering from Indian Brook.

48.20 Flirtation Walk to west. (See item 23 under West Point article, ERM 47.35, for details.)

48.20 Sheridan Monument to west. On Gees Point. Philip Henry Sheridan (1831–1888) was a Union general in the Civil War. He was a member of the class of 1853 at West Point. He distinguished himself at Perryville and in the Chattanooga Campaign and Wilderness Campaign. He beat Lee at Five Forks and cut him off at Appomattox Courthouse. On Sherman's retirement in 1883, he was made commanding general of the United States Army.

48.20 Gees Point on west. Also Gee's Point. Possibly a corruption of "Geese" Point. There is a lighthouse here. There is 88 feet of water just off the point and the river bends sharply to the west. There is also a fog bell here.

48.25 Warner Ridge to east.

48.25 Saint Basil's Academy to east. Now a Greek Orthodox seminary. Present building is Tudor style, ca. 1920. At about the turn of the century, this property belonged to M. M. Gouverneur and later to Jacob Ruppert, the brewer.

48.35 Dick's Castle to east.

On top of a high hill in the midst of the city of Granada, Spain, rises a complex of buildings referred to as the "Alhambra." Parts of the structure date back to the ninth century. The palace has no archi-

LIGHTHOUSE AT GEE'S POINT, West Point c1870. Cro'nest and Storm King Mountains in background. Magazine Point of Constitution Island at far right. Drawing by Harry Fenn. Author's collection.

AERIAL VIEW OF EXTERNALLY COMPLETED DICK'S CASTLE, 1989. Photo: Courtesy Ames Brown and Moorish Castle Corporation.

DICK'S CASTLE UNCOMPLETED SOUTH FRONT, 1979. Photo: Courtesy of Anton Chmela.

tectural unity but consists of a series of halls and courtyards built at need. The walls and ceilings were adorned with geometric designs, and the ornamental stone lions guarding many of the fountains are heresies of Christian influence that came during the fifteenth century.

Dick's Castle is not a replica of the Alhambra, but the flavor of Moorish architecture and Christian motifs has been preserved in a structure that was caught in the renaissance of new building ideas in the United States between 1900 and 1930. The late Mrs. Evans R. Dick was impressed with the

Alhambra and decided to build a residence here in Garrison that would have been the "showplace of the Hudson Valley." Her dream was short-lived, when in 1911 after six years of construction, her husband's financial means were destroyed by a stock market slump initially indicated by the earlier 1907 crash. The Dick family had spent close to $3,000,000 when building was halted, and had their vision been completed some $7,000,000 would have been spent.

Although work had stopped, Mrs. Dick refused to sell the castle for any price. Years passed and no one looked after the building. Vandals broke in and destroyed the inner courtyard. Ornamental figurines were torn from the walls. In 1944 the castle was finally purchased from the Dick family by an Austrian engineer, named Anton Chmela.

Work is presently under way to finish one wing of the castle. Plans call for a museum which will house a collection of items, mostly models, that will illustrate the history of American industry. The courtyard will be restored preserving the Moorish style that first prompted Mrs. Dick to begin a venture which the present owners hope to finish.

(Brochure privately printed by Anton Chmela ca. 1975.)

The writer visited with Mr. Chmela and observed work in progress. There are many exquisite details and it is altogether a very romantic place. The castle is located on a hill with an elevation of about 400 feet. The views from the upper floors are outstanding.

Upon Mrs. Chmela's death in 1979, the property was sold to the Dia Art Foundation, who planned to use the castle as a museum, exhibiting the works of Hudson Valley artists.

Dia's plans never completely materialized, and after further construction work the castle was acquired by the Moorish Castle Corporation, who are rushing the project to completion. A recent visit by the author disclosed a new tile roof and a great deal of interior and exterior finish. The owners are seeking either a private purchaser for the completed castle or a good use such as a museum, conference center, hotel, or some appropriate combination thereof. In any case, the castle will definitely be completed and put to good appropriate use. It is also being marketed under the name "Castle at Garrison."

48.40 Cat Hill to east (elevation 800 feet).

48.40 Warren's Landing to east. At mouth of Indian Brook. Used by Van Tassel's sloop until building of railroad in 1850 made it unusable.

48.40 Indian Brook to east. Rises in Catfish Pond south of Moneyhole Mountain, east of Cat Hill. It first flows northwest for about one mile where it turns southwest after receiving the waters of Loch Lyall, via Loch Lyall Brook. This bend is near the Albany Post Road (Route 9). It then flows southwest for two miles through very picturesque ravines and over waterfalls. After passing under a high viaduct on Route 9D, it flows into a shallow bay opposite Gees Point. This bay is virtually shut off from the Hudson by the causeway of the New York Central Railroad. This bay also collects the waters from several small brooks flowing from Dale's Pond, Lath's Pond, and Cat Pond, and through the meadows separating Constitution Island from the mainland. The north bank of Indian Brook is followed by a scenic and picturesque narrow dirt road between Route 9D and Route 9. The falls on this stream are very picturesque and were a popular place of resort in the nineteenth century. They were dubbed "Fanny Kemble's Bath" after a noted incident in 1832 or 1833 when this famous and attractive young actress got soaked and almost killed herself climbing them.

46.50 World's End. Mid-channel between Gees Point and Constitution Island. This is the deepest place in the Hudson River—202 feet.

48.50 Site of chain across river 1778–1779. This chain was installed under the direction of Captain Thomas Machin. It was manufactured at forges in the Ramapo mountains. The links were made of iron bars, 2½ inches square. Their average length

was a little over two feet and their weight about 140 pounds each. According to Lossing:

The chain was stretched across the river at the narrowest place, just above Gee's Point (the extreme rocky end of West Point) and Constitution Island. It was laid across a boom of heavy logs, that floated near together. These were sixteen feet long, and pointed at each end, so as to offer little resistance to the tidal currents. The chain was fastened to these logs by staples, and at each shore by huge blocks of wood and stone. This chain and boom seemed to afford an efficient barrier to the passage of vessels; but their strength was never tested, as the keel of an enemy ship never ploughed the Hudson after the fleet of Vaughan passed up and down in the autumn of 1777, and performed its destructive mission.

(Lossing, *The Hudson*, pp. 227–228.)

The chain was installed in April of 1778. It was protected by a "chain battery" at West Point. Part of the chain is on display at Trophy Point.

48.50 Constitution Island to east. A rocky island with a maximum elevation about 100 feet, it is bounded on the north by Foundry Cove, on the west and south by the main channel of the Hudson, and on the east by marshes traversed by small brooks flowing from Dale's Pond, Lath's Pond, and Cat Pond. Its eastern side is traversed from south to north by the New York Central Railroad, which attains it by means of long causeways across the mouth of Indian Brook and Foundry Cove. It belongs to the United States Military Academy and is not open to the public except on special tours operating from the ferry landings at West Point and Garrison. Advance reservations are required.

It is claimed that a French family by the name of Martelaire lived here about 1720. In any event, it was acquired by the Philipse family from the first subdivision of the Highland Patent in 1754 until 1836, when it was purchased by Henry Warner. The stretch of the Hudson here is called the Martelaer's Rack, or Martyr's Reach. It is possible that this derived from the early settler Martelaire. However, Lossing has another possible explanation: "It was called by the Dutch navigators Martelaer's Island, and the reach in the river between it and the Storm King, Martelaer's Rack, or Martyr's Reach. The word martyr was used in this connection to signify "contending" and "struggling," as vessels coming up the river with a fair wind would frequently find themselves, immediately

HUDSON RIVER SHIP *DAYLINER* passing Trophy Point at West Point. View is looking north. The *M. V. Dayliner* was operated by the Hudson River Day Line between Manhattan and Poughkeepsie between 1972 and 1989. Photo: © Edward Grant.

after passing the point of the island into this reach, struggling with the wind right ahead." As the name seems to have been in use from very early times, the story of the Frenchman Martelaire seems just a bit too pat to ring true.

The island was fortified early in the Revolution at the suggestion of Bernard Romans. It was first garrisoned on September 21, 1775, and the fort was called "Constitutional Fort," in honor of the British Constitution. It soon became simply Fort Constitution. A block house or powder house was built near the high western tip of the island, and its ruins can still be seen. It was the eastern terminus of the great chain from West Point. Washington's bodyguards were mustered out here in December of 1783.

After the Revolution, it generally became known as Constitution Island, although the Warner Family used the old name of Martelaer's Rock well into the twentieth century.

Henry Warner, who purchased the island in 1836, was a New York City lawyer. He had financial reverses shortly after purchasing the island and retired here to a simple house he called "Wood Crag." This house was built of stone and clapboard, with parts dating back to before the Revolution. A large addition was put on about 1845. His household consisted of his sister and his two daughters, Susan (1819–1885) and Anna (1827–1915). They lived a simple life here. The girls were very religious and never married. They conducted Bible classes and befriended homesick cadets. Aside from a rare trip to Boston or New York, they never left the island. However, they did attain a wide fame.

In 1850 G. P. Putnam published a novel by Susan Warner entitled *The Wide Wide World*, which turned out to be a tremendous best-seller, selling hundreds of thousands of copies. It went through thirty editions. The book was quite sentimental, but struck the popular note. A second novel entitled *Queechy* sold almost as well, and its name was even given to a lake in Columbia County near the foothills of the Berkshires. Susan used the pen name of Elizabeth Wetherell. Anna Warner also tried her hand at writing, with some substantial success. She wrote under the name Anna Lothrop and specialized in children's books. In 1876 the two collaborated on a novel entitled *Wych Hazel*.

The sisters always wanted the island to go to the military academy and refused large offers for it. However, Congress would never appropriate the small price they asked—and needed for their maintenance. In 1908 Anna and Mrs. Russell Sage gave the island to the government. The gift was accepted at the direction of President Theodore Roosevelt. The terms of the gift provided for Anna Warner to live

there until her death (1915) and for the maintenance of the island and house "as is" forever. These wishes have been followed out substantially ever since. At the time of writing the boat leaves from West Point South Dock and the Garrison Marina on Tuesday and Wednesday afternoons, June through September. Phone 914-446-8676 (Mon–Fri. 10–11:30 A.M.) for reservations.

48.50 Targes Rock to east. Also called Powder House Point and Magazine Point.

48.60 Valley Point to west. Referring to Washington Valley. (ERM 48.90)

48.60 Trophy Point and Battle Monument to west. This was the site of Roe's West Point Hotel in the nineteenth century. There are unexcelled views northward from here. Besides the Battle Monument (see item #17 in West Point article, ERM 47.35) there are various other old cannon and mortars on display. Former site of Fort Sherbourne.

48.60 West Point North Dock to west or south. This was the original West Point landing where Fulton's steamboat docked.

48.60 West Point Post Exchange to west or south. A large modern brick building.

48.60 Mount Independence and Fort Putnam to south. (Refer back to ERM 47.50.)

48.60 Cadet Chapel to south. At 300 feet above the river, this is the dominant structure on the reservation. Designed by Cram, Goodhue & Ferguson, it was completed in 1910. It is built of granite in neo-Gothic style and cruciform in plan. There is a high buttressed tower at the crossing of the nave and transepts. The aisle walls of the nave are solid masonry, but the clerestory walls are all glass except

MAGAZINE POINT, CONSTITUTION ISLAND, known as "World's End." View looking south from steamer *Robert Fulton*. Hudson River Day Line photo, courtesy Alfred V. S. Olcott, Jr.

VIEW NORTH FROM MAGAZINE POINT. On left are Cro'nest and Storm King Mountains (with scar of highway clearly visible). Mountains on right are Breakneck and Mt. Taurus (Bull Hill). Photo: © Gretchen McHugh.

for stepped stone buttresses. The interior decoration is lavish and allegorical in nature. The magnificent pipe organ has 12,500 pipes. The service is interdenominational, but similar to that of the Episcopal church.

48.65 Constitution Island Marsh to east.
This separates Constitution Island from the mainland. Marshes are an important part of the estuary's ecosystem. They provide a nursery for young fish and unique habitats for many species of plants and wildlife. This marsh is brackish and is drained twice daily by the fall of the tide. Many years ago there were ill-advised attempts to permanently drain the marsh by digging ditches which are still visible. It is owned and maintained by the Audubon Society.

48.65 Boscobel Restoration to east. This was originally at River Mile 35.25. (Please refer back.) Restoration of eighteenth-century home of States Morris Dyckman (1755–1806), with fine collections of

CONSTITUTION ISLAND AND MARSH from Cro'nest Mountain. Cold Spring and Foundry Cove at left. U.S. Military Academy at West Point in right foreground. Photo: Alfred V. S. Olcott.

English china, silver, books, and period furnishings. The house is in the style of Robert Adam. The gardens are extensive and beautiful. The house is open daily except Tuesdays, Thanksgiving, Christmas, and January and February. It is located on Route 9D. Boscobel is now the home of the Hudson River Shakespeare Festival. Aside from Shakespearean works, this organization also mounts classic and contemporary plays, often in new and provoking stagings. Boscobel is within reasonable taxi distance from both Garrison and Cold Spring Metro-North commuter railroad stations. For information and reservations telephone 914-265-3638.

48.90 Crow's Nest Brook to west. Rises in a bog at 1,200-foot level of Crow's Nest Mountain.

48.90 Murray's Ravine to west. It is near the shore of the Hudson. Crow's Nest Brook flows through it.

48.90 Washington Valley to west. This is a long, broad valley along the southern foot of Crow's Nest Mountain, Hill of Pines, Mose Gees Mountain, and Mount Rascal, at the northern end of the United States Military Reservation. It is traversed by Routes 293 and 218. The West Point golf course is at its eastern end. As with so many other places, it takes its name from the fact that Washington used to stay in a house here when visiting West Point, winter of 1779. Moore House, now demolished.

49.00 Foundry Cove to east. It was named for former West Point Foundry which operated here between 1817 and 1884. During the War of 1812, President James Madison ordered the creation of four foundries in different parts of the country. Cold Spring was chosen as one, as it could be protected by West Point. James Kirke Paulding, the writer, was serving as secretary of the board of naval commissioners at the time and gave the direction of the foundry to Gouverneur Kemble (1786–1875). The foundry was a pioneer in much technology and built America's first iron ship, the revenue cutter *Spencer.* Its greatest fame came from the "Parrott gun," much used in the Civil War, and invented by Robert P. Parrott, who was one of the directors of the firm. There were very close ties between the firm and the administration of West Point. For many years it operated a fleet of seven sloops plying between Cold Spring and New York City. The *Victorine* was supposedly the fastest on the river. The foundry ultimately closed down because it could not compete with more modern plants. Some of the iron used was mined behind Mt. Taurus. The Putnam County Historical Society maintains a museum. The only remaining building is the foundry office, dating from 1865.

Foundry Cove is the outlet of Foundry Brook, which rises east of Schofield and Breakneck Ridges in Cold Spring Reservoir and Jacox Pond and flows southwest to just south of Cold Spring.

The Foundry Cove is bounded on the south by Constitution Island, on the east by a marsh, and on the north by bluffs on the south side of Cold Spring. Formerly there was a wharf used by the foundry on the north side, but only a few stones remain. The Cove is crossed by a causeway of the New York Central Railroad with a low, short bridge in the center. It is mostly shoal water only two to four feet deep, with the exception of a few holes.

To the east of it is the Boscobel Restoration. Just to the north of Boscobel is the mid-nineteenth century Victorian mansion of the painter Thomas Prichard Rossiter (1818–1871), who lived here from 1859 until his death. The mansion of Gouverneur Kemble is also nearby on the north side of the Cove, as is the Roman Catholic Chapel of Our Lady of Cold Spring, brick, in style of Etruscan temple, ca. 1834, on a bluff looking out over the water.

49.00 Town of Philipstown to east. Name derives from early patent and includes such villages as Cold Spring, Garrison, and Manitou. At Philipsburg, where the Continental Army was encamped, almost every soldier was innoculated with the kine-pox, to shield him from the ravages of smallpox. This was before Jenner, and considered a dangerous maneuver. Jenner's first cow-pox vaccination was in 1796.

49.30 Falls Brook to west.

49.40 Rose's Brook to west.

49.50 Crow's Nest Mountain to west (elevation 1,396 feet). Also frequently shortened to "Cro' Nest." This name is also given to a huge hollow among the summits of these hills, which suggests the idea of an enormous crow's nest. It has inspired several local poets:

> *Where Hudson's waves o'er silvery sands*
> *Winds through the hills afar,*
> *And Cro' Nest like a monarch stands,*
> *Crowned with a single star.*
>   George Pope Morris
>   (*Poems of George Pope Morris*, p. 233)

> *'Tis the middle watch of a summer night,*
> *The earth is dark, but the heavens*
>   *are bright,*
> *The moon looks down on old Cro' Nest—*

> *She mellows the shade on his shaggy*
>   *breast,*
> *And seems his huge grey form to throw*
> *In a silver cone on the wave below.*
>   from "The Culprit Fay"
>   by Joseph Rodman Drake

Crow's Nest is bounded on the south by Washington Valley, on the west by Mount Misery and Whitehorse Mountain, and on the north by Storm King Valley and Storm King Mountain. The southern peak has an elevation of 1,403 feet, although in early days the northern peak, with 1,396 feet elevation, was considered the true Crow's Nest. It is traversed by both Old and New Storm King Highways. The southern portion is within the United States Military Reservation. The northern portion belongs to the Palisades Interstate Park Commission, and some of the western part belongs to Harvard's Black Rock Forest Preserve. In the early days West Point trainees and trial artillerists at the West Point Foundry used the southern and eastern escarpments for target practice. One major reason why the Military Academy makes its part of the mountain out of bounds to the public is that there are believed to be substantial numbers of unexploded shells on the mountainside.

49.50 Site of former Foundry Dock to east. North of Foundry Cove.

49.50 Our Lady of Cold Spring R. C. Church to east. This church is in the form of an Etruscan temple, ca. 1834.

49.50 Cold Spring Village to east. This attractive residential village takes its name from a large cold spring at which, it is said, boats plying the Hudson used to fill their water butts. In the nineteenth century the West Point Foundry gave impetus to the town's growth, and many small-scaled eighteenth and nineteenth-century structures survive in a good state of preservation. Gouverneur Kemble and the painter Thomas Prichard Rossiter lived here, and the locality was a popular resort of such literary lights as Fitzgreen Halleck, Washington Irving, and Joseph Rodman Drake, who was inspired to write his lyrical quasi-epic while taking a moonlight walk along the shore here.

The waterfront remains a lovely and lively place with its tree-shaded nineteenth-century bandstand and stone mooring walls. The Hudson View Inn at the landing is charming and has been continuously dispensing hospitality since 1837. It is a fine place to watch the boats passing by of an afternoon, or to visit on a full moonlit evening when the Hudson looks like burnished silver.

49.55 Undercliff to east. On southern slopes of Mount Taurus. This was the home of the noted publisher and poet George Pope Morris (1802–1864). Built by John C. Hamilton, son of Alexander Hamilton.

49.55 Old Storm King Highway to west. Between West Point and Cornwall, carved from the cliffs of Crows Nest and Storm King Mountains, it affords magnificent views. It is narrow and winding.

49.55 New Storm King Highway to west. Going across the tops of Crow's Nest and Storm King further inland, it affords quite a different set of fine views. Used by Route 9W, completed ca. 1940, it is a modern all-weather highway.

50.00 Kidd's Plug Cliff to west. This must have been destroyed either by quarrying or construction of the Old Storm King Highway—or possibly by artillery practice. I give Benson Lossing's description in 1865:

High up on the smooth face of the rock, is a mass slightly projecting, estimated to be twelve feet in diameter, and by form and position suggesting, even to the dullest imagination, the idea of an enormous plug stopping an orifice. The fancy of some one has given it the name of Captain Kidd's Plug, in deference to the common belief that that noted pirate buried immense sums of money and other treasures somewhere in the Highlands. Within a few years ignorant and credulous persons, misled by pretended seers in the clairvoyant condition, have dug in search of those treasures in several places near West Point; and some, it is said, have been ignorant and credulous enough to believe that the almost mythical buccaneer had, by some supernatural power, mounted these rocks to the point where the projection is seen, discovered there an excavation, deposited vast treasures within it, and secured them by inserting the enormous stone plug seen from the waters below. It is plainly visible from vessels passing near the western shore. Kidd's Plug Cliff is a part of the group of hills which form Cro' Nest....
(Lossing, *The Hudson*, pp. 217–218.)

50.50 Little Stony Point to east (elevation 13 feet). Until recently, this was the site of a stone crusher, tipple, and barge loading dock of the Hudson River Stone Corporation who had a quarry on the lower southwestern slopes of Mt. Taurus. The point is now State parkland with a swimming beach with reasonably clean water.

50.50 Quarry to east. (See article above.) This was the last of the notorious stone quarries operating in

the Hudson Highlands. The Hudson River Stone Corporation started blasting here in 1931.

50.55 Mount Taurus or Bull Hill to east (elevation 1,420 feet). According to Wallace Bruce,

The mountain opposite Cro' Nest is Bull Hill, or more classically, Mt. Taurus. It is said that there was formerly a wild bull in these mountains, which had failed to win the respect and confidence of the inhabitants, so the mountaineers organized a hunt and drove him over the hill, whose name stands a monument to his exit.
(Bruce, *Hudson by Daylight*, p. 130.)

Table Rock, at the 1,000-foot level, is a popular lookout point on the hiking trail over the mountain. As described in the preceding two articles, this mountain was subject to quarrying until quite recent times. In 1970 the Taconic State Park Commission acquired Mount Taurus and included it, along with neighboring Breakneck Ridge and Sugar Loaf, in the Hudson Highlands State Park. Catskill Aqueduct passes under in a mile-long tunnel.

Benson Lossing tells us that "It is the old 'Bull Hill' which in Irving's exquisite story of 'Dolph Heyliger,' 'bellowed back in the storm' whose thunders had 'crashed on the Donder Berg, and rolled up the long defile of the Highlands, each headland making a new echo.'"

51.00 The Clove to west. Also known as Storm King Valley, Mother Cronk's Cove, and Donderbarrack (Thunder-chamber) and Valley of Hope.

This clove is situated between Crows Nest Mountain to the south and Storm King Mountain to the west and north. Formerly there was a considerable cove in the Hudson River, but this has been largely cut off and turned into a shallow backwater by the causeway of the West Shore Railroad, which has caused much of it to silt up. The Old Storm King Highway follows around the clove at the 200-foot level and the new one at the 1,000-foot level. Storm King Brook rises between Whitehorse Mountain and Crow's Nest and flows generally northeasterly through the clove. Stillman's Spring is near the 200 foot level. The area is heavily timbered.

There was a pre-Revolutionary settlement at the foot of the clove. It is recorded that a family named Cronk had a small farmstead on the mountaintop back of the clove, and this may account for the old name "Mother Cronk's Cove." Lossing tells us that a New York City resident named Lambertson had a solitary summer retreat here in 1865. Somewhat later, part of this land belonged to Dr. Matthew Beattle of Cornwall, who sold it to Dr. Earnest C.

Stillman of Cornwall. He, in turn, gave much of his land further inland to Harvard University for forestry research. The Clove now belongs to the Palisades Interstate Park Commission.

In 1824 the sloop *Neptune* capsized here, drowning thirty-five persons. The name "Donder-barrack" or "Thunder Chamber" comes from the old Dutch belief that the storm-goblins stored their thunder here. The name "Valley of Hope" has a rather interesting history. During the Revolution, West Point was thought of as the Gibralter of America. When the question came up of a national capital much thought was given to its security from enemy attack. Consequently, serious consideration was given to this valley as our national capital, because of its mountain ramparts and easy access by the Hudson. Speculators soon bought up the property in this Valley of Hope. The hopes fell flat when Washington was created in the District of Columbia. It is quite difficult to picture what would have happened if the capital had been located here. As the nation grew, probably the expansion would have been around Cornwall and Newburgh.

51.25 Breakneck Brook to east. Between Mount Taurus and Breakneck Ridge.

51.25 Storm King Station to east. Nathaniel Parker Willis convinced the New York Central Railroad to give this name to the small way-station once located here. Formerly Ferry to Cornwall. In 1988 Metro-North restored limited service to accommodate weekend hikers.

51.50 Breakneck Mountain to east. This is actually the western end of a long ridge running southwest to northeast. Its highest elevation is 1,213 feet. Breakneck Brook and Mount Taurus are to the south, Sugarloaf Mountain to the north. A popular hiking trail runs along the ridge.

According to the old legend, the bull that was chased over Mount Taurus was finally chased onto the top of this ridge and fell off a cliff, breaking his neck.

This ridge was subjected to extensive quarrying of the dark granite at a relative early date, and still bears ugly scars. Lossing tells us that:

Several years ago (1846) a powder blast, made by the quarriers high up on the southern declivity of the mountain, destroyed an object interesting to voyagers upon the river. From abreast the Storm King, a huge mass of rock was seen projected against the eastern sky in the perfect form of a human face, the branches of a tree forming an excel-

BREAKNECK MOUNTAIN FROM LITTLE STONY POINT. Anonymous engraving. Author's collection.

lent representation of thick curly beard upon the chin. It was called the TURK'S HEAD.... Its demolition caused many expressions of regret, for it was regarded as a great curiosity, and an interesting feature in the Highland scenery on the river.

(Lossing, *The Hudson*, p. 209.)

The name Turk's Face Mountain was used into the twentieth century. However, in 1901 Wallace Bruce tells us that it was called St. Anthony's Face. There seems to have been some confusion with Anthony's Nose. The mountain is now part of Hudson Highlands State Park. The pressure tunnel of the Catskill Aqueduct comes up at the northwestern foot of the mountain, near the shore, and then passes beneath Breakneck in a 1,000-foot-long tunnel. The tip of the ridge is pierced by tunnels of the New York Central and Route 9D. There is hikers' access parking at the north end of the tunnel, where the trail starts up the ridge. There are tremendous cliffs in the old quarry section on the southwest face.

51.50 Breakneck Point on east.

51.50 Wey-Gat. This is Dutch for "Wind Gate," the name for that part of the river between Storm King Mountain and Breakneck Mountain. In the nineteenth century this place was called the Northern Gate of the Highlands.

51.50 Storm King Mountain to west (elevation 1,340 feet). This is the northeastern buttress of the

STORM KING MOUNTAIN AND WEST SHORE RAILROAD TRAIN c1900. Hudson River Day Line photo. Courtesy Alfred V. S. Olcott, Jr.

Hudson Highlands, with Butter Hill to the southwest and Storm King Clove and Whitehorse Mountain to the south. The Old Storm King Highway traverses the cliffs above the Hudson on a narrow ledge at the 200-foot level, offering magnificent views. The New Storm King Highway climbs the back of the mountain to the 900-foot level, offering more limited views.

The earliest name given to this mountain by Europeans was Klinkersberg (so-called by Henry Hudson, from its glistening and broken rock). Lossing tells us that:

The Storm King, seen from the middle of the river abreast its eastern centre, is almost semicircular in form, and gave to the minds of the utilitarian Dutch skippers who navigated the Hudson early, the idea of a huge lump of butter and they named it "Boter Berg" or "Butter Hill." It had borne that name until recently (1865), when Mr. Willis successfully appealed to the good taste of the public by giving it the more appropriate and poetic title of Storm King.
(Lossing, *The Hudson*, p. 208.)

The western extension of the ridge is still called Butter Hill. There was a named train on the West Shore called the "Storm King." It was a mid-afternoon express from Albany to Weehawken.

> *... when the Storm King smites his*
> *   thunderous gong,*
> *Thy hills reply from many a bellowing*
> *   wave;*
> *And when with smiles the sun o'erlooks*
> *   thine brow,*
> *He sees no stream more beautiful*
> *   than thou.*

                                                    Anon.

In the nineteenth century the Storm King Mountain House, a resort, sanitarium, and later private club, operated on the north slope at the 1,200 ft. level.

51.55 Catskill Aqueduct. The aqueduct passes beneath the river here in an inverted siphon 1,100 feet below the river, in solid rock. The tunnel is horseshoe shaped, being 17 feet high and 17½ feet wide—

large enough for a railroad train to pass through. The water flows at a rate of 4 m.p.h. and passes 500,000,000 gallons per day. Granite towers can be seen on either side of the river atop the tunnel shafts. On the east side the water continues through another 1,000-foot tunnel beneath Breakneck Mountain and another, a mile long, beneath Mt. Taurus. The aqueduct tunnel is 1,400 feet below the high water mark. It was completed in 1919.

51.55 Dutchess County to east (1990 population 259,462). For the next 47 miles to just above Tivoli, the eastern shore belongs to Dutchess County. Dutchess is one of the original ten counties erected in 1683 and is named in honor of the wife of the Duke of Albany and York, later King James II. It has an area of 816 square miles and extends inland from the Hudson sixteen miles to the Taconic Mountains. It is bounded on the west by the Hudson River, on the north by Columbia County, on the east by Salisbury, Litchfield, and Fairfield Counties in Connecticut, and on the south by Putnam County, New York, which was taken from Dutchess in 1812. It is comprised of twenty townships and the incorporated cities of Beacon and Poughkeepsie. The townships are Red Hook, Milan, Pine Plains, Northeast, Rhinebeck, Clinton, Stanford, Amenia, Washington, Pleasant Valley, Hyde Park, Poughkeepsie, La Grange, Unionvale, Dover, Pawling, Beekman, East Fishkill, Wappinger, and Fishkill. Principal towns and cities are Poughkeepsie, Beacon, Pawling, Millbrook,

Millerton, Tivoli, Red Hook, Rhinebeck, and Hyde Park.

Principal mountain ranges are the Taconics along the Connecticut border and the Fishkill Range, including North and South Beacon Mountains in the northern Hudson Highlands. There are several north–south ridges of hills parallel to the Hudson and the Taconics. Principal watercourses are the Roeleff Jansen's Kill, Wappinger's Creek, and Fishkill Creek, flowing west to the Hudson. Principal lakes are Whaley Lake, Quaker Lake, Lake Walton, Sylvan Lake, Tamarack Lake, Hunn's Lake, Swift Pond, Indian Lake, Strauss Marsh, Round Lake, Upton Lake, Long Pond, Silver Lake, Spring Lake, Halycon Lake, Miller Pond, Thompson Pond, and Stissing Pond. Principal parks are Taconic State Park, Rudd Pond Area, and Margaret Lewis Norrie State Park. The Taconic State Parkway, a toll-free scenic highway, runs the length of the county from north to south about five miles inland from the Hudson. Principal railroads are the main line of the New York Central, along the Hudson River; the former New Haven lines from Poughkeepsie Bridge to Pawling and Brewster and from Fishkill Junction to Hopewell Junction; and the Harlem Division of the former New York Central along the base of the Taconics from Brewster and Pawling north to Dover Plains, Amenia, Millerton, and Copake Falls (the northern section largely defunct), all presently in the Conrail System. Both MTA and Amtrak operate over the Hudson River Line. The county is largely rural with

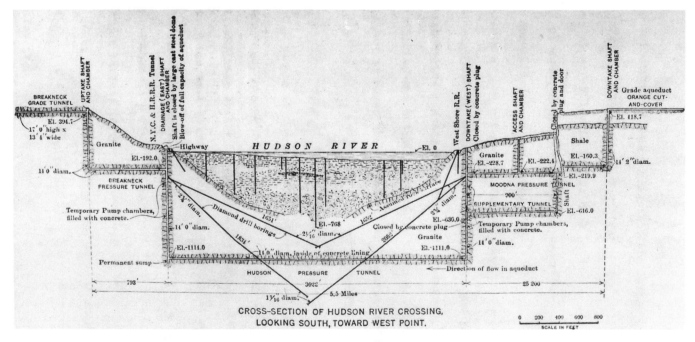

CROSS-SECTION OF HUDSON RIVER CROSSING,
LOOKING SOUTH, TOWARD WEST POINT.

CROSS-SECTION OF HUDSON RIVER crossing Catskill aqueduct. Courtesy Alfred V. S. Olcott, Jr.

many truck and dairy farms and large private estates. Poughkeepsie is the county seat.

The area was originally populated by the Wappinger Indians. On February 8, 1682, a license was granted to Francis Rombout, Jacobus Kipp, and Gulian Ver Planck to purchase land from the Indians. On August 8, 1683, they purchased a tract of 85,000 acres from Nimham, chief of the Wappingers. They in fact cheated the Indians. First they bargained to purchase for a given price "all the land they could see," and then conducted the Indians to the top of South Beacon Mountain, the highest elevation between the Catskills and the seacoast and indicated a tract of land sixteen miles back from the Hudson to the Taconics. The Indians honored this bargain for many years, but in 1740 Chief Daniel of the Wappingers sought to have it set aside in a celebrated law trial—to no avail. This large patent was known as the Rombout Patent. Gulian Ver Planck died before the patent was issued, but his place was taken by Stephanus Van Cortlandt. Jacobus Kipp married Ver Planck's widow, thereby succeeding to the share of his defunct partner. Letters of patent were granted by King James II to Rombout, Van Cortlandt, and Kipp. In 1698 Lt. Colonel Henry Beekman had a large patent centering on Rhinecliff. The Schuyler Patent of 1688 included tracts north and south of Poughkeepsie and Cruger's Island. To a large extent Dutchess County remained under the manorial system until the mid-nineteenth century. Much of the eastern portion of the county was settled by Quakers and Yankees from New England. Only limited industrial development came with the steamboats and railroads. For many years drovers would herd their cattle to the steamboats at Poughkeepsie for shipment to New York City, and consequently the main roads developed running from east to west. In the later nineteenth and early twentieth centuries, Dutchess was favored by the wealthy for country estates, and some of the finest face on the Hudson River. There was a limited iron and steel industry at Poughkeepsie in the mid-nineteenth century. Commercial impetus was given by construction of the Poughkeepsie Railroad Bridge in 1886. The principal industry in Dutchess County today is International Business Machines (IBM), with principal plants at Poughkeepsie and Fishkill.

52.30 Cornwall-on-Hudson to west. A former resort area, now a residential village at the northern foot of Storm King Mountain, south of Moodna Creek, much of the town is on a plateau or terrace affording fine views over Newburgh Bay and many attractive homesites. It was the home of such well-known nineteenth-century literary figures as Lyman Abbott,

E. P. Roe, and Nathaniel Parker Willis, whose estate Idlewild became well known through his magazine writings and his book *Outdoors at Idlewild.* Idlewild was designed by Calvert Vaux, then practicing at Newburgh. After Willis's death in 1867 the property passed to the novelist Edward Payson Roe. The New York, Ontario & Western Railway branched off westward from the West Shore at Cornwall. In 1892 the N.Y.O. & W. built a large pier here for the transfer of coal to barges. The former village of Canterbury is now the principal shopping section of Cornwall. The Museum of the Hudson Highlands, one of the East's finest nature museums and interpretative centers, is located here at the base of Storm King Mountain on The Boulevard. 914-534-7781.

52.80 Site of New York, Ontario & Western pier to west.

52.80 Sugarloaf Mountain to east (elevation 900 feet).

52.80 Pollepel Island to east. Also variously called Pollepel's Island, Pollepel Eiland, Polly Pell's Island, Pot Ladle Island, and, at an earlier time, Cheese Island. An Indian tribe called it Menahtis, meaning a small island. The Polypus is the name of a prickly pear of the cactus family which once grew abundantly on the island. The Dutch Poptlepel or Polopel means spoon or potladle.

The island is mostly rock and covers 6¾ acres with a maximum elevation of 115 feet. It is 1,010 feet from the eastern shore of the Hudson, but the breakwaters forming the small harbor come to within 650 feet from shore. There are flats of shallow water both north and south of the island, but a channel deep enough for steam tugboats between it and the mainland.

BANNERMAN'S ISLAND ARSENAL. Photo: © Gretchen McHugh.

BANNERMAN'S ISLAND. Photo: © Gretchen McHugh.

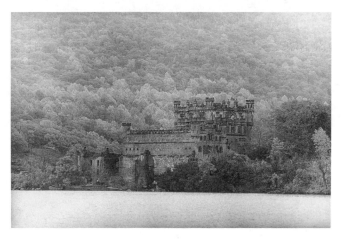

BANNERMAN'S ISLAND. Photo: © Gretchen McHugh.

A chevaux-de-frise was constructed between the island and Plum Point on the western shore in 1776.

The Indians believed the island was haunted and would not stay on it at night—which made it somewhat of a refuge for those fleeing from them. The early Dutch mariners believed the island marked the northern limit of the domain of the goblins of Dunderberg. New sailors to the Hudson were inoculated against the Heer of Dunderberg by being ducked in the river as their boats passed the island when entering the highlands. In 1866 Benson Lossing told of a lone fisherman who lived on the island with his insane wife. Later another fisherman named Ward, a relative of Henry Ward Beecher, lived on the island. At one time Matthew Vassar wanted to acquire the island as a site for a monument to Henry Hudson, but he failed to arouse interest or backing. Since the Revolution, the island belonged to William Van Wyck from 1788 until his devisees sold it to Walter C. Anthony in 1888. That same year it was deeded to Mary G. Taft, who sold it to Francis Bannerman on December 5, 1900.

Francis Bannerman VI was born in Dundee, Scotland, in 1851, and came to America when he was three years old. His family settled in Brooklyn, and his father established a business selling articles acquired at Navy auctions. His son followed in his footsteps and entered the business in a large way after the Civil War. Francis Bannerman was descended from one of the few MacDonalds to survive the massacre at Glencoe in 1692. He was a Scottish patriot, a founder of the Caledonian Hospital in Brooklyn, a member of the St. Andrew's Society, and a strict Presbyterian. After his purchase of Pollepel Island in 1900, Francis Bannerman commenced construction of a Scottish castle for a summer retreat and an arsenal for his business. He built the present structure with its crennelations, turrets, moats, battlements, etc., with the intent to be both romantic and functional at the same time. It was still incomplete at the time of his death in November of 1918.

The Bannerman family continued to use the island arsenal. The main place of business was at Broadway in New York City, but it was moved to Blue Point, Long Island, in 1959. The island was used for storage of ammunition, arms, and explosives. It was the center of a worldwide business.

For many years the great castle of Bannerman's Island Arsenal attracted the attention of travellers on the river steamers and the New York Central Railroad and Route 9D. In 1967 the Bannermans sold the island to the people of the state of New York. They removed all the old military merchandise, giving much of it to the Smithsonian Institution for their museum. The Taconic State Park Commission took possession on July 1, 1968. For a short while they offered public tours of the island. On the night of August 8, 1969, a great fire destroyed all the buildings. Only romantic ruins remain.

53.20 Moodna Creek to west. Its Indian name was Wooraneck, but it was later known as Murderer's Creek because of legends of Indian treachery in the immediate neighborhood. The name was changed at the behest of N. P. Willis, whose estate Idlewild abutted the stream. It rises in Tomahawk Lake near Blooming Grove and flows northeast to near Washingtonville, where it is joined from the northwest by the waters of the Otter Kill. It then flows east, by the northern end of Schunnemunk Mountain, to Salisbury Mills and Mountainville, where it turns north past Firthcliffe and then turns east after receiving the waters of Silver Stream from the northwest. It flows into the Hudson through tidal marshes south of Plum Point. It gives its name to a great high viaduct of the Erie Railroad near Salisbury Mills, and flows through some of the most idyllic scenery in the eastern United States. Its pollution by several paper mills became a cause célèbre, but the stream is now relatively pure.

53.30 Sloop Hill to the west. In 1988 this was acquired by Scenic Hudson as a nature preserve. Sand mining operations have almost cut the height of this hill in half, but vegetation is returning and the footpaths offer unexcelled views over the water and beaches still in their natural state.

53.40 Plum Point to west. Also variously called Plumb Point and Nicoll's Point, it was settled in 1684 by an individual named Patrick MacGregorie. During the Revolution, it was fortified with a battery of fourteen guns. The Georgian Colonial mansion was the home of Alfred P. Sloan of General Motors. Today the point has been cut up and intensively developed for row-type housing.

54.00 Wade's Brook to east. Also called Cascade Brook.

54.10 Gordon's Brook to east. This brook flows into and from Melzingah Reservoir, which is named in honor of "The Cascade of Melsingah," a poem by William Cullen Bryant, published in *The Talisman* of 1828.

54.50 New Windsor to west (population 22,937). A residential suburb of Newburgh, this little town is best known as a cantonment site for the Revolutionary Army—particularly after the cessation of active hostilities. Washington made his headquarters at the Ellison House here between June 22 and July 21, 1779, and between December 1, 1779 and June 25, 1780. Generals Knox, Greene, and Gates and Colonels Biddle and Wadsworth also had headquarters nearby. In neighboring Vail's Gate, Generals St. Clair and Gates used the Edmonston House as headquarters, and General Lafayette used the Brewster House. The New York Military Academy, a preparatory school for West Point and one of the oldest in New York State, is located here. Its brick and concrete Gothic buildings cover a 350-acre campus. The New Windsor Cantonment was one of three winter camps occupied by the Continental Army for eight months in 1782–1783. It is also called Temple Hill from the Temple, a large meeting hall wherein Washington refused a crown. The Masonic Order maintains a shrine here.

54.90 Dutchess Junction to east. A defunct railroad junction between main line of New York Central and the Newburgh, Dutchess & Connecticut R. R., it has been superseded by Fishkill Junction.

55.00 Fishkill Bay and Creek to east. The Bay has extremely shallow shoal water; depths range from one-half to four feet. It is separated from main body of Newburgh Bay on the north by Denning Point. Fishkill Creek rises behind Beacon Ridge and flows generally southwest to the Hudson. Name from the Dutch Vischer's Kil, or Fisherman's Creek (Indian name: Mawanassigh).

55.00 Denning Point to east. Named for Captain William Denning, a patriot officer. Eastern terminus of Revolutionary period ferry to Newburgh and New Windsor and eastern terminus for Erie Railroad rail car ferry, this was also known as Fishkill Hook. There were burial grounds of the Wiccapee and Shenandoah Indians here.

Formerly the Fishkill Branch of the New Haven R. R. terminated here at the car ferry. A model of the large sidewheel railroad car ferry *William T. Hart,* which operated on this route, may be seen at the Hudson River Maritime Center Museum in Kingston. The Point has recently been acquired as an environmental preserve through the efforts of Scenic Hudson Preservation Conference.

56.00 Mount Beacon to east. Highest point(s) in the Fishkill Mountain Range, it actually has two summits: North Beacon (elevation 1,531 feet) and South Beacon (1,635 feet). These are the highest points between the Catskills and the seacoast. It was formerly called Grand Sachem Mountain, in the Wequehache, or Endless Hills. Its present name comes from beacon fires used as signals during the Revolution. The gigantic fires were built up of rectangular pyramids thirty feet high built of logs filled with brush wood. James Fenimore Cooper set some of the most exciting action of his novel, *The Spy,* on the slopes of this range.

The summit of North Beacon could formerly be reached by the abandoned and ruined Mount Beacon Incline Railway. This unique cable railway was the steepest of its length in the world with an

CAR ON MOUNT BEACON INCLINE RAILROAD. Author's collection.

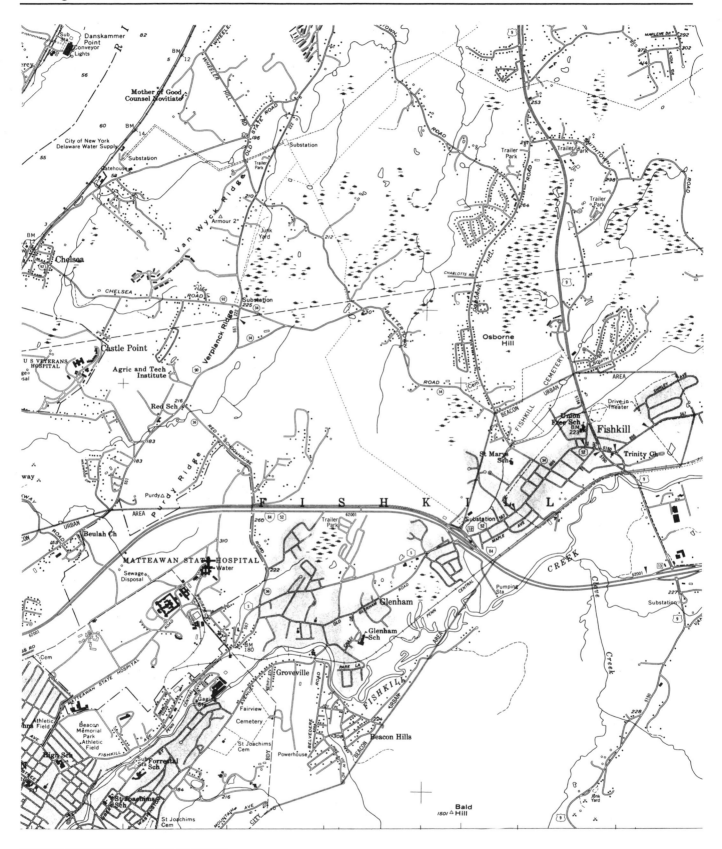

NEWBURGH/WAPPINGER'S FALLS SOUTH

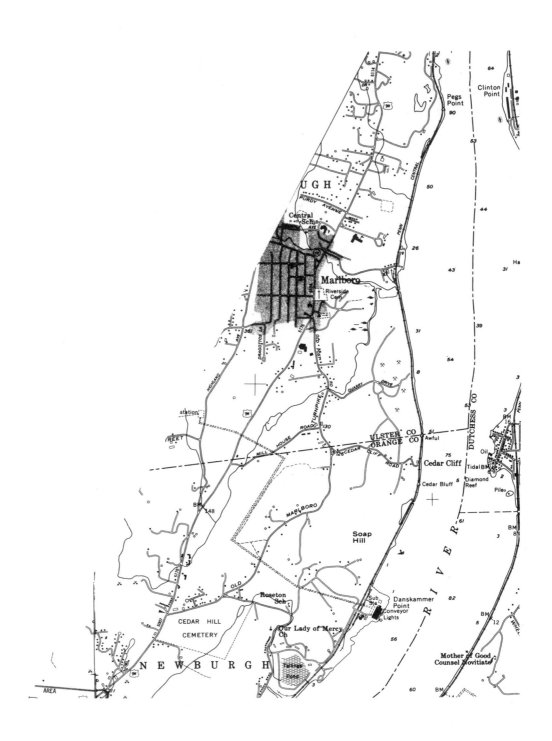

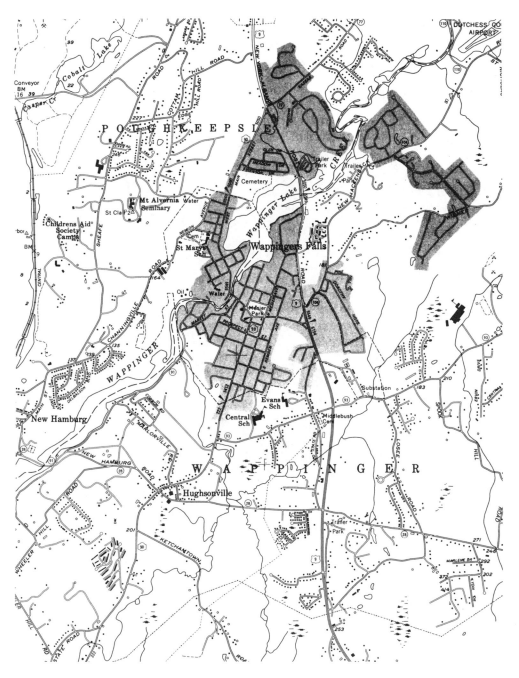

NEWBURGH/WAPPINGER'S FALLS NORTH

average gradient of 64%. The track, which is also built on a curve, is 2,364 feet long. In the middle is a double track section known as the Brown Patent Turn-Out, where the two cars pass each other. The railway was designed by the Otis Elevator Corporation, who also built the machinery. The roadbed was built by the Mohawk Construction Company, and the cars were built by the Ramapo Iron Works at Hillburn, NY. Total lift is 1,200 feet. The two cars each seat fifty-four passengers and travel at a rate of 500 feet per minute—one car ascending while the other descends. Motive power comes from powerful electric motors turning a drum at the top around which is wound the cable. The cars have a 10,000 lb. load capacity. The 1⅜-inch-thick steel cable has a capacity of sixty-two tons. The system was designed with a twelve-times safety factor. Safer than most modern office building elevators, the Otis Double Grip Safety Device, activated by a centrifugal governor, can hold 50,000 lbs. There are also hand brakes on the cars and on the cable drum. In normal operation, the cars are controlled by Otis Electric Limit Stops, as in most modern elevators. The system was opened on May 30, 1902, and has operated since without accident. It was long operated by the Mount Beacon-on-Hudson Association. In 1909 it carried 70,000 passengers. There were some summer homes and a dance hall and casino at the top. The line also carried some freight and has served as a ski lift. At various times there has been talk of building a hotel or motel atop the incline. The view is spectacular.

56.00 Quassaic Creek to west. It rises south of Plattekill and flows generally south by southeast past Savilton, Cronomer Valley, and Glenwood Park; thence behind Newburgh. Here it turns east and flows into the Hudson south of Newburgh. Principal tributaries are Bushfield Creek (Orange Lake) and Gidneytown Creek.

56.00 Newburgh to west (population 26,454). An industrial and residential city located along the river edge and on a plateau 300 feet above the river, it was first settled in 1709 by German Palatinates, who established the Palatine Parish by Quassaic under the Lutheran Minister Joshua Kocherthal. The town was named after Neuberg-on-Rhine. However, the Palatinates were almost penniless and, by 1762, most had moved west into Pennsylvania to find richer farmlands. They were superseded by Scots and Englishmen who modified the name of the town to Newburgh, in honor of Newburgh-on-Tay in Scotland. George Washington had his headquarters here toward the end of the Revolution, from March 31, 1782, until late August 1783. He established his headquarters in the house of the Huguenot Jonathan

Hasbrouck. This is now preserved as an historic site and museum. While at Newburgh, Washington received the infamous Newburgh letter. It was anonymous but threatened revolt by the army if their pay was not immediately forthcoming. Washington shamed the would-be rebels into being patient by remarking that his eyesight had grown dim in the service of his country. Here he also received the Nicola letter offering him the crown. This, too, he scorned. It was at Newburgh that the Continental Army was finally disbanded upon signing of the Treaty of Paris in 1783.

After the Revolution, Newburgh developed as a trading center for the rich agricultural area further inland. Produce was shipped from here to New York City. By 1798, Major Isaac Belknap and three other entrepreneurs had established four lines of sloops trading between Newburgh and New York City. Construction of the Newburgh & Cochecton Turnpike quickened the growth of this "gateway city" on the new road to western expansion. Ultimately the road was to go on to Canandaigua, but construction of the Erie Canal in 1825 diverted the path of western trade to Albany. The Erie Railroad opened a branch from Chester on its main line in 1850, reaching the Hudson via the Valley of the Moodna and the Quassaic Creek Ravine. It was planned to establish a railroad car ferry to Fishkill, where connections further east were to be maintained by the Dutchess & Columbia Railroad and the New York & New England. This route was later superseded by construction of the railroad bridge at Poughkeepsie in 1886.

Newburgh was incorporated as a city in 1865. During the early nineteenth century, Newburgh was a whaling port and home of China and ivory traders—a true seaport. In the mid-nineteenth century the famous landscape architect Andrew Jackson Downing lived and worked here, as well as his younger associates Calvert Vaux, Frederick Law Olmstead, and Frederick C. Withers. The school of Hudson River Bracketed Architecture was indigenous to Newburgh. By 1842, industry had grown to such an extent that there were three flouring mills, three plaster mills, an extensive brewery, a rotary pump manufactory, and factories manufacturing floor cloths, soap, candles, morocco leather, buckskin, ploughs, combs, tobacco products, chairs, carriages, guns, whips, and sashes and blinds. There were also two iron foundries, two tanneries, four lumber yards, six coal yards, two ropewalks, two freestone and marble yards, a steam engine factory and general machine shop, a steam boiler factory, two ship yards, a marine railway, an extensive brick yard, and three printing offices.

In later years Newburgh produced major quantities of flannels, overalls, paper boxes, iron products, hats, wire products, furniture, building supplies, paints, soap, electric motors, reed chairs, flour, feed, wallpaper, and lawn mowers. The West Shore Railroad was put through town in 1883. There was a ferry service to Fishkill-Beacon from 1743 until 1963. In the late nineteenth and early twentieth century, the Orange Traction Company operated local streetcars and the electric interurban Newburgh & Wallkill Valley Railway to Orange Lake and Walden. Newburgh was a major steamboat landing, and the Marvell Shipyard here built many of the most famous Hudson River steamers, including the *Hendrick Hudson* and *Robert Fulton*, not to mention innumerable steam ferryboats.

Downing Park was designed as a memorial to Andrew Jackson Downing by Vaux & Olmstead, and its beautiful grounds offer fine prospects of the surrounding countryside. Newburgh is the seat of Mount Saint Mary College. Of particular interest architecturally are the Orange County Courthouse (1841) by Thornton M. Niver; St. George Episcopal Church (1819), Greek Revival; and the Dutch Reformed Church (1830), Greek Revival, by Alexander Jackson Davis.

Newburgh is a city in decline. Regressive tax policies have driven industry away. The steamboat industry died after World War I, and Newburgh lost its importance as a point of transshipment. Discontinuation of the ferry in 1963 and its replacement by a new bridge north of town diverted more trade from the area, as did the cessation of West Shore passenger trains and elimination as a landing by the Hudson River Day Line because of decay of the dock. The construction of a new dock in 1973 was futile, as it is too delicate to withstand the impact of a large ship against the bulkheads. There has been chronic unemployment with a staggering welfare load. When an aggressive city manager attempted to limit welfare, he got into serious trouble. The major stores have moved out to the suburbs as has industry and the middle class population. Crime is rampant and many people in Orange County who used to shop in Newburgh are afraid to go there. Most of the county administration has moved to Goshen and Middletown. An ill-advised urban-renewal policy has demolished much of the precious architectural heritage, which might have made Newburgh into a nineteenth-century Williamsburg. While some restoration work and renewal programs are going forward, the future of this once attractive city is still very much undecided.

While most of the foregoing negative statements unfortunately remain true, there has, however, been some substantial forward movement. An attractive new waterfront drive has opened up extensive magnificent views and gradually new housing is being built. In the writer's opinion they don't take maximum advantage of the splendid setting, but they are clean, new, and decent, and provide homes and increase civic pride. Let us hope that the good work continues of reviving this once proud city to its former attractiveness.

56.10 Hasbrouck House and Washington Monument Belvidere to west. The Hasbrouck House was built in 1724 and was enlarged in 1750–1753 when it was purchased by Jonathan Hasbrouck. It is in the Dutch Colonial style with a low roof, but has similarities to the typical Huguenot stone house. It had reached its present form in 1770. George Washington and his wife lived here from April 4, 1782, until August 18, 1783. It was here that Washington wrote his famous "crown letter" rejecting a monarchy, and here, on June 7, 1783, that he parted with his guard. His army lay in camp five miles westward at New Windsor. Knox and Lafayette were frequent visitors. In 1850 the State of New York purchased the house from the Hasbrouck family. This was the first historic preservation effort by any state or federal agency.

The grounds include a large lawn, well and well-sweep, flagpole, museum building (erected in 1910), and the grave of Usual (Uzal) Knapp, a member of Washington's life guard, who died in 1836 at the age of ninety-six.

The Washington Monument Belvidere was completed in 1888. I quote from the report of the committee to erect the monument:

…the committee, after much reflection, had come to the conclusion that the most appropriate monument to carry out the spirit of the joint resolution

HASBROUCK HOUSE, Washington's headquarters, Newburgh. Photo: Alfred H. Marks.

would be a structure of rude but imposing nature, built of the native stone. Such a structure would typify the rugged simplicity of the times and personages it was intended to commemorate.

In addition to this, the site of the proposed monument afforded an opportunity for distant display, which could not well be ignored. The grounds are on a bluff overlooking the river, and in full view of travelers on the cars and passing steam-boats. The monument therefore should be of sufficient proportions to attract the eye of the millions who annually pass up and down the river.

Another fact to which the attention of the committee was called was that these Headquarters are visited every year by thousands of excursionists from the city of New York and tourists from all parts of the world. A very natural, and probably the first, impulse of strangers visiting a monument is to ascend it, and for this reason the committee was of opinion that if the structure to be erected could be surmounted by an accessible outlook it would be a very desirable feature.

...the committee commissioned Mr. Maurice J. Power, of New York, who has had a wide experience and great success in monumental structures, to prepare a design. Mr. Power called to his aid Mr. John H. Duncan, of New York, artist and architect.

The design prepared by Mr. Duncan and adopted by the committee represents a Tower of Victory, built of native stone, of a rectangular form. The dimensions or ground lines are 37 by 32 feet, with a total height of 53 feet. Four large archways open into the atrium, one on each side. In the center of the atrium, upon a polished pedestal of red granite, will stand a life-size bronze statue of Washington, modeled by the sculptor O'Donovan. (Note: This statue was not a success and has been removed to the museum.)

From the ground floor two commodious circular stair-cases (one for ascent and the other for descent) lead to a belvedere, or open outlook, capable of holding over three hundred persons.

The view from the belvedere will prove a very attractive feature to the thousands of strangers who visit these Headquarters every year. (Note: It is presently closed to the public.) *It embraces a broad expanse of river and mountain scenery, with outlying valleys. North and South Beacon, upon whose towering tops the signal fires were lit during the Revolution, are directly in front, whilst to the right will be seen the Northern Gate to the Highlands and West Point in the distance.*

("The Centennial Celebration and Washington Monument at Newburgh, N.Y.," Report of the Joint Select Committee Washington, Government Printing Office, 1889.)

56.10 Site of former Marvell Shipyard to west. Along riverfront below the Hasbrouck House park.

56.20 Site of former Newburgh-Beacon ferry terminal.

56.25 Site of former steamer landing.

56.30 West Shore Railroad passenger terminal to west. Classic red brick ca. 1900.

56.30 Fishkill and Beacon to the east (Beacon population 13,243; Fishkill Village 1,957; Fishkill Township 17,655). A residential city with light manufacturing, the present city of Beacon was incorporated in 1913 and incorporated the former villages of Fishkill Landing and Matteawan. The name Matteawan is Indian, and its derivation is somewhat confused. It means either "country of good fur" or "confluence of streams," which would in effect denote good beaver and other furbearing animal country. (The name is not uncommon elsewhere, and usually the location fits this description.) The area was originally populated by the Pachami branch of the Wappinger Indians, although Wiccapee and Shenandoah tribes had burial grounds on nearby Denning Point.

The present village of Fishkill is two miles inland and incorporates the former villages of Glenham and Wolcottville. It derives its name from the Dutch name for the local creek—Vischer's Kil, or Fisherman's Creek.

The entire neighborhood was part of the Rombout Patent of 1682. (See article on Dutchess County for more details—ERM 51.55.) Other partners in the patent were Gulian Verplanck, Jacobus Kipp, and Stephanus Van Cortlandt. Catharyna, daughter of Francis Rombout, was born in New York City in 1687. At the age of sixteen, she married Roger Brett, a lieutenant in the English navy. They settled here in 1714 and built the house at 50 Van Nydeck Avenue, Beacon, which is still standing and is now a museum. After her husband's death, Madam Brett, as she was locally called, became an active businesswoman. Her mill was the principal local industry. Unlike most other landowners, it was her practice to sell her lands rather than lease them. This led to commercial development. She died in 1764 and is buried in the old Reformed Church at Fishkill.

Gulian Verplanck also built a large home known as Mount Gulian between 1730 and 1740, on land purchased by his grandfather (also named Gulian) and Francis Rombout from the Wappinger Indians in 1683.

During the Revolution it was used as headquarters

by Gen. Baron von Steuben, and here, on May 13, 1783, General Knox and other Continental Army officers founded the Society of the Cincinnati.

Mount Gulian has always remained in the Verplanck family, although the house was largely destroyed by fire in 1931. The Mount Gulian Society was formed in 1966 by descendants of Gulian Verplanck in order to restore the house and preserve it as a site of historic interest. Reconstruction was completed in 1976. It is approximately ¼ mile north of the intersection of Routes 9D and I-84 at the Newburgh Beacon Bridge. It is open to the public. Call 914-831-8172 for visitation hours and information on special events.

During the Revolution, Fishkill became a major supply depot and hospital area. It was first used as such after the Battle of White Plains. Many American Revolutionary soldiers are buried in the area. Part of Washington's army was encamped here from March of 1782 until August 1783. The Van Wyck House, which served as headquarters for Gen. Israel Putnam, served as the model for the Wharton House in Cooper's *The Spy*, of which many of the most exciting actions take place in this neighborhood. The Brinckerhoff House served as Washington's headquarters. The ferry, which had been established in 1743, served as a vital communications link inside the American lines.

After the Revolution, there was considerable commercial development. Between 1812 and 1816 the Long Wharf and ferry slips were built and an inn was established at the wharf. After 1814 John Jacob Astor, Peter Schenck, and Philip Hone, attracted by waterfalls on the Fishkill, built a cotton mill and foundry. Bricks, cotton goods, silk, machinery, wagons, and hats were also made here. About 1872 Alexander T. Stewart established his Beacon Piece and Dye Works, which was originally called the Groveville Mills. It produced carpets. The workers' homes are well preserved and provide a good example of a nineteenth-century industrial community.

The Fishkill-Beacon area also attracted wealthy estate owners. Tioranda was built in 1859 by Richard Morris Hunt for George Joseph Howland, a shipping magnate. It is Gothic-Victorian with contrasting black and white glazed bricks. It is now known as Craig House and is used as a sanitarium.

Also part of the Craig Sanitarium is Wodenethe, the former estate of Henry Winthrop Sargent, to whom Andrew Jackson Downing dedicated his *Architecture of Country Houses*, in 1850. The house was built in 1825 and was extensively remodeled by Calvert Vaux in 1853. It is painted yellow with white trim and is three-story with a hipped roof.

Mount Gulian, the Verplanck family home, burned in 1931. This was the home of Gulian Crommelin Verplanck (1786–1870). He was admitted to the bar in 1807 and took part in politics, writing against the Clinton faction. His verse satires are collected in *The Bucktail Bards* (1819). Verplanck served in the New

NEWBURGH BEACON BRIDGE, 1963. View is looking eastward. Twin span has since been erected to the south. Courtesy New York State Bridge Authority.

York legislature and in the U. S. House of Representatives. From 1821 to 1824 he was a professor at the General Theological Seminary, and wrote *Essays on the Nature and Uses of the Various Evidences of Revealed Religion* (1824). He was associated with William Cullen Bryant and R. C. Sands in writing the annual *Talisman*. However, Verplanck is best remembered for his three-volume edition of Shakespeare's plays in 1847, and he remains among the greatest of Shakespeare scholars.

The 900-acre estate of his former neighbor John J. Scanlon has been taken over by the state of New York for the Matawan Correctional Facility, formerly referred to as Matteawan State Hospital for the Criminally Insane.

The principal local industry is IBM. There is also a major Veteran's Administration Hospital.

56.30 Newburgh Bay. Eight miles long, extending from Cornwall on the south to Chelsea at the north, its widest section (1.6 miles) is opposite the mouth of Moodna Creek north of Cornwall. The eastern shore is largely shoal water, the principal channel being nearer the western shore.

56.35 New Newburgh Steamboat Landing to west.

57.00 Sherman's Dock on west.

57.20 Newburgh-Beacon Bridge. A unit of the New York State Bridge Authority, it opened to traffic November 2, 1963. This is a combination deck truss and continuous deck bridge, designed by Modjeski & Masters. Principal contractors were Frederick Share Corporation, Dravo Corporation, and Bethlehem Steel Corporation. Overall length is 7,855 feet. Length of main span is 1,000 feet. The bridge has a two-lane roadway. Vessel clearance is 135 feet and the highest point of steel above water is 252 feet. The highest point of roadway slab above water is 192 feet. There are 24 spans, 23 piers, and 2 abutments. The deepest foundation goes 165 feet below the surface of the water. Actual construction was started in March 1961. Total cost was $70,000,000. It carries Interstate 84. A toll is charged. A twin structure was opened in 1985.

57.30 Matawan Correctional Facility to east. Formerly referred to as the Matteawan State Hospital for the Criminally Insane.

58.00 Balmville to west. Named for the "Balm of Gilead tree," also known as the Bonville oak tree, the oldest living thing in Orange County. This tree was a seedling in 1699. It is 90 inches in diameter with a circumference of 25 feet, 5 inches. A "protected" tree, it is surrounded by a fence.

5

The Central Hudson

58.00 Brockway to east. This is the site of a former brick yard.

58.50 Purdy Ridge to east (elevation 342 feet).

58.50 Cronomer Hill to west (elevation 728 feet).

59.50 Castle Point--U. S. Veterans Hospital to east (elevation 170 feet). Opened in 1924 for care of tubercular war veterans, it can accommodate 400 patients. It is a series of light red brick buildings with a tall water tower.

59.75 Mud Hole to west. A shallow cove now cut off from the river by the West Shore railroad tracks, so named because it seemed to the railroad builders that this took so much fill that it was a bottomless hole.

60.00 Middle Hope to west. This village is inland on Route 9W.

60.25 Low Point to east.

60.25 Van Wyck Ridge to east (elevation 393 feet).

60.25 Chelsea to east. This was formerly called Carthage Landing. There is an active yacht club here which is home to a considerable fleet of small sailboats. The Delaware Aqueduct Tunnel is here, and an intake station.

61.00 Roseton to west. Here was the home of Sen. John Bailey Rose, owner of the Rose Brick Co. The house was later Beau Rivage Restaurant and overlooked the river. It was two-story Greek Revival clapboard with Ionic columns, ca. 1810. Roseton is a station on the West Shore Railroad.

61.25 Clay Pitts to west. Jova brickyard.

62.00 Danskammer Point to west. A low, flat, rocky point jutting out into water 36 feet deep, it was long a menace to navigation. Formerly there was a projecting point. This was broken off when it was run into by the large steamer *Cornell* one misty morning in 1890. The present lighthouse was built on the fragments which fell into the water. It takes its name from the Dutch "teufel's danskammer," or "devil's dancehall." This name was given it by Lt.

Cowenhoven in 1663, who saw Indians doing ceremonial dances there by firelight. This was a usual meeting place for Indians to hold their ceremonial dances, and Henry Hudson witnessed such a ceremony on his first visit. It is recorded that one of the dances was called the "kintikaeye."

Benson Lossing tells us that

On this rock the Indians performed their peculiar semi-religious rites, called pow-wows, before going upon hunting and fishing expeditions, or the warpath. They painted themselves grotesquely, built a large fire upon this rock, and danced around it with songs and yells, making strange contortions of face and limbs, under the direction of their conjurors or 'medicine men.' They would tumble, leap, run and yell, when, as they said, the Devil, or Evil Spirit, would appear in the shape of a beast of prey or a harmless animal; the former apparition betokened evil to their proposed undertaking, and the latter prophesied of good. For at least a century after the Europeans discovered the river these hideous rites were performed upon this spot, and the Dutch skippers who navigated the Hudson, called the rock Den Duyvel's Dans Kamer. Here it was that Peter Stuyvesant's crew were "most horribly frightened by roystering devils," according to the veracious Knickerbocker.

(Lossing, *The Hudson*, p. 196.)

More recently the point has been the location of large power plants of Central Hudson Electric Company and large oil barges are anchored immediately along-shore in deep water.

62.75 Hughsonville to east. This village is inland on Route 9D. The landing was formerly known as Farmer's Landing.

62.75 Soap Hill to west. Its prominent cliffs rise to an elevation of 320 feet.

63.00 Wappinger's Creek and Falls to east.
This is also the name of a town about a mile up the creek. Wappinger's Creek takes its rise in several lakes in Clinton and Stanford townships east of Staatsburg and Hyde Park. The stream first takes its

proper name just south of Willow Brook Village, at the confluence of Hunn's Lake Creek and Willow Brook. It then flows southwest past Hibernia to Salt Point, where it is joined from the north by the waters of Little Wappinger's Creek. It continues southwest past Pleasant Valley, Rochdale, and Manchester Bridge to the neighborhood of New Hackensack, and forming the boundary between Poughkeepsie and La Grange townships. North of the village of Wappinger's Falls, it forms Wappinger's Lake. Here it goes over a seventy-five-foot fall to tidewater. Near its outlet to the Hudson, it is crossed by a highway bridge and a bascule bridge on the New York Central Railroad. The village (population 5,607) is on a plateau with an elevation of 116 feet. Local industries included a bleachery and an overall factory. The name comes from the local powerful tribe of Wappinger Indians.

63.20 Diamond Reef in midstream. This rocky reef with only five feet depth surrounded by water sixty-two feet deep to west and sixty-eight feet deep to east is also known as New Hamburg Reef. It is known for excellent striped bass fishing.

63.20 Cedarcliff to west. It was formerly known as Hampton and Hampton Ferry. It is a local station on the West Shore Railroad. The large and beautiful historic Cedar Hill Cemetery is also located here off Route 9W.

63.30 New Hamburg to east. This is a local station for Wappinger's Falls on New York Central Railroad. It is an old Palatinate settlement.

63.50 Hampton Point to west. Also known as Peck's Dock, it is noted for fine white cedar trees. Dolomite (magnesium limestone) is quarried on both sides of the river for concrete and road building. The quarries here belong to the New York Trap Rock Division of Lone Star industries.

63.75 Site of former Indian fishing encampment to west.

64.00 Vineyards to west.

64.20 Site of area's earliest settlement (ca. 1695) to west. This later became an important textile manufacturing center.

Three-quarters of a mile west of here is Mill House, built in 1714 by Daniel Gomez. He had built a mill nearby in 1711. The house has the distinction of being the oldest standing dwelling house in North America built by a member of the Jewish faith. Gomez was quite prosperous and the Maune Kill was also known as Jew's Creek from his mills. In

1772 he sold his house to Wolfert Acker, who expanded the house. The third owner was Henry Armstrong, a novelist. He wrote a Civil War novel called *Rutledge* while living here.

64.50 Maune Kill to west. Formerly known as Jew's Creek from the mills of "Gomez the Jew" in the eighteenth century, it rises on the eastern slopes of the Marlboro or Plattekill Mountains and flows over falls in the village of Marlboro.

64.50 Marlboro to west. It is also spelled Marlborough. This is the name of both a village and a town in Ulster County. It is a station on the West Shore Railroad and a formerly active steamboat landing. There was once a profusion of arbor vitae trees in the area. This was a fruit-growing center until the 1930s. This landing used to dispatch a boatload of raspberries daily to New York City in season. It is alleged that the aroma would spread over the river for miles. Here was the home of Col. Lewis DuBois, of 5th Regiment of the Continental Line (1728–1802). His home (ca. 1763) is believed to be the first clapboard house built in Ulster County. Washington visited here. The hotel was built in 1858. McCourt House (brick) dates back to ca. 1830. There are wineries in this area.

64.50 Ulster County to west. From here to West Camp (Wanton Island, ERM 100.50) the west bank is occupied by Ulster County.

Ulster was one of the ten original counties established in 1683 and was named in honor of the Duke of York's earldom in Ireland. It has a present area of 1,143 square miles but has lost some area in the south to Orange. It presently consists of twenty townships: Hardenburgh, Denning, Shandaken, Woodstock, Olive, Hurley, Marbletown, Rochester, Wawarsing, Shawangunk, Gardiner, New Paltz, Plattekill, Marlborough, Lloyd, Esopus, Rosendale, Kingston, Ulster, and Saugerties. The city of Kingston is the county seat. Other principal towns are Saugerties, New Paltz, Rosendale, and Ellenville.

Principal watercourses are Esopus Creek, rising near Slide Mountain in the Catskills and flowing east to the Hudson at Saugerties; Rondout Creek, rising in the high Catskills and also flowing east to the Hudson at Kingston; and the Wallkill River, rising in Lake Mohawk in northern New Jersey and flowing northeast through Orange County to Ulster County at Wallkill. It continues northeast past New Paltz to a junction with Rondout Creek just east of Rosendale.

Principal lakes are Rondout Reservoir and the large Ashokan Reservoir, both belonging to the city of New York. There are three principal groups of mountains. The Catskills occupy the western half of the county. The Shawangunk Mountains are in the southwestern part of the county and the Plattekill Mountains parallel the Hudson River.

The county was settled very early. Henry Hudson made his voyage of discovery in 1609. By 1614 there was an active trading post at Kingston, before the landing of the pilgrim fathers at Plymouth Rock. Early settlement was by the Dutch, with a strong infusion of French Huguenots in the Hurley and New Paltz areas.

In 1708, during the governorship of Lord Cornbury (1702–1708), Queen Anne granted a patent of approximately two million acres to Major Johannis Hardenbergh, Esq., formerly "High Sheriffe of Ulster Countie," and six other grantees. This patent covered most of present-day Ulster, Delaware, Sullivan, and Greene Counties. As most of this area was mountainous and unfit for farming, the major had difficulty finding settlers. Among the first were German Palatinate refugees from the Rhineland. (The Palatinates, victims of the French in the religious wars in Europe, had sought help from England. Queen Anne, sympathetic to their plight and, among other things, aware of the Hardenbergh patent in the Catskills and the need for settlers, agreed to help them.) They first were settled along the Hudson River (1710–1711) and unsuccessfully attempted the manufacture of tar and pitch. After much suffering, they took up farming. Others moved south and settled at Newburgh.

Vagueness about the boundaries of the patent caused decades of litigation, particularly pertaining to the western one which was variously construed as being the Bear Kill at one extreme and the West Branch of the Delaware at the other. In 1749 Ebenezer Wooster surveyed the property and divided it into large sections called Great Lots, averaging between 10,000 and 30,000 acres. By the time matters were settled, most of the original grantees for whom Major Hardenbergh was fronting were long dead. For many years the heirs of the original grantees cherished their "titles" and speculated with them, but few enjoyed any substantial benefit.

In 1672 a smaller patent entitled the Fox Hall Patent had been granted to Capt. Thomas Chambers. This was located above Esopus. It soon lapsed because of lack of heirs. Much of the land around Kingston belonged to the Kingston Commons. The mountainous nature of the territory and confusion over titles and boundaries inhibited settlement of much of Ulster County. The remaining area, unlike that on the east bank of the Hudson, was settled by small freeholders.

Most of eastern Ulster County is devoted to farming—largely orchards and vineyards. The balance is devoted to watershed purposes, forest preserves, parklands, and the resort industry. Principal early industries were tanning and bluestone quarrying. Building of the Wallkill Valley, Ulster & Delaware, and West Shore Railroads did much to foster the resort industry. Tourism remains the county's principal industry. There is an IBM plant at Kingston and other light industry at Kingston, Woodstock, and Ellenville. Kingston serves mainly as an administrative and shopping center.

64.50 Howland to east.

64.70 Casper Creek to east. It flows southwest into Hudson from southeastern section of Poughkeepsie. It was formerly called Casperkill or Jan Casper's Kill; Indian names were Thanakonok and Pietawick-quasseick.

64.70 Young estate to west. This was a point of deep-channel shipping of fruit in the late nineteenth and early twentieth centuries.

64.90 Quarry and crusher to east. Lone Star industries.

64.90 Channingville to east. This is about one mile inland.

64.90 Lake Pontusco to east. Also known as Cobalt Lake, it is located on Casper Creek.

64.90 Pegg's Point to west.

65.00 Clinton Point to east.

65.00 Stoneco Post Office to east. Here is located the New York Trap Rock dolomite quarry.

65.10 Sand pit to west: behind Peggs Point.

65.50 Quarry to east.

65.50 Old landing to west. The *Trojan* was burned here in a local labor war in 1940. This was a winter lay-up berth for river steamboats.

66.00 Barnegat to east. Helen Wilkinson Reynolds tells us, in her *Dutch Houses in the Hudson Valley Before 1776:*

> From the oysterbeds along the Atlantic coast shell-lime was ... obtained to add to the filling for the walls (of houses) and, later, limestone ridges in the Hudson Valley were exploited, as for example at Barnegat (the "fire-hole") in the town of Poughkeepsie, a place which earned its name in the eighteenth century from the flames flaring out of the many kilns in which limestone was calcined there.

The property where the present quarries are located was once the site of DeWitt Clinton's country home.

66.00 Gallaudet Home for Aged and Infirm Deaf-Mutes to east. This home is located on a 100-acre estate established in 1872 by Dr. Thomas G. Gallaudet (1822–1902), son of Thomas H. Gallaudet (1787–1852), who initiated systematic education of the deaf in America. It is inland from the quarry region.

66.50 Camelot to east. Formerly called Milton Ferry, it was once a local railroad station under its present name.

66.75 Goose Cove to east. Behind railroad embankment. Largely silted up.

66.75 Spackenkill to east. This stream flows through the southern sections of Poughkeepsie and empties into Goose Cove. It is eulogized by local Poughkeepsie author William F. Gekle.

66.50 Cliffs to west. These cliffs are named Lange Rack on the Coast and Geodetic Service navigation chart #283. The name Lange Rack properly applies to the Long Reach of the Hudson hereabouts, rather than to any land features.

67.00 Van Keurens to east.

67.00 Elderhoj art colony to west. This is a stuccoed building in Moorish style, early twentieth century.

67.10 Captain Sherbourn Sears House to west. This two-story clapboard, mid-eighteenth century house was modernized in mid-nineteenth century. This was formerly the property of "Father Devine," alias Joe Baker, born in Savannah, Georgia, in the 1890s. This flamboyant personality set himself up as a prophet. He came to New York in 1915 with twelve disciples and set up a commune in Brooklyn. Later he moved to Harlem. His adherents claimed he was God Himself. His followers went by the names of children and angels and dedicated all their property and earnings to the commune. He owned many businesses—a number of them in Ulster County.

67.25 Rudco to east.

67.25 Spring Brook to east. Benson Lossing tells an interesting story about this location:

About four miles below Poughkeepsie is an ancient stone farmhouse and a mill, at the mouth of Spring Brook, at the eastern terminus of the Milton Ferry. Here, during the old war for independence, lived Theophilus Anthony, a blacksmith, farmer, miller, and staunch Whig, who used his forge for most rebellious purposes. He assisted in making a great chain that was stretched across the Hudson in the Highlands at Fort Montgomery, to prevent the British ships of war ascending the river and carrying invading troops into the heart of the country. For this offence, when the chain and accompanying boom were forced, and vessels of Vaughan carried the firebrand to Esopus or Kingston, the rebel blacksmith's mill was laid in ashes, and he was confined in the loathsome "Jersey" prisonship at New York, where he had ample time for reflection and penitence for three weary years. Alas! the latter never came. He was a sinner against ministers, too hardened for repentance, and he remained a rebel until the close of his life. Another mill soon arose from the ashes of the old one, and there his grandsons, the Messrs. Gill were grinding wheat when we were there for the descendants of both Whigs and Tories, and never inquired into the politics of the passengers upon their boat at the Milton Ferry. (1860)

(Lossing, *The Hudson*, p. 193.)

67.50 Milton to west. Formerly known as Milton Ferry, this town was once the center of a Quaker intellectual colony. It once shipped large quantities of strawberries, raspberries, currants, and grapes. It was the home of novelist Mary Hallock Foote. Several active wineries are located here. This is a major orchard area.

67.60 IBM plant to east. Its water towers are visible.

67.65 Sand's Dock to west. This is the site of the Ward family shipyard.

68.00 Long Point to east.

68.80 Locust Grove to east. This is the former home of Samuel F. B. Morse (1791–1872), inventor of the telegraph. It is a two-story Italian villa with wings, begun in 1830 and renovated in 1852, on a 100-acre estate. It is now known as the Young-Morse Historic Site, at 370 South Road (Route 9) Poughkeepsie and open to the public. Telephone 914-454-4500.

69.10 Southwood Estate to east. This is a two-story brick house with tower and mansard roof (ca. 1865). Sunfish Cove is to east.

69.15 Mine Point to east. Distinguished by a tomb, it is in the grounds of the Poughkeepsie Rural Cemetery. It is also known as Lookout Point.

69.20 Blue Point to west. This is the site of the Hudson Valley Winery, and was formerly called Juffrouw's Hoeck (Madam's Point).

70.10 Fox Point to east.

70.10 Vassar Brothers' Hospital to east. This institution in a group of red-brick buildings was founded by two nephews of Matthew Vassar.

70.40 Oakes to west.

70.45 Lewisburg to west.

70.50 Mid-Hudson Bridge. A unit of the New York State Bridge Authority, this beautiful suspension bridge was opened to traffic on August 25, 1930. The bridge has an overall length of 3,000 feet, with a main span of 1,500 feet. It carries two vehicle lanes and two pedestrian sidewalks. Vessel clearance is 135 feet. The east pier was carried down to a record depth of 135 feet below water to reach solid rock. Principal building contractors were American Bridge Company, Blakeslee-Rollins Corporation, David Schoentag, Inc., and Scott Brothers Construction Company. Total cost was $5,890,000.

The bridge was designed by Ralph Modjeski (1861–1940), partner in the firm of Modjeski & Moran, engineers. This noted bridge designer was born in Cracow, Poland, and came to the United States in 1876, after studying engineering in Paris. He was perhaps the leading bridge designer of his day. Other principal spans of his are the Huey P. Long Bridge at New Orleans, the Iowa-Illinois Memorial Bridge at Davenport, Iowa, the Ben Franklin Bridge over the Delaware at Philadelphia, and large structures for the Southern Pacific Railroad over the Columbia and Willamette Rivers. In later life he resided at Saugerties. His partner was Daniel E. Moran.

His mother was the famous tragic actress Helena Modieska (1844–1909). After a successful European career, she came to the United States in 1877. She was best known for her Shakespearean roles.

70.50 Poughkeepsie to east. The "Queen City" of the Hudson. The city is partly upon a hillside, sloping to the river, but chiefly upon an elevated plain, back of which is College Hill, whose summit is 500 feet above the town. The plain has a 200-foot elevation.

MID-HUDSON BRIDGE, POUGHKEEPSIE. Beautiful towers the masterpiece of bridge designer Ralph Modjeski (1861–1940). Photo: Courtesy New York State Bridge Authority.

There are several theories as to the derivation of the name Poughkeepsie. One is that it comes from the Indian "Pooghkepesingh," meaning "where the water breaks through or falls over," possibly referring to the rapids on the Fall Kill. Another theory is that it means "reed-covered lodge by the little water place." The most likely is the theory propounded by Benson J. Lossing (a native of this vicinity) in his book *The Hudson:*

The name is a modification of the Mohegan word, Apo-keep-sinck, signifying "safe and pleasant harbour." Between two rocky bluffs was a sheltered bay (now filled with wharves [1860] near foot of Main Street), into the upper part of which leaped, in rapids and cascades, the Winnakee, called Fall Kill by the Dutch. The northerly bluff was called by the Dutch "Slange Klippe," or Adder Cliff, because of the venomous serpents which were abundant there in the olden time. The southern bluff bears the name of Call Rock, it having been a place from which the settlers called to the captains of sloops or single-masted vessels, when passage in them was desired. With this bay, or "safe harbour" is associated an Indian legend, of which the following is the substance:—Once some Delaware warriors came to this spot with Pequod captives. Among the latter was a young chief, who was offered life and honour if he would renounce his nation, receive the mark of the turtle upon his breast, and become a Delaware brave. He rejected the degrading proposition with disdain, and was bound to a tree for sacrifice, when a shriek from a thicket startled the executioners. A young girl leaped before them, and implored his life. She was a captive Pequod, with the turtle on her bosom, and the young chief was her affianced. The Delawares debated, when suddenly the war-whoop of some fierce Hurons made them snatch their arms for defense. The maiden severed the thongs that bound her lover, but in the deadly conflict that ensued, they were separated, and a Huron chief carried off the captive as a trophy. Her affianced conceived a bold design for her rescue, and proceeded immediately to execute it. In the character of a wizard he entered the Huron camp. The maiden was sick, and her captor employed the wizard to prolong her life, until he should satisfy his revenge upon Uncas, her uncle, the great chief of the Mohegans. They eluded the vigilance of the Huron, fled at nightfall, with swift feet, towards the Hudson, and in the darkness, shot out upon its bosom, in a light canoe, followed by blood-thirsty pursuers. The strong arm of the young Pequod paddled his beloved one safely to a deep

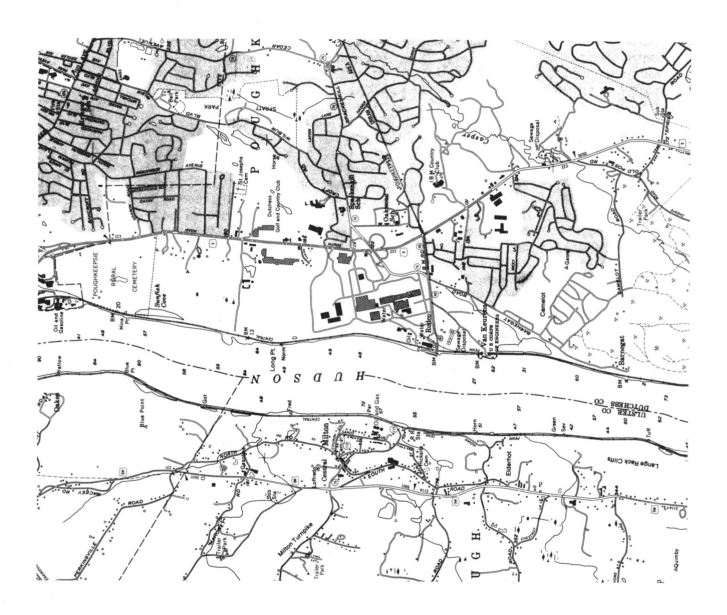

rocky nook near the mouth of the Winnakee, concealed her there, and with a few friendly Delawares whom he had secured by a shout, he fought, conquered, and drove off the Huron warriors. The sheltered nook where the maiden lay was a "safe harbour" for her, and the brave Pequod and his friends joyfully confirmed its title to Apo-keep-sinck.
(Lossing, *The Hudson*, pp. 187–188.)

A very nice tale if you can swallow it! More possibly, it simply referred to a safe canoe anchorage. Another derivation of Call Rock is from the Dutch "Kaal" Rock, signifying barren or bald.

Lossing gives a list of various spellings as found in records and maps: Pakeepsie, Pacapsey, Pakepsey, Paughkepsie, Pecapesy, Pecapsy, Pecapshe, Pochkeepsinck, Poeghkeepsing, Poeghkeeksingk, Poeghkeepsink, Pochkeepsey, Pochkeepsen, Pochkeepsy, Pochkepsen, Pochkyphsingh, Pockeepsy, Pockepseick, Pockepseng, Pokepsing, Poghkeepsie, Poghkeepsinck, Poghkeepsing, Poghkepse, Poghkepsen, Poghkeepsink, Poghkeepson, Poghkeepse, Pokeepsigh, Pokeepsingh, Pokeepsink, Pokeepsy, Pokepsinck, Pokkepsen, Poughkeepsey, Poukeepsie, Poukeepsy, Pikipsi, Picipsi, Pokepsie, Pokeepsie, Poughkeepsie. Total— 42.

The area was originally populated by the Wappinger or Wappingi Indians. In 1683 Chief Massany gave a deed to two Hollanders, and the first settlement was made in 1687. Baltus Van Kleek built a substantial home near the mouth of the Fall Kill in 1705. This stood until 1835. This house was pierced with loopholes for musketry, near the roof, that being a necessary precaution against Indian attacks. The New York legislature met here during two sessions in 1777 and 1778 when New York was held by the British and after Kingston had been burned by Vaughan.

The township of Poughkeepsie was incorporated in 1788. That same year, in June, a State Convention met here to consider the Federal Constitution. Among the members were Alexander Hamilton, George Clinton, John Jay, and Chancellor Livingston. They voted to accept it by one vote. This, and passage by Virginia of ratification, put the Federal Constitution into effect on July 26, 1788.

The village of Poughkeepsie was formed in 1799, and incorporated as a city in 1854. It is the county seat of Dutchess County.

Joel Benton, a local writer, tells us that Poughkeepsie:

...soon became the center of a large trade running in long lines east and west from the river.

Dutchess county had at this time but a sparse population. There was a post-road from New York to Albany; but the building of the Dutchess Turnpike from Poughkeepsie to Sharon, Connecticut, connecting with one from that place to Litchfield, which took place in 1808, was a capital event in its history. This made a considerable strip of western Connecticut tributary to Poughkeepsie's trade.

Over the turnpike went four-horse Concord stages, with berailed top and slanting boot in the rear for trunks and other baggage. Each one had the tin horn of the driver; and it was difficult to tell upon which the driver most prided himself—the power to fill that thrilling instrument, or his deft handling of the ponderous whip and multiplied reins. Travelers to Hartford and Boston went over this route; and an east and west through and way mail was a part of the burden. A sort of overland express and freight line, styled the Market Wagon, ran in and out of the town from several directions. One or more of these conveyances started from as far east as the Housatonic River and they frequently crowded passengers in amongst their motley wares.

Speaking of the stage-driver's horn recalls the fact that when the steamboat arrived—which was so solitary an institution that for some time it was distinctly called "The Steamboat" the tin horn did duty also for it. When it was seen in the distance, either Albanyward or in the New York direction, a boy went through the village blowing it to arouse those who wished to embark on it. It is said the expectant passengers had ample time, after the horn was sounded, to make their toilets, run down to the river (or walk down) and take passage on it.

Poughkeepsie honored in May 1824, the arrival of Lafayette, and dined him, besides exchanging speeches with him, both at the Forbus House, on Market Street, very nearly where the Nelson House now stands, and at the Poughkeepsie Hotel. It was one of Poughkeepsie's great days when he came. Daniel Webster has spoken in her Court House; and Henry Clay, in 1844, when a presidential candidate, stopped for a reception.

In 1844, the New York State Fair was held here somewhere east of what is now Hooker Avenue. It was an occasion thought important enough then to be pictured and reported in the London Illustrated News. Two years after the telegraph wires were put up in this city, before they had yet reached the City of New York. Considering the fact that Prof. S. F. B. Morse, the telegraph inventor, had his residence here, this incident was not wholly inappropriate.

("Vignettes of Poughkeepsie," in *The Four Track Series*, published by the New York Central System, No. 36, Jan. 1902, p. 20.)

Thus go Mr. Benton's reminiscences. The New York Central railroad came through in 1849. The large railroad bridge across the Hudson was built in 1886, thus making Poughkeepsie an important railroad center.

In *Picturesque America*, edited by William Cullen Bryant, E. L. Burlingham gives the following description of Poughkeepsie.

The "rural city," as one of our writers has called it, lies very pleasantly upon its group of gentle hills, and overlooks a bright and sunny portion of the riverview. By day, one may quarrel a little with the smoke of its busy founderies, but by night these become the most strangely beautiful and striking feature in many miles of the Hudson's scenery. They light the river like weird beacons, and the sound of their great furnaces comes across the water in the stillness, as the panting of giants that toil when the weaker forces of the world are all asleep. (p. 3.)

Other nineteenth-century industries included Adriance, Platt & Co., who manufactured the famous Buckeye Mowers and Reapers; the Phoenix Horsehoe Company; the Knitting-Goods Establishment; and various shoe, shirt, silk thread, and hardware factories.

More modern industries have produced ball bearings, cream separators, dairy equipment and office machinery, coughdrops, candy, and computers. Important local firms are the DeLaval Co., International Business Machines, and Smith Brothers Cough Drops. This last named firm was established in 1850 by William Wallace Smith and Andrew Smith, of the flowing beards, who used their photographs printed upon each box of cough drops. They were commonly known throughout the land as "Trade" and "Mark." The present factory was built in 1914, and the cough drops are still popular both as candy and as an effective medicinal. The Smith Brothers also long operated a good restaurant on Market Street. The writer can remember accompanying his father on business trips when a small boy and eating there. It had old fashioned wooden paneling and paddle fans. We would arrive from Newburgh on the Dayline steamer (these were the days of gas rationing during World War II) and take a bus up Main Street from the Landing and put up overnight at the old Nelson House. Poughkeepsie was a busy place at that time, and the proximity of President Franklin D. Roosevelt's home at Hyde Park and the wartime projects of IBM gave the town considerable importance.

For many years, from 1895 until 1950, the Intercollegiate Rowing Association regatta was held on the Hudson here. It was finally removed to Marietta on the Ohio River. Excursion trains full of fans would be parked on the high bridge for viewing. The winning crews would paint their initials on the rocks along the western shoreline. Some faint ones can still be made out.

Poughkeepsie is an educational center. The Dutchess Community College, Marist College, and Vassar College are all located here. Also, for many years, Poughkeepsie was the seat of the famous Eastman College, a popular business and commercial school. Matthew Vassar (1792–1868) was born in England and came to America with his father in 1796. The family operated successful breweries in Poughkeepsie. In 1861 he founded the Vassar Female College, "where women can learn what is useful, practical and sensible." He gave more than $800,000 to the school. Today the school is coeducational.

In recent years Poughkeepsie has seen considerable economic decline. The city became a "two-industry town," i.e., De Laval and IBM, with both the advantages and disadvantages of such a limited economic base. River shipping has declined to zero and its importance as a railroad junction was diminished first by the creation of Penn Central and Conrail, and then by the "temporary" closing of the railroad bridge and the trade route it upheld after a fire several years ago. The bridge was not repaired, although several industrial associations and the Interstate Commerce Commission agitated to make Conrail repair and reopen it. Much of the river-slope part of town has been torn down to make way for urban renewal. New parks have been built along the waterfront and a fine automobile expressway takes through traffic off the local streets. There have been new public housing projects, a new civic center and mall and auditorium and other major physical improvements. The dilapidated steamboat landing has been removed and the waterfront generally cleaned up.

However, with the lack of activity, this is like the mortician's "prettying up" the corpse. For lack of a proper landing place, the day boats no longer put in at Poughkeepsie. There is still a crying need for additional diversified industry. There is too much unemployment in the area.

There are many interesting eighteenth and nineteenth century homes and commercial buildings. Among the most interesting are the following:

1. A group of Greek Revival houses on Mill Street (ca. 1840-50)
2. Commercial buildings on Main Street (mid-nineteenth century)

3. Vassar Brothers' Institute, two-story brick Georgian (ca. 1765)
4. Victorian and Greek Revival townhouses on Mill Street
5. Home of George Clinton, two-story brick Victorian (ca. 1765)
6. Glebe House, brick Georgian (ca. 1767)
7. Old Ladies' Home, Greek Revival (1836)
8. Soldiers' Fountain, South Avenue and Montgomery Street (1870): Civil War memorial, cast iron, at entrance to Eastman Park
9. Eastman House, three-story brick, Italianate Victorian (ca. 1870)
10. Frear House, one-story stone (eighteenth century)
11. *Springside*: summer home of Matthew Vassar, board and batten (ca. 1850). House and grounds designed by Andrew Jackson Downing. This is considered the best remaining example of Downing's residential landscape architecture.

Old churches include:

1. Church of St. Peter (R.C.), Italianate Victorian (1853)
2. Episcopal Church of the Holy Comforter, stone Gothic Revival (1860), designed by Richard Upjohn
3. Second Baptist Church, clapboard Greek Revival (ca. 1840).

Poughkeepsie is the northern terminus of the MTA Hudson Line suburban rail service and an express stop for Amtrak. It was once the northern terminus of Hudson River Day Line excursion service. After dilapidation of the dock, the boats only cruised to Poughkeepsie without landing.

70.50 Call Rock to east. It is at the eastern foot of the Mid-Hudson Bridge. See Poughkeepsie article for derivation of name.

70.51 Site of former steamboat landing to east. At the foot of Main Street. Now removed.

70.52 Fall Kill to east. Formerly Winnakee Brook, it rises in northeastern section of Poughkeepsie township and flows southwest to Hudson through northern portion of the city.

70.52 College Hill to east. (elevation 365 feet). It was formerly property of Sen. Morgan and William Smith, who gave it to the city as a park.

70.52 Adder or Snake Cliff to east. Formerly the Dutch "Slange Klippe," it was named for the former profusion of snakes.

70.52 Railroad Cantilever Bridge. This bridge was begun in 1873. It was designed by John Flack Winslow (1810–1895), president of the Poughkeepsie & Eastern Railway. Construction was halted by the Panic of 1873, but resumed in 1886 under the Union Bridge Company's direction. Steelwork was finished on August 29, 1888, and the first train operated across on December 29, 1888. There has been considerable misinformation spread in recent years by the Penn-Central Railroad and Conrail, to the effect that the bridge is constructed of iron upon wooden pilings. In fact, this bridge was the first major structure constructed of Bessemer steel in the United States. James Winslow, in his capacity of civil engineer and metallurgist, was the first person to use such steel and manufacture it in the United States, and it was used in the famous "ironclad" Union gunboat *Monitor* in 1862 in the Civil War. Winslow was quite familiar with the virtues of Bessemer steel by the time he designed this bridge. Only a very minimal use was made of iron, in such minor uses as handrails. The foundations are actually cyclopian concrete, firmly reaching to bedrock.

POUGHKEEPSIE RAILROAD BRIDGE. Hudson River Day Line steamer *DeWitt Clinton* and two ferryboats visible to left. Hudson River Day Line photo, courtesy Alfred V. S. Olcott, Jr.

The total length of the bridge, including approach trestles, is 6,676 ft., of which 3,093 ft are cantilever construction. The distance over water is 2,606 ft. and distance between the shore piers 2,692 ft. The center span is 546 ft, with the two adjacent channel spans 525 ft. each and the two spans adjacent to the shore each 548 ft. The track is 212 ft. above the water, with a vessel clearance of 165 ft. beneath the center span. The cost of the bridge was $10,000,000. It was built for railroad use only. Originally it carried two tracks, but has been reduced to single track because of increasing weight of trains. For many years it was operated by the Philadelphia & Reading Rwy, Central New England RR, New York, New Haven & Hartford RR, and Penn-Central RR. On May 8, 1974, there was a fire on the tracks which destroyed many track ties and put the bridge out of service. For competitive reasons Penn-Central chose not to repair the bridge and return it to service. When Penn-Central was merged into Conrail the bridge was still out of service. Conrail subsequently tore up the connecting tracks on either shore for many miles and sold the bridge to an entity called Railway Management Associates, of St. Davids, Pennsylvania, Gordon Schreiber Miller, Agent, for $1.00—less than the cost of removing the bridge. The writer has spoken with Mr. Miller, and indeed has personally inspected the deed from Conrail at the writer's home the day it was recorded at the Dutchess and Ulster County courthouses. Mr. Miller had several uses in mind for the bridge; apparently none of them have come to fruition and the bridge is gradually falling into dilapidation, much to the consternation of local officials. The Central Hudson Electric Company removed their power lines from the bridge in 1987 in favor of a submarine cable just to the south of the bridge. It is presently fenced off at both ends to keep people from going out upon it and possibly getting hurt, and some of the track has been removed from the eastern end to prevent loose track hardware from falling down onto Poughkeepsie streets and homes. Nobody knows exactly what the owners have in mind at time of writing, and there are many conjectures afloat, including development of a tourist train or trolley ride. The writer once crossed the bridge on an excursion years ago. The views are tremendous, but the bridge vibrates beneath a train to a terrifying degree. The bridge is on the Register of National Historic Sites and is thus protected. Let us hope that a good, profitable use can be found for this grand old structure.

71.50 Marist College to east.

71.50 Water intake and Purification plant to east.
City of Poughkeepsie.

71.50 Illinois Mountain to west (elevation 1,129 feet).

71.50 Twaalfskill Creek to west.
It rises west of Blue Point and flows northeast to the Hudson through a picturesque ravine.

71.50 Highland to west.
Originally called New Paltz or Elting's Landing, the village of New Paltz is several miles inland in the Wallkill Valley; and the village of Highland uphill overlooking the Hudson River. In 1678 a group of displaced Huguenots, living then in the Palatinate, purchased a 39,0000-acre tract, stretching from the Hudson River to the Shawangunk Mountains, west of the Wallkill River, from the Esopus Indians. The purchase was confirmed by a Patent from the English governor Edmund Andros that same year. The first settlement was inland at New Paltz on the Wallkill River. Over the years Elting's Landing became the main route to the outside world, with a ferry to Poughkeepsie operating from 1793 until 1941. The landing was bombarded by British ships in 1777. Interesting buildings are the Ferryman Inn, or Yelverton House (eighteenth-century frame saltbox), Mid-Hudson Hotel (1850) with stepped gables, and Davis Place (ca. 1830). The Yelverton House is at 39 Maple Avenue, and is the oldest frame house in Ulster County, still standing without extensive renovations. Raising fruit has always been the main occupation. Today there are many orchards and wineries. The blooms in the spring and beautiful fruit in the fall make this a delightful area to visit. Large coolers and processing plants are on the farms further inland. Mariner's Harbor Restaurant on the water's edge is an excellent place from which to view the river traffic, and is noted for its seafood. From 1894 to 1925 a trolley line operated to New Paltz from the landing, and in later years operated from the Poughkeepsie streetcar line tracks and over the railroad bridge. This was operated by the New Paltz, Highland & Poughkeepsie Traction Co.

72.00 Site of Woodcliff Amusement Park to east.
Long defunct.

72.75 Hudson River State Hospital to east.
This mental hospital, founded in 1871 on property purchased from James Roosevelt, has a brick Victorian Gothic main building designed by Vaux & Withers. Its grounds have grown from 208 to 1,730 acres. Now there are 83 buildings.

72.75 Lange Rack Cliffs to west.
This is the former start of a four-mile course of intercollegiate crew races. Some faded painted trophies may still be seen on the rocks.

73.20 Roosevelt to east. This is a former local New York Central station.

73.20 Dog Head Cove Point to west. Site of early nineteenth-century Coe House.

73.80 Culinary Institute of America to east.
Red brick Gothic buildings with white trim dating from 1903, with a five-story main building on a seventy-acre campus, this was formerly St. Andrews-on-the Hudson, a Jesuit seminary and monastery. Since 1972 it has been the home of America's premier school for commercial chefs and food service personnel. The school was founded in 1946 in New Haven, Connecticut. Offering exclusive training for cooks in the broadest sense, the institute is the only facility of its kind awarding a degree for purely vocational training in the culinary arts. The degree is awarded upon completion of four trimesters of courses and a trimester of externship. This private non-profit, educational facility has a curriculum that is known and respected throughout the world.

The school operates the Escoffier Restaurant and Rabelais Grill, as well as a coffee shop and diner. All are open to the general public, but the gourmet Escoffier Restaurant requires reservations (telephone 914-452-9600).

The famous French scientist and philosopher Pierre Teilhard de Chardin is buried on the grounds in the old Jesuit Cemetery, still beautifully maintained by the Culinary Institute, and this site has become a pilgrimage shrine for those interested in the philosophy of science and religion.

74.00 Maritje Kill to east. It rises south of East Park and flows southwest to the Hudson.

74.25 Crum Elbow Point to west. Also called Krumm Elbow. There are several possible derivations, both from the Dutch. The more popular one is from "Krom Elleboge" or "crooked elbow." However, the original Dutch name for the location was Kromme Hoek, or "rounded point." Father Divine once owned a 500-acre estate here which was called Negro Heaven. It was operated as a communal farming project. There was a large pavilion and boathouse.

74.75 "Springwood" home of Franklin Delano Roosevelt to east. The following is taken from the brochure of the National Park Service:

Franklin D. Roosevelt, 32nd President of the United States was born in this home on January 30, 1882. He was the only child of James and Sara Roosevelt.

Franklin Roosevelt spent much of his life here.

Here Franklin—the toddler, the little boy, the young man—was shaped and grew to maturity. Here he brought his bride, Eleanor in 1905, and here they raised their five children. From here he began his political career that stretched from the New York State Senate to the White House. Roosevelt was a State senator, 1911–13, Assistant Secretary of the Navy under Woodrow Wilson, 1913-20, and unsuccessful vice-presidential candidate in 1920. Then, in 1921, he contracted infantile paralysis. During his struggle to conquer the disease he spent much time here. He refused to become an invalid and reentered politics. He was elected Governor of New York in 1928 and 1930 and President of the United States in 1932. As Governor and President, he came here as often as he could for respite from the turmoil of public life. On April 15, 1945, three days after his death in Warm Springs, Georgia, President Roosevelt was buried in the family rose garden. Seventeen years later, on November 10, 1962, Mrs. Roosevelt was buried beside the President.

The central portion of the building, the oldest section, dates to the early 1800s. When James Roosevelt bought the house, then called "Spring Wood," in 1867, it had a clapboard exterior.

The main house has undergone many renovations and additions with the passage of years. In 1916 it assumed its present form. The central part, its clapboards removed, was covered with stucco and fronted by a porch with a sweeping balustrade and a small colonnaded portico. On each end, the Roosevelts added a two-story wing.

The house was designated a National Historic Site on January 15th 1944. A gift from President Roosevelt, the site then consisted of 33 acres containing the home, outbuildings, and the grave site. The site was formally dedicated on April 12, 1946, the first anniversary of the President's death, and now contains 188 acres.

The Franklin D. Roosevelt Library and Museum, which are NOT part of the National Historic Site, are located nearby. They contain the President's books, papers, ship models, gifts, and personal belongings.
(National Park Service, GPO 1974-585-454/7.)

The Roosevelt Historic site is located at 249 Albany Post Road (Route 9) in Hyde Park. Telephone 914-229-9115.

75.25 Crum Elbow Point Light to east.

75.50 Rogers Point to east.

75.50 Mt. Hymettus to west. (elevation 900 feet.) John Burroughs gave it this name because of his luck in finding many bees, beehives, and wild honey on its slopes. Mount Hymettus near Athens in Greece is famous for its fields of flowers, many bees, and honey.

76.00 Plattekill Hills to west.

76.40 Santa Maria Novitiate to west. Two-story brick Italianate Victorian building, mid-nineteenth century.

76.40 Hyde Park to east. Originally called Stoutenburgh after Jacobus Stoutenburgh who lived here in 1741. However, as early as 1705, Peter Fauconier, private secretary of Edward Hyde, Viscount Cornbury, royal governor of New York, obtained a patent for land in this vicinity. Subsequently the name was changed from Stoutenburgh to the more aristocratic Hyde Park. Of particular architectual interest in the town are the railroad station, with bracketed overhang, and the Eymard Seminary. This building, originally a private mansion named Crumwald, dates from 1889 and is Romanesque in style with towers and dormers. Saint Peter Julian Eymard was the founder of the congregations of the Fathers of the Blessed Sacrament and of the Servants of the Blessed Sacrament. He was born at La Mure d'Isere, France in 1811 and early evinced a great sensitivity to the Real Presence in the Blessed Sacrament. He devoted his entire life founding an order devoted to perpetual adoration of the Blessed Sacrament. He died in 1868.

76.40 East Park to east. Inland from Hyde Park.

76.60 Crum Elbow Creek to east. It rises near East Park and flows generally west to the Hudson, through several small ponds near the Vanderbilt Mansion.

76.60 Frothingham Dock to west. This is the western terminus of a former horse-powered ferry to Hyde Park.

77.00 Vanderbilt Mansion National Historic Site to east. The following article is taken from the brochures of the National Park Service which administers the site:

The history of the 211 acre grounds goes back much further than that of the mansion. The grounds had been maintained as a country seat by prominent individuals since colonial days. The fine old trees and spreading lawns had been carefully developed for generations.

Hyde Park, as the estate was first called, is said to have been named by Peter Fauconnier, the private

VANDERBILT MANSION, HYDE PARK. Photo: © Gretchen McHugh.

secretary of Edward Hyde, Viscount Cornbury, later third Earl of Clarendon and Governor of New York from 1702 to 1708. Fauconnier held office in the colony as collector and receiver general and also owned extensive tracts of land, including a part of the patent of Hyde Park. This patent was granted in the reign of Queen Anne on April 18, 1705. The town of Hyde Park, established in 1821, took its name from the estate.

Dr. John Bard, noted physician and pioneer in hygiene, acquired the entire Hyde Park patent during the two decades following the death of Fauconnier in 1746. Dr. Bard lived principally in New York City until about 1772, when he moved to Hyde Park. He built a house just north of the present St. James Church and began to develop the virgin land of the estate. After the Revolution, Dr. John Bard returned to private practice in New York. There he assisted his son, Dr. Samuel Bard, as attending physician to George Washington, then in his first term as President of the United States. Dr. John Bard retired to Hyde Park again in 1798, and there, a year later, he died.

Dr. Samuel Bard received the property by transfer shortly before his father's death. Educated at King's College (now Columbia University) and at

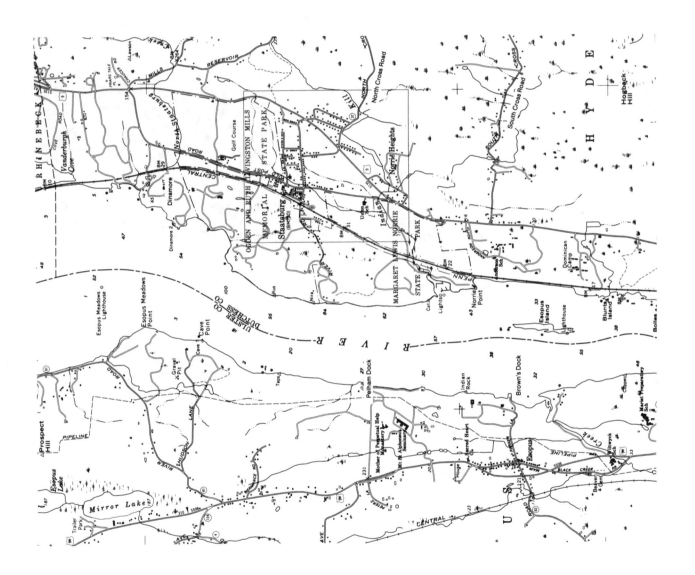

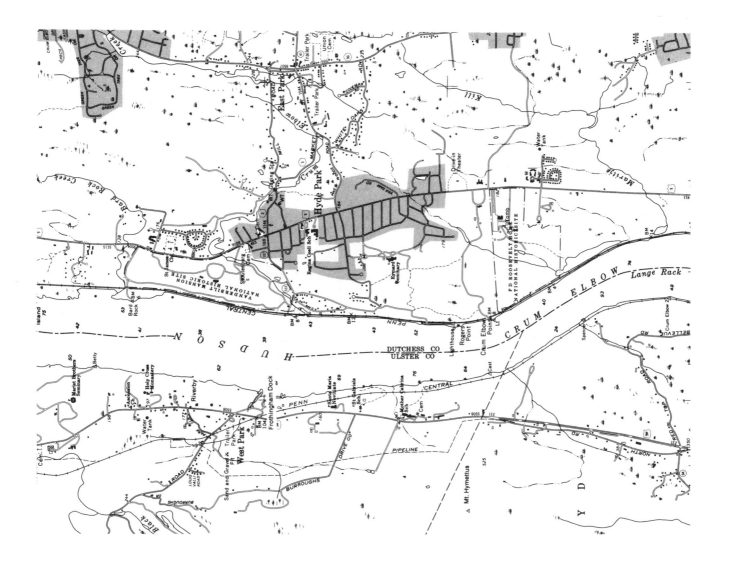

Edinburgh, he, like his father, was an eminent physician.

The younger Dr. Bard built a new mansion at Hyde Park. This was a large house on the high elevation rising about 300 feet above the Hudson River and commanding a superb view of this beautiful stream, of the Shawangunk Range to the west, and of the Catskill Mountains to the north. Continuing to improve the grounds, Dr. Bard also undertook experiments in horticulture and farming. He imported small fruits from England, larger ones from France, melons from Italy, and vines from Madeira. Dr. Bard and his wife lived at Hyde Park until 1821, when they died within a day of each other.

Their only surviving son, William Bard, inherited Hyde Park, which had been reduced by land sales to 540 acres, but lived there only until about 1828. In that year he sold the estate to Dr. David Hosack of New York City. Dr. Hosack, who had been a professor of natural history at Columbia College, was a former partner of Dr. Samuel Bard, and received the latter's medical practice when he retired.

Dr. Hosack, who was deeply interested in plants, flowers, and trees, revived horticultural experimentation and gardening at Hyde Park. He engaged André Parmentier, a Belgian landscape gardener, to lay out roads, walks, and scenic vistas. This work was probably done between 1828 and 1830. The rare and exotic specimens which grace the lawns and park appear to date principally from that time.

In 1840, 5 years after the death of Dr. Hosack, John Jacob Astor bought the mansion tract from the heirs. Mr. Astor almost immediately made a gift of the estate to his daughter, Dorothea Astor Langdon, and her children. Walter Langdon, Jr., a son, became the sole owner of the estate in 1852. He continued to live at Hyde Park until his death in 1894. During this period the greenhouses and flower gardens were enlarged and the farmland east of the Albany Post Road was reunited with the property by purchase in 1872.

The Langdons had no children, so Hyde Park was offered for sale in 1895. It was purchased by Frederick William Vanderbilt, the grandson of Commodore Cornelius Vanderbilt who had founded the family fortune.

Mr. Vanderbilt had the Langdon House torn down. On its site he erected the present structure, which was completed in 1898 at a cost of $660,000 without furnishings. Care was used in choosing the furnishings; Continental motifs, especially Italian and French, predominate. Mr. Vanderbilt greatly improved the grounds and built new farm buildings, carriage houses, and entranceways.

The Vanderbilts occupied the mansion during the spring and autumn. Entertaining at the large mid-Hudson Valley estates during the early 1900's was usually limited to weekends. Mr. Vanderbilt died in 1938, having willed the estate to Mrs. Vanderbilt's niece, Mrs. Margaret Van Alen, now Mrs. Louis Bruguiere.

Vanderbilt Mansion was designated a national historic site on December 18, 1940, following Mrs. Van Alen's gift of the estate to the United States for that purpose. The site consists of 212 acres of beautiful grounds overlooking the Hudson River together with the mansion house and related buildings. Vanderbilt Mansion is a symbol of an era. It is a magnificent example of the great estates built by wealthy financial and industrial leaders between 1880 and 1900.

The stately mansion of Indiana limestone is the focal point of the Vanderbilt estate. Designed by McKim, Mead and White, this 3-story American "royal palace," built at a cost of $660,000, is one of the finest examples of Italian Renaissance architecture in the United States and a fitting symbol of the Gilded Age.

When Frederick Vanderbilt (1857–1938) purchased the estate from Walter Langdon, Jr. in 1895, he was influenced by its proximity to New York City and its scenic charm. Also, his neighbors would be the Rodgerses, the Roosevelts, the Millses, and, farther upriver, the Astors—all families of prominence and wealth. But more importantly, Vanderbilt found the land ideal for pursuing his interests in purebred livestock and horticulture. The grounds of the estate were enlarged in 1905 when Vanderbilt purchased the Sexton estate adjoining his property on the north.

In 1895 the Vanderbilts had the Pavilion constructed and lived there while the mansion was built (McKim, Mead and White in Classic Greek style). The Langdon House was torn down in 1896 and that October Vanderbilt began construction of his 54-room mansion. It was finished in December 1898. During the next few months furnishings were installed and in May 1899 the first of many gala parties was given. The Vanderbilts looked forward to returning each spring and fall to their Hudson River estate. Their summers were spent elsewhere, but in winter they came here on weekends and at Christmas, living in the Pavilion, for the mansion was closed. During these visits they took particular delight in sleighing.

The mansion was lavishly furnished in continental motifs, mostly Italian and French. Noted decorators Georges A. Glaenzer and Ogden Codman designed the decor of some of the rooms, while McKim, Mead *and White did the others. Cost was no hinderance to the Vanderbilts.*

Like other wealthy families along the Hudson, the Vanderbilts entertained lavishly. Gala balls were held in the 30 by 50 foot drawing room, and refreshments were served in the spacious oval reception hall with its large fireplace imported from a European palace. Guests included nobility and leaders in business, politics and the arts such as the Duke of Marlborough, who was Vanderbilt's niece's husband, and Franklin D. Roosevelt.

The Vanderbilts played an important role in the economy of the community hiring local residents when possible, to work in the mansion, on the grounds, the farm, coachhouse, and Italian gardens. When the Vanderbilts were at Hyde Park, 17 household helpers were needed at the mansion alone. They also took an active interest in the welfare of nearby villages.

Much of these activities ceased after Louise Vanderbilt's death in 1926. Frederick, though a power in the business world, was a quiet and reserved man who cared little for social life, preferring walks on the mansion grounds, yachting and overseeing the care of his gardens and purebred livestock. When he died in 1938, the mansion and grounds were left to Louise Vanderbilt's niece, Margaret Van Alen (the late Mrs. Louis Bruguiere), since the Vanderbilts had no children.

(Vanderbilt Mansion-National Historic Site
United States Department of the Interior—
Form 1962 0-625246)

The mansion is open daily from 9 a.m. to 5 p.m. except New Year's Day and Christmas. This is a must for the serious tourist. Telephone 914-229-9115.

77.20 West Park to west. This was the home of the author and naturalist John Burroughs (1837–1921). He was born in Roxbury, New York, the son of a farmer. He later taught school in Olive Bridge and worked as a Treasury Clerk in Washington and as a journalist. In 1874 he designed and built his home, *Riverby*, in West Park, and gave himself over to horticulture and pomology, and most importantly to the writing of the many nature essays for which he is best known. Much of this writing was done in his "bark study" overlooking the Hudson, where he was visited by Walt Whitman, John Muir, and Theodore Roosevelt. He also had a retreat on the southern slopes of Shaupeneak Mountain called *Slabsides,* and maintained a summer home near Clump Mountain west of Roxbury in the Catskills, which he called *Woodchuck Lodge.* Primarily an essayist, he was

also a poet and an avid explorer, and the first to make a recorded visit to the summit of Slide Mountain, highest of the Catskills. He is buried near Roxbury.

His son Julian Burroughs (d. 1954) also lived at West Park, and his home was called *The Nest.* He was an architect and designed the elaborate stables for the estate of Colonel Oliver Hazard Payne, for whom he also served as estate manager between 1914 and 1918.

The Payne estate is now the Marist Brothers novitiate. The main mansion was built in 1910 from designs by Carrere & Hastings, of New York, best known for the Main Branch of the New York Public Library on Fifth Avenue. The mansion is a chateau in the French style with 36 rooms. It makes extensive use of marble and California tile. Mr. Payne was an oil magnate and an associate of John D. Rockefeller.

The Church of the Ascension (Episcopal) on Route 9W was built in 1842. It has two ogee windows and is of unusual charm. The West Shore Railroad leaves the riverbank and cuts inland for the rest of the way to Albany just south of West Park.

77.75 Bard's Rock and Creek to east. It rises west of Hogback Hill and flows southwest to the Hudson.

78.30 Bolle's Island to east. Formerly called Shad Island, it is now joined to the mainland.

78.50 Hogback Hill to east (elevation 364 feet).

78.75 Blunt's Island to east. It is now joined to the mainland.

78.75 Site of Placentia to east. This was the country seat of James Kirke Paulding (1779–1860), one of the Knickerbocker school. He was a popular novelist and best known for his *The Dutchman's Fireside.* He also wrote the interesting *New Mirror For Travellers & Guide To The Springs* in 1828, one of the earliest Hudson River guidebooks. He was also active in politics and served as Secretary of the Navy under Martin Van Buren. He lived at *Placentia* in elegant retirement for many years, enjoying his books, his pictures, and his friends, among whom was Washington Irving. After his death, the estate was sold to Robert T. Lord and was renamed *Gros Bois.*

79.00 Esopus Island. It is just east of midstream and has channels on either side.

79.25 Black Creek to west. It rises on the western slopes of Illinois Mountain and flows north into Chodikee Lake (Grote Binnewater) (also known as Black Pond). Then it continues over several waterfalls and through some narrow gorges before turning northeast by north to enter the Hudson below the town Esopus. Its waters are dark with tannin from cedar and hemlock trees—thus its name.

79.50 Esopus to west. Formerly known as Van Pelt's, this town was founded in 1811. On the riverfront is located *Rosemont,* the former home of Alton B. Parker (1852–1926), New York State jurist and 1904 Democratic Presidential candidate. The house dates from before the Revolution and is two-story clapboard.

79.50 Brown's Dock to west.

79.75 Indian Rock to west. This was the site of the Walter P. Seaman House (1870), a two-story clapboard building.

79.75 Norrie Point to east. This is a state park with a public yacht basin and marina. It is part of Margaret Lewis Norrie State Park.

79.75 Shaupeneak Mountain to west (elevation 910 feet).

79.90 Indian Kill to east. Formerly Ficket's Creek, it rises in Staatsburg Reservoir and flows southwest to the Hudson north of Norrie Point.

79.90 Mt. St. Alphonsus Seminary to west. Of the Roman Catholic Redemptorist order, its massive 211-room gray stone building was erected in 1900. It is 4½-story Romanesque, with a 100,000-volume library. Grounds cover 400 acres.

80.25 Pelham Dock to west. It is also known as Pell's Dock. Here was the 1,200-acre model orchard and fruit farm of Robert L. Pell, Esq. He had over 25,000 trees in his orchards and was one of the largest fruit shippers in the world. He shipped apples to Queen Victoria, as well as large quantities of table grapes, currants, and small fruits. His estate was known as *Cliffwood.*

81.20 Staatsburg to east. It is inland and is not seen from the river. It was first settled by Dr. Samuel Staats and Dirck Van der Burgh. In the 1850s large ice storage sheds were erected here, and the Staatsburg Ice Tool Works was established in 1858.

St. Margaret's Episcopal Church was built in 1891, designed by Richard Upjohn. It is Gothic style and has two three-panel stained glass windows of the thirteenth century taken from Chartres Cathedral. They were the gift of Ogden Mills, Sr., as a memorial to his wife, Ruth Livingston Mills.

81.50 Cave Point to west. Inland and not visible from the river is the village of Ulster Park.

81.60 Mills Mansion State Historic Site to east. Lo-cated in Mills Memorial State Park, this is operated by the Taconic State Park Commission. The following is taken from the official descriptive brochure:

The Mills Mansion, with grounds, architecture and furnishings still intact, is an elegant relic of the turn of the 20th century. Its story, however, extends back a century earlier in the state's history. In 1792 General Morgan Lewis, New York's third governor purchased the land and built a home on the present mansion site. Governor Lewis was married to Gertrude Livingston, the sister of Chancellor Robert P. Livingston of Clermont, and the house has had close associations with the Livingston family ever since.

When the original mansion burned in 1832, Morgan Lewis and his wife immediately had it rebuilt in the popular Greek Revival style of their day. At the end of the 19th century, the home was in the possession of Ruth Livingston Mills, great-granddaughter of the original builder and wife of Darius Ogden Mills (1884–1937) a wealthy financier and philanthropist. At this time the old Greek Revival building was heavily remodeled in accordance with designs prepared by the prestigious architectural firm of McKim, Mead and White. Two large wings were added to the existing central core and the exterior was embellished with balustrades, pilasters and swags. The interior, decorated in the style of Louis XV and Louis XVI, remains rich with marble fireplaces, oak paneling and gilded ceiling and wall decorations installed at that time.

The Mills family usually came to Staatsburg in the autumn when, with their neighbors and house guests, they could sail on the river, ride horses kept in their large stable, or play golf at a course installed behind the house. The household staff numbered about 25 and many more were employed in the gar-

MILLS MANSION, STAATSBURG. Photo: © Gretchen McHugh.

dens, greenhouses, and extensive farming enterprises.

In 1937, Mrs. Henry Carnegie Phipps, in memory of her parents Ruth and Ogden Mills, gave the house and its grounds to New York State. The exterior is encased in white marble in the French Renaissance style. It has 65 rooms and cost $500,000. It is now open as a museum.

(Undated, anonymous, information leaflet issued by Taconic State Park and Recreation Commission—no form number)

The entrance is on Old Post Road in Staatsburg. Telephone 914-889-4100.

81.70 Lewis Pier to east.

81.75 Dinsmore or the Locusts to east. This is the estate of William B. Dinsmore, who, with Alvin Adams, founded the Adams Express Co. in 1840.

81.80 Dinsmore Point to east. There is currently a serious error in this matter. The current Coast & Geodetic Survey Navigation Chart #283 incorrectly labels Esopus Meadows Point, on the west shore, as Dinsmore Point. Consequently the name has been transferred in popular usage.

82.30 Esopus Meadows Lighthouse near mid-river to west of shipping channel. Esopus Meadows is a shallow area of the Hudson on the west side, with weedy shoals and water only a single foot or so deep. It is treacherous, and even very small craft can easily be wrecked. The main channel here is curved close to the Eastern shore. There are sharp reefs. It is protected by Esopus Meadows Light (1872) at the south end. The lighthouse is of Victorian design on an artificial island. It is one-story clapboard with tower.

82.30 Esopus Meadows Point to west. This point is incorrectly labeled Dinsmore Point on the U. S. C. and G. Navigation Chart #283.

82.75 Vanderburgh Cove to east. Cut off from river by New York Central Railroad causeway, it is an outlet of Fallsburg Creek and Landsman Creek.

82.75 Fallsburg Creek to east. It rises south of Rhinebeck and flows southwest to Vanderburgh Cove. The former Beekman's Mills dock is near its mouth. It is also known as Dow's Dock.

82.80 George Holliday Mansion to east.

82.90 Landsman Kill to east. Also known as Landsman Creek and Vanderburgh Creek, it rises southwest of Rhinebeck and flows south to

Vanderburgh Cove. It was named for Casper Landsman, first miller on stream.

83.00 Mirror Lake to west. Out of sight, inland on a plateau, it is also known as Binnewater Pond.

83.10 Prospect Hill to west (elevation 360 feet).

83.10 Jones Point to east.

83.10 Linwood to east. Ancestral home of the late Col. Jacob Ruppert. He was a wealthy brewer, real estate owner, and onetime owner of the New York Yankees baseball team. *Linwood* has been more recently owned by his nephew, J. Ruppert Schalk. It is now owned by the sisters of St. Ursula.

83.20 Ruins of Wyndcliffe to east. This brick Victorian mansion (1852) was described in the novels of Edith Wharton, whose aunt, Elizabeth Schermerhorn Jones, lived here, and whom she often visited.

83.20 Jones island to east. This is a tiny islet just off Jones Point.

83.30 Hemlock Point to west.

83.30 Wildercliff to east. Built by a famous Methodist preacher, Rev. Freeborn Garrettson (1752–1827) in about 1799. It had many distinguished guests, including Bishop Asbury and other dignitaries of the Methodist Church. He married Catherine Livingston (1752–1849). Their daughter, Mary Garrettson (1794–1879), lived here until her death. The house later passed to E. R. Jones and A. Frinck. It is a two-story clapboard with gambrel roof. The wings are later additions.

83.50 Wilderstein to east. This is a Victorian mansion with minaret-like towers and similar details. It was originally built in the Italian villa style by John Warren Ritch for Thomas Suckley in 1852. Additions in the Queen Anne style were made by Arnout Cannon in 1888. The interiors are very elaborate with extensive use of leaded glass and were designed and executed by Tiffany. The extensive grounds covering 40 acres were landscaped by Calvert Vaux. Until 1991 it was occupied by members of the Suckley family. Although in a state of some dilapidation, it is currently undergoing restoration and on special occasions is open to the public. For visiting information contact Wilderstein Preservation, Box 383, Rhinebeck, NY 12572. Telephone 914-876-4818.

83.80 Swan Plot to east. This is a long shallow reef of one- and two-foot depth, parallel to the eastern shore. There is a channel of between a twenty-one- and a twenty-six-foot depth between it and the shore, but it is open to deep water only at the southern end. There are only seventeen feet at the northern end.

83.80 Ellerslie Dock to east. The railroad passes through a tunnel here.

84.40 Big Rock Point to west.

84.50 Hussey's Mountain to west (elevation 1,005 feet). It is also called Huzzy Hill.

84.50 Ellerslie to east. This was the hilltop estate and palatial summer home of former Vice President Levi P. Morton (1824–1920). The 600-acre estate was owned earlier by the Hon. William Kelly. Later it was the Farley Military Academy and it is now the Pius XII School.

85.00 Sturgeon Point to east.

85.25 Port Ewen to west. This village was built entirely by the Pennsylvania Coal Company and was named in honor of its president, John Ewen. It was laid out in 1851 and had a population of about 1,400, most of whom worked on, or built, the company's coal barges. The Gurney Brickyard and a large ice storage yard were also located here. The shrine of Our Lady of the Hudson is located here.

86.00 Sleightsburg to west. This is an old river town, popular with retired rivermen. Capt. William O. Benson (d. 1986), well-known historian and writer on the Hudson River and steamboats, resided here. This was the former southern terminus of the cable ferry across Rondout Creek.

86.25 Rhinecliff to east. Formerly known as Shatzell's Dock, Rhinecliff is the station and landing for Rhinebeck, about a half mile inland. It is not seen from the river. The name derives from the name of the Rhine River and "beck," which means cliffs. William Beekman came from the Rhine in Germany in 1647 and purchased the area around Rhinebeck from the Indians. He gave homes to several poor families who came with him. The area closer to the river was originally called Kipsbergen. The families of the Kips purchased lands extending four miles along the river. The original deed, signed by three Esopus Indians, is dated July 28, 1686. A confirming Royal Patent is dated June 21, 1688. On May 26, 1702, the land of the patent was divided among five partners. Kipsbergen was absorbed into Rhinebeck Precinct on December 16, 1737. The Rhinebeck area is noted for the violet-growing industry and the Beekman Arms Hotel, established in 1700 and claimed to be the oldest continuously operating hotel in the United States. The Long Dock used to be the terminus of the Rondout Ferry. It was also formerly known as

Hoffman's Landing. It is presently an Amtrak stop. This was also formerly the western terminus of the Hartford & Connecticut Western Railroad, later the Rhinebeck Branch of the Philadelphia & Reading.

86.25 Rondout Creek to west. It rises south of Slide and Rocky Mountains in the Catskills and flows generally southeast through Peekamoose Lake, Rondout Reservoir, and Honk Lake to the vicinity of Napanoch. It then turns northeast along the northwestern foot of the Shawangunk Mountains, past Kerhonkson, Port Jackson, St. Josen, Accord, Alligerville, Kyserike, and High Falls. Here it breaches the Shawangunk Mountains and continues past Rosendale, Creeklocks, Bloomington, and Eddyville, where it falls to tidewater—the head of navigation from the Hudson. The portion between Napanoch and Eddyville was paralleled by the defunct Delaware & Hudson Canal. Just above Creeklocks, it receives the waters of the Wallkill River, which rises in northern New Jersey.

Below Eddyville, it broadens out with tidal marshes and with Gumaer Island in the middle. Barges come up this far to be loaded with aggregate. There were lime kilns along the shore here and bluestone yards at Wilbur, the next town downstream. Here the creek is crossed by the 1,200-foot long, 150-foot high truss bridge of the West Shore Railroad, built in 1883. Further toward the Hudson are the old canal villages of Connelly and Sleightsburg on the south bank, and Rondout on the north bank. These formerly were connected by a cable ferry, since replaced by the Route 9W suspension bridge. Immediately west of the road bridge is the famous Island Dock where, in past years, immense piles of coal were unloaded from canal boats prior to reshipment in river and coastal barges and schooners. On the north bank is the Strand section of Rondout, which was the former commercial center of the central Hudson valley. Here was located the ferry terminal of the Rhinecliff Ferry and the home port of the Cornell tug and barge fleet, the *Mary Powell, Baldwin,* and *Romer.* Still further toward the Hudson, on the north bank, are former limestone quarries, later used as mushroom-growing caves, and the Ponckhockie Cliffs and neighborhood of Ponckhockie. There were formerly many ship and boatyards in the vicinity. Jetties extend out into the Hudson River on either side, with mud flats to the north and south. There is a navigation light at the tip of the south jetty, and a two-story brick lighthouse tower, built in 1915, at the tip of the north jetty. Just north of this, across some mud flats, is Kingston Point. The Hudson River Maritime Center Museum is located on the creek at Rondout, and the excursion boat Rip Van Winkle of Hudson River Cruises operates from the creek.

86.30 Kingston Point to west. Formerly called Columbus Point, it used to be an important river landing and transfer point to the trains of the Ulster & Delaware Railroad. For many years, the Hudson River Day Line maintained a pleasure park here. Now there are oil depots and a public park. The point is now part of Kingston Urban Cultural Park and recreational facilities are being upgraded. The Trolley Museum of New York has restored the Ulster & Delaware tracks between Rondout and Kingston Point and offers trips out to the point. The point is a delightful picnic place and the train ride is inexpensive and recommended. On the north side of the point, reached from Delaware Avenue, Kingston, there is a sandy public bathing beach. (914 331-3399)

86.30 Delaware & Hudson Canal to west. This canal extended from Honesdale, Pennsylvania, to Rondout. It was built to carry coal. (Functioned 1828 to 1904.)

86.30 Ponckhockie to west. Inland from Kingston Point, this is a neighborhood of Kingston. Its name is also spelled Ponk Hockie, signifying "burial grounds" in Indian language. The name also applies to Manlius limestone cliffs on the north shore of Rondout Creek, known as the Vlightberg. An old cement mine here was called the Glory Hole.

86.30 Rondout to west. Originally a separate city at the junction of Rondout Creek (formerly called the Wallkill River at this place) with the Hudson River, it was originally called Bolton. Rondout was merged into the city of Kingston in 1878, along with neighboring Ponckhockie and Wilbur. This was a major steamboat center, being the home port to the famous Mary Powell and the paddlewheel tow-boats Norwich and Austin, which used to pull long tows of coal barges from the outlet of the Delaware & Hudson Canal here to New York City. There were ferries to Rhinecliff, Sleightsburg, and Connelly. The waterfront area was called the Strand. Ulster & Delaware passenger trains used to originate both at Kingston Point and Rondout, before climbing the steep hill to the Union Station in upper Kingston. Urban renewal is fast clearing away the typical old "river town" type commercial buildings, although there are still quite a few fine older churches and homes on the slopes above the town.

Since 1980 the banks of Rondout Creek in Rondout and Ponckhockie have been part of the Kingston Urban Cultural Park. Many of the remaining old buildings have been beautifully restored,

including Sampson's Opera House (Freeman Building) and the Mansion House Hotel. New stores and restaurants have moved into the area and parks have been landscaped and developed along the waterfront and the port has become an active center again for excursion and coastal cruising ships. The key element in the revitalization is the Hudson River Maritime Center Museum, opened on July 4, 1980. The museum is dedicated to the preservation of the maritime heritage of the Hudson River. It is also the Visitor's Center for the UCP. Telephone 914-338-0071.

Another complementary key element is the Trolley Museum of New York, based on the former Ulster & Delaware RR tracks. It has old streetcars on display and offers rides between The Strand in Rondout and Kingston Point. Telephone 914-331-3399. The large modern excursion boat Rip Van Winkle regularly operates from Rondout landing and is operated by Hudson River Cruises. 914-255-6515.

86.30 Kingston to west. This is the seat of Ulster County. The Indian name for the area where the city now stands was At-kar-karton, the great plot or meadow on which they raised beans and corn. It was the location of a settlement of the Esopus Indians, largely an agricultural tribe. According to Wallace Bruce, "all of the countryside in this vicinity was known as Esopus, supposed to be derived, according to Ruttenber, from the Indian word "seepus," a river. A "sopus Indian" was a Lowlander, and the name is intimately connected with a long stretch of territory from Esopus village, near West Park, to the mouth of the Esopus at Saugerties.

Although traders had operated from the Rondout area as early as 1614, the first permanent settlers came to the area about 1652. The area near the waterfront was first simply called Redoubt, but was later corrupted to Rondoubt and finally Rondout. The later settlers built on a high piece of ground overlooking the fertile Esopus Flats meadowlands, to the northwest. This area had been used previously by the Indians to grow maize and was prime farmland. Although the settlers purchased the land from the Indians, their gradual encroachment caused resentment and, in 1659, the First Esopus War broke out and caused the settlers to request a garrison to defend them. At this time the settlers were rather thinly spread out on individual farms. In 1658, Governor Peter Stuyvesant directed that a stockaded town be erected at Wiltwyck ("wild place"), as the settlement was then known. This area was bounded by the present North Front, Green, and Main Streets, and Clinton Avenue. According to Wallace Bruce:

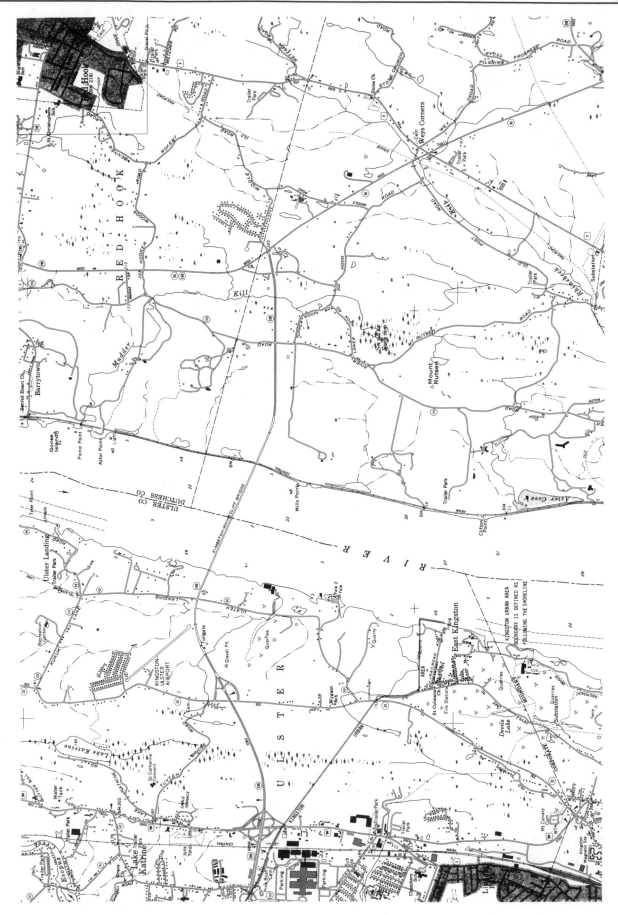

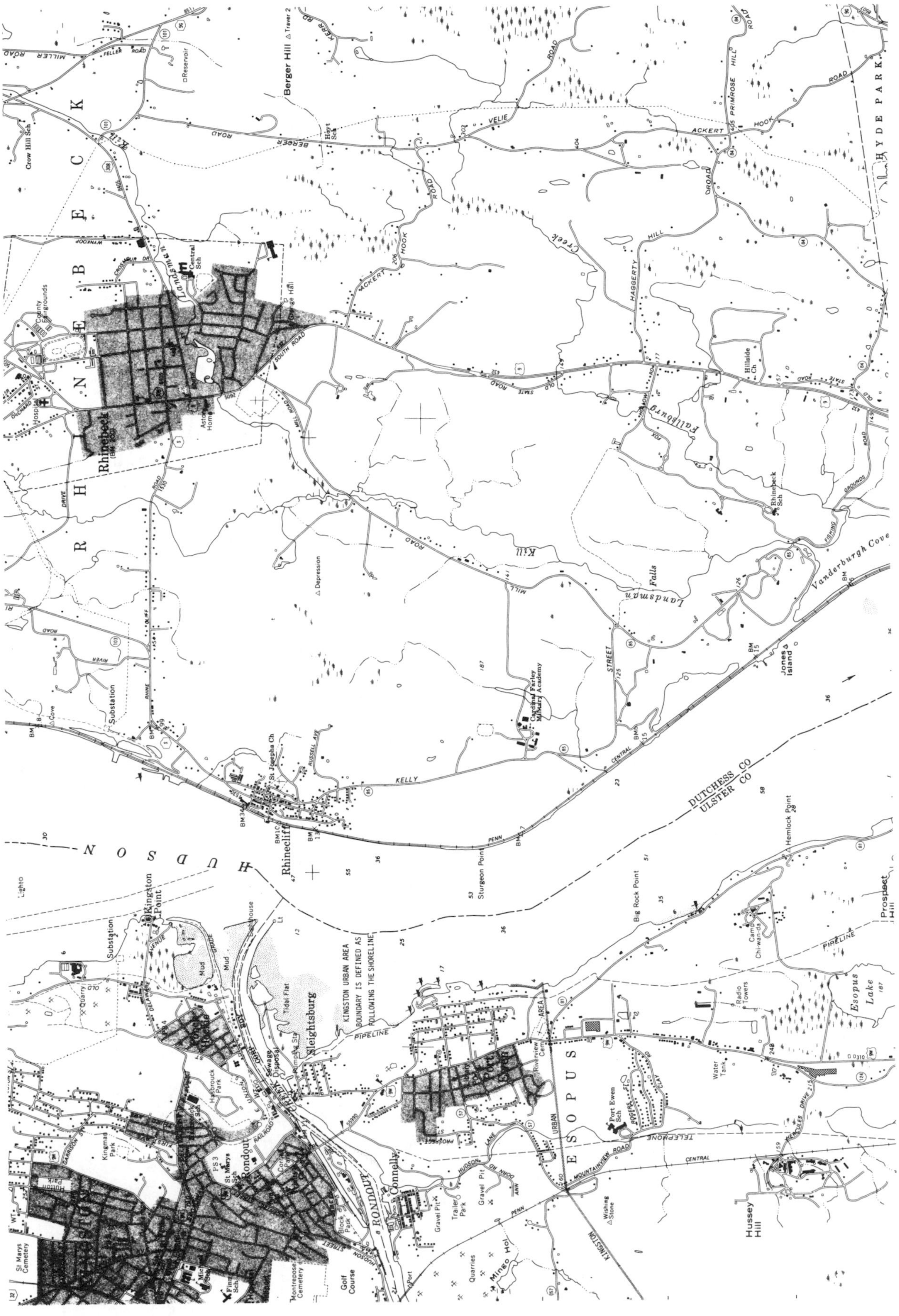
RHINEBECK
Rhinebeck
Rhinecliff
HUDSON
Kingston Point
Rondout
Connelly
Sleightsburg
Port Ewen
ESOPUS
Esopus Lake
Hussey Hill
Prospect Hill
Hemlock Point
Sturgeon Point
Big Rock Point
Jones Island
Vanderburgh Cove
Landsman Kill
Fallsburg
DUTCHESS CO
ULSTER CO
HYDE PARK
Berger Hill
Crow Hill Sch
Cardinal Farley Military Academy
St Josephs Ch
KINGSTON URBAN AREA BOUNDARY IS DEFINED AS FOLLOWING THE SHORELINE
Tidal Flat
Hasbrouck Park
Kingman Park
Golf Course
Montrepose Cemetery
St Marys Cemetery
Mingo Hol
Quarries
Camp Chi-wan-da
Radio Towers
Water Tank
Wishing Stone
Hillside Ch
Rhinebeck Sch
County Fairgrounds
Hospital
Astor Home
Substation
Depression

KINGSTON EAST

*The east, north and west fronts ran along eleva-
tions overlooking the lowlands and having a varying
altitude of from twenty to thirty feet. The enclosure
comprehended about twenty-five acres of land.
There were salients, or horn works at each end of
the four angles, with a circular projection at the
middle of the westerly side, where the elevations
were less than upon the northerly and easterly sides.
The church standing upon the ground . . . was
enclosed with a separate stockade, to be used as the
last resort in case of disaster, and, projecting from
this separate fortification, a strong block-house commanded and enfiladed the approaches to the southerly side, which was a plain.*

(Bruce, *Hudson by Daylight*, p. 182.)

*The fortifications included a guard house, barracks,
and blockhouse. The stockade consisted of a
wooden palisade made of spike-topped logs. There
were tunnels running from the basements of the
buildings inside the stockade to the low-lying
meadows roundabout.*

*The Dutch Reformed Church was organized in
1659. The first was built of logs, and has been succeeded by five later buildings. The present fine
Gothic structure, designed by Minard Lefever, was
built in 1852, according to Dr. Van Slyke, one of the
pastors. This church claims a distinction which does
not belong even to the Collegiate Dutch Churches of
Manhattan Island, and, by a peculiar history, stands
identified more closely with Holland than any other
of the early churches of this country When every
other church of our communion had for a long time
been associated with an American Synod, this
church retained its relations to the Classis of
Amsterdam, and, after a period of independency and
isolation, it finally allied itself with its American sis-
terhood as late as the year 1808.*

(Bruce, *Hudson by Daylight*, p. 199.)

It is still considered the Mother Church of the Dutch
Reformed Church in America. Dominie Blom was
the first preacher.

A formal charter was granted to Wiltwyck in 1658,
and work on the stockade was completed in 1661.

On June 7, 1663, a band of Indians attacked
Wiltwyck and neighboring Hurley and massacred
many inhabitants. This was the outbreak of the
Second Esopus War. In November, a punitive expedition was mounted which finally broke the power of
the Indians.

In 1665 the colony came under English rule. English troops garrisoned here under the command of
a Capt. Daniel Brodhead behaved obnoxiously.
When the citizens remonstrated they were accused

of causing what was called the Esopus Mutiny. Governor Nicolls intervened, and the "mutiny" devolved
into legal squabbles and was finally forgotten.

Dutch rule was restored between 1673 and 1674.
Under the English there was peaceful development.
The name of the settlement was changed to
Kingston in 1679. During the French and Indian Wars
(1754–1760), Kingston served as a base for frontier
military operations. During this period the name
Esopus was frequently used instead of Kingston.
This became more the case after the outbreak of the
Revolution in 1775.

During the Revolution, Kingston served as capital
of the state of New York, and was the first meeting
place of the New York State senate in 1777. After
the defeat of Gen. Burgoyne at Saratoga, Gen. John
Vaughan sailed up the Hudson on a punitive expedition. On October 13, 1777 he burned Esopus, sparing
only one house. The inhabitants fled to Hurley,
where a small force of Americans hanged a messenger who was caught carrying dispatches from
Gen. Clinton to Burgoyne. The constitution was formally announced at Kingston on April 22, 1777. The
first court was held here on September 9 and the
first legislature on September 10. Adjourning on October 7, they convened again August 18, 1779, and
again in 1780 from April 22 to July 2, and also for
two months beginning January 27, 1783.

Consequently, it can be seen that Kingston was a
hotbed of patriot activity. Wallace Bruce states that:
"The burning of Kingston seemed unnecessarily
cruel, and it is said that Vaughan was wide of the
truth when, to justify the same, he claimed that he
had been fired upon from dwellings in the village." In
any event, this was the last military action in the
area. The stone-walled buildings were quickly rebuilt,
and development continued after the war. Many of
the settlers were Huguenots, who intermarried with
the Dutch and English. The present courthouse was
built in 1818 on the site of a previous one, in which
the New York State Constitution was adopted in
1777. George Clinton, who was born in 1739, was
inaugurated as the first governor of the state of New
York at Kingston in 1777. The ceremony took place
outside the court house. Clinton was surrounded by
the Council of Safety and a square formed by two
companies of soldiers. He was proclaimed governor
by Egbert Dumond, the sheriff of the county, reading
his proclamation from the top of a barrel, and closing
it with the words, "God save the people," for the first
time taking the place of "God save the king." In 1812,
Governor Clinton was buried in the yard of the
Dutch Reformed Church, across the street.

Fulton's first successful steamboat of 1807 began
the development of neighboring Rondout as an im-

portant river port. Completion of the Delaware & Hudson Canal in 1828 added to the importance of the port. Kingston developed as a transport and finance center for the tanning, ice, brick, and bluestone industries, as well as into a farm produce marketing center.

The coming of the railroads increased Kingston's importance as a transport center. The Wallkill Valley Railroad was completed to a junction with the Erie Railroad at Montgomery in 1872. In 1875 the New York, Kingston & Syracuse (later the Rondout & Oswego and the Ulster & Delaware) was completed from Kingston Point to Stamford, in the western Catskills. It was later extended to a junction with the Delaware & Hudson Railroad at Oneonta. In 1883 the West Shore Railroad from Weehawken to Albany was completed through Kingston. The Ellenville & Kingston branch of the New York, Ontario & Western reached Kingston in 1902. For many years Kingston boasted a union terminal served by four steam railroads and an electric traction line.

The turn of the present century was the high point of Kingston's prosperity. Kingston was merged with neighboring Rondout and Wilbur in 1878. There was ferry service from Rondout across Rondout Creek to Sleightsburg and Connelly and across the Hudson to Rhinecliff, where there were connections with the Hudson River Railroad (New York Central) and Hartford & Connecticut Western. Steamers of all lines stopped at Kingston Point until 1953. An electric streetcar line ran along Broadway, connecting uptown Kingston with the ferry to Rhinecliff at Rondout. The union terminal, city hall, Y.M.C.A., library, and hospital were all located along Broadway. Many fine mansions were built on the heights overlooking Rondout. During this era, the Cornell and Coykendall families were prominent in business and public improvements.

Then the decline began. In 1904 the Delaware & Hudson Canal was abandoned, being superseded by railroads bypassing Kingston. This ended the great coal transfer activity at island dock and eliminated the need for the many towboats and barges. People began driving to the Catskills rather than traveling by boat and train. Ulster & Delaware passenger service, long only a pathetic remainder, ended in 1954. In 1957 the New York, Ontario & Western was totally abandoned, its passenger service having been discontinued many years earlier. In 1958 the last West Shore passenger train left town. The Rondout Creek ferry was discontinued after completion of the Route 9W suspension bridge in the 1930s. The Rhinecliff ferry stopped upon completion of the Kingston–Rhinecliff bridge in 1957. Construction of the New York Thruway outside of town diverted still more activity from Kingston. Only the coming of the light-aggregate industry and IBM brought any new activity to the area. Although still the principal trading town on the west bank of the Central Hudson Valley, Kingston is a relatively quiet place today. However, it is becoming more and more recognized as a place of historic interest because of its many well-preserved old buildings and interesting nineteenth-century residential, ecclesiastical, and commercial architecture. There is presently talk of building an authentic "Steam Town" here, with steam train excursions on the scenic Ulster & Delaware.

Kingston is the tourist center of a county in which tourism is the principal industry. Certainly the creation of the maritime center and railroad and trolley museums make a fitting memorial to a city that saw its greatest glory as a steamboat and railroad center.

The Senate House Museum is at 312 Fair Street. Telephone 914-338-2786. Walking Tours of the Historic Stockade District are operated by Friends of Historic Kingston and led by costumed guides from May through September. Call 914-338-1004.

88.00 Astor Cove to east. This cove is cut off from the river by a railroad causeway. The former Hartford & Connecticut Western Railroad cut inland here. The William Astor estate was near here, as was the Beekman Manor House.

88.25 Clifton Point to east. Formerly Rutsen's Landing, here was located *Ferncliff,* the country residence of Vincent Astor, son of John Jacob Astor.

88.25 East Kingston to west.

88.00 to 91.00 The Flats. This is an extensive and continuous shallow area just west of mid-stream. There are navigation channels on either side. Depths average two and three feet.

FERNCLIFF, ASTOR ESTATE, RHINECLIFF. Built by Colonel John Jacob Astor. Photo: author's collection.

88.75 Mt. Rutsen to east (elevation 350 feet).

89.45 Whiskey Point to west.

89.60 Mills Point to east. This is also known as Mill Dock.

89.60 Flatbush to west.

90.00 Kingston–Rhinecliff Bridge. A unit of the New York State Bridge Authority, it carries New York State Route 199. Opened to traffic February 2, 1957, it was designed by D. B. Steinman. Principal contractors were Harris Structural Steel and Merritt, Chapman & Scott. The bridge is of the continuous deck design and has an overall length of 7,793 feet. The main span is 5,200 feet with a vessel clearance of 152 feet. There are two vehicle lanes. A toll is charged eastbound.

91.00 Heath to the west.

91.00 Lake Katrine to west. Further inland. A jewel of a mountain tarn, it also gives its name to a station on the West Shore RR.

91.20 Rokeby to east. This famous and historic estate is not visible from the river. The original house was

built in 1815 by General John Armstrong and his wife Alida Livingston, on ancestral lands of her family. The original house was a two-story structure of stuccoed stone in the Federal style. In the mid-nineteenth century it was acquired by William B. Astor, whose wife was THE Mrs. Astor. He made enlargements, including a magnificent octagonal Gothic Revival library. A mansard roof and tower were later added. In 1895 Stanford White re-worked the entire fabric into the present imposing and picturesque, but not architecturally unified, structure. At present the house stands in need of considerable renovation. A start was made in 1986 by the architect Raymond Ruge, but work stopped upon the death of the architect. In recent generations Rokeby has been the home of the Aldrich family, who are related to the Astors. It is a private home and not regularly open to visitation.

In his 1866 book *The Hudson*, Benson J. Lossing gives us the following description:

...Rokeby, the seat of William B. Astor, Esq., who is distinguished as the wealthiest man in the United States. (1866) It was formerly the residence of his father-in-law, General John Armstrong, an officer in the war for independence, and a member of General Gates's military family. Armstrong was the author of the celebrated addresses which were privately circulated among the officers of the Continental Army lying at Newburgh, on the Hudson, at the close of the war and calculated to stir up a mutiny, and even a rebellion against the civil power. The feeble Congress had been unable for a long time to provide for the pay of the soldiers about to be disbanded and

KINGSTON-RHINECLIFF BRIDGE. Photo: Courtesy New York State Bridge Authority.

ROKEBY MANSION AT BARRYTOWN. This has been the ancestral home of the Armstrong, Astor, Chanler, and Aldrich families. View shows west front. The Gothic library occupies the octagonal tower. Drawing by Benson Lossing, 1866. Author's collection.

sent home in poverty and rags. There was apathy in Congress and among the people on the subject, and these addresses were intended to stir up the latter and their representatives to the performance of their duty in making some provision for their faithful servants, rather than to excite the army to take affairs into their own hand, as was charged. Through the wisdom and firmness of Washington, the event was so overruled as to give honor to the army and benefit the country. Washington afterwards acquitted Major Armstrong of all evil intentions, and considered his injudicious movement (instigated, it is supposed, by Gates) as a patriotic act.

Armstrong afterwards married a sister of Chancellor Livingston, and was chosen successively to a seat in the United States senate, an ambassador to France, a brigadier-general in the army, and secretary-of-war. He held the latter office while England and the United States were at war, in 1812–14. He was the author of a "Life of General Montgomery," "Life of General Wayne," and "Historical Notices of the War of 1812." Rokeby, where this eminent man lived and died, is delightfully situated, in the midst of an undulating park, farther from the river than the other villas, but commanding some interesting glimpses of it, with more distant landscapes and mountain scenery. Among the latter may be seen the range of the Shawangunk, in the far southwest. Here Mr. Astor's family reside about eight months of the year.

(Lossing, *The Hudson*, pp. 175–177.)

91.25 Astor Point to east.

91.35 Mudder Kill to east.

91.40 Picnic Point to east. Also known as Chanler Island.

91.50 Goose Island to east. Formerly Daisy Island.

91.50 Sylvania to east. Inland from Goose Island. This Georgian Revival Mansion was designed by Charles Adams Platt in 1905 and is of two-story stucco construction. It is the center of the extensive Sylvania Farms in Barrytown. The house was built by John Jay and Elizabeth Chanler Chapman, and later was the home of Chanler and Olivia Chapman.

91.50 Ulster Landing to west. Here is located *Wrongside*, a two-story brick and clapboard mansion dating from about 1825. Its name was given to the estate by the Livingstons, who felt their relative who built it should have done so on the east bank of the river.

91.55 Tyler Point to west.

91.75 Barrytown to east. Formerly known as Lower Red Hook Landing, after the town of Red Hook which is located several miles inland. This is a local railroad station. Wallace Bruce tells us that: "It is said when General Jackson was President, and this village wanted a post office, that he would not allow it under the name of Barrytown, from personal dislike to General Barry, and suggested another name; but the people were loyal to their old friend, and went without a post office until a new administration." The present writer thinks this story is apocryphal, as he can find no references to a "General Barry." However, William T. Barry was Postmaster General during Jackson's administration. It is easy to see how the facts might have been mixed up. Actually Barry was a good friend of Jackson's. Did the residents get their post office only on condition of naming it after Mr. Barry? The location is notable for possessing a pair of octagonal houses designed by Alexander Jackson Davis, about 1860.

91.75 Edgewater to east. This graceful two-story Federal style mansion, designed by Robert Mills, faces the river and is located, as its name would indicate, right on the edge of the river, with the railroad running close behind it. The original building dates from 1820 and was built by Margaret Livingston and her husband, Lowndes Brown. When the railroad was built in 1851, Mrs. Brown, then a widow, was indignant and sold the house and moved to Europe. In the mid-nineteenth century the house and landscape was modified from its original Greek Revival style to Federal by Alexander Jackson Davis. In recent years the house has belonged to Gore Vidal, the author, and Richard H. Jenrette, its present owner, who is a preservationist and serves as Chairman of Historic Hudson Valley. It is strictly private.

92.30 Trap Cliff to east.

92.35 Hog's Back. Slightly to east of mid-channel, this is a reef with as little as four feet of water, marked by a flashing white light, with channels on either side.

92.35 Glenerie to west. Inland on Esopus Creek.

92.35 Washburn Brothers Brick Yards to west.

92.75 Turkey Point to west.

92.75 Montgomery Place to east. This is one of the most interesting estates along the Hudson because of its sad history. This is best told by Benson Lossing:

Adjoining Annandale is Montgomery Place, the residence of the family of the late Edward Livingston, brother of the Chancellor, who is distinguished in the annals of his country as a leading

MONTGOMERY PLACE, ANNANDALE-ON-HUDSON. Photo: ©
Gretchen McHugh.

*United States senator, the author of the penal code
of the State of Louisiana, and ambassador to France.
The elegant mansion was built by the widow of General Richard Montgomery, a companion-in-arms of
Wolfe when he fell at Quebec, and who perished
under the walls of that city at the head of a storming
party of Republicans on the 31st of December 1775.
Montgomery was one of the noblest and bravest
men of his age. When he gave his young wife Janet
a parting kiss at the house of General Schuyler, at
Saratoga, and hastened to join that officer at
Ticonderoga, in the campaign that proved fatal to
him, he said, "You shall never blush for your Montgomery." Gallantly did he vindicate that pledge. And
when his virtues were extolled by Barre, Burke, and
others in the British parliament, Lord North
exclaimed, "Curse on his virtues: he has undone his
country."*

*The wife of Montgomery was a sister of Chan-
cellor Livingston. With ample pecuniary means and a
good taste at command, she built this mansion and
there spent fifty years of widowhood, childless, but
cheerful. The mansion and its 400 acres passed into
the possession of her brother Edward, and there, as
we have observed, members of his family now
(1866) reside. Of all the fine estates along this portion of the Hudson, this is said to be the most perfect in its beauty and arrangements. Waterfalls, picturesque bridges, romantic glens, groves, a
magnificent park, one of the most beautiful of the
ornamental gardens in this country, and views of the
river and mountains, unsurpassed, render
Montgomery Place a retreat to be coveted, even by
the most favoured of fortune.*

(Lossing, *The Hudson*, pp. 173–174.)

The following sequel is told in Stone's History of
New York City:

*In 1818 the Legislature of New York—DeWitt
Clinton, Governor—ordered the remains of General
Montgomery to be removed from Canada to New
York. This was in accordance with the wishes of the
Continental Congress, which in 1776, had voted the
beautiful cenotaph to his memory that now stands in
the wall of St. Paul's Church, fronting Broadway.
When the funeral cortege reached Whitehall, N. Y.,
the fleet stationed there received them with appropriate honors; and on the 4th of July they arrived in
Albany. After lying in state in that city over Sunday,
the remains were taken to New York, and on
Wednesday deposited, with military honors, in their
final resting place, at St. Paul's. Governor Clinton had
informed Mrs. Montgomery of the hour when the
steamer "Richmond," conveying the body would
pass her home. At her own request, she stood alone
on the portico. It was forty years since she had
parted from her Richard, to whom she had been
wedded but two years when he fell on the heights
of Quebec; yet she had remained faithful to the
memory of her "soldier" as she always called him.
The steamboat halted before the mansion; the band
played the "Dead March," and a salute was fired; and
the ashes of the venerated hero, and the departed
husband, passed on. The attendants of the Spartan
widow now appeared, but, overcome by the tender
emotions of the moment, she had swooned and
fallen to the floor.*

(Bruce, *The Hudson by Daylight*, p. 193.)

In her *Biographies of Francis Lewis and Morgan
Lewis*, Julia Delafield gives the following interesting
description of Janet Montgomery:

*Mrs. Montgomery's eyes had the peculiarity of
being always half shut. The lid was probably too
long. In a miniature that the General had taken to
send to Ireland, she is represented looking down,
reading a letter. It gives the idea of a handsome
woman. Her complexion, even in her old age, did
honor to her Scotch descent. She had a noble head,
well placed on her shoulders, and like her sisters,
Mrs. Garretson and Mrs. Lewis, she was above the
middle height, and extremely graceful. Sprightly
sense, sweetness of temper, and overflowing good
humor attracted round the sisters men of the highest
position as well as talent.*

(Julia Delafield, *Biography of Francis Lewis &
Morgan Lewis*, New York: Scribners, 1877.)

Mrs. Montgomery originally called Montgomery Place
the Chateau de Montgomery. Edward Livingston
lived from 1764 to 1836. He had the grounds landscaped by Andrew Jackson Downing and the house

enlarged by Alexander Jackson Davis. The building is a two-story Federal mansion. The remodeling was done in 1840 and again in the 1860s. In 1900 the property belonged to Carleton Hunt and his sisters. In 1940 it was the property of General John Ross Delafield, the great-grandson of Edward Livingston.

In 1986 the property was purchased by Sleepy Hollow Restorations, now called Historic Hudson Valley, helped by a gift from J. Dennis Delafield. The task of restoring the mansion was very difficult as termites, water, and rot had taken great toll. The east portico was propped up by two-by-fours with only one of its four Corinthian columns intact.

The mansion, built between 1804 and 1805, sits on a terrace 160 feet above the river, surrounded by black locust trees, and with grand views westward over the Hudson to the distant Catskill Mountains. It is located upon a 434-acre estate with 22 miles of carriage roads and walking paths, a 150-acre orchard with over 5,000 peach, pear, and apple trees under active cultivation, and a hardwood forest untouched since 1700, making it the oldest stand of forest along the Hudson. There are a conservatory, coach house, greenhouse, and arboretum containing rare trees, and a series of formal and informal gardens. The estate includes the working Montgomery Place Orchards & Farms, with a farmstand on Route 9G. The estate also includes the entire hamlet of Annandale-on-Hudson, which is also being restored.

In June 1988 the restoration was finally opened to the public along with a new visitor's center. The 23-room mansion is still undergoing restorations but is now open to visitors. The entrance is located on River Road (Route 103) and the telephone is 914-758-5461 This is one of the grand "must visit" places in the Hudson Valley.

92.75 South Bay to east. This bay is now cut off from the river by a railroad causeway. It is very shallow, only one and two feet deep. *Blithewood* and *Montgomery Place* face onto South Bay. South Bay is part of the Hudson River National Estuarine Research Reserve.

92.75 Skillpot Island to east. This island is in South Bay, inside the railroad causeway. Skillpot was an old Dutch term for a large turtle. This is a very small island.

92.80 Sawkill Creek to east. This creek empties into South Bay.

92.80 Annandale-on-Hudson to east. This is a small hamlet a half-mile inland. The neighborhood embraces such major features as *Montgomery Place*, *Blithewood*, Bard College, and Ward Manor Estate campus of Bard College.

92.80 Whale's Back to east (elevation 300 feet).

92.85 Blithewood to east. *Blithewood* is an estate established in 1795 by Gen. John Armstrong (1758–1843), whose history has been given under the heading of *Rokeby* (ERM 91.20). He married Alida, the sister of Chancellor Livingston. In 1810, he sold *Blithewood* and moved to *Rokeby*. *Blithewood* was then purchased by John Cox Stevens (1785–1857), another brother-in-law of Chancellor Livingston. He was a yachtsman and a founder of the New York Yacht Club and a backer of *America*, leading to the creation of the America's Cup. In 1835 Robert Donaldson acquired *Blithewood*. During his tenure, the grounds were landscaped by Andrew Jackson Downing, who also designed the gatehouse. It is recorded that Dr. John Bard lived here after 1853.

The present late Georgian style mansion was designed by Francis F. V. Hoppin and was erected by Andrew C. Zabriskie in 1899.

92.90 Bard College (main campus) to east. This college was founded by Dr. John Bard in 1960 as St. Stephen's College for Sons of Episcopal Clergyman. Since 1928 it has been a unit of Columbia University. There are two main campuses. One is immediately north of the center of Annandale-on-Hudson, and the other on the former Robert B. Ward estate, further north. At the main campus a most notable structure is the Chapel of Holy Innocents, designed in 1860 by Charles Babcock, an associate of Richard Upjohn. It is built on the site of an earlier church built in 1857, which burned in 1858. The interior has been redecorated by Ralph Adams Cram. The *Blithewood* estate and mansion, slightly to the south, is now part of Bard College and used as a study center in economics.

93.75 Cruger Island to east. Formerly called Magdalen Island, Cruger Island is also called Cruger's

BLITHEWOOD, ANNANDALE-ON-HUDSON. This mansion is now the home of the Jerome Levy Economics Institute of Bard College. Photo: courtesy of Bard College.

Island, and is now joined to the mainland. Wallace Bruce tells us that:

> There is an old Indian legend that no person ever died on this island, which a resident recently (1900) said still held true. It is remarkable, moreover, in possessing many antique carved stones from a city of Central America built into the walls of a temple modeled after the building from which the graven stones were brought. The "ruin" at the south end of the island is barely seen from the steamer hidden as it is by the foliage, but it is distinctly noted from the windows of the New York Central in the winter season. Col. (John Church) Cruger has spared no expense in the adornment of his grounds, and a beautiful drive is afforded the visitor. The bogus ruins were built about 1840 to simulate the Romantic atmosphere of Thomas Cole's paintings. The island was later given by William B. Ward to the New York Association for Improving the Condition of the Poor for use as a summer camp and health resort.

93.80 Ward Manor Estate to east. This is now a part of Bard College, a unit of Columbia University. This 2,000-acre estate called Ward Manor was the former home of Robert B. Ward, the prominent baker. The Ward Mansion is a two-story stuccoed Tudor building dating from 1918. There is an interesting gatehouse dating from 1915, which is a two-story castellated structure with a tower.

94.25 Saddle Bags. West of the main vessel channel in the river, these are treacherous reefs in roughly the shape of a pair of saddle bags. Depths are between five and thirteen feet.

94.50 Beckwith Hill to east (elevation 400 feet).

94.50 Glasco to west. Located at the eastern terminus of the Glasco Turnpike from Woodstock, at the base of the Catskill Mountains, it takes its name from a large sign originally painted on a wharf warehouse which a glass company formerly used to transship its products. The glass was made between 1809 and 1855 at Shady, near Woodstock, and brought here over the Glasco Turnpike for transfer to boats. The area was originally settled by Palatinates.

94.50 North Bay to east. Formerly called De Koven's Cove or Bay, it is cut off from the river by a railroad causeway, and is now almost completely silted up. Benson Lossing gives us the following interesting information, which is at the root of the popular but incorrect story that Fulton built the *Clermont* at North Bay. It was actually built at New York City and Hoboken:

> *Mr. Livingston's chief honour as a man of science, and promoter of useful interests, is derived from his aid and encouragement in efforts which resulted in the entire success of steam navigation. As early as 1797, he was engaged with an Englishman named Nesbit in experiments. They built a steamboat on the Hudson River, at a place now known as De Koven's Cove, or Bay, about half a mile below Tivoli, or Upper Red Hook Landing. Brunel, the engineer of the Thames Tunnel, and father of the originator and constructor of the "Great Eastern" steamship, was the engineer. The enterprise was not successful. Livingston entered upon other experiments, when he was interrupted by his appointment as United States minister to the court of France. In Paris he became acquainted with Robert Fulton's experiments there.*
>
> (Lossing, *The Hudson*, p. 169.)

Upon returning to America, Fulton did spend some time at *Clermont* nearby, perfecting his designs for the North River Steamboat. Thus it is easy to see how the confusion has arisen.

North Bay is part of the Hudson River National Estuarine Research Reserve.

94.80 Stony Creek to east. It flows into northern end of North Bay.

94.80 Magdalen Island to east. Also spelled Madalin and Madaline, it was formerly called Goat Island and Slipsteen Island. A great depth of 47 feet of water is immediately offshore. It would be possible to draw a steamboat up alongside and tie it to a tree.

95.30 Sycamore Point to east.

95.80 Catskill Mountains to west.

95.80 Tivoli to east. Formerly known as Upper Red Hook Landing. Between 1798 and 1802, a Frenchman by the name of Peter de Labigarre built a home here which he called the Chateau de Tivoli. He hired an itinerant draftsman named Charles Balthazar Julien

TUG *MARY TURECAMO* AND LIGHTLY LOADED BARGE. Kaaterskill High Peak seen in distance. Photo: © Gretchen McHugh.

Fevret de Saint-Memin, who was an expatriot officer of the Guard of King Louis XVI. He was also a portrait painter. In any event, he drew up impractical plans of a town with 60-feet-wide streets in a grid-iron pattern. Of these streets, only Flora and Diana remain today. The speculation was a failure, and the lots did not sell. Monsieur DeLabigarre died in 1807 and Chancellor Livingston bought them all at a fore-closure sale.

The *Callendar House*, two-story frame in the Federal style with wings and quoins (ca. 1790) was formerly the property of Johnston Livingston. *Sunning Hill* and *The Pynes*, a two-story clapboard mansion, date from about 1790. St. Paul's Protestant Episcopal Church on Wood Road dates from 1868. It was designed by Robert E. Livingston, grandson of the Chancellor. It is Victorian Gothic in style and was modified in 1922 by the addition of eight burial vaults to receive the remains of the Livingstons.

96.00 Rose Hill to east. This is a two-story brick Italianate Victorian villa, ca. 1870. Wallace Bruce gives us this information:

The residence of J. Watts De-Peyster stands on a commanding bluff north of the railway station and it was beside his open fireside many years ago that he told the writer how his house was saved from Vaughan's trip up the river to burn the Livingston Manor House. Rose Hill, the home of his ancestors, was mistaken for "Clermont," but a well-stocked cellar mollified the British Captain. "Rose Hill" was named after the old Watts Mansion in Edinburgh, which has recently (1900) been removed to make room for a railway.

Rose Hill projects so far out into the river that it is beyond the Islands two miles below, which, at one time, were about in the center of the wide expanse of water between the main shores. To give a better idea, however, of the projection, steamboats which pass down to the front have to sheer in so far in making their landing at Tivoli, a quarter of a mile below, that they disappear from sight of those looking southward and watching them from the piazza of the mansion. Rose Hill itself has grown like one of the old English family houses, with the increase of the family until, in strange but picturesque outline—the prevailing style being Italian, somewhat in the shape of a cross—it is now 114 feet long by 87 feet deep. The tower in the rear, devoted to library purposes, rises to the height of about sixty feet. This library, first and last, has contained between twenty and thirty thousand volumes. Such indefinite language is used, because the owner has donated over half this number to the New York Historical Society, the

New York Society Library, and a number of other similar organizations in different parts of the United States. As a working library, replete with dictionaries and cyclopaedias, in many tongues and on almost every subject, it is a marvel. It is likewise very valuable for its collections on military and several other special topics. From it was selected and given to the New York Historical Society, one of the finest possible collections on the History of Holland, from the earliest period down to the present time. In spite of all these donations it is still a curiosity shop; not only for the bibliophile, but for a curio-seeker.

(Bruce, *Hudson by Daylight*, p. 199.)

96.25 Long Pier to west. This is a former steamboat landing south of the mouth of Esopus Creek. It was also formerly known as Saugerties Landing.

96.50 Esopus Creek to west. Rising on the slopes of Panther and Slide Mountains in three branches, the combined stream begins near the settlement of Slide Mountain Post Office. The principal source is Winnisook Lake. Blossom Falls are on the middle branch. From Slide Mountain, the stream flows in a big curve first west, and then north, through the Big Indian Valley to the village of Big Indian. Here it turns southeast to Phoenicia, Mount Pleasant, and Boiceville and finally enters Ashokan Reservoir. Below the dam at Olive Bridge it continues southeast to Lomontville, where it makes a bend to the northeast and flows through broad fertile flats between the Catskill foothills and the northern tip of the Shawangunks. It passes the early Dutch settlements of Marbletown, Hurley, and Kingston. It continues north through marshes, past the village of Lake Katrine, to a junction with Plattekill Creek above Glenerie Falls. It turns sharply right under the West Shore Railroad and goes over Glenerie Falls. It then turns sharply north at the foot of the falls and flows through a gorge which is straight, rugged, and very narrow, to the vicinity of Saugerties. Here it is dammed just below the Route 9W bridge and forms a fair size lake. In the nineteenth century, the falls were used for water power for the paper mills. Below the dam the creek flows through another deep gorge and makes a sharp turn to the east, where it becomes still tide water. The shores are lined with marinas and boatyards for the final short stretch to the Hudson, which it enters between tidal flats and jetties on either side. There is a Coast Guard station and lighthouse on the Washburn's Point jetty on the north side.

96.50 Washburn's Point to west. This lighthouse is two-story brick with a tower. It was built in 1869.

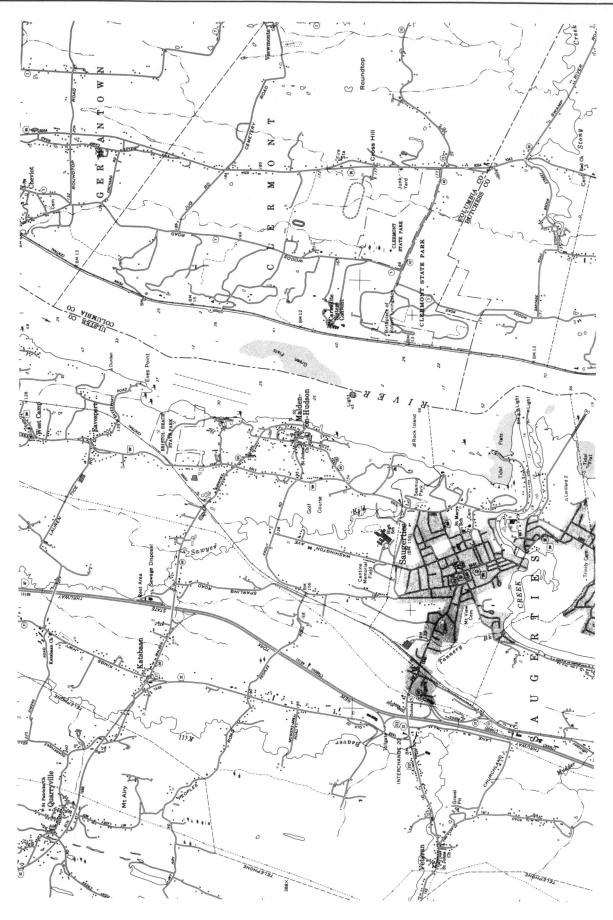

SAUGERTIES LIGHTHOUSE, SOUTH SIDE. Photo: © Gretchen McHugh.

96.50 Saugerties to west. The first known settler in the township was Cornelius Lambertson Brinks who settled near Mt. Marion in 1688. The name Saugerties derives from "Da Zaagertijis," which is Dutch for "saw mills." The first one was built in 1663 on the Sawyerkill by Cornelius Vogel.

The remains of a similar one, presently in progress of restoration, can be seen on the Sawyer's Kill near Seamon Memorial Park, north of the village. Settled by the Dutch, it was developed by the Livingstons. It once had extensive lumbering, white lead, and paper industries and shipped much blue-stone. Principal among the paper companies were the Sheffield Paper Company, the Barkley Fibre Company (pulp wood), and the Martin Company (cardboard).

Saugerties in around 1800 is well described by Cooper in his novel *Afloat and Ashore*. The following describes the Mynderse House and grounds almost perfectly, with its main house built in 1690 and "new" wings of 1743:

My father died on the farm on which he was born, and which descended to him from his great-grandfather, an English emigrant that had purchased it of the Dutch colonists who had originally cleared it

from the woods. The place was called Clawbonny, which some said was good Dutch, others bad Dutch; and now and then a person ventured a conjecture that it might be Indian. Bonny it was in one sense at least, for a lovelier farm is not on the whole of the wide surface of the Empire State. What does not always happen in this wicked world, it was as good as it was handsome. It consisted of three hundred and seventy-two acres of first-rate land, either arable or rich river bottom in meadows, and of more than a hundred of rocky mountain side, that was very tolerably covered with wood. The first of our family who owned the place had built a substantial one-story stone house, that bears the date of 1707 on one of its gables; and to which each of his successors had added a little, until the whole structure got to resemble a cluster of cottages thrown together without the least attention to order or regularity. There were a porch, a front door, and a lawn, however; the latter containing half a dozen acres of a soil as black as ones hat, and nourishing eight or ten elms that were scattered about as if their seeds had been sown broadcast. In addition to the trees and a suitable garniture of shrubbery, this lawn was coated with a sward that, in the proper seasons, rivalled all I have

SAUGERTIES LIGHTHOUSE, EAST SIDE. Photo: Walter Plankl.

read or imagined of the emerald and shorn slopes of the Swiss valleys.

Clawbonny, while it had all the appearance of being the residence of an affluent agriculturist, had none of the pretension of these later times. The house had an air of substantial comfort without, an appearance that its interior in no manner contradicted. The ceilings were low, it is true, nor were the rooms particularly large; but the latter were warm in winter, cool in summer, and tidy, neat, and respectable all the year round. Both the parlors had carpets as had the passages and all the better bed-rooms; and there were an old-fashioned chintz set-tee, well stuffed and cushioned, and curtains in the "big parlor," as we called the best apartment; the pre-tending name of drawing-room not having reached our valley as far back as the year 1796 or that in which my recollections of the place, as it then ex-isted are the most vivid and distinct.

We had orchards, meadows, and ploughed fields all around us; while the barns, granaries, stiles, and other buildings of the farm were of solid stone, like the dwelling, and all in capital condition.

There was a mill, just where the stream that runs through our valley tumbles down to a level below that on which the farm lies, and empties itself into a small tributary of the Hudson. This mill was on our property, and was a source of great convenience and of some profit to my father. There he ground all the grain that was consumed for domestic purposes for several miles around; and the tolls enabled him to fatten his porkers and beeves, in a way to give both a sort of established character. In a word, the mill was the concentrating point for all the products of the farm, there being a little landing on the margin of the creek that put up from the Hudson, whence a sloop sailed weekly for town. My father passed half his time about the mill and landing, superintending his workmen, and particularly giving directions about the fitting of the sloop, which was his property also, and about the gear of the mill.

There had been a generation of sloops which bore

the name of Wallingford, as well as generations of men, at Clawbonny, and this every riverman knew. In point of fact, we counted four generations of men and six of sloops. Now, none of these vessels was worthy of being mentioned, but this which my father had caused to be built, but she had a reputation that extended to everybody on the river

I had a dozen slaves, also; negroes who, as a race, had been in the family almost as long as Clawbonny. About half of these blacks were singularly laborious and useful, namely, four males and three of the females; but several of the remainder were enjoying otium, and not altogether without dignitate, as heirlooms to be fed, clothed, and lodged, for the good or evil they had done. There were some small-fry in our kitchens, too, that used to roll about on the grass, and munch fruit in the summer, ad libitum, and stand so close in the chimney-corners in cold weather, that I have often fancied they must have been, as a legal wit of New York once pronounced certain eastern coal mines to be, incombustible. These negroes all went by the patronymic of Clawbonny, there being among them Hector Clawbonny, Venus Clawbonny, Caesar Clawbonny, Rose Clawbonny and Julietta, commonly called Julee, Clawbonny—who was black as a crow—and Romeo Clawbonny; who were the Pharaoh, Potiphar, Samson and Nebuchadnezzar, all Clawbonnys in the last resort. Neb, as the namesake of the herbivorous King of Babylon was called, was about my own age, and had been a sort of humble playfellow from infancy; and even now, when it was thought proper to set him about the more serious toil which was to make his humble career, I often interfered to call him away to be my companion with the rod, the fowling-piece, or in the boat, of which we had one that frequently descended the creek and navigated the Hudson for miles at a time, under my command. The lad, by such means, and through an off-hand friendliness of manner that I rather think was characteristic of my habits at that day, got to love me as a brother or comrade. It is not easy to describe the affection of an attached slave, which has blended with it the pride of a partisan, the solicitude of a parent, and the blindness of a lover. I do think Neb had more gratification in believing himself particularly belonging to Master Miles, than I ever had in any quality or thing I could call my own. Neb, moreover liked a vagrant life, and greatly encouraged Rupert and myself in idleness, and a desultory manner of misspending hours that could never be recalled. The first time I ever played truant was under the patronage of Neb, who decoyed me away from my books to go nutting on the mountain, stoutly maintaining

that chestnuts were just as good as the spelling-book, or any primer that could be bought in York.

We were all four of us seated on a rude bench that my mother had caused to be placed under the shade of an enormous oak that stood on the most picturesque spot, perhaps, on the whole farm, and which commanded a distant view of one of the lovliest reaches of the Hudson. Our side of the river, in general, does not possess as fine views as the eastern, for the reason that all our own broken, and in some instances magnificent, background of mountains, fills up the landscape for our neighbors, while we are obliged to receive the picture as it is set in a humbler frame; but there are exquisite bits to be found on the western bank, and this was one of the very best of them. The water was as placid as molten silver, and the sails of every vessel in sight were hanging in listless idleness from their several spars, representing commerce asleep.

(James Fenimore Cooper, *Ashore and Afloat* pp. 2, 3, 5, 23.)

At the southern end of town, on Route 9W, there are several sharp bends in the road and bluestone walls are layed up along the roadside. Several old houses and churches in this neighborhood are reminiscent of the following extract from Cooper's *Miles Wallingford* (p. 137).

St. Michael's churchyard is beautifully ornamented with flourishing cedars. These trees had been cultivated with care, and formed an appropriate ornament for the place. A fine cluster of them shaded the graves of my family, and a rustic seat had been placed beneath their branches, by order of my mother who had been in the habit of passing hours of meditation at the grave of her husband.

This scene describes the grave of Grace Wallingford, "The Lily of Clawbonny," a character quite obviously patterned after Cooper's own beloved sister who had died young. The scene might equally well fit the Church of the Ascension in West Park.

The old commercial neighborhood, and falls of the Esopus, as well as Barclay Heights with its mansions, are worth a visit. Seamon's Park has extensive floral displays and an annual autumn Chrysanthemum Festival. The Wede Marine Museum is located here.

96.75 Sawyer's Kill to west. This creek flows south from the Great Vly Swamp southwest of the Kalkberg to the Hudson. It was named for the saw mills along its banks. The first mill here was built in 1663 by Cornelius Vogel.

96.75 Columbia County to east. From here to mile 126.60, opposite Barren Island, the eastern bank is occupied by Columbia County. It occupies an area of 643 square miles and is largely devoted to agriculture and dairy operations. It was taken from Albany County in 1786 and named in honor of Christopher Columbus. Hudson is the county seat. Chatham and Hillsdale are the only other two towns of any size. It is bounded on the west by the Hudson River, on the north by Rensselaer County, on the east by Massachusetts, and on the south by Dutchess County. The Taconic range of the Berkshire Mountains runs along the eastern border. The county is drained to the east by the Green River, which flows into the Housatonic, and to the west, or Hudson, by the Roeliffe Jansen Kill (also known as Livingston Creek and Ancram Creek) and by Claverack Creek and Stockport Creek (also known as Major Abraham's Creek or Kinderhook Creek). The Hudson River Railroad runs along the Hudson and is now part of the Conrail Mainline. The former Boston & Albany Railroad runs from the Massachusetts State Line to Castleton, cutting through the townships of Chatham and Kinderhook in Columbia County. The Harlem Division of the former New York Central (now defunct) runs from Copake Falls in Dutchess County to Chatham. Formerly a line of the Rutland Railroad came down to Chatham from Renssalaer County. The New England Branch of the New York Thruway parallels the Boston & Albany, and the Taconic State Parkway, coming up from Dutchess County, terminates at the Thruway, just north of Chatham. Principal lakes are Queechy Lake, Copake Lake, and Knickerbocker Lake. Formerly there was a considerable iron industry centered near Hudson and Ancram.

97.50 Rock Island to west. Near the shore, it is small and surrounded by shallow water of one- and two-foot depth.

97.90 Clermont Wharf to east.

97.90 Clermont to east. Formerly the estate of the Livingston family, it is now maintained as Clermont Mansion State Historic Site by the Taconic State Park & Recreation Commission.

The history of the mansion and estate with the Livingston family and the entire history of this part of New York State are a single story, best told by giving the history of the family.

The Livingstons are of Scottish ancestry, of the family of the Earls of Linlithgow. Robert Livingston (1654–1728) was descended from Mary Livingston, one of the "four Marys" who attended Mary Queen

CLERMONT MANSION FROM FORMAL GARDENS. The Livingston family seat near Tivoli. Photo: © Gretchen McHugh.

of Scots during her childhood and education in France. He was born at Roxburghshire, Scotland, and lived in Holland until coming back to the British Isles at the age of nine. After the death of his father, he came to America in 1673 and settled in the Albany area. He married Alida Van Rensselaer, a widow, and a daughter of the Schuyler family. He soon became wealthy through his active trading ventures and influential family connections. He is said to have been a friend of Captain Kidd, and a powerful promoter of his enterprises. Between 1684 and 1715, he made many purchases from the Indians of land on the eastern bank of the Hudson. These lands ran along the Hudson for twelve miles and back eastward, fanning out to a breadth of thirty miles. He later purchased tracts on the western shore, which were part of the Hardenburgh Patent. A patent was granted for the eastern lands by Gov. Thomas Dongan in 1686 under the name, "the Lordship and Manor of Livingston." This was confirmed by King George I. In 1710, Gov. Robert Hunter helped Livingston consolidate his various holdings which then came to a total of 162,248 acres. He paid to the King's treasury "an annual rent of twenty-eight shillings, lawful money of New York," or about $3.50. Benson Lossing tells us that: "This magnificent estate was constituted a manor, with political privileges. The free-holders upon it were allowed a representative in the colonial legislature, chosen by themselves, and in 1716 the lord of the manor, by virtue of that privilege, took his seat as a legislator. He had already built a manorhouse, on a grassy point upon the banks of the Hudson, at the mouth of Roeliffe Jansen's Kill." (Lossing, *The Hudson*, pp. 166–167.)

This Manor House was called *Linlithgow* after the city in Scotland. It was later taken down by his greatgrandson. He was Secretary of Indian Affairs from

1695 to 1728 and served as representative to the New York Provincial Assembly (1709–11 and 1715–25), becoming its speaker in 1718. He had two sons:

1) Philip Livingston (1686–1749) established the senior branch of the family. He married Catharine Van Brugh and had three sons. This senior branch retained possession of the manor at Linlithgow. His sons were:

    a) Peter Van Brugh Livingston (1710–1792). In 1775, he was elected president of the First Provincial Congress.

    b) Philip Livingston (1716–1778). A signer of the Declaration of Independence and an active member of the Continental Congress.

    c) William Livingston (1723–1790). He moved to New Jersey in 1772. He was a member of the First and Second Continental Congress, and was elected the first Governor of New Jersey in 1777.

2) Robert L. Livingston (1688–1775) established the junior branch of the family. Although his father had given his older brother, Philip, the major part of his estate, coming to 247,000 acres and the manor house at Linlithgow, he provided for young Robert by giving him an estate of 13,000 acres south of the Roeliffe Jansen Kill, which was known as the Lower Manor. Young Robert built a fine mansion which he called *Clermont*, as was also called the small village further inland. He had five daughters (all of whom made advantageous or distinguished marriages) and one son, Robert R. Livingston (1718–1775).

Robert R. Livingston, Sr. (1718–1775) was often called "the Judge," as he served as judge of the Admiralty Court from 1759 to 1763 and as judge of the Supreme Court of the colony from 1763 to 1775. He was an active patriot and a member of the Stamp Act Congress and writer of the letter of protest sent by that congress to the king. He also established powder mills which supplied Washington's army. He was the chairman of the New York Committee of Correspondence. His son was also an active patriot and had a distinguished public life.

Robert R. Livingston, Jr. (1746–1813) became famous as "Chancellor Livingston," as he served in that capacity from 1777 to 1801. Next to governor, this was the most powerful post in the new state of New York. He was a strong advocate of the rights of the colonies and, as a member of the Second Continental Congress, was one of the five elected to draft the Declaration of Independence. The Revolution reached his home of *Clermont* in October of 1777 when a British landing party sailed up the Hudson, burned Kingston, and proceeded on to burn *Clermont*. The family and servants escaped after burying or hiding their valuables. After the war, as

Chancellor, he administered the oath of office when Washington became the first president of the United States in 1789. In 1781 Livingston became First Minister of Foreign Affairs, and later served as Minister to France under Jefferson, when he negotiated with Napoleon for the Louisiana Purchase. While in France, he met Robert Fulton and became his partner in the successful development of the steamboat. The *North River Steamboat* of *Clermont* stopped at the Chancellor's dock on her maiden voyage up the Hudson in 1807. In 1794 the Chancellor finished a new home just south of *Clermont*, which he called *Arryl House*. This burned in 1908, but the ruins are still visible. It was an elegant, French-inspired building and became the showplace of the Hudson.

Judge Livingston's younger son, Edward Livingston (1764–1836) served as the first Secretary of State of the United States and had a long and distinguished career.

Old *Clermont* continued to be a home to the Livingston family through the years until 1962, when the property was given to New York State as an historic site. The center part of the house was built shortly after the British burned the original house in 1777, and part of the walls from the earlier building were incorporated into it. The north wing was added in 1802 as an office where the tenants could pay their rent. The south wing was added in 1830 to give the family more room. It was again enlarged in 1893. The steep, chateauesque roof was added in 1874.

The house and grounds are now open to the public. The entrance is off Woods Road (County Route 5) and the junction of Columbia County Route 40 in Germantown. The Clermont State Historic Site has been completely restored. Telephone 518-537-4240.

97.90 Cross Hill to east (elevation 322 feet).

97.91 Roundtop to east (elevation 341 feet).

97.92 Little Roundtop to east (elevation 300 feet).

98.00 Green Flats. These are slightly to east of midstream. The main vessel channel is to the west. Depths are between one-half and seventeen feet. It is also known as Lower Flats—Middleground.

98.25 Canoe Hill to west.

98.25 Bristol to west. Bristol Beach is an undeveloped county park of seventy-three acres with a sandy beach in a protected cove. The water is clean. From the twenty-two-acre beach area you can wade out 600 feet before reaching the main channel.

98.50 Malden-on-Hudson to west. Site of Staples House (ca. 1837) and a Methodist Church in the bracketed style dating from 1867, it was the home town of John Bigelow (1817–1911), noted editor, author, and diplomat. From 1848 to 1861, he shared with William Cullen Bryant in the ownership and editing of the *New York Evening Post.* His antislavery and free-trade editorials were especially vigorous. In 1861 he was appointed consul general at Paris and served as United States minister to France from 1865 to 1866. He is credited for preventing French recognition of the Confederacy.

99.00 Bigelow Blue Stone Company dock and quarry to west.

99.25 The Maelstrom. Slightly to east of the western vessel channel, between Green Flats and Upper Flats, is a narrow but rather deeper channel (eleven- to sixteen-foot depths) between the shallow flats of one-half and one-foot depths, that connects the main channel, on the west of the flats, with the secondary deepwater channel to the east of the flats. During the change of tide, the waters rush through here in eddies and whirlpools. *The American College Dictionary* defines maelstrom as follows: 1) a famous whirlpool off the NW coast of Norway, 2) any great or violent whirlpool, 3) a resistless confusion of affairs, or influence.

99.60 Eve's Point to west.

99.61 Evesport to west.

100.00 Upper Flats (Livingston Flats). These are to the east of mid-stream. The vessel channel is to the west. The flats are covered with grass and are only one-half to one foot deep.

100.00 Livingston Channel to east. East of upper flats, this is a secondary channel along the eastern shore, petering out at the northern end. Access is only from southern end. Depths are between twenty-one and forty-one feet.

100.25 West Camp Landing to west.

100.30 West Camp to west. Queen Anne of England sent Palatinate refugees here in 1710 in an unsuccessful attempt to manufacture turpentine.

100.50 Wanton Island to west. A battle here established the hegemony of the Iroquois Nation over the Mahicans.

100.50 Greene County to west. From here to Barren Island, at mile 126.60, the western shore is occupied by Greene County. It has an area of 653 square miles. Catskill is the county seat. It was taken from Albany and Ulster Counties in 1800 and named in honor of Revolutionary War general Nathaniel Greene, of Rhode Island, who had been given lands

in the towns of Windham, Ashland, Jewett, and parts of Lexington and Hunter, to the eastern base of the mountains. He established a cloth factory at Red Falls. Presently the county consists of the townships of Halcott, Prattsville, Ashland, Lexington, Jewett, Durham, Hunter, Catskill, Cairo, Athens, Greenville, Coxsackie, and New Baltimore. The eastern portion of the county consists of low ridges, interspersed with fertile valleys parallel to the Hudson. The western part of the county is comprised of the Catskill Mountains and a high plateau, drained to the northwest by Schoharie Creek, and the East, West, and Batavia Kills. The eastern escarpment of the Catskills and lowlands are drained by Kaaterskill Creek, Lake Creek, Basic Creek, Potic Creek, and Catskill Creek—all emptying into the Hudson via Catskill Creek. The county is bordered by the Hudson River on the east, Albany and Schoharie counties on the north, Delaware County on the west, and Ulster County on the south.

Principal bodies of water are North, South, and Black Lakes. The West Shore Railroad runs parallel to the Hudson, as does Route 9W and the New York Thruway. Principal east-west routes are State Routes 81, 145, 23, and 23A. Principal towns are Catskill, Athens, Coxsackie, Cairo, Palenville, Greenville, Tannersville, Windham, Hunter, and Prattsville. Much land is devoted to state parks and forest preserves. Recreation is the principal industry, and this was the classic area of the Catskill Mountains. There is considerable quarrying for Portland cement along the Hudson.

100.50 Cheviot to east. This is a characteristic nineteenth-century farm and river village.

100.90 Cementon to west. Formerly Smith's Landing, it was named for the many cement plants in the neighborhood.

101.25 East Camp to east. I quote from Benson Lossing: "In the year 1710 Governor Hunter, by order of Queen Anne, bought of Mr. Livingston 6,000 acres of his manor, for the sum of a little more than £200, for the use of Protestant Germans then in England, who had been driven from their homes in the Lower Palatinate of the Rhine, then the dominions of a cousin of the British Queen. About 1,800 of them settled upon the manor lands, and at a place on the opposite shore of the river, the respective localities being known as East and West Camp." (Lossing, *The Hudson,* p. 167.) They were expected to produce tar, turpentine, and other naval stores. However, they were inexperienced, and the local trees were not suited to produce such products. Robert Livingston contracted to furnish bread and beer for 6¢ per day

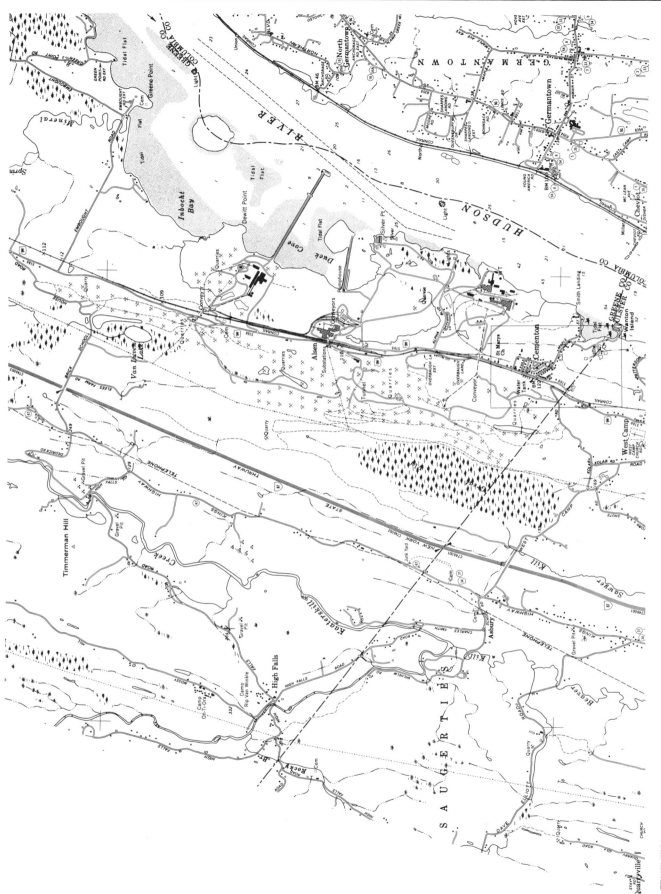

CEMENTON

for adults and 4¢ for children. He also sold them flour and meat and gave them cash advances. Everybody lost by the transaction and the colonies were disbanded in 1712. Many of the Palatinates settled elsewhere in the Hudson Valley and Catskills.

101.50 Germantown to east. It has a local railroad station. (See above for history.)

102.45 Sliver Point to west. There were formerly ice houses here.

102.50 Duck Cove to west. Here there is grassy shoal water.

102.65 Marsh Island to west. There are trees on the island.

102.65 Alsen to west. Inland on Route 9W and West Shore RR, it has large cement works.

102.90 Long pier to west. Here are elaborate facilities for loading cement barges. There are six hoppers.

03.00 North Germantown to east.

103.25 Dewitt Point to west.

103.25 Tree-covered shoals to west. These are immediately offshore at DeWitt Point.

103.40 Post Creek to west.

103.50 Inbocht Bay to west. Also called Embought Bay, it has grassy water of one-half-foot depth. It is fed by Mineral Spring Brook and Post Creek.

CEMENT SILOS AT SILVER POINT, CEMENTON. Photo: © Gretchen McHugh.

104.00 Mineral Spring Brook to west. It flows south from swale between Kykuit Hill and the Kalkberg Cliffs into north shore of Inbocht Bay.

104.00 Greene Point to west. At the north end of Inbocht Bay, this is the site of Van Arden House, a two-story clapboard mansion, mid-nineteenth century.

104.00 Nine Mile Tree to east. This is an oldtime navigational sighting point.

105.00 Burgett Creek to west. This creek drains marshes south of Catskill and east of Kykuit Hill.

105.25 Roeliffe Jansen's Kill to east. The Indians called it Saupenak, and it formed the boundary between the Mohegans to the north and the Wappingers to the south. The present name is derived from Killaen Van Rensselaer's estate overseer around 1630. It was also known as Livingston Creek and Ancram Creek. It rises near Hillsdale in eastern Columbia County and flows south into Dutchess County, whence it turns and takes a northwesterly course to the Hudson.

105.25 Linlithgo to east. Robert Livingston built his first manor house on a grassy knoll on the north bank of Roeliffe Jansen's Kill near its outlet into the Hudson about 1699. This building burned about 1800 and was immediately replaced by one slightly to the east. This too burned in 1918. These manor houses were always occupied by the senior branch of the Livingston family, according to primogeniture. The first eight generations of the Livingstons were buried in vaults of the Livingston Memorial Chapel (Dutch Reformed), which was built in 1722 and rebuilt in 1870.

The name Linlithgo is a corruption of Linlithgow. The Livingstons were descended from the earls of Linlithgow in Scotland. Linlithgow is the county town of West Lothian (formerly Linlithgow), and near the south shore of Loch Linlithgow and west of Edinburgh. The burgh was a residence of Scottish kings; Linlithgow Palace, on an elevated promontory above the loch, was the birthplace of James V and Mary Queen of Scots. The parish church of St. Michael was founded by King David I of Scotland. Linlithgow was the scene of the murder of James Stuart, first earl of Murray.

A bit farther inland from the Hudson are the remains of the works of the Hudson River Ore & Iron Company, which were worked in conjunction with the Iron Mountain Mines between 1875 and 1898. The Burden Iron Works were also in the vicinity.

105.45 Linlithgo Station to east. This was formerly Livingston Station.

105.50 Washburn Dock to east. This is a ruined long pier with trees growing on it.

105.50 Mount Tom to east (elevation 519 feet).

106.00 Foxes' Creek to east. Rising near Mt. Tom, its course was followed by a railroad spur leading to the Burden Iron Works.

106.20 Burden Dock to east. A former trans-shipment point for iron and iron goods, it is now a ruin.

106.35 Oak Hill Landing to east.

106.35 Oak Hill to east. The hill has an elevation of 265 feet. The mansion is two-story, brick construction with a mansard roof and verandah. It was built in 1763 by John Livingston. At present *Oak Hill* is the home of Henry H. Livingston, the present "Lord of the Manor," and head of the Livingston family.

106.40 Blue Hill to east (elevation 660 feet).

106.50 The Kalkberg to west. This is derived from the Dutch for "chalk rock." The name has also been corrupted to "Callabarrachs," "Collar Back," and "Calderberghs." It is a long limestone ridge of about 250 feet elevation parallel to the Hudson running from Cementon on the south to Quarry Hill, west of Catskill, at the north. Van Luven Lake sits atop the ridge at 213 feet. In the nineteenth century it was a popular scenic drive from Catskill, as good views were obtained of both the Catskill Mountains and the Berkshires, as well as of the Hudson River. Subsequent quarrying for the cement plants has despoiled large areas and placed much of it off limits. It represents the easternmost reach of the Catskills.

106.50 Ramshorn Creek to west. This is a short crooked creek through the marshes east of Kykuit Hill.

106.50 The Fly to west. Corruption of the Dutch Da Vly, this means "the swamps or marshes."

106.50 Kykuit Hill to west. This is roughly translated from the Dutch as "beacon hill." The early settlers used it as such to warn of the approach of Indians. John Overbagh settled here in 1722.

107.20 Greendale to east. A local railroad station and former terminus of steam ferry to Catskill, it was also formerly known as Oak Hill Station and Catskill Station. *Oak Hill*, a two-story brick mansion with mansard roof and veranda, was built in 1763 by John Livingston (1750–1822). It is in the Federal style and was extensively remodeled in the mid-nineteenth century.

107.25 Catskill Creek to west. Catskill Creek rises near Franklinton in Schoharie County and flows southeast past Livingstonville, Preston Hollow, Cooksburg, Oak Hill, East Durham, Freehold, South Cairo, and Leeds, to a confluence with the Kaaterskill Creek at Cauterskill. It is the dividing line between the Helderberg Mountains to the north and the Catskill Mountains to the south. It was followed by the early, unsuccessful Canajoharie & Catskill Railroad, which was never extended west of Cooksburg, and by the Susquehanna and Schoharie Turnpikes. At Leeds it is crossed by the historic old stone bridge. Above Cauterskill it flows through the picturesque Austin's Glen, which is crossed by a bridge on the New York Thruway just south of Exit 21. Formerly the narrow-gauge Catskill Mountain Railroad followed it through the Glen. East of Cauterskill, it is crossed by the high trestle of the West Shore Railroad (1883) and what is now a footbridge, but was formerly used by the Catskill Mountain Railroad, at a lower level. It flows through the village of Catskill where it is crossed by the vehicular Uncle Sam bascule bridge. Below this is the old port where the Catskill Evening Line boats used to tie up. After flowing past the promontory of Hopp's Nose on the south bank, it flows into the Hudson south of Catskill Point. Hopp's Nose, also known as Hop-O-Nose, is a rock formation projecting into the stream and is said to have caused many steamboat accidents. It was named for the prominent nose of a local redman named Hopp. Claes Uylenspiegel, a fur trader, had a cabin here prior to 1650.

Principal tributaries are Basic and Potic Creeks on the north and the Shingle Kill and Kaaterskill Creek on the south.

Kaaterskill Creek

This is probably the most famous waterway in the Catskills. It rises in a marsh west of the village of Haines Falls, near which it flows over a 160-foot cataract at the head of Kaaterskill Clove. In mid-clove it is joined from the north by the waters of Lake Creek, which rises in North and South Lakes and then flows over the scenic Kaaterskill Falls and Bastion Falls. After going over many rapids and waterfalls, it leaves the clove at Palenville. A bit further east it goes over Kaaterskill High Falls and then dips down into Ulster County. It then turns decisively north through deep picturesque valleys to Cauterskill, where it flows into Catskill Creek.

107.25 Catskill to west. With a population of 5,317, Catskill is the seat of Greene County. It is one of the alleged home towns of the legendary Rip Van Winkle. It is the actual home town of Samuel Wilson, who, as a sutler in the War of 1812, became known as "Uncle Sam." Wilson resided in a house on West Main Street from 1817 to 1824. In that same house,

Martin Van Buren (later eighth president of the United States, and a native of Kinderhook across the Hudson) had married Hannah Hoes in 1807.

The first recorded visit of a white man to Catskill was by Henry Hudson in 1609, when he found "a very loving people." He traded with the local Mahican Indians, who had recently been ignominiously defeated by the neighboring warlike Mohawks in a battle on Rodgers Island, just above the mouth of Catskill Creek. After this, the Mohawks claimed hegemony over the Mahicans, who shortly thereafter dispersed.

The first recorded settlement is that of Claes Uylenspiegel, a fur trader who had a cabin at Hop-O-Nose before 1650. Also prior to 1650, Hans Vos, after whom is named the Vosenkill, established a mill on that stream. Jan Jansen van Bremen also built on the present site of the Van Veighten House beneath Jefferson Heights, at the ford across Catskill Creek on the King's Highway. In the late seventeenth century, Marte Gerritse Van Bergen settled in the neighborhood of Leeds, which was the original Old Kaaterskill. In 1677 Capt. Sylvester Salisbury, an officer of the British troops that took over New Netherlands from the Dutch, acquired many thousands of acres along Catskill Creek. In 1705 Francis Salisbury erected a handsome two-story mansion at Leeds.

With the development of river commerce, the center of activity shifted down the hill from Jefferson Heights to Het Strand, or the landing, on the present site of Catskill village. The town was incorporated in 1806. Impetus for this was given by completion of the Susquehanna Turnpike (ca. 1800) to Wattle's Ferry (Unadilla) on the Susquehanna River. An eastern segment extended from Salisbury, Connecticut, to Greendale, across the Hudson from Catskill. This made Catskill the natural ferry place for westward migration from New England. It was also a good place for shipping the produce of the interior down-river to New York City. In 1838 the steamboat *Frank* began plying regularly between Catskill and the City. The ferry also soon came under steam. The *Frank* was soon followed by the *Utica, Washington, Thomas Powell, New Champion, Andrew Harder, Kaaterskill, Catskill, William C. Redfield, Thomas McManus,* and *Onteora.*

As if all this road and river activity was not enough to assure prosperity, the Canajohrie & Catskill Railroad was built and operated between Catskill and Cooksburg from 1840 to 1842, when it was closed down after an accident. The tanning industry in the mountains made Catskill a busy deepwater port for the receipt of raw hides for tanning and the shipment of tanned hides. As the tanning business declined, the Catskill Mountain House (1824), high atop South Mountain on the great wall of Manitou, with its tremendous view over the Hudson River Valley, began to attract many travelers. Prior to 1824, Erastus Beach of Catskill had been operating stagecoach lines up and down the Hudson Valley and into the interior. His relative, Charles L. Beach, soon assumed control of these operations and also acquired the Catskill Mountain House. He then turned it into the "Yankee palace in the clouds." He also improved the old mountain turnpike starting at Catskill.

The work of the landscape painter Thomas Cole (1801–1848), who settled in Catskill shortly after his first visit in 1825, and Washington Irving's tale of *Rip Van Winkle,* and William Cullen Bryant's poem "Kaaterskill Falls," focused interest on the Northern Catskills. It was halfway between the metropolis and the pleasure meccas of Saratoga Springs and Ballston Spa. Catskill became the natural gateway to the Catskills, and Catskill Point, where through steamers stopped, was developed. This was an important landing for both Night and Day Line boats until the final Day Line sailing in 1953. The Catskill Evening Line, eventually controlled by Beach interests, sailed right up Catskill Creek into the village. Completion of the Hudson River Railroad on the east shore of the Hudson in 1851 made Greendale, sometimes called Catskill Ferry, an important location.

To complete this transport nexus, in 1882, Beach interests completed the narrow-gauge Catskill Mountain Railroad from Catskill Point to Palenville, with a branch to Cairo. Eventually, connections were built to the top of the mountain via the Otis Elevating Railway and the Catskill & Tannersville Railway, another narrow-gauge line built by the Beaches. There were three stations in Catskill: the Point, the Village, and a station near the West Shore Railroad depot, which was up above on a hill, south of the trestle over Catskill Creek. The Catskill Mountain Railroad operated until 1918. The West Shore had come through town in 1883. Changing vacation patterns and the automobile killed the resorts and the steamboats and little railroads that served them. Later the New York Thruway also bypassed Catskill.

Around the turn of the century the shale brick industry was extensive and also provided paving materials for New York City. As early as 1808 there was an iron foundry. Today liqueurs and cement products are manufactured. At the turn of the century Catskill boasted its own fine resort, the Prospect Park Hotel, on a terrace north of the village and overlooking the river. Its broad verandahs commanded a fine view of the Hudson and the distant Berkshires.

107.25 Catskill Point to west. This is a former important steamboat landing and terminus of ferry to Greendale and of the Catskill Mountain Railroad.

107.30 Prospect Park Hotel site to west. Now occupied by St. Anthony's Friary, this hotel opened in the 1860s. It is described by Wallace Bruce as follows:

Just out of the village proper, on a beautiful outlook, stands the charming Prospect Park Hotel, unrivaled in its beauty of location. It has a most delightful piazza, four hundred feet long, sixteen feet wide, supported by Corinthian pillars twenty-five feet high, with many private balconies, and charming views from every room. The main building is two hundred and fifty feet front, with wing one hundred and fifty feet by forty, situated in a large and beautiful park. This handsome park adjoins the best residence portion of the village, thus affording miles of elegant shady walks and drives near at hand. The views and scenery from the "Prospect" are unsurpassed....

108.00 Church's Hill and Olana Castle to east (elevation 500 feet). The home of landscape painter Frederick Edwin Church (1826–1900), this unique house in the Persianesque style was designed by the world-renowned painter of the Hudson River School as a three-dimensional presentation of his ideal of beauty. He consulted with architect Calvert Vaux on "practical matters."

Perched atop a hill with extensive views of the Hudson River and Catskill Mountains, Olana is extravagantly beautiful, alive with color, drama and detailing of the Eastern art that entranced Church. The name Olana means "our castle on high." It is now a state historic site and open to the public. The castle has thirty-five rooms and was completed in 1872. The entrance is on Route 9G in Hudson. Telephone 518-828-0135.

108.50 Rogers Island to east of main vessel channel. Formerly known as Vastrack Island, this is a large, low-lying island, separated from the eastern shore by a shallow channel obstructed by a submerged dike called Hallenbeck Creek. Wallace Bruce tells us that on Rogers Island,

...the last battle was fought between the Mahicans and Mohawks and it is narrated that "as the old king of the Mahicans was dying, after the conflict, he commanded his regalia to be taken off and his son

OLANA CASTLE. Home of Hudson River School painter Frederick Edwin Church, near Hudson. Phogo: © Gretchen McHugh.

put into the kingship while his eyes were yet clear to behold him. Over forty years had he worn it, from the time he received it in London from Queen Anne. He asked his son to kneel at his couch, and, putting his withered hand across his brow, placed the feathery crown upon his head, and gave him the silver-mounted tomahawk—symbols of power to rule and power to execute. Then, looking up to the heavens, he said, as if in despair for his race, "The hills are our pillows, and the broad plains to the west our hunting-grounds; our brothers are called into the bright wigwam of the Everlasting, and our bones lie upon the fields of many battles; but the wisdom of the dead is given to the living." This battle was in 1625.

(Bruce, *Hudson by Daylight*, p. 220.)

108.60 Rip Van Winkle Bridge. This is a unit of the New York State Bridge Authority. A cantilever bridge costing $2,500,000 and opened on July 2, 1935, it was built by the Frederick Share Corporation.

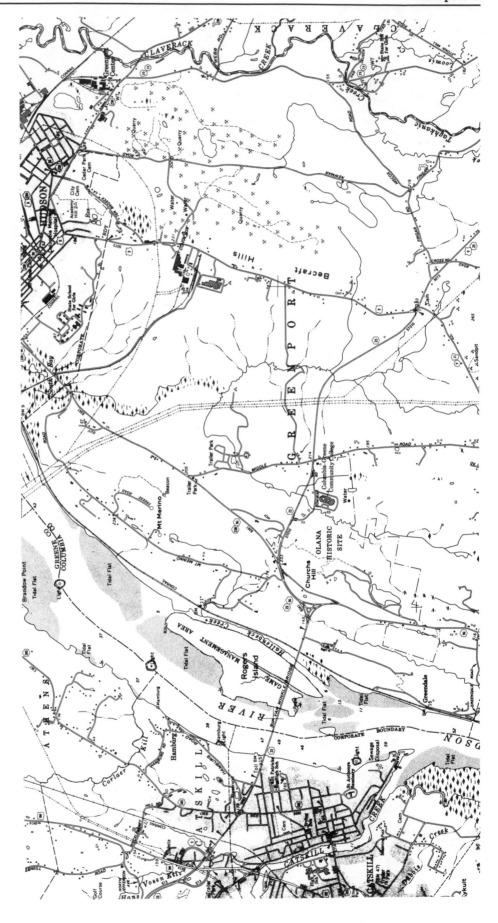

HUDSON SOUTH

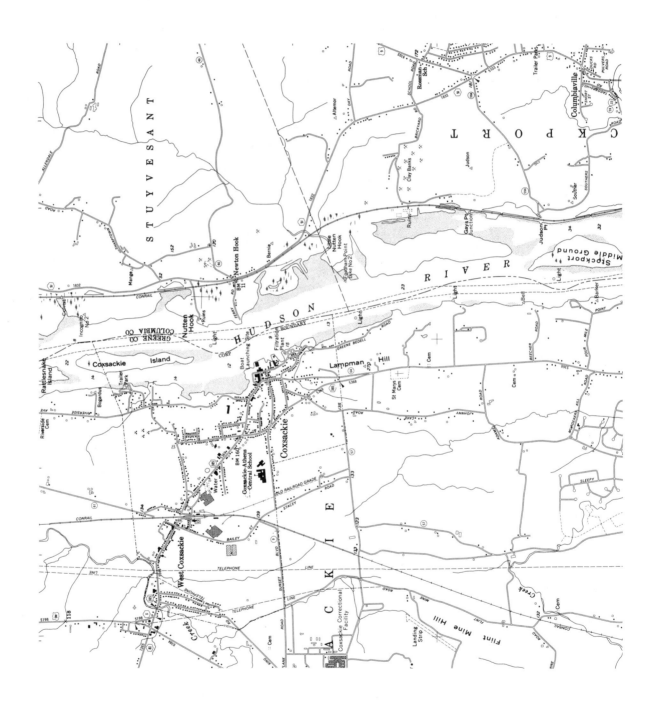

HUDSON NORTH

RIP VAN WINKLE BRIDGE AT CATSKILL. Photo: Courtesy New York State Bridge Authority.

There are two vehicle lanes; vessel clearance is 145 feet. The bridge is 5,041 feet long with a main span of 800 feet. A toll is charged eastbound.

108.75 Hamburg to west. This is a fishermen's settlement.

109.25 Corlaer Kill to west.

109.25 Moreno Point at north end of Rogers Island.

110.00 Brandow Point to west.

110.00 Mount Merino to east (elevation 540 feet). This is one of the first places to which Merino sheep were brought in this country.

110.90 Overhead power cables (clearance 145 feet).

111.25 Hudson Light. On an island to the west of the navigation channel, it is a brick Victorian structure with gambrel roof and tower (1874).

111.25 South Bay to east. Now largely filled in, this was the site of the Hudson Iron Works in the mid-nineteenth century. Its chief business was the conversion of the crude ore into "pigs" ready for the manufacturer's use. Two kinds of ore were used: hematite from West Stockbridge and magnetic from the forest of Dean Mines, in the Hudson Highlands. In 1860 it produced about 16,000 tons of pig iron.

111.25 New York State Reformatory for Women to east.

111.25 Hallenbeck Hill to west (elevation 304 feet).

111.25 Swallow Rocks. These rocks are at southern end of Middle Ground Flats, between the main navigation channel on the east and the secondary western channel. The western channel was formerly used for navigation. This was formerly called Doper's

ATHENS-HUDSON LIGHTHOUSE. Photo: © Gretchen McHugh.

Island and Noah's Brig. There are interesting stories associated with the place.

In 1845 the steamer *Swallow*, while racing with two other boats, *Express* and *Rochester*, from Albany to New York, rammed these rocks, broke up, and caught fire. Fifty of the three hundred passengers were killed. Currier and Ives circulated a lurid lithograph of the disaster. Later Ira Buchman hauled the wreckage seven miles inland and built himself a two-story home known as the Swallow House.

The other story may be apochryphal and concerns a certain Captain Noah. According to the story, on one foggy twilight Captain Noah, with a fleet of rafts, sighted "a dark object riding the waters." It looked like a brig under sail. "Brig Ahoy!" he shouted. No answer. "Brig Ahoy! Answer, or I'll run you down!" No reply. Captain Noah kept to his course. Suddenly there was a crash and wood crunched on rock. Captain Noah had mistaken two trees on the island for masts with sails set.

111.25 Athens to west. Originally called Loonenburg or Lunenburg, it was first settled in 1686, but there is evidence that prehistoric Indians mined flint stones at Flint Hill 12,000 years ago, at a site now belonging to the New York Archeological Association. The old Indian village of Potick was located a short distance back from the river. The Looneburg Patent of 17,500 acres, running from Coxsackie to Catskill Creek and embracing the Athens area, was purchased by Adrian Van Loon, a Walloon whose family had come to America in 1581, shortly after Jacques Cartier had first explored the St. Lawrence in 1534. They had migrated down through the Adirondacks into the Hudson Valley about 1598. Jan Van Loan built a house in Athens in 1708, although a previous owner of the patent had acquired an Indian deed from a certain Caniskeek on April 30, 1665.

The Zion Lutheran Church was organized in 1703, and its first pastor, the Rev. Justus Falkner, was the first Lutheran minister ordained in America.

Isaac Northrup is credited with moving for incorporation of the village in 1805. Athens soon became a port for merchant sailing ships and whalers and supported a considerable shipbuilding industry. The natives favored classic-style architecture. This all reflects the "Yankee culture" of the many settlers from New England. A steam ferry to Hudson was established prior to 1836, and in 1867 Athens became the southern terminus of the Saratoga & Hudson River Railroad, known as "the white elephant line," because it never made a profit. Its route along Murderer's Creek northwest of town became the Athens Branch of the West Shore Railroad in 1883. It is now abandoned. Other parts of the Saratoga & Hudson

River survive as bits of the West Shore Main Line, Conrail, South Bethlehem branch, and the Delaware & Hudson. The Van Loan & Magee Co. built steamboats. Steamboats connecting Athens with New York City were the *John Taylor*, and *Erastus Corning* of the John H. Starin Line. Starin later became prominent in Long Island Sound and coastal shipping. The Starin boats to Athens carried cattle as well as passengers. In 1873 the Athens steamboat terminal suffered a disastrous fire, and the business declined from then on.

The Schoharie Turnpike was completed to Cooksburg in 1802, starting from Athens. However, the Susquehanna Turnpike starting from Catskill, and the short-lived (1840–1842) Canajoharie & Catskill Railroad, offered strong competition to the Athens route.

Development of faster steamboats which did not stop at Athens, completion of the West Shore Railroad (1883), Hudson River Railroad (1851), Delaware & Hudson Railroad (1868), and the Rip Van Winkle Bridge (1935) all served to divert traffic from this once important transportation center. Ice harvesting and brickmaking were the last major industries in the area.

During its heyday Athens had cultural pretensions, with fine architecture and an opera house which can still be seen on Second Street (now known as the Brooks building). Located west of town are the once-popular picnic resorts of Black, Green, and Hollister Lakes. There are many well-preserved fine old buildings in the town. The Haight-Gantley-Van Loan Mansion (1812), with its Oval Ballroom, built by Gen. Samuel Haight, is particularly elegant.

Middle Ground Flats
112.00 to 113.75

This is a low flat island in mid-stream. The main shipping channel is to the east.

112.00 Hudson to the east. With a population of 8,940, Hudson is the seat of Columbia County. It is the western terminus of the Hudson & Chatham Branch of the Boston & Albany Railroad, also known as the Claverack Branch of the New York Central. It is an Amtrak passenger stop today. Formerly ferries to Athens and to Catskill left from here.

Jan Frans Van Hoesen purchased land here from the Indians in 1662. However, the story of its permanent settlement is best told by Benson Lossing:

About thirty miles below Albany, lying upon a bold, rocky promontory that juts out from the

FEDERAL STYLE HOUSE AT HUDSON. Photo: © Gretchen McHugh.

*eastern shore at an elevation of fifty feet, with a
beautiful bay on each side, is the City of Hudson, the
capital of Columbia County, a port of entry, and one
of the most delightfully situated towns on the river.
It was founded in 1784 by thirty proprietors, chiefly
Quakers from New England. Never in the history of
the rapid growth of cities in America has there been
a more remarkable example than that of Hudson.
Within three years from the time when the farm on
which it stands was purchased, and only a solitary
storehouse stood upon the bank of the river at the
foot of the bluff, one hundred and fifty dwellings,
with wharves, storehouses, workshops, barns, etc.,
were erected, and a population of over fifteen hundred souls had settled there, and become possessed
of a city charter.*

(Lossing, *The Hudson,* p. 146.)

Most of the settlers came from Nantucket and Providence. One of the reasons for the rapid growth was
that they brought prefabricated buildings with them.
This was a remarkable innovation at the time. The
original settlement was called Claverack Landing.
Even at this early date, the city had a mill, a shipyard, two tanneries, and a covered ropewalk. In
1790, twenty-five schooners, including both whalers
and traders, showed Hudson as their registered
home port. A city charter was granted in 1785—the
third in the state.

Parade Hill, or Promenade Hill, a public park atop
the riverfront bluffs, was granted to the Common
Council in 1795 by the "proprietors." It commands
extensive views of the Helderbergs and the Catskills.
Today machinery, woolen knit goods, ginger ale,
shirts, matches, dresses, and flypaper are manufactured, and there are large cement plants at the
southeastern end of town.

112.00 Prospect Hill to east (elevation 375 feet).

112.00 Greenport Center to east. It is inland from
the Hudson.

112.50 North Bay to east. This bay is cut off from
the river by a railroad causeway.

113.00 Murderer's Creek to west. This creek rises
south of Coxsackie and flows southeast into the
western channel of the Hudson north of Athens.

113.80 Priming Hook to east.

113.80 Hasbrouck Hill to east (elevation 205 feet).

Stockport Flats to east
114.00 to 118.00

These are part of the Hudson River National Estuarine
Research Reserve.

114.25 Stottville to east.

114.30 West Flats to west. Shoal water.

115.45 Fourmile Point to west. Here is located an
early nineteenth-century stone lighthouse with clapboard wings. Formerly called "Chaney Tinker."

115.45 Vosburgh Swamp to west. Inland from
Fourmile Point.

115.75 Stockport Creek to east. Formed by the junction of Kinderhook Creek from the north and
Claverack Creek from the south, it was formerly
called Major Abraham's Creek. Abram Staats built a
one-story stone house in 1664 on the north bank of
the creek near its junction with the Hudson,
replacing one of 1654 that had been burned by Indians.

115.80 Stockport Station to east. Henry Hudson
landed here on September 17, 1609.

Stockport Middle Ground
116.20 to 116.80

There are channels to either side and a main vessel
channel to the west. This is part of the Hudson River
National Estuarine Research Reserve.

116.45 Columbiaville to east. It cannot be seen from
river.

116.75 Judson Point to east.

117.00 Gay's Point to east.

117.35 Fitch's Wharf to west.

117.35 Unnamed man-made island to east of main channel.

118.00 Lampman Hill to west (elevation 270 feet). This hill is the property of Leonard Bronck Lampman.

118.00 Fordham Point to east.

118.20 Little Nutten Hook to east.

118.50 Coxsackie lower landing to west.

118.75 Coxsackie to west. Pronounced "Cook-sackie," its name is from the Indian Kaak-aki. Authorities are divided on the meaning of the term. Some say it means "place where geese gather," others "place of owls," and others "cut banks." Still another theory is that it is a corruption of the Dutch "Koeksrackie," meaning "Cook's Little Reach."

Coxsackie was settled in 1661 by Pieter Bronck of Albany, who built a house somewhat inland near Route 9W in 1663, which is now used as a museum by the Green County Historical Society.

On May 17, 1775, 225 men gathered in the house of Leendert Bronck, who was a member of the Committee of Correspondence and Safety, to sign what has been called the Coxsackie Declaration, prior to the signing of the national Declaration of Independence, stating that "Americans would not consent to be ruled, save by themselves," and "never to become slaves," and to oppose the "arbitrary and oppressive Acts of the British Parliament." It was signed in the wake of the news of the battles of Lexington and Concord as committee couriers sped along the King's Highway in front of the Bronck homestead.

In about 1824, the Robert Owen-inspired Forestville commonwealth, a communal socio-religious community, was established here. The town of Coxsackie was incorporated in 1867. Today there are granite works, and valves are manufactured. There was formerly a ferry to Newton Hook.

118.80 Nutten Hook to east. This was formerly known as Newton Hook or Newton Hook Station. It once had a ferry to Coxsackie. The large Stack icehouse is located here.

119.00 Coxsackie Upper Landing to west.

119.50 to 120.20 Coxsackie Island to west of main vessel channel. There is a secondary channel to the west of the island with depths of 10 to 22 feet. It was formerly known as Hauver Platte and Budd's Island.

120.50 Rattlesnake Island to west. The main channel lies to the east of the island. There is a lighthouse at the northern end. It used to be called Coxsackie Lighthouse, and the island was Lighthouse Island. For many years, this lighthouse was staffed by two spinsters and the informal name of Old Maids' Light was used among the rivermen.

121.00 Kinderhook Point to east. Name means "children's point."

121.45 Stuyvesant to east. This is a local railroad station. Henry Hudson landed here. This was the original location of the village of Kinderhook. However, the settlement was soon moved inland because of the mosquitoes and malaria.

121.50 Coxsackle Creek to west. It rises in West Coxsackie and flows northeast to the Hudson River It is fed from the northwest just before entering the Hudson by Sickles Creek, originally called Clove Kill.

121.50 Robinson Hill to west (elevation 558 feet).

122.00 Kinderhook Village to east It is inland and cannot be seen from the river. It is on Kinderhook Creek. The original settlement was on the Hudson at the site of the present Stuyvesant. In the churchyard of the Dutch Reformed Church, north of the village, is the grave of Edmond Charles "Citizen" Genêt (1763–1834), who married the daughter of Gov. George Clinton and became an American citizen. He was the French minister to the United States in 1793, and his activities caused some embarrassment to George Washington.

Kinderhook was the birth and burial place of Martin Van Buren (1782–1862), eighth president of the United States. His home, *Lindenwald,* was built in about 1810. He lived here after his presidency until his death. The house, called the "house of history," is open as a museum. It contains some items which belonged to Van Buren as well as period furniture and historical portraits.

The Van Ness House was built by Peter Van Ness who served in the colonial wars and commanded a regiment at Saratoga. He was a member of the state convention which adopted the federal Constitution.

The Luycas Van Alen House is a Dutch-style brick house dating from 1736. It also is open as a museum. Kinderhook is rich in well-preserved old houses, as is neighboring Valatie.

Martin Van Buren National Historic Site. 518-758-9689.

Luycas Van Alen House, Route 9H. 518-758-9265.

121.50 to 122.75 Bronck Island to west. This island is now joined to the mainland.

123.20 Mill Creek to east. There was an early settlement at its mouth.

124.00 to 126.50 Houghtaling Island to the east of main vessel channel. It is now joined to the mainland at its northern end by Lower and Upper Schodack Islands. A shallow (minimum seven foot depth) channel to the east of the island leads to Schodack Landing.

124.30 Matthew Point to west.

125.50 New Baltimore to west. This is the home of former sloop and barge building industries. In 1800, Paul Sherman was building schooners here. Later, local boatyards built canal boats and repaired smaller vessels. Many Quakers settled here in the early nineteenth century. Neat white houses and a New England atmosphere make this a popular retirement place for sea and river captains. There are many eighteenth-century and Victorian houses in the area. Most of the village is on a plateau 100 feet above the Hudson. The 1939 movie *Little Old New York* was filmed here.

126.50 Hannacroix Creek to west. Also spelled Hannacrois Creek, it rises in the southern Helderbergs and flows through a ravine three miles long and eighty feet deep and over Dickinson Falls southeast to Alcove Reservoir (city of Albany), thence east and northeast to the Hudson River.

126.50 Former channel between Lower Schodack and Houghtaling Islands to east.

126.60 Barren Island to west. Formerly Bear Island, it is now joined to the mainland. A sewage plant is located here. The name is a corruption of the Dutch "Beam Island." This is the site of the famous "Rensellaerstein" described by Washington Irving in his *Knickerbocker History of New York.*

126.60 Albany County to west. From here north to the Mohawk River, we have Albany County on the western bank. It has an area of 531 square miles and is bounded on the east by the Hudson River, on the south by Greene County, on the west by Schoharie County, and on the north by Schenectady County and Saratoga County. The central and southwestern part of the county is taken up by the Helderberg Mountains. Principal drainage is by Catskill and Hannacroix Creeks and the Mohawk River into the Hudson. The largest bodies of water are Alcove and Basic Reservoirs. Principal rail lines are the West Shore from Ravena to Rotterdam Junction, the New York Central Mainline from Albany to Schenectady, and the Delaware & Hudson from Duanesburg to Albany and thence north to Cohoes. The New York

Thruway parallels the West Shore Railroad. Albany was one of the original ten counties formed in 1683, and named in honor of one of the titles of the Duke of Albany and York, later King James II. It is comprised of the towns of Rensselaerville, Westerloo, Coeymans, Bethlehem, New Scotland, Berne, Knox, Guilderland, Green Island, and Colonie and the city of Albany. Principal towns are Albany, the county seat and capital of the state of New York, Menands, Watervliet, and Cohoes.

126.60 Rensselaer County to east. This county runs along the eastern bank from here to mile 164.30, opposite Stillwater in Saratoga County. It is bounded on the south by Columbia County, on the west by the Hudson River, on the north by Washington County, and on the east by the states of Vermont and Massachusetts. Troy is the county seat. It has an area of 665 square miles and was taken from Albany County in 1791. It was named in honor of the early patroons.

It is an area of undulating hills. The principal watercourse is the Hoosic River, flowing northwest into the Hudson near Schaghticoke. Principal bodies of water are Tomhannock Reservoir, Babcock Lake, Long Pond, Dyken Pond, Wager Pond, Snyder's Lake, Crooked Lake, and Burden Lake.

The New York Central Railroad runs along the Hudson north to Rensselaer, where the main line crosses to Albany. A branch continues north to Troy. The Boston & Albany has a line from Chatham to Albany, and the Boston & Maine formerly had a line from Troy to Eagle Bridge. The main line of the Boston & Maine cuts across northern Rensselaer County, following the Hoosic River, from Mechanicville to Williamstown, Massachusetts. There is passenger service only on the New York Central and Boston & Albany mainline. Rensselaer-Albany is an Amtrak station with service to New York, Boston, Montreal, Buffalo, Detroit, and Chicago.

The main highways are Route 7 from Troy to Bennington, Vermont, and Route 2 from Troy to Williamstown, Massachusetts.

Principal towns are Troy, Rensselaer, and Hoosick Falls.

126.50 to 128.75 Lower Schodack Island to east of main navigation channel. Shallow secondary channel east of island. Now joined to Houghtaling Island at the south and Upper Schodack Island at the north. The name Schodack means "place of fire," referring to the permanent council fire which the Mohican Indians maintained near here.

127.50 Coeymans to west. Pronounced "queemans," it was settled in 1673 by Barent Pieterse Coeymans. It is a typical sleepy old Dutch river town and is well described by James Fenimore Cooper, under the name of Willow Cove, in his novel *Miles Wallingford*. This was once a major ice-cutting center. The Sutton & Suderley brick plant is still active.

127.50 Mull Island to east. It is now incorporated into Lower Schodack Island.

127.55 Coeymans Creek to west. It rises near South Bethlehem and flows southeast to the Hudson at Coeymans.

127.55 Ravena to west. Inland to west of Coeymans, on Route 9W, Thruway, and West Shore Railroad.

127.55 Schodack Landing to east. Located on mainland, east of Lower Schodack island, at head of navigability of the eastern channel, it was formerly a local railroad station.

128.00 Roah Hook to west.

128.00 Little Schodack Island to east. This is a very small island in the eastern channel, here known as Hell Gate.

128.50 Mull Plaat to east. Now incorporated into northwestern shoreline of Lower Schodack Island, its name refers to "mill plot."

129.00 Former site of Hell Gate to east. Now filled in, this was a narrow channel between Upper and Lower Schodack Islands.

129.00 to 130.50 Upper Schodack Island to east. The main navigational channel is west of the island. On the east side is shallow, tidal Schodack Creek, the outlet of Muitzes Kill. Upper Schodack Island is now connected with the mainland at the northern end and Lower Schodack Island at the southern end.

129.00 Schodack Creek (outlet of Muitzes Kill) to east. It is located east of Upper Schodack Island.

129.80 Alfred H. Smith Memorial Bridge. This steel and concrete railroad bridge was named after a former president of the New York Central Railroad. It was built for freight trains running between the former Hudson River Railroad and the Boston & Albany Railroad and the large classification yard at Selkirk, two miles west of here, where connection is made with the West Shore line. The bridge is a mile long, including approaches. It is a through truss bridge, with two major river spans. The eastern one is 600 feet long and the western one 400 feet. The bridge crosses not only the main channel of the Hudson, but also Shad Island and the Binnen Kill. Clearance is 135 feet. It cost $20,000,000. Built between 1926 and 1928 by the Hudson River

Connecting RR, a subsidiary of the New York Central RR.

129.90 Castleton-on-Hudson Bridge. This bridge carries the Berkshire section of the New York State Thruway to a connection with the Massachusetts Turnpike. The mile-long Castleton bridge is 5,330 feet long. Its deck provides for two separated traffic lanes in each direction, with a thirteen-foot-wide raised steel center mall. The bridge consists of relatively short continuous-plate girder approach spans on each side of the main and anchor spans. The main spans are of cantilever-truss design. The bridge pavement is 144 feet above the river, and there is 135 feet clearance between the river and the bottom of steel. The two main towers are 256 feet above the river. The substructure is composed of two abutments and forty-two reinforced concrete bents. These are comprised of two tall vertical columns stiffened with an intermediate strut and capped with a heavy concrete beam. The supporting columns range from five feet in diameter to fourteen feet for those supporting the main span.

A fog horn with a one-mile range blasts northward whenever the visibility is less than 2,000 feet. Ships approaching from the south are warned by a similar system on the neighboring railroad bridge, 400 feet to the south.

The substructure was built by Arthur A. Johnson Corporation and P. Kiewit Sons Co. of New York. Structural steel super-structure was built by Harris Structural Steel Co. of New York. Total cost of the bridge was $17,000,000. The bridge was designed by Madigan Hyland Consulting Engineers. and opened to traffic on May 26, 1959.

129.80 Shad Island to west.

129.80 Binnen Kill to west. It separates Shad Island from the mainland.

130.50 Baker Creek to west. It separates Shad island on the west from Schermerhorn Island on the east.

130.50 to 131.30 Schermerhorn Island to west. It is virtually joined to the mainland.

131.25 Vlockie Kill to east.

131.25 Selkirk to west. Inland, this is the site of a major railroad junction and freight classification yard.

131.50 Castleton-on-Hudson to east. This is an oldtime small river town. Named after the castle-like appearance of the steep bank upon which it is built. It was settled ca. 1630 and incorporated 1827. Paper boxes are manufactured here. Between 1860 and 1923 Castleton had thirteen ice houses harvesting millions of tons of ice. Some authorities think

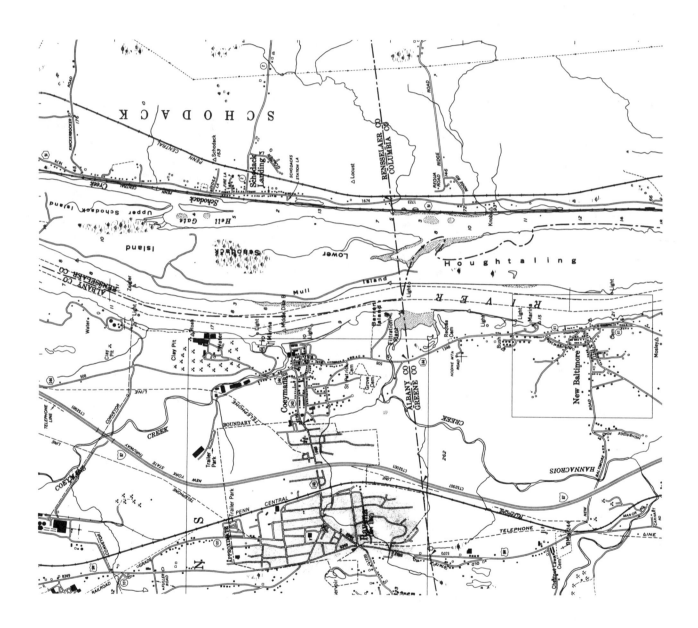

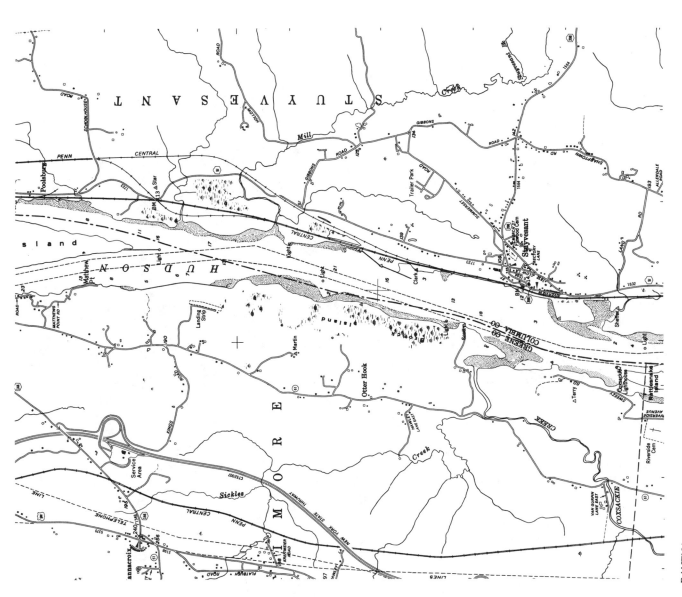

RAVENA

SOUJOURNER TRUTH TOWING *WOODY GUTHRIE* beneath New York State Thruway and Conrail Railroad bridges below Castleton. Photo: ©
Gretchen McHugh.

Castleton might have been the site of the Mahican's "Ever-burning Council Fire."

131.50 Poplar Island to west. It is now joined to the mainland.

132.35 Vloman Kill to west.

132.35 Cow Island to east. It is now joined to the mainland.

132.50 Moordener Kill to east. In English, its name means Murderer's Creek. There is a legend of a girl tied to a horse by Indians and dragged through the valley.

132.50 Brookview to east.

132.50 Papscanee Creek to east. Also known as Dead Creek, it separates Campbell, Pixtaway, and Papscanee Islands from the mainland.

132.60 to 134.00 Campbell Island to east. It is separated from the mainland by Papscanee Creek and from Pixtaway Island by a small stream.

132.70 Cedar Hill to west.

132.70 Stony Point to east. This point is on the mainland.

133.00 Schodack to east. This is a former principal settlement of the Mahican Indians.

133.20 Vandenburgh Hill to east (elevation 268 feet).

133.20 Parda Hook to west. It is said a horse once drowned here in a horse race on the ice. "Pard" is an old name for a spotted horse.

133.50 Pixtaway Island to east. Between Campbell Island on the west and Papscanee Creek on the east, it is joined to Papscanee Island at its northern end.

133.75 Vierda Kill to east. It flows into Papscanee Creek.

133.80 Bear Island to west. This island is now joined to mainland.

134.00 to 137.00 Papscanee Island to east. The main channel passes to the west. It was formerly called Staat Island.

134.10 Frothingham Lake to west. The lake lies inland. There is a small racetrack on Route 144.

134.35 Staat Point to east. On Papscanee Island.

134.50 Wemple to west.

135.00 Van Wies Point to west.

135.25 Lighthouse to west.

STAATS HOUSE, STAATS ISLAND. Photo: Alfred H. Marks.

135.25 Frothingham to west.

135.50 East Greenbush to east.

135.60 Cooper Kill to east. On Papscanee Island, it drains southwest into the main channel of the Hudson.

136.30 Island Creek to west. Separating Beacon, Cabbage, and Westerloo Islands from the mainland, it receives waters of the Norman's Kill at its northern end.

136.35 Beacon Island to west. This island is in the mouth of Island Creek.

136.40 Bethlehem Center to west.

136.50 Glenmont to west.

136.50 Grandview Hill to east. This was called "Schoti-ack," place of the ever-burning council fire of the Mahicans. Its elevation is 420 feet.

136.50 Cabbage Island to west. This was formerly called Parr's Island.

136.50 Overslaugh Bar. We quote at length from Wallace Bruce, writing for publication 1901:

The Castleton Bar or "overslaugh," as it was known by the river pilots, impeded for years navigation in low water. A. Van Santvoord, Esq., President of the Hudson River Day Line, and other prominent citizens along the Hudson, brought the subject before the State Legislature, and work was commenced in 1863. In 1868 the United States Government, very properly (as their jurisdiction extends over tidewater), assumed the work of completing the dykes, and they now stretch for miles along the banks and islands of the upper Hudson. Here and there along our route between Coxsackie and Albany will be seen great dredges deepening and widening the river channel. Mr. Charles G. Weir, U. S. Engineer in charge of the Hudson river improvements, in a recent report, says that the work of removing shoals and other obstructions that are a menace to navigation is progressing satisfactorily, and that dredges are at work deepening the channel from Coxsackie to the State Dam at Troy, in accordance with the act of Congress of September 19, 1890, which calls for a channel 12 feet deep and 400 feet wide from Coxsackie to the foot of Broadway, Troy, and thence 12 feet deep and 300 feet wide to the State Dam.

The plan provides for a system of longitudinal dykes to confine the current sufficiently to allow the ebb and flow of the tidal-current to keep the channel clear. These dykes are to be gradually brought nearer together from New Baltimore toward Troy so as to assist the entrance of the flood-current and increase its height.

The engineers report that the greater part of the material carried in suspension in the Hudson river above Albany is believed to come from the Mohawk river, and its tributary the Schoharie river, while the sands and gravel that form the heavy and obstinate bars near Albany and chiefly between Albany and Troy, come from the upper Hudson.

The discharge of the Hudson between Troy and Albany at its lowest stage may be taken at about 3,000 cubic feet per second. The river supply, therefore, during that stage is inadequate in the upper part of the river for navigation, independent of tidal flow.

The greatest number of bars is between Albany and Troy, where the channel is narrow, and at least six obstructing bars, composed of fine and coarse gravel and coarse and fine sand, are in existence. In many places between Albany and Troy the navigable depth is reduced to 7 ½ feet by the presence of these bars.

From Albany to New Baltimore the depths are variable, the prevailing depth being 10 feet and over, with pools of greater depth separated by long crossover bars, over which the greatest depth does not exceed 9 or 10 feet.

(Bruce, *Hudson by Daylight*, p. 233.)

Even after completion of the above-described work, the river between Albany and Hudson was cluttered with small islands, and until 1930 only twelve feet deep at low tide. This presented a serious problem to navigation. The channel was later dredged to a depth of twenty-seven feet, enabling large sea-going vessels to proceed to Albany, independent of the tides. Albany was thus made a seaport. In 1954, Congress authorized further deepening of the channel to thirty-two feet.

By the 1960s, the channel had been improved to 34 feet depth and 400 feet width.

137.00 Teller Hill to east (elevation 407 feet).

137.25 Teller Crossing to east.

137.30 Turning Basin to east. It has a 25-foot depth.

137.75 Norman's Kill to west. It rises near East Berne in the Helderbergs and flows east through the Normanskill Ravine, or the Vale of Ta-Wa-sentha ("place of many dead" or of "waterfalls") to Island Creek, west of Westerlo Island. It was named for an early Albany settler who erected a mill near the mouth of the stream. The Delaware & Hudson follows the Norman's Kill through the ravine. The Vale of Ta-Wa-sentha is one of the supposed dwellings of the legendary Hiawatha.

137.75 Greenbush Banks or Heights to east (elevation 300 feet).

137.75 Westerlo Island to west. Site of the Port of Albany with heavy shipping and rail facilities, it incorporates the former Marsh Island.

137.75 Dow's Point to east. This is the former estate of V. P. Douw.

137.75 Hazelwood to west.

137.75 Kenwood to west.

138.00 Bogart Island to west. Now incorporated into Westerlo Island.

138.00 Clinton Heights to east.

138.50 Port of Albany to west. Port for oceangoing vessels.

138.75 Niagara Mohawk Power Company Kenwood Generating Station to west. This is a large steam generating station with tall smokestacks.

138.75 Westerloes to west.

138.75 Cuyler Dike to east.

139.00. Island Creek to west. This is the northern part of a former creek, now canalized. It no longer connects with the southern portions inside Cabbage and Westerlo Islands, as Westerlo Island is now joined to the mainland.

139.00 Greenbush Heights to east.

139.40 Site of former Parker Dunn Memorial Bridge. Operational from 1933 to 1974, when it was removed, it was named in honor of Parker F. Dunn (1890–1918), a hero of World War I. It had the heaviest known lift span and served as the principal highway crossing at Albany.

139.50 Mill Creek to east. It is now largely covered over.

139.50 to 140.00 Van Rensselaer Island to east. It is now part of the mainland and has been partially dredged away.

139.50 Albany to west. With a population of 115,781, this is the capital of the state of New York and the seat of Albany County.

Albany was visited by Henry Hudson on September 19, 1609. The first settlement was in 1614 when Fort Nassau was built on Castle Island to protect fur traders. It was under the command of Hendrick Christiaensen. This fort was destroyed by a flood in 1617.

In 1623, the Dutch West India Company sent thirty Walloon families to settle in the Albany area. They built another fort, called Fort Aurania (Fort Orange in English), on Castle Island in 1624.

The first large grant of land was made in 1629, to Killaen Van Rensselaer, a pearl and diamond merchant of the Netherlands. This tract centered on Fort Orange and was on both sides of the Hudson River. It covered an area twenty-four by forty-eight miles. Killaen Van Rensselaer was the uncle of Wouter Van Twiller, a director of the Dutch West India Company, and later the third governor of New Netherlands. Van Rensselaer himself did not venture to the New World, but sent his relative Roelf Janssen as overseer. The tenants had to buy all supplies from the commissary and have their grain ground at the

RE-CREATION OF HENRY HUDSON'S SHIP *HALVE MAENE* at Albany. Photo: © Bob Hansen.

patroon's mill. By 1637 the patent covered 700 square miles. On April 8, 1680, Van Rensselaer had purchased from King Aepgin of the Mahicans "all that tract of country on the west side of the Hudson, extending from Beeren Island up to Smack's Island, and in breadth two day's journey." In 1642 the Van Rensselaers built Fort Crailo at Greenbush. This area was then known as Crawlier. Later this house served as the upper manor. The lower manor, called Claverack, or "clover pasture," was built in 1685 and was active until 1783. A western manor was located at the north end of present-day Albany. In later years it was taken down and moved to Williamstown, Massachusetts. In 1664 or 1670, Richard Van Rensselaer built another house called De Vlackte, or "the flats," opposite Breaker Island south of Watervliet. This house was later sold to Philip Pietersen Schuyler.

By the time of the governorship of Peter Stuyvesant (1647–1664), Killaen Van Rensselaer thought himself so powerful that he instructed his

ALBANY WATERFRONT. Delaware & Hudson Building in foreground. Photo: Alfred H. Marks.

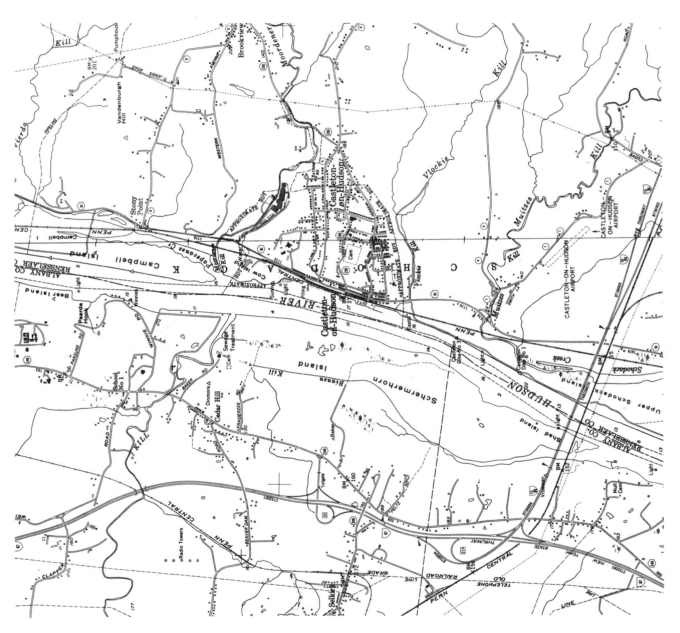

DELMAR/EAST GREENBUSH

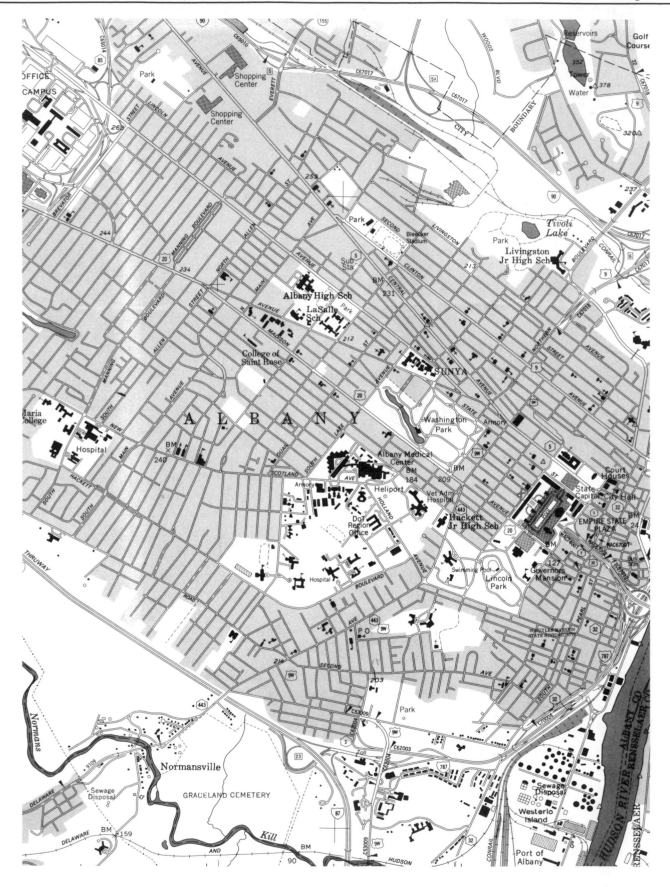

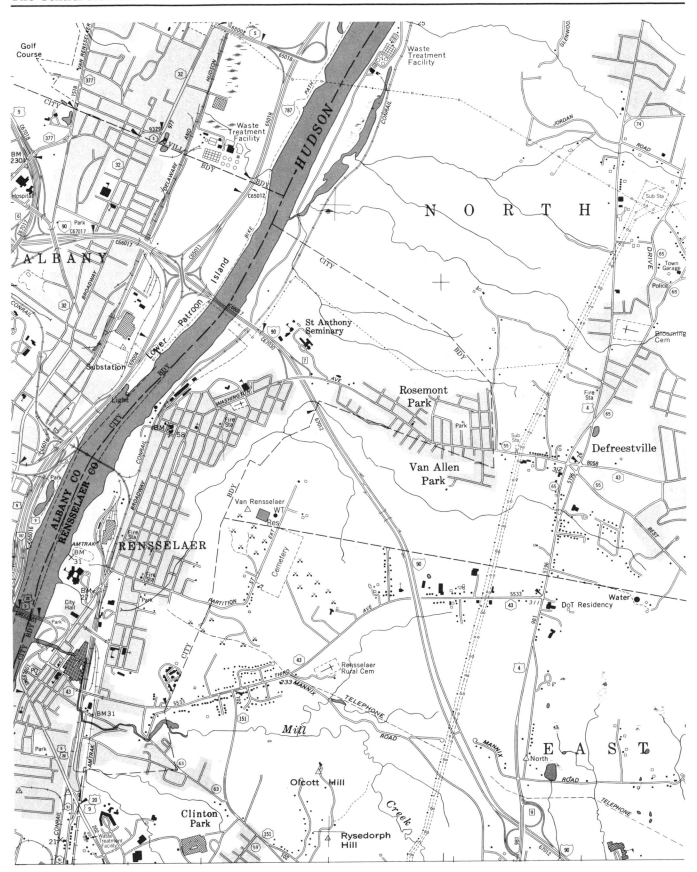

henchman Nicholas Koorn to build a fort, Rensellaerstein, on Barren Island and demand tribute tolls from passing vessels by *wapen recht*. The power of the Van Rensselaers was becoming intolerable to the company, and director general (governor) Peter Stuyvesant ordered the laying out of the town of Beverwyck adjacent to Fort Orange. This was to be considered company property and was placed under the jurisdiction of three magistrates, completely independent of the manor of Rensselaerwyck, which surrounded it for miles on all sides. This was the nucleus of the present city of Albany.

Later, in 1685, Killaen's grandson was confirmed in his rights to the manor of Rensselaerwyck by the English. This was the only one of the major Dutch patroonships to survive under later English domination, and indeed lasted on past the American Revolution. Two hundred years later, in 1838, there were still between 60,000 and 100,000 tenants on farms owned by the sixth lord of the manor, Stephen Van Rensselaer III, known as the "good patroon." He had acceded to the title at the ripe old age of five years.

After the English conquest in 1664 the name of the town was changed from Fort Orange to Albany, in honor of the Scottish title of the Duke of Albany and York, later King James II. In 1686, it was chartered as a city by Gov. Thomas Dongan—the second city to be chartered in the present United States.

During the French and Indian War, a congress was held at Albany, which was attended by such dignitaries as Benjamin Franklin. Members drew up in 1754 the so-called "Albany plan of union." This served as an important example for later developments before and during the Revolution.

After the Revolution, commercial development began in earnest. Capt. Stewart Dean of Albany sailed his sloop *Experiment* around the world to Canton, China, via Cape Horn, between 1785 and 1787. In 1785 a stagecoach line to New York was chartered. The New York State Legislature established itself here in 1797, renting a house for Gov. John Jay—thus making Albany the State Capital.

The greatest impetus came with the development of the steamboat in 1807. The Champlain Canal was completed in 1822 and the great Erie Canal in 1825. The large Cruttendon's Hotel was opened about 1827. The Mohawk & Hudson Railroad was completed in 1831, and the Hudson River Railroad in 1851. Among later important commercial developments were the improvement of the New York State Barge Canal in 1918 and opening of the $13,000,000 Port of Albany in 1932, with facilities covering 217 acres, including a large grain elevator, and accommodating sea-going ships of twenty-seven foot draft.

Any review of the history of Albany must make

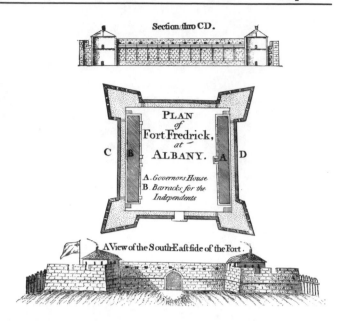

FORT FREDERICK AT ALBANY. From *A set of plans and forts in America, reduced from actual surveys*, London, 1763.

mention of its greatest native son. General Philip Schuyler (1733–1804) was fourth in descent from an ancestor who had come to Beverwyck from Holland in 1650. He was born at Albany and served in the French and Indian Wars. He married Catherine Van Rensselaer, thus uniting with the family of the Patroon. He served in the Provincial Assembly and the Continental Congress in 1775 and 1779. Between 1775 and 1777 he served as Major General of the Northern Department under Washington. He later served as the first United States Senator from New York. After the Battle of Saratoga, he was host to the captive Gen. John Burgoyne at his mansion in Albany. His daughter, Elizabeth Schuyler, married Alexander Hamilton in December 1780. He owned an extensive estate at Schuylerville further up the Hudson near Saratoga.

Important buildings in Albany not described elsewhere are:

1. New York State Office Building. Located west of the capitol, it has thirty-three stories. It was built of limestone and granite in 1930 at cost of $6,500,000.
2. Roman Catholic Cathedral of the Immaculate Conception, Madison and Eagle Streets. In Gothic style with spires similar to those at Cologne, it was built in 1852.
3. New York State Bank Building. On the northeast corner of State and Pearl Streets, it is a seventeen-story red brick built in 1927, designed by H. I. Cobb. It incorporates Adam-style elements of the original building of 1803 by Philip Hooker.
4. New York State Court of Appeals Building. On Eagle

EMPIRE STATE PLAZA AND SOUTH FRONT STATE CAPITOL at Albany. Photo: © Gretchen McHugh.

Street between Pine and Columbia, it is in Greek Revival style. It has a portico with six Ionic columns of white Sing-Sing marble, and was built between 1835 and 1842. Henry Rector was the architect.

5. Albany County Courthouse. On Eagle Street between Pine and Columbia, it is a granite and limestone Ionic-Neoclassic building, 1916.

6. Gen. Philip Schuyler Monument. Located in front of City Hall, this monument is by J. Massey Rhind.

7. Statue of General Philip Sheridan (1831–1888). This Civil War general led cavalry under Grant. He was born in Albany. The statue is by John Quincy Adams Ward. It was completed by Daniel Chester French.

8. "Arbor Hill" Ten Broeck Mansion. Designed by Phillip Hooker, this historic mansion is on a five-acre site bounded by Ten Broeck Street, Ten Broeck Place, and Livingston Avenue, and is operated by the Albany County Historical Society since it was donated in 1947 by the Olcott family, a prominent Albany banking family who occupied the house for 100 years. This Georgian brick mansion was built in 1797 by Abraham Ten Broeck, a hero of the Revolution, wealthy Albany merchant, and former Albany Mayor for two separate terms. Located at 9 Ten Broeck Place, it is open to visitors. Telephone 518-436-9826 for visiting hours and information.

6

From the Capital Area to the Adirondacks

139.50 Albany. The tide here is 4½ feet.

139.50 Rensselaer to east. With a population of 10,136, Rensselaer was formed in 1897 by the union of the villages of East Albany, Greenbush, and Bath-on-the-Hudson, also known as Rensselaerwyck. This was the early seat of the Van Rensselaer family.

Fort Crailo, actually a fortified manor house, is located on Riverside Street, south of Columbia. It is open as a free museum. It was built in 1704 as the home of Hendrick Van Rensselaer, whose grandfather was patroon of a huge estate encompassing

most of what is now Rensselaer and Albany counties. The rear wing was built in 1762. During the French and Indian War, the house served as temporary headquarters to Gen. James Abercromby (1706–1781) on his way to Ticonderoga. During his visit in 1758, it is alleged that a Dr. Richard Shuckburgh, who was attached to Abercromby's staff, was struck by the very bedraggled appearance of the colonial militia while sitting on the edge of a well. In an idle moment he penned the poem "Yankee Doodle." Thus Fort Crailo came to be called the "Yankee Doodle home."

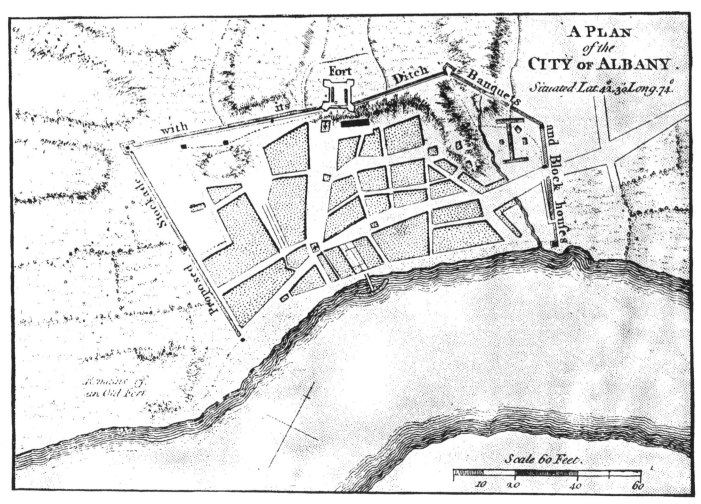

CITY OF ALBANY PLAN. Circa 1763.

During the Revolution, twelve of the Crailo Van Rensselaers served the patriot cause, and early in the war, colonial troops assembled on Fort Crailo's grounds.

Beverwyck, on Washington Avenue opposite Eighth Street, now St. Anthony's Seminary, was built between 1840 and 1843. It was the manor house of William Paterson Van Rensselaer, younger son of Stephen Van Rensselaer. It is a 2½-story structure built of stone with Greek Revival details including an Ionic portico. Frederic Diaper was its architect. It has been a Franciscan seminary since 1912.

Dyes, chemicals, felts, and woolens are manufactured here. It is a major junction for railroad passenger service, with lines running to New York, Boston, Montreal, and the west. It is the location of Amtrak's Albany station.

139.65 Quackendary Kill to east. It is now largely covered over.

139.65 New highway bridge. This bridge connects with Interstate 787.

139.80 Site of former railroad bridge. This bridge formerly led to Union Station, Albany, and was used by all passenger trains.

140.50 Railroad bridge. This bridge was formerly for freight only. It is presently used by all freight and passenger trains.

140.75 Tivoli Lakes to west, on Patroon Creek.

140.75 Bath-on-the-Hudson to east. This was an early health resort because of the many mineral springs in the area and is named for the famous spa resort of Bath in England. Today the area is entirely

ST. JOHN'S R. C. CHURCH, RENSSELAER. A notable Byzantine style landmark. Photo: Alfred H. Marks.

residential and it became part of the City of Rensselaer in 1897. From 1831 to 1904 it was the eastern terminal of the old North Ferry to Albany.

140.75 Defreestville to east. Beyond Bath, it is located on Quackendary Kill.

140.80 Patroon Creek to west. This creek is followed by the line of the New York Central Railroad.

140.80 to 142.00 Lower Patroon Island to west. The main vessel channel lies to the east.

141.50 Interstate 90 bridge.

141.50 North Albany to west. At the turn of the century this was the largest lumber market in the Eastern United States. White pine from the Adirondack Region was the principal commodity. Much of this wood was brought down to North Albany by canal boats and shipped out by oceangoing ships or rail. Gigantic stacks of lumber, up to sixty feet high, were erected along the river bank.

141.80 Filtration plant to west.

141.80 Unnamed inlet to east. This inlet is separated from the main channel by Bath Dike.

142.25 to 142.80 Patroon Island to west. The vessel channel lies to the east.

142.65 Overhead power cables (authorized clearance 155 feet).

FORT CRAILO AT RENSSELAER. Photo: Alfred H. Marks.

142.80 to 144.80 Little River to west. Separating Breaker Island from the mainland, it has depths of from three to ten feet. It is open to small craft from the Hudson only at its northern end.

142.80 to 144.80 Breaker Island to west. Formerly Cuyler's Island, it was the site of the Park Island race course in 1894. In the early twentieth century there was a large amusement park on Cuyler's Island.

143.00 Menands to west.

143.00 Loudonville to west (beyond Menands). This village, with a population of 9,299, is named in honor of John Campbell, 4th Earl of Loudon (1705–1782), commander in chief of the British forces in North America in 1757 during the French and Indian Wars. He became governor of Virginia in 1758.

143.50 Moordenaer's Kill to west. This creek flows into Little River.

143.80 Overhead power cable. (authorized clearance 138 feet).

143.90 Kromme Kill to west. This creek flows into Little River.

143.90 Hillhouse Island to west. This island was formerly known as Breaker Island, and is incorporated into the present Breaker Island. There was formerly a foundry here served by the small Breaker Island RR, a subsidiary of the Delaware & Hudson RR.

143.90 Mix's Island to west. It is now incorporated into Breaker Island.

144.25 Highway lift bridge. (Route 378): horizontal clearance 301 feet, vertical clearances 62 feet closed, 139 feet open. The bridge is now in a permanently lowered position. The large concrete counterweights were found to be corroded and have been removed.

SCHUYLER HOUSE AT THE FLATS (Vlackte) by Benson Lossing.

This bridge is popularly known locally as "The Menands Bridge," an unofficial name.

144.25 South Troy to east.

144.50 Wynant's Kill to east.

144.50 Albia to east (atop ridge).

144.50 Burden's Point to east.

144.50 Former Immaculate Conception Monastery to east. Now part of Hudson Valley Community College.

144.80 Port Schuyler to west.

144.80 Burden's Iron Works to east.

145.30 Watervliet to west (population 12,404).

145.30 Watervliet Arsenal to west. This arsenal was established in 1813 during the War of 1812. Its historic structures include: Quarters No. 1: two-story, stone officer's home built 1845; Building No. 24: a three-story trimmed stone enlisted men's barracks with two-story columned porch, built in 1843; Building No. 38: the "cast-iron building," built in 1839 from decorative cast-iron components cast in New York City; and Building No. 110: the Big Gun Shop, a gigantic brick factory building, built in 1889, enlarged in 1918 and 1942.

145.30 Smart's Pond to east.

145.60 Poesten Kill to east.

146.00 Ida Lake to east.

146.00 Mount Ida to east (elevation 360 feet). This mount consists of Cambrian rock and glacial clay. It is in the center of Troy Municipal Prospect Park.

146.25 West Troy to west. This is now part of Watervliet.

146.25 Troy to east. With a population of 62,918, this city runs seven miles along the river to the east. The Indian name for the vicinity was Pa-an-pa-ack, which means "field of standing corn." It is included in the tract granted to Killaen Van Rensselaer by the Dutch West India Company in 1629. Gradually the area grew up as a market center for Dutch and Palatinate farmers along the Mohawk Valley, as this was the head of tidewater navigation on the Hudson River. As late as 1785, most of the area in the present city was owned by three farmers, all descendants of Derick Vanderheyden. The land immediately to the north belonged to the Lansing family. This area is now called Lansingburgh, but was called New City before the Revolution. The section near downtown

TROY NORTH

Troy was called Ashley's Ferry or Ferry Hook, after Capt. Stephen Ashley who ran a tavern here. The name Troy was adopted in 1789. In 1796, a post office was established. In the 1790s, bricks and paper were manufactured along the Poestenkill. Troy was incorporated as a village in 1798. It had been surveyed as a town in 1786.

The nineteenth century was Troy's golden age of commercial development. The Troy–Schenectady Toll Road was opened in 1802. The first steamboats arrived shortly after 1807. The Champlain Canal came in 1822 and the Erie Canal in 1825. In 1822, Henry Burden established his iron works to manufacture iron plate, bells, and stoveplates. In 1825 Mrs. Hannah Lord Montague invented the "detachable" collar and gave birth to an important local industry. Construction started on the Schenectady & Troy Railroad in 1838 and was completed in 1842. With the coming of the railroad, Charles Veasie and Orasmus Eaton opened railroad coach works here. In 1835, the first bridge across the Hudson was opened to Green Island by the Rensselaer & Saratoga Railroad. Ebenezer Brown attempted commercial production of detachable collars in 1829. In 1834 Lyman Bennett opened the first successful collar factory. In 1845 he added cuffs to his line. Business boomed with the introduction of the sewing machine in 1852. The former Cluett-Peabody plant on River Street was the largest producer of men's shirts in the world. Until 1989 this nine-story plant produced the famous Arrow shirt and housed an interesting collar museum.

By 1852 fancy clothes, horseshoes, iron products, coal tar, ammonium sulphate, phenol, and benzol were important products. The iron plates for the *Monitor* were manufactured at Troy. Horatio Winslow's Troy Iron Works were the first in the United States to use the Bessemer Process. Troy was the iron and steel center of the country until Andrew Carnegie opened his mills near Pittsburgh in 1873. The Troy Furnace of Republic Steel is still in operation.

Neighboring Lansingburgh, which was joined to Troy in 1901, was the home of Poor & Co. which manufactured rail joints. Other industries still active today include the manufacture of coke, engineering and surveying instruments, women's wear, and valves and fire hydrants (Ludlow Co.). Immigration of French Canadians about 1860 led to the development of knitting mills.

Troy was an early center of liberal social action and unionism. It was also a center of abolitionist activity. During the fugitive slave trial of Charles Nalle on April 27, 1860, Harriet Tubman led a riot which enabled Nalle to escape.

During the War of 1812, Troy added to Hudson folklore. Samuel Wilson (1766–1854), a former brickmaker and slaughterhouse operator, had military contracts. He was what was then called a sutler. Later Wilson lived in Catskill. During his Troy sojourn, it was his business to pack and consign meat to a certain Elbert Anderson, who was in charge of a cantonment at Greenbush. He would brand the meat with the initials "EA-US," standing for Elbert Anderson-United States. The "U.S." soon came to refer to "Uncle Sam" Wilson.

Troy was an educational center from early times. In 1814 Emma Willard founded the Troy Female Seminary. This was later called the Emma Willard School. In 1916, Mrs. Russell Sage founded Russell Sage College for women, in honor of her late husband (1816–1906), a merchant and congressman. He is buried in Oakwood Cemetery.

The Rensselaer Polytechnic Institute, an engineering college, was founded in 1824 by Stephen Van Rensselaer "for the purpose of instructing persons in the application of science to the common purposes of life." Amos Eaton (1776–1842) was appointed senior professor. The original buildings were of Georgian design and built of brick and limestone. Today R.P.I. is one of the nation's top engineering schools, with a worldwide reputation.

St. Joseph's Seminary, next to R.P.I., was founded in 1856. Its fine buildings are built of brick in the Romanesque revival style. There is a Gothic chapel built in 1933.

The Hudson Valley Community College is also located at Troy.

Major parks include Prospect Park, Frear Park, and Beman Park, as well as Sage Park and areas along the Wynantskill and Poestenkill and Lake Ida.

Other buildings of interest include:

1. The First Baptist Church, on Third Street between Congress and State. This is a red brick structure with six Ionic columns and a pediment of white wood. It has a tower and tall spire, and dates from 1846.
2. St. Paul's Episcopal Church at the northeast corner of State and Third Streets, is the oldest church in the city. In English-Gothic style, it dates from 1827. It is built of limestone with wood trim.
3. The Emma Willard School is of English Collegiate-Gothic style (with Tudor and early English details). Built of Schoharie limestone, 1821. It has an octogonal tower with gargoyles and open tracery.
4. The Betsy Hart House, 59 Second Street, was built in 1827 for railroad magnate Richard P. Hart. Its style is Georgian colonial. It was built of marble and has 13 rooms. The house is now owned by the

FIRST BAPTIST CHURCH, TROY. Built 1846. Photo: © Bob Hansen.

Rensselaer County Historical Society and is operated as a museum.

On May 10, 1862, a great fire destroyed most of Troy. At noon that day, a fire broke out on the Rensselaer & Saratoga Railroad bridge to Green Island, and the burning sparks were driven by a strong northwest wind into the heart of the city. It was thought that the fire was started by a spark from a locomotive igniting the wooden bridge. People were burned to death in the streets, and 507 buildings were destroyed by 6 P.M. when the fire died down.

In its heyday, Troy was served by freight and passenger trains of the Boston & Maine, Delaware & Hudson, and New York Central Railroads. The overnight Montreal Limited between New York and Montreal used to operate via Troy and the Green Island bridge. Today only the tracks of the former New York Central (now Conrail) still reach Troy. There is no passenger service.

At the head of ship navigation, Troy was an important steamboat port. Several lines of large steamers terminated here. There was also a local steamer to Albany.

146.30 Route 7–Nineteenth Street bridge. The old swing type bridge has been replaced with a new high-level fixed span.

146.40 South branch or sprout of Mohawk River enters from the west.

146.40–149.00 Green Island to west. Formerly called Tibbett's Island, this was the site of important railroad locomotive and car shops.

146.50 Center Island to west of vessel channel. This was formerly called Starbuck Island. The channel to its west between it and Green Island has only one and two foot depths.

146.50 Mount Olympus to east (elevation 535 feet).

146.75 Green Island Bridge. A former railroad, and later road bridge, the pioneer wooden railroad bridge of the Rensselaer & Saratoga Railroad was the first bridge across the Hudson River. It opened on October 6, 1835 and burned on May 10, 1862. The second bridge was a lift bridge with horizontal clearance of 160 feet and closed vertical clearance of 24 feet and open clearance of 129 feet. It was built by the Delaware & Hudson Railroad in 1884 and was rebuilt in 1925. It was of lattice truss and through plate girder design, and had an overall length of 625 feet. Rail operations ceased in 1963, and the bridge was conveyed to the counties of Albany and Rensselaer for use as an automobile bridge. The bridge collapsed in March 1977.

A new bridge has been completed on the site of the one that collapsed in 1977. The new bridge is a giant lift bridge for automobiles and pedestrians only. The counterweight housings are sheathed in metal with a very "moderne" appearance. This is the third impressive bridge at this location.

CLUET PEABODY PLANT, TROY. Photo: Alfred H. Marks.

147.10 New high level highway bridge Green Island to Troy. This is a fixed position bridge similar to the Route 7–Nineteenth Street span.

147.20 Adams Island in mid-stream (channels either side). It was formerly called Big Stony Island.

147.50 Stony Island to west. West of navigation channel, offshore of Green Island.

147.75 Troy government lock and dam. This is the head of tidewater navigation. The lock is near the eastern shore. On the western shore is a hydro-electric plant built by Thomas A. Edison and still in operation. Adjacent to it is the former Ford Motor Company automobile assembly plant.

148.25 Jan Gowson Island to west. This small island is offshore of Green Island.

149.00 Main sprout or branch of Mohawk River to west.

149.00–150.00 Van Schaick's Island to west. Formerly Cohoes Island, this was the site of the Northern Inland Navigation Co. canal, an unsuccessful project sponsored by Philip Schuyler in 1795. The Van Schaick House was built in 1777; two-story brick with gambrel roof. There was a military encampment on the island during the Revolution. In 1799 Col. Goose Van Schaick went into the "central wilderness" to destroy villages of the Onondaga.

149.80 Cohoes to west. The name means "canoe falling," with possible reference to the falls of the Mohawk located here. Another interpretation is "the island at the falls." The author's preference is that it refers to the Indian word for salmon or shad, which were caught in the falls and rapids here.

In *Picturesque America*, edited by William Cullen Bryant in 1872, R. E. Garczynski writes:

At Cohoes there is a great fall; about a mile above the falls, the river, broad and deep as it is, has been hemmed in by a dam, and a great portion of its waters drawn off by a waterpower company. The little town of Cohoes is entirely manufacturing. It is the Lowell of New York. Here are the great Harmony Cotton-Mills; and here, also, are some twenty-five woolen-mills, besides paper-factories and other industries.

The falls of Cohoes are quite close to the Harmony Mills; and a capital view can be obtained of them, either from the bank in rear of one of the mills, or from an island in the river at some distance below. Very much depends upon the season of the year as regards the impression which the falls make upon the mind of a traveller. In the dry season there

is but little water, and hence the upper part of the falls appears like a series of grand rapids. In the early summer there is one tremendous descent of water, falling over seventy feet. The banks on either side are high and shaly, crowned generally with dark pines at the summit, and showing, below, a diagonal stratification, as if they had been upheaved.

(*Picturesque America*, edited by William Cullen Bryant, p. 465.)

Another interesting description of the falls of the Mohawk is given by Benson Lossing in his book *The Hudson* of 1866:

The scenery about the mouth of the Mohawk, particularly in the vicinity of Cohoes Falls, is exceedingly picturesque, and at some points really grand. A highway bridge, nine-hundred feet in length, and a railway viaduct still longer, cross the river over the rapids a short distance below the falls. From the former a fine distant view of the cataract and the rapids below may be obtained, but the best places to observe them in all their beauty and grandeur, are at the Cataract House, in the village of Cohoes, which stands upon the summit verge of a precipice one hundred and seventy feet in height. Down a steep slope of that precipice, for about fifty feet, the proprietor has constructed a flight of steps, and upon the top of a broad terrace at their foot he has planted a flower garden, for the enjoyment of visitors. Around its edge, from which may be obtained a view of the entire cataract, is a railing with seats, and there the visitor may contemplate at ease the wild scene on every hand. On his left, as he gazes up the river, rush large streams of water from the top of the precipice above him, in almost perpendicular currents, from the waste-sluices of a canal, which, commencing at a dam almost two miles above the falls, conveys water to numerous mill-wheels in the village. By this means immense hydraulic power is obtained and distributed.

The water-power at Cohoes is under the control of a stock company, who rented it to the proprietors of mills and factories. The entire fall of water controlled by the company is one hundred and twenty feet; and the minimum supply of water is one thousand cubic feet each second. The estimated value of the various articles manufactured here is nearly three millions of dollars per annum.

Below the fall, the water rushes over a rocky bed, in foaming rapids between high banks, to the plain, where the islands divide it into channels, and through these it flows gently into the Hudson.

(Lossing, *The Hudson*, pp. 109–111.)

FALLS OF THE MOHAWK AT COHOES. Photo: © William M. Rau.

FALLS OF THE MOHAWK 1866. Drawing: Benson Lossing.

Cohoes was settled by the Dutch and incorporated in 1869. Knitted goods, paper products, and shoddy are manufactured here. Its population is 18,653. Here are located the great brick mill buildings of the Harmony Mill and Star Woolen Mill with their mansard roofs and towers dating from between 1837 and 1845. There are also many old workers' tenement houses, some dating from the 1870s. This is a typical late nineteenth-century industrial city.

Cohoes is served by the Delaware & Hudson Railroad.

149.80 Mohawk River to west. Originally called the Maaquas River, after the Indians dwelling along it. It rises near Rome, in central New York State, and flows 140 miles eastward into the Hudson at Cohoes. For most of this distance, it is canalized as part of the New York State Barge Canal. Earlier the Erie Canal had paralleled it, as did the later railroads and highways. From Rome it flows east past Utica, Herkimer, Little Falls, Canajoharie, Fonda, Fultonville, Auriesville, Tribes Hill, Fort Hunter, Amsterdam, Schenectady, and Crescent to the power dam above

Cohoes Falls. In the early nineteenth century, this was the site of a pleasure resort with terraces and gardens. With the building of the Harmony Mill in 1837, the water was diverted and large mill buildings and row houses were erected for the workers. The area remains industrialized today, and only a trickle of water flows over the falls. After going over more rapids, it flows into the Hudson's West Channel near Simmons and Van Schaick Islands. It receives the waters of the large Schoharie Creek, which rises in the Catskills at Fort Hunter, near Tribes' Hill.

149.50 Lansingburg to east. Formerly New City, before the Revolution. It was incorporated into Troy in 1901.

149.90 Simmons Island to west. In mouth of Mohawk River. Van Schaick Island to its east and Peobles Island to its north. Not visible from Hudson.

149.90 Route 470 highway bridge. This is a gracefully arched double-draw bascule bridge. However, the mechanism is now inoperable and for practical purposes it is now a fixed span.

150.50 Peeble's (or Peeble's) Island to west. Formerly called Van Hover's Island. It separates the Middle and North Sprouts of the Mohawk. It is

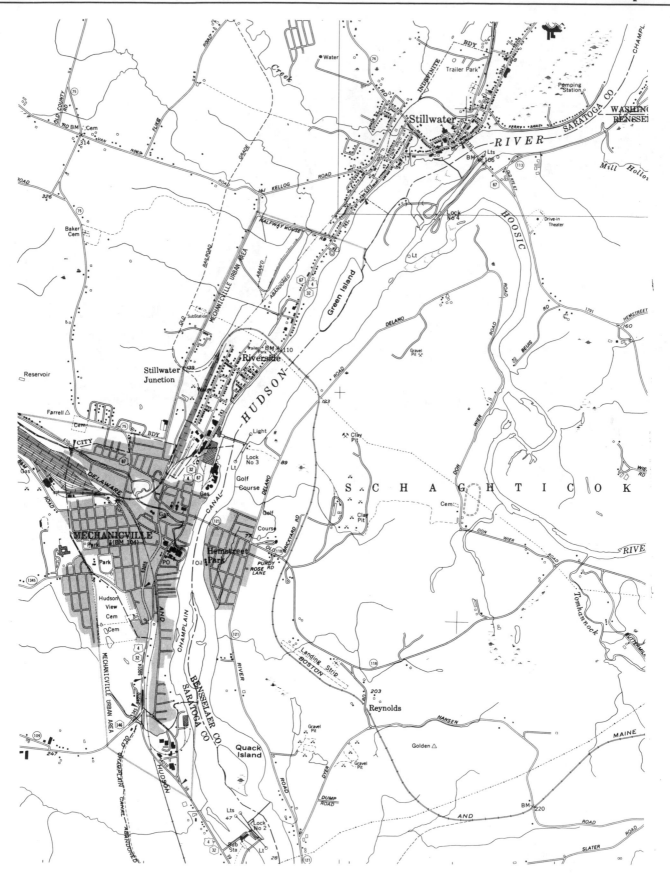

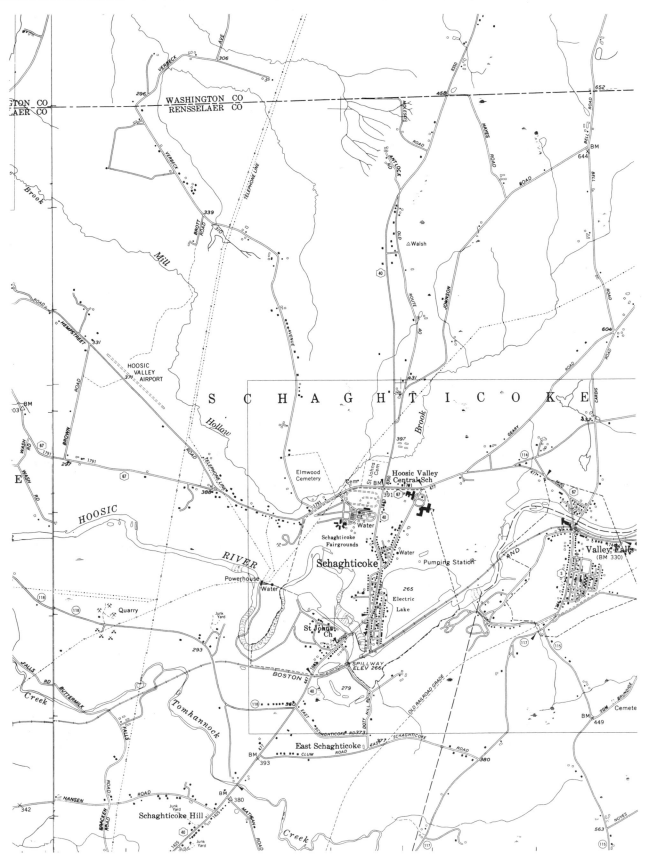

MECHANICVILLE/SCHAGHTICOKE SOUTH

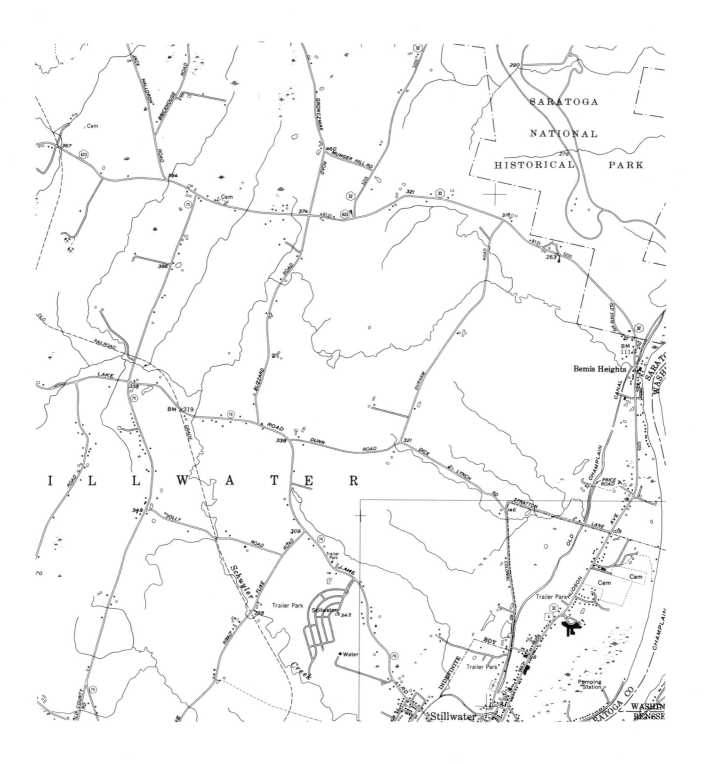

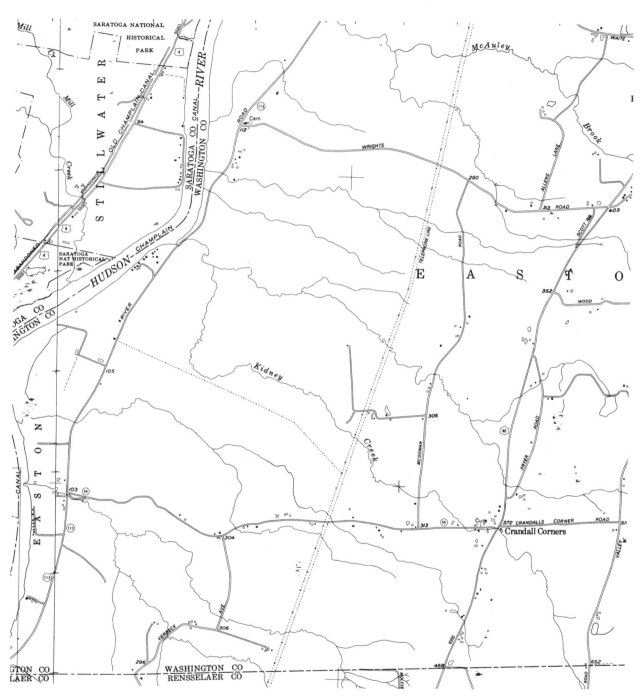

MECHANICVILLE/SCHAGHTICOKE NORTH

STANDARD MANUFACTURING COMPANY, LANSINGBURGH. Photo: Alfred H. Marks.

largely hidden from the Hudson River by the northern end of Van Schaick Island. It is now called Peebles Island State Park and is reached by a footbridge from Waterford, over the North Sprout and entrance to the Barge Canal.

150.54 Second Island to west. Not visible from Hudson River, this is in the North Sprout of the Mohawk River between Peoble's Island, which hides it from the Hudson, and Goat Island, further west, between it and the mainland—also in the North Sprout. It is not readily accessible. May be seen from streets on north end of Simmons Island off Route 470.

150.55 Goat Island to west. In the North Sprout of the Mohawk River, between Second Island and Mainland. Same comments as for Second Island.

150.60 Bock Island to west. In North Sprout of Mohawk River between Peoble's Island and Mainland, north of Goat Island. Not reached by bridges.

150.60 Buttermilk Falls on Middle Sprout of Mohawk River to west. Separates Van Schaick Island on the south from Peoble's Island to the north.

151.00 Revolutionary War breastworks to west. On the northern end of Peoble's Island.

151.00 North Sprout or Channel of Mohawk River to west. Hidden by Peoble's Island, which it separates from the mainland, it empties into the inlet of the New York State Barge Canal.

146.75 to 151.00 The Green Island Branch of the Delaware & Hudson Railroad, formerly the Rensselaer & Saratoga Railroad, ran north from the Green Island bridge at Troy to Waterford along the Hudson, on Green, Van Schaick, and Peoble's Islands. This route was used by the Montreal Limited, which

ran by Troy and bypassed Albany and Cohoes, on the main line. The great Gilbert Car Works were located on Green Island.

151.00 Entrance of New York State Barge Canal (Erie Canal) and locks to west.

151.40 Waterford to west. This is a former important point on the Erie Canal.

151.40 U. S. Route 4 bridge.

151.50 Saratoga County. The western bank from here to Glens Falls is occupied by Saratoga County. Its county seat is Saratoga Springs, its area 814 square miles. It was taken from Albany County in 1791.

152.00 Pleasantdale to east.

153.75 Campbell Island.

155.00 Half Moon to west.

156.60 Lock No. 1.

157.00 McDonald Creek to west.

159.00 Lock No. 2.

159.35 Quack Island.

LAUGHLIN TERBLE MILL, WATERFORD. Photo: Alfred H. Marks.

OUTLET NEW YORK STATE BARGE CANAL, WATERFORD. Photo: Alfred H. Marks.

161.00 Mechanicville to west. With a population of 6,247, it was settled before 1700, incorporated as a village in 1859, and made a city in 1915. There are railroad shops here and bricks, paper, and knit goods are manufactured. This is the home of Elmer Ephraim Ellsworth (1837–1861), a Civil War hero. There is an important junction of the Boston & Maine, and Delaware & Hudson Railroads here.

161.00 Anthony Kill to west.

161.25 Highway Bridge.

161.25 Hemstreet Park to east. A small residential community fronting on the Hudson River.

161.25 Schaghticoke to east. This is five miles inland beyond Hemstreet Park on Route 118. It is hidden by hills from the Hudson River. It is a much larger community than Hemstreet Park and is situated on the Hoosic River.

161.75 Lock No. 3.

162.00 Stillwater Junction to west. The Boston & Maine, and Saratoga & Schuylerville Railroads used to meet here. The Saratoga & Schuylerville is now abandoned.

162.40 Riverside to west.

162.50 Boston & Maine Railroad bridge. Built by the Boston, Hoosac Tunnel & Western Railway Co. in

LOCK # 3—CHAMPLAIN CANAL. Photo: Alfred H. Marks.

1879, it is on the present mainline between Boston and Rotterdam Junction, N.Y.

163.00 Green Island. It is located to the west of the navigation channel.

163.50 Hoosic River to east. Originally called the Walloomsac, and also spelled Hoosac and Hoosick, it is the Indian name for "place of stones." It rises in Cheshire Reservoir in the Berkshire Mountains of Massachusetts, south of Adams. Then it flows north past Adams and North Adams, thence west to Williamstown, where it is joined from the south by the Green River. It then turns northwest and enters Vermont near Pownal. After passing North Pownal,

Vermont, it enters New York and flows past North Petersburg, Hoosick, Hoosick Falls, and North Hoosick to Eagle Bridge. Here it turns directly west and flows past Buskirk, Johnsonville, Valley Falls, and Schaghticoke before entering the Hudson.

164.00 Lock No. 4. In east channel.

164.30 Stillwater to west.

164.30 Schuyler Creek to west.

164.30 Route 67 bridge across Hudson River.

164.30 Washington County to east. It has an area of 837 square miles. Hudson Falls is the county seat. It was taken from Tryon County in 1784 and was named in honor of George Washington. Tryon County had been established in 1772 and named for Gov. William Tryon of New York. It was taken from Albany County and included all settlements west and southwest of Schenectady as well as the present Washington County. Tryon County no longer exists, all its area having been assigned to other counties.

165.30 Mill Hollow Brook to east.

168.00 Bemis Heights to west.

168.00 Site of rope ferry, operational in 1860.

168.20–171.20 Saratoga National Historical Park to west. On October 17, 1777, General Horatio Gates, with a varied collection of troops calling themselves an American army, defeated an invading British force under Gen. John ("Gentleman Johnny") Burgoyne and prevented British control of the strategic Hudson Valley. This was the turning point of the American fortunes, and directly led to French intervention on the American side.

It was the grand strategy of the English to gain control of the Hudson Valley between Canada and New York City and thus split New England from the other colonies. To prevent this, Washington determined to hold the Highlands of the Hudson and the upper Hudson Valley at all costs. In the great British campaign of 1777, the chief strategy was for Gen. John Burgoyne to march down from Canada via Lake Champlain and hook up with Sir William Howe and Sir Henry Clinton, who were to move up from New York, and with Barry St. Leger, who was to march from the west via Oswego and the Mohawk Valley. Burgoyne was halted at the Battle of Saratoga and St. Leger at the Battle of Oriskany. For reasons undetermined, Howe and Clinton failed to move north from New York according to schedule. Thus the campaign was abortive, and the American victories were a turning point in the long war. The British never did succeed in splitting the colonies, although

they made a foray as far north as Clermont on the Hudson in 1777 and burned Kingston.

Generals Philip Schuyler, Benedict Arnold, and Gates led the American side. The Hessian Baron Reidesel and Generals Phillips and Simon Fraser served under Burgoyne.

There is a visitors' center and nine miles of drives with site markers. A free folder maps the battlefield route. Demonstrations are offered afternoons in July and August.

168.50 Mill Creek to west.

169.30 Kidney Creek to east.

170.00 Kroma Kill to west.

171.20 McAuley Brook to east.

171.21 Site of Powers-Briggs rope ferry.

172.45 Site of Sarles rope ferry (operational from the early nineteenth century to about 1930).

172.60 Schuyler Brook to east.

172.80 Wilbur's Basin to west. This is an old Champlain canal basin.

173.00 Ensign Brook to east.

174.90 Holmes Hill to west.

175.00 Flately Brook to east.

175.80 Coveville and The Cove to west. This was formerly called Do-ve-gat and Van Vechten's Cove.

176.50–178.00 Site of American fortifications of 1777 on hill to east.

177.00 Fryer Brook to east.

178.25 Site of Fort Clinton to west. This is a French and Indian War fortification.

178.25 Victory Mills to west. Beyond fortifications, located on Fish Creek.

178.50 General Phillip Schuyler House to west. On the south side of Fish Creek, this is a restored two-story clapboard structure dating back to 1777. The original house was burned at the time of the Battle of Saratoga.

In 1745, there stood a brick mansion on this site, owned and occupied by a kinsman of Philip Schuyler. This house was attacked by a band of Frenchmen and Indians, and the owner was shot and his body consumed by flames. This property was then bequeathed to his nephew Philip, who built a country mansion on the site. In 1777 Gen. Burgoyne ordered the house burned—an act which he later came to regret upon making the personal acquain-

SCHUYLER HOUSE, SCHUYLERVILLE. Photo: Author's collection.

tance of Gen. Schuyler, who treated him very well when his prisoner. Schuyler built the present house as replacement soon thereafter, and used it as his country seat until his death in 1804.

178.80 Greenwich to east. Inland from river and not visible.

178.80 Fish Creek or Fish Kill to west.

178.80 Schuylerville to west. The village occupies the site of Gen. Burgoyne's entrenched camp at the time he surrendered. The Bullard Paper Mills were operating here in about 1870. Formerly, a bridge of the Greenwich & Johnsonville Railroad (now defunct) crossed the Hudson from here to Thomson. It was washed out and was never replaced.

178.80 Route 29 bridge.

179.00 Site of Fort Hardy to west. This dates back to the French & Indian Wars.

179.00 Fort Saratoga to east.

180.00 Batten Kill to east. The Di-On-On-Deh-O-Wa or "great falls" of the Batten Kill are a short way up-stream. The Batten Kill rises near Ludlow, Vermont, and flows south past Danby, Mount Tabor, Manchester, and Arlington. Here it turns west and flows past West Arlington and into New York State. It continues west past Shushan, East Greenwich, Battenville, Greenwich, and Middle Falls to the Hudson.

180.10 Lock No. 5 to west.

180.10 Site of Hessian camp of 1777 to east.

180.50 Site of crossing of British forces in 1777.

180.60 Clarks Mills to east.

180.75 Stark's Knob to west. Site of key battery that blocked British in 1777.

SARATOGA BATTLE MONUMENT. Photo: Author's collection.

181.00 Dam.

181.30 Northumberland to west.

181.30 Thomson to east.

181.40 U.S. Route 4 bridge.

182.00 Bacon Hill to west.

183.00 Van Antwerp Creek to east.

184.00 Slocum Creek to east.

184.25 Saratoga Dam.

184.25 Lock No. 6 to east.

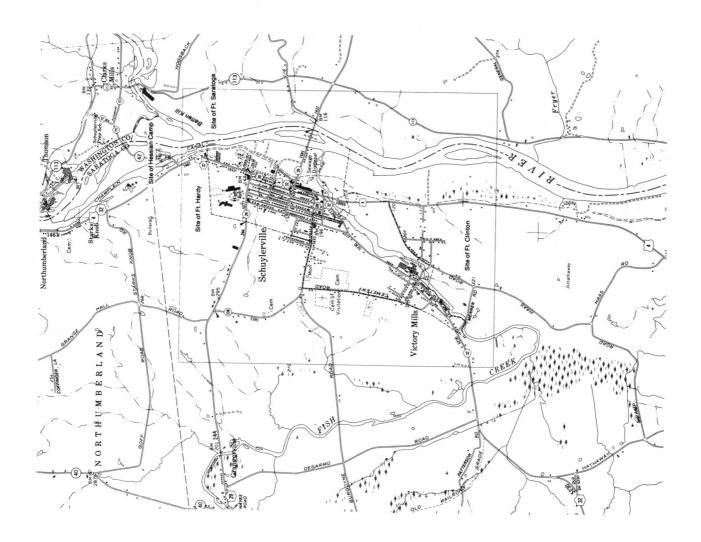

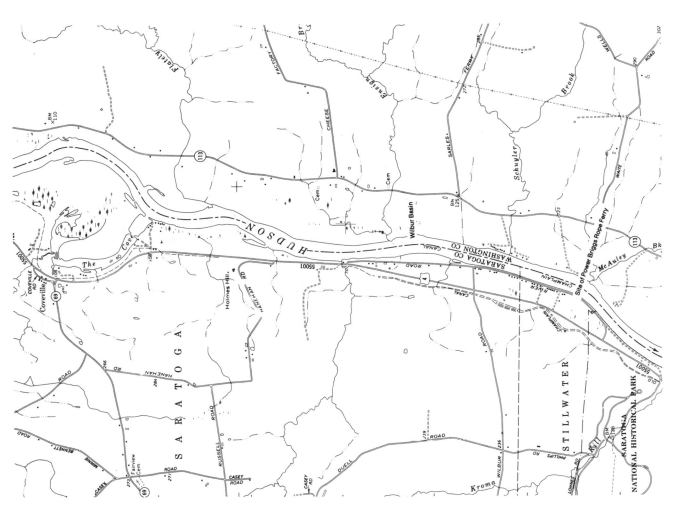

SCHUYLERVILLE

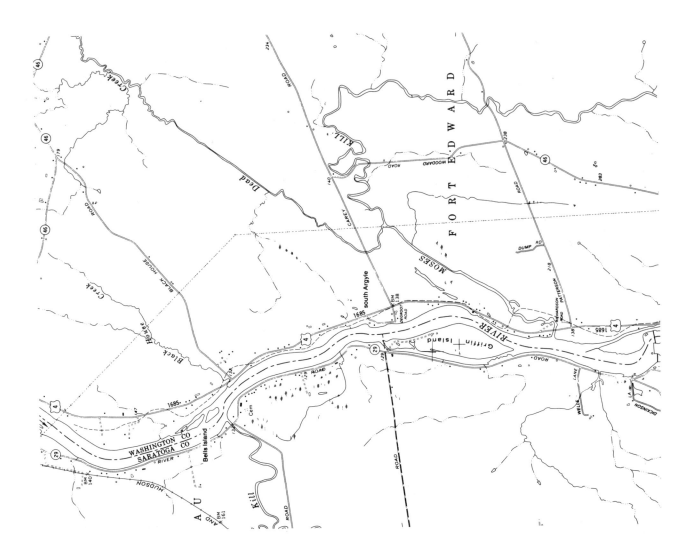

FORT MILLER

185.00 Fort Miller to east. This is a small community. There was a small fort on the west shore of the Hudson in the French and Indian War. There are no remains.

186.00 Payne's Island.

186.45 Dams.

186.50 Normal Pool.

187.00 Gansevoort to west (inland on Route 32).

187.25 Galusha's Island

187.75 Thompson Island.

188.00 Moses Kill to east.

188.25 Griffin Island.

188.50 South Argyle to east.

189.50 Black House Creek to east.

189.60 Snook Kill to west.

189.90 Bell's Island.

190.25 Fort Edward Center to east. Here are located the Gansevoort Mill House of 1781 and the Fort Edward Center Friends' Meeting House (clapboard, early nineteenth century).

190.25 Munro's Island.

192.20 Lock No. 7 of Champlain Canal. This canal leaves the Hudson here and follows Bond Creek to the northeast and Whitehall, at the southern tip of Lake Champlain.

192.20 Bond Creek to east.

192.25–193.00 Roger's Island. Armies were encamped here during the French and Indian War. This island was associated with Maj. Robert Rogers.

FORT MILLER MEETING HOUSE. Photo: Alfred H. Marks.

192.50 Site of Fort Edward to east. One of the largest garrisons in North America during the French and Indian Wars. It has left no significant remains. Built by Phineas Lyman in 1755, it was briefly occupied by Burgoyne in 1777.

192.50 Fort Edward to east. It was incorporated in 1849. Paper milling is the principal industry. There is a Delaware & Hudson (Amtrak) passenger station here.

192.80 Delaware & Hudson Railroad bridge. The first railroad bridges here were built in 1876 and 1880. The present bridge was built in 1924 and reconstructed in 1941. It was engineered by the D. & H. engineering department and was built by AmBridge Company. It carries the main line to Canada.

192.90 Route 197 bridge.

193.00 McCrae House to east. This is a clapboard, late-eighteenth-century structure. There is a famous legend associated with this locality. I shall quote at length from Benson Lossing's *The Hudson:*

Fort Edward was strengthened by the republicans, and properly garrisoned, when the revolution broke out in 1775. When General Burgoyne, with his invading army of British regulars, hired Germans, French, Canadians and Indians, appeared at the foot of Lake Champlain, General Philip Schuyler was the commander in Chief of the republican army in the Northern Department. His headquarters were at Fort Anne, and General St. Clair commanded the important post of Ticonderoga. In July, Burgoyne came sweeping down the lake triumphantly. St. Clair fled from Ticonderoga, and his army was scattered and sorely smitten in the retreat. When the British advanced to Skenesborough, at the head of the lake, Schuyler retreated to Fort Edward, felling trees across the old military road, demolishing the causeways over the great Kingsbury marshes, and destroying the bridges, to obstruct the invader's progress. With great labour and perseverance Burgoyne moved forward, and on the 29th of July he encamped upon the high bank of the Hudson at the great bend where the village of Sandy Hill now stands.

At this time a tragedy occurred near Fort Edward, which produced a great sensation throughout the country, and has been a theme for history, poetry, romance, and song. It was the death of Jenny M'Crea, the daughter of a Scotch Presbyterian clergyman, who is described as lovely in disposition, graceful in manners, and so intelligent and winning in all her ways, that she was a favourite of all who

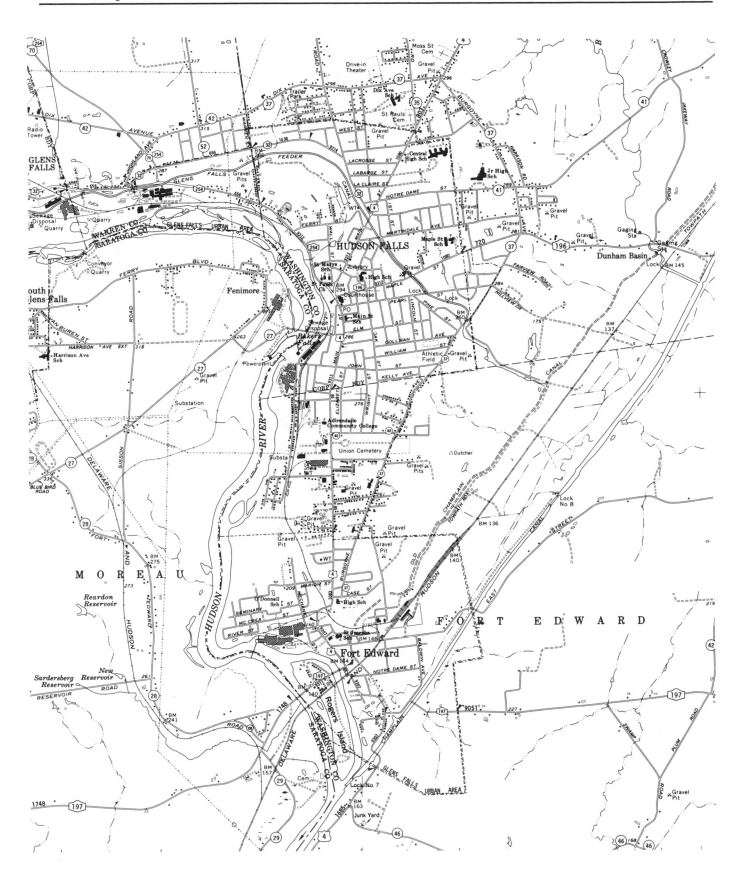

HUDSON FALLS

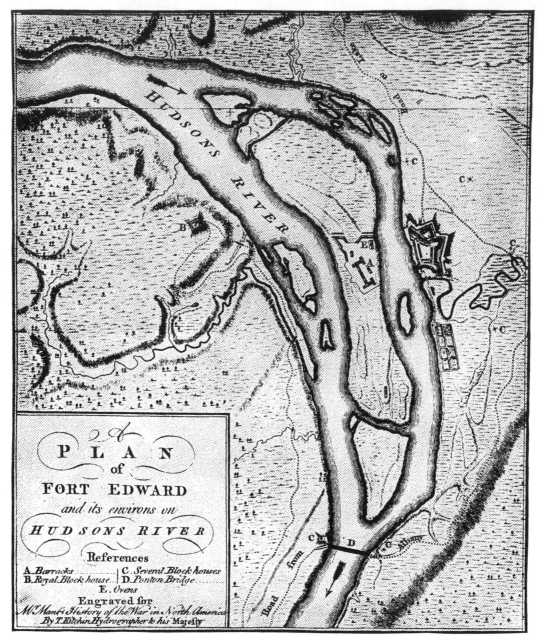

FORT EDWARD and its environs on Hudson River circa 1755.

knew her. She was visiting a Tory friend at Fort Edward, at this time, and was betrothed to a young man of the neighborhood, who was a subaltern in Burgoyne's army. On the approach of the invaders her brother, who lived near, fled, with his family, down the river and desired Jenny to accompany them. She preferred to stay under the protection of her Tory friend, who was a widow, and a cousin of General Fraser of Burgoyne's army.

Burgoyne had found it difficult to restrain the cruelty of his Indians. To secure their cooperation he had offered them a bounty for prisoners and scalps, at the same time forbidding them to kill any person

not in arms for the sake of scalps. The offer of bounties stimulated the savages to seek captives other than those in the field, and they went out in small parties for the purpose. One of these prowled around Fort Edward early on the morning after Burgoyne arrived at Sandy Hill, and, entering the house where Jenny was staying, carried away the young lady and her friend. A negro boy alarmed the garrison, and a detachment was sent after the Indians, who were fleeing with their prisoners toward the camp. They had caught two horses, and on one of them Jenny was already placed by them, when the detachment assailed them with a volley of musketry. The savages were unharmed, but one of the bullets mortally wounded their fair captive. She fell and expired, as tradition relates, near a pine-tree, which remained as a memorial of the tragedy until a few years ago. Having lost their prisoner they secured her scalp, and with her black tresses wet with her warm blood, they hastened to the camp. The friend of Jenny had just arrived, and the locks of the maiden, which were of great length and beauty, were recognized by her. She charged the Indians with her murder, which they denied, and told the story substantially as it is here related.

This appears, from the corroborating circumstances, to be the simple truth of a story which, as it went from lip to lip, became magnified into a tale of darkest horror, and produced a widespread indignation. General Gates, who had just superseded General Schuyler in the command of the northern army, took advantage of the excitement which it produced, to increase the hatred of the British in the hearts of the people, and he charged Burgoyne with crimes utterly foreign to the gentleman's nature. In a published letter, he accused him of hiring savages to "scalp Europeans and the descendants of Europeans"; spoke of Jenny as having been "dressed to meet her promised husband, but met her murderers" employed by Burgoyne; asserted that she with several women and children, had been taken "from the house into the woods, and there scalped and mangled in a most shocking manner," and alleged that he had "Paid the price of blood!" This letter so untruthful and ungenerous, was condemned by Gates's friends in the army. But it had the desired effect; and the sad story of Jenny's death was used with power against the ministry by the opposition in the British parliament.

The lover of Jenny left the army, and settled in Canada, where he lived to be an old man. He was naturally gay and garrulous, but after that event he was ever sad and taciturn. He never married, and avoided society. When the anniversary of the tragedy approached, he would shut himself in his room, and refuse to see his most intimate acquaintances; and at all times his friends avoided speaking of the American revolution in his presence. The body of Jenny was buried on her brother's land; it was re-interred at Fort Edward in 1826, with imposing ceremonies; and again in 1852, her remains found a new resting-place in a beautiful cemetery, half-way between Fort Edward and Sandy Hill. Her grave is near the entrance; and upon a plain white marble stone, six feet in height, standing at its head, is the following inscription:

Here rest the remains of Jane M'Crea, aged 17; made captive and murdered by a band of Indians,

while on a visit to a relative in the neighbourhood, A.D. 1777. To commemorate one of the most thrilling incidents in the annals of the American revolution, to do justice to the fame of the gallant British officer to whom she was affianced, and as a simple tribute to the memory of the departed, this stone is erected by her niece, Sarah Hanna Payne, A.D. 1852.
(Lossing, The Hudson, pp. 76–79.)

194.00 Gravel pits to east.

194.00 Moreau Township to west.

195.30 Power plant to west.

195.50 Baker's Falls. The river here is about 400 feet in width. The entire descent of the water, in the course of a mile, is between 70 and 80 feet.

195.60 Sewage disposal plant to east.

195.60 Road bridge.

196.00 Hudson Falls to east. With a population of 7,917, this is the seat of Washington County. Originally called Sandy Hill, it was settled in 1761 and incorporated in 1810. Papermaking is the principal industry. It is on the Glens Falls (formerly Lake

HUDSON'S FALLS. Building on right is the General Electric plant, source of PCB contamination. Photo: © Gretchen McHugh.

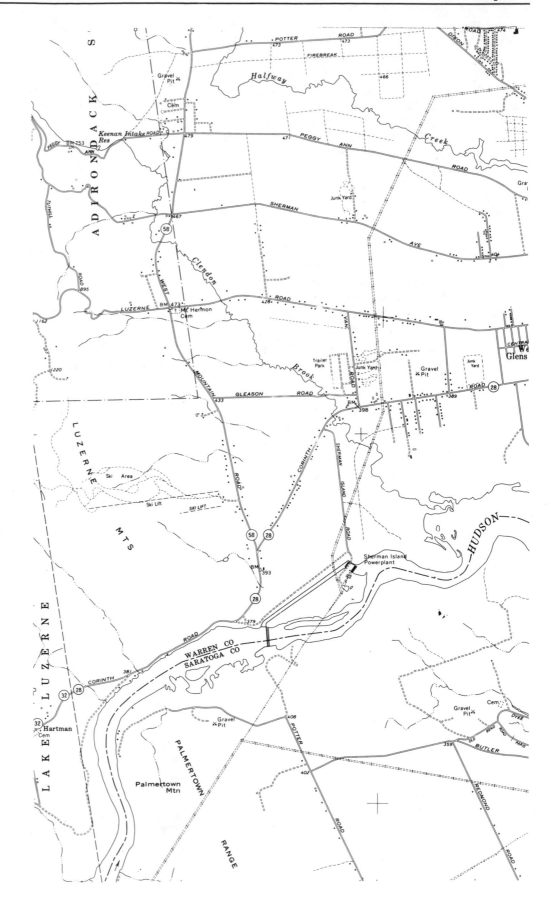

GLENS FALLS

GLENS FALLS. Photo: Alfred H. Marks.

George) branch of Delaware & Hudson Railroad. There is a very attractive town square here.

196.00 Fenimore to west.

196.50 Big Bend. Here the river bends to the west.

197.00 Gravel pits to north.

197.50 Quarries to north and south.

198.00 Sewage disposal plant to north.

198.50 Quarry to north.

198.50 Paper mills to north.

199.00 Cooper's Cave. In island in midstream in rapids.

199.10 Glens Falls (dam and power canals on sides). Again we will quote from Benson Lossing's *The Hudson:*

Glen's Falls consist of a series of rapids and cascades, along a descent of about eighty feet, the water flowing over ragged masses of black marble, which here form the bed and banks of the river. Hawkeye, in Cooper's "Last of the Mohicans," has given an admirable description of these falls, as they appeared before the works of man changed their features. He is standing in a cavern, or irregular arched way, in the rock below the bridge, in the time of the old French war with Uncas and Major

LOG POND AND DAM AT GLENS FALLS. Photo: © Gretchen McHugh.

FINCH PRUYN MILL, GLENS FALLS. Photo: Alfred H. Marks.

Heywood, and Cora and Alice Munro, the daughters of the commandant at Fort William Henry, on Lake George, when Montcalm with his motley horde of French and Indians was approaching. "Ay," he said, "there are the falls on two sides of us, and the river above and below. If you had daylight, it would be worth the trouble to step up on the height of this rock, and look at the perversity of the water. It falls by no rule at all: sometimes it leaps, sometimes it tumbles; there it skips—here it shoots; hereabouts, it pitches into deep hollows, that rumble and quake the 'arth, and thereaway it ripples and sings like a brook, fashioning whirlpools and gullies in the old stone, as if 'twere no harder than trodden clay. The whole design of the river seems disconcerted. First, it runs smoothly, as if meaning to go down the descent as things were ordered; then it angles about and faces the shores; nor are there places wanting where it looks backward, as if unwilling to leave the wilderness to mingle with the salt!

The falls had few of these features when we visited them (1866). The volume of water was so small that the stream was almost hidden in the deep chan-

nels in the rock worn by the current during the lapse of centuries.

(Lossing, *The Hudson*, pp. 67–68.)

Lossing's final comment is still true in 1991. Most of the water is diverted to side canals. Only after a heavy rainfall, or during the spring runoff of melting snows in the Adirondacks, can a fine flow of water be seen. When the writer was a boy, it used to be possible to descend to the rocks in the falls by means of a staircase from the Route 9 bridge. This is now closed off, and it is quite difficult to see the falls today.

199.10 Route 9 bridge.

199.10 South Glens Falls to south.

199.10 Glens Falls to north. With a population of 17,222, this place was called Chepontuo by the Indians, meaning "a difficult place to get around." The area was part of the 23,000-acre Queensbury Patent. It was first settled in 1763. In 1780 it was destroyed by the British. In 1788 Col. John Glen of Schenectady acquired and built mills here. It was incorporated as a village in 1839 and as a city in 1908. The manufacture of shirts and cellulose was started in 1879. Principal industries are pulp and paper mills and the manufacture of clothing. Glens Falls is the birthplace of Charles Evans Hughes (1862–1948), lawyer, jurist, statesman, and Chief Justice of the United States Supreme Court.

200.00 Pruyn's Island.

200.00 Log Pool. In past years a great boom was strung across the river here to collect the logs sent downriver during the drives and prevent their going over the falls and being splintered.

314.00 Lake Tear of the Clouds (elevation 4,322 feet). On the slopes of Mount Marcy, elevation 5,344 feet. This is the highest source of the Hudson.

7

Excursion Information

Southbound Express Route to Start of Lower West Side Route

0.00 (−0.25 E.R.M.) Start at east end of Lincoln Tunnel, Eighth Avenue and West 39th Street, Manhattan. Enter Lincoln Tunnel westbound. Take Interstate 495 to the New Jersey Turnpike.

−4.00 Interstate 95. Enter Turnpike at Secaucus.

−6.00 Snake Hill on right. Mentioned by Washington Irving in his *Knickerbocker History of New York*, it is now almost totally destroyed by quarry operations.

−6.75 Cross Hackensack River. Cross New York & Greenwood Lake Railroad (now N. J. Transit). You have been running parallel to the former Pennsylvania Railroad main line on the left. This is now Amtrak's Northeast Corridor Route.

−8.50 Cross the Morris & Essex Division of the former DL&W RR, now N. J. Transit, former P.R.R. lines, now Amtrak, and former Hudson & Manhattan Railroad, now PATH.

−8.55 Cross Passaic River. Newark is to the right.

−9.00 Pass beneath the Pulaski Skyway, named after Polish patriot Casimir Pulaski (1747–1779), who fought in the American Revolution. A nobleman by birth, he came to America with a letter of introduction to George Washington from Benjamin Franklin. He fought in the battles of Brandywine and Germantown. In 1778 he resigned his cavalry command rather than serve under Anthony Wayne. He formed his own cavalry unit, the Pulaski Legion, and was mortally wounded while leading a cavalry charge in the attack on Savannah, Georgia. The Pulaski Skyway carries U. S. Routes 1A and 9A and provides panoramic views.

−11.25 Exit for Newark International Airport, a facility of the Port Authority of New York and New Jersey. Operated under a lease from the city of Newark dating from 1948, it was first opened on October 1,

1928 and then consisted of only 68 acres. Today it has 2,300 acres. There are three major runways and more than twelve miles of seventy-five-foot-wide taxiways. Newark is regularly served by scheduled airlines with flights to all parts of the world. The beautiful, new passenger terminals A, B, and C were completed in 1972, 1973, and 1988 respectively. The airport is fully equipped with the most modern navigational equipment. In 1987 the airport handled 368,000 plane movements, 23,475,000 commercial passengers, 325,000 tons of air cargo.

−11.25 Exit for bridge across Newark Bay to Bayonne and Holland Tunnel.

−12.25 Port Newark on left. Parallel railroad on left is former line of Central Railroad of New Jersey, now Conrail.

−13.25 Elizabeth–Port Authority Marine Terminal on left. Port Newark was opened by the city of Newark in 1915 and came under Port Authority operation in 1948. There is berthing space with 23,387 lineal feet of wharfage and 848 acres of shoreside staging area. The port handled 1,873,955 long tons in 1975. There are thirteen miles of roadway and thirty-eight miles of railroad tracks and three major container ship terminals. Facilities include public cold storage warehouses, a frozen meat inspection building, a wine terminal, a fumigation building, seventy miscellaneous service buildings, a public truck scales, a Waterfront Commission Employment Center, a Seamen's Church Institute Recreation Center, and two commercial bank buildings. Major container ship facilities belong to the Maersk Red Star Line and Universal Terminal and Stevedoring Corp. The Elizabeth-Port Authority Marine Terminal is the major container port of the United States. Twenty-two container cranes serve the same number of container ship berths—16,934 linear feet of wharfage. Port Authority operation began in 1958. In 1975 8,099,841 long tons of cargo were handled. Major steamship lines operating from the port are Sea-Land Service, Inc.; Puerto Rico Maritime Shipping Authority; Atlantic Container Line, Ltd. Smaller lines are served by the stevedoring facilities of International Operating Co., Pittston Stevedoring Corp. and Maher Terminals, Inc.

-15.20 Spires of St. Patrick's R. C. Church, built 1887, prominent on the left.

- 15.25 Elizabethport. Cross former main line of Central Railroad of New Jersey, now Conrail.

- 15.50 Elizabeth to right. The tall building is the Union County Courthouse (1903) by Ackerman & Ross.

- 16.50 Cross Elizabeth River.

- 16.75 Pass beneath western approach to Goethal's Bridge. See article on Arthur Kill. Staten Island to left.

- 17.25 Cross Morse's Creek.

- 19.75 Cross Rahway River.

- 20.25 Raritan Arsenal on right. Carteret on left.

- 22.50 Port Reading on left.

- 23.75 Sewaren on left.

- 23.80 Cross Woodbridge Creek. Woodbridge on right.

- 24.00 Cross former Pennsylvania Railroad Perth Amboy Branch, now New Jersey Transit, used by North Jersey Shore trains.

- 25.00 Exit 11: Leave New Jersey Turnpike. Enter Garden State Parkway, southbound.

- 27.00 Perth Amboy to left.

- 28.00 (- 20.00 E.R.M.) Cross Raritan River on Alfred E. Driscoll Memorial Bridge, named for a former New Jersey governor.

- 29.00 Pay toll.

- 36.50 Exit 117, Matawan; *exit from* Parkway. Enter Route 36 east.

- 49.50 Highlands: *turn right* off Route 36 onto Portland Road, just before coming to drawbridge.

- 49.51 *Turn right immediately* on Highland Avenue.

- 49.55 *Bear left uphill* on Lighthouse Road.

- 49.70 Twin Lights (- 23.00 E.R.M.). See article on River Route.

Lower West Side Road Route

0.00 (- 23.00 E.R.M.) Historic Twin Lights. Start downhill on Light House Road.

0.20 *Turn right* on Highland Avenue.

0.30 Cross Portland Road.

0.40 *Turn left* under bridge. Navesink River on right.

0.41 *Turn left* again up onto Route 36 West.

0.45 Gertrude Ederle Park on right.

0.50 *Turn right* on Route 36 West, Memorial Drive.

1.60 *Turn right* on Scenic Road.

1.80 *Bend right* on Scenic Road.

2.10 Mt. Mitchell scenic overlook on right. Extensive views of Sandy Hook and Lower Bay. Eastpointe Apartments to the right. Adequate parking.

2.60 Viewpoint on right. Bachert's Hofbrauhaus on left.

3.20 *Bear right.*

3.50 View of Raritan Bay on right.

3.60 Atlantic Highlands town line.

4.30 *Turn right* on First Avenue.

5.10 *Turn around:* foot of First Avenue and Sutton Walk. Site of former combined steamboat and railroad pier and terminal. Adequate parking and public rest rooms available.

5.15 *Turn left* on Ocean Boulevard.

6.00 Cross bridge.

6.10 *Turn left* on Lawrie Road.

6.15 *Bear left* on Hilton Road.

6.30 *Bear left* on Bayside Road.

6.40 Historic Henry Hudson Spring on left. Henry Hudson replenished his ship's water supply at this spring in 1609. It was used for similar purposes by ships through the early twentieth century.

8.00 Road turns to good gravel pavement.

8.20 Hard pavement resumes.

9.50 *Bear left.*

9.60 *Turn right* on Shore Drive (large willow tree and Marie Manor Apartments on right).

9.80 *Turn left* on Water Witch Avenue.

9.90 *Turn right* on Bay Avenue, Route 8.

10.70 Go under bridge.

10.80 *Turn right up hill on Highland Avenue.*

10.90 *Turn sharp right* onto Route 36 East and bridge.

11.00 Cross Navesink River. Seawall and Atlantic Ocean straight ahead.

11.20 *Turn right* around cloverleaf to Sandy Hook.

11.60 Gateway National Recreation Area, Sandy Hook.

11.90 Fishing Area No. 1, dunes.

13.30 Ocean bathing area No. 1.

13.50 Spermaceti Cove Visitor Center on right.

13.60 Ocean bathing area No. 2.

13.70 *Turn around.* End of open public road. Entrance to Fort Hancock. Worth visiting when open.

13.70 (-21.50 E.R.M.) See Sandy Hook article.

16.40 Cross Navesink River. Continue on Route 36 West, Memorial Drive.

20.10 *Turn right* on First Avenue, Atlantic Highlands.

20.30 *Turn left* on West Highland Avenue.

20.50 Cross brook.

21.30 *Turn right* on Leonard Avenue.

21.70 *Turn left* on Beach Avenue.

21.90 Leonardo Beach. *Turn around.* State Marina.

22.10 Conover Beach Beacon.

22.10 *Turn right* on Leonard Avenue.

22.60 *Turn right* on Route 36 West.

22.70 Pass beneath U.S. Government Railroad, which connects the U.S. Naval Ammunition Depot at Earle with the Navy long pier at Leonardo on Sandy Hook Bay.

22.80 Entrance Naval ammunition depot.

SEABROOK HOMESTEAD AT PORT MONMOUTH. Land side view. Photo: Alfred H. Marks.

23.60 *Turn right* on East Road.

24.10 *Turn right* on Main Street. Belford.

24.50 Boatyards on Compton Creek. Repair facilities for the fishing fleet. *Turn around.* Middletown Public Dock.

24.60 *Turn right* on Broadway.

24.70 Cross Compton Creek.

24.90 *Turn right* on Main Street.

25.10 *Turn left* on Port Monmouth Road.

25.30 Seabrook Homestead on right, at foot of Wilson Avenue. Now houses Shoal Harbor Marine Museum with displays of the fishing and shipping trades. Maintained by the Middletown Township Historical Society, this house was built ca. 1664–1668 by Thomas Whitlock, who moved here from Long Island. From 1696 until 1910 it was the homestead of the Seabrook family. In the late eighteenth century, it also served as a stagecoach tavern. As this was the only house on the dunes at the time of the Revolution, the British believed that the owners were spying on their ships. Actually, the spy was Col. John Stilwell, who was stationed on a high hill above the beach. The house was also known as the "Spy House."

25.30 *Turn left* on Wilson Avenue.

25.90 *Turn right* on Main Street.

26.30 *Turn right* on Bray Avenue.

26.80 Cross Pew's Creek.

27.80 Ideal Beach.

27.80 *Turn left* on Seabreeze Avenue.

28.00 *Bear right* on Shore Boulevard.

28.00 Keansburg.

28.60 (-21.00 E.R.M.)

28.61 *Turn right* on Main Street.

28.70 *Bear left* on Beachway.

29.00 Point Comfort-Keansburg (-21.00 E.R.M.); former steamboat pier.

30.50 *Bear left* onto Laurel Avenue.

30.60 *Turn right* on Route 36 West.

31.70 Cross Thorne's Creek.

31.72 Natco Lake on right.

31.75 Union Beach.

31.75 *Turn right* on Shore Road.

32.00 *Turn left* on Jersey Avenue.

32.10 *Turn right* on Union Avenue.

32.40 Cross Flat Creek.

32.70 View of Raritan Bay, Staten Island, Verrazano Bridge.

32.70 Road becomes Front Street.

33.10 Coneskonk Point.

33.10 *Turn left* on Dock Street.

33.50 *Turn right* on Florence Avenue.

33.90 Cross brook.

34.10 *Turn right* on Broadway.

34.40 Cross Chingarora Creek.

34.50 *Bear right* on First Street.

35.10 Keyport.

35.10 *Turn right* on Broad Street.

35.20 View of Raritan Bay and Matawan Creek.

35.20 *Turn left* on American Legion Drive.

35.50 *Turn right* on West Front Street.

35.60 Cross Luppatatcong Creek.

35.90 Cross Matawan Creek.

37.10 Cliffwood Beach Development on right.

39.10 Cross Whale Creek, Madison township line.

39.10 Leave Monmouth County. Enter Middlesex County.

39.35 Florence Harbor Section of Cliffwood Beach.

39.40 Pirate Ship Building on left. An old landmark.

40.50 Cross Marquis Creek.

40.50 Laurence Harbor line.

41.40 Cross Cheesecake Creek; extensive view to right.

41.65 Cross New York & Long Branch Railroad, Conrail system, New Jersey Transit.

42.00 Morgan.

42.40 *Bear right* on South Pine Avenue.

43.50 *Turn right* on Bordentown Avenue.

43.60 Cross Raritan Valley Railroad (independent short line, running from South Amboy to New Brunswick).

43.70 *Turn left* on South Stevens Avenue.

44.10 South Amboy. Population 7,863.

44.10 *Turn right* on Main Street.

44.30 Public Service Electric & Gas Co. power plant on right.

44.40 Pass under Camden & Amboy Railroad (formerly Pennsylvania Railroad; now Conrail system). New Jersey's first railroad—1831.

45.30 Traffic circle.

45.30 *Bear right* on Route 35.

45.90 Begin Victory Bridge across Raritan River.

46.20 Thomas A. Edison Bridge (Route U.S. 9) and Alfred E. Driscoll Bridge (Garden State Parkway) to left.

46.20 New York & Long Branch Railroad bridge to right.

46.50 End of Victory Bridge.

46.70 *Turn right* on Main Street (formerly Smith Street).

46.70 Perth Amboy. Settled in 1683 and incorporated in 1718, it was the capital of East Jersey from 1686 until the union of East and West Jersey, and thereafter, for a time, alternate capital with Burlington. Great growth came after 1876, when it became the tidewater terminal of the Lehigh Valley Railroad, and much coal was shipped from here. It is still the seat of the General Proprietors of the Eastern Division of New Jersey. This organization still holds shares and meets regularly to distribute any new lands discovered in its portion of New Jersey. The population is 41,967. Principal industries are the smelting and refining of metals. Formerly there was an extensive brick, tile, pottery, and terracotta industry here.

47.00 *Turn right* on Bertrand Street.

47.10 *Turn left* on Market Street.

47.50 Cross over the New York & Long Branch Railroad (Conrail system), New Jersey Transit.

47.50 Perth Amboy railroad station on left.

48.00 Traffic circle.

48.00 *Turn right* on High Street.

48.40 *Turn left* on Sadowski Parkway.

48.40 Waterfront Pavilion: view of Raritan Bay and River and railroad hopper car dumpers in South Amboy across the river.

48.60 Street becomes Water Street.

48.60 Arthur Kill on right.

48.90 *Turn right* on Gordon Street.

48.95 *Turn left* on Front Street.

49.00 Former ferry to Tottenville, Staten Island.

49.00 *Turn left* on Smith Street.

49.20 *Turn right* on High Street.

49.70 *Turn left* on Buckingham Avenue.

49.90 *Turn right* on State Street.

50.50 *Turn left* on Hall Avenue.

50.55 Cross over New York & Long Branch Railroad.

50.70 *Turn right* on Amboy Avenue.

50.90 *Turn right* onto Grove Street.

50.95 Enter Outerbridge Crossing across the Arthur Kill to Staten Island.

50.95 Route 440 East.

51.20 Begin bridge.

52.00 Cross Arthur Kill. Extensive views of Raritan Bay area.

52.00 Tottenville. The southernmost town on Staten Island and in New York State, this is the southern terminus of the Staten Island Rapid Transit line to Saint George. Former ferry to Perth Amboy. Settled ca. 1680 as manor of Tottenville, granted to Christopher Billop by Gov. Thomas Dongan. The property immediately adjacent to the Outerbridge Crossing was settled ca. 1712 by members of the Dissosway (Dusachoy, Dusochany, Dusway, etc.) family. They were descendants of the Huguenot Marc du Sauchoy who came to the New Netherlands shortly before 1655.

52.90 End of bridge (pay toll eastbound only). Staten Island, New York. Get into far right lane before toll booths for immediate sharp right turn exit beyond toll booths.

53.00 *Turn right* on Page Avenue exit.

53.10 *Turn right* on Boscombe Avenue.

53.20 *Turn left* on Page Avenue.

53.30 *Turn right* on Richmond Valley Road.

53.50 *Turn left* on Arthur Kill Road.

53.60 Cross creek.

53.60 Nassau Smelting and Refining Co. plant on left. This division of Western Electric Co. melts down old telephone equipment and cables to retrieve copper and brass for reuse.

53.80 Cross Staten Island Rapid Transit railroad.

53.80 *Bear right*.

54.40 *Turn left* on Main Street, Tottenville.

54.50 *Turn right* on Craig Avenue.

54.80 Cross Amboy Road. Continue on Craig Avenue.

55.20 *Turn left* on Hylan Boulevard. Named for John Francis Hylan (1868–1936), a political leader and mayor of New York City 1918–1925. He was born in Greene County, New York, and attended New York Law School. He was an opponent of Tammany Hall and was known as "Red Mike" Hylan. Hylan Boulevard is the main thoroughfare along the eastern shore of Staten Island.

55.20 There is an interesting short sidetrip here. By turning right on Hylan Boulevard for 1/10 mile we come to the end of the road at the Billopp Conference House, at Ward's Point (−20.00 E.R.M.). This is the southernmost point in New York State. There are extensive views of Perth Amboy, New Jersey, and the junction of the Arthur Kill and the Raritan River at the head of Raritan Bay. The Billopp Conference House is a National Historic Landmark in Conference House Park. It was the early home of Christopher Billopp, a pioneer settler. Here Benjamin Franklin, John Adams, and Edward Rutledge met with Lord Howe and Sir Henry Strachey on September 11, 1776 in an unsuccessful conference to settle with the British.

56.30 Tottenville Pool on right. Continue on Hylan Boulevard.

57.10 Mount Loretto on left. These are the burned-out ruins of Mission of the Immaculate Virgin—Mount Loretto, a home for children founded by Father Drumgoole.

57.50 Prince's Bay on the right was an important oyster port until 1916.

58.20 Cross Wolfe's Brook.

58.50 Seguine Point to right.

58.90 (−18.00 E.R.M.) Wolfe's Pond Park on right.

59.60 Arbutus Lake on right. Huguenot Beach on right.

59.65 St. Joseph-by-the-Sea on right.

60.15 Seaside.

60.25 Sea Breeze House on right.

61.40 (− 15.50 E.R.M.)

61.40 Great Kill's Bay and Crooke's Point to right.

62.70 Great Kill's Park on right.

63.10 Great Kill's Section of Gateway National Recreation Area on right. Extensive natural areas, beaches, and public bath houses.

63.60 *Turn left* on Guyon Avenue. (E.R.M. -14.60)

64.60 Cross Staten Island Rapid Transit Railway. Oakwood Heights Station on right.

65.20 *Turn left* on Amboy Road.

65.30 *Turn right* on Clarke Avenue.

66.90 Richmondtown Historic area. A 100-acre site established in 1952, the restoration of the former County Center by the Staten Island Historical Society, and the city of New York, this area features demonstrations of weaving, spinning, dyeing, printing, pottery, and carpentry in July and August. There is also a museum.

67.40 Parking lot and Staten Island Historical Museum on right.

67.50 *Turn right* on Arthur Kill Road.

67.60 Voorlezer's House on left.

67.60 *Turn right* on Richmond Road.

68.70 *Turn left* on Rockland Avenue.

68.90 High Rock Nature Conservation Center on right.

69.20 *Turn right* on Manor Road.

69.20 (− 14.00 E.R.M.)

69.20 LaTourette Park on left.

69.30 Sea View Hospital on left.

70.50 Junction with Brielle Road on left.

70.70 *Turn right* on Ocean Terrace.

71.00 *Turn right* on Todt Hill Road.

71.70 *Turn left* on Four Corners Road.

72.00 *Bear left.*

72.30 *Turn left* on Richmond Road.

72.40 Perine House on right, 1476 Richmond Road, Dongan Hills. The house consists of two connecting buildings. The rear stone house is believed to have been erected ca. 1680 by Thomas Stillwell, an important man on Staten Island—constable, sheriff, magis-

trate, captain of the militia, and member of the colonial assembly. The stone house nearer the road is believed to have been erected ca. 1713 by Nathaniel Britton, Stillwell's son-in-law. Two wooden additions date from 1749 and 1758. In 1746 Britton's widow sold the house to Walter Dongan, nephew of Sir Thomas Dongan. In 1749 his son sold the house to Joseph Holmes, innkeeper. Holmes kept an inn here until his death in 1759. Ultimately the house passed to his daughter Ann Holmes, wife of Edward Perine. The house remained in the Perine family for over one hundred years. Hamilton Britton Perine sold the house to Donald C. Craig in 1913, and in 1915 it was purchased by the Staten Island Antiquarian Society, now the Staten Island Institute of Arts and Sciences. During the Revolution, British soldiers were quartered here.

72.50 *Turn right* on Delaware Avenue.

73.10 Go under Staten Island Rapid Transit.

73.30 *Turn right* on Hylan Boulevard; get into left lane.

73.50 *Turn left* on Seaview Avenue.

74.70 *Turn left* on Father Capodanno Boulevard, formerly called Seaside Boulevard. Franklin Delano Roosevelt Boardwalk is now on our right.

74.90 (− 12.80 E.R.M.)

74.90 Hoffman Island on right.

75.20 Parking area on right.

76.20 *Bend left* on Lily Pond Avenue.

76.75 St. Joseph's Hill Academy on left.

76.80 Pass beneath Interstate 278, Entrance to the Verrazano Narrows Bridge.

76.90 Road now becomes School Road.

77.30 Vandeventer's Point.

77.30 U. S. Army Fort Wadsworth on right. The oldest continually manned fortification on American continent, its museum exhibits depict the history of the U. S. Army. (Free, open Sunday, Monday, Thursday, Friday from 1–4 P.M., Saturday 10–9.)

77.30 *Turn left* on Bay Street.

77.35 Von Briesen Park on right: view of Verrazano Bridge. (− 11.00 E.R.M.)

77.95 Cross Hylan Boulevard.

78.00 (− 10.00 E.R.M.) Rosebank Section.

78.30 Pouch terminal on right. (− 9.70 E.R.M.)

78.50 Go under Staten Island Rapid Transit.

78.60 Bayley Seton Hospital on left. Formerly belonged to the U. S. Public Health Service. (-9.65 E.R.M.)

79.00 Tappen Park on left.

79.20 Stapleton Section, formerly Doyle's Ferry. (-9.60 E.R.M.)

79.70 Tompkinsville section.

79.70 *Bear right* on Bay Street.

80.00 St. George.

80.00 U. S. Coast Guard on right.

80.00 Ducksberry Point. (-8.50 E.R.M.)

80.00 Manhattan Ferry and Staten Island Rapid Transit Terminals on right.

80.00 *Bear left* on Richmond Terrace.

80.10 Richmond Borough Hall on left. This structure has four stories with a clock tower. In the style of a French town hall, it was built in 1906 by Carrère & Hastings, architects.

80.60 Staten Island Museum on left (corner of Wall Street). Art, photography, American Indian and local archeology, science, and natural history exhibits are here. (Tuesday–Saturday 10–5, Sunday 2–5.)

80.60 (-8.25 E.R.M.)

80.60 Robbins Reef and Constable Hook, Bayonne, on right.

80.60 Kill Van Kull right.

80.90 Pavillion Restaurant on left, in Greek Revival style.

81.60 Sailor's Snug Harbor on left: A group of Greek Revival buildings, in Ionic style, 1831–1833, by Martin E. Thompson, architect. Founded by Captain Robert R. Randall in 1833, it contains over fifty buildings. The marine paintings in the lobbies are interesting, as is a statue of Capt. Randall by August Saint-Gaudens, unveiled in 1884. This home for retired seamen is supported largely by revenues from extensive land holdings in Manhattan.

83.30 Cross Clove Road.

83.35 Cross Clove Brook (in a corrugated pipe culvert).

83.40 *Bear right* on Richmond Terrace.

83.50 Pass beneath Staten Island Rapid Transit.

SAILOR'S SNUG HARBOR, STATEN ISLAND. Greek Revival complex dating 1831–1833 by Martin E. Thompson. Photo: Author's collection.

83.50 Port Richmond.

84.00 Former ferry to Bayonne on right.

84.00 *Turn left* on Nicholas Avenue.

84.15 Pass beneath Staten Island Rapid Transit.

84.60 *Turn right* on Hooker Avenue.

84.70 *Turn right* on Trantor Place.

84.70 Elm Park.

84.70 Entrance to Bayonne Bridge.

85.00 Pass toll booths.

85.10 Begin Bayonne Bridge. (See article in river section.)

85.75 Cross Kill Van Kull.

86.40 End Bayonne Bridge.

86.50 *Turn right* on West 7th Street, Bayonne.

86.90 *Turn right* on Avenue C.

87.40 Bergen Point. Site of Revolutionary Fort DeLancey. (Former ferry to Staten Island.)

BAYONNE BRIDGE. Built in 1931, the bridge gives a channel clearance of 150 ft. The arch is 1,675 ft long. Photo: © Uta Gore.

87.40 Kill Van Kull Park. Site of former amusement area along waterfront on right.

87.40 *Turn left* on First Street. Kill Van Kull on right.

87.60 Site of former LaTourette on right.

87.60 *Turn left* on Broadway.

87.80 Pass East 3rd Street. Herbert House, a fine example of a typical nineteenth-century Bayonne home, is on right. Note the fence.

88.20 Pass under Central Railroad of New Jersey (Conrail).

88.20 *Turn right* on West 8th Street.

88.30 Road becomes Avenue E.

89.00 *Turn right* on East 21st Street (becomes Hook Road).

89.05 Pass under Central Railroad of New Jersey.

89.50 Refinery area.

89.80 *Bend left*, merge into 22nd Street.

90.00 Exxon refinery on right.

90.10 *Bend left* on Avenue J.

90.20 *Turn right* on Route 169.

90.40 *Turn right* on Hook Road.

90.70 *Turn left:* Commerce Street.

90.80 Port Johnson.

90.80 Constable Hook. (−8.20 E.R.M.) *Turn around.*

90.90 *Turn right* on Hook Road.

91.20 *Turn left.* Cross railroad track. Get onto Route 169 North.

91.70 Pass 22nd Street on left. Continue straight on Route 169.

92.90 (−7.75 E.R.M.)

92.90 Military Ocean Terminal on right.

94.30 Pass under New Jersey Turnpike Extension and cross over Central Railroad of New Jersey (Conrail).

94.50 Cross Garfield Avenue.

94.70 *Turn left* on Avenue C.

94.85 Pass under New Jersey Turnpike Extension.

95.20 St. Vincent's Church (1927) on right. It is in Romanesque style.

95.30 *Turn right* on 44th Street.

95.50 *Turn left* on Kennedy Boulevard.

95.70 *Turn right* into Bayonne Park, Belvidere.

95.80 *Turn right* on Park Road.

96.10 Circle left around Monopteros.

96.50 Continue straight.

96.60 *Turn right* on Park Road.

96.80 *Turn right* again on Park Road.

97.00 Lagoon on right. View of Newark Bay and Turnpike Bridge.

97.10 *Turn left* on Park Road.

97.10 Port Newark across bay on right. Parking available.

97.20 *Bend left* on Park Road.

97.30 *Turn right.*

TYPICAL VICTORIAN PERIOD HOMESTEAD IN BAYONNE. This view is highly typical of Bergen Point up until a few years ago, and was taken in 1979. Photo: Alfred H. Marks.

THE MONOPTEROS AT BAYONNE PARK. Photo: Alfred H. Marks.

97.40 Exit from Bayonne Park.

97.40 *Turn left* on Kennedy Boulevard. For many years this road was known as Hudson County Boulevard, and follows the route of an old road from colonial days which went from Jersey City to Philadelphia via Staten Island.

97.50 World War I monument and statue of "Doughboy" on right.

97.50 *Turn right* on Dillon Drive, becomes West 40th Street.

97.60 Fountains and small park.

97.70 *Turn left* on Avenue C.

98.20 *Turn right* on 51st Street.

98.40 *Turn left* on Broadway.

98.60 Bayonne-Jersey City line.

98.60 Broadway becomes Garfield Avenue.

98.60 Pass beneath Turnpike Extension.

98.80 Pass beneath Lehigh Valley and Pennsylvania Railroads (Conrail), electrified line.

99.40 Bayview Cemetery on left. New York Bay Cemetery on right.

99.60 (− 6.50 E.R.M.)

99.60 Entrance to Caven Point Terminal on right.

100.00 Dingson Ryan Memorial Park (formerly Bayside Park) on right.

100.30 *Turn right* on Bayview Avenue.

100.50 Statue of Liberty visible ahead.

100.70 *Bear right* on Morris Pesin Drive.

101.60 Statue of Liberty Park. This area, formerly known as Black Tom, was an important railhead and terminal. It was owned by National Docks Co. and served by Lehigh Valley and Pennsylvania Railroads. It was the site of a tremendous ammunition explosion during World War I. In August of 1916, German saboteurs allegedly blew up a munitions plant here. Six months previously they had destroyed the Kingsland (New Jersey) Arsenal. The United States government brought suit, and the German government was finally ordered to pay $50,000,000 damages in 1940.

101.60 *Turn around* at overlook lot. (− 4.50 E.R.M.)

102.60 *Turn right* on Freedom Way.

105.00 (− 4.80 E.R.M.)

LAST UNDEVELOPED STRETCH OF SHORELINE on Upper New York Bay. This view, seemingly of nothing, was taken in 1979 and is significant as showing the pristine condition of most of the great developed area on the western shore of the bay. Photo: Alfred H. Marks.

105.00 Ellis Island on right.

105.50 Former Central Railroad of New Jersey, Baltimore & Ohio and Reading Co. coach and pullman yards on right. Science Center on left.

105.60 *Turn right* on Audrey Zapp Drive. (Formerly called Johnston Avenue.)

106.00 Former Central Railroad of New Jersey passenger and ferry terminal on right. It has been restored for use as a visitors' center.

106.00 (− 3.74 E.R.M.)

106.00 Morris Canal Basin on left. View of lower Manhattan ahead.

106.00 *Turn around.*

107.30 *Turn right* on Pacific Avenue.

107.60 *Turn right* on Grand Avenue.

108.30 St. Peter's Preparatory School on left.

108.40 Site of fortification on Powle's Hook.

108.40 *Turn right* on Washington Street: "Liberty Tree Corner."

108.60 *Turn left* on Essex Street.

108.70 HEALTH WARNING: The following stretch of our route through Jersey City, Hoboken, Weehawken, West New York, Guttenberg, Edgewater, and Fort Lee is frequently covered by a foetid miasma of noxious fumes from the many diesel buses and trucks crowding our route. Many people suffer burning eyes, nausea, and difficult breathing and headache from breathing these fumes. They are worst during commuter rush hours 7–10

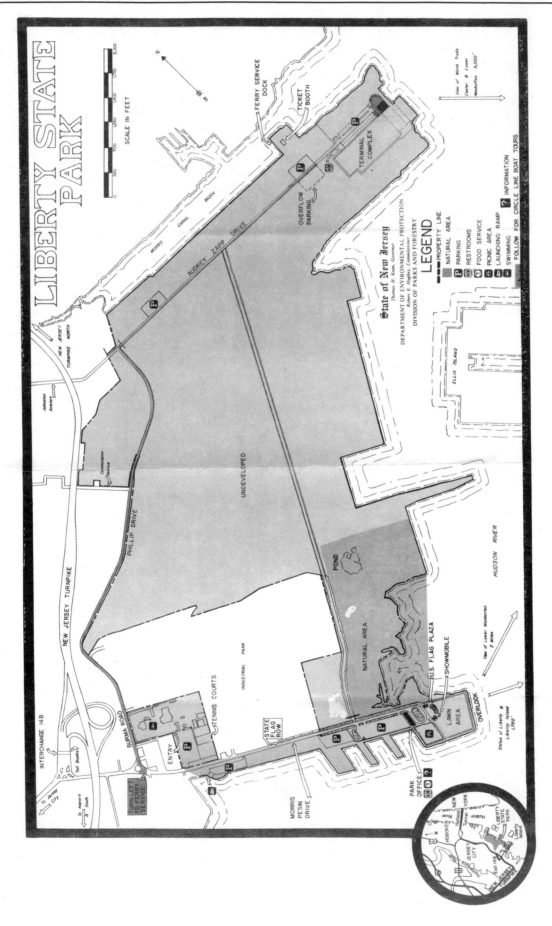

A.M. and 3–7 P.M. and we suggest planning your tour through this section outside those times. Furthermore, the lighter traffic will make your touring safer and pleasanter.

108.80 *Turn left* on Greene Street.

108.90 *Turn right* on York Street.

108.95 *Turn left* on Hudson Street.

109.00 Exchange Place. (– 3.70 E.R.M.)

109.00 Former terminal site of Fulton's pioneer ferry on right.

109.00 Site of former Pennsylvania Railroad passenger and ferry terminal straight ahead and on right (also early Cunard piers).

109.00 *Turn left* on Exchange Place, which becomes Montgomery Street.

109.20 United States Post Office on left. Pass Washington Street.

109.25 New Jersey Title Guarantee and Trust Co. Building (Nos. 83–85) on left. This yellow brick structure with cast terracotta ornaments and Art Deco portal was built in 1888. Its portal dates from 1931. It has been converted to an apartment house.

109.50 Jersey City City Hall ahead. Of limestone and granite in eclectic style, it was designed by Lewis H. Broome and built in 1835. In the days of Frank Hague, this building became laughingly known for the fact that, prior to election time, there was always a major fire in the basement Hall of Records.

109.50 *Turn right* on Luis Munoz Marin, formerly Henderson Street.

109.60 *Bend right* on Luis Munoz Marin.

109.70 *Bend left* on Luis Munoz Marin; Harborside Terminal Development on right.

110.00 *Turn right* on Newport City Drive.

110.00 Newport City development area.

110.30 Site of former Erie Railroad passenger and ferry terminal on left. This was the site of the former Long Dock Co. property. The Pennsylvania Railroad (Conrail) Harsimus Cove freight yards were on the right. A good view of lower Manhattan ahead.

110.30 *Turn left.* (– 2.50 E.R.M.)

110.80 Holland Tunnel ventilator tower to right, at end of Pier 9, formerly used by American President Lines as both origin and terminus of its Around-the-World freight and passenger service. The tickets for the longest cruise available in the world used to read simply: "Jersey City to Jersey City."

112.20 *Turn right* off Newport City Drive onto Henderson Street.

112.30 Pass beneath Delaware, Lackawanna & Western Railroad (Erie-Lackawanna; N. J. Transit).

112.40 *Turn right* on Observer Highway.

112.80 Former Erie-Lackawanna Railroad offices on right. Former Railway Express Co. terminal.

112.80 Hoboken.

112.80 *Turn left* on Hudson Street.

112.90 *Turn right* on Hudson Place. A former elevated railway and trolley terminal is on right, now used as a bus terminal.

112.95 Lackawanna Terminal.

112.95 (– 2.00 E.R.M.)

112.95 N. J. Transit's suburban passenger terminal is on right. The former ferry terminal and offices are straight ahead. There is a PATH station here. The statue is of Samuel Sloan, former president of Delaware, Lackawanna & Western Railroad. This is also the site of the original Hoboken Ferry.

112.95 *Turn left* on River Street.

113.15 (– 1.80 E.R.M.)

113.15 Hoboken–Port Authority Marine Terminal on right. Being demolished.

LACKAWANNA PLAZA AT HOBOKEN. The Delaware, Lackawanna & Western Railroad ferry and train terminal, built in 1907 by Kenneth M. Murchison, dominates the Plaza, sarcastically called the "Piazza San Lackawanna" by the late Christopher Morley. There was formerly a campanile tower copied after that of St. Marks in Venice. Photo: © Gretchen McHugh.

113.20 Hudson Square Park on left.

113.30 *Bend right* on Fourth Street—Sinatra Drive— and cross Hoboken Shore Railroad.

113.25 *Bend left* on Sinatra Drive.

113.60 Castle Point. (− 1.50 E.R.M.)

113.60 Stevens Institute of Technology on left. Hoboken Shore Railroad tracks formerly paralleled this road. Now inactive, they may be abandoned. The former *S.S. Stevens*, an oceangoing passenger liner, was used as a dormitory and anchored on the right until August 26, 1975.

113.70 Site of Sibyl's Cave on left.

114.00 (− 1.00 E.R.M.) Elysian Park on left. Former Pennsylvania Railroad marine shops stood on right.

114.10 *Turn right* on Hudson Street.

114.20 Sit of former Maxwell House Coffee plant on right.

114.30 Site of former Bethlehem Steel shipyard on right.

114.40 Site of former Lackawanna 14th Street Ferry Terminal on right.

114.40 *Turn left* on 14th Street.

114.60 *Turn right* on Park Avenue.

114.80 Cross bridge over Jersey Junction Railroad (Conrail).

115.00 Weehawken.

115.00 Lincoln Harbor Development on right. (− 0.50 E.R.M.)

115.60 *Bear right* on Boulevard East.

VIEW LOOKING SOUTH FROM CASTLE POINT, HOBOKEN. Photo: © Gretchen McHugh.

115.60 Entrance to Lincoln Tunnel on left.

115.80 Pass Baldwin Avenue on right. (Note: This is the turnoff for a rather rough alternate route along the foot of the cliffs to the foot of Pershing Avenue at the site of the former West Shore Railroad and Ferry Terminal. This alternate route is paralleled on the left by tracks of the Jersey Junction Railroad (Conrail) and passes on the right large banana docks, which occupy the former site of the Delaware & Hudson Canal Co. dockyard. The famous Weehawken dueling grounds occupied a small bench or plateau part way up the cliffs on the left, which was blasted away at time of construction of the railroad. The Electric Ferry operated from the foot of Baldwin Avenue. The bluff here is known as King's Bluff. A double-track trolley line paralleled Pershing Avenue to the top of the cliffs. The portal to the tunnel of the Guttenberg Steam Railroad division of the North Hudson Railroad can be seen high up on the cliffs under the present roadway.)
THIS IS NOT A PUBLIC ROAD. IT BELONGS TO ARCORP PROPERTIES AND PORT IMPERIAL FERRY-BUS SYSTEM.

115.80 Lincoln Tunnel Administration Building on right.

115.80 (− 0.25 E.R.M.)

116.40 King's Bluff area.

116.40 *Turn right* on King Street.

116.50 *Turn left* on Hamilton Place.

116.55 Bust of Alexander Hamilton on right. This is immediately above the former Weehawken Dueling Grounds.

116.55 (− 0.15 E.R.M.)

116.70 *Continue straight* onto Boulevard East.

116.80 Hamilton Plaza Park on right.

117.20 Cross 48th Street, Weehawken to left. Pershing Avenue to right. This leads to site of former West Shore Railroad and Ferry Terminal to 42nd Street and Cortlandt Street, Manhattan. The old terminal site is now redeveloped by Arcorp Corporation under the name of Port Imperial, after their President, Arthur Imperatore. They operate a new ferry service to West 38th Street in Manhattan and also to downtown, with parking facilities in Weehawken and a free Manhattan crosstown bus connection. The ferries are for passengers only—no vehicles. Please note: The alternate route suggested on mile 115.80 is now on private property and may not be open.

117.20 End of Lower West Side road route. Starting point of West Side road route.

VIEW LOOKING NORTH FROM CASTLE POINT, HOBOKEN. Photo: © Gretchen McHugh.

West Side Road Route

0.00 Start West Side Road route. (0.50 E.R.M.) Corner of Boulevard East, Pershing Avenue and 48th Street, Weehawken, New Jersey. Head north on Boulevard East.

0.10 Small Park on right.

0.30 West New York City line.

0.50 Donnelly Park on right.

Alternate Route (shore line)

0.60 At this point, Boulevard East crosses what is called 60th Street to the left and Hillside Road to the right.

0.60 *Turn right* on Hillside Road. Descend Palisades. Slough's Meadows are seen at the foot of the cliffs to the right. There are good views of Manhattan and passenger liner piers and far down Hudson River. Large new apartment buildings are on the bluff to the left.

0.80 Road bends left at the site of former New York Central Railroad Marine shops, and West New York Ferry on right.

0.90 River View Park atop cliff to left.

1.00 Entrance to Port Imperial Ferry on right. Site of former N.Y.O. & W. Railway coal docks.

1.10 Guttenberg city line. Becomes River Road. (1.50 E.R.M.)

1.11 Ferry Road to left. Site of former Guttenberg Ferry on right.

1.35 North Bergen city line. Note: From mile 1.00 to mile 5.80, River Road is paralleled on the right by abandoned tracks of the New York, Susquehanna & Western Railway.

2.00 Bull's Ferry. Blockhouse Point on right. (2.45 E.R.M.) This is the site of a former ferry. Bull's Ferry Road comes down cliff on left.

2.00 Rejoin main route; continue straight on River Road.

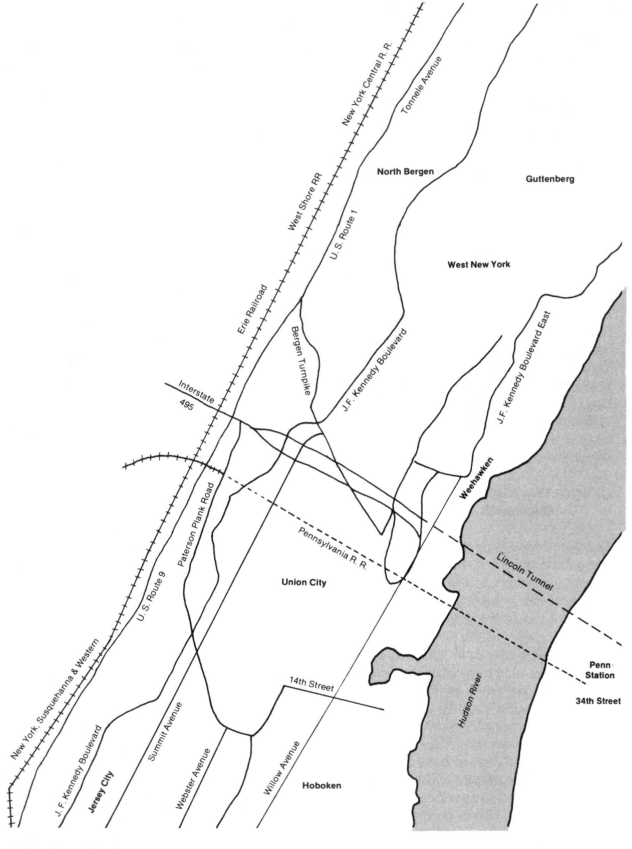

Hudson County, New Jersey.

SLOUGH'S MEADOW, WEEHAWKEN. Manhattan is seen in the distance. This picture, taken in 1989, is most unusual. In the 1880s this area was covered by busy railroad freight yards and the shoreline with giant docks and grain elevators. These all have now been removed, but the area is slated for redevelopment with residential and commercial structures. Photo: © Gretchen McHugh.

Main Route (atop Palisades)

0.60 Cross 60th Street–Hillside Road and continue straight on Boulevard East.

0.80 Auf Der Heide Park on right, named for former West New York mayor Oscar Auf Der Heide. Formerly called River View Park.

1.10 Guttenberg city line. (1.50 E.R.M.)

1.35 North Bergen city line.

2.30 *Turn left* into North Hudson Park.

2.60 *Bear left* on Park Road.

2.90 *Bear left* on Park Road.

3.20 *Turn left* on 79th Street. Leave North Hudson Park.

3.40 *Turn left* on Boulevard East.

3.45 *Turn sharp right* on Bull's Ferry Road.

3.50 Go down steep hill.

3.80 Bull's Ferry. Blockhouse Point straight ahead. (2.45 E.R.M.)

3.80 *Turn left* on River Road (alternate rejoins main route here).

3.81 Edgewater town line. Leave Hudson County, enter Bergen County.

3.90 Lever Brothers' factory on right.

4.10 Shadyside area of Edgewater. (3.00 E.R.M.)

4.20 *Bear right* on River Road: Route 505.

4.40 Former Ford assembly plant on right, now Tri-Terminal. (3.30 E.R.M.)

4.70 Cross bridge over New York, Susquehanna & Western Railway. The entrance of the railroad tunnel under the palisades is visible to left. Former Sea Train terminal on right.

5.00 Site of former Hills Bros. coffee plant on right.

5.20 Sunnyside area of Edgewater. (4.30 E.R.M.)

5.40 Former Alcoa (Aluminum Company of America) plant on left was being redeveloped as condominiums, but has had to be abandoned because of PCB contamination.

5.40 Binghamton's Restaurant on right. The restaurant is the former Delaware, Lackawanna & Western Hoboken ferryboat *S.S. Binghamton*. (4.40 E.R.M.)

5.80 Site of the former Jack Frost sugar refinery on right.

5.80 Site of the former U.S. Postal Service mailbag repair facility on right.

FERRYBOAT *BINGHAMTON* AT EDGEWATER. Now operates as a floating restaurant, but formerly on the Hoboken Ferry routes. This view taken in 1989. Photo: © Gretchen McHugh.

5.80 End of N.Y.S. & W. Railway tracks on right.

6.00 Edgewater. (4.80 E.R.M.)

6.00 Cross Edgewater Plaza. The former 125th Street ferry terminal was on the right. The trolley terminal was located here with carbarns on left.

6.10 *Bear right* at junction with Route 5. Continue on River Road.

7.10 Undercliff section of Edgewater. (5.00 E.R.M.)

7.50 Tillie Tudlem (section of Edgewater also known variously through the years as Tilly Toodlum, Pleasant Valley, Burdett's Ferry, and Fort Lee Park. A former steamboat landing and resort). (7.10 E.R.M.)

7.50 Junction with Henry Hudson Drive on right.

Alternate No. 1—Undercliff

(This route can be used in either direction but is closed in winter.) This route is the preferred scenic route but is frequently closed to motor traffic in favor of bicycle traffic.

7.50 Corner of Henry Hudson Drive and Hudson Terrace (Main Street), Fort Lee town line.

7.50 *Turn right* on Henry Hudson Drive. Enter Palisades Interstate Park.

7.80 DuPont Dock or Powder Dock on right. (7.15 E.R.M.)

8.00 Hazard's Dock on right. (7.20 E.R.M.)

8.10 Pass beneath George Washington Bridge. (7.30 E.R.M.)

8.30 Carpenter's Beach on right. (7.50 E.R.M.)

8.40 Turnoff for Ross Dock recreation area on right. Boat ramps are here.

9.50 Allison Park atop cliffs to left.

9.60 The Miraculous Gully to left. (8.00 E.R.M.)

9.70 Allison Point to left. (8.10 E.R.M.)

9.80 Site of former Dyckman Street ferry terminal on right.

9.80 Englewood Cliffs landing. (9.70 E.R.M.)

9.80 Englewood Yacht Club on right.

9.80 Entrance to parking and picnic area to right (pay area).

9.80 *Bear left*, uphill.

10.20 Bloomer's Dock to right. (9.75 E.R.M.)

10.20 Devil's or Fiddler's Elbow—hairpin turn. (9.70 E.R.M.) Junction of Palisades Avenue, which continues to top of the cliffs and Palisades Interstate

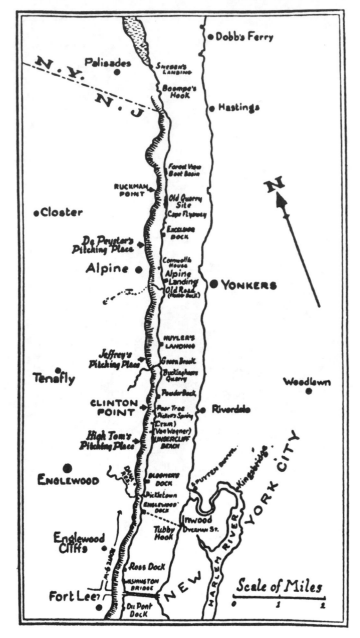

PALISADES REGION FEATURES. Author's collection.

Parkway and Route 9W, and Henry Hudson Drive. Sometimes the Drive is open to this point in winter.

10.20 *Bear right* on Henry Hudson Drive.

10.50 High Tom on left. (9.80 E.R.M.)

10.50 Frank's Rock on shoreline—lowest point on drive.

10.80 Undercliff (under the mountains). A former active settlement of farmers, pear arborists, quarrymen, woodcutters, and fishermen, it was heavily populated in the Dutch era. Remains of a cemetery may be seen in the area west of the drive. (10.30 E.R.M.)

11.20 Powder Dock on right. Clinton Point on left (10.75 E.R.M.).

12.30 Lambier Dock on right. (12.20 E.R.M.)

12.60 Cross bridge over Greenbrook Falls to left. (12.30 E.R.M.)

13.00 Huyler Landing on right. (13.00 E.R.M.)

13.75 Traffic circle. Bear left up to cliffs. (13.50 E.R.M.)

Optional sidetrip

13.75 *Bear right* down cliffs.

14.05 Alpine Grove—former Yonkers Ferry terminal. It now has boat docks, picnic facilities, pay parking area. (14.40 E.R.M.)

14.05 *Turn around.*

14.35 *Turn sharp right* up hill at circle—rejoin main route.

Alternate No. 1 (continued)

14.20 Riverview landing to right at foot of cliffs. (14.40 E.R.M.)

14.40 Cape Fly Away to right. (14.50 E.R.M.)

14.50 Palisades Interstate Park Commission Headquarters on right. This is in a fine mansion formerly belonging to the Oltman family.

14.55 *Bear left* and pass under Palisades Interstate Parkway.

14.60 *Turn right* on Route 9W North. Junction with Alternate 2—Overcliff Route.

Alternate No. 2--Overcliff

(Works best northbound. Open all year.)

7.50 Tillie Tudlem—Junction of River Road, Henry Hudson Drive, and Hudson Terrace (sometimes also called Main Street here).

7.50 Continue left uphill on Hudson Terrace. (7.10 E.R.M.)

7.50 Fort Lee town line.

7.70 Restoration of Fort Lee on right. (E.R.M. 7.30)

7.80 Pass beneath approach to George Washington Bridge. (E.R.M. 7.30)

8.00 Linwood section of Fort Lee. Large apartments on left. (E.R.M. 8.00)

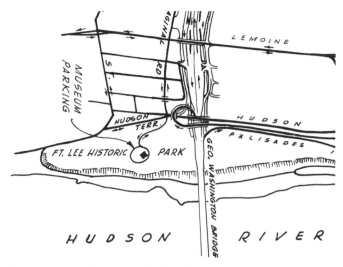

Historic park at Fort Lee. Author's collection.

8.60 Victorian cottages on left. Remains of stone walls belonging to earlier estates are visible between Hudson Terrace and the Palisades Interstate Parkway on the right.

8.90 Prentice Hall Publishing Co. on left.

9.30 *Turn right* beneath parkway.

9.40 *Turn right* on Allison Park Road.

9.60 *Turn left.* Enter Allison Park. (E.R.M. 7.80) This is a very special portion of the Palisades Interstate Park System. It was originally privately endowed and administered by the trustees under the will of William Outis Allison (1849–1924), a lifelong resident of the immediate area. The park is entirely fenced and opens at 9 A.M. for the daylight hours only. The park is much more formal than most sections of the Interstate Park System and features "formal-rustic" landscaping, manicured lawns, tar paths, and a spectacular clifftop walk with extensive views embracing Manhattan, the Hudson, Spuyten Duyvil Creek, George Washington and Henry Hudson Bridges, and the Cloisters. There are extensive plantings of pine, rhododendron, and mountain laurel. Many wooden and stone benches (one a unique natural stone bench) are located around the grounds. Facilities include paved parking area, a granite Dutch Colonial style rest room building, drinking water fountains, and caretaker's lodge.

9.60 *Circle left* on Park Road.

9.70 Exit Allison Park.

9.70 *Turn right* on Allison Park Road.

9.90 *Continue straight.*

10.00 Enter grounds of St. Michael's Villa and St. Peter's College. When entering grounds, note faces carved in dead tree trunk straight ahead. Bear left on two-way drive and circle around to exit. The four-story, turreted, orange brick main building was formerly St. Joseph's Orphanage. There are attractive statues of the Blessed Virgin, St. Joseph, and the child Jesus in the center of the turn-around drive. The grounds feature attractive hydrangea plantings, and are at the top of the gully known as the Miraculous (long before any religious orders occupied the site—origin of name is unknown). (E.R.M. 8.20) Circle around and exit villa grounds. Site of former Palisades Mountain House. See article E.R.M. 8.05.

10.40 *Turn right* back under parkway.

10.50 *Turn right* on Hudson Terrace.

10.80 *Turn right* on Palisades Avenue (Englewood Cliffs). (9.70 E.R.M.)

10.81 Pass beneath parkway.

10.82 *Turn left* onto Palisades Interstate Parkway Northbound.

11.80 Rockefeller Lookout (available northbound only). Elevation 400 feet. Paved parking area. 20 minute limit. This point offers extensive views embracing Manhattan, Henry Hudson Bridge, Spuyten Duyvil Creek, Bronx V. A. Hospital, Baker Field, Long Island Sound, and Westchester County. There is a memorial dedication plaque to John D. Rockefeller, Jr., who dedicated much land to the Palisades Interstate Park Commission and who envisioned the Palisades Interstate Parkway. Coin-operated binoculars are available. There are low stone walls along the cliff tops—caution is urged. There are several dangerous open cliff tops but no fences. Beware of policemen who have been convicted of bullying, mistreating, and robbing motorists in 1991.

13.50 *Pass over* entrance road to Greenbrook Sanctuary from Route 9W. The Greenbrook Sanctuary incorporates a wild and rugged area with a 6.5 acre pond (source of Greenbrook) known as "the Kelders," Dutch for "the cellars." The sanctuary is open only to members of the Palisades Nature Association, P.O. Box 155, Alpine, New Jersey 07620.

14.60 Alpine Lookout (available northbound only). This viewpoint with 430 feet elevation, opposite Riverdale and Yonkers, features Chimney Rock. There are many sheer drops but also a substantial fence along the clifftop. Paved parking area with 20-minute limit.

15.50 Armstrong FM radio transmission tower visible ahead to left. This was built in 1938 by FM radio pioneer Maj. Edwin Armstrong, who taught at Columbia University. It is 485 feet high with triple arms and broadcasts over a range of 100 miles. It was the first FM radio station, but has since been discontinued.

15.80 Cross small bridge.

16.20 *Exit right* onto Old Closter Dock Road. (This is the Alpine approach road to Route 9W North.)

16.40 *Circle right* under parkway.

16.50 *Turn right* onto Route 9W North. Junction with Alternate 1, Undercliff Route. Future mileages are based upon the Alternate No. 1.

Combined Route (continued)

14.60 *Head North* on Route 9W.

15.10 Former Ringling family (circus) estate on right.

16.30 *Turn right* on side road to State Line Lookout. This is located at Exit 3 of the Palisades Interstate Parkway.

16.45 State Line Lookout. Elevation 522 feet (E.R.M. 17.70.) Paved parking. Light refreshments available in season. *Turn around.*

16.60 *Enter* Palisades Interstate Parkway Northbound.

17.40 *Exit* from Parkway at Exit 4, onto Route 9W North.

17.70 New Jersey/New York State line. (E.R.M. 18.00)

17.75 Skunk Hollow on right.

17.90 Entrance to Columbia University Lamont Geological Observatory on right. This is a seismological recording station and teaching facility. It is located on the former estate of Dr. John Torrey, noted botanist, and incorporates his former red sandstone mansion and gardens, as well as those of the neighboring estate Niederhurst, ca. 1860, a Victorian Italianate mansion. The property is not open to the public.

18.30 Long Path on right. Blue blazes.

18.50 Palisades. (E.R.M. 18.90)

18.50 Pass Washington Spring Road. A 1.5-mile round trip to the right to Sneden's Landing (Old Paramus) is suggested for those interested in old houses. The native stone house in Pennsylvania Dutch style atop the cliffs is a modern reproduction built in 1937.

19.50 Rockland Country Club and golf course on left.

19.80 Tallman Mountain Park on right, a unit of the Palisades Interstate Park System. A loop drive around the park is recommended as a short side trip. There are two picnic areas. The northern one offers superior views of the Tappan Zee, Piermont Village, Erie Pier, Tappan Zee Bridge, Crumkill Creek Meadows, and Sparkill Creek. Recreational facilities include picnic areas, swimming pool, athletic fields, tennis, handball, badminton, basketball, football, softball, children's play area. Rest rooms are available. No pets are allowed. The park closes at 9 P.M.

20.00 Pass junction Route 340 on left. Continue straight on Route 9W.

20.10 Palisades/Piermont town line.

20.20 Start Sparkill Creek Viaduct. (E.R.M. 20.80)

20.50 End Sparkill Creek Viaduct.

20.60 *Turn left* at second traffic light—Hickey Street.

20.70 *Turn right* on King's Highway.

20.80 Large Dutch Colonial home with Ionic columns on verandah on right.

21.10 *Turn right* and enter Rockland Cemetery, established 1847. Drive to grave of Gen. John C. Frémont (1813–1890), "Pathfinder of the West," atop Mt. Nebo. There are good views. Just keep following cemetery roads to top of mountain. Circle back to the entrance. This is a 2.1-mile round-trip.

23.20 *Turn right* back onto King's Highway.

23.50 Closed-off back entrance driveway to Dominican Convent and St. Agnes Home and School for Children on left.

23.70 Back entrance to St. Thomas Aquinas College on left.

24.20 Olde Stonehouse Inn on right (ca. 1728).

24.30 *Turn right* on Route 303.

24.50 *Turn right* on Greenbush Road.

24.51 Bell-Ann Factory on right.

24.55 Dutch house on right.

24.60 Volkswagen building on right on former Rockland County Fairgrounds.

25.20 *Turn right* up ravine on Clausland Mountain Road.

25.50 Town of Orangetown Park on left.

26.40 *Turn right* on Tweed Boulevard.

26.70 Expansive view of Tappan Zee on left. Top of Clausland Mountain (E.R.M. 22.00).

27.50 *Turn right* into town of Orangetown Park.

27.85 Parking. Views both east and west. *Turn around.*

28.20 *Turn right* on Tweed Boulevard.

29.20 Driveway to *Castlewood* on right. This is a private home; do not enter. This former home of Eleazar Lord, first president of the Erie Railroad, is a three-story field-stone structure, ca. 1850, extensively remodeled by McKim, Mead & White.

29.30 *Turn right* on Route 9W.

29.40 Pass Castle Road on right.

29.90 *Turn right* at second light—Route 340.

29.90 Sparkill.

30.00 *Turn left* off Route 340 onto Piermont Avenue at Erie Railroad crossing.

30.05 *Turn right* on Valentine Avenue.

30.15 Christ Episcopal Church on right: a nineteenth-century, stone crenellated Gothic structure.

30.30 St. Charles A.M.E. Zion Church on right. Stone, built in 1865, rebuilt in 1893.

30.30 Park, lily pond (former ice pond), and Route 9W trestle on left.

30.40 *Turn left* on Ferdon Avenue.

ANCIENT BRIDGE ACROSS THE SPARKILL. This old moss-covered masonry structure dates from the early 19th century and is typical of much local stonework. Note icebreaking center abutment. Photo: Alfred H. Marks.

30.50 Pond and dam and former Tappan Landing on Sparkill Creek on left.

30.50 Pass under Route 9W trestle.

30.70 Sparkill/Piermont town line.

30.90 Ferdun-Blauvelt house on right: a two-story Greek Revival with Ionic temple facade and fluted columns (ca. 1840) on the southwest corner of Rockland Road.

30.90 Crescent Ribbon Factory on left; red brick with Gothic ornamentation; originally a silk mill.

31.10 First Reformed Church on right, established in 1839.

31.20 Tallman Park drive on right. Closed to all but official vehicles.

31.20 Old chain drawbridge across Sparkill Creek on left; one-way in the opposite direction.

31.20 *Bear right* and cross Sparkill Creek on new bridge.

31.20 View of Carroll Castle across the river in Tarrytown on right.

31.25 *Turn right* at light on Paradise Avenue.

31.30 *Turn around*—area of mid-nineteenth-century houses undergoing restoration.

31.35 *Turn right* at light onto Piermont Avenue.

31.45 Cross former Erie Railroad mainline (now an industrial spur).

31.50 Piermont Village. (E.R.M. 21.25)

31.50 Former Clevepac Corp. paper carton plant on right.

31.50 Former Erie Railroad pier on right. (E.R.M. 21.20)

OLD COTTAGE c1700 at Piermont. Photo: Alfred H. Marks.

CHAINBRIDGE ACROSS THE SPARKILL at Piermont. Photo: Alfred H. Marks.

LOWER LANDING ON THE SPARKILL at Piermont. Photo: Alfred H. Marks.

32.00 Area of old houses. (E.R.M. 21.25)

    a) Onderdonk Dutch House on left, 756 Piermont Avenue.

    b) Garrison Colonial House on left, 800 Piermont Avenue.

    c) House with gingerbread vergeboards and fluted Corinthian columns on left, 830 Piermont Avenue.

    d) Victorian house with mansard roof on left, 840 Piermont Avenue.

    e) Bracketed house on left, 850 Piermont Avenue.

    f) Colonial house with Victorian modifications on right, 867 Piermont Avenue.

    g) Victorian House with mansard roof on left, 870 Piermont Avenue.

    h) House with trellised porch in Hudson River Gothic Style on right, facing St. John's R. C. Church.

32.30 Piermont/Grand-View-on-Hudson town line. Cross brook. Name of road changes to River Road. Area of more old homes.

PARADISE AVENUE, Piermont. Photo: Alfred H. Marks.

ONDERDONCK HOUSE, Piermont. Photo: Alfred H. Marks.

   a) Hudson River Gothic cottage on left, 251 River Road.
   b) Federal period mansion on left, 245 River Road.
   c) Colonial cottage on right, 242 River Road.
   d) Bracketed mansion on left, 225 River Road.
   e) Bracketed cottage on left, 221 River Road.
   f) Victorian mansard roof villa on left, 217 River Road.
   g) Several Hudson River Gothic bracketed villas on both sides.

33.30 Double cottage in bracketed style, batten board construction on right (ca. 1820), 108 and 110 River Road.

33.50 Bracketed house on left, 81 River Road.

33.60 Grand View Springs and pool on left, 55 River Road.

33.70 Canaday Eagle Spring Water Co. on left, 35 River Road.

GOTHIC COTTAGE, Grand View. Photo: Alfred H. Marks.

33.80 Stone hermitage style Hudson River Gothic cottage on right (with red sandstone stepped gables). It was formerly the Wayside Sunday School, 1860. 24 River Road.

33.90 Pass under Tappan Zee Bridge. (E.R.M. 23.20)

34.00 Grand-View-on-Hudson/Nyack town line.

34.10 Salisbury Manor Apartments and Cornelison Point on right. (E.R.M. 23.60)

34.70 *Turn left* at light on Clinton Avenue.

34.80 *Turn right* at light on Broadway.

35.00 St. Paul's Methodist Church on left; Romanesque, limestone with dark sandstone trim.

35.10 Christian Science Church on right; Hudson River Gothic board and batten.

35.10 *Turn right* on Cedar Hill Avenue.

35.20 *Turn left* on Piermont Avenue.

35.25 *Bear right.*

35.25 Hudson House on left, 50 Piermont Avenue. Former DePew House, 1836, Hudson River Gothic with late Victorian additions, square cupola.

35.35 St. John's Deliverance Tabernacle on right, 35 Piermont Avenue. Doric style Greek Revival.

35.40 *Turn left* on Burd Street.

35.60 *Turn right* on South Broadway.

35.80 First Reformed Church on left; red brick Gothic with clock in tower.

36.00 Federal mansion on right, 63 South Broadway.

36.10 First Baptist Church on left; brick with Gothic elements, built in 1857, rebuilt in 1881.

36.20 Large Victorian House behind high brick wall, ca. 1846, 235 S. Broadway.

36.30 Upper Nyack town line. (E.R.M. 25.25)

36.50 Empire Fire Company No. 1 on left.

36.70 Old Stone Church on right. Built in 1813, it is the oldest church in Rockland County.

36.85 *River Plum* on right; stuccoed Hudson River Gothic.

36.90 Cross brook.

37.10 Fellowship of Reconciliation Center on right; Federal-style mansion with Ionic elements, red brick, 523 Broadway. It was formerly called *Shadow Cliff*.

37.40 View of Hook Mountain Cliffs ahead.

37.40 *River House* on right, 531 Broadway, a French Provincial chateau.

37.80 Old Carriage House and view of Hudson River on right.

37.80 Entrance to Nyack State Park.

37.80 *Turn around.*

37.90 *Turn right* on Larchdale Street.

38.00 *Turn left* on Midland Avenue.

38.00 Mary Dell Convent and outdoor chapel on right.

38.70 *Turn right* on Old Mountain Road.

38.90 Spook Hollow.

39.10 *Turn right* on Route 9W.

39.60 Turnout located on right for footpath atop Hook Mountain. It is inconspicuous and is located just south of a driveway.

40.10 Nyack/Rockland Lake town line.

40.50 *Turn right.*

40.50 Rockland Lake State Park (acquired by Palisades Park Commission in 1958); swimming, golf course, picnic areas. (E.R.M. 28.65)

40.70 Follow road along east side of Rockland Lake.

41.90 Rockland Lake Village.

41.90 Road to Trough Hol and Rockland Lake Landing on right. This is a dead end; official vehicles only. It is a very steep hill; bicycles must be walked.

41.90 *Bend left.*

42.15 Gethsemane Cemetery on right.

42.40 *Turn right.*

42.50 *Turn right* on Route 9W.

42.60 Swarthout Lake on left.

44.10 Junction with Route 303 from left.

44.30 View of Upper Hackensack Valley on left.

44.30 West portal of West Shore Railroad tunnel below on left.

44.50 New York Trap Rock Co. High Tor Quarry seen ahead.

44.60 Junction Route 304 on left.

44.70 Enter Long Clove. (E.R.M. 31.50)

44.70 Haverstraw town line.

44.90 André monument on right.

44.90 East portal of West Shore Railroad tunnel on right below.

45.10 Lookout pulloff on right. Extensive view of Haverstraw Bay and Highlands.

45.50 Pass over traprock conveyor.

45.55 Short Clove on left, traffic light. (E.R.M. 32.40)

45.60 *Turn right* on Short Clove Road and cross railroad.

45.60 High Tor on left. (E.R.M. 33.00)

45.70 Former brick yards on right.

46.10 Old wooden tenements on left. You are now on Maple Avenue.

46.10 *Turn right* on Fairmont Street.

46.11 *Turn right* on West Street. (This seems almost like just one turn.)

46.20 Marina on right.

46.30 *Turn left* on Canal Street.

46.40 *Turn left* on First Street (also called Front Street) "Captains' Row." Widest part of Hudson River.

46.40 B.P.O.E. building on right; Victorian ca. 1860.

46.40 Area of interesting old houses on left:
a) 52 First Street at corner of Van Houten Street: Van Houten House, 1790.
b) 44 First Street: Major Welch House, two-story brick Victorian with mansard roof and brackets, mid-nineteenth century.
c) 42 First Street: two-story Hudson River Bracketed, mid-nineteenth century.
d) 34 First Street: Captain Woolsey House, three-story brick with Ionic portico, ca. 1845.

e) 20 First Street: Hudson River Gothic cottage.

f) 10 First Street: Ionic Greek Revival, ca. 1840.

46.45 *Emeline* Dock on right.

46.50 River View Boat Club and old ferry slip on right.

46.50 Cross Main Street, Haverstraw. (E.R.M. 33.25)

46.51 Hudson River Gothic mansion (ca. 1840) on right, 7 First Street.

46.55 Former Cornell Steamboat Co. dock on right.

46.60 *Turn left* on Broad Street.

46.70 *Turn right* on Rockland Street.

46.80 *Turn left* on Division Street; area of row houses.

46.80 View of Bowline Point and lagoon to right.

46.90 *Turn right* on Broadway.

46.90 View of High Tor to left.

47.10 *Continue straight* at light. Entrance to Bowline Point power plant and park on right. Suggested two-mile side trip to end and back.

47.10 St. Peter's R. C. Church on left.

47.40 *Bend right* on Samsondale Avenue.

47.60 Cross Minisceongo Creek.

47.65 *Turn right* on Tanneyann's Lane.

47.90 *Turn right* on Railroad Avenue.

48.00 *Turn left* on Grassy Point Road. Power plant on right.

48.50 Cross Minisceongo Creek.

48.60 A cove of the Hudson is on the right. Minisceongo Creek is on the left.

49.40 Grassy Point: former steamboat landing is on the right.

49.40 *Turn left*.

49.60 Old Roman Catholic Church on left, 1889.

49.70 U.S. Gypsum plant on left.

49.70 Minisceongo Yacht Club on right.

49.90 Cross Minisceongo Creek, Penny Bridge.

49.90 View of High Tor to left; Stony Point Bay, Stony Point, and Verplanck Point to right.

49.95 *Turn right* on Beach Road.

50.40 *Turn left* under railroad (limited clearance).

50.60 *Turn right* on Farley Drive.

50.90 *Turn right* on Jackson Drive.

51.00 *Bear left* on Jackson Drive. This becomes Lincoln Oval. Continue around.

51.20 *Turn right* on Georgian Drive (downhill).

51.30 *Turn right* on Park Road.

51.40 Enter Stony Point Battlefield Park, Memorial Arch and bridge over the railroad. Park is closed Mondays and Tuesdays.

51.75 *Turn around* parking area. (E.R.M. 36.20)

52.10 Leave Battlefield Park.

52.20 *Turn right* on Park Road North, up ravine.

52.40 *Turn right* on Route 9W.

52.50 Tomkin's Cove town line.

52.80 *Stay straight* on Route 9W. Buckberg Mountain Road on left.

53.00 *Turn right* on Elm Street.

53.30 *Turn left* on Elm Street.

53.40 *Turn left* on Spring Street.

53.40 View of Orange & Rockland Lovett power plant on right. (E.R.M. 37.37)

53.50 *Turn left* on Church Street (gravel road) uphill.

53.60 *Turn right* on Route 9W.

53.60 Old schoolhouse, now library, on left.

53.70 Boulderberg Manor, former Calvin Tomkins House, on right.

54.00 Entrance drive to Boulderberg Manor on right.

BOULDERBERG MANOR, Tompkins Cove. Built in 1858 by Calvin Tomkins out of poured concrete. Very innovative for its time. Design inspired by Andrew Jackson Downing. Photo: Author's collection. Courtesy Boulderberg Manor.

54.20 Pass under power transmission line. (E.R.M. 37.40) View of Indian Point.

54.40 Indian Point Atomic Power Plant across river. (E.R.M. 38.25)

54.45 Old graveyard on right.

55.40 Hudson River Reserve Fleet Monument on right. (E.R.M. 38.00 for article)

55.70 *Turn right* on Old Ayers Road (marked dead end).

56.20 *Turn right,* then *left* along railroad.

56.30 Jones Point. View of Peekskill. (E.R.M. 38.50)

56.30 *Turn around.* It is possible to walk along the tracks to Kidd's Point.

56.50 *Turn left.*

56.60 Site of former Jones Point depot. (E.R.M. 38.45)

56.65 Cross cement street at diagonal.

56.70 Tabernacle Church on right.

56.90 *Turn right* on Route 9W.

56.95 Hiker's parking on left. Dunderberg-Suffern trail head.

57.30 Dunderberg Mountain. Scenic pulloff on right. (E.R.M. 40.00) View of Peekskill on right.

57.90 Vista—Bear Mountain on left with tower. Anthony's Nose, Iona Island, and The Race.

59.20 Old road to Doodletown on left. (E.R.M. 41.60)

60.60 Entrance to Bear Mountain Park on left. Site of former Knickerbocker Ice Co. storage depot on right. Doodletown Bight on right. (E.R.M. 42.10)

60.60 Bear Mountain Bridge seen ahead. Anthony's Nose to right.

61.50 Entrance to Bear Mountain Inn on left. (E.R.M. 42.40)

61.60 Swimming pool down to right.

61.80 Hessian Lake on left. (42.40 E.R.M)

61.85 Site of Fort Clinton on right. (E.R.M. 42.40)

61.85 Rockland/Orange County Line. (See article E.R.M. 42.60)

61.95 Bear Mountain Circle. Continue around going north on Route 9W. This is the junction of Palisades Interstate Parkway, Route 9W, Route 202, and Route 6. Bear Mountain Bridge to right. (E.R.M. 42.50)

62.00 *Continue north* on Route 9W.

62.20 Start of Popolopen Creek viaduct. (E.R.M. 42.60)

62.40 End of Popolopen Creek viaduct.

62.45 Site of Fort Montgomery on right. Reached by narrow footpath. (E.R.M. 42.65)

62.45 *Turn left* on Old Route 9W.

62.80 *Turn left* on Mine Torne Road.

63.00 Pass trail entrance to Hell Hole on left.

63.05 Trail to Brooks Lake on right.

63.10 *Turn around.* Trail to Popolopen Torne on right. Hell Hole on left. Entrance to U.S. Military Academy straight ahead.

63.10 Site of former Queensboro furnace down on left.

64.50 *Cross* old Route 9W. Continue straight on Mine Dock Road.

64.50 *Bear right* downhill.

64.60 *Bear right.*

64.70 Pass beneath Route 9W viaduct.

64.80 *Turn around.* Fort Montgomery depot. Sandy Beach. General Wayne left here for Stony Point on July 15, 1779. It offers a view of Anthony's Nose. (E.R.M. 42.75) The present owners of this location are inhospitable to visitors and have guard dogs.

65.90 Pass beneath viaduct again.

66.00 *Bear left.*

66.10 *Turn right* on Old Route 9W.

65.50 *Turn left* on present Route 9W.

66.70 Garrison Pond on right. Randall House on left (ca. 1770). (E.R.M. 43.40)

67.30 *Turn right* on Route 218.

67.80 Sugarloaf visible across river.

67.90 Union Cemetery on right.

67.90 Highland Falls town line.

68.30 Margaret Corbin monument, reading "Molly, Margaret Corbin, Heroine of Fort Washington, passed her last days on the former Morgan Estate near by." (E.R.M. 44.80)

68.40 Cragston Residential Park on right. Former entrance gate to Morgan Estate on left, also stone walls. (E.R.M. 45.00)

68.60 Junction with cutoff to Route 9W on left. Continue straight.

69.10 Ondora Residential Park on right.

70.10 *Turn right* on Havens Road, off Main Street.

70.30 *Bear sharp left.*

70.40 *Bear sharp right.*

70.50 *Turn around.* View across river to Beverly Dock. (E.R.M. 45.70)

70.50 *Bear right* uphill.

70.70 *Turn right* on Main Street.

70.80 *Bear right.* Leave Route 218.

70.90 Cross Highland Brook at top of Buttermilk Falls. (E.R.M. 46.20) This is at the corner of Webb Lane, on private property.

71.05 Site of former Ladycliff College on right. Also previous sites of former Cozzens and Cranston's Hotels. Property is no longer a college and is being redeveloped as a museum and visitors' center by the U. S. Military Academy.

71.10 *Turn right* on Station Hill.

71.40 Spring on overhanging rock on left.

71.45 *Turn around.* Site of former Cranston's Station-Highland Falls Depot, now a private residence. (E.R.M. 46.70)

71.80 *Turn right* on Main Street.

71.90 Enter gates of United States Military Academy, West Point. As we go to press there are rumors that the grounds of the U. S. Military Academy may be closed to touristical motor traffic because of overcrowding. In such event, use Routes 9W and Route 218 as a bypass. No doubt adequate arrangements will be provided for visitors.

71.95 Hotel Thayer on right, built in 1924. (E.R.M. 46.75)

NOTE: From here to 73.40 the roads are frequently closed and motorists must use a more inland detour by Michie Stadium. If road is closed, we recommend parking in lot across from Hotel Thayer and taking a walking tour as far as Trophy Point and back. (Walk = 1.70 miles round trip.)

72.20 *Bear right.*

72.30 Go under building. Viewpoint parking on right.

72.40 Thayer Hall on right. (E.R.M. 47.50)

72.50 Parking on roof of former Riding Academy on right.

72.55 Officer's Mess.

72.60 Cullum Hall on right; Ionic neo-classic with hipped roof, designed by Stanford White of McKim, Mead & White in 1896.

72.70 *Bear right and right again* on Clinton Place.

72.90 Ruins of Fort Clinton on left, built in 1779, formerly Fort Arnold.

72.90 Kosciuszko monument on left. (E.R.M. 47.76)

72.95 Monument on right. Parade Grounds on left.

73.05 Trophy Point on right. Site of former West Point Hotel. (E.R.M. 48.60) The Battle Monument was designed by Stanford White.

73.15 Chapel visible on hill to left. (See article E.R.M. 48.60)

73.25 *Go straight.* Post Exchange and good view to right.

73.35 Old officers' houses on left.

73.40 Catholic Chapel of the Most Holy Trinity on left.

73.40 Road becomes Washington Road.

73.40 Continue north on Washington Road.

73.70 Old Cadet Chapel and burial ground on right. This Greek Revival building was built in 1836 of native stone and has been moved several times. It is now used for funerals. The cemetery dates from 1816 and contains the graves of Generals Winfield Scott, Custer, and Goethals.

73.70 Margaret Corbin grave and marker on right.

73.80 *Bear straight right* at fork.

74.00 *Bear left* on Washington Road.

74.30 New Hospital and Cro' Nest Mountain on right.

74.60 Leave U. S. Military Academy, West Point. Washington Gate.

74.65 Washington Valley (E.R.M. 48.90)

74.65 *Turn right* on Route 218.

75.60 Pass Lee Gate on right.

75.70 Begin Old Storm King Highway. Built by Gen. George Washington Goethals (1858–1928).

75.80 Cross Falls Brook.

76.30 Cross Rose's Brook.

76.40 Cliff on left. Cro' Nest Mountain. Ahead, across the river, are Breakneck Mountain and Mount Taurus (Bull Hill). View ahead of Storm King Mountain on west bank.

76.80 Parking on right. The valley here is called Mother Cronk's Cove. View ahead of Newburgh Bay and Pollepel's Island. (E.R.M. 51.00)

77.00 Stillman's Spring on left.

77.05 Cross Storm King Brook.

77.20 Parking on right. View of Breakneck Mountain across river.

77.30 Cross stream, No. 1.

77.31 Cross stream, No. 2.

77.50 Cliffs of Storm King Mountain on left. View ahead of Breakneck Mountain and Mount Taurus.

77.80 Point of Storm King Mountain. Road is 200 feet above river. Parking on right. View north of Cornwall, Newburgh Bay, city of Newburgh, Pollepel's Island, Beacon Range, across river, and Shawangunk and Catskill mountains to the north-west. (E.R.M. 51.50)

78.10 Cross stream, No. 3.

78.20 Parking on right.

78.30 Cross stream, No. 4.

78.40 Cross stream, No. 5

78.40 End of Old Storm King Highway.

78.40 Cornwall village line. Road now called Bayview Avenue.

78.80 Camp Olmstead on left. Note Victorian gatehouses.

79.10 *Turn right* on Hudson Terrace. (E.R.M. 52.30)

79.15 Cross brook.

79.20 *Turn sharp right* on River Street.

79.20 Spring and park on right.

79.30 Cross West Shore Railroad.

79.31 Cornwall Landing. (E.R.M. 52.80) Cornwall Yacht Club on right. Site of former N.Y.O.&W. Railway docks and coal trestle. View across river to South Beacon and Breakneck Mountain. It is near here that Consolidated Edison Co. proposed construction of a pumped storage inlet.

79.31 *Turn left.*

79.40 Cross West Shore Railroad again.

79.80 Go straight on Shore Road.

80.10 *Turn right* on River Avenue. Cornwall Depot.

80.11 Cross former New York, Ontario & Western Railway tracks.

80.40 Overgrown drive up hill to left went to *Idlewild,* home of Nathaniel Parker Willis. His water gardens were located to the right near outlet of Moodna Creek.

80.50 Cross Idlewild Brook.

80.70 New Windsor town line.

80.70 Moodna Creek on right. (E.R.M. 53.20)

80.90 *Bear right.*

81.00 *Turn right* at stop light on Route 9W.

81.10 Cross Moodna Creek.

81.40 Pass road to Sloop Hill on right. Colonie Funeral Home on left. Former Leonard D. Nicoll House, 2½-story Ionic Greek Revival, 1843.

81.70 *Turn right* on Old Route 9W.

82.00 Pass drive to former Oakland Academy on right.

82.00 St. Thomas Episcopal Church on left. Stone with crenellated bell tower, mid-nineteenth-century.

82.05 Plum Point on Hudson Condominiums on right. Scenically inappropriate.

82.10 Junction with Quassaick Avenue on left. (Southbound turn here to get on Route 9W southbound.) The road now becomes River Road.

82.15 Thomas Ellison House site on right, with historical marker. Used as headquarters by Washington at various times between 1779–1781, it was demolished in mid-nineteenth century.

82.20 Enter Historic New Windsor area; many early nineteenth-century buildings.

82.30 Texaco petroleum depot on right.

82.40 Citgo petroleum depot on right (Cities Service Oil Co.).

82.45 Amoco depot on right (American Oil Co.–Standard Oil of New York).

82.47 Affron Tank Terminal on right.

82.70 Exxon Corp. petroleum depot on right.

82.80 Sunoco petroleum depot on right (Sun Oil Co.).

83.10 Mobil Oil Corp petroleum depot on right.

83.30 Cross Quassaic Creek. (E.R.M. 56.00)

83.30 Newburgh city line. Mount Beacon is across the river. The West Shore Railroad underpass beneath the Erie Railroad branch from Greycourt Junction is on right. This is the site of the former Marvel shipyard, on right, now Steel Style Corp.

83.40 Pass under Erie Railroad.

83.60 *Turn left* on Renwick Street.

83.90 *Turn right* on Liberty Street.

84.05 Pass Lafayette Street.

84.10 Hasbrouck House on right. (E.R.M. 56.10)

84.15 *Turn right* on Washington Street.

84.20 Belvidere on right. Mount Beacon across river.

84.20 *Turn left* on Washington Place.

84.40 *Turn left* on Broadway. (E.R.M. 56.20)

84.50 *Turn right* on Grand Street.

84.55 St. Patrick's R. C. Church on left; greystone, ca. 1855, by Rembrandt Lockwood.

84.60 Ebenezer Baptist Church on right (down First Street); red brick, Hudson River Gothic with clock tower and belfry.

84.65 Associated Reform Church on left; clapboard, Federal style, ca. 1790.

84.65 Newburgh Library on right; three-story brick Victorian, ca. 1865.

84.70 St. George's Episcopal Church on left; stone, 1819.

84.75 Newburgh City Club on right; (restored) two-story brick, ca. 1845. Designed by Andrew Jackson Downing and Calvert Vaux, later remodeled by Henry Hobson Richardson.

84.75 Newburgh Court House on left; brick Greek Revival with Ionic entablature, ca. 1830.

84.77 New Library on right; former site of Palatine Hotel.

84.77 Spire of First Methodist Church up Third Street to left; Gothic Revival, mid-nineteenth-century, designed by Rembrandt Lockwood.

84.78 Dutch Reformed Church on right; Greek Revival, ca. 1830, by Alexander Jackson Davis.

84.80 Westminster Presbyterian Church on left; brick, ca. 1890.

85.00 Calvary Presbyterian Church on left; ca. 1890, fieldstone Gothic with red tile, patterned roof and stone spire, heavy cast iron fence, and cemetery. It is now a Seventh Day Adventist Church.

85.10 *Turn left* on Clinton Street.

85.20 *Turn right* on Liberty Street.

85.30 St. Mary's Villa on left.

85.60 *Turn left* on Carobene Court.

85.80 *Turn left* on Elmwood Place.

85.85 *Turn left* on Powell Avenue.

86.00 Mount St. Mary's College on left; grounds an example of late nineteenth-century Victorian landscape architecture.

86.40 Chapman Steamer No. 1 firehouse on right.

86.50 Street now called DuBois Street.

86.50 Downing Park on right. Designed by Frederick Law Olmstead in honor of Andrew Jackson Downing in 1892.

86.60 *Turn right* on Third Street.

86.61 *Turn right* on City Terrace.

86.85 *Bear left and then right.* Formal gardens undergoing volunteer restoration.

86.90 Hilltop. Views of river. *Turn around* at loop.

87.10 *Bear right.*

87.15 *Bear right* onto Carpenter Avenue.

87.40 *Turn right* off Carpenter Avenue onto Gidney Avenue.

87.80 *Turn right* on Liberty Street.

87.85 *Turn left* on South Street.

88.00 *Turn left* on Grand Street.

88.10 *Turn right* on Clinton Street.

88.20 *Turn right* on Montgomery Street.

88.20 Crawford House on right; three-story clapboard, Ionic columns, ca. 1830. Built for David Crawford in Federal style. Home and museum of the Historical Society of Newburgh Bay and the Highlands, 189 Montgomery Street.

88.30 *Turn left,* downhill, on South Street.

88.35 *Turn left* on Water Street.

88.50 *Bear left* on Leroy Place.

88.90 *Turn right* on Balmville Road.

89.00 Johnes Home on left.

89.10 Cross over Interstate 84, Newburgh-Beacon Bridge to right. (E.R.M. 57.20.)

89.30 Powelton Country Club on left; one of oldest golf courses in United States, rebuilt in 1929.

89.40 Chadwick House on right; mid-nineteenth-century.

89.60 Eastman House on right; two-story brick cottage. Downing type with jig-saw ornamentation, mid-nineteenth-century.

89.90 St. Agnes Church on right; red brick and clap-board, Hudson River Gothic (ca. 1870).

89.92 Balmville—Balm of Gilead Tree (also known as Bonville Oak Tree). (E.R.M. 58.00.)

89.93 *Bear straight right* to River Road. Follow signs to Beau Rivage.

90.20 *Bear right.*

90.20 Reese House on left; rusticated Victorian with Andrew Jackson Downing influences, ca. 1859.

90.40 Our Lady of Hope Seminary on right; Oblates of Mary, Tudor Style, ca. 1890.

92.60 Site of former Rose House on right. For many years operated as Beau Rivage Restaurant. (E.R.M. 61.00)

92.70 Roseton. (E.R.M. 61.00)

92.90 Hess Oil Co. Roseton Terminal on right.

93.40 Roseton Generating Plant–Danskammer Point on right. (E.R.M. 62.00)

93.60 Our Lady of Mercy R. C. Church on left; brick, ca. 1890.

93.60 The power plants in this area are a joint venture of Central Hudson Power, Consolidated Edison Co., and Niagara Mohawk, built 1973. Many transformer yards and transmission lines are in this vicinity.

94.20 Cedar Hill Cemetery is on left.

94.40 *Turn right* on Old Marlboro Turnpike, also called Old Post Road.

95.70 Orchards.

95.80 Quarries near Cedar Cliff are visible on right. (E.R.M. 63.20)

96.10 Quarry Road on right. New York Trap Rock Div. Lone Star Industries.

96.12 Pond and dam with waterfall on left.

96.40 Bracketed mansion on right.

96.70 Christ Episcopal Church on right.

96.75 *Turn right* onto Route 9W off Old Post Road.

96.80 Marlboro village. (E.R.M. 64.50)

96.80 St. Mary's R. C. Church on left.

96.85 Riverside Cemetery on right.

97.20 Cross Maune Kill, falls on left. (E.R.M. 64.50)

97.21 *Turn right* on Dock Road.

97.25 Foundations of nineteenth-century Marlboro Winery on right.

97.70 Former depot and landing. *Turn around.* (E.R.M. 64.50.)

98.20 *Turn right* on Route 9W.

98.30 Marlboro Middle School on left.

98.32 Elementary school on right.

98.33 Young estate on right at end of Young Avenue. (E.R.M. 64.70)

98.50 Marlboro town line, Pegg's Point to right. (E.R.M. 64.90)

100.10 Hepworth Farms on left, reputed to be the first fruit stand in the Hudson Valley.

100.70 Milton town line.

100.71 *Turn right* on South Road.

100.80 *Turn right* on Old Indian Road. Micajiah Lewis homestead on left; one-story stone, pre-1760, remod-eled.

101.70 Former Milton Railroad depot and landing on right. Now operated as Kedem Royal Winery. View of I.B.M. tower across river. (E.R.M. 67.50)

101.80 *Turn left* uphill on Dock Road.

102.20 *Turn right* on Main Street (end of Dock Road).

102.25 *Turn right* on Church Street.

102.30 Presbyterian Church on left; creosote shingle Gothic, bracketed, ca. 1890.

102.30 United Methodist Church on right; clapboard, ca. 1850, cemetery.

102.30 *Turn around.*

102.35 *Turn right* on Main Street.

102.50 Locust Grove Fruit Farm and vineyard, both sides.

102.50 Yellow Victorian barn on right.

102.90 Cross brook; picturesque orchards.

103.00 *Bear right* on North Road.

103.40 Sunnycrest on right; mid-nineteenth-century. Home of (Civil War) Gen. Peter Wanzer.

103.45 White colonial home on right.

103.50 *Turn right* on Route 9W off Main Street, North Road.

104.60 Pass Blue Point Road on right. Hudson Valley Wine Co. orchards and winery are at end of road. (E.R.M. 69.20.)

105.70 Junction Routes 44 and 55. Mid-Hudson Bridge to right. (E.R.M. 70.50.)

106.00 End of interchange.

106.10 Cross over former Central New England Railroad (New Haven-Conrail) right of way leading to the Poughkeepsie Railroad Bridge. Track removed and right of way obscured by new vegetation.

106.20 Highland town line. (E.R.M. 71.50)

106.40 *Turn right* off Route 9W onto White Street.

106.70 *Turn right* on Vineyard Avenue.

106.80 *Bear left* downhill, along Twaalfskill Creek.

106.90 Mid-Hudson Hotel on left; ca. 1850, brick with stepped gable ends.

106.92 Cross West Shore Railroad tracks. Former ferry slips to left.

107.10 Cross railroad tracks again. Here is former Highland depot remodeled as a small copy of Lake Mohonk Mountain House.

107.15 Elting's Landing historical marker on right. Bombarded by the British in 1777. The ferry was established by Noah Elting in 1793. A horse-powered flat boat was used in 1819, and the Dutchess & Ulster Steam Power Ferry was established in 1830.

107.20 Continue along river on Oakes Road, under bridges.

107.90 *Turn around.* Oakes. (E.R.M. 70.40)

108.90 Mid-Hudson Hotel on right. Continue uphill on Vineyard Avenue, the right fork.

109.40 *Turn right* on Bellevue Road.

110.60 *Bear right* at fork.

110.80 *Bear right* at fork.

111.30 View of Culinary Institute of America across river. (E.R.M. 73.80)

111.80 Small Binnewater Pond on right.

112.40 Krum Elbow on right. (See article E.R.M. 74.25)

112.90 Orchard area. Road now called Red Top Road.

113.20 *Turn right* on Route 9W—divided highway.

113.25 Plant and offices of Staff Lighting on right.

113.80 New York State Police Station on right.

114.60 End of divided highway.

114.90 Mother Cabrini School on right; two-story stone with later Carpenter Gothic elements, 1820. St. Francis Xavier Cabrini (Mother Cabrini) (1850–1917) was born in Italy and came to the United States in 1889. She founded the order of Sisters of the Sacred Heart of Jesus and devoted herself to founding orphanages. She was canonized by Pope Pius XII in 1946—the first U.S. citizen to be canonized.

115.40 West Park town line.

115.50 Site of former St. Gabriels School on right.

115.60 Santa Maria Novitiate (Christian Brothers) on right; two-story brick Italianate Victorian mid-nineteenth-century.

116.00 View of Vanderbilt mansion across river. (E.R.M. 77.00)

116.10 Cross over West Shore Railroad.

116.40 "Aberdeen," Greek Revival house on right; ca. 1835, clapboard with temple facade.

116.40 The Hedges Restaurant on left; French Provincial building (Gillhooley's house).

116.50 Van Benschoten House on right; two-story stone and shingle.

116.52 Rustic gateway on right.

116.60 *Riverby* on right; home of John Burroughs, two-story stone, ca. 1873, designed and landscaped by Burroughs. (See article E.R.M. 77.20)

116.80 Holy Cross Episcopal Monastery on right.

116.90 Church of the Ascension (Episcopal) on right; stone, 1842, with two ogee windows; Hudson River Gothic stone parsonage.

117.30 Wildwycke Village on left (entrance). An abandoned shopping center utilizing the stone stables designed by Julian Burroughs in Tudor style. The barn has a bell and clock. Formerly part of the Oliver Hazard Payne estate.

117.30 Marist Brothers Novitiate entrance on right. Former estate of Oliver Hazard Payne. (See article E.R.M. 77.20)

117.50 Old mill ruins on left; mid-nineteenth-century.

117.52 Ascension Church Cemetery on left.

117.70 *Turn left* on Black Creek Road.

117.75 Cross Black Creek.

117.80 Former Wiltwyck School on right. Stone buildings now converted to condominiums.

118.30 Cross Route 9W at grade. Be careful. It is here called Broadway.

118.30 You are now on Main Street, Esopus.

118.50 *Turn right* on Parker Avenue at Motts Garage.

118.80 Rosemont Mansion on left. (See article E.R.M. 79.50)

119.00 *Turn around* at Indian Rock. Private boat landing and launching site. (E.R.M. 79.75)

119.50 *Turn right* on Main Street.

119.70 Esopus Methodist Church on right; ca. 1845, clapboard, Greek Revival elements.

119.80 *Turn right* on Route 9W (Broadway).

120.10 Mount St. Alphonsus on right; Redemptorist Father's Major Seminary, a massive 4½-story Romanesque gray stone building, 1900. (E.R.M. 79.90)

120.60 Mother of Perpetual Help Monastery on right, Redemptorist Nuns.

120.70 Ulster Park town line.

121.40 Dutch Reformed Church on left; brick with Gothic Revival elements and bell tower, 1827.

121.60 *Turn right* on River Road, Ulster County Route 24.

121.60 Orchard area. Husseys Mountain to west.

121.80 Old Red Schoolhouse with belfry to left.

123.10 Riverfront. Esopus Meadows on right. Lighthouse. (See article E.R.M. 82.30)

124.40 View upriver to Catskill Mountains and Kingston-Rhinecliff Bridge.

125.60 *Bend left.*

125.70 *Turn right* off River Road onto Route 9W.

125.70 Village of Port Ewen. (E.R.M. 85.25)

125.72 Cemetery on right.

125.30 View of Catskill Mountains ahead.

126.50 *Turn right* on North Broadway.

126.50 Sleightsburg. (See article E.R.M. 86.00)

127.00 *Turn around.* Southern terminus of former Skillipot cable ferry to Rondout, across Rondout Creek. View of Ponckhockie Cliffs.

127.10 *Turn left* on First Avenue.

127.20 *Turn right* on Parsell Street.

127.30 View of Rondout Lighthouse on left. (E.R.M. 86.25)

127.32 *Turn right* on Second Avenue.

127.40 *Turn left* on North Broadway.

127.70 *Go straight* at light onto Old Route 9W.

128.00 Begin Suspension Bridge across Rondout Creek.

128.20 End bridge. You are on Wurts Street, Rondout. (E.R.M. 86.30)

128.30 Trinity Methodist Episcopal Church on left; 1867, yellow brick, Hudson River Gothic, with slate spire.

128.30 Veterans' Memorial on right.

128.40 Corner of Spring Street. Abandoned First Baptist Church on left; brick Gothic, fine spire, 1861.

128.45 St. Mark's A.M.E. Church on right; fieldstone Gothic Revival with Tudor influences, ca. 1870, slate roof, crennelated belfry.

128.45 St. Peter's R.C. Church on left; yellow brick Hudson River Gothic with Romanesque belfry, 1871.

128.50 *Turn right* on Rogers Street.

128.50 Redeemer Lutheran Church on right; fieldstone Tudor with crennelated square belfry, ca. 1900.

128.60 *Turn right* on Broadway.

128.60 Ponckhockie Cliffs on left.

128.90 Strand area of restored nineteenth century commercial buildings. Building on right was former Samson Opera House, later known as Freeman Building. Now home of Mary P's Restaurant.

128.90 *Turn left* on The Strand, now also known as Rondout Landing.

129.00 Pass beneath new Route 9W Bypass Bridge. Rondout Landing on right. Homeport of Hudson River Cruises. Operates *M/V Rip Van Winkle* to West Point and other landings up and downriver during summer season.

RONDOUT LANDING, Kingston. The author was President of the Hudson River Maritime Center at Rondout Landing when this picture was taken on July 8, 1983. Tugboat *Anthony McAllister* is seen maneuvering the world's largest floating crane, the *Century*, into position as she delivers the historic steam tugboat *Mathilda* to become a permanent exhibition. The *Mathilda* has since been somewhat restored and is on exhibit. Photo: © Carmen Schettino.

129.05 McAllister Corporation former St. Lawrence River steam tugboat *Mathilda* on right. Undergoing restoration.

129.06 Hudson River Maritime Center on right.

129.10 Site of old Rhinecliff Ferry House on right.

129.15 Trolley Museum on left. Rides to Kingston Point.

129.30 Ruins of old limestone furnace on left.

129.60 *Bend left* on North Street, Ponckhockie.

130.00 *Turn right* on Delaware Avenue.

130.10 Cross Ulster & Delaware railroad track.

130.40 Kingston Point. *Turn around.* (E.R.M. 86.30) Area of old Dayline Park and lagoon where replica of *Clermont* was anchored.

130.60 *Turn right* into park. Good view upriver.

130.80 *Turn right* on Delaware Avenue.

131.00 Continue uphill on Delaware Avenue.

131.20 Victorian school house on left.

131.20 *Turn right* on Lyndsley Avenue.

131.30 Cordt's House on right; 1873, twenty-two-room Victorian mansion.

131.30 *Turn around.* Good view looking south.

131.40 *Turn right* on Delaware Avenue.

131.50 *Turn left* on Abruyn Street.

131.55 Union Congregational Church on right; cast concrete, Hudson River Gothic, late nineteenth-century, formerly known as "The Children's Church," Ponckhockie, 1780.

131.60 *Turn right* on Walnut Street. Ponckhockie Cliffs ahead.

131.70 *Turn right* on Gill Street.

131.75 *Turn left* on Yeoman Street.

131.80 *Turn left* on East Union Street (Tompkins).

131.90 *Turn right* on East Strand.

132.40 *Turn right* on Broadway.

132.70 St. Mary's Church on right; brick Tudor, ca. 1910, with square belfry.

133.80 *Turn right* on Broadway, Route 9W. Continue uphill.

133.90 *Turn right* on East Chestnut Street.

134.00 *Turn left* on Livingston Street.

134.01 Emanual Evangelical Lutheran Church; Hudson River Gothic, green brick with spire, ca. 1860.

134.10 *Turn right* onto Delaware Avenue and then immediately *bear left* onto Route 9W North.

Optional Side Trip to Old Kingston

(4.5 miles round trip).

0.00 Corner of Livingston Street and Delaware Ave. Turn left on Delaware Avenue and then right on Broadway. (NOTE: No left turns are allowed onto Delaware Avenue. *Turn right* and seek a turnaround.)

0.10 Kingston Hospital on right.

0.20 Kingston Library on left; red brick, composite style, ca. 1900.

0.20 Old Kingston City Hall on right; nineteenth-century, by Arthur Crooks. Modeled after Palazzo Vecchio in Florence, ca. 1875, mansard roof.

0.25 Kingston High School on left; yellowbrick, Ionic Neo-Classic, ca. 1900.

0.30 Kingston Municipal Auditorium on left. (Corner of Hoffman.)

0.40 Bus terminal on left.

0.50 Y.M.C.A. on left; three-story red brick, ca. 1900.

0.60 Go under West Shore Railroad and Greenkill Avenue.

0.80 Junction Routes 28–32–213.

0.90 Octagon House on left; corner of Elmendorf Avenue, two-story red brick.

1.10 *Turn left* on Park Avenue. View of Catskill Mountains ahead.

1.20 First Baptist Church on right; stone, Hudson River Gothic with spire, fieldstone, ca. 1890.

1.30 Governor Clinton Hotel on right; red brick Georgian with temple portico, ca. 1910, now apartments.

1.30 *Turn right* on Clinton Avenue. Entering Stockade area, original part of town.

1.50 Senate House on left (Colonel Wessel Ten Broeck House), 1676. This was the first meeting place of the New York State Senate in 1777.

1.50 *Turn left* on North Front Street.

1.80 *Turn left* on Green Street.

2.10 *Turn left* on Pearl Street.

2.20 *Turn left* on Wall Street.

2.25 Old Dutch Church on right; fieldstone with spire, 1852, by Minard Lefever. Governor George Clinton (1739–1812) is buried in the churchyard.

2.30 Old courthouse on left; 1818, on site of earlier one.

2.40 *Turn right* on North Front Street.

2.50 *Turn right* on Fair Street.

2.51 Senate House Museum on left.

2.70 *Turn left* on Pearl Street.

2.80 Continue straight on Park Avenue.

3.00 *Turn right* on Broadway (Routes 28 and 32).

3.20 Octagon House on right.

3.50 Pass under Greenkill Avenue and West Shore railroad.

4.10 *Turn left* on Delaware Avenue.

4.50 *Turn left* onto Route 9W North.

End of sidetrip.

Old Houses in the Stockade Area.

1. Converse Street and Frog Alley
   Pieter Cornelise Louw-Bogardus site, ca. 1668, earliest documented house in city.
2. St. James Street
   No. 84: Van Keuren House.
3. Wall Street
   No. 97: Van Steenbergh House, 1700, the only house that escaped burning by General Vaughan in 1777.
   No. 225: Cornelius Elmendorf House, before 1777.
4. Green Street
   No. 7: Tobias Van Bruen House.
   No. 135: Col. Abraham Hasbrouck House.
   No. 138: Gerrett Van Keuren House.
   No. 145: Rachel DuMond House, frame, late eighteenth century.
   No. 147: Egbert DuMond House, Federal style.
   No. 175: Jacobus Coenradt Elmendorf House.
5. Main Street
   No. 63: John Sudam House (also known as Van Leuven) ca. 1820, Federal style.
   No. 74: Tobias Swart House, Colonial style.
   No. 77: Dr. Elmendorf House.
   No. 78: Brick House, ca. 1840.
6. Crown Street
   No. 10: Cornelius Tappen House, First Post Office.
   No. 42: Petrus Franciscus Rogan House, ca. 1750, also known as Franz House, Swiss settlers.
   No. 43: Matthew Jansen House.
   No. 53: Abraham DeWitt Lowe House (ca. 1750), Coffee House.
   Corner of North Front Street: Jacobus S. Bruyn House, ca. 1750.
7. John Street
   No. 20: DeWitt House, ca. 1830
   No. 74: Jan Hendrickse Persen House, 1700s.
   Corner of Green Street: Luke Kiersted House, 1700s, frame.
8. Pearl Street
   No. 26: The Columns (Reverend Hoes House), Greek Revival, served as a rectory.
   No. 109: Cornelius Masten House (1725), stone.

Corner of Wall Street: Johannes Masten House, frame.

9. Maiden Lane

No. 88: Coonradt Elmendorf Tavern. The Committee of Safety met here.

No. 129: John McLean House, before 1730.

10. Clinton Avenue

No. 308: Abraham Masten House.

11. North Front Street

No. 3: Tremper House, 1801

No. 61: Anthony Freer House.

Corner of Green Street: Martinus Hoffman House (1660), also known as Jan Gacherie House (now operating as "Hoffman House" restaurant).

12. Road to Hurley: Tjerck Claessen DeWitt House (1669).

There are many other old and interesting buildings in the Stockade area and a leisurely walking tour is greatly recommended.

Continue Main Route

135.50 *Turn right* on Route 32.

135.52 Town of Ulster line.

135.60 You are on Old Flatbush Road. (E.R.M. 89.60)

135.80 Quarries on both sides.

136.10 View of Kingston-Rhinecliff Bridge to right.

136.40 *Turn right* on Route 37, Ulster Landing Road.

136.60 Town of Ulster Park. Riverside picnic ground and boat launching site, entrance on right.

137.80 Driveway to *Patroon Hill* on right; two-story clapboard with tower, 1835.

138.00 Pass under Kingston-Rhinecliff Bridge. (E.R.M. 90.00)

138.90 *Turn right.*

139.40 Entrance to Wrongside on right; two-story brick and clapboard, ca. 1825. Name given to the estate by the Livingstons, who felt their relative who built it should have done so on the east bank of the river.

141.80 Ulster Landing. (E.R.M. 91.50)

142.20 St. George's camp on right.

142.70 Ulster County Park. St. George's bathing beach entrance on right.

143.20 View of Catskill Mountains.

143.30 Pass road to Turkey Point on right.

143.70 *Turn right* on Route 32. (E.R.M. 92.85)

143.70 Flatbush Center.

143.71 One-room red brick schoolhouse on right.

144.20 Flatbush Reformed Church on right; organized in 1807, present building 1808, fieldstone with square belfry.

144.20 Good view of Catskill Mountains; left to right, Overlook Mountain, High Peak, Wall of Manitou.

144.40 Old stone house and well house on right.

145.20 Glasco town line.

145.80 Glasco Center.

145.80 *Turn right* on Glasco Turnpike also called Delaware Avenue.

146.40 *Turn around* at site of former glass warehouse at corner of Hudson Street. (E.R.M. 94.50.)

147.00 *Turn right* on Route 32.

147.00 Overlook Mountain and Kaaterskill High Peak seen ahead.

147.50 *Turn right* on Route 9W; Barclay Heights.

148.40 Saugerties town line.

148.40 St. Mary of the Snow Cemetery on left.

148.50 *Turn right* on Spaulding Lane.

148.60 Schoonmaker House on right; one-story stone, eighteenth century.

148.61 *Turn left* on Simmons Street.

148.90 *Turn left* on Barclay Heights.

149.10 *Turn right* on Burt Street.

149.30 *Bear right.*

149.35 *Turn right* on Ferry Street.

149.40 Esopus Creek and marinas on left. (E.R.M. 96.50)

149.70 *Turn around* at Saugerties Power Boat Association.

150.05 *Bear left* uphill.

150.30 *Turn right* on Route 9W.

150.40 *Turn right again* on Route 9W.

150.40 Trinity Church and Catskill Mountains on left. Hudson River on right.

150.60 *Turn left* on Route 9W. Kaaterskill High Peak seen ahead.

150.62 Old Red Brick School on right.

150.70 Cross Esopus Creek on Truss Bridge, above the dam.

150.90 *Turn right* on Route 9W, Partition Street.

151.00 *Turn right* on Dock Street.

151.00 Pull off to right. Overlook point. Gorge and falls of the Esopus.

151.00 *Turn around.*

151.10 *Turn right* on Route 9W, Partition Street.

151.30 *Turn right* on Route 9W, Main Street.

151.40 Reformed Church and Parsonage on left.

151.50 Kiersted House on left; one-story stone with small wing, pre-Revolutionary.

151.70 Schoonmaker Homestead on left; one-story stone with smaller wings, pre-Revolutionary.

151.80 *Turn right* on Mynderse Street.

152.00 Salt Box House on right; ca. 1820.

152.00 Mynderse House on left; one-story stone, early eighteenth century. This is the possible setting for "Clawbonny" in Cooper's *Afloat and Ashore.* The original house dates from 1690, with new wings dating from 1743.

152.30 *Bear left* on Lighthouse Drive.

152.40 Esopus Creek on right; old mills.

152.60 Capt. John Field House on left; two-story brick, Greek Revival mansion with fluted Doric columns, ca. 1840.

152.60 Marinas on right.

153.00 Coast Guard Station on right.

153.10 Rock Point. Private estate.

153.10 *Turn around.* View of lighthouse. (E.R.M. 96.50) Washburn's Point.

153.80 *Turn right* uphill on Mynderse Road (no street sign).

153.90 View to left of Saint Marys of the Snow R. C. Church; light gray, Hudson River gothic, with spire.

154.10 Continue straight onto Route 9W.

154.20 Entrance to Seamon Park on right; extensive floral displays, annual autumn Chrysanthemum Festival.

154.40 Sawyer's Mill and Falls on Sawyer Kill to right; old mill undergoing restoration.

154.40 Cross Sawyer Kill. View of Catskill Mountains to left.

154.80 *Bear right* off Route 9W.

155.30 Malden-on-Hudson. Methodist Church; brick bracketed, with tall spire, 1867.

155.60 Battleship Maine Memorial, 1898; an old cannon.

155.60 *Turn right* on unnamed street. Loop around, *bearing right* all the time to Malden Landing, an old Hudson River village.

155.90 *Bear right* again back onto the main road.

155.90 Victorian gingerbread cottage with large cast-iron floral urn ahead.

156.00 Pass Maine Memorial again on left.

156.00 *Bear left.*

156.30 *Turn right* on Route 9W.

156.80 Cross bridge over West Shore Railroad.

157.40 *Turn right* on Emerick Road.

157.50 *Bear right.*

157.70 Cross grade crossing of West Shore Railroad.

157.70 *Bear left.*

157.90 Cross bridge over brook.

158.00 *Turn around,* bearing left; Eve's Point. (E.R.M. 99.60)

158.70 *Bear left.*

158.75 *Turn right* on Route 9W.

158.90 Good view of Catskill Mountains to left; Overlook, High Peak, Cloves.

158.92 Enter village of West Camp. (E.R.M. 100.30)

158.92 *Bear right* on Route 9W.

159.20 St. Paul's Lutheran Church and Old Stone House on right.

159.90 *Bend right* under West Shore Railroad.

160.00 *Turn sharp left* on Route 9W. Enter township of Catskill.

160.00 Village of Cementon.

160.50 St. Mary's R. C. Church and Alpha Portland Cement Plant to right.

160.50 Enter Greene County. (E.R.M. 100.50)

161.00 Entrance to Alpha Cement Plant on right.

161.20 Alsen. (E.R.M. 102.65)

161.20 Lehigh Portland Cement Co. to right.

161.21 *Sharp left* and *right* under West Shore Railroad.

161.22 Kalkberg on left. (E.R.M. 106.50)

161.70 Pass under cement conveyor.

162.70 *Turn right* on Embought Road.

162.80 Cross West Shore Railroad at grade.

162.80 Kalkberg, behind.

163.50 View of Inbocht Bay to right. (E.R.M. 103.50)

163.80 Cross Mineral Spring Brook. (E.R.M. 104.00)

163.90 *Bend left.*

164.60 *Bear left* at corner of Greenpoint Road. (E.R.M. 104.00)

165.10 *Bear left* at Anbach Lane.

165.40 Fine view of Catskill Mountains to left, beyond the Kalkberg.

165.70 Kykuit Hill. (E.R.M. 106.50)

165.70 Clauland House on right; 1½-story stone with one-story attachment, 1740.

166.30 Village of Catskill town line. (See E.R.M. 107.25)

166.30 Embought Road becomes Broome Street.

166.70 *Turn right* on Grand View Avenue.

166.80 Victorian red brick mansion on left.

167.20 *Turn left* on West Main Street.

167.40 Driveway to Hudson View House to right.

167.60 Hop O'Nose on right.

167.80 Old Mill on right. Union Cotton Mills, ca. 1860, two-story brick with tower.

167.90 Catskill Creek on right. Marinas.

168.10 Uncle Sam House on left. Two-story stucco, early nineteenth century. Martin Van Buren, eighth president of United States, was married here in 1807. Also, Sam Wilson ("Uncle Sam") lived here between 1817 and 1824.

168.11 *Turn right* on West Bridge Street.

168.15 Cross Catskill Creek on "Uncle Sam" bascule bridge.

168.20 *Turn right* on Water Street.

168.20 Site of Catskill Evening Line dock on right.

168.30 *Turn left* on Bronson Street.

168.35 *Turn right* on Hill Street.

168.40 *Turn left* on Greene Street.

168.50 *Turn right* on Main Street.

168.50 Dr. Albuisson House on southwest corner; two-story brick with stepped gable, fine doorway, and later bracketed cornice, ca. 1825.

168.70 Site of shale brick company; office building, two-story clapboard, ca. 1840, on creek to right.

168.90 Rip Van Winkle Bridge seen on left. (See E.R.M. 108.60)

169.00 Catskill Landing. Catskill Point. (E.R.M. 107.25)

169.00 County Highway Department garage. Former site of terminus of Greenbush Ferry, Catskill Mountain narrow gauge railway, and wharf of Hudson River Day Line.

169.00 *Turn around.*

169.80 First Reformed Church on right; red brick, Hudson River Gothic.

169.85 First Baptist Church on left; red brick Hudson River Gothic, two spires.

169.85 Greene County Courthouse on right; Ionic style with dome and frieze pediment entablature.

170.20 *Bear left.*

170.30 *Turn right* up Summit Avenue.

170.35 *Bear right* and *left* again.

170.40 *Turn right* on Grand Street.

170.45 *Turn right* on North Street.

170.70 *Turn left* on Thompson Street.

171.00 *Turn right* on Spring Street.

171.20 *Turn right* on William Street.

171.25 Great view of Catskill Mountains.

171.25 St. Luke Episcopal Church on left; stone with slate roof and spire, bracketed style.

171.50 *Turn left* on Main Street.

171.60 Howard Slide on left.

171.65 *Turn left* on Bridge Street.

171.70 *Turn left* on Franklin Street.

171.72 Christ Presbyterian Church and Old Courthouse on right; mid-nineteenth century with Corinthian columns made in same pattern as those used on the former Catskill Mountain House. First Court House, two-story brick, Palladian window, ca. 1812, now a Masonic Temple.

171.72 Howard Slide on left.

171.80 *Turn right* on William Street.

171.90 *Turn right* on Spring Street.

171.98 *Turn right* on Bridge Street (Route 385).

172.05 *Turn left* on Liberty Street.

172.05 St. Patrick's Church; red brick Hudson River Gothic with spire, 1885.

172.10 *Turn left* on Harrison Street.

172.20 *Turn right* into grounds of St. Anthony's Friary.

172.20 Site of former Prospect Park Hotel. (E.R.M. 107.30) Circle around building. View of Rip Van Winkle Bridge.

172.50 Exit friary grounds. Turn right on Harrison Street.

172.51 *Turn left* on Prospect Avenue.

172.70 *Turn right* on William Street.

172.70 Ionic-style Greek Revival house on left; ca. 1840.

172.80 *Turn left* on Woodland Avenue.

172.81 Picturesque roofed gateway on right.

173.10 *Turn left* on High Street.

173.20 *Turn right* on Spring Street.

173.30 Former home and studio of artist Thomas Cole on right.

173.40 *Turn right* on Route 23. Rip Van Winkle Bridge ahead. (E.R.M. 108.60)

173.70 *Turn left* on Hamburg Road.

174.30 Hamburg Village. (E.R.M. 108.75) View across river of Olana Castle and Mount Merino.

174.90 *Turn right* on Route 385.

175.00 Athens Village line. (E.R.M. 111.25)

175.80 Lighthouse on right. (E.R.M. 111.25)

176.90 *Turn left* on Fifth Street.

176.91 *Bear right.*

176.9.1 Van Loan-Haight-Gantly House on left, 38 Franklin Street. Two-story yellow brick, Federal style, built in 1812 for Gen. Samuel Haight, it has an oval ballroom and was very elegant for its day.

176.92 *Turn right* on Franklin Street.

177.10 *Turn right* on Third Street.

177.20 *Turn left* on South Washington Street.

178.30 House with conservatory on left; Clark House, ca. 1865.

178.31 *Turn left* on Second Street.

178.31 House with stepped gables.

178.40 Brooks Building, 1893. Formerly the Opera House.

178.80 *Turn right* on Leeds Road (South Vernon Street).

178.90 *Turn right* on First Street.

179.10 *Turn right* on South Montgomery Street.

179.20 *Turn left* on Third Street.

179.30 *Turn left* on Washington Street (Route 385).

179.90 Zion Lutheran Church.

180.10 Old yellow brick schoolhouse, Hudson River Gothic.

180.30 Athens Boat Launching site.

180.40 Cross Murderers' Creek. (E.R.M. 113.00)

180.60 *Turn right* on Brick Row. Group of row houses for railroad workers. Three-story brick, mid-nineteenth century.

180.70 *Turn left* along Brick Row.

181.80 *Turn around.* Go back to Route 385.

182.10 *Turn right* on Route 385.

182.10 View of Catskill Mountains to left and Berkshire and Green Mountains of Vermont on right.

182.30 Large yellow farmhouse with Mansard roof on left. Orchard area.

183.20 Entrance to Sleepy Hollow Lake Development on left.

183.90 *Turn right* on Fourmile Point Road.

184.60 Klinkenburg House on left; two-story stone with brick ends, early eighteenth century.

184.90 Pond on right.

185.30 Fourmile Point (E.R.M. 115.45). Lighthouse of stone with clapboard wings, early nineteenth century.

185.30 *Turn around.*

186.70 *Turn right* on route 385.

186.80 Old cemetery on right.

187.00 Groesback House on right; two-story clapboard, early nineteenth century.

187.00 Extensive view of Catskill Mountains to left.

187.10 Mansion on knoll at right; two-story brick Victorian, ca. 1870.

187.20 Elmcrest Farm on right. Lampman House, two-story clapboard, ca. 1800. Later enlarged and renovated with mansard roof and brackets.

187.20 Lampman Hill. (E.R.M. 118.00)

187.20 *Turn right* on Ely Street, Coxsackie.

188.00 House with stepped gable to right.

188.00 *Turn right* on New Street (one way).

188.01 *Turn right* on South River Street.

188.01 Old foundry on left.

188.60 *Turn around.* (E.R.M. 118.50)

188.90 *Bear right.*

189.20 Old brick stores in area.

189.20 Boat launching site. (E.R.M. 119.00)

189.20 *Turn around.*

189.30 *Turn right* on Reed Street.

189.40 *Turn right* on Ely Street (becomes Mansion Street).

189.40 Heermance Memorial Library.

189.70 Large red brick school house, corner of Elm Street.

189.80 *Turn right* on Washington Avenue.

189.80 St. Mary's Catholic Church on left.

190.20 *Turn left* on Lafayette Avenue.

190.50 Van Dyk House on right; built by Abraham Van Dyk in early nineteenth century. Two-story brick, Federal style.

190.60 *Turn right* on Mansion Street (Route 385).

190.70 *Turn right* on Lawrence Avenue, Greene County Route 61 (just before West Shore Railroad bridge).

190.80 Old brick farmhouse.

191.20 Cross Coxsackie Creek. (E.R.M. 121.50)

191.30 One-room schoolhouse on left. Now private home.

194.30 *Turn right* down Mill Street, New Baltimore. (E.R.M. 125.50)

194.60 *Turn left* on Main Street (Alton Civil Institute).

194.65 *Turn around* at Church Street.

194.70 *Turn right* at Parsons-Bronck House; 1½-story eighteenth century.

194.90 Old clapboard church, now a private home.

195.00 Continue straight on Route 144.

195.70 Requea Cemetery on right.

195.90 Greene/Albany county line. (See E.R.M. 126.60)

196.10 Cross Hannacroix Creek. (E.R.M. 126.50)

196.20 Coeymans. Bronck House to right; 1½-story stone, mid-eighteenth century.

196.25 Road to Barren Island on right (closed to public). (E.R.M. 126.60)

196.40 Coeymans. You are on Main Street.

196.70 Large Doric Greek Revival house.

196.90 Continue straight on Main Street. (E.R.M. 127.50)

197.00 *Bear right* across bridge over Coeymans Creek. (E.R.M. 127.55)

197.05 *Turn right* downhill.

197.20 Ariantje Coeymans House on right; two-story stone, ca. 1728.

197.30 Ravena Yacht Club—boat sheds, launching ramp, view of Castleton Bridges.

197.30 *Turn around.*

197.60 *Turn right* on Main Street, Route 144.

197.70 Powell & Minnock Brick Works to right.

197.70 *Bear left.* View of Castleton bridges.

197.90 Coeymans town line.

198.50 Pass beneath conveyor.

199.20 New York Thruway visible to left.

200.20 Cross over New York Central Castleton cutoff line (Conrail). (E.R.M. 129.80)

200.30 Pass beneath New York Thruway Berkshire branch. (E.R.M. 129.90)

201.30 Junction Route 396. Continue on Route 144.

201.70 Baker Farm on right; two-story clapboard, 1791.

201.80 Thruway entrance on left.

202.00 Cedar Hill town line.

202.90 Cross Vloman Kill. (E.R.M. 132.35)

202.91 *Turn right* on Lyons Road.

203.10 Old mill site on right.

203.60 *Turn left* along picnic area.

204.00 Boat launching area.

204.20 *Turn sharp right.*

204.40 Winne House to right; brick Victorian, white with mansard roof, ca. 1860.

204.50 Parda Hook (E.R.M. 133.20); site of Barent-Winne Docks, active in the nineteenth century, especially in the Albany rice trade.

204.50 *Turn around.*

204.60 *Turn right* on Winne Road.

204.80 Pryor House (B.P.O.E.) on right; Italianate Victorian, ca. 1900.

204.90 *Turn right* on Route 144.

204.92 Town of Bethlehem line.

205.00 Old Schoolhouse on left; brick, 1859, enlarged in 1907.

205.90 Our Lady of Angels seminary on right.

206.30 Old racetrack on left.

206.30 Halfway House on right; one-story stone, late eighteenth century.

206.30 Frothingham Lake on right.

206.40 *Turn right* on Mosher Road.

206.60 Town House on right; Italianate Victorian, ca. 1870.

206.70 *Bear left.*

206.90 *Bear right.*

207.00 *Bear left.*

207.20 Site of former icehouse on right.

207.40 Van Wies Point. (E.R.M. 135.00)

207.40 Van Wies House on right; clapboard with some early stone elements, 1679. Hendrick Gerritse Van Wie, Dutch colonist in Fort Orange in 1664, built a house here in 1679.

207.40 Road now becomes Wheeler Road, or Van Wies Point Road.

208.20 *Turn right* on Route 144.

208.25 Van Wies Point School on left; one-room brick, mid-nineteenth century, now shingled.

208.50 Exxon tank farm to left.

208.70 Texaco tank farm.

209.00 Niagara Mohawk Kenwood generating station to right. (E.R.M. 138.75)

209.40 Cross West Shore Railroad Albany Branch (Conrail).

209.90 Glenmont.

210.00 *Turn left* on Retreat House Road.

210.10 Corning Hill on left; former estate of Erastus Corning, railroad magnate and mayor of Albany.

210.60 *Turn right* on Corning Hill Road.

210.60 Kenwood.

210.70 *Turn left* on Route 144.

210.80 Cross Norman's Kill.

211.10 Pass beneath Delaware & Hudson Railroad.

211.30 Academy of the Sacred Heart to left; Victorian eclectic with Gothic and mansard elements; Victorian yellow brick gatekeeper's cottage.

211.40 Housing development on right.

211.60 Pass beneath Interstate 787.

211.70 You are on South Pearl Street, Albany.

211.70 Cherry Hill on left; 1787 two-story clapboard with gambrel roof. Until 1963, Cherry Hill served as the home of Philip Van Rensselaer and his descendants. Today it features many of the original furnishings, documents, and china and silver collections. 523 South Pearl Street. 518 434-4791.

211.90 Entrance to port of Albany on right. (E.R.M. 139.00)

212.00 *Turn left* on 4th Avenue.

212.10 *Turn right* on Elizabeth Street.

212.30 *Turn right* on Catherine Street.

212.40 *Turn right* on Clinton Street.

212.40 Schuyler Mansion on right, also called *The Pastures*; two-story brick Georgian, 1762, built by Philip Schuyler, a descendent of one of Albany's earliest settlers. With Schuyler's active role in the Revolutionary War and in the formation of the new nation, the mansion became a headquarters where such notables as the Compte de Rochambeau, General Washington, General Lafayette, Benjamin Franklin, and Aaron Burr were entertained. Several years after the war, Schuyler's daughter Elizabeth was wed to Alexander Hamilton in the mansion's drawing room.

Open daily except holidays.
32 Catherine Street. 518 434-0834.

212.45 *Turn left* on Schuyler Street.

212.50 *Turn left* on South Pearl Street.

212.60 *Turn right* on Ferry Street.

212.70 *Turn left* on Green Street.

212.80 St. John's Catholic Church.

212.85 Restored row houses.

213.20 *Turn right* on Madison Avenue.

213.60 *Turn left* on Broadway.

213.90 Former Day Line building on right (l'Auberge des Fougères); Dutch Revival, 1907.

214.00 Delaware & Hudson Building on right; now State University of New York. Built for the Delaware & Hudson Railroad Co. in 1918 (Marcus T. Reynolds architect), it is in Flemish-Gothic style with steep slate roofs, ornamented dormers. It is built of granite, four-story, with thirteen-story central tower with large bronze weather vane styled after Henry Hudson's *Half Moon*. A one-story vaulted arcade runs across the front. Major renovation was undertaken in 1975. (E.R.M. 139.50)

214.00 *Bear right* around rotary to *turn left* up State Street.

214.00 Federal Office Building on right; stone, Victorian eclectic, 1870.

214.20 St. Peters Church on right; stone, 1802, later Gothic elements.

214.30 *Turn right* on Eagle Street.

214.31 Albany City Hall on right; modified French Romanesque, 1882, by Henry Hobson Richardson, with sixty-bell carillon (largest bell weighs 11,200 lbs.). Statue of Philip Schuyler by J. Massey Rhind.

214.31 Site of former Fort Frederick to left.

214.32 New York State Capitol building to left; a gigantic French chateau, built between 1867 and 1898 at a cost of $25,000,000. Its design is eclectic. Thomas W. Fuller, Leopold Eidlitz, Henry Hobson Richardson, and Isaac G. Perry all worked on the building.

214.35 *Turn left* on Washington Street.

214.40 New York State Museum-State Education Building on right; with thirty-six Corinthian columns across the facade, built in 1912, designed by Palmer, Hornbostel & Jones, at a cost of $4,000,000.

ALBANY CITY HALL. Designed by Henry Hobson Richardson in 1882. Photo: © Bob Hansen.

214.70 *Turn left* on Dove Street.

214.80 *Turn left* on State Street.

215.00 New State Office Buildings on right.

215.50 *Turn right* on Broadway.

215.55 *Circle left* around rotary to head north on Broadway.

215.70 *Turn right* (north) on Broadway.

215.90 Former Union Station on right, now converted to headquarters of Norstar Bancorp. The pioneer Mohawk & Hudson Railroad was chartered in 1826 to run between Albany and Schenectady, and opened to traffic in 1831. It was financed by the State Bank of Albany, founded in 1804—a predecessor of the present Norstar Bancorp. The original Albany depot was atop the hill to the west of town. Later the Mohawk & Hudson became a part of first the New York Central System, and later Penn-Central and then Conrail. Today passenger trains are operated by Amtrak.

ALBANY UNION STATION. Seen in recently restored glory in 1989. Photo: © Bob Hansen.

The predecessor depot on the North Broadway, Albany, site was built in 1872. Traffic rapidly grew to such proportions that a new and larger terminal was required. The present building was designed by Shepley, Rutan & Coolidge of Boston, who also designed Boston's massive South Station. This architectural firm was successor to the firm of Henry Hobson Richardson, who designed the New York State Capitol and Albany City Hall. Norcross Brothers of Springfield, Massachusetts, were the general contractors. The building is described by the architects as in the "creative eclectic style, consisting of elements of Beaux Arts Classical and Second Renaissance Revival styles." It is built of pink Milford granite. It was opened for service on December 17, 1900. It was purchased by the State of New York on December 14, 1966. The *Twentieth Century Limited* made its last stop here on December 3, 1967. The last passenger train stopped here on December 29, 1968, on which date operations were transferred to a modern smaller depot across the river in Rensselaer, and called Albany-Rensselaer. The new station has much more convenient parking space and is well served by new roads and better suited to present train operations operated by Amtrak. The new station was recently enlarged and modernized. The Albany Union Station is listed on the National Register of Historic Places. Over the years it served trains of the New York Central, West Shore, Boston & Albany, and Delaware & Hudson railroads, and ultimately fell into dilapidation after service was transferred.

In April 1984 it was purchased by Norstar Bancorp for conversion to corporate headquarters. The architectural and engineering firm of Einhorn, Yaffee & Prescott of Albany was retained to undertake restoration and conversion. The original waiting room had a ceiling 56 feet high. This space was used by

moving the walls inward 15 feet on both east and west sides and building new intermediate floor levels around the perimeter of a new smaller atrium retaining the architectural detailing of the original waiting room—thus preserving the design character and also gaining useful modern office floor space. The building has won a great amount of professional architectural recognition as a masterpiece of adaptive reuse and visitors are welcome during normal business hours.

216.40 Pass beneath New York Central mainline (Conrail).

216.80 A statue of "Nipper," the Victor "his master's voice" dog, an R.C.A. trademark, is prominent on the roof of a building to right. The building is now occupied by SONY and the dog's ear now has an aircraft obstruction light in it.

217.30 Pass beneath Interstate 90. (E.R.M. 141.50)

217.70 Albany International Co.—Felt Division factory on right.

217.80 Albany/Menands city line. (E.R.M. 143.00)

218.00 Old Erie Canal bed parallel to right. D. & H. railroad also parallel to right.

218.40 Junction Route I-787.

218.50 Montgomery Ward Building on left; 9-story concrete.

218.60 Cross over Delaware & Hudson Railroad.

218.60 Former Van Rensselaer estate to left.

219.00 Menands Manor on left.

219.30 Junction Route 378. Bridge to Troy on right. (E.R.M. 144.25)

219.70 St. Agnes Cemetery and Albany Rural Cemetery on left. Cemetery is on site of former estate of William Howard Hart called *Fernwood*.

219.80 Doric-style mansion to left.

219.90 Watervliet/Menands city line.

220.00 Jermain House on left; two-story clapboard, Doric temple front, ca. 1840.

220.20 *Take right fork.*

220.50 Continue straight on Third Avenue.

220.80 Entrance to Watervliet Arsenel on left.

220.90 *Turn left* at light.

221.00 Old Arsenel buildings on left.

221.50 Watervliet City Hall on left. (E.R.M. 146.25)

221.70 Continue straight on Broadway.

221.90 Pass beneath highway.

222.00 Junction I-787. Continue straight.

222.20 *Turn right* on Twenty-fifth Street, traffic light.

222.25 Pass beneath I-787.

222.30 Cross ditch (which is the west channel of Hudson River).

222.31 Green Island. The street is now called Albany Avenue.

222.50 Bridge to Troy on right (former D. & H. Railroad bridge). (E.R.M. 146.75)

222.70 St. Mark's Chapel on right.

223.10 Park with view of dam and lock on right. (E.R.M. 147.75)

223.20 *Turn left* on Tibbits Avenue.

223.30 Cross D. & H. Railroad track.

223.50 *Turn right* on Cohoes Avenue.

224.30 City of Cohoes line.

224.40 *Turn right* at Proctor & Schwarz Mill.

224.40 One block before traffic light, you are riding in bed of old Erie Canal.

224.80 Remains of lock and bridge footing on left.

224.90 *Turn right* on Bridge Street.

225.00 Cross sprout or channel of Mohawk River. (E.R.M. 149.00)

225.00 View of Simmons Island to left.

225.10 Van Schaick Island.

225.11 *Turn right* on First Street.

225.20 *Turn left* on Hudson Avenue.

225.40 Cross Park Avenue and enter park.

225.42 Golf course on right. Site of Revolutionary encampment on left.

225.45 *Bend left.*

225.50 *Turn right* on Old Military Road.

225.60 Cross D. & H. Railroad (former Rensselaer & Saratoga Railroad).

225.70 *Turn left.*

226.00 Van Schaick House on left; two-story white brick with gambrel roof, 1777.

226.10 View of Hudson River to right.

226.30 View of Route 470 bridge across Hudson to right.

226.40 *Turn left* on Ontario Street, Route 470.

226.50 *Turn right* on Park Avenue (at light).

226.60 *Turn left* on Heartt Avenue.

226.65 View of lower Cohoes Falls, railroad and highway bridges across Mohawk River, and Harmony Mill.

226.70 *Turn left* on River Street.

226.71 *Turn right* on Ontario Street, Route 470.

226.72 Cross bridge over sprout of Mohawk River.

226.72 Rapids visible to right.

226.80 Simmons Island.

226.90 Cross west channel of Hudson and rapids, sprout of Mohawk River.

227.00 Cohoes. (E.R.M. 149.80)

227.20 Cross bed of old Erie Canal.

227.21 *Turn right* on Saratoga Street (light).

227.30 *Turn left* on Oneida Street. Mill area.

227.40 Cross main line of Delaware & Hudson Railroad.

227.45 *Turn right.*

227.47 *Turn left* on New Courtlandt Street.

227.50 View of Mohawk River to right.

227.60 Junction with Mohawk Street. Harmony Mills to left.

227.80 Site of finding of Cohoes Mastodon; found in 1866, now in New York State Museum.

228.00 *Turn right* on Front Street. East Harmony tenements.

228.10 *Turn left* on Cataract Street.

228.20 *Turn left.* View of falls to right.

228.22 *Turn left* on School Street. Power pond on right.

228.25 *Turn right* on North Mohawk Street.

228.30 *Bear right* at light.

228.50 Upper view of Mohawk Falls. Cohoes Falls to right.

228.70 *Turn left* on Cascade Street and *make U-turn.*

228.70 *Turn right* on North Mohawk Street.

229.20 *Bear left* at light.

229.30 Tenements on left.

229.80 *Turn right* on Mohawk Street.

229.90 *Turn left* on Oneida Street (light).

230.00 Cross Delaware & Hudson main line.

230.10 *Turn left* on Saratoga Street (Route 32).

230.20 Cross Mohawk River. (E.R.M. 150.45)

230.20 D. & H. railroad viaduct and falls to left.

230.20 Van Schaick Island to right.

230.50 Mansfield House on right; two-story clapboard, full Greek facade, ca. 1840.

230.60 Town of Waterford.

230.60 Waterford Museum to right.

230.70 Cross New York State Barge Canal. View of locks to left and right. (E.R.M. 151.00)

230.80 *Bear right* on Broad Street, Route 32. (E.R.M. 151.40)

230.90 Cross water-filled section of old Erie Canal and Lock No. 2.

231.00 *Turn left* on 3rd Street, Route 32 and 4N (light).

231.60 Good view of Hudson River to right.

231.90 Halfmoon. (E.R.M. 155.00)

233.50 Champlain Canal Lock No. 1 to right.

234.50 Brookwood to right; Greek Revival with full temple facade and Ionic columns, ca. 1840.

237.00 Lock No. 2 to right. Melville hydro plant. (E.R.M. 159.00)

237.50 Leeland House.

237.50 Ten Broeck House; two-story clapboard, late eighteenth century.

238.00 *Bear right.*

238.60 Town of Mechanicville. (E.R.M. 161.00)

239.60 Cross Anthony Kill. (E.R.M. 161.00)

239.80 Lock No. 3 and bridge across Hudson to right. (E.R.M. 161.75)

240.40 Boston & Main Railroad bridge across Hudson. (E.R.M. 162.50)

240.50 Stillwater town line.

242.00 Village of Stillwater. Octagon houses.

242.30 *Bear right.*

242.70 Lock No. 4 and bridge to canal park to right. (E.R.M. 164.00)

242.70 Historic sites: Fort Ingoldsby, 1709. Fort Winslow, 1756. Montressor's Blockhouse. Storehouse and barracks, 1758. Schuyler supply depot, 1777.

244.20 Leave Stillwater.

244.90 Bemis Heights. (E.R.M. 168.00)

245.20 Junction Routes 32 and 4. Continue straight on Route 4 to right.

247.10 Enter Saratoga Battlefield Historical Park.

247.20 Historical Park drive on left. Keep straight on Route 4.

247.60 *Turn right* on River Road.

251.50 Town of Saratoga line. (E.R.M. 171.70)

251.80 Continue straight on River Road.

252.60 *Turn right* on Route 4.

254.50 Greek Revival farmhouse on left.

256.70 Victory Mills, site of Fort Vrooman and Fort Clinton on left.

257.60 Site of surrender of Gen. Burgoyne to Gen. Gates.

257.90 Village of Schuylerville. (E.R.M. 178.80)

257.92 Philip Schuyler House on right, 1777.

257.92 Site of oldest cotton mill in New York State.

258.10 Cross Fish Creek. Enter village. (E.R.M. 178.80)

258.15 Junction Route 32.

258.20 Burgoyne Street, leading to battlefield and monument on left.

258.30 Junction Route 29 and bridge across Hudson on right. (E.R.M. 178.80)

258.60 Junction Route 29 to Saratoga Springs on left.

258.60 Site of camp of Gen. Burgoyne.

259.10 Lock No. 5 to right. (E.R.M. 180.00)

259.30 Northumberland town line.

260.30 *Turn left* on Route 32. Stark's Knob to left. (E.R.M. 180.75)

261.20 Bacon Hill. (E.R.M. 182.00)

SARATOGA SPA IN 1958. Spa has since fallen into disrepair. Photo: Arthur G. Adams.

261.20 *Turn right* on Saratoga County Route 29.

263.90 Fort Miller across river to right. (E.R.M. 185.00)

264.40 *Bear right.*

265.60 Old cemetery on left.

266.00 *Bear right.*

266.70 John McCrea House on left.

268.90 Continue straight on West River Road.

270.10 Villa (ca. 1820) to left. (E.R.M. 192.25)

270.30 Cross Delaware & Hudson main line.

270.50 *Turn right* on Route 197.

270.52 *Turn left* on Route 28—Fort Edward Road.

272.60 *Turn right* on Sisson Road.

272.90 Cross roadbed of former D & H Railroad Fenimore Branch. (E.R.M. 192.80)

273.20 *Turn right* on Bluebird Road.

274.00 Continue straight.

274.30 Fenimore. Large water tower to left with Chase written on it. (E.R.M. 196.00)

274.30 *Bear left.* Road becomes Ferry Boulevard.

274.50 *Turn left* on Sisson Road.

274.60 *Turn right* on Harrison Avenue Extension.

275.00 *Bear right* on Van Buren Avenue.

276.00 South Glens Falls village line.

276.40 Cross South Glens Falls branch of D. & H. Railroad.

276.50 *Turn right* on Spring Street.

277.90 *Turn left* on First Street.

277.00 *Turn right* on Hudson Street.

277.05 *Turn left* on River Street.

277.10 *Turn right* on Main Street, Route 9W.

277.10 Federal style house on left, with palladian window (ca. 1810).

277.20 Cross Hudson River above Glens Falls and Cooper's Cave.

277.30 Glens Falls. (E.R.M. 199.10)

277.30 End.

GRAND UNION HOTEL, Saratoga. Author's collection.

Southbound Express Route to Start of Lower East Side Route

0.00 Start at corner of 42nd Street and West Side Highway, 12th Avenue. Head South on 12th Avenue, West Side Highway. (E.R.M. 0.00)

−**4.00** (−3.28 E.R.M). Enter Brooklyn-Battery Tunnel. Ole Singstad was the tunnel's designer and chief engineer. It is a facility of the Triborough Bridge and Tunnel Authority. Construction started October 28, 1940, and halted for three and a half years during World War II. The tunnel was opened to traffic May 25, 1950. The length between portals is 9,117 feet. The tunnel has two separate tubes, each with 21'4" roadways with two traffic lanes in each tube. Fifty-three large exhaust fans supply 4,150,000 cubic feet of fresh air each minute, completely changing the air every one-and-a-half minutes. There is a large ventilation tower at the eastern edge of Governor's Island (no vehicular outlet). The tubes have a diameter of thirty-one feet and are of cast iron and were shield-driven under the East River through rock and earth. The land sections were con-structed by cut and cover. Tolls are collected at the southern portal.

−**5.50** Exit Brooklyn-Battery Tunnel.

−**6.50** *Bear right* on Gowanus Expressway—becomes Belt Parkway. Starting in 1996 the elevated Gowanus Expressway will be completely closed for reconstruction for a number of years. Follow posted detour signs.

−**9.25** Owl's Head Park on left. Begin Shore Parkway. (−8.25 E.R.M.)

−**11.75** Fort Hamilton. You are now on Shore Parkway, also known as Belt Parkway. (−11.20 E.R.M.)

−**19.00** Exit 11S Flatbush Avenue. *Turn right.*

−**20.50** Marine Parkway bridge. Toll each way. (−15.00 E.R.M.)

−**21.00** *Turn right* Breezy Point Exit.

−**23.05** Gatehouse to Rockaway Point. Security check. Rockaway Point is a private residential development. Entry to the grounds is strictly limited to the main road and entirely at the discretion of the security guard on duty. We suggest you seek entry only if you have a very serious interest so as not to abuse the owners' courtesy. Similar excellent ocean views are obtainable at the Jacob Riis Park boardwalk.

— **24.25** Corner Bay 227th Street and Rockaway Point Boulevard. (− 21.50 E.R.M.)

Lower East Side Road Route

Northbound Scenic Route—Rockaway Point to Forty-second Street Manhattan.

0.00 Start Tour: corner Bay 227th Street and Rockaway Point Boulevard. (− 21.50 E.R.M.)

Rockaway Point. You are in Queens County on a barrier sand bar parallel to the southern shore of Long Island, and separated from it by Jamaica Bay Inlet. There is a lighthouse here. Coney Island lies to the north. The view is across Lower New York Bay to Sandy Hook and Atlantic Highlands, both in New Jersey. Normally many ships can be seen from here entering or leaving the Narrows.

0.10 Rockaway Point Boulevard and Bay 222nd Street.

1.00 Rockaway Point Village. Bay 204th Street.

1.20 Rockaway Point Gatehouse.

Private residential development. View of Marine Parkway Bridge ahead to left. Former site of abandoned apartment house project on right. In 1979 these high-rise structures were demolished in thirty seconds by the use of explosives. This was the first use of this method in the New York City area. Remains were two twenty-foot-high hills of rubbish.

1.90 Fort Tilden on right.

2.50 Roxbury Village. Residential development.

2.80 Coast Guard base on left.

2.90 Beach 169th Street.

3.00 *Bear left* onto Marine Parkway Bridge.

3.20 View of Rockaway Inlet and Riis Park bathing pavilion.

Jacob Riis Park. This large recreation park and ocean bathing beach, with large public parking areas and bath houses, was named for the Danish-American journalist and philanthropist Jacob August Riis (1849–1914). His book *How the Other Half Lives*, subtitled *Studies Among the Tenements of New York* (1890), brought attention to the wretched living conditions of the poor in New York and ultimately led to reforms. A reprint, with many historical photographic illustrations, is available from Dover

Publishing of New York City. Riis became a lifelong personal friend of Theodore Roosevelt.

3.30 Begin Marine Parkway Bridge. Be cautious of unusual pavement.

The Rockaway Peninsula is ten miles long and has a residential population of over 125,000. The Marine Parkway Bridge is the main access route for commuters.

Marine Parkway Bridge—A facility of the Triborough Bridge and Tunnel Authority, across Rockaway Inlet. Construction was started in June of 1936, and the span was opened to traffic on July 3, 1937. The bridge was designed by Wardell Hardesty. Emil Praeger was chief construction engineer. The total length of bridge, including viaducts, is 4,022 feet. The length of the lift-truss span is 540 feet, the length of each side truss span is 540 feet. Normal clearance at lift span above mean high water is 55 feet. Raised position under clearance is 150 feet. There are four traffic lanes. Tolls are collected at the northern end. (− 15.00 E.R.M.) View of Coney Island and Staten Island to left. Jamaica Bay to right.

4.10 North end of bridge. Enter Brooklyn.

4.30 Pay toll. Start of Flatbush Avenue Extension, Brooklyn.

4.40 Floyd Bennett Field on right. Dunes on left. This airport is named for a pioneer American aviator who flew over the North Pole and participated in several Arctic expeditions. He lived from 1890 until 1928.

4.60 Dead Horse Bay on left.

4.90 Boat basin on left. Deep Creek on left.

MARINE PARKWAY BRIDGE. Photo: Courtesy Triborough Bridge & Tunnel Authority.

5.80 *Turn* onto Belt Parkway *westbound*. Also called Route 27-A.

6.80 Cross Gerritsen Inlet.

6.90 You are on Plum Island.

7.30 Plum Beach on left. Shell Bank Creek and Plum Beach channel on right. There are extensive tidal flats on left.

7.60 *Turn off* at Exit 9—Knapp Street.

7.60 Western end of Brooklyn Marine Park.

7.90 *Turn left* on Knapp Street. Cross over parkway.

8.00 *Turn right* on Emmons Avenue. (If heading southbound, enter Parkway East here.)

8.30 Sheepshead Bay on left. Home port to many commercial fishing, party, and private pleasure boats. Excursion boats and small passenger ferries operate from here to Breezy Point and Rockaway Point Village.

8.60 Breezy Point ferry terminal on left.

8.70 F.W.I.L. Lundy Brothers' Seafood Restaurant on right founded by Frederick, William, Irving, and Louis Lundy. This large, ornate building has long been a Brooklyn institution. It has excellent seafood and is well worth a stop. Formerly, the waiters acted in a very independent manner. This was traditional and wasn't to be taken personally.

8.80 Footbridge over Sheepshead Bay to left. (Ocean Avenue Footbridge.) This footbridge is actually located at 19th Street, although officially called the Ocean Avenue Footbridge.

9.00 *Turn left* on Shore Boulevard. Head of Sheepshead Bay.

F. W. I. L. LUNDY'S SEAFOOD RESTAURANT, Sheepshead Bay. Frederick, William, Irving, and Louis Lundy's seafood emporium, long a Brooklyn landmark serving freshly caught fruit del mare. This view c1979. Photo: Alfred H. Marks.

9.10 *Turn left* again on Shore Boulevard.

9.30 The footbridge you passed before is now on your left again.

10.00 Dead End. *Turn around.* Kingsborough Community College.

Manhattan Beach Air Force Base. You are now in the Manhattan Beach section of Brooklyn. This was a great society summer resort in the nineteenth century with the great Manhattan Beach Hotel, which was open only in the summertime. John Philip Sousa, the "March King," dedicated a famous march to this popular pleasure mecca. Let us read how William H. Bishop described this resort in *Scribner's Magazine* in 1880:

We emerge from the train in a station forming part of the hotel itself. A Coney Island hotel of consequence has its railway station, and two or three special lines of land and water transportation, as an-

SHEEPSHEAD BAY HARBOR. This view shows docks for fishing fleet and party boats. The passenger ferryboat to Breezy Point is seen in the background. c1979. Photo: Alfred H. Marks.

MANHATTAN BEACH HOTEL. Photo: Library of Congress. Author's collection.

other might have elevators or steam-heating. We pass through a wide corridor wainscoted and ceiled up (as are all the interiors that meet the eye in the neighborhood) with cheerful, varnished pine, and out upon the enormous piazza. A multitude of people are dining at little tables on it, set with linen, glass and silver, and others are moving up and down in close procession.

Thalatta! Thalatta! what a charming glimpse of the sea! A wide esplanade between is green with turf and gay with flowers—geranium, heliotrope, lobelia, coleus, the queenly, tropical leaves of the Canna Indica—all growing finely out of the two feet of earth the careful gardeners have put down for their sustenance. They have a peculiar value from their situation; a lively fancy makes a species of jewels of them instead of flowers, in their setting of silvery white sand. In the center is a music stand shaped like a scallop shell. Benches are scattered profusely along;—the beach below is full of parasols and summer costumes bright against the water, pink-legged children with their skirts very much tucked up, are wading in it, reflected in the shallows....

(*Scribners Magazine*, May 1880, New York/Article "Manhattan Beach," by William H. Bishop)

These hotels were of monstrous size and built of wood. They sported mansard roofs, spires, steeples, oriental style towers and much gingerbread wood carving. None are left.

Other famous hotels were the Hotel Brighton and Oriental Hotel—a name perpetuated in Oriental Boulevard.

10.10 *Turn left* on Norfolk Street.

10.20 *Turn right* on Oriental Boulevard.

10.30 Manhattan Beach Park on left.

11.00 *Bear right* on Corbin Place.

11.10 Chambers Square.

11.10 *Bear left* on Gerald Street.

11.15 *Bear right*. Road becomes Brighton Beach Avenue.

11.35 Brighton Beach on left. (Former site of Hotel Brighton and Carousel.)

11.45 Pass Coney Island Avenue.

11.45 Elevated railway trestle overhead.

11.90 *Turn left* under concrete arches, onto Ocean Parkway.

12.00 Seaside Park on right.

12.10 *Turn right* on Surf Avenue.

12.10 Famous Coney Island Boardwalk on left.

12.40 New York City Aquarium on left.

12.60 Enter amusement area.

12.70 Cross Stillwell Avenue.

12.70 *The* Original Nathans Hot Dogs on left.

12.80 Site of former Dreamland Park on left.

This adult amusement park featured gigantic sculpture, gaudy recreations of scenes from Wagner's operas, such as "The Dragon's Gorge," and fun-house type attractions. It was very gaudy and greatly popularized by the well-known popular ballad, "Meet Me Tonight in Dreamland."

13.00 Site of once-famous Steeplechase Park.

Steeplechase Park, known as "the funny place,"

ORIENTAL HOTEL, CONEY ISLAND. Photo: Library of Congress. Author's collection.

DREAMLAND PARK, CONEY ISLAND. Photo: Library of Congress. Author's collection.

was a twenty-five-acre amusement park founded by George C. Tilyou in 1897. It burned to the ground in 1907, but was rebuilt in 1908 and operated until 1964 when the site was purchased for a housing project. Many of the amusements were located inside a six-story-high steel shed. The park was named for its most popular ride—a sort of roller-coaster arranged with multiple tracks. On each track was a wooden steeplechase horse, much like those on a carousel. At the start of the ride all the horses were lined up at the top of the highest elevation. When the operator released the brakes the horses would start off over the long, winding course—zooming past one another in a simulation of a genuine steeplechase. Other rides were the ferris wheel and great parachute jump ride. Riders were given a close simulation of an actual parachute free fall of over 100 feet from atop a steel tower.

13.00 Abe Stark Center on left.

13.00 Cross West 21st Street.

13.00 Site of former Luna Park on right.

Luna Park was the third of the great Coney Island adult amusement parks. It was modeled after the Great White Way of the Chicago World's Fair and was rather similar to the still-existing Tivoli Gardens in Copenhagen, Denmark. Luna Park was opened by Thompson and Dundy in 1903. It burned down with considerable loss of life after World War II. Luna Park was beautiful and fantastic. Among the attractions were Mundy's Menagerie and Wormwood's Monkey Theater and the "Shoot the Chutes." This was a ride where you coasted down a roller coaster track into a pool of water with a great splash. The writer remembers visiting Luna Park as a child and getting stuck in a dark underground tunnel in a little cart pulled by a donkey. The ride was called "The Coal Mine," and the little cart jumped the track on a curve, and we had to sit for about an hour until the custodian came searching for us with a kerosene lamp.

13.90 Gatehouse to Seagate—a private residential area. (E.R.M. – 13.00) (Atlantic Highland to west.)

13.95 *Turn right* on West 37th Street. Make sure car doors are locked. This is a rough neighborhood, and motorists are often mugged. Do not allow yourself to get "bottled up" behind traffic on any narrow Brooklyn street as this is often a deliberate move preliminary to attacking and breaking into a car which cannot move ahead. Let the tourist beware. Avoid this tour after dusk and during height of rush hours.

14.20 *Turn right* on Neptune Avenue.

15.10 *Turn left* on West 17th Street—becomes Cropsey Avenue.

15.20 Cross bridge over Coney Island Creek.

15.30 *Turn left* onto Belt Parkway Westbound at (Bay 50th Street).

15.50 Gravesend Bay on left.

15.55 Dreier Offerman Park on left.

16.20 Pass Exit 5 for Bay Parkway.

16.20 New Utrecht. (– 12.20 E.R.M.)

16.20 Bensonhurst Park on left.

16.50 Dyker Beach Park on right. Exit 4. (– 11.25 E.R.M.)

16.70 View of Gravesend Bay, Lower New York Bay, and Verrazano Narrows Bridge to left.

17.60 Fort Hamilton. Veterans' Administration Hospital to right.

18.50 Pass beneath Verrazano Narrows Bridge. (– 11.00 E.R.M.)

18.55 Fort Lafayette site on left. The Narrows. (– 10.75 E.R.M.)

20.00 View of Statue of Liberty and World Trade Center.

20.70 Owl's Head Park on right. (– 8.25 E.R.M.)

20.75 *Bear left* on Interstate 278—Brooklyn-Queens Expressway.

20.90 Cross above 69th Street.

21.00 Start of Gowanus Elevated Highway.

21.30 Cross above former Bay Ridge terminal tracks of New York Connecting Railroad.

21.50 Brooklyn Army Terminal on left. Bay Ridge section. (– 8.10 E.R.M.)

21.70 Bush terminal on left. (– 7.00 E.R.M.)

21.90 Williamsburg Savings Bank building visible ahead.

21.90 *GET OFF* expressway at 38th Street Exit.

22.10 *Turn left* on Fourth Avenue.

22.30 *Turn right* on 33rd Street (Burger King on corner).

22.50 *Turn left* on Fifth Avenue. (Southbound use 32nd Street between Fifth and Fourth Avenues.)

22.50 Greenwood Cemetery on right.

22.80 Entrance to Greenwood Cemetery (corner 5th Avenue and 24th Street).

Greenwood Cemetery. One of the nation's most famous cemeteries and among the most beautiful, it is one of the finest remaining examples of the Romantic landscape tradition. The statues are some of the best Victorian sculpture extant in America. The first burial was held here in 1840, and Greenwood soon rose to be the most fashionable cemetery in America. Among the famous buried here are Nathaniel Currier, James M. Ives, Rev. Henry Ward Beecher, DeWitt Clinton, Mayor William Jay Gaynor, Peter Cooper, Horace Greeley, William Marcy "Boss" Tweed, Samuel F. B. Morse, Duncan Phyfe, James Renwick Jr. (architect of St. Patrick's Cathedral), and Lola Montez (mistress of King Ludwig I of Bavaria). (Sightseeing is permitted on weekdays only.)

Wealthy families who erected large tombs and mausoleums were the Whitneys, Lorillards, Aspinwalls, Schermerhorns, Howlands, Havemeyers, and Pierreponts. Two famous graves bear statues of their owners. That of seventeen-year-old Charlotte Canda, who was killed in a carriage accident returning home from a ball, and of a certain sea captain named Correja attracted particular attention during the Victorian age. The tomb of the wealthy theatrical entrepreneur William Niblo (owner of the famous Niblo's Garden in Manhattan) is among the loveliest. It is in Gothic style and at the edge of beautiful little Crescent Water with its smooth reflections and gracefully swimming swans and ducks. The sections, roads, and paths bear such poetic names as Sylvan Water, Valley Water, Twilight Dell, Green Bough Avenue, Fern Avenue, Ocean Hill, Woodbine Path, Cedar Dell, etc. The largest tomb is that of the multimillionaire Stephen Whitney on Ocean Hill. It is an eight-sided Gothic chapel surrounded by rhododendron, ivy, and ornamental trees. There is an example of the rare Egyptian Revival architecture in the tomb of Dr. James Anderson on Cliff Path overlooking Sylvan Water.

The main entrance gate at Fifth Avenue and 24th Street has been called "the culmination of Gothic Revival." It was built entirely of brownstone and is a collection of pointed arches, medieval sculpture, and elaborately carved towers massed vertically to turn the visitor's thoughts heavenward. It was designed in 1861 by Richard Michell Upjohn, who also designed the Connecticut state capitol. He was the son of the leading proponent of Gothic Revival architecture in America.

Greenwood Cemetery comprises 478 acres, including Gowan's Heights, Brooklyn's highest spot, with an elevation of 216 feet. This was an important locality in the Battle of Long Island and is described in some detail by N. P. Willis in his *American Scenery*.

The area embraced by the cemetery was a glacial moraine with the usual erratic boulders scattered about. This prompted the minor poet Wendell Phillips Garrison (1840–1907), son of William Lloyd Garrison, to write the following poem, which is included in his *Post Meridian Sonnets* of 1898:

At Greenwood Cemetery
Here was the ancient strand, the utmost
  reach,
Of the great Northern ice-wave; hitherto
With its last pulse it mounted, then
  withdrew,
Leaving its fringe of wreckage on
  the beach:
Boulder and pebble and sand-matrix-each
From crag or valley ravished, scanty clues
To its old site affording in its new,
Yet real, as the men of science teach,
Life hath not less its terminal moraine:
Look how on that discharged from
  melting snows
Another rears itself, the spoil of plain
And Mountain also, marked by stones
  in rows,
With legend meet for such promiscuous
  pain:
"Here rests—Hier ruhet, or ici repose."
(*An American Anthology*, edited by Edmund Clarence Stedman, Boston: Houghton Mifflin Co., 1900, p. 794.)

Alternate Route 1—Around cemetery on streets

22.80 Corner Fifth Avenue and 24th Street. Continue straight on Fifth Avenue.

23.00 *Turn right* on 19th Street.

23.75 *Turn right* on Tenth Avenue.

23.80 *Turn left* on McDonald Avenue.

24.30 *Turn left* on Caton Avenue.

Alternate Route 2—Through cemetery

22.80 Enter cemetery at Fifth Avenue and 24th Street gateway.

Inside cemetery follow signs to Fort Hamilton entrance. Owing to vandalism problems public visitation to Greenwood Cemetery is now discouraged and strictly limited. Permission to enter is now rarely granted and then only by advance application and to visitors with an authentic and serious interest and with good credentials. Write or phone them well in advance for permission and set a definite time so that you are expected. Please do not abuse this limited privilege by requesting entry unless you have a serious purpose for visiting the grounds. We are sorry that such a situation has had to come about.

24.00 Leave cemetery at Fort Hamilton entrance.

24.00 *Turn left* on Fort Hamilton Parkway.

24.10 *Turn right* on Caton Avenue at intersection with McDonald Avenue.

Continuation of Combined Route

24.10 Corner of Caton Avenue and McDonald Avenue.

24.20 *Bend right* on Caton Avenue.

24.60 *Bend left* on Caton Avenue.

24.70 *Turn left* on Coney Island Avenue.

24.80 *Turn right* on Parkside Avenue.

25.10 Parade Grounds on right.

25.10 Prospect Park on left—covers 526 acres and was designed by Vaux and Olmsted in 1857.

25.40 *Turn left* on Ocean Avenue.

25.90 *Bear right.*

26.00 *Turn left* on Flatbush Avenue.

26.10 Lefferts Homestead on left.
   This house was built by Pieter Lefferts (1753–1791) to replace one accidentally burned down on August 22, 1776 when the Americans were burning adjacent grain fields prior to the Battle of Long Island so that the grain would not fall into British hands. It originally stood at 563 Flatbush Avenue, but was later moved to its present site in Prospect Park. It is open as a museum and is maintained

by the Daughters of the American Revolution. Pieter Lefferts was a delegate to the Constitutional Convention, a lieutenant in the American Army, and later a senator.

26.30 Brooklyn Zoo on left.

26.40 Brooklyn Botanic Garden on right.
   This is among the world's finest botanical gardens and has an international reputation. It is extremely beautiful and the rose display is exceptional. The gardens cover fifty acres with a large conservatory and museum. Special gardens include the Japanese Garden, Cranford Rose Garden, Fragrance Garden, Rock Garden, Iris Garden, Shakespeare Garden, Children's Garden, Ryoanji, Roji, and Tallman Gardens. Althouth the Botanic Garden is a cultural institution affiliated with the City of New York, it is a private institution. Twenty percent of the support of the garden comes as a subsidy from the city. The rest comes from gifts of private citizens. Every tree, shrub, and flower is purchased with private funds.
   Generally speaking, the gardens are open daily except Mondays (unless the Monday is a holiday, in which case the garden will be open).
   Do not plan your picnic lunch or rest break here. Go to Prospect Park instead. The Botanic Garden is only for study and contemplation.

26.70 Brooklyn Public Library on right.

26.80 Grand Army Plaza and Triumphal Arch.
   The Plaza was designed in 1866 by Olmstead, Vaux & Company. The Memorial Arch is the entrance to Prospect Park and is located south of

LEFFERTS HOMESTEAD. Located on Flatbush Avenue, Brooklyn. Photo: Alfred H. Marks.

ARCH AT GRAND ARMY PLAZA, BROOKLYN. Designed by Olmstead & Vaux in 1866. Photo: Alfred H. Marks.

the traffic circle where Flatbush Avenue, Vanderbilt Avenue, Prospect Park West, Eastern Parkway, and Union Street all converge. The Soldiers and Sailors Memorial Arch is an 80-foot-high neo-classical monument designed by John H. Duncan to honor Union Troops who fought in the Civil War. There are two bronze bas-relief panels over the doorways. The horses were modeled by Thomas Eakins and the figures of Ulysses S. Grant and Abraham Lincoln were modeled by William O'Donovan. The group of Navy sailors on the east facade, the group of Army soldiers on the west facade, and the quadriga on the top were designed by Frederick MacMonnies. Atop the arch are figures of two herald angels announcing peace and an allegorical figure of Columbia.

26.80 *Bear left* around circle.

27.00 *Turn right* off circle onto Prospect Park West.

27.10 *Turn right* on President Street.

27.20 *Turn right* on Eighth Avenue.

27.30 *Turn right* on St. John's Place.

27.40 *Turn right* on Plaza Street.

27.45 Montauk Club on right.
    Designed by Francis H. Kimball in 1891 in the Venetian Gothic style, built of yellow brick and terra cotta, it found its inspiration in the Ca d'Oro at Venice.

27.60 *Turn right* on Prospect Park West.

28.00 Litchfield Mansion on left.
    Located inside Prospect Park. It was designed in the modified Italianate style in 1855–1856 by Alexander Jackson Davis. The classic collonade has unusual corncob capitals.

LITCHFIELD MANSION, BROOKLYN. On Prospect Park West, this modified Italian Style villa was designed by Alexander Jackson Davis in 1855. Photo: Alfred H. Marks.

MONTAUK CLUB, BROOKLYN. Landmark Venetian Gothic clubhouse designed by Francis H. Kimball in 1891. Photo: Alfred H. Marks.

28.50 *Turn right* on 15th Street. Make sure car doors are locked and that you always have room to move ahead. Attacks on motorists are common in this area.

28.70 Park Slope area. Armory on right.

29.50 *Turn right* on Hamilton Avenue, under viaduct.

29.70 Cross Gowanus Canal. (-6.52 E.R.M.)

30.10 Stay on Hamilton Avenue. *Do not enter tunnel.*

30.30 Stay on Hamilton Avenue. *Do not enter tunnel.*

30.80 Former site of India Wharf and Atlantic Basin on left. View of Manhattan and Governor's Island. (E.R.M. − 5.10)

30.80 *Turn right* on Van Brunt Street.

30.90 *Turn right* on Union Street.

31.00 Entering Brooklyn Heights/downtown area. Many of the streets in this area are named for prominent local residents, including Robert Fulton, merchant Hezekiah Pierrepont, John Hicks, Jacob Middagh Hicks, John Middagh, Henry Remsen, and Teunis Joralemon.

31.20 *Turn left* on Hicks Street.

31.60 St. Peter's Church; red brick, Hudson River Gothic.

31.80 *Turn right* on Atlantic Avenue.

32.10 *Turn left* on Boerum Place.

32.40 *Turn left* on Fulton Street.

32.40 Borough Hall on left; Greek Revival, ca. 1846–1848, Ionic details, Gamaliel King, architect.

32.40 Municipal Building on right; modified Roman eclectic, 1924. McKenzie, Voorhees, Gmelin and Walker, architects.

32.50 Cross Court Street; you are now on Joralemon Street.

32.60 Packer Collegiate Institute, 170 Joralemon Street; ivy-covered Gothic Revival, 1854, Minard Lafever, architect.

3.2.61 *Turn right* on Clinton Street.

32.70 St. Anne's Episcopal Church on left; Victorian Gothic, 1867-69, Renwick and Sands, architects.

32.80 *Turn right* on Cadman Plaza West.

33.00 *Turn right* on Montague Street.

33.10 Franklin Trust Building on left; Romanesque Revival skyscraper. Tile mansard roofs and dormer windows. George L. Morse, architect, 1888.

33.30 *Turn right* on Hicks Street.

33.50 *Turn left* on Clark Street.

BROOKLYN BOROUGH HALL. Greek Revival. Designed by Gamaliel King in 1846. Restored in 1986. Photo: Alfred H. Marks.

PACKER COLLEGIATE INSTITUTE. On Joralemon Street, Brooklyn. Gothic Revival, 1854, by Minard Lefever. Photo: Alfred H. Marks.

33.60 *Turn right* on Brooklyn Heights Terrace.

33.60 Columbia Heights.

33.65 *Turn right* on Pineapple Street.

33.70 *Turn right* on Willow Street.

33.90 *Turn left* on Pierrepont Street.

34.10 Monroe Unitarian Church on left, formerly named Church of the Saviour; Gothic Revival, 1844, Minard Lafever, architect.

34.15 *Turn left* on Clinton Street.

34.20 *Turn right* on Cadman Plaza West.

34.20 Main Post Office on left; French Renaissance with Romanesque Revival forms and German Renaissance details, 1885–1891, Mifflin E. Bell, architect.

34.40 *Turn right* on Joralemon Street.

34.70 *Turn right* on Hicks Street.

34.70 Grace Episcopal Church on left; Gothic Revival, Richard Upjohn, architect, 1847–1848.

34.80 *Turn left* on Montague Street.

34.90 *Turn left* on Montague Terrace.

35.00 *Turn right* on Remsen Street.

35.05 View of Lower Manhattan and Upper New York Bay. Flagpole. (-5.00 E.R.M.)

35.05 *Turn around.*

35.05 *Continue* back East on Remsen Street.

35.40 *Turn left* on Court Street.

35.60 Supreme Court Southern District of New York on right.

35.65 Post Office on right.

35.65 *Turn right* on Tillary Street. *Get into left lane immediately.*

35.70 *Turn left* on Adams Street. *Stay in center lane* for Brooklyn Bridge.

35.90 Begin Brooklyn Bridge.

36.20 Begin suspension span.

36.90 End suspension span. (E.R.M., – 4.5)

Brooklyn Bridge, the oldest, and by many considered the most beautiful, major suspension span in the United States, was built between 1869 and 1883 by John A. Roebling (1806–1869) and his son Washington Augustus Roebling (1837–1926). The elder Roebling was born in Mulhouse, Alsace, and studied engineering in Berlin. He came to America in 1831 and developed a strong type of steel cable, opening a plant in Trenton, New Jersey. Early suspension spans included the Allegheny Bridge at Pittsburgh, several aqueduct bridges for the D. & H. Canal, a

BROOKLYN POST OFFICE. At corner of Cadman Plaza and Pierrepont Street. Designed by Mifflin E. Bell in 1885. Photo: Alfred H. Marks.

bridge between Cincinnati and Covington across the Ohio River, and the great Niagara Falls Suspension Bridge of 1855. The Brooklyn Bridge was his greatest achievement. Early in its construction he suffered a serious injury on a ferry boat while supervising the work, and died a few days later. His son supervised completion of the bridge, but he also was a victim of his work. He was stricken with caisson disease in 1872 as a result of continuous underground work. Although an invalid, he supervised from his bed in Brooklyn Heights until the bridge was opened to traffic in 1883. In 1888 he took over supervision of the Roebling Plant in Trenton.

The Brooklyn Bridge has an overall length of 6,775 feet with a center span of 1,595 feet. Total suspended sections equal 3,450 feet with a width of 85 feet. The vertical clearance above water is 133 feet. There are four main cables of 15¾″ diameter, each comprised of 5,700 wires. The two major towers are built of dressed stone with twin pointed archways. Their style is Gothic Revival with crowning mouldings somewhat reminiscent of the Egyptian style. Box girder spans are supported by four main cables with much cross bracing, which creates an attractive gossamer effect.

It was opened for traffic on May 24, 1883. On May 30, a great panic took place when someone among the crowd of strollers screamed that the bridge was giving way. People fought to get off and became jammed together in the stairways. Forty people were injured, and twelve were crushed to death.

The bridge, as originally built, carried two dual-width vehicle roadways, two horse-car tracks and a wide boardwalk in the center. During later years it also carried electric streetcars and rapid transit railway trains. Various authorities give the initial cost as between $13,000,000 and $15,000,000. However, within the first twenty-six years in service, increasing

MANHATTAN FROM BROOKLYN HEIGHTS, 1979. This view shows why Brooklyn Heights has become such a popular residential area. Photo: Alfred H. Marks.

loads—particularly electric trains—made it necessary to spend an additional $15,000,000 on partial reconstruction and strengthening. Twenty workmen lost their lives in the construction of the bridge. Today it carries only motor traffic and pedestrians. It was overhauled in 1983.

36.90 Manhattan end suspension span. *Take exit* to Park Row South.

37.30 New York City Hall seen straight ahead; Federal style with French influence, 1803–1812, John McComb Jr. and Joseph François Mangin, architects.

37.30 New York Municipal Building to right. Topped by gilded statue of "Civic Fame" by Adolph A. Weinman.

37.40 *Turn left* on Broadway.

37.40 Woolworth Building straight ahead, 233 Broadway. This is a Gothic skyscraper built 1911–1913, its exterior clad with self-washing terra-cotta. The architect was Cass Gilbert. The interior has much exquisite detailing and art work. With 60 stories and a height of 792 feet, it was world's tallest when built.

37.50 Western Electric corporate headquarters on left, 222 Broadway.

37.50 St. Paul's Chapel. A unit of Trinity Episcopal Parish, and the oldest church structure in Manhattan, Georgian style structure, built in 1764–1766, Thomas McBean, architect. The steeple was built in 1793–1794 by James C. Lawrence. George Washington worshiped here regularly during his residence in New York. On the right.

37.55 American Telephone and Telegraph Building, 195 Broadway, on right; Roman eclectic, built in 1913, William Welles Bosworth, architect.

37.60 *Turn left* on John Street.

38.00 *Turn right* on South Street.

38.00 South Street Seaport Museum on left.

38.10 *Turn right* on Wall Street.

38.20 *Turn left* on Water Street.

38.30 *Turn right* on Hanover Square.

38.35 India House on left; Classic Revival, ca. 1837, architect unknown. It is assumed to have been erected by Richard F. Carman as an office block after a disastrous fire in 1835. It later housed the New York Cotton Exchange and the Hanover Bank, and is presently a private club. It houses a superb maritime museum.

38.40 *Bear left* on Beaver Street.

HANOVER SQUARE AND INDIA HOUSE. This square and handsome classic revival building c1837 captures the atmosphere of older commercial New York. Photo: Alfred H. Marks.

38.40 Delmonico's Restaurant on left.

38.50 *Turn right* on Broad Street.

38.60 New York Stock Exchange on left; Beaux Arts eclectic, 1901-1904, George B. Post, architect. The pediment group of statuary is by John Quincy Adams Ward, assisted by Paul W. Bartlett.

38.65 Cross Wall Street. Continue straight on Nassau Street.

38.65 Federal Hall on right (formerly U.S. Subtreasury). A national memorial, built in 1834–1842 in Greek Revival style by Town and Davis and S. Thomson and Frazee, it is now a museum. It stands on the site of the older Federal Hall, which was a Georgian-style building, remodeled by Charles Pierre L'Enfant from New York's Second City Hall into a Federal Capitol. On April 30, 1789, George Washington was inaugurated as the first President of the United States on the front portico of this older building.

38.70 U. S. Federal Reserve Bank seen straight ahead; Italian Renaissance eclectic, 1928, York and Sawyer, architects.
Chase Manhattan Bank on right. Marine Midland Bank on left. World Trade Center seen down Cedar Street, to left.

38.70 *Turn left* on Cedar Street.

38.80 *Turn left* on Broadway.

38.83 Monument on right; Revolutionary Prisoners' Monument.

38.90 Wall Street on left.

38.90 Trinity Church on right. This is the third Episcopal church on this site, built in 1840–1846 by Richard Upjohn in Gothic Revival style. The bronze doors in Italian style, depicting Biblical scenes, were carved by Karl Bitter under the supervision of Richard Morris Hunt.

39.00 Bowling Green, site of early recreation ground.

39.10 United States Customs House on left; Beaux Arts eclectic, 1901–1907, Cass Gilbert, architect. Sculptured figures on north facade are by Daniel C. French. The interiors are also very fine, but the building is not open to the general public on a regular basis.

39.10 Cross Battery Place; Broadway becomes State Street.

39.20 Castle Garden and Battery Park on right. (– 3.85 E.R.M.)

39.30 Shrine of St. Elizabeth Seton on left (Our Lady of the Rosary), 7 State Street; Federal style with Ionic trim. The east wing dates back to ca. 1793; there is a colonnaded west wing (1805). The architect is unknown. This was once the private home of Elizabeth Ann Seton (1774–1821) and her husband William Magee Seton, a wealthy merchant. Born Elizabeth Ann Bayley, she came from a prominent and well-to-do family and knew George Washington socially in her youth. She married William Seton in 1794, lived in this house and had five children. She was widowed in Pisa, Italy, in 1803 and introduced to the Catholic doctrine by the Filicchi family of that city. Although brought up in the Episcopal faith, she entered the Catholic Church at St. Peter's Church, Barclay Street, upon her return home in 1805. She was disowned by her family because of her conversion and ran a school in this house to support her children. She later entered religious orders and moved to Emmitsburg, Maryland, in 1809. She subsequently founded the order of the Sisters of Charity, which now numbers 7,500 members. She was canonized Saint Elizabeth Ann Seton at Rome on September 14, 1975—the first native-born American saint.

39.30 Staten Island Ferry Terminal on right. (– 4.20 E.R.M.)

39.30 *Bend left* on State Street.

39.35 *Turn left* on Whitehall Street.

39.40 United States Army building on right. Granite and red brick in Gothic Revival style.

39.50 *Turn left* on Pearl Street.

39.65 *Turn right* on State Street.

39.70 *Turn left* on Battery Place.

39.75 Whitehall Building on right.

39.80 Pier A on left. (E.R.M. – 3.84)

39.85 *Turn right* on West Street (West Side Highway).

39.90 Battery Park City development on left.

39.90 Downtown Athletic Club on right.

40.10 Brady Building on right. Gothic styled skyscraper designed by Cass Gilbert as a trial of that style prior to designing the Woolworth Building. Former headquarters of the Delaware, Lackawanna & Western Railroad.

40.10 Pass foot of Cedar Street.

40.20 Pass foot of Liberty Street. Jersey Central Railroad ferries formerly landed to the left.

40.30 Foot of Cortlandt Street. (E.R.M. – 3.71) Fulton's first commercial voyage of the *North River Steamboat of Clermont* departed from here. This was also the site of the first steam ferry to Jersey City, and later terminal of Pennsylvania Railroad and West Shore Railroad ferries. Now considerably inland owing to landfilling out to pierhead line.

40.30 World Trade Center on right.

40.31 Vista International Hotel on right. World Financial Center office complex on left on landfill.

40.35 Pass foot of Vesey Street. Former site of Washington Market.

40.40 New York Telephone Co. building, 140 West Street, on right. It is built in vertical modern style. Designed by McKenzie, Voorhees and Gmelin, Architects, it was completed between 1923 and 1927.

40.45 Foot of Barclay Street. Site of former Lackawanna Railroad ferry to Hoboken on left.

40.60 Foot of Chambers Street. Site of former Erie Railroad ferry to Jersey City on left.

41.00 Foot of Vestry Street.

41.10 Foot of Desbrosses Street. Former Pennsylvania Railroad, West Shore Railroad ferries, and Hudson River Day Line terminals on left.

41.20 Foot of Canal Street. (E.R.M. – 2.50)

41.40 Former New York Central Railroad St. Johns Park Freight Terminal on right.

42.80 Chelsea.. (E.R.M. – 1.20) Foot of West 23rd Street.

43.20 Foot of 30th Street. (E.R.M. – 1.00) Heliport on left.

43.40 Foot of West 34th Street. (E.R.M. − 0.50) Javits Convention Center.

43.50 Ferry to Port Imperial, Weehawken, on left. Foot passengers only. No vehicles carried. (West 38th Street)

43.60 Yellow brick Lincoln Tunnel ventilator tower on left.

43.80 Foot of West 42nd Street. (E.R.M. 0.00) Base Line.

East Side Road Route

0.00 Start East Side Road Route, corner of West 42nd Street and 12th Avenue, New York City (Manhattan). Former West Shore Railroad ferry terminal for Weekhawken and West New York was situated at foot of West 42nd Street. The Hudson River Day Line, Pier 81, is slightly to the south, and the Circle Line, Pier 83, is slightly to the north.

Head north on 12th Avenue. (E.R.M. 0.00)

0.30 New passenger liner terminal on left. West 49th Street. (E.R.M. 0.30)

0.50 DeWitt Clinton Park on right between West 52nd and West 54th Streets.

0.75 Pass West 57th Street on right.

0.80 Go up onto elevated highway ("Miller highway").

This elevated highway originally started just north of the exit of the Brooklyn Battery Tunnel, and has been largely demolished and removed to the south of here. The original elevated structure began to literally fall apart from corrosion several years ago owing to delayed and improper maintenance and damage from salt used to melt ice and snow.

1.20 Site of former New York Central car-float slips on left and freight yards on right.

1.50 *Turn right* on West 72nd Street exit. Note elegant older apartment houses and townhouses.

1.60 *Turn left* on Riverside Drive. Townhouses and apartments on right. Riverside Park on left. This was the most fashionable residential street in the city in 1910.

1.90 Cross West 79th Street. Yacht Basin to left. (E.R.M. 1.85)

2.30 Cross West 86th Street on right.

2.40 Soldiers' and Sailors Monument on left. (2.45 E.R.M.)

3.60 Cross West 110th Street, Cathedral Parkway.

Note: Two blocks to the East (.20 mile), at the corner of 110th Street and Amsterdam Avenue is the Cathedral Church of Saint John the Divine (Episcopal). Although still uncompleted, this is the largest church structure in the United States. It is the largest Gothic Cathedral in the world and will hold 40,000 standees. Construction was started in 1892. The choir, apse, and original crossing were designed by Heins & LaFarge (won in competition) in Romanesque Eclectic style, and completed in 1907. After 1911 a contract was awarded to Ralph Adams Cram of Cram & Ferguson for completion of the nave, final crossing, and transept, in French Gothic eclectic. The cathedral is in use but still unfinished, and there are various differing plans for the ultimate completed design.

The high area between 110th Street and 125th Street to the south and north, and Morningside Avenue on the east and the Hudson River on the west, is known as Morningside Heights. In the early twentieth century, after the relocation of Columbia University here, it was known as the "Acropolis of America."

Columbia University is located between Broadway and Amsterdam Avenue and 116th and 120th Streets. It was founded in 1754 as King's College by grant of King George II and located downtown. In 1784 it was reorganized as Columbia College, and in 1912 the name was changed to Columbia University, although this name was used unofficially from 1896. Around the turn of the century the university moved to its present site. The medical school was founded in 1767.

4.10 Cross West 120th Street.

4.10 Riverside Church and Inter-church Center on right. (E.R.M. 4.30)

4.20 Grant's Tomb on left. (E.R.M. 4.40)

4.30 Site of former Claremont Inn on left.

In later years this was an elegant restaurant located immediately north of Grant's Tomb. It had formal gardens and delicate small arbors and pavilions. Its history is told by Benson Lossing in his *The Hudson,* of 1866:

"Upon a high promontory overlooking the Hudson, on the south side of Manhattanville, is Jones's Claremont Hotel, a fashionable place of resort for the pleasure-seekers who frequent the Bloomingdale and Kingsbridge roads on pleasant afternoons. At such times it is often thronged with visitors, and presents a lively appearance. The main, or older portion of the building, was erected, I believe, by the elder Dr. Post, early in the present century, as a summer residence, and named by him Claremont [Editor's note: Actually it was built in 1797.] *It still* [1866] *belongs to the Post family. It was an elegant country mansion, upon a most desirable spot, overlooking many leagues of the Hudson. There, more than fifty years ago, lived Viscount Courtenay, afterwards Earl of Devon. He left England, it was reported, because of political troubles. When the War of 1812 broke out, he returned thither leaving his furniture and plate, which were sold at auction. The latter is preserved with care by the family of the purchaser. Courtenay was a great lion in New*

York, for he was a handsome bachelor, with title, fortune, and a reputation—a combination of excellences calculated to captivate the heart-desires of the opposite sex.

Claremont was the residence, for a while, of Joseph Buonaparte, ex-king of Spain, when he first took refuge in the United States, after the Battle of Waterloo and the downfall of the Napoleon dynasty. Here, too, Francis James Jackson, the successor of Mr. Erskine, the British minister at Washington at the opening of the War of 1812, resided a short time. He was familiarly known as "Copenhagen Jackson," because of his then recent participation in measures for the seizure of the Danish fleet by the British at Copenhagen. He was politically and socially unpopular, and presented a strong contrast to the polished Courtenay."

The restaurant remained a resort of society on into the mid-twentieth century, much as described by Lossing, and the writer remembers being taken there for refreshments on Sunday afternoon. It was burned and demolished by the city in 1951.

On the grounds is a small grave marked with the simple inscription, "Here lies an amiable child." It was sometimes surmised that this was a "natural" child of Viscount Courtenay, although there is no evidence to support this opinion.

4.45 South end of Harlem Valley Viaduct. (E.R.M. 4.75)

4.60 Cross above West 125th Street on right.

4.80 North end of Harlem Valley Viaduct (E.R.M. 5.00), Manhattanville.

4.80 Cross West 135th Street on right.

4.80 New sewage treatment plant on riverfront to left. (E.R.M. 5.00.)

6.00 Trinity Parish Cemetery on right, between West 153rd and West 155th Streets.

6.60 Cross West 165th Street. Carmansville. (See E.R.M. 7.00.)

6.60 Columbia Presbyterian Medical Center on right. (See E.R.M. 7.10.)

6.80 Pass beneath George Washington Bridge (See E.R.M. 7.30.)

6.80 Jeffrey's Hook and lighthouse to left under Bridge. (E.R.M. 7.30)

7.50 Pavilion Overlook on left. Fort Washington Park on hill on right. (See article in River section under E.R.M. 7.30.)

7.60 Fort Tryon Park on right. (See E.R.M. 8.20.)

7.90 *Turn right* on Fort Tryon and Cloisters Exit. (Note: This short sidetrip is possible headed northbound only.)

8.10 The Cloisters. (See E.R.M. 8.30.) Circle around and go back to Riverside Drive northbound.

8.37 Cross over Dyckman Street on low viaduct. Former ferry to Englewood on left. (E.R.M. 8.70)

8.38 Tubby Hook on left. (E.R.M. 8.70)

8.40 Inwood Park on right. (E.R.M. 8.75)

8.40 Road now becomes Route 9A.

9.00 Stop. Pay toll.

9.10 South end of Henry Hudson Bridge over Spuyten Duyvil Creek. Henry Hudson Monument seen ahead.

9.50 North end of Henry Hudson Bridge. Riverdale.

9.55 *Turn right* Exit 18, Kappock Street.

9.62 *Turn right* on Palisade Avenue.

9.90 Pass under Henry Hudson Bridge. (E.R.M. 9.70)

10.20 *Northbound—Continue straight* on Palisade Avenue.
Southbound—Turn left on Kappock Street to enter Henry Hudson Bridge.

11.00 Riverdale Park on left.

11.30 *Turn right* on West 248th Street.

11.40 *Turn left* on Independence Avenue.

11.50 Wave Hill. An historic mansion and extensive grounds including formal and rustic gardens owned by the City of New York. We quote from the brochure they issue: "Wave Hill House was built in 1843 by jurist William Lewis Morris. Publisher William Henry Appleton purchased the property as a summer home in 1866. Between 1893 and 1911 George W. Perkins, a financier and associate of J. P. Morgan, assembled several separate properties into Wave Hill, an eighty acre estate."

Wave Hill's quiet beauty has nurtured an unusual number of distinguished temporary residents including Samuel Clemens, Theodore Roosevelt, Arturo Toscanini, and Bashford Dean. Dean, the first Curator of Armor at the Metropolitan Museum of Art, was the builder in 1928 of the Armor Hall at the north end of the Wave Hill House. During the 1950s the Wave Hill House was the residence of Sir Gladwyn Jebb, British delegate to the United Nations.

In 1960 the Perkins-Freeman Family gave twenty-eight acres of the original estate to New York City for use as a horticultural garden and cultural and educational institution. Today, Wave Hill retains its former domestic ambience in its new role as a public garden. Within this unique setting, visitors can enjoy concerts, summer outdoor theater, an acclaimed outdoor sculpture show, varied indoor exhibits, planted exhibitions, weekly garden and forest walks—all set off by the backdrop of the Hudson River and The Palisades. They also maintain an active Hudson River Program with an annual Hudson River Day.

In planning your itinerary we urge you to allow at least a half-day if possible to enjoy this beautiful and unique attraction. There is a nominal entrance fee to the grounds.

11.55 Site of Villa Pauline on left. The home of conductor Arturo Toscanini from 1940 to 1957, it had five acres of grounds and half-timbered Tudor house with porte cochere. The house commanded a fine view of the Hudson River and Palisades, of which Toscanini was very fond.

Toscanini was very fond of the writings of Washington Irving, and he was a frequent visitor to the *Sunnyside* restoration. The tie that bound the American author and the famous conductor was their mutual love for the Hudson River.

Tapes and recordings of every performance the maestro ever conducted that was broadcast or recorded were carefully stored at the Villa Pauline.

Villa Pauline was demolished several years ago. The Toscanini collection is now housed at Wave Hill, where the maestro also resided for a considerable time.

11.70 *Turn left* on West 252nd Street.

11.75 *Turn right* on Sycamore Avenue.

11.77 *Turn left* on 254th Street (Riverdale Railroad Station at end of street).

11.80 *Turn right* on Palisade Avenue.

12.10 Riverdale Center for Religious Research on left. Home of famous contemporary cosmologist and historian-philosopher Thomas Berry.

12.20 Passionist Fathers' Retreat House on left. Visitation Monastery on right.

12.50 *Turn right* on 261st Street. (Mount St. Vincent Railroad Station, end of street.) Mount St. Vincent College on left. Former Font Hill home of Edwin Forrest on left. (12.20 E.R.M.)

12.65 *Turn left* on Riverdale Avenue.

12.80 Entrance to Mount St. Vincent College on left.

12.90 Pass 263rd Street—New York City/Yonkers city line.

13.00 *Turn left* on Valentine Place (P.S. 27 on left). (12.30 E.R.M.)

13.20 *Turn right* on Hawthorne Avenue.

13.45 Hawthorne High School on right.

13.70 Pass Ludlow Street (Ludlow Railroad station end of street). (13.00 E.R.M.)

14.10 *Turn right* on Vark Street.

14.20 *Turn left* on Riverdale Avenue.

14.60 Cross Main Street (Municipal Pier at end of street. (14.10 E.R.M.)

14.65 Cross Dock Street (Yonkers Railroad station at end of street). Cross over Nepperhan River—now in underground sewer.

14.65 Philips Manor restoration on left.

14.65 Street name changes to Warburton Avenue. Continue straight.

15.70 Trevor Park on left; twenty-three-acre former private estate of John B. Trevor. *Glenview*, the Trevor mansion, is in Victorian Gothic style and now serves as the home of the Hudson River Museum. There is also a modern planetarium. Open daily except Mondays. (14.60 E.R.M.)

16.83 Greystone section. (16.10 E.R.M.) (Greystone Railroad station at end of Odel Avenue to left.)

17.90 Cross Brook. Yonkers city line. Enter village of Hastings-on-Hudson.

18.70 Cross Washington Street.

18.78 Cross over viaduct.

18.82 Cross Main Street (Hastings-on-Hudson Railroad station at end of street).

19.10 *Turn left* on Broadway (Route 9). (Southbound *turn right* on Warburton Avenue.)

19.15 Pass Edgar's Lane on right; site of Revolutionary skirmish.

19.40 Dobbs Ferry/Hastings-on-Hudson town line. (18.65 E.R.M.)

19.60 St. Christopher's School on left; Gothic Revival mansion by Alexander Jackson Davis, built for E. B. Strange, a New York silk merchant.

19.80 Sacred Heart School on left.
Note: Here Broadway goes uphill to the right. Livingston Avenue drops downhill straight ahead. *Bear right* on Broadway.

20.20 Former Summerfield Methodist Church on left, 303 Broadway. This orange brick building with dark stone trim was built in 1894. It has been used subsequently as a Greek Orthodox Church, an art gallery, and an apartment house.

20.25 *Estherwood* (now the Masters School) on right up Clinton Avenue; a large mansion built in 1890 by James Jennings McComb.

20.50 *Turn left* on Broadway, Route 9.

20.50 Sacred Heart Church on left; ca. 1890, fieldstone.

20.70 Dobbs Ferry School on left; three stories, red brick Tudor style, ca. 1900.

20.90 Mount Mercy College on left.

21.00 Dobbs Ferry/Irvington town line.

21.10 *Nuits*, the Cottenet mansion on left; 1892.

21.20 *Turn left* on Ardsley Avenue.
  Bear left on Hudson Road. Note railroad station ca. 1890 on right.
  Bear left on Hudson Road East. This is Ardsley-on-Hudson. (E.R.M. 20.10)

22.30 *Turn left* on Broadway.

22.50 Pass Ardsley Avenue again. This time *go straight*.

22.50 Cyrus W. Field gatehouse on right, southeast corner of Ardsley Road and Broadway.

22.50 *Nevis* on left (1835), former home of James Alexander Hamilton, third son of Alexander Hamilton, now a laboratory and arboretum belonging to Columbia University.

23.00 O'Dell Tavern on left; ca. 1690.

ESTHERWOOD AT DOBBS FERRY. Built as a residence by J. J. McComb, this wedding cake is now the home of the Masters School. Photo: © Carolyn Hovick Abrahams.

OCTAGON HOUSE AT IRVINGTON. This mansion, built according to the concepts of Orson Fowler, was once the home of noted Hudson River historian Carl Carmer. The Scenic Hudson Preservation Conference was organized at a meeting here. Photo: © Gretchen McHugh.

23.20 Pass Station Road on left. Irvington railroad station at end of street. (E.R.M. 20.80)

23.40 Pass Main Street, Irvington on left.

23.50 St. Barnabas Episcopal Church on left; stone gothic, 1853.

23.60 Irvington Presbyterian Church on left; 1869, James Renwick architect, Romanesque style, windows designed by Louis Comfort Tiffany.

23.80 Abbotsford section.

23.90 Penny Bridge over Sunnyside Brook, Sunnyside Monument.

23.90 Washington Irving Monument on left. Consists of bronze and marble panels over a bridge with bas reliefs in bronze of Rip Van Winkle and Boabdil, the last king of Granada, two characters immortalized by Irving, facing a central marble shaft topped by a bust of Irving. Sculpture by Daniel Chester French (1850–1931), best known for his statues of the Minuteman at Concord, Massachusetts, and Lincoln, in the Lincoln Memorial at Washington.

23.90 *Turn left* on Sunnyside Lane.

24.60 Cross Old Croton Aqueduct (now a footpath).

25.00 Sunnyside Restoration parking lot. (See article E.R.M. 21.45.)

25.00 *Turn around* and return to Broadway, Route 9.

25.80 *Turn left* on Broadway.

25.85 Irvington/Tarrytown town line.

25.85 *Shadow Brook* estate on left.

26.00 David Maun cottage on right; 1826 clapboard saltbox.

26.00 *Belvedere* Estate on left.

26.10 *Lyndhurst* on left. (See article E.R.M. 22.25.)

26.70 Hilton Inn on left. Carroll Castle on hill to right.

26.80 Cross over New York State Thruway, Tappan Zee Bridge to left. (E.R.M. 23.20)

27.30 Hopkins gatehouse on right; brick, Victorian, mansard roof, mid-nineteenth century.

27.50 Washington Irving School on left; two stories.

27.60 First Baptist Church on right.

27.61 Christ Church on left; 1837, brick Gothic with crenellated tower. Washington Irving was a vestryman here.

27.80 Cross Main Street, Tarrytown. Railroad station at end of street. Half-timbered commercial block on northwest corner.

27.90 Second Reformed Church on right; 1837 Greek Revival, Ionic portico.

27.95 Lovett House on right; clapboard, gabled roof, ca. 1890.

28.00 Warner Library on left. See description under Tarrytown article. (E.R.M. 24.00.)

28.10 Patriots' Park and monument to captors of Major André on left. This is the spot where Major André was captured.

28.10 Cross André Brook.

28.10 Tarrytown/North Tarrytown line.

28.20 Church of the Immaculate Conception on left. Formerly St. Mark's Church, it is a gray stone Gothic mid-nineteenth-century structure.

28.30 First Reformed Church (ca. 1870); red brick Gothic.

28.40 *Bear left* downhill on Route 9, North Broadway.

28.60 *Turn left* here for .10 mile to Philipsburg Manor Restoration. (E.R.M. 24.50) See Pocantico River article for full description.

28.70 Cross Pocantico River on Washington Irving Memorial Bridge. This is Sleepy Hollow. The old Head-

LYNDHURST MANSION, TARRYTOWN. Landward view. Photo: Courtesy National Trust for Historic Preservation.

PHILLIPSBURG MANOR—UPPER MILLS. This is located on the Pocantico River at North Tarrytown. Photo: © Gretchen McHugh.

less Horseman Bridge, where Icabod Crane met the Headless Horseman, was slightly to the west.

28.70 Kingsland Point Park to the left.

28.75 Sleepy Hollow. This is the area immortalized by Washington Irving in his Legend of Sleepy Hollow.

28.75 Old Dutch Reformed Church of Sleepy Hollow on right. Parking for church and grave of Washington Irving behind church. According to Irving, the Dutch called this area "die Slapering Haven." This church was greatly beloved by Irving. The weather vane is marked "V. F. (Verdyk Flypse) 1700." The bell was cast in Holland in 1685 and is marked: "Si Deus pro Nobis, Quis Contra Nos-1685." The Church was built by Frederick Philipse I in 1697 or 1699 (the records are not clear). Its walls are thirty inches thick. A popular Currier and Ives print of 1867 made this quaint church familiar to millions. The adjoining churchyard contains the graves of such locally notable families as the Van Tassels, Eckers, Van Werts, Swartwouts, Beekmans, and Buckhouts.

29.25 Sleepy Hollow Cemetery main gate on right. This is a large and beautifully landscaped cemetery containing the graves of such notables as Washington Irving, Carl Schurz, Robert G. Ingersoll, Andrew Carnegie, and Whitelaw Reid.

29.25 Philipse Manor section of North Tarrytown on left.

29.55 North end of Sleepy Hollow Cemetery on right.

29.75 Sleepy Hollow Manor on left.

31.00 Phelps Memorial Hospital on left.

31.10 Junction with Route 117.

31.60 Archville. Cross Old Croton Aqueduct.

SLEEPY HOLLOW CHURCH AT NORTH TARRYTOWN. This famous and historic church was built by Frederick Philipse I c1697–1699 and was beloved and immortalized by Washington Irving, who is buried in its churchyard. Photo: © Gretchen McHugh.

32.10 I.B.M. entrance on left.

32.20 Sleepy Hollow Country Club entrance on right. (E.R.M. 26.50) Brick and limestone mansion in Renaissance style built in 1895 by McKim, Mead & White for Elliott Shepard.

32.25 St. Mary's Episcopal Church on right; Scarborough. Built in 1851, it was copied from the fourteenth-century Gothic church of St. Mary in Scarborough in Yorkshire. Stained glass windows by John Bolton of Pelham, who popularized the craft in America in the mid-nineteenth century. Washington Irving planted the ivy on the church.

32.50 Sleepy Hollow Country club exit on right.

32.60 Clear View School on left.

32.90 *Rosemond* on right. Home of John L. Worden, commander of the *Monitor*. It is a two-story brick Greek Revival building, ca. 1840. (E.R.M. 27.00)

32.90 Corner of Scarborough Road on right.

32.90 Scarborough Presbyterian Church on right. Free-stone and smooth sandstone are combined in this neo-Baroque structure, built in 1893. The high tower is surmounted by a belfry and cupola.

33.25 Beechwood on left; two-story frame, 1835.

33.30 Sparta Burying Ground on left; pre-Revolutionary time to present.

33.60 Ossining town line. (E.R.M. 28.65)

34.80 Ossining United Methodist Church on right; ca 1860, fieldstone Gothic with elaborate campanile.

34.90 The Mud House on left; two-story cement block Victorian house with mansard roof, ca. 1870.

34.95 First Presbyterian Church on left; Hudson River Gothic, red brick with large clock, ca. 1880.

35.10 Site of Union Hotel.

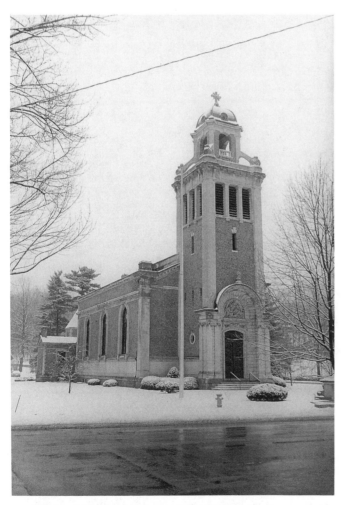

SCARBOROUGH PRESBYTERIAN CHURCH. This neo-Baroque landmark dates from 1893. Photo: © Gretchen McHugh.

35.10 First Baptist Church on left; red brick Hudson River Gothic, bracketted with wooden belfry.

35.12 Westchester County Savings Bank on left. (E.R.M. 28.75)

35.12 Trinity Episcopal Church on right; Gothic, ca. 1880.

35.15 Junction Route 133. Continue straight on Route 9.

36.20 Mariandale Dominican Sisters Nursing Home on left.

36.20 Crawbuckie Point on left. (E.R.M. 29.50)

36.30 Sheraton Inn on left.

36.60 Junction Route 9A. Continue on Route 9.

36.90 Crotonville.

37.00 Cross Croton River. (E.R.M. 30.25)

37.40 *Turn right* at exit.

37.50 *Turn right* on Croton Point Avenue.

37.60 *Turn right* on South Riverside Avenue.

37.80 Van Cortlandt Manor Restoration. (E.R.M. 30.25) This manor house was the center of the great 86,000-acre Van Cortlandt Manor Estate which was erected in 1697. It ran twelve miles along the Hudson from the Croton River to Anthony's Nose. The history of the Van Cortlandt dynasty is as follows:

Oloff Stevenson Van Cortlandt, father of the first proprietor of the estate, was a lineal descendant of the Dukes of Courland in Poland. His ancestors emigrated to Holland when deprived of the Duchy of Courland. The family name was Stevense or Stevensen, van (or from) Courland. They adopted the latter as a surname, the true orthography of which in Dutch is Korte (short), and Landt (land), a term expressing the form of the ancient Duchy of Courland. He emigrated to New Amsterdam in 1637 and soon became rich and powerful. He was colonel of the burghery, president of the "nine men," Schepen of the city, and eventually became burgomaster from 1655 till the end of the Dutch regime in 1664.

His son, Stephanus Van Cortlandt (1643–1700), first Lord of the Manor, assembled a large estate along the Hudson by 1687. His eldest son, Johannes Van Cortlandt, had built a rough stone house, or trading post and hunting lodge on the site of the present manor house in 1683. This was the nucleus of the present structure. This was used by Gov. Thomas Dongan as a hunting lodge in the duck hunting seasons. Stephanus Van Cortlandt was granted manorial rights in 1697, which included the rights of Courts Baron and Court Leet, and the right to send his own representative to the provincial assembly. He paid an annual rent to the Crown of forty shillings on the Feast of the Annunciation of the Blessed Virgin Mary. At the age of 34, he became the first American-born Mayor of the City of New York. He also served as Chief Justice of the Province and was a member of the Governor's Council. He married Gertrude Schuyler and had eleven children.

His son, Philip Van Cortlandt (1683–1746), second Lord of the Manor, married Catherine DePeyster. They used the manor house only as a summer home, residing principally in New York City.

Philip's son, Pierre Van Cortlandt (1721–1814), third Lord of the Manor, established his permanent home here in 1749 and greatly enlarged and improved the old stone structure. Pierre served as Lieutenant Governor of New York from 1775 to 1795.

The Van Cortlandt family were pro-American during the Revolution, and this provoked the ire of the British, who partially burned the manor in 1777. It was restored in 1780. Benjamin Franklin, John Jay, General Lafayette, Baron von Steuben, Rochambeau, and George Washington were all guests at Van Cortlandt manor. The great preacher George Whitefield preached from the front verandah, and it is claimed that he could be heard across the Hudson.

The house has rubblestone walls three feet thick and with loopholes. Notable features are the double stairs that climb to the verandah and the broad paneled Dutch door.

The manor house was lived in by Van Cortlandts for 260 years—seven generations. Anne Stevenson Van Cortlandt, who died in 1940, was the last direct descendant to live here. After her death, the house deteriorated for thirteen years and was in danger of being demolished when it was purchased by John D. Rockefeller, Jr. The present restoration, by Sleepy Hollow Restorations, includes the ferry house, ferry house kitchen, a smokehouse, the necessary, a red-brick long walk between the manor and ferry houses, and colonial gardens of herbs, flowers, and fruit trees.

37.80 *Turn around.*

38.00 *Turn left* on Croton Point Avenue.

38.00 View of Croton Bay on left.

38.20 Pass under Route 9.

38.30 Cross trestle over New York Central/Conrail Railroad tracks.

38.30 Croton-Harmon station to left. Amtrak and M.T.A. service.

38.35 Harmon car shops on right; ca. 1860.

38.70 Pass sand pits.

39.10 Croton Point Park. (E.R.M. 30.50) *Turn around* at traffic circle.

39.90 Cross railroad trestle.

40.00 Pass under Route 9.

40.10 *Turn right* onto Route 9 North.

40.40 Prickly Pear Hill appears ahead.

40.40 Croton-on-Hudson on right.

40.50 Senasqua Beach on left.

40.70 Junction Route 129 (Municipal Place). (E.R.M. 32.00)

41.15 Croton North station on left. (E.R.M. 32.40)

42.70 Old Oscawana on left. (E.R.M. 33.25)

43.30 *Get off expressway* at Montrose Exit, Route 9A. (Southbound—Enter Route 9.)

43.40 *Turn left* on Route 9A (New York and Albany Post Road).

44.20 *Turn left* on Cruger's Station Road.

44.80 Cruger's Station—original site of Boscobel—on right. (35.00 E.R.M.)

44.80 *Turn left* on Cruger's Avenue.

45.00 Name of road changes to Cortlandt Street.

45.30 Cross Furnace Brook, Oscawana Park.

45.40 Oscawana Island on right. (E.R.M. 34.65)

45.70 *Turn left* on Furnace Dock Road (E.R.M. 33.50)

46.40 *Turn left* on Albany Post Road.

46.40 Chimney Corners.

46.50 Cross Furnace Brook.

46.52 *Turn left* on Route 9A (New York & Albany Post Road).

46.60 Pass under Route 9.

47.41 Cross over New York Central Railroad (Conrail).

47.80 Franklin D. Roosevelt V. A. Hospital on left. (E.R.M. 35.25)

47.90 *Turn left* on Dutch Street, Montrose. Keep to right of traffic divider.

48.60 *Turn right* on Sunset Road (Bony Hollow Road). Entrance to George's Island County Park and Montrose Point are on the left. Entrance fee.

49.00 Episcopal Church of the Divine Love on right. Brick, 1869.

49.00 Cross Montrose Point Road. (E.R.M. 35.75)

49.40 *Turn left* on King's Ferry Road.

49.60 Town of Cortlandt line.

49.60 Post Hannock House. The owner operated the King's Ferry in 1664. It served as Col. Livingston's Headquarters in 1781, and, in 1782, Washington presented medals here to the captors of Major André.

49.70 Green Cove on left. Henry Hudson anchored here. Many Indians came down to the ship and one of them was killed in an affray. (E.R.M. 36.25)

49.70 Lake Meahagh on right. Also called Knickerbocker Pond. (E.R.M. 36.50)

49.80 *Turn left* on Riverview Avenue.

50.10 Cross Broadway. *Bend right.* Street becomes Hardie Street.

50.20 Verplanck Point; launching ramp, view of Stony Point.

50.50 Old King's Ferry Wharf. View of Stony Point, Buckberg Mountain, and Tomkins Cove. *Turn around.* (E.R.M. 36.75)

50.90 *Turn left* on Broadway.

51.80 St. Mary's R. C. Cemetery on right (St. Patrick's).

51.80 Georgia-Pacific Co. Gypsum Division Buchanan Plant on left.

52.00 Village of Buchanan line.

52.20 Pass under power line.

52.20 South gate Indian Point atomic power plant on left.

52.30 Main gate Indian Point atomic power plant on left. This is the visitors' entrance. (E.R.M. 38.25)

52.60 Pass Bleakley Avenue (Indian Point Road) on right.

52.70 Lent's Cove Park on left. Charles Point visible across cove.

52.70 Cross Dickey Brook. (E.R.M. 39.00)

52.90 Road becomes John Walsh Boulevard.

53.00 Charles Point. Site of Westchester RESCO incinerator. Good views of Peekskill Bay and lower gate to the Highlands. Charles Point Marina and headquarters National Maritime Historical Society.

53.35 *Turn right* on Louisa Street.

53.90 *Turn left* on Lower South Street. Watch out for large, fast, wild-driving garbage trucks.

54.20 Travis Point on left. (E.R.M. 39.45)

54.30 Mount St. Francis Church on left.

54.60 Railroad Station to left.

54.70 *Turn right* on Hudson Avenue and immediately turn right again to get onto Route 9, North.

54.80 Main Street Peekskill exit, pass.

54.80 Peekskill Bay, Jones Point, and Dunderberg Mountain to left. (E.R.M. 39.50)

55.00 Fort Hill on right. (St. Mary's School) (E.R.M. 39.60).

55.10 Manitou Mountain ahead.

55.20 Scenic parking area (available southbound only).

55.40 *Turn left* on Routes 202 and 6, across bridge.

55.50 Cross Annsville Creek. (E.R.M. 39.75)

55.60 Begin traffic circle.

55.80 *Turn right* on Route 9 North.

Optional Sidetrip

55.80 *Turn right* on Route 9 North.

56.20 Confluence of Peekskill Hollow Brook and Annsville Creek with Canopus Creek (here called Sprout Brook) on right.

57.50 Cross Annsville Creek.

57.50 Wallace Pond on left.

58.40 Westchester/Putnam county line.

59.30 Cross Appalachian Trail. Continental Village over hill to right.

59.40 Graymoor: Mount of Atonement Monastery. Founded in 1898 by Father Lewis Wattson and Mother Lurana White, an Anglican priest and nun. On October 30, 1909, the entire religious community was received at once into the Roman Catholic Church, Father Wattson taking the new name of Father Paul James Francis. Father Paul in later years became known as the "prophet of reunion" because of his work for Anglican-Roman unity. He died in

1940. The Christopher Inn is a halfway house for the rehabilitation of unfortunate men.

59.40 *Turn right* uphill.

59.50 Convent on left.

59.70 Christopher Inn on left.

59.80 Main buildings atop hill.

60.40 Take loop road around top of hill.

60.50 Christopher Inn on right.

60.70 Convent on right.

60.80 *Turn left* on Route 9 South.

60.90 Cross Appalachian Trail.

64.40 Traffic Circle. *Bear right.* End of sidetrip.

Return to Main Route

55.80 Continue around traffic circle on Routes U. S. 6 and U. S. 202 West.

55.95 End of circle. Take Routes U. S. 6 and 202 West.

56.20 Entrance to Camp Smith on right. (E.R.M. 40.30)

56.20 Peekskill Bay and Dunderberg Mountain on left. (E.R.M. 40.00)

56.40 Roa Hook on left. (E.R.M. 40.30)

57.40 Fish Island on left. (E.R.M. 40.75)

57.60 Manitou Mountain on right.

57.80 Round Island on left. (E.R.M. 41.00)

58.10 Iona Island on left. (E.R.M. 41.50)

58.40 Cross Broccy Creek. (E.R.M. 41.60)

58.75 Scenic lookout parking on left. Bear Mountain across river.

59.30 Anthony's Nose on right. (E.R.M. 42.40)

59.45 Entrance to Bear Mountain Bridge. *Bear right* on Route 9D (E.R.M. 42.50)

59.65 Westchester/Putnam county line. North end of Camp Smith Reservation.

60.25 Appalachian trail on right.

60.70 Pass Manitou on left. It is .50 mile to the Manitou railroad station. There is a marker here stating the first chain across the river was forced by the British on October 17, 1777.

60.75 Cross Copper Mine Brook. (E.R.M. 44.40)

61.00 South Mountain Pass on right.

62.37 Canada Hill on right. (E.R.M. 44.40)

62.65 Former Garrison Inn Restaurant on left.

63.00 St. James Chapel on left. Painted red, Gothic, ca. 1860, now an antique dealer.

63.20 Manitoga Nature Conservancy on right. This is an 80-acre forest preserve with four miles of walking trails, sponsored by the Nature Conservancy, a national non-profit land conservation organization.

63.90 St. Francis Retreat House on left.

64.10 Sugarloaf Mountain on right. (E.R.M. 45.50)

64.40 Site of Beverly Robinson House on right. (E.R.M. 45.70)

64.50 Entrance drive to *Wing and Wing* on right (1857).

64.60 Glenclyffe. (E.R.M. 45.65)

64.70 Capuchin Franciscan friary and Sisters of the Cross convent on left (ca. 1890 and 1932). (E.R.M. 46.40)

64.80 *Castle Rock* on top of hill to right. Built in 1881 for William H. Osborn. (E.R.M. 46.40)

64.90 Highlands Country Club on left. Home of Xavier's restaurant (top rate!).

65.10 Garrison town line.

65.20 Junction NY Route 403 on right. *Turn left* off Route 9D towards riverfront.

65.20 Jacob Mandeville House (1737) on right.

65.30 *Turn sharp blind right.*

65.40 *Bend to right.*

65.60 Arden Point on left across railroad tracks. (E.R.M. 46.75)

65.80 *Turn left* on bridge across railroad tracks.

65.81 *Turn left.*

65.82 Golden Eagle Hotel (1840) on right. Now apartments.

65.85 Garrison Village. (E.R.M. 47.35)

65.86 Old horse-watering trough on right. Now a flowerpot.

65.90 New Railroad Depot (ca. 1880) on left.

65.90 *Turn around.* Excellent view across river to West Point South Dock. There is a foot-passenger ferry here. The new railroad depot is now also used as a theater. A park with bandstand gazebo is near the river bank. Old auto ferry slips are visible. The Garrison Yacht Club has deepwater docking berths.

65.95 Old yellow clapboard depot (ca. 1853) on left, now a store.

66.00 *Turn right* over bridge across railroad. Continue straight up hill.

66.20 Glover House (ca. 1850) on left.

66.30 St. Josephs R.C. Church on left; white frame Hudson River Gothic.

66.40 *Turn left* on Route 9D.

66.50 St. Philip's Church in the Highlands on left; Episcopal, 1863, by Richard Upjohn, who is buried in adjoining graveyard. The architect was a vestryman of this church. The parish was founded in 1770. Multicolored slate roof, buttressed tower.

66.80 Cross Philips Brook. (E.R.M. 47.70) Site of Connecticut camps on right.

66.90 Garrison town line.

67.30 William Moore House (1847), now Malcolm Gordon School, on left; yellow brick Gothic by Richard Upjohn.

67.50 Entrance to St. Basil's Academy on left; former Jacob Ruppert mansion, Tudor style, ca. 1920. (E.R.M. 48.25)

67.90 Entrance to Dick's Castle on right. (E.R.M. 48.35) (Garrison Hall development.)

67.90 Start across Indian Brook Viaduct. (E.R.M. 48.40)

68.00 End Indian Brook Viaduct.

68.50 Entrance to Boscobel on left. (E.R.M. 48.65)

68.90 Thomas Rossiter House on left (1860).

68.95 Plumbush Inn on right.

69.00 Cross viaduct over Foundry Brook.

69.10 *Turn left* on Old Road.

69.20 Foundry Brook on left. (E.R.M. 49.00)

69.35 Putnam County Historical Society on left.

69.40 West Point Foundry Museum on left.

69.45 *Continue straight* on Route 9D (Chestnut Street).

69.60 St. Mary's Church in the Highlands on left; Episcopal, 1868, by George E. Harney—bluestone walls,

BOSCOBEL. Now located near Cold Spring, this mansion was moved here from its original site near Cruger's Station. It was the home of States Morris Dyckman (1755–1806). Photo: Courtesy Boscobel Restorations.

simple gable roof, stone spire, modeled upon an English parish church.

69.70 *Turn left* on Main Street, Cold Spring. Manitou Hotel on NE corner now called Henry's On Hudson.

69.80 Salmagundi Book Store on right.

70.00 *Turn left* on Lunn Terrace.

70.10 *Turn right* across railroad bridge.

70.15 *Turn right* immediately after crossing bridge.

70.20 *Turn left* on Main Street.

70.30 Circle around bandstand on riverfront. Turn around at Front Street, Cold Spring. (E.R.M. 49.50) Historic Hudson House hotel (1837) is on the left. The view across the river extends to West Point, Washington Valley, Cro' Nest Mountain. Retrace route back over railroad to corner of Lunn Terrace and Main Street.

70.60 *Turn right* on Main Street.

70.70 *Turn left* on Fair Street.

71.30 *Run back into* Route 9D. Continue straight. (Southbound: continue straight right onto Fair Street. Do not go uphill on Route 9D.)

71.30 Little Stony Point and Mother Cronk's Cove on left. (E.R.M. 50.50 and 51.00)

71.40 Old stone crusher area.

71.70 Mount Taurus (Bull Hill) on right. (E.R.M. 50.55)

72.50 Site of former Storm King railroad station on left. (E.R.M. 51.25)

72.50 Enter tunnel under Breakneck Ridge (E.R.M. 51.50)

72.70 Exit tunnel.

72.70 Putnam/Dutchess county line.

72.80. Catskill Aqueduct pumping station on left. (E.R.M. 51.55)

73.60 Pollepel Island (Bannermans Island) on left. (E.R.M. 52.80)

74.00 Dutchess Manor Restaurant (ca. 1870) on left.

74.00 Sugarloaf Mountain on right.

74.80 Dutchess Junction on left. (E.R.M. 54.90)

75.70 City of Beacon line.

76.10 Craig House (Tioranda) on left. Built in 1859 by Richard Morris Hunt for shipping magnate George Joseph Howland, it is Gothic-Victorian with contrasting black and white glazed bricks. It now serves as a sanitarium.

76.10 Route 9D here called Howland Avenue.

76.40 Mount Beacon inclined railway base depot on right. (E.R.M. 56.00)

76.40 Turn left on Route 9D, Wolcott Avenue.

76.70 St. Luke's Episcopal Church on right: 1868 by Frederick C. Withers, stone English Gothic. The churchyard has the grave of Chancellor James Kent. (E.R.M. 55.00)

76.80 Cross Fishkill Creek.

76.90 Cross New Haven Railroad, now Conrail.

77.50 Continue straight west toward the river.

77.60 *Turn left* on Wolcott Avenue to site of railroad station (Amtrak and Metro-North Commuter RR). Former terminal of Newburgh-Beacon Ferry on left. (E.R.M. 56.30) This location formerly called Fishkill Landing. Printing and carton plant of Federal Paper Board Co. is to the south. Good view of Newburgh Bay and Northern Highlands. *Turn around* to corner of Wolcott Avenue and Beekman Street.

78.35 *Turn left* uphill on Beekman Street.

78.40 *Turn left* on Route 9D, North Avenue.

78.80 Southern Dutchess Country Club on left.

79.00 Beacon town line.

79.20 Cross Interstate 84. Newburgh-Beacon Bridge to left. (E.R.M. 57.20)

79.50 Site of Mount Gulian, former home of Verplanck family, on left.

79.60 Entrance to Fishkill Health Related Center, on right. Formerly called Matteawan State Hospital. (E.R.M. 57.30)

80.00 Purdy Ridge on right. (E.R.M. 58.50)

80.80 Entrance to Castle Point U. S. Veterans' Hospital on left.

80.90 *Turn left* on Castle Point Road.

81.00 Cross Hospital private road.

82.00 *Bend sharp right* on River Road South.

82.40 Castle Hill Veterans' Hospital on right. (E.R.M. 59.50)

82.90 *Turn right* on Spring Street.

83.50 *Turn left* on Market Street. Chelsea. (E.R.M. 60.25)

83.70 Continue straight along railroad on North River Road.

84.40 City of New York Delaware Aqueduct tunnel and intake station on left. (E.R.M. 60.30)

84.40 View of Danskammer Point and Soap Hill across river, to left.

84.80 Continue on North River Road. Derick Brinkerhoff House to left; 1½-story clapboard, ca. 1820.

85.20 *Turn left* on Old State Road.

86.30 *Turn left* on Wheeler Hill Road.

87.10 *Turn sharp left* on New Hamburg Road, Route 28.

87.50 Cross Wappinger's Creek. (E.R.M. 63.00)

87.70 New Hamburg depot on left.

87.80 *Turn left* on Bridge Street.

87.85 Cross Main Street.

87.95 *Bear left* on Bridge Street.

88.00 Cross railroad bridge.

88.05 *Turn left* on Main Street.

88.10 *Turn right* on Railroad Avenue.

88.15 *Turn right* on River Street. (E.R.M. 63.30)

88.35 *Turn right* on Point Street.

88.70 *Turn right* on Reed Road. Cross railroad bridge.

89.00 *Turn left* on Channingville Road.

89.30 *Turn left* on Sheafe Road.

89.50 Bowdoin County Park on left.

91.00 Entrance George Clinton estate on left.

91.40 Lone Star Industries on left.

SPRINGWOOD—HOME OF FRANKLIN DELANO ROOSEVELT at Hyde Park. Photo: © Gretchen McHugh.

92.70 *Turn right* on Old Post Road.

92.90 *Turn left* on Route 9.

93.00 I.B.M. Country Club on right.

93.40 I.B.M. plant on left. (E.R.M. 67.60)

94.80 *Locust Grove* on left. (E.R.M. 68.80)

95.00 *Southwood* on left. (E.R.M. 69.10)

95.60 Poughkeepsie Rural Cemetery on left. (E.R.M. 69.15)

95.90 *Turn right* off Route 9 onto Academy Street.

95.90 Central Hudson Power Company headquarters on left.

96.10 Entrance to *Springside* on right; summer home of Matthew Vassar, with grounds landscaped by Andrew Jackson Downing.

96.40 *Turn left* on Montgomery Street.

96.50 *Turn right* on South Street. Eastman Park on left.

96.60 Soldiers' Memorial Fountain on left.

96.75 Brick Armory on right.

97.00 Bardavon Theater on right. Site of former Nelson House Hotel on left.

97.20 Civic Center on left.

97.25 Post Office on right.

97.25 *Turn left* on Mansion Street.

97.30 *Turn right* on Washington Street (Route 9G).

98.50 Poughkeepsie city line.

98.50 Marist College on left. (E.R.M. 71.50)

98.70 Mid-Hudson Business Park on right.

99.00 Hudson River Psychiatric Center on right. Formerly called Hudson River State Hospital. (E.R.M. 72.75)

100.00 South entrance Culinary Institute of America on left. (E.R.M. 73.80)

100.10 North entrance Culinary Institute of America on left.

101.10 Hyde Park town line.

101.10 Cross Maritje Kill. (E.R.M. 74.00)

101.90 Franklin D. Roosevelt National Historical Site on left. (E.R.M. 74.75)

104.80 *Turn left* on Main Street.

104.90 Vanderbilt Stables on right.

105.00 *Turn left* on Curry Lane.

105.40 *Turn sharp right* on River Road.

105.70 Hyde Park depot and landing on left. (E.R.M. 76.40) Street becomes Main Street.

106.10 *Bear left* on West Market Street.

106.30 *Turn left* on Route 9.

106.30 Federal style mansion on left.

106.50 Entrance to Vanderbilt Mansion National Historical Site to left.

106.50 *Turn left* into driveway. (E.R.M. 77.00)

106.70 Cross pond to parking area.

107.50 Exit north gate.

107.50 *Turn left* on Route 9.

107.50 St. James Episcopal Church on right; stone Gothic, 1844, by Augustus Thomas Cowman, architect. The parish was founded in 1811 by Dr. Samuel Bard and Gen. Morgan Lewis. The first minister was Rev. John McVickar (1787–1868). Franklin D. Roosevelt was senior warden. In 1939 King George VI and Queen Elizabeth worshiped here.

107.55 Vanderbilt Barns on right; ca. 1900, Stanford White, architect.

107.60 Cross Bard Rock Creek. (E.R.M. 77.75)

110.00 *Turn left* onto Old Post Road.

110.10 Margaret Lewis Norrie State Park on left. (E.R.M. 79.75) Park roads offer excellent views of Indian Kill and Norrie Point. Beautiful marshes and

VIEW FROM HYDE PARK. Drawn by William Bartlett c1836 for publication in N. P. Willis's *American Scenery*. It is taken from grounds of the Vanderbilt Estate National Historic Site. From author's collection.

woodlands. Picnicking and boat launch facilities. Home of Norrie Point Yacht Club. Recommended sidetrip.

112.05 Cross Indian Kill.

112.60 Staatsburg village center. (E.R.M. 81.20)

112.70 St. Margaret's Episcopal Church on right.

113.10 *Turn left* into Ogden Mills State Park.

113.20 Cross over railroad tracks.

113.90 Mansion. Circle around. (E.R.M. 81.60)

113.90 *Turn left* on Old Post Road.

114.90 Dinsmore golf course on right. This is possibly the second oldest in United States.

115.70 *Turn left* on Route 9.

116.00 *Turn left* on South Mill Road.

116.60 Cross Landsman Kill. (E.R.M. 82.90)

117.00 Linwood (Sisters of St. Ursula) on left. (E.R.M. 83.10)

117.10 Ruins of Wyndcliffe on left. (E.R.M. 83.20)

117.20 Keep bearing left.

117.50 Wildercliff on left. (E.R.M. 83.30)

117.80 *Turn sharp left* on Route 85. (Southbound—*sharp right* on South Mill Road.)

117.80 Old Schoolhouse on right. one-story Carpenter Gothic, now a residence.

118.00 Wilderstein on left. (E.R.M. 83.50)

VANDERBILT MANSION AT HYDE PARK. Landside view. Photo: © Gretchen McHugh.

118.80 Pius XII School on right; formerly Cardinal Farley Military Academy, and earlier Ellerslie, home of Levi P. Morton. (E.R.M. 84.50)

119.60 Rhinecliff town line. Road becomes Kelly Street.

120.50 Amtrak Rhinecliff depot on left.

120.70 Leave Rhinecliff.

121.50 *Turn left* on River Road. County Route 103.

122.50 Entrance to *Ferncliff*, Carmelite Sisters Nursing Home. (E.R.M. 88.25)

123.00 Astor estate gatehouse on left; stone Victorian mansard ca. 1860.

123.80 Former Mary Astor chateau on left.

123.80 Mount Rutsen on right. (E.R.M. 88.75)

124.90 Entrance to *Leacote Farm* on left; stone Gothic Revival based on design of Lyndhurst, ca. 1880.

125.00 *Orlot* estate on left.

125.10 Cross Route 199. Kingston-Rhinecliff Bridge to left. (E.R.M. 90.00)

125.20 Eighteenth-century stone house on left.

125.50 Gatehouse to *Steen Valetje* on left—now called *Mandara*.

126.00 *Rokeby* on left; two-story stuccoed stone, Federal style, ca. 1815, later mansard roof, tower, and other renovations. (E.R.M. 91.20)

126.00 Road becomes Annandale Road.

127.10 *Turn left* on Dock Road.

127.90 Cross railroad.

128.00 Barrytown depot and landing. *Turn around.* (E.R.M. 91.75)

128.10 Cross railroad.

128.40 Sacred Heart Church on left; carpenter Gothic, 1874.

128.80 *Turn left* on Annandale Road.

129.00 St. John's Church on right; Episcopal, Carpenter Gothic, mid-nineteenth century.

129.20 Moore House on left; pre-revolutionary stone and brick with gable ends.

129.40 Drive to Montgomery Place on left. (E.R.M. 92.75) *See article.*

129.70 Cross Saw Kill.

129.70 Annandale-on-Hudson. (E.R.M. 92.80)

129.75 *Bear left* at fork.

130.10 *Blithewood* Gatehouse on left. Gatehouse by A. J. Davis. The neo-classical mansion and Italianate garden were designed in 1899 by Francis F. V. Hoppin on ground laid out by A. J. Downing.

130.30 Bard College on right.

130.40 Bard Hall; two-story stone Gothic, ca. 1860, on right.

130.50 Bard College library, two-story brick with Ionic columns, copy of a classic Greek temple, 1893, on right.

130.70 Chapel of the Holy Innocents on left. Stone Gothic, ca. 1860.

131.10 Ward Manor gatehouse straight ahead; two-story stone castellated structure with tower, 1915.

131.10 *Turn right* on Route 103 (Cruger Road to the left). (E.R.M. 93.75)

131.40 *Turn left* on Manor Road.

131.50 Ward Mansion; two-story stuccoed Tudor-style, ca. 1918. (E.R.M. 93.80)

131.50 *Turn around* at circle.

131.70 *Turn left* on Route 103.

131.80 *Turn left* on Route 9G.

132.50 Beckwith Hill on right.

133.30 *Turn left* on Kidd Lane.

134.10 *Turn right* over bridge across Stony Creek.

134.30 Mansion on left; ca. 1850. You are now on Washburn Avenue.

134.90 *Turn left* on Broadway, Route 402.

134.90 Tivoli.

135.80 Tivoli Depot. View of Saugerties across river. (E.R.M. 95.80.)

135.80 *Turn around.*

136.30 *Turn left* on Woods Road, Route 35.

136.50 St. Paul's Church on left. Brick with bell tower, ca. 1850. Tombs of Livingston family.

136.90 Tivoli town line.

137.60 Enter Clermont State Park.

137.80 *Turn left* on Park Road.

138.10 *Clermont*: Livingston Mansion. (E.R.M. 97.90)

138.10 *Turn around* (parking available here).

138.40 Continue straight on Route 35 after leaving park.

138.50 *Turn left* on Route 35.

139.10 *Ridgely*; Carmelite Sisters' convent on left, the former Thomas Hunt mansion, late nineteenth century.

139.30 *Chiddingstone* on left; two-story brick mansion, bracketed, ca. 1890.

139.50 *Southwood on* left; two-story, brick and stone mansion, mansard roof and brackets, late nineteenth century.

139.50 *Clermont Farm* on right.

139.60 *Midwood* on left; Two-story clapboard home with bracketed cornice, mid-nineteenth century. Built by Robert R. Livingston Clarkson.

140.10 *Oaklawn* on left; childhood home of Eleanor Roosevelt, mid-nineteenth century, much altered.

140.20 *Holcroft* on left; two-story brick mansion, ca. 1890.

140.50 *Northwood* on left; two-story brick house with mansard roof, mid-nineteenth century.

141.30 *Turn left* on Cheviot Road.

141.35 Cheviot Cemetery on right. Site of East Camp. (E.R.M. 101.25)

141.60 Cheviot depot. (E.R.M. 100.50)

141.60 *Turn around.*

141.80 *Turn left* on Cheviot Road Extension.

142.10 *Turn left* on Route 35.

142.60 Mansion on right; two-story brick, ca. 1850.

142.75 *Turn left* onto Routes 35 and 9G.

142.80 Views of Catskill Mountains and Kaaterskill Clove to left.

142.90 *Turn left* at light. To Germantown.

143.00 Site of Diell Rockerfeller Grist and Saw Mill, 1751.

143.30 Site for former Germantown depot. (E.R.M. 101.50) *Turn around.*

143.70 *Turn left* on Route 9G.

144.50 Germantown town line.

144.60 Shapp's Landing Road on left (1684).

144.90 *Turn left* on Route 35A.

145.20 North Germantown line. (E.R.M. 103.00)

145.90 Extensive view to left; includes cement works at Alsen, Duck Cove, DeWitt Point, Inbocht Bay, and Kalkberg—also distant Catskills.

145.90 You are on Northern Boulevard.

146.40 North Germantown.

146.40 Peary House on left; board and batten Carpenter Gothic, mid-nineteenth century (Crawford).

146.50 Cross narrow bridge.

146.70 North Germantown town line.

146.90 *Turn left* on Route 9G.

147.70 Germantown/Livingston township line.

147.70 Cross Roeliff Jansen's Kill. (E.R.M. 105.25)

147.90 *Turn right* on Route 10, formerly called "Ye Waggon Road from Manor House."

148.50 Linlithgo. (E.R.M. 105.25)

148.50 Livingston Memorial Chapel; parts from 1722, rebuilt 1870, Dutch Reformed. Tombs of first eight generations of Livingstons.

148.50 *Turn around.*

149.10 *Turn right* on Route 9G.

149.90 Cross Fox Creek culvert.

151.50 *Turn right* into drive of *Olana Castle.*

151.80 Lake on right.

152.50 *Olana Castle.* (E.R.M. 108.00) Parking area.

152.50 *Turn around.*

153.50 *Turn right* on Route 9G.

154.20 Church Hill on right.

154.40 Rip Van Winkle Bridge on left. (E.R.M. 108.60)

154.40 Junction Routes 9G and 23. *DO NOT CROSS BRIDGE.*

154.50 *Turn left* onto Mt. Merino Road.

154.50 Extensive views to left: panorama of entire Great Wall of Manitou. From south to north: Overlook Mountain, Indian Head Mountain, Twin Mountain, Kaaterskill High Peak, Round Top, South Mountain, North Mountain, Acra Point, Mount Thomas Cole, Windham Mountain.

156.40 Pass beneath power lines.

156.40 Mount Merino on right. (E.R.M. 110.00)

156.50 Mansion on right; 2½-story brick, ca. 1840.

157.00 *Turn left* off Mount Merino Road, onto Routes 9G and 23B.

157.10 Hudson city line.

157.30 Cross brook. Road becomes South 3rd Street.

157.50 *Turn left* on Warren Street.

157.80 *Turn right* on Front Street.

157.80 Washington Hose Company No. 3.

157.80 The Parade on left. (E.R.M. 112.00) Panoramic views.

158.00 *Turn right* on State Street.

158.50 Hudson Library on left. It is located in an old brick schoolhouse.

158.60 Brick armory on left.

158.70 Row houses.

159.00 Junction Routes 9G and 23B. *Turn left* on Green Street, Route 9.
(Southbound—*turn right* on State Street.)

159.40 Junction Routes 23B and 9. *Turn left* on Route 9, Fairview Avenue.
(Southbound—*turn right* on Green Street.)

159.70 Hudson city line. Cross railroad track.

160.00 Fireman's home on left.

162.10 Stottsville town line. Greenport/Stockport town line.

162.10 *Bend left* on Route 9.
(Southbound—*bend right* on Route 9G, Fairview Avenue.) (E.R.M. 114.25)

162.40 Green water tower on right.

162.40 Views of Taconics on right and Catskills on left.

163.40 Columbiaville Falls. (E.R.M. 116.45)
Columbiaville was incorporated in 1812. There were a cotton factory and saw, paper, and grist mills.

163.50 Cross Stockport Creek.

163.50 *Turn left* on Southers Road, Route 22.

163.70 Greek Revival house on right.

163.90 *Turn left* to Stockport.

164.60 Site of former Stockport Station. (E.R.M. 115.80) *Turn around.*

164.65 Maj. Abram Staats House on left; one-story stone, ca. 1664, much altered.

165.30 *Turn left* on Southers Road.

166.40 SOUTHBOUND ONLY *turn sharp left.*

166.50 Road to former Stockport Landing and Judson Point on left. (E.R.M. 116.75)

166.70 SOUTHBOUND ONLY *bear left.*

167.80 *Turn left* on Route 9J.

168.10 View of Catskills to left.

169.40 Stockport-Stuyvesant line. Patent granted to Arent Van Dendbergh in 1666. Sold to Hans Hendricksen in 1667.

169.60 Greek Revival house on right.

170.20 Nutten Hook (E.R.M. 118.80) and site of former Newton Hook Station on left. Former ferry to Coxsackie.

172.70 Town line.

172.90 Powell Patent marker on left (southwest corner). Patent granted in 1664.

173.20 Stuyvesant Landing. (E.R.M. 121.45)

173.40 Junction with Route 398 on right.

173.40 Wendover Mansion on left; two-story brick, early nineteenth century, with possible earlier portions.

173.50 Van Schaack houses; built in 1790 and 1820, in brick Federal and Italian villa styles, now Stuyvesant Home.

173.70 Stuyvesant town line.

173.90 Henry Hudson landed here September 19, 1609.

174.00 Northwest corner of Powell Patent of 1664.

174.20 Bracketed villa on right.

174.40 View of Catskills to left.

175.00 Go under New York Central Railroad loop track to Alfred H. Smith Memorial Bridge.

175.30 Cross brook.

175.70 Cross brook.

175.90 Go under railroad loop track to bridge.

178.80 Columbia/Rensselaer county line. Cross brook. (E.R.M. 126.60)

180.00 Schodack Landing. (E.R.M. 127.55)

180.10 Ten Eyck House on right; 1½ story brick, gambrel roof, mid-nineteenth century.

180.80 Schodack Island to left. (E.R.M. 129.00)

181.50 Pass beneath Alfred H. Smith Memorial Bridge. This single-track railroad bridge was named in honor of former president of the New York Central Railroad. (E.R.M. 129.80)

181.60 Pass beneath New York Thruway Berkshire Branch Bridge. (E.R.M. 129.90)

182.70 Cross Muitze's Kill.

183.00 Cross Vlockie Kill. (E.R.M. 131.25)

183.50 Junction Route 150 to right.

183.50 Castleton-on-Hudson. (E.R.M. 131.50)

183.60 House with stepped gable on right.

183.80 Resurrection Rest Home on right.

184.20 Castleton town line.

184.40 Cross Moordener Kill. (E.R.M. 132.50)

185.00 Becker House on right; two-story clapboard, rebuilt after fire ca. 1860.

185.20 Cross Vierda Kill. (E.R.M. 133.75)

186.20 Staats Island Road on left.

186.60 Schodack/East Greenbush town line.

187.00 East Greenbush, Hayes Road on right. (E.R.M. 135.50)

187.00 Genet Schoolhouse on right; Carpenter Gothic, ca. 1850.

189.60 Port of Albany and Sunoco tank farm on left.

189.60 Niagara Mohawk Kenwood generating station to left. (E.R.M. 138.75)

190.70 *Turn left* onto Route 9, Columbia Turnpike. (SOUTHBOUND—*turn right* onto Route 9J.)

190.80 Cross bridge over New York Central Railroad (Conrail).

191.10 *Turn left* on Akin Avenue.

191.20 *Turn left* on Nelson Avenue.

191.30 *Turn right* on Belmore Place.

191.40 *Turn left* on Riverside Avenue.

191.80 *Turn around* at foot of Riverside Avenue.

191.80 BASF plant on east. Port of Albany on south.

192.20 Fort Crailo on right; two-story brick, ca. 1700, renovated. One of the early buildings of Rensselaerwyck, it is now a museum. 518 463-8738.

192.40 Cross over Routes 9 and 20. Go north on Broadway.

192.60 Pass entrance of bridge to Albany. (E.R.M. 139.65)

192.70 Cross Quackendary Kill.

192.75 St. John's Byzantine-style church seen uphill on right. Unique campanile, a Rensselaer landmark.

192.90 Amtrak Albany-Rensselaer Depot across tracks on right.

194.20 *Turn right* on Washington Avenue.

194.30 *Bear left* uphill.

194.40 Continue straight ahead.

194.80 Cross over Interstate 90.

194.90 St. Anthony-on-Hudson on left.

195.00 Franciscan Mission House on left.

195.90 North Greenbush/Rensselaer town line. Road becomes Washington Avenue Extension.

196.40 *Turn left* on Route 4.

196.40 Defreestville. (E.R.M. 140.75)

198.10 Junction Route 136 on right.

199.20 Troy/North Greenbush town line.

199.50 Hudson Valley Community College on right.

199.50 Former Immaculate Conception Monastery on left. Now part of Hudson Valley Community College.

199.60 Cross Wynants Kill. (E.R.M. 144.50)

200.30 Junction Route 378 on left.

200.30 *Turn right* on Route 4, Burden Avenue. (SOUTHBOUND—*bend left* on Route 4.)

200.60 *Turn right* on 4th Street, Troy. (E.R.M. 144.80)

201.40 Cross Poesten Kill. (E.R.M. 145.60)

202.20 New Liftbridge to Green Island on left.

202.70 Former Cluet-Peabody plant on left.

204.30 Green Island on left, across river.

204.30 Continue north on Route 4, here called River Street and later Second Avenue.

204.40 Go beneath Route 787.

205.10 Junction Route 470. Van Schaick Island on left, across river. (E.R.M. 149.90)

205.50 Old Lansing Inn on right. Lansingburgh.

205.80 Standard Manufacturing Company mill on right.

ST. PAUL'S EPISCOPAL CHURCH, TROY. Dates from 1827 in the Gothic Revival style. Photo: © Bob Hansen.

206.20 Junction Route 142. *Go straight.*

206.30 Route 4 here turns left across the bridge to Waterford. (E.R.M. 151.40)

206.30 *Continue straight* on a series of self-guiding local roads leading immediately into each other under the following names: River Road, Marion Avenue, Houghney Road, Irish Road. Much of the old River Road is now blocked off, requiring a detour inland, but offering in return some fine panoramic views. The large building on the left is the old streetcar barn, now used for buses. At several points sections of the former Boston & Maine Railroad Troy Branch are crossed at grade—now abandoned and tracks torn up.

207.20 Troy city line.

208.10 Pleasantdale town line.

211.00 *Turn left* on Route 40.
   (SOUTHBOUND—*turn right* on Irish Road).

212.00 *Turn left* on Calhoun Road.
   (SOUTHBOUND—*turn right* on Route 40).

213.00 *Turn right* on River Road.
   (SOUTHBOUND *turn left* on Calhoun Rd.)

215.00 Quack Island and Lock No. 2 on left. (E.R.M. 159.00 & 159.35)

216.50 Enter Hemstreet Park.

216.50 *Turn left* on Locust Avenue.

216.60 *Turn right* on Hudson Street.

216.70 *Bear right* on Maple and South Washington Streets.

216.80 *Turn right* on Howland Avenue (Route 67).

216.90 Turn left on Linden Street. This begins a semi-circular sidetrip to the confluence of the Hudson River and the Hoosic River through some verdant farmland with many fine panoramic views. There are several sections of well-graded gravel road. The name of the road changes from section to section under the names Linden Street, Delano Road, Don Wier Road, and Knickerbocker Road, but ultimately rejoins Route 67. Just follow your nose and stay on the main route. There is a very low-clearance, narrow underpass beneath the Boston & Maine Railroad two-track mainline. Do not attempt this loop with high and wide vehicles or trailers. As of 1988 the road was smooth and comfortable driving. High and wide vehicles should continue straight east on Howland Avenue, Route 67, to junction with Route 40 and continue tour from there.

217.00 Lock No. 3 to left. (E.R.M. 161.75)

218.10 Pass beneath Boston & Maine Railroad (narrow and low). This is their main, two-track freight line between Boston and Rotterdam Junction, near Schenectady. It crosses the Hudson River at E.R.M. 162.50.

219.80 *Bend sharp right.* Hoosic River now on left. Confluence with Hudson River. (E.R.M. 163.50)

222.55 Site of Fort Schaghticoke on left. Early eighteenth century fortification. You are now on Knickerbocker Road.

222.60 Turn left onto Route 67, here called Schaghticoke Road.
   (SOUTHBOUND—*turn right* onto Knickerbocker Road.)

224.95 Cross bridge over Boston & Maine RR mainline.

225.60 *Turn left* on Route 40. (SOUTHBOUND—*turn right* on Route 118, Schagticoke Road, runs into Route 67.)

226.10 Cross Bridge over Boston & Maine RR mainline.

226.20 Cross Hoosic River.

226.30 *Bear left* uphill.

227.00 Village of Schaghticoke.

227.10 *Turn left* on Main Street, Route 121.

227.40 Rensselaer County Fairgrounds on left.

227.40 Elmwood Cemetery on right.

231.40 *Turn right* on River Road, Route 120. (SOUTHBOUND—*turn left* on Route 121.)

232.30 Rensselaer/Washington county line. River Road becomes Washington County Route 113.

238.30 Sarles Ferry site on left. (E.R.M. 172.45)

243.70 Saratoga Battle Monument visible on hill across river to left.

243.70 Cross Route 29.

243.70 Bridge to Schuylerville on left. (E.R.M. 178.80)

245.10 Cross Batten Kill. (E.R.M. 180.00)

245.20 *Turn left.*

245.50 Site of Hessian Camp of 1777 on left.

245.70 *Turn right.*

245.70 Site of British camp and river crossing of 1777 on left.

245.90 *Turn left.*

246.80 Thomson. (E.R.M. 181.30)

247.00 *Turn left* off Route 113. Then *immediate right* on Route 4.

248.60 *Turn left* at fork.

248.80 *Turn left* over bridge at Lock No. 6. (E.R.M. 184.25)

248.90 Fort Miller. (E.R.M. 185.00)

249.40 *Turn right.*

249.80 *Turn right.*

249.90 Cross bridge over Champlain Canal.

250.00 *Turn left* on Route 4.

251.50 Lock floodgate on canal to left.

252.20 Cross Moses Kill. (E.R.M. 188.00)

253.10 South Argyle. (E.R.M. 188.50)

254.60 Fort Edward Center; original burial place of Jenny M'Crea. (E.R.M. 190.25)

256.60 Cross Champlain Canal, Lock No. 7. (E.R.M. 192.20)

256.70 *Turn right.*

256.75 Enter town of Fort Edward.

256.80 Old Fort House Museum.

256.90 Junction Route 197. Continue on Route 4.

257.30 Old Fort Edward area on left. (E.R.M. 192.50)

257.50 Pass beneath Delaware & Hudson Railroad main line. New Amtrak depot moved a block north from this former depot site. (E.R.M. 192.80)

257.60 Junction Route 197 on left. Continue straight. (E.R.M. 192.90)

257.80 United Methodist Church on left.

257.85 Cross railroad grade crossing, D. & H.

257.90 Cross bridge over railroad, D. & H.

258.00 *Bear left* on Route 4.

258.50 Union Cemetery on right.

258.50 Fort Edward village line.

259.00 Union Cemetery on right.

259.25 Adirondack Community College on left.

259.50 Mullen Mansion on right, ca. 1800.

259.90 Washington County Courthouse on right. Brick Victorian, 1878.

260.10 Junction Routes 4 and 254.

MULLEN MANSION AT FORT EDWARD. Built c1800. Photo: Alfred H. Marks.

260.10 *Turn left* on Route 254.

260.10 Hudson Falls town square. (E.R.M. 196.00)

260.70 Washington/Warren county line. Warren County has area of 883 square miles. Taken from Washington County in 1813, it was named for Gen. Joseph Warren, killed at Battle of Bunker Hill. Lake George is the county seat.

261.40 Junction Routes 254 and 32.

261.40 *Go straight* on Route 254.

261.60 Southbound, take far right fork at traffic light onto Route 254.

261.90 Glens Falls city line.

262.00 Pass beneath Delaware & Hudson Glens Falls branch.

262.20 Southbound, *bear left* on Route 32.

262.20 Routes 32 and 254 become Warren Street.

262.20 Flintcote Plant on left.

VILLA AT HUDSON FALLS. Typical Italianate 19th century home. Photo: Alfred H. Marks.

METHODIST CHURCH AT HUDSON FALLS. A typical "North Country" public building. Photo: Alfred H. Marks.

VILLAGE SQUARE AT HUDSON FALLS. Photo: Alfred H. Marks.

Side Trip

262.20 *Turn left* on Prospect Street for one block down the hill to the pulp log dump of the Finch-Pruyn paper mill. This is a unique sight and smell. Beware of large and fast-moving log trucks and trac-

PULP YARD AT GLENS FALLS. Typical of the areas surrounding pulp mills in the Upper Hudson Valley. Photo: Alfred H. Marks.

tors. *Turn around* and return uphill and *turn left* on Warren Street to continue tour.

262.20 Center of Glens Falls.

262.90 *Turn left* on Route 9.
   (SOUTHBOUND—*turn right* on Warren St., Route 32.)

263.00 Finch-Pruyn paper mill on left.

263.10 Cooper's Cave and Glens Fall on Hudson River on right. Route 9 Bridge across Hudson River. (E.R.M. 199.10)

263.10 End.

East Side Railroad Route

Service on this line is provided from Grand Central Terminal in Manhattan as far north as Poughkeepsie by the Metropolitan Transit Authority, making all local stops. Through trains to Albany and beyond are operated by the National Railroad Passenger Corporation, Amtrak. The route is over the former tracks of the New York & Harlem, Hudson River Railroad, and New York Central Railroad. In later years, these lines have been operated by the New York Central & Hudson River Railroad, the New York Central Railroad, Penn Central Railroad, and Conrail—who still own much of the track.

M. T. A. Route
(Metro-North Commuter Railroad)

Our trip commences at Grand Central Terminal on Forty-second Street in Manhattan, at Park Avenue—which here actually passes through an upper level of the terminal. The original station was built in 1871 and expanded in 1884 and 1900. The present terminal was built between 1903 and 1913. It is in the Beaux Arts eclectic style and was designed by Warren, Wetmore, Reed and Stem. Col. William J. Wilgus was the principal engineer. Grand Central has two levels of tracks. Forty-one tracks carry through traffic on the upper level, and suburban trains use tracks on the lower level. On the upper level there is a run-around loop track. In consequence of an accident in the Park Avenue tunnel in 1902, the legislature passed an act requiring trains to be operated through the tunnel by electric traction. Beneath both levels is the giant power plant that moves the trains and lights and heats the buildings. Tracks and switches in underground caverns carved out of solid rock stretch out for seventy-nine acres.

0 Grand Central Terminal. The train remains in a tunnel beneath Park Avenue for 3½ miles, and then comes out on an elevated trestle above Park Avenue in the Harlem section of Manhattan.

4 125th Street Station—an elevated station. After leaving 125th Street, the line crosses the Harlem River on a large vertical lift bridge.

5 The Bronx (138th Street). Beyond here the Hudson division splits to the west from the Harlem division, which continues straight to White Plains, Brewster, and a connection with the Boston & Albany at Chatham. Local trains also use this line to Woodlawn Junction to reach the former New York, New Haven & Hartford line to Boston.

7 Sedgwick Avenue.

8 High Bridge, West 169th Street, Bronx. Pass beneath the High Bridge of the Old Croton Aqueduct. Parallel Harlem River and Spuyten Duyvil Creek to Spuyten Duyvil Station.

9 Morris Heights, West 177th Street, Bronx.

10 University Heights, West 207th Street, Bronx. Former Putnam Division splits off at Kingsbridge.

10 Marble Hill, West 225 Street.

11 Spuyten Duyvil. Junction with West Side Manhattan line, former southern end of Hudson River Railroad.

Amtrak Route

0 Penn Station (former Pennsylvania Station), 32nd Street and Seventh Avenue. The present terminal used by Amtrak's Northeast Corridor and Hudson Valley trains, New Jersey Transit, and the Long Island Rail Road, was built in 1964 on the site of the former palatial terminal of the same name built in 1906 by the former Pennsylvania Railroad. The original terminal was designed by McKim, Mead and White, with Charles Follen McKim as partner-in-charge. It was built in Roman style and modelled after the Baths of Caracalla. The great pit made by the excavation for the tracks was comparable to the building of the Panama Canal. All above-ground vestiges of the original terminal have been removed and replaced by strictly limited utilitarian facilities. Destruction of the original building was one of the greatest acts of vandalism in modern times. The new Madison Square Garden and Penn Center office building are above the modern station.

After leaving Penn Station, Amtrak Hudson River Line trains run north through a series of open cuts and tunnels beneath Riverside Drive for 4.5 miles to 122nd Street, where the tracks run on an elevated trestle inland and parallel to the West Side Highway.

5 Cross 130th Street — Former Manhattan station of Hudson River RR

Tracks gradually descend to sea level and follow the shoreline of the Hudson with excellent views over the water of Edgewater and Fort Lee, New Jersey, and the Palisades.

7 Pass beneath George Washington Bridge.

8.4 Cross Dyckman Street (Tubby Hook). Englewood Cliffs, NJ across river. Run along western edge of Inwood Hill Park Manhattan.

10 Cross Spuyten Duyvil Creek. (See articles River mile 9.70.)

10.5 Berian's Neck—Junction with line from Grand Central Station.

13 Riverdale.

13 Mount St. Vincent.

14 Ludlow.

15 Yonkers.

16 Glenwood.

18 Greystone.

19 Hastings-on-Hudson.

20 Dobbs Ferry.

21 Ardsley-on-Hudson.

22 Irvington.

23 Sunnyside restoration.

25 Tarrytown.

26 Philipse Manor.

29 Scarborough.

31 Ossining. (Here tracks pass through tunnel beneath Sing Sing prison.)

33 Croton-Harmon. End of electrification for through trains. Cross Croton River south of station.

34 Croton-on-Hudson.

35 Croton-North Station.

36 Oscawana.

37 Crugers. (Tracks cut inland to Peekskill.)

39 Montrose.

41 Peekskill. (Tracks cross Annsville Creek north of station.)

45 Manitou.

47 Glenclyffe.

49 Garrison.

52 Cold Spring.

54 Storm King.

56 Dutchess Junction.

58 Beacon.

62 Chelsea.

64 New Hamburg. (Cross Wappinger's Creek south of depot.)

67 Camelot.

73 Poughkeepsie.

76 Roosevelt.

78 Hyde Park.

83 Staatsburg.

88 Rhinecliff.

94 Barrytown Station. A miniature Greek temple, now a bookstore.

98 Tivoli.

104 Germantown.

105 North Germantown.

109 Greendale.

114 Hudson.

118 Stockport. (Cross Stockport Creek south of depot.)

121 Newton Hook.

124 Stuyvesant.

130 Schodack Landing.

134 Castleton-on-Hudson.

142 Rensselaer (Now Albany-Rensselaer—the present Amtrak station for the Albany area.)
    The main line crosses the Hudson River here, as do Montreal-bound trains operating further north via the Delaware & Hudson Railroad.

143 Albany. (Union Station is now out of service. Trains use the upper railroad bridge formerly used for freight only. The lower bridge to Union Station has been removed.)

Albany & Troy Branch of Conrail
(freight service only)

0 Albany.

1 Rensselaer.

5 Iron Works.

6 Madison Street, Troy.

6½ Adams Street, Troy.

7 Troy, Union Station (formerly connections with D & H and B & M).

Amtrak Route Albany–Rensselaer to Montreal via Schenectady

Over lines of former New York Central (Now Conrail) and Delaware & Hudson Railroads.

142 Albany-Rensselaer Amtrak Station

143 Cross Hudson River on moveable bridge. Views of Albany to left. Former Albany Union Station to left.

145 Run uphill through rock cut.

160 Schenectady Union Station—Leave NY Central-Conrail Lines. Commence D & H trackage.

Delaware & Hudson Route

0 Schenectady Union Station. Union College Campus to left.

1.6 Cross Mohawk River.

2.1 Alplaus.

2.3 Glenville—Mohawk Yard.

4.7 Glenville Junction Line to right goes to Mechanicville.

10.0 BW Cabin—connection from New England from east.

10.5 Ballston Lake Station—actual lake 1 mile to east.

16.7 Cross Kayaderosseras Creek—flows to Hudson south of Schuylerville.

16.7 Ballston Spa (old line from Albany via Mechanicville enters from east).

23.0 Saratoga Station—one mile from town and spa.

35.0 Gansevoort (cross Snook Creek). Enters Hudson near Fort Edward.

40.9 Cross Hudson River on fixed deck truss bridge.

41.4 Fort Edward (Glens Falls branch off to west).

43.8 Begin to parallel Champlain Canal to Whitehall.

48.9 Smith's Basin.

52.8 Fort Ann.

56.7 Comstock. (Putnam Mtn. to west, 1827 ft.) (Pilot Knob west, 2078 ft.)

59.8 Start to parallel Wood Creek to east. Flows to Lake Champlain.

63.4 Whitehall—(formerly Skenesborough). Rutland, VT branch to east.

63.9 Cross very narrow southern end Lake Champlain. Commence to run north along western shore of lake.

64.5 Black Mountain to west, 2,665 ft.

69.7 Clemens. Elephant Mountain west, 1,954 ft. Bald Mountain east, 1,045 ft.

73.2 Dresden.

78.2 Putnam.

81.0 Cummings.

83.0 Wrights.

85.5 Ticonderoga (Historic Fort) Ferry to Larrabee Pt., VT.

85.9 Addison Junction (branch to Baldwin at north end of Lake George to west).

94.9 Crown Point (former fortifications and monument). Bridge across Lake Champlain to Vermont for autos.

101.3 SR Cabin—Line cuts inland from lake.

101.7 Sherman (formerly Burdicks).

102.3 Bulwaggan Bay to east.

102.6 Port Henry (formerly iron mining industry here).

107.8 Mineville, Jct. Bald Mountain west, 2,055 ft. Line cuts inland.

113.6 Westport Station one-half mile west of town, inland.

113.6 Campbell Mountain to west, 2,000 ft.

116.4 Wadham's Mills.

117.3 Coon Mountain to east, 1,015 ft.

118.1 Merriam (formerly Whallonsburgh). Split Rock Mountain east, 1,035 ft.

123.1 Essex Station (1 mile west of Essex). Bouquet Mountain west, 1,240 ft.

127.8 Willsboro.

130.8 Red Rock Cliffs. Track runs on high ledge above lake with spectacular views.

132.3 Willsboro Bay to east. Rattlesnake Mountain west, 1,300 ft.

135.8 Douglas. Trembleau Mountain west, 950 ft. Trembleau Point east.

140.3 Port Kent. Ferry to Burlington, VT.

142.2 Cross Ausable River (Ausable Chasm to west).

146.2 Valcour.

148.6 South Junction (former line to west to Ausable Forks).

150.0 Bluff Point (site of former Hotel Champlain, now Bellarmine College to east, overlooking lake).

153.2 Plattsburgh.

157.4 Beekmantown.

158.7 Spellmans.

162.7 West Chazy.

169.0 Chazy.

172.8 Cooperville.

176.7 Rouses Point (on lakefront). Former railroad bridge to Alburg, VT. This is at northern end of the Richelieu River, which is the outlet for Lake Champlain. The Richelieu flows into the St. Lawrence at Sorel, Que. Rouses Point is the Canada/United States Customs stop.

Napierville Junction Railroad— Canadian Pacific Route

180.0 Cross into Canada—begin Napierville Junction RR.
Lacolle, Que.
Napierville
St. Edouard
St. Mathieu
Delson

226.0 Enter tracks of Canadian Pacific Railroad.

227.0 Cross St. Lawrence River.

228.0 Montreal West.

231.0 Westmount.

232.0 Montreal, Windsor Station.
End NVJCT—CP Route.

Canadian National Railroad— Amtrak Route

Cross into Canada

181.7 Cantic, Que. (Canadian Customs).

223.0 Cross St. Lawrence River on Victoria Bridge (good view of Falls of St. Lawrence and Port of Montreal).

225.0 Montreal, Central Station.

Delaware and Hudson Glens Falls Branch (freight only)

0 Fort Edward.

2 Hudson Falls.

6 Glens Falls.

15 Lake George. (Track abandoned between Glens Falls and Lake George.) Formerly connection with Lake George Steamboat Co. to Bolton Landing, Sabbath Day Point, Huelet's Landing, Hague, Silver Bay, and Baldwin (Ticonderoga).

West Side Railroad Route

Over lines of the New Jersey Junction Railroad and the West Shore Railroad, now Conrail.
Presently freight service only. Any excursions would probably operate from Erie-Lackawanna Terminal at Hoboken. The Weehawken Terminal is entirely gone.

-4 Hoboken Terminal. Switch onto tracks of New Jersey Junction Railroad and run along foot of Palisades to Weehawken. Pick up West Shore tracks.

0 Weehawken. Formerly ferries to West 42nd Street and Cortlandt Street. One-mile-long tunnel beneath Palisades to the Hackensack Meadows. New ferry to West 38th Street.

2 North Bergen.

5 Cross Overpeck Creek.

6 Little Ferry. (Tracks of New York, Susquehanna & Western Railway are parallel on the left. Hackensack River to left.)

7 Ridgefield Park.

8 West View. The dome of the Bergen County Courthouse, across the river in Hackensack, is visible. Neoclassic style by J. R. Gordon, 1912.

9 Bogota.

10 Teaneck.

11 West Englewood.

12 Bergenfield. Formerly, along with Dumont, part of town of Schraalenberg. Railroad shortened name to Bergen Fields. Old South Dutch Reformed Church visible to left.

13 Dumont. Northern part of Old Schraalenburgh. Old North Dutch Reformed Church visible to right.

Former end of much local commuter service. Extensive coach yards were north of station. World War I Camp Merritt was to the east of here.

15 Haworth. Exclusive residential area.

16 Harrington Park. Former summer resort. Town layed out by Vaux & Olmsted. Exclusive residential town. The Oradell Reservoir on the Hackensack River is to west.

18 West Norwood, New Jersey.

20 Tappan, New York. Treason Hill, where Major André was hung, is just west of tracks. He was tried here.

21 Orangeburg. Large Rockland State Hospital (mental) west of here. This was the site of the large World War II Camp Shanks, used for embarkation and mustering out.

22 Blauvelt.

25 West Nyack.

26 Cross bridge over New York Thruway.

27 Lake De Forest on Hackensack River to west.

27 Valley Cottage. In 1753 a large tract here was sold to John Ryder by Peter Geslar.

29 Congers-Rockland Lake. Named for Abraham B. Conger, who settled here in 1840. Home of wireless inventor A. Frederick Collins.

30 Tunnel beneath Palisades to Hudson Valley.

31 Views of Haverstraw Bay to right.

33 Haverstraw.

34 West Haverstraw. This is the former end of suburban service. It was formerly a junction with the New Jersey & New York Railroad.

35 Stony Point.

37 Tomkins Cove.

40 Jones Point. Dunderberg Mountain, Snake Creek.

41 Iona Island. Doodletown Bight.

42 Bear Mountain. Steamboat docks. Anthony's Nose across river. Cross Popolopen Creek. Bear Mountain Bridge above.

43 Tunnel.

43 Fort Montgomery.

46 Buttermilk Falls to left.

47 Highland Falls.

48 West Point (South Dock).

48 Tunnel beneath Parade Grounds and Trophy Point.

49 Cro' Nest Mountain to left.

51 Mother Cronk's Cove.

52 Storm King Mountain to left.

53 Cornwall. Formerly New York, Ontario & Western Railway cut off here to the west, toward Oswego.

54 Cross Moodna Creek.

57 Newburgh.

61 Roseton.

64 Cedarcliff.

65 Marlborough.

69 Milton.

73 Highland. Mid-Hudson and Poughkeepsie Railroad bridges above.

78 Railroad leaves the river and cuts inland to Glenmont.

79 West Park.

81 Esopus.

83 Ulster Park.

86 Port Ewen. Explosive storage yards south of depot.

87 High Wilbur trestle over Rondout Creek.

88 Short tunnel beneath Montrepose Cemetery.

89 Kingston Union Station. Former junction with Ulster & Delaware and New York, Ontario & Western, Ellenville & Kingston Branch.

91 Lake Katerine. I.B.M. plant to south of depot. Views of Catskill Mountains to west.

96 Mount Marion. The mountain is to the west. The railroad now parallels the New York Thruway.

97 Cross Esopus Creek above Glenerie Falls to right.

101 Saugerties.

102 Malden-on-Hudson.

105 Alsen (Cementon). Kalkberg to west. Inbocht Bay to east.

108 Kykuit Flats and Hill to east.

111 Catskill.

112 High trestle above Catskill Creek.

115 West Athens.

121 Coxsackie.

125 New Baltimore.

128 Ravena (station for Coeymans). Main line of West Shore cuts off to northwest. Train enters the Albany Branch.

133 Selkirk. Cross the Boston & Albany, Castleton Bridge Line.

136 Wemple.

138 Glenmont.

139 Kenwood. Enter trackage of Delaware & Hudson line from Binghamton. Former Albany & Susquehanna Railroad.

139 Cross Norman's Kill. Vale of Tawasentha to west.

140 Port of Albany to right.

142 Albany. Former Union Station. Connections north to Delaware & Hudson main line and west to former New York Central main line to Buffalo and Chicago, Conrail.

OTHER REGIONAL RAILROAD ROUTES:

A) Delaware and Hudson North Creek Line
(freight and excursion service only)

0.0 Saratoga

16.9 Corinth

21.9 Hadley (Lake Luzerne)

29.5 Stony Creek

35.2 Thurman

43.6 The Glen

49.5 Riverside

57.1 North Creek

—— North River

—— Aiden Lair

90.1 Tahawas (Titanium Mines) (Sanford Lake)

B) Staten Island Rapid Transit
(frequent service)

St. George Ferry Terminal

Tompkinsville

Stapleton

Clifton

Grasmere

Old Town

Dongan Hills

Jefferson Avenue

Grant City

New Dorp

Oakwood Heights

Bay Terrace

Great Kills

Eltingville

Annadale

Huguenot Park

Princess Bay

Pleasant Plains

Nassau

Atlantic Station

Tottenville

C) New Jersey Transit—North Jersey Coast Line
(frequent passenger service)

0.0 Penn Station, New York City

10.0 Penn Station, Newark, NJ

15.5 Elizabeth

20.8 Rahway

24.5 Woodbridge

28.0 Perth Amboy

29.0 Raritan River Bridge

30.0 South Amboy

31.7 Morgan (Laurence Harbor)

34.0 Cliffwood

35.2 Matawan

37.0 Hazlet

41.2 Middletown

45.0 Red Bank

47.4 Little Silver-Oceanport

49.0 Monmouth Park

49.9 Branchport

51.0 Long Branch

This is route of former New York & Long Branch RR.

D) Conrail Elizabethport–Perth Amboy Line—Former CRR of NJ.
(freight and excursion service only)

0.0 Elizabethport

0.9 Elizabeth Avenue

1.8 Bayway

3.9 Tremley

7.3 Port Reading

8.4 Sewaren

9.6 Barber

11.5 Perth Amboy

E) New York & Putnam RR (Former New York Central)
(largely abandoned)

0.0 Sedgwick Avenue (Bronx)

4.0 Kings Bridge

5.0 Van Cortlandt Park

7.0 Lincoln

8.0 Dunwoodie

10.0 Bryn Mawr Park

11.0 Nepperhan

11.5 Gray Oaks

12.0 Nepera Park

13.0 Mount Hope

14.0 Chauncey

15.0 Ardsley

18.0 Elmsford

21.0 East View

24.0 Graham

26.0 Briarcliff Manor

29.0 Millwood

31.0 Kitchawan

32.0 Croton Lake

34.0 Croton Heights

36.0 Yorktown Heights

37.0 Amawalk

39.0 Granite Springs

41.0 Baldwin Place

43.0 Lake Mahopac

44.0 Mahopac

46.0 Crafts

48.0 Carmel

53.0 Brewster

F) Metro-North Commuter Railroad– New York & Harlem Line
(frequent passenger service to Brewster. Sporadic commuter service to Pawling. Largely abandoned north of there, but there are plans to reopen for passenger service to Chatham.)

0 Grand Central Station, New York City

4 125th Street

5 Bronx (138th Street)

6 Bronx-Melrose (E 162nd St.)

7 Morrisania (E 168th St.)

8 Tremont (E 177th St.)

9 Fordham (E 190th St.)

10 Botanical Garden (E 200th St.)

11 Williams Bridge (E 210th St.)

12 Woodlawn (E 233rd St.)

13 Wakefield (E 241st St.)

13 Mount Vernon

14 Fleetwood

15 Bronxville

16 Tuckahoe

17 Crestwood (Eastchester)

19 Scarsdale

21 Hartsdale

22 White Plains

24 Holland Avenue (North White Plains)

24 White Plains (North Station)

25 Valhalla

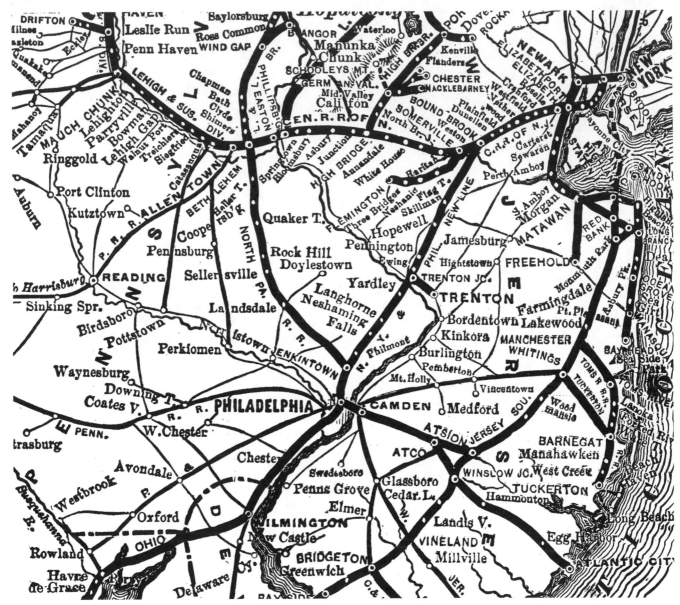

Rail lines in Northern New Jersey, New York Bay area, at time of maximum buildout (1896). From Central Railroad of New Jersey map. Author's Collection.

77 Dover Plains

79 State School

81 Wassaic

85 Amenia

93 Millerton

105 Copake Falls (Bishbash Falls)

109 Hillsdale

112 Craryville

119 Philmont

127 Chatham

G) Northern Railroad of New Jersey
(presently freight only served by Conrail. New Jersey Transit plans to return to passenger service as a light rail line.)

0 Pavonia Avenue (Jersey City) (Newport City)

10 Ridgefield, NJ

11 Palisades Park

12 Leonia

14 Nordhoff

15 Englewood

16 Highwood (Hudson Avenue)

17 Tenafly

18 Cresskill

19 Demarest

20 Closter

21 Norwood

22 Northvale

24 Sparkill, N.Y.

26 Piermont

27 Grand View

28 South Nyack

29 Nyack

Bibliography

Adams, Arthur G. *The Catskills: A Guide to the Mountains and Nearby Valleys.* Fleischmanns, N.Y.: Purple Mountain Press, 1988.

Adams, Arthur G. *The Catskills: An Illustrated Historical Guide with Gazetteer.* New York: Fordham University Press, 1990.

Adams, Arthur G., with Roger Coco and Harriet and Leon R. Greenman. *Guide to the Catskills With Trail Guide and Maps.* New York: Walking News, Inc., 1975. 2nd Ed. 1987.

Adams, Arthur G. *The Hudson River in Literature,* Revised Edition with maps and illustrations. New York: Fordham University Press, 1988. (First Ed. SUNY Press 1981 non-illus.)

Adams, Arthur G. *The Hudson Through the Years,* Revised and Expanded 3rd Edition. New York: Fordham University Press, 1996. (First Edition, Lind Publications, 1983.)

Adams, Arthur G., with Raymond J. Baxter. *Railroad Ferries of the Hudson: and the Stories of a Deckhand.* Woodcliff Lake, N.J.: Lind Publications, 1987.

Adams, Arthur G. *Tour Guide to the Catskills.* (Updated version of *The Catskills: A Guide to the Mountains and Nearby Valleys,* 1988.) Fleischmanns, N.Y.: Purple Mountain Press, 1993.

Bailey, Rosalie Fellows. *Pre-Revolutionary Dutch Houses and Families In Northern New Jersey and Southern New York.* New York: Dover Publications, Inc., 1968.

Beebe, William. *Report on the Eleventh Expedition, the Department of Tropical Research of the New York Geological Society.* New York: Geological Society, 1928.

Beers, F. W., C. E. *Atlas of the Hudson River Valley from New York City to Troy.* New York: Watson & Co., 1891. Reprinted by Martin Wehle, Churchville, N.Y.: 1979.

Beers, F. W. *County Atlas of Ulster New York.* New York: Walker & Jewett, 1875. Reprinted by Martin Wehle, Churchville, N.Y., 1978.

Beers, J. B. & Co. *History of Greene County, N.Y.* New York: 1884. Reprinted by Hope Farm Press, Cornwallville, N.Y., 1983.

Best, Gerald M. *The Ulster & Delaware Railroad Through the Catskills.* San Marino, California: Golden West Books, 1972.

Birmingham, Stephen. *America's Secret Aristocracy.* Boston: Little, Brown & Co., 1987.

Boyle, Robert H. *The Hudson River: A Natural and Unnatural History.* New York: W. W. Norton & Co., Inc., 1969.

Brandt, Clare. *An American Aristocracy: The Livingstons.* Garden City, N.Y.: Doubleday & Co., Inc., 1986.

Bruce, Wallace. *The Hudson by Daylight.* New York, Bryant Literary Union, 1901 & 1907. Reprinted by Walking News, Inc., New York, 1982.

Bryant, William Cullen, Ed. *Picturesque America.* New York: D. Appleton, 1872.

Burroughs, John. *Our River.* Article in Scribners Magazine, New York, 1880.

Burroughs, Julian. *Hudson River Memories* (Edited from memoirs of the author by his daughter Elizabeth Burroughs Kelley.) West Park, N.Y.: Riverby Books, 1987.

Carmer, Carl. *The Hudson.* (Originally published 1939.) 50th Anniversary edition, New York: Fordham University Press, 1989.

Cawley, James and Margaret. *Exploring the Little Rivers of New Jersey.* New Brunswick, N.J.: Rutgers University Press, 1961.

Cole, David. *History of Rockland County.* New York: J. B. Beers & Co., 1884.

Cooper, James Fenimore. *Leatherstocking Edition of Complete Novels.* New York, G. P. Putnam Sons, Undated, Limited Edition. His following novels contain material pertinent to the Hudson River: *Ashore and Afloat; The Chain-bearer; Homeward Bound; Home as Found; The Last of the Mohicans; The Pioneers; The Red-Skins; The Spy; Satanstoe; Water-Witch.* Extensive excerpts from the above novels are included in the author's anthology: *The Hudson River in Literature,* New York: Fordham Univ. Press, 1988.

Cudahy, Brian J. *Over and Back: A History of Ferryboats in New York Harbor.* New York: Fordham University Press, 1989.

Davis, Alexander Jackson. *Sketches of Montgomery Place,* c 1840. Sleepy Hollow Press, distributed exclusively by Fordham University Press, New York, 1989.

De Lisser, R. Lionel. *Picturesque Catskills—Greene County,* 1894. Reprinted by Charles E. Dornbusch, Cornwallville, N.Y., 1971.

De Lisser, R. Lionel. *Picturesque Ulster.* Originally published in eight numbered parts, Kingston, NY, 1896 to 1905. Reprinted in one volume by Twine's Catskill Bookshop, Woodstock, N.Y., 1968.

Doherty, Joan F. *Hudson County: The Left Bank.* Northridge, California: Windsor Publications, Inc., 1986.

Downing, Andrew Jackson. *The Architecture of Country Houses,* 1850. Republished by Dover Publications, New York, 1969.

Downing, Andrew Jackson. *Pleasure Grounds and A Visit to Montgomery Place* (1847). Republished in a combined edition by Sleepy Hollow Press, distributed exclusively by Fordham Univ. Press, New York, 1989.

Duffy, Francis J., with William H. Miller. *The New York Harbor Book.* Falmouth, Maine: TBW Books, 1986.

Elting, Irving. *Dutch Village Communities on the Hudson River.* Baltimore: Johns Hopkins University, 1886. Reprinted New York, Johnson Reprint Corporation, 1973.

Evers, Alf. *The Catskills: From Wilderness to Woodstock.* Garden City, N.Y.: Doubleday & Company, Inc., 1972.

Fogarty, Catharine M., with John E. O'Connor and Charles F. Cummings. *Bergen County: A Pictorial History.* Norfolk, Va.: The Donning Company, 1985.

Fried, Marc B. *The Early History of Kingston & Ulster County, N. Y.* Marbletown, Kingston, N.Y.: Ulster County Historical Society, 1975.

Gekle, William F. *A Hudson Riverbook.* Poughkeepsie, N.Y.: Wyvern House, 1978.

Gekle, William F. *The Lower Reaches of the Hudson River.* Poughkeepsie, N.Y.: Wyvern House, 1982.

Helmer, William F. *Rip Van Winkle Railroads.* Berkeley, California: Howell-North Books, 1970.

Hilton, George W. *The Night Boat.* Berkeley, California:, Howell-North Books, 1968.

Hope, Jack, with photographs by Robert Perron. *A River for the Living—The Hudson and Its People.* Barre, Mass.: Barre Publishing, 1975. Distributed by Crown Publishers, New York.

Howat, John K. *The Hudson River and Its Painters.* New York: Penguin Books, 1978. First published by the Viking Press, 1972.

Howell, Charles, with Allan Keller. *The Mill at Phillipsburg Manor, and A Brief History of Milling.* Sleepy Hollow Press. Exclusively distributed by Fordham University Press, New York, 1989.

Howell, William Thompson. *The Hudson Highlands.* New York: Walking News, Inc., 1982.

Ingersoll, Ernest. *Handy Guide to the Hudson River and Catskill Mountains* (1910). Republished by J. C. & A. L. Fawcett, Inc., Astoria, N. Y., 1989.

In The Hudson Highlands. New York Publication Committee of the New York Chapter of the Appalachian Mountain Club, 1945. Reissued by Walking News, Inc., New York, 1979.

Irving, Washington. *A History of New York—From the Beginning of the World to the End of the Dutch Dynasty,* by Diedrich Knickerbocker. The Kinderhook Edition of *The Works of Washington Irving.* New York, G. P. Putnam's Sons, 1880. Also included, of Hudson River interest, are Irving's *Rip Van Winkle; The Legend of Sleepy Hollow; Wolfert Webber,* or *Golden Dreams; Dolph Heyliger.* NOTE: The above Irving works are also included in the author's anthology: *The Hudson River in Literature,* New York: Fordham University Press, 1988.

Hamlin, Talbot. *Greek Revival Architecture in America* (1944). Reissued by Dover Publications, New York, 1964.

Johnson, Harry, with Frederick S. Lightfoot. *Maritime New York in Nineteenth-Century Photographs.* New York: Dover Publications, Inc., 1980.

Keller, Allan. *Life Along the Hudson.* Tarrytown, Sleepy Hollow Press, 1976. Currently available through Fordham University Press, New York, 1989.

Kelley, Elizabeth Burroughs. *A West Parker Remembers When.* West Park, N.Y.: Riverby Books, 1987.

Kobbé, Gustav. *The New Jersey Coast & Pines* (1885). Reissued by Walking News, Inc., New York, 1982.

Lossing, Benson J. *Field Book of the American Revolution.* New York: Harper & Brothers, 1852. Reissued by Charles E. Tuttle Co., Rutland, Vt., 1972.

Lossing, Benson J. *The Hudson: From Wilderness to the Sea.* Troy, N.Y.: H. L. Nims & Co., 1866. Reissued by Ira J. Friedman Division of Kennikat Press, Port Washington, N. Y., 1972.

McCabe, John B. *Hiking With History in the Hudson Highlands.* New York: Carlton Press, Inc., 1977.

Mack, Arthur C. *The Palisades of the Hudson* (1909). Reissued by Walking News, Inc., New York, 1982.

Miers, Earl Schenck. *Where the Raritan Flows.* New Brunswick, N.J.: Rutgers University Press, 1964.

New York Walk Book. New York-New Jersey Trail Conference and The American Geographical Society, Garden City, N.Y.: Doubleday-Natural History Press, 1971.

Nutting, Wallace. *New York Beautiful* (1927). Reissued by Garden City Publishing Co., Garden City, N.Y., 1936.

O'Brien, Raymond J. *American Sublime: Landscape and*

Scenery of the Lower Hudson Valley. New York: Columbia University Press, 1981.

Oechsner, Carl. *Ossining, New York.* Croton-on-Hudson, N.Y.: North River Press, 1975.

Paulding, James Kirke. *New Mirror For Travellers; and Guide To The Springs.* New York: G. & C. Carvill, 1828.

Paulding, James Kirke. *The Dutchman's Fireside—A Tale.* New York: J. &. J. Harper, 1831. NOTE: Sections of the above Paulding works descriptive of the Hudson River are included in the author's anthology: *The Hudson River in Literature,* New York: Fordham University Press, 1988.

Reynolds, Helen Wilkinson. *Dutch Houses in the Hudson Valley Before 1776.* Originally published in 1929 by Payson and Clarke, Ltd. for the Holland Society, New York. Reissued, New York: Dover Publications, 1965.

Rifkind, Carole and Carol Levine. *Mansions, Mills and Main Streets.* New York: Schocken Books, 1975.

Ringwald, Donald C. *Hudson River Day Line: The Story of a Great American Steamboat Company.* Berkeley, California, Howell-North Books, 1965. Reissued by Fordham University Press, 1990.

Savell, Isabelle K. *Wine & Bitters.* New City, N.Y.: Historical Society of Rockland County, 1975.

Scull, Theodore W. *Hoboken's Lackawanna Terminal.* New York: Quadrant Press, 1987.

Serrao, John. *The Wild Palisades of the Hudson.* Woodcliff Lake (Westwood), N.J.: Lind Publications, 1986.

Shaughnessy, Jim. *Delaware & Hudson.* Berkeley, California: Howell-North Books, 1967.

Simpson, Jeffrey, with photographs by Ted Spiegel. *An American Treasure—The Hudson River Valley* (A color photo essay). Sleepy Hollow Press, Tarrytown, 1986. Available through Fordham University Press, New York, 1989.

Simpson, Jeffrey. *The Hudson River 1850-1918: A Photographic Portrait.* Tarrytown, N.Y.: Sleepy Hollow Press, 1981.

Simpson, Jeffrey. *Officers and Gentlemen: Historic West Point in Photographs.* New York: Fordham University Press, 1989.

Smith, Karl Beckwith III. *Hudson Heritage—An Artist's Perspective on Architecture.* Cold Spring, N.Y.: Salmagundi Press, 1989.

Van De Water, Frederic F. *Lake Champlain and Lake George.* New York: Bobbs-Merrill Co., 1946.

Van Rensselaer, Mariana Griswold. *Henry Hobson Richardson and His Works.* New York: Dover Publications, 1969.

Van Zandt, Roland. *The Catskill Mountain House.* New Brunswick, N.J.: Rutgers University Press, 1966.

Van Zandt, Roland. *Chronicles of the Hudson: Three Centuries of Travellers' Accounts.* New Brunswick, N.J.: Rutgers University Press, 1971.

Wakefield, Manville B. *Coal Boats to Tidewater.* South Fallsburg, N.Y.: Steingart Associates, 1965.

Westervelt, Francis A., Ed. *History of Bergen County New Jersey 1630-1923.* New York: Lewis Historical Publishing Co., 1923, 3 Vols.

Whitson, Skip. *The Hudson River One Hundred Years Ago.* Albuquerque, N.M.: Sun Publishing Co., 1975.

Whitson, Skip. *New York City 100 Years Ago.* Albuquerque, N.M.: Sun Publishing Co., 1976.

Whitson, Skip. *Old Long Island.* Albuquerque, N.M.: Sun Publishing Co., 1976.

Willis, Nathaniel Parker. *American Scenery.* London: George Virtues, 1836. (With plates by William Bartlett.)

Willis, Nathaniel Parker. *Out-Doors at Idlewild; or the Shaping of a Home on the Banks of the Hudson.* New York: Charles Scribner, 1855.

Willis, Nathaniel Parker. *Rural Letters.* Auburn, N.Y.: Alden, Beardsley & Co., 1853. NOTE: Excerpts from the above Willis works specifically dealing with the Hudson River are included in the author's anthology: *The Hudson River in Literature,* New York: Fordham University Press, 1988.

Wilstach, Paul. *Hudson River Landings.* Port Washington, N.Y.: Ira J. Friedman, Inc., 1969. Original edition: New York: The Bobbs-Merrill Company, 1933.

Winsor, Justin. Ed. *Narrative and Critical History of America,* 8 Vols. Boston: The Riverside Press; Cambridge, Houghton, Mifflin and Company, 1889.

Wyckoff, Jerome. *Rock Scenery of the Hudson Highlands and Palisades.* Glens Falls, N.Y.: Adirondack Mountain Club, 1971.

Index

Keys to understanding this index:

RM   Indicates River Mile. These may be negative or positive. The base line 0.00 is at 42nd Street, New York City. Numbers run negatively south from there and positively north from there. Used for all features visible from the water.

ERM   Equivalent River Mile. Used as a useful cross reference for some inland points.

WR   Mileage from base point on the western road route. Run positively north.

ER   Mileage from base point on the eastern road route. Run positively north.

WRR   Mileages positively north along western railroad route from Weehawken.

ERR   Mileages positively north along eastern railroad route from Grand Central and/or Penn Station.

LWR   Lower western road. Run positively north from Atlantic Highlands to base line at Weehawken, 48th Street.

LER   Lower eastern road. Run positively north from Rockaway Point to 42nd Street, Manhattan.

LEEXP   Lower east express route. Run negatively south from base line at 42nd Street Manhattan to Rockaway Point.

LWEXP   Lower west express route. Run negatively south from Manhattan to Atlantic Highlands.

D&H   Delaware & Hudston (Amtrak) routes run positively north from Albany to Montreal.

CN   Canadian National Railroad (Amtrak) routes run positively north from Albany to Montreal.

CP   Canadian Pacific Railroad (Amtrak) routes run positively north from Albany to Montreal.

NPJR   Napierville Junction Railroad. Routes run positively north from Albany to Montreal.

A&T   Albany & Troy Railroad. Route runs positively north from Albany to Troy.

LGSTBT   Lake George Steamboat Company. Runs positively north from Lake George Village (Caldwells) to Baldwin Landing, near Ticonderoga.

Spellmans, N.Y., D&H 158.70; 382
Spermaceti Cove (Sandy Hook), RM −21.50, LWR 13.50; 28, 30, 303
Spencer (revenue cutter), 185
Sphagnum Pond, *174*
Spitfire (galley), 131
Spitzenberg Mountains, RM 37.00; 149
Split Rock Mountain (Adirondacks), 381
Spook Hollow (Upper Nyack), WR 38.90; 322
Spring Brook, RM 67.25; 206
Springside (Vassar estate), RM 70.50, ER 96.10; 212, 369
Springsteels Farm (Stony Point), RM 36.20; 153
Spring Valley, N.Y., 42, 126
Springwood (Roosevelt Mansion at Hyde Park),RM 74.75; 214, *369*
Sprout Brook, RM 39.75, ER 56.20; 365
Sprouts of the Mohawk, *274, 277, 278, 279,* 280
Spuyten Duyvil Creek, RM 9.70, ER 9.30, ERR 10–11; *102, 112, 113, 114, 119,* 131, 358, 379, 380
Spuyten Duyvil Station, ERR 11; 379
Spy House (Seabrook Homestead, Port Monmouth, N.J.), 30, *303*
Spy, The (Cooper), quoted, 120, 163
Squirrelwood (Highland Falls), 171
Staat Island, RM 134.00–137.00, ER 186.20, *261,* 374
Staats, Abram, House, RM 115.75, ERR 118, ER 164.65; *254, 261,* 313
Staats, Dr. Samuel, 220
Staatsburg, N.Y., RM 81.20, ERR 83, ER 112.60; 220, 370, 380
Staatsburg Reservoir, 220
Stack Icehouse, RM 118.80; 255
Stadthuys in New York, 1679, 82
Stamp Act Congress, 240
Stamford, N.Y., 227
Standard Manufacturing Co. Mill, RM 205.80; *284,* 374
Standard Oil of New Jersey, 35, 57
Staples House (Malden-on-Hudson), 240
Stapleton (S.I.), RM −9.60, LWR 79.20; 38, 39, 57, 307
Starbuck Island, RM 146.50; 277
Starin, John H., 253
Starkes Knob, RM 180.75, WR 260.30; 287, 342
Starret-Lehigh Warehouse (Manhattan), RM −1.10, LER 43.10; 91, 355
State Line Rock, RM 18.00, WR 16.45, 17.75; *118, 124,* 318
Staten Island, RM −8.50–−17.00, LWR 52.90–84.70; *25,* 39
Staten Island Antiquarian Society, 306
Staten Island Ferry and Train Terminal, LWR 83.50; 34, 38, 305; Brooklyn, LER 39.30; *83,* 355
Staten Island Historical Society, 39, 306
Staten Island Museum, LWR 80.60; 307
Staten Island Rapid Transit Railroad, LWR 53.80–83.50; passim, 34, 38, 305
Staten Island Zoo, 39
State University of New York Building (Albany), WR 214.00; *263*
Station Rock, RM 18.00, WR 16.45; *118,* 124
Status Eylandt (S.I.), 37
Steamtown Foundation, 227
Steel Style Corporation, WR 83.30, RM 56.10; 327
Steen Valetje (Stony Valley), ER 125.50; 371
Steeplechase Park site (Coney Island), LER 13.00; 44, 56, 347
Sterling Iron Works, 166
Sterling Lake (Orange Co.), 169
Steinman, D. B., 228
Steuben, Gen. Frederick William Augustus, Baron von, 201
Stevens, Gen. Ebenezer, 68
Stevens, Edwin Augustus, 89, 91
Stevens, John Cox, 41, 89, 90, 231
Stevens, Robert L., 91
Stevens (site of former berth) (Hoboken), LWR 113.60; 312
Stevens Insitute of Technology, RM −1.50, LWR 113.60; 90, 91, 312
Stevens Point, RM −1.50, LWR 113.60; *312*
Stewart, Alexander, T., 201
Stewart, Maj. John, 153
Stewart Airport (Newburgh), RM 56.10
Stillman, Dr. Ernest, 187
Stillman's Spring, WR 77.00; 326
Stillwater, N.Y., RM 164.30, WR 240.50–244.20; *280, 282, 283,* 286, 342
Stillwater Junction, RM 1162.00; 285
Stillwell, Col. John, 303

Stillwell, Thomas, 306
Stillwell Lake, RM 42.60; 169
Stillwell-Perine House (S.I.), 39, 306
Stirling, Col., 105
Stirling, N.J., 40
Stockport Creek, RM 115.75, ERR 118, ER 163.50; 239, *251,* 254, 373, 380
Stockport Flats, 14, 354
Stockport Landing, RM 116.75, ER 166.50; 254, 373
Stockport Station, RM 115.80, ERR 118, ER 164.60; 254, 373
Stoffelsen, Jacob, 86
Stoneco Post Office, RM 65.00; 205
Stony Creek, RM 94.80, ER 134.10; 1 *3,* 232, 371
Stony Island, RM 147.50; 278
Stony Lonesome (West Point), RM 47.35; *174,* 178
Stony Point (ferryboat), 86
Stony Point (Greenbush), RM 132.70; 261, 383
Stony Point (Bay, Lighthouse, and Battlefield Park), RM 35.75, ER 50.20, WR 49.90–52.50, WRR 35; *142,* 152–154, 323
Storm King Brook and Clove, RM 51.00, WRR 51.00, WR 77.05; 189, 326
Storm King Mountain, RM 51.50, WRR 52, WR 76.40, 77.05–78.40; *174, 185,* 188, *189,* 326, 383; State Park, *174;* pumped storage plant, 16, 18, 189
Storm King Station, RM 51.25, ERR 54, ER 72.50; 188, 368, 380
Storm King Valley, RM 51.00, WRR 51.00, WR 76.80, ER 71.30; 187
Storm Ship (legend), 131, 161
Stottville, N.Y., RM 114.25, ER 162.10; 254
Stoudinger, John, 41
Stoughton, Charles W. & Arthur A., 99
Stout, Richard, 30
Stoutenburgh, Jacobus, 215
Stoutenburgh, N.Y., RM 76.40, ER 102.80; 215
Stoutenburgh-Bergh House (Hyde Park), ER 102.80; 369
Strachey, Sir Henry, 305
Strand, Het (Catskill), 246
Strand, Het (Rondout), RM 86.25, WR 128.90; 330
Strand (Manhattan), 84
Strange, E. B., 359
Strawberry Hill, 129
Strykers Bay (Manhattan), RM 3.30; 99
Stuart, James, 1st Earl of Murray, 244
Sturgeon Point, RM 85.00; 222
Stuyvesant, Gov. Peter, 37, 65, 89, 11a2, 223, 263, 268
Stuyvesant, N.Y., RM 121.45, ERR 124, ER 173.20; 250, 255, *259,* 373, 380
Subtreasury Building (Manhattan), LER 38.65; 82
Subway Grounds, RM −26.00; 22
Suckley, Thomas, 221
Sudam, John, 332
Suffern, N.Y., 126
Suffolk County, L.I., 24
Sugarloaf Hill, RM 45.50, ER 64.20, WR 67.80; 171
Sugarloaf Mountain, RM 52.80, ER 74.00; *176,* 191, 366, 368
Sunfish Cove, 206
Sunning Hill (Tivoli), RM 95.80; 233
Sunnycrest (Milton), WR 103.40; 329
Sunnyside, N.J. (Edgewater), RM 4.30, WR 5.20; 99, 315
Sunnyside (Washington Irving's home, Tarrytown), RM 21.45, ERR 23, ER 25.00; 131, *133, 134,* 360, 380
Sunnyside Brook (Tarrytown), ER 23.90; 360
Sunoco Depot (East Greenbush), ER 189.60; 374
Sunoco Depot (New Windsor), WR 82.80; 326
Sunset Park (Brooklyn), 51
Sunset Park (Highlands), 155
Superintendant's Quarters (West Point), RM 47.35, WR 73.08; 173, 178, 325
Susquehanna Railroad, see New York Susquehanna & Western Rwy.
Susquehanna River, 246
Susquehanna Turnpike, RM 107.25; 245, 246, 253
Sussex County, N.J., 40
Sutherland Pond, 174
Sutton & Suderley Brickyard (Coeymans), RM 127.50; 257
Suycker Broodt (Sugar Loaf "Hill"), 171
Swallow (steamboat), 253